EYEWITNESS TRAVEL

# KENYA

KU-757-117

ETHIOPIA

Moyale

Marsabit

Wajir

NORTHERN KENYA

Garissa

SOMALIA

**Northern Kenya**
Pages 338–357

**Central Highlands**
Pages 312–337

**Northern Coast**
Pages 230–255

Hola

Mutomo

NORTHERN
COAST

*Indian
Ocean*

Garsen

Lamu

SOUTHEASTERN
SAVANNAHS

Voi

Malindi

Watamu

SOUTHERN
COAST

Kwale

Mombasa

Shimoni

**Southern Coast**
Pages 202–229

**Southeastern
Savannahs**
Pages 180–201

EYEWITNESS TRAVEL

# KENYA

Main Contributors **Philip Briggs and Lizzie Williams**

**DK**

DK

LONDON, NEW YORK,
MELBOURNE, MUNICH AND DELHI
**www.dk.com**

**Managing Editor** Aruna Ghose
**Editorial Manager** Ankita Awasthi
**Design Managers** Sunita Gahir, Kavita Saha
**Project Editor** Arundhti Bhanot
**Project Designer** Mathew Kurien
**Editors** Sandhya Iyer, Yasmin Rahman
**Designers** Stuti Tiwari Bhatia, Amisha Gupta
**Senior Cartographic Manager** Uma Bhattacharya
**Cartographer** Mohammad Hassan
**DTP Designer** Azeem Siddique
**Senior Picture Research Coordinator** Taiyaba Khatoon
**Picture Researcher** Shweta Andrews

**Contributors**
Philip Briggs, Lizzie Williams

**Photographers**
Demetrio Carrasco, Nigel Hicks, Linda Whitwam

**Illustrators**
Chapel Design and Marketing Ltd, Chinglemba Chingtham,
Arun Pottirayil, T. Gautam Trivedi

Printed and bound in China

First published in Great Britain in 2009
by Dorling Kindersley Limited
80 Strand, London WC2R 0RL

15 16 17 18 10 9 8 7 6 5 4 3 2 1

**Reprinted with revisions 2011, 2013, 2015**

Copyright © 2009, 2015 Dorling Kindersley Limited, London
A Penguin Random House Company

ISBN 978-0-2410-0700-6

Front cover main image: A Lion in Masai Mara at sunrise

◀ Maasai *moran* (warrior) framed by an *Acacia tortilis* tree with Mount Kenya behind

Flamingoes at Lake Nakuru National Park

# Contents

Elaborate Swahili wooden door,
Lamu town

Samburu people in their colourful
traditional costume

# Wild Kenya

# Kenya Area
# by Area

Traditional sailing dhow,
Lamu waterfront

Two of the four sculpted giant tusks that
are Mombasa's leading landmark

# Travellers' Needs

# Survival Guide

The imposing Fort Jesus in Mombasa

# HOW TO USE THIS GUIDE

This travel guide helps you to get the most from your visit to Kenya. It provides both detailed practical information and expert recommendations. *Introducing Kenya* maps the country, sets it in its historical and cultural context, and describes events through the entire year. *Wild Kenya* is an extensive guide to wildlife viewing in Kenya and includes practical information on parks and reserves. *Kenya Area by Area* describes important sights, with maps, photographs and illustrations. Restaurant and hotel recommendations can be found in *Travellers' Needs*. The *Survival Guide* has tips on everything from transport to using the telephone system.

## Wild Kenya

*The Safari Experience* focuses on the activities on offer while on a safari and gives tips on locating and viewing wildlife through the year. *Habitats* gives an overview of the landscapes of Kenya. The *Field Guide* is an introduction to the wildlife of Kenya, from the Big Five to all the keenly sought primates, large and small mammals, reptiles and birdlife.

**Key Facts** provides details for each animal species, including habitat, top places to see and sighting tips.

## Kenya Area by Area

In this book Kenya has been divided into eight regions, each of which has a separate chapter. The most interesting places to visit have been numbered on a *Regional Map* at the beginning of each chapter.

**1 Introduction**
The landscape, history and character of each region is outlined here, showing how the area has developed over the centuries and what it offers to the visitor today.

**Each area of Kenya** can be quickly identified by its colour coding, shown on the front flap.

**2 Regional Map**
This map shows the road network and gives an illustrated overview of the region. All the sights are numbered and there are also useful tips on getting around.

**Sights at a Glance** lists the chapter's sights by category.

## 3 Street-by-Street Map
This gives a bird's-eye view of the key area in each chapter.

**A suggested route** for a walk is shown in red.

**Stars indicate** the sights that no visitor should miss.

**The information block** provides the details needed to visit each sight. Map references locate the sights on the *Road Map of Kenya* on the inside back cover.

## 4 Detailed Information
All the important sights in Kenya are described individually. They are listed in order following the numbering on the *Regional Map* at the start of the chapter.

**Features** explore themes specific to the region.

## 5 Kenya's Top Sights
These are given two or more full pages. Historic buildings are dissected to reveal their interiors; national parks have maps showing facilities and trails; museums have colour-coded floorplans to help locate interesting exhibits.

## 6 Travellers' Needs and Survival Guide
These sections cover areas such as shopping, entertainment, activities, health, security, communications, banking and currency and travel.

**Directory boxes** give contact information for services and venues mentioned in the text.

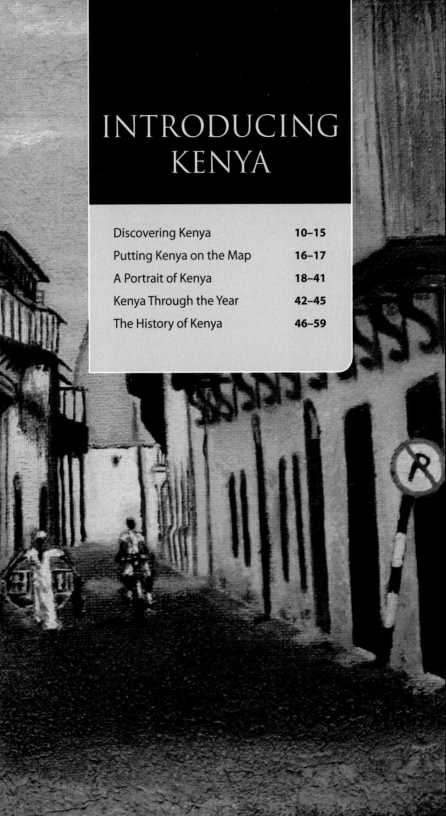

# INTRODUCING KENYA

# DISCOVERING KENYA

Kenya is a vast country, and the focus is not on urban sightseeing or even beach tourism, but on exploring wild national parks and other safari destinations, many accessible only by air or by rough and time-consuming gravel roads. As such, it is advisable not to cram too much into your stay (a two- or three-night stay is a minimum for the more remote national parks), or you risk spending most of your time travelling rather than viewing wildlife. Bearing this in mind, the following tours have been designed to take in as many highlights as possible, while keeping long-distance travel to a minimum. First up are three two-day tours of places that offer a large number of attractions in a compact area: the capital Nairobi, the scenic Lake Naivasha, and the coastal resorts of Malindi and Watamu. These are followed by a 12-day driving safari and a two-week fly-around safari, both supplemented by suggestions for those who want to extend their stay.

**Lake Nakuru**
The millions of flamingoes that gather periodically at Lake Nakuru are one of the main highlights for visitors.

## 12-Day Road Safari West and North of Nairobi

- Encounter a hunting cheetah or fresh lion kill on the central plains of the world-famous **Masai Mara National Reserve**.

- Watch thousand-strong flocks of flamingoes soar above beautiful **Lake Nakuru** in the heart of the Rift Valley.

- Take a guided game walk in search of rhinos in **Laikipia Plateau**.

- Stay up all night waiting for giant forest hog and other forest nocturnals to visit **Serena Mountain Lodge**.

- Marvel at the spectacular dances performed by the traditional pastoralists after which **Samburu National Reserve** is named.

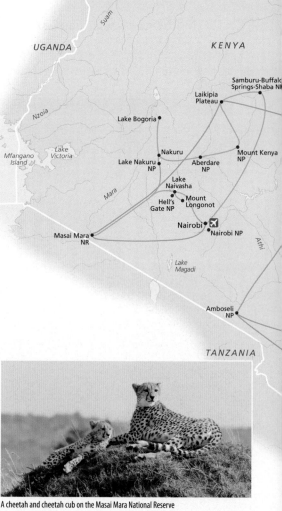

A cheetah and cheetah cub on the Masai Mara National Reserve

◀ A contemporary painting by a Kenyan artist depicting traditional houses with fretwork balconies in Mombasa

**Key**

West and North of Nairobi tour

Fly-in Safari and Beach tour

```
0 miles        75
0 kilometres        75
```

**Amboseli National Park**

The impressive snowcapped peak of Kilimanjaro rises above Amboseli National Park and provides a stunning backdrop to the lakes, plains, swamps, forests and wildlife that are found here.

**Fort Jesus**

This well-preserved structure, built to protect Mombasa harbour, is a fine example of a Portuguese military fortification from the 16th century.

## 2-Week Fly-in Safari and Beach Tour

- See the renowned wildebeest migration from on high in a serene balloon safari above the **Masai Mara National Reserve**.

- Take a night drive in search of leopard, genet and bushbaby on the **Laikipia Plateau**.

- Go in search of rhino in the dense riverine forests of **Meru National Park**.

- Watch elephants march across the plains of **Amboseli National Park** below the majestic snowcapped peak of Kilimanjaro.

- Wander the aromatic alleys of **Mombasa** Old Town below the towering buttresses of Fort Jesus.

## 2 Days in Nairobi

*The largest and most cosmopolitan city in East Africa also hosts the region's finest museum and borders the superb Nairobi National Park.*

- **Arriving** International flights and domestic flights on large aircraft land at Jomo Kenyatta International Airport (JKIA), 15 km (9 miles) southeast of the city centre. Light aircraft to safari destinations typically use the central Wilson Airport. Taxis are available at both airports.

- **Transport** The safest way to explore most sites is with a recognized tour operator or by taxi. Public transport can be crowded and time-consuming, and is unavailable for Nairobi National Park, which can be visited on a day tour or in a rented vehicle.

### Day 1
**Morning** Allow at least two hours to make your way around the two-storey **Nairobi National Museum** *(pp162–3)*, highlights of which include a photographic exhibition documenting the early days of Nairobi, a gallery dedicated to the hominine fossils unearthed in Kenya's Rift Valley, and fascinating ethnographic and natural history displays. The

Exhibition of wildlife models at Nairobi National Museum

museum gardens, set on a green hill north of the city centre, also incorporate a great little snake park and open-air sculpture gallery. From here, head downhill along Uhuru Avenue to the city centre, stopping at the bustling **City Market** *(p160)*, before heading to the historic **City Square** *(p159)* then out to the leafy western suburb of Karen for a lunch break.

**Afternoon** A popular first stop in Karen is the **Karen Blixen Museum** *(p172)*, whose centrepiece is the meticulously restored farmhouse where its namesake, the Danish-born author of *Out of Africa*, lived from 1914–32. Head on to the **AFEW Giraffe Centre** *(p172)* for an eye-fluttering encounter with the world's tallest land animal, then around the corner to **Nairobi Mamba Village** (feeding time 4:30pm Sun; *p172*) for close-up views of Nile Crocodile and ostrich, the world's largest reptile and bird respectively.

### Day 2
**Morning** An early start is recommended for **Nairobi National Park** *(pp166–7)*, since wildlife – in particular the lions, cheetahs and other large predators that stalk the plains – tends to be most active in the early morning. Wildlife spotting is a hit-and-miss activity, so you might see anything anywhere, but Narogoman Dam is a top spot for birds, while the grassland of Hyrax Valley often supports plenty of grazing ungulates.

**Afternoon** If you like your wildlife wild, spend the full day exploring the park, heading southeast with a picnic lunch to the open **Athi Plains** *(p169)* and tangled riverine scrub and hippo pool on the Athi River Track. Alternatively, the **Safari Walk** *(p166)* and the **Animal Orphanage** *(p166)* at the entrance to the park offer a great opportunity to stretch your legs and see animals up close and these are always a great hit with children.

White-necked cormorants, one of many species of bird to visit at Lake Naivasha

## 2 Days at Lake Naivasha

*This beautiful lake northwest of Nairobi is most alluring to active travellers seeking to walk or cycle in Kenya's safari country.*

- **Arriving** Around two hours' drive from Nairobi, depending on traffic, Lake Naivasha can be reached in a rented vehicle, on an organized tour, or by bus.

- **Transport** For those who arrive without transport, distances are too great to walk between sites, but public transport runs along the Moi South Lake Road (connecting most sites below) and bicycles can be rented near the entrance to Hell's Gate.

### Day 1
**Morning** Take a boat (or, when water levels are low, stroll across) from the south shore to pedestrian-friendly **Crescent Island Game Park** *(p272)*, home to giraffe, zebra, various antelope and plentiful birds. Enjoy lunch at any of the lakeshore hotels.

**Evening** Heading west for another 16 km (10 miles) brings you to **Elsamere** *(pp272–3)*, the former home of conservationist Joy Adamson that is now maintained as a museum. The house is surrounded by a fever tree forest that is teeming with birds and regularly visited by the

For practical information on travelling around Kenya, see pp414–19 lovely black-and-white colobus monkey. Another 10 km (6 miles) further northeast, the **Crater Lake Game Sanctuary** *(p273)* is a private reserve centred on a beautiful green crater lake whose shallows are often tinged pink with flamingoes.

**Day 2**
**Morning** Cycle or walk through **Hell's Gate National Park** *(pp274–5)*, which protects a spectacular volcanic landscape teeming with large herds of peacefully grazing wildlife and more occasionally visited by the likes of lion and elephant. A scenic highlight, about 1 km (0.6 miles) from the entrance gate, is **Fischer's Tower** *(p275)*, an isolated volcanic plug that stands sentinel between the tall basaltic cliffs for which the park is named.

**Afternoon** Hell's Gate has more than enough trails to keep cyclists or hikers busy for a full day, provided they carry all the food and water they need. Otherwise, give your weary legs a break relaxing over a drink at your hotel swimming pool or bird-watching along the lakeshore.

> **To extend your trip...**
> Only suitable for reasonably fit and agile travellers, the steep day hike to the 2,776 m (9,108 ft) rim of volcanic **Mount Longonot** *(p265)* is among the most spectacular in East Africa.

## 2 Days at Malindi and Watamu

*The twin towns of Malindi and Watamu provide a microcosmic introduction to the cultural, historic and natural charms of the beguiling Swahili Coast.*

- **Arriving** Flights connect Malindi to most other major tourist centres in Kenya. Watamu lies 20 km (12 miles) south of Malindi by road.

- **Transport** Malindi is small enough to explore on foot. Other sites can be visited using public transport taxis, or on the day tours offered by most hotels.

**Day 1**
**Morning** Begin a walking tour of Malindi's old centre at **Uhuru Gardens** *(p244)*. Head north a few paces along Mama Ngina Road to the **Friday Mosque** *(p244)* and its celebrated pillar tombs. Pop in opposite at the **Malindi Tourist Market** *(p244)*, or continue straight ahead to the **Malindi Museum** *(p244)*. From here, a 1.5-km (1-mile) stroll east along the waterfront takes you past a modest but appealing **Portuguese Chapel** *(p245)* built in 1542, and the **Vasco da Gama Cross** *(p245)* erected in 1499. Return the same way to enjoy a relaxed lunch at one of the waterfront Italian or seafood restaurants near the museum.

Remains of a medieval Swahili city at the Gedi Ruins, Malindi

**Afternoon** Take an afternoon snorkelling trip in a glass-bottomed boat to the stunning coral gardens of **Malindi Marine National Park** *(p236)*, offshore of Malindi and Watamu.

**Day 2**
**Morning** At least 2 hours, ideally longer, is required to explore the haunting **Gedi Ruins** *(pp242–3)*, which consist of the well-preserved jungle-bound remains of a medieval Swahili city set about 1 km (0.6 miles) inland of Watamu. If time permits, on your way out pop into the fascinating **Kipepeo Butterfly Project** *(p241)* next to the entrance gate.

**Afternoon** Energetic nature lovers will enjoy a guided or unguided walk in the **Arabuko Sokoke Forest Reserve** *(pp238–41)*, whose shady interior supports plenty of mammals and birds that are unique to the region. If that sounds too daunting, a more relaxed way to spend the afternoon would be lazing on the beach or swimming in **Watamu** *(p236)*, set on scenic Turtle Bay.

> **To extend your trip...**
> An important site for shorebirds, **Mida Creek** *(p236)*, 7 km (4 miles) from Watamu, hosts a community-based tourist project aimed at keen birders. The local community also oversees tourist visits to the more remote **Hell's Kitchen** *(p237)*, a spectacularly eroded sandstone valley north of Malindi.

Sandy beaches and shallow waters covering coral reefs, Watamu

## 12-Day Road Safari West and North of Nairobi

- **Arriving** The start and end point of this tour is Nairobi, which is serviced by numerous international carriers, landing at Jomo Kenyatta International Airport (JKIA), a short drive from the city centre. Unless your flight in lands very early or your flight out leaves late in the day, plan on spending a night (or if you prefer, longer) in Nairobi at the start and end of the trip.

- **Transport** Although some individual sites are accessible on public transport, most are not. Most people would do the trip as a guided tour with a reputable operator, but it would also be possible to self-drive in a rental vehicle, ideally with good clearance and 4WD.

### Day 1: Nairobi
Depending on when your flight lands, pick a day, or half a day, from the Nairobi itinerary on p12.

### Day 2: Lake Naivasha
Situated a comfortable driving distance from Nairobi, **Naivasha** *(p265)* is a lovely spot in which to spend some time before reaching **Lake Naivasha** *(pp270–71)*. Relax alongside the scenic bird-rich water or visit one of the sites mentioned in the itinerary on pp12–13.

> **To extend your trip…**
> Allocate a second night in Naivasha so you can stretch your legs cycling through **Hell's Gate** *(pp274–5)* or climbing volcanic **Mount Longonot** *(p265)*.

### Days 3–5: Masai Mara National Reserve
A bumpy, dusty half-day drive south from Naivasha brings you to the entrance gate to Kenya's most famous and arguably finest safari destination. The **Masai Mara National Reserve** *(pp266–9)* isn't a place to explore

in a hurry, and the most rewarding roads for wildlife spotting will depend on which lodge you stay at, the time of year, and a fair amount of luck. But over three days, you can be sure of seeing lion, elephant and plenty of other wildlife. Budget permitting, try to slot in an early morning **balloon safari** *(p266)* over the wildlife-rich plains.

### Day 6: Lake Nakuru National Park
Head back to the Rift Valley to **Lake Nakuru** *(pp280–81)*, the centrepiece of a small but very scenic national park famed for the aggregations of up to one million flamingos that frequently colour its shallows pink. The lake's southern floodplain is a reliable spot for white rhino sightings, and also home to large flocks of pelican.

> **To extend your trip…**
> Most tours include just one night in Nakuru. But a second night allows time to explore the park's far south (good for black rhino and lion), and to take a day trip to **Lake Bogoria** *(pp284–7)* if, as is sometimes the case, Nakuru's flamingoes have relocated there.

### Day 7: Mount Kenya or the Aberdares
For a complete change of pace, stay overnight at one of the two "tree hotels" in **Aberdare National Park** *(pp320–21)*, or the similar **Serena Mountain Lodge** *(p329)* bordering **Mount Kenya National Park** *(see pp326–9)*, both of which offer excellent

nocturnal game viewing in a forested highland environment that hosts very different wildlife to the plains.

### Days 8–9: Laikipia Plateau
Sticking to the Central Highlands north of Nairobi, the vast **Laikipia Plateau** *(pp322–5)* is protected in a patchwork of private wildlife sanctuaries that collectively support wildlife densities comparable only to the Masai Mara and form an important stronghold for the endangered African wild dog, black and white rhino, and the introduced chimpanzees of Sweetwaters. Other attractions include guided walking and horseback safaris, low tourist volumes and night drives.

### Days 10–11: Samburu-Buffalo Springs-Shaba National Reserves
Set in the arid badlands stretching northward from Mount Kenya to the Ethiopian border, but bisected by the perennial Ewaso Nyiro river, the near-contiguous **Samburu-Buffalo Springs-Shaba National Reserves** *(see pp346–50)* are known for their harsh semi-desert scenery, leopard sightings, and a wealth of localized large mammals not found elsewhere in the country. Samburu has the best wildlife, while Shaba is the pick for those who want to escape the crowds. Make sure to include a visit to a traditional Samburu village in your itinerary.

### Day 12: Nairobi
After a morning game drive, head back to the capital for one last night.

A diverse array of wildlife gathered at Lake Nakuru National Park

Volcanic landscape at Hell's Gate National Park

## 2-Week Fly-in Safari and Beach Tour

- **Arriving** This tour starts and ends at Nairobi (see p12), and again it is best to schedule a first and last night in the city. The itinerary could be changed to begin and end at Mombasa's Moi International Airport instead.

- **Transport** Scheduled light aircraft flights connect all sites on this itinerary, and are the most efficient way to get between them, though you may sometimes need to change aircraft at Nairobi's Wilson Airport. Any good operator will ensure you are booked into lodges that offer a full package including airport pick-ups, game drives and other activities.

### Day 1: Nairobi
Depending on when your flight lands, pick a day, or half a day, from the Nairobi itinerary on p12.

### Days 2–4: Masai Mara National Reserve
Three days is the minimum required to make the most of Kenya's most famous **Masai Mara National Reserve** (pp266–9) and its plentiful wildlife. For fly-in visitors, the lodges and camps in the relatively untrammelled **Central Plains** (see p269) and **Mara Triangle** (see p269) are strongly recommended over those in the reserve's more heavily touristed east. Your driver/guide will

know the best areas for seeing wildlife locally. An early morning **balloon safari** (p266) over the reserve is recommended.

### Days 5–7: Laikipia Plateau
See itinerary for days 8–9 on the facing page.

### Days 8–9: Meru National Park
The wildest and least densely touristed of Kenya's major national parks, **Meru National Park** (pp334–7) is home to one of the country's most spectacular luxury bush lodges in the form of **Elsa's Kopje** (see p335). Game drives offer an opportunity to see "northern specials" such as reticulated giraffe and gerenuk, as well as rhino, while other attractions include the wild riverine scenery along the Tana river that includes prehistoric-looking doum palm trees.

> **To extend your trip...**
> Arrange to be driven to the coast over two or three days, stopping at scenic **Lake Chala** (p194), then taking a road safari through the vast **Tsavo East and West National Parks** (pp186–91).

### Days 10–11: Amboseli National Park
**Amboseli** (pp198–201) is a scenic national park set at the northern base of magnificent **Kilimanjaro** (see p195), a 5-km- (3-mile) high volcanic mountain whose snowcapped peak dominates the skyline even though it lies across the border

in Tanzania. The best game circuit is around **Ol Tukai** (p199), which is surrounded by swamps dense with birdlife and massive tuskers, while the view from **Observation Hill** (p198) is truly spectacular.

### Days 12–14: Diani Beach
Kenya's premier beach destination, **Diani** (p214) is lined with resorts catering to most tastes and budgets. Many people are content to laze around the hotel swimming pool or beach, but there is also plenty to occupy more active travellers: snorkelling and diving at Funzi Island offshore of **Shirazi** (p219), a day trip to the historic **Mombasa Old Town** (pp210–11) abutting the imposing **Fort Jesus** (pp212–13), or a mini-safari in search of sable antelope and coastal forest wildlife in **Shimba Hills National Reserve** (pp220–23).

Palm-fringed white sands and turquoise sea at Diani Beach

# Putting Kenya on the Map

Flanked by a tropical 480-km (300-mile) coastline on the Indian Ocean in the south-east, bordering South Sudan, Somalia and Ethiopia in the arid north and Uganda and Tanzania in the south-west, Kenya straddles the equator. Roughly the size of France, it covers 586,000 sq km (226,196 sq miles), of which about 10,700 sq km (4,130 sq miles) is taken up by Lakes Victoria and Turkana. Estimated at 45.5 million in 2014, Kenya's population has been bolstered by the influx of immigrants from neighbouring conflict-torn countries. About 75 per cent live in an agricultural belt running northwest from Nairobi to the Ugandan border. The rest reside in Nairobi, Nakuru, Kisumu and Mombasa.

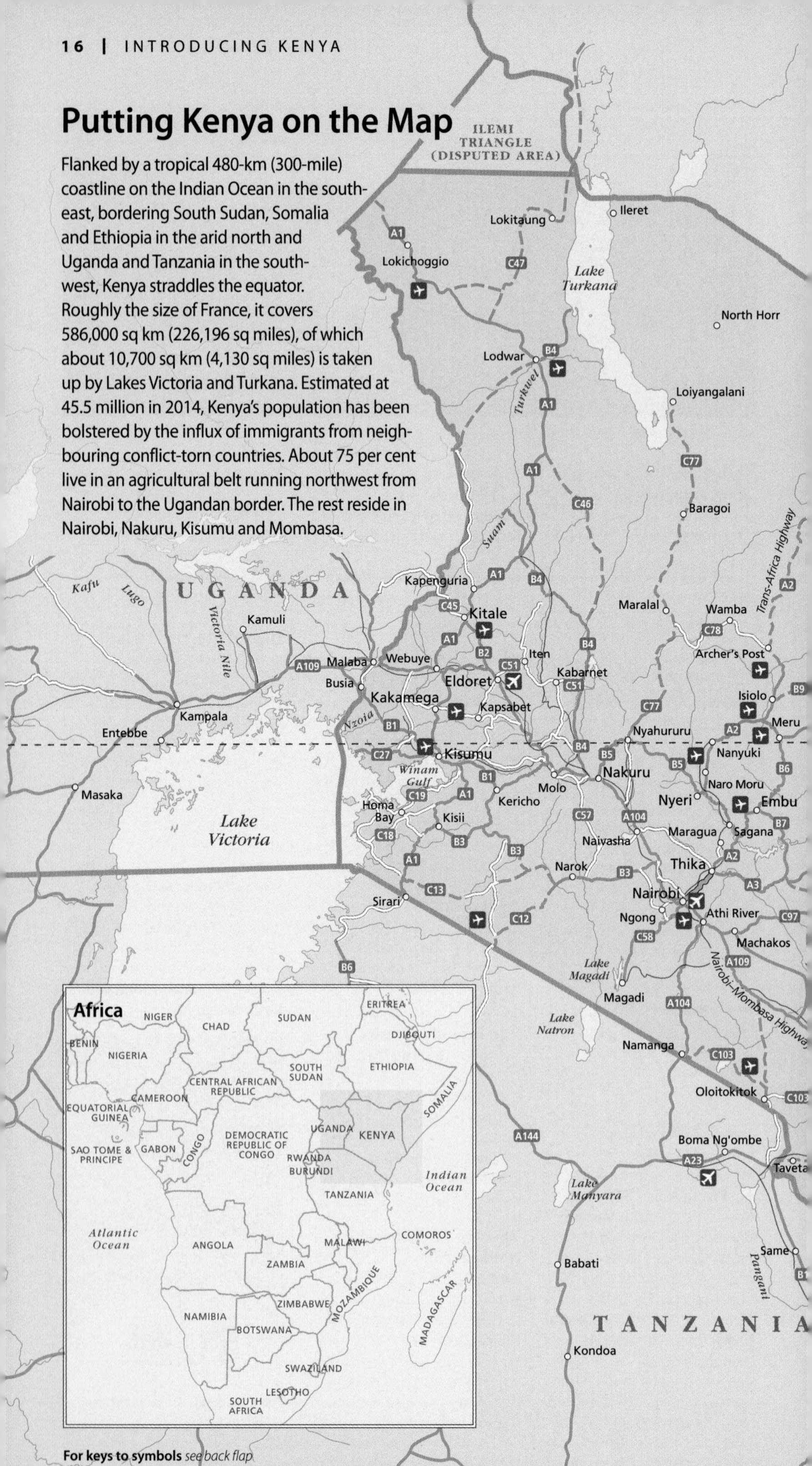

ILEMI TRIANGLE (DISPUTED AREA)

Lokitaung    Ileret

Lokichoggio    A1    C47    Lake Turkana

North Horr

Lodwar    B4    Loiyangalani

A1    C77

C46    Baragoi

Trans-Africa Highway

Kapenguria    A1    B4    Maralal    Wamba

Kamuli    Kitale    C45    C51    C78    Archer's Post

UGANDA    A1    B2    Iten    Kabarnet    Isiolo    B9

Malaba    Webuye    Eldoret    C51    C77    A2    Meru

A109    Busia    Kakamega    Kapsabet    Nyahururu    Nanyuki

Kampala    Victoria Nile    B1    Nzoia    B4    B5    B5    Naro Moru

Entebbe    C27    Kisumu    B1    Molo    Nakuru    Nyeri    Embu

Masaka    Winam Gulf    C19    Kericho    C57    A104    Sagana    B7

Homa Bay    Kisii    Naivasha    Maragua    A2

Lake Victoria    C18    B3    Narok    Thika    A3

A1    B3    Nairobi    C97

Sirari    C13    C12    Ngong    Athi River    Machakos

B6    C58    A109

Lake Magadi    Magadi    Nairobi–Mombasa Highway

A104

Lake Natron    Namanga    C103

A144    Oloitokitok    C103

Boma Ng'ombe    A23    Taveta

Lake Manyara    Pangani    Same

T A N Z A N I A    Kondoa

Kafu    Lugo    Kampala    Turkwel    Suam    B4

## Africa

NIGER    CHAD    SUDAN    ERITREA

BENIN    DJIBOUTI

NIGERIA    SOUTH SUDAN    ETHIOPIA

CENTRAL AFRICAN REPUBLIC

CAMEROON

EQUATORIAL GUINEA    UGANDA    KENYA    SOMALIA

SAO TOME & PRINCIPE    GABON    CONGO    DEMOCRATIC REPUBLIC OF CONGO    RWANDA    Indian Ocean

BURUNDI

TANZANIA    COMOROS

Atlantic Ocean    ANGOLA    MALAWI

ZAMBIA    MOZAMBIQUE    MADAGASCAR

ZIMBABWE

NAMIBIA    BOTSWANA

SWAZILAND

LESOTHO

SOUTH AFRICA

**For keys to symbols** see back flap.

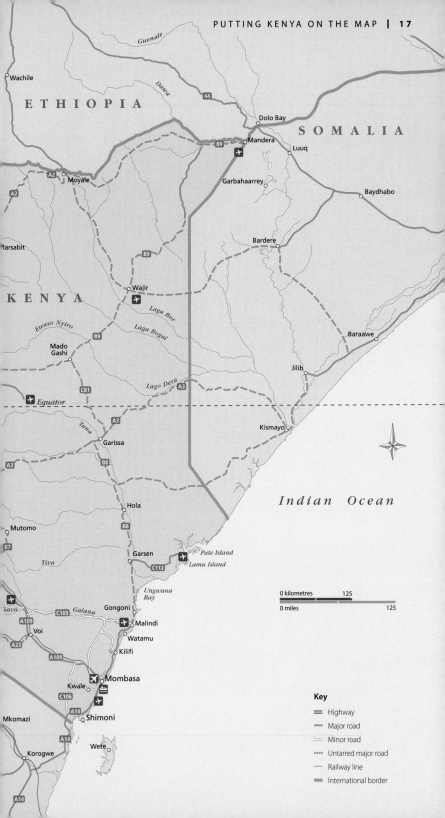

# A PORTRAIT OF KENYA

With outstanding natural beauty, prolific wildlife, a gorgeous tropical coastline and a gorgeous tropical coastline and a rich and diverse ethnic tapestry, Kenya has plenty to offer visitors. Thrilling safaris on the broad savannahs of the Rift Valley are the biggest draw, while the palm-backed white-sand beaches along the Indian Ocean coast are ideal for a relaxed holiday.

Covering a considerable chunk of East Africa, Kenya is neatly girthed across the middle by the equator and bisected by the southerly course of the jagged Rift Valley. The country has a varied altitude featuring lofty mountains and escarpments, open plains and stony deserts, fertile rolling hills and forested valleys and a beautiful 480-km (300-mile) tropical coastline. This wealth of natural habitat is protected in over 50 national parks and reserves, and many more private conservancies. Together, these cover about 10 per cent of the 580,400-sq-km (224,000-sq-mile) country. With the exception of the great apes, Kenya is home to a full complement of East African animals and is also one of the best places on the continent for bird-watching. The long sunny days and the azure Indian Ocean, with its colourful marine life, ensure a perfect environment for a laid-back holiday on the coast.

Kenya's character has been shaped by its long history, from the emergence of mankind some 6 million years ago to the colonial days of hunters, settlers and adventurers. Its rich ethnic heritage is evident from the traditionally dressed Maasai and Samburu people tending their livestock, while a long Swahili tradition has left its mark in the architecture and Islamic way of life on the coast and in the Kiswahili language.

A group of lionesses resting on a tree trunk

◄ Maasai men playing the game *bao* in a village in the Amboseli National Park, Rift Valley

Flamingoes congregating in the algae-rich waters of Lake Nakuru

## Land and Ecology

Kenya is a land rich in biodiversity. Its natural environment is split into many distinct zones, from rainforest, high moorland and wetlands to semidesert, thornbush scrub and grassland savannah. These habitats harbour over 7,000 species of plants and trees, more than 25,000 species of animals and in excess of 1,000 species of birds. This concentration and variety of flora and fauna is greater than that in many other African countries, owing largely to Kenya's two life-giving rainy seasons.

The impact of humans in this region dates back millions of years, and there is archaeological evidence to show the existence of hominids (early man). Over time, they were followed by migrant hunter-gatherer tribes, who roamed across the land in search of resources, and eventually pastoralists, who introduced agriculture. In the late 19th century, agriculture was boosted by the advent of European settlers, who were attracted by Kenya's climate and fertile soil. They laid out plantations and terraced fields in the verdant western hills and valleys. As a result, wildlife was forced into the agriculturally unproductive savannah, where big-game hunters depleted substantial herds of large animals. By the 1940s, the need to establish national wildlife reserves was recognized, not only to protect big game, but also to protect natural habitats and maintain large areas for water catchment.

Wildlife numbers were further decimated during the poaching scourge that plagued East Africa during the 1970s and 1980s. In 1989, President Moi set alight a huge stock of confiscated ivory (see p165) in a much publicized and successful bid to stamp out poaching; this contributed to a subsequent worldwide ban on ivory trade. Kenya Wildlife Service (KWS) was formed in 1990 to take on the poachers, and it now employs thousands of officers in game management, anti-poaching and conservation activities. Animal numbers have steadily increased in national parks and private conservancies, which have contributed to wildlife protection and increased the mobility of animals on migratory routes.

Rhino calf being fed at Lewa Wildlife Conservancy

## Economy

On becoming independent in 1963, Kenya had a good transport infrastructure and an economy dominated by agriculture. Today, it is one of the world's leading producers of tea and coffee and exports exotic vegetables and fresh flowers to Europe. In fact, Kenya is the world's largest exporter of roses, and tea alone generates an income of about US$1 billion.

In the 1970s, when long-haul destinations grew in popularity with European holiday-makers, tourism became increasingly important to the Kenyan economy. While Kenya once attracted fearless adventurers and big-game hunters, today its wildlife, natural attractions and location – only a 9-hour flight from Europe – ensure that it is one of East Africa's principal holiday destinations with a good tourism infrastructure that supports tens of thousands of jobs. In good years, tourism can earn Kenya in excess of US$1.2 billion, which makes the sector the country's biggest foreign exchange earner. Tourism experienced a slump after the terrorist bombings in Nairobi in 1998, and in Mombasa in 2002 as well as post-election violence in 2007, but the industry recovered quickly and, by 2011, Kenya received 1.2 million visitors. The sector continues to expand and visitors now have a greater choice of destinations and activities.

A tea picker at work near Kericho

Kenya's economy has experienced a number of cycles of growth followed by downturns and stagnation, caused by anything from drought to political instability and corruption. Nevertheless, given that Kenya does not rely on mineral wealth like other countries in the region and has been under pressure from an influx of refugees and conflits over its borders, its economic growth has been overall steady. Per capita income grew at least fourfold between 1975 and 2011. Kenya was removed from the International Monetary Fund's list of countries requiring debt relief in 2005, and today it is considered a self-sufficient developing nation. One of its most phenomenal success stories is the information and communication technology sector, taking into account its vibrant telecoms industry which pioneered mobile payments technology and exported the innovation across Africa and around the world. Nairobi, the capital, is now the primary communications and financial hub of East Africa. A wide range of foreign firms have branches in the city, and foreign investment in turn further supplements economic growth.

Hot-air balloon floating over the Masai Mara Game Reserve

## Government and Politics

Kenya is a republic and multiparty state with a unicameral National Assembly. The president is both head of state and head of government, and appoints the vice president and cabinet. From independence in 1963, Kenya's politics was dominated for nearly 40 years by the terms of two presidents. President Jomo Kenyatta, who governed from 1963 to 1978, is often referred to as the Father of the Nation for his contribution to Kenya's independence. His successor, Daniel arap Moi, governed from 1978 to 2002 but was criticized both for reverting Kenya to a one-party state for a time and for excessive corruption.

Maasai warriors performing a traditional dance

In 2002, Mwai Kibaki succeeded Moi as president, but his legitimacy was questioned when his 2007 election win was reputedly rigged and his main contender, Raila Odinga, was believed to be the legitimate winner. The dispute led to violence across the country, resulting in deaths and a downturn in the economy. The United Nations stepped in and by mid-2008 an agreement for a coalition government between Kibaki and Odinga had been negotiated and a new constitution was passed in 2010 that granted citizens a bill of rights. Uhuru Kenyatta, the son of Jomo Kenyatta, became Kenya's fourth president in 2013.

## People and Society

The diversity in Kenya's ethnic groups today is derived from a long history of migration, settlement and fusion of older cultures. Thousands of years ago, the Cushite, Bantu and Nilotic peoples roamed East Africa and settled into hunter-gatherer and pastoral communities. The first millennium saw the intermingling of Persians and Arabs with tribes on the coast, which gave rise to Swahili culture, while the 19th and 20th centuries witnessed the arrival of white settlers from Europe and indentured labour from India. Since the early 2000s, refugees from strife-torn, neighbouring Somalia and South Sudan have filtered into Kenya. Some indigenous communities retain a way of life in scattered settlements that has changed little over the centuries. Each group has its own social and political organization, and a deep sense of kinship that governs individual behaviour, rites of passage and marital customs.

Former President Mwai Kibaki inspects a guard of honour

By contrast, since the arrival of the colonists, many other ethnic groups have adopted a Western way of life. The result is a multicultural society, and while ethnic Africans dominate, there are pockets of Indian traders, farmers of European descent and a multinational community of businesspeople.

Kenya has one of the fastest rates of population growth in the world – since independence in 1963, the population has risen from nine million to an estimated 45.5 million. Settlements are distributed unevenly around the country, with the arid north being more sparsely populated than the fertile west. The urban population, about 25 per cent of the total, is concentrated in the cities of Nairobi, Mombasa, Nakuru and Kisumu.

Kenya's constitution guarantees freedom of worship, and a majority of Kenyans are actively religious. Christianity was introduced by early missionaries in the 19th century and today some 70 to 80 per cent of the population is Christian. Most are regular churchgoers and Protestant, Anglican and Roman Catholic churches

Friday prayers at Jamia Mosque, Nairobi

are prolific across the country. Islam was introduced during the centuries of trade with the Arabian Peninsula and people on the coast are mainly Muslim. There are also substantial communities of Hindus and Sikhs among the Indian populace in urban areas.

## Arts and Sports

In recent decades, Kenya has produced a number of internationally acclaimed musicians, writers and sportspeople. These include Kikuyu pop star Joseph Kamaru, who has sold over half a million records worldwide, and Ngũgĩ wa Thiong'o, a noted novelist and playwright since the 1960s.

The introduction of cricket, rugby and golf during the colonial years has made sport a popular activity among Kenyans. They love playing football, although the national team, Harambee Stars, has never qualified for the FIFA World Cup. However, Kenya is best known for its world-class distance runners. At the 2008 Beijing Olympics, Kenya scooped up 14 medals and at the 2012 London Olympics, they won 11 medals, including a gold in the men's 800 m (half a mile) by David Rudisha, the men's 3,000 m (2 miles) steeplechase and a silver in the men's marathon by Abel Kirui. Kenya also hosts the Lewa (Safaricom) Marathon (see p394). Other popular sports include car rallies, horse racing and deep-sea fishing events.

Athletes celebrating Kenya's victory at the 2008 Beijing Olympics

# The Landscape of Kenya

Kenya's regions all have markedly diverse landscapes. The coast is fringed with coral reefs and islands, backed by a gradually rising dry coastal plain of savannah and thorny bush. The country is neatly bisected from north to south by the Great Rift Valley, which is broad and shallow in the north and deepens further south where it is walled by towering escarpments. The arid north's flat expanse forms three-fifths of Kenya. By contrast, the Central Highlands support the Aberdares, Mount Kenya and many other mountains. Nairobi is located on a 1,500-m- (5,000-ft-) high plateau. West of the Rift Valley, savannah plains descend to Lake Victoria.

**The pristine coral reefs** that stretch along the palm-lined beaches of the coast are among Kenya's biggest attractions.

## Indian Ocean Coastline

Kenya's tropical coastline boasts a string of fine, palm-backed beaches with soft white sands, gentle breezes and mangrove forests. The colourful offshore reefs are home to a host of marine life, while the temperate waters offer good diving and snorkelling. A wide variety of wildlife inhabits the coastal forests.

## Western Escarpments

Western Kenya's Rift Valley, characterized by its cliffs and escarpments, is home to several soda lakes fringed with pink thanks to the flocks of flamingoes that feast there on fish and algae. The escarpments give rise to gentle hills and bright-green tea plantations, which descend to the sandy shores of Lake Victoria.

**Mangrove forests** cover some 40 per cent of the coast. This salt-tolerant tree is found on sheltered shores and deep into river estuaries.

**The lilac-breasted roller** has a distinctive bold white forehead with a pale-purple chest and throat. Fairly common, it can be seen on bare branches in dry, open woodland.

**Sea turtles** nest at a number of sites along the coast. The females dig holes with their flippers and lay as many as 100 eggs at a time.

**Tea**, an important export commodity, is grown in the highland areas near the Rift Valley at altitudes above 1,500 m (4,900 ft).

**Starfish**, urchins, parrotfish, lionfish and angelfish are some of the more colourful marine species that inhabit Kenya's coral reefs.

**Acacia trees** are straight-stemmed evergreen forest trees with broad branches and dense, glossy foliage. They are a popular habitat for leopards.

## Northern Deserts

The north of Kenya is a region of arid, stony, sun-baked deserts, where the people live a harsh existence. This is Kenya at its wildest. Across the shimmering Chalbi Desert lies Lake Turkana, often called the Jade Sea due to its brilliantly turquoise waters, which are surrounded by a lunar landscape of extinct volcanoes and lava beds.

**Camels** are kept by nomadic pastoralists in the north. They are used to carry goods between remote settlements that trucks cannot reach.

**The gerenuk** is one of a number of desert-adapted animals that are not found in the south of Kenya. An unusual antelope, it stands on its hind legs to feed on thorn trees.

**Crocodiles** are abundant in Lake Turkana. The lake's Central Island, in particular, is a favourite breeding ground.

## Central Highlands

A temperate plateau of lush agricultural and game-rich land, the Central Highlands lie on the lower slopes of Mount Kenya, Africa's second highest mountain. Laikipia Plateau consists of grasslands and dense cedar and olive forests, while the Aberdares have a landscape of undulating moors and primeval forests.

**The giant lobelia** is a plant that only grows at high altitudes on the slopes of East Africa's mountains. When in bloom, it produces numerous greenish-white flowers.

**The bongo** is a shy mountain antelope with a reddish coat that has distinctive white stripes. It lives in bamboo forests and swampy glades.

**Red hot pokers**, with their distinct vibrant colours, can be frequently seen in mountain glades after the long rains.

## Southern Savannahs

The most popular region for safari trips, southern Kenya has the largest reserves in the country, which are home to a full host of East African animals. Tsavo and Amboseli are famous for great herds of elephant while the Masai Mara has gentle undulating hills and riverine forests along the Mara river.

**Wildebeest** move around the Masai Mara's southern plains in an annual migration in search of fresh pasture.

**Secretary birds**, often seen on open plains, may be named for the plumes on their crest, which resemble quills tucked behind the ears of old-fashioned secretaries.

**Whistling thorn acacia** stud the open grasslands. Ants pierce the thorns with tiny holes, which make a whistling sound when the wind blows through them.

# The Great Rift Valley

A geographical and geological fissure, the Great Rift Valley extends approximately 8,700 km (5,400 miles) from Lebanon to the lower Zambezi River Valley in Mozambique. The valley was formed by a rifting of the earth's crust some 10–20 million years ago, which forced up volcanic activity that altered the landscape. Its width varies from about 30 km (19 miles) to 150 km (93 miles) across. It is an important archaeological site, and fossils of bones of animals and early humans have been found at several places in the Rift Valley; the high alkaline level in the soil and sediments of volcanic ash are ideal components in the process of fossilization.

**Key**
■ The Great Rift Valley

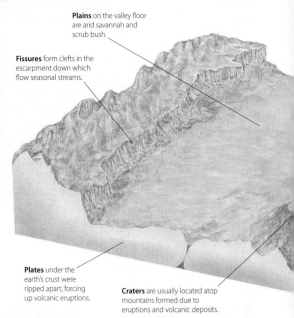

**Plains** on the valley floor are arid savannah and scrub bush.

**Fissures** form clefts in the escarpment down which flow seasonal streams.

**Flamingoes** are attracted to feed on the algae in the Rift Valley lakes. Many lakes contain high levels of sodium carbonate caused by alkalinity from the surrounding volcanic rock and evaporation.

**Plates** under the earth's crust were ripped apart, forcing up volcanic eruptions.

**Craters** are usually located atop mountains formed due to eruptions and volcanic deposits.

**The bubbling geysers and steam jets** that line the shores of Lake Bogoria are caused when water is heated close to boiling point by volcanic gas and hot rocks underground.

**Mount Elgon** is an extinct volcano on the Kenya–Uganda border and, at about 15 million years, is thought to be the oldest volcano overshadowing East Africa's Rift Valley. Of its several peaks, the 4,321-m (14,178-ft) Wagagai is the highest.

**Menengai Crater**, located on the floor of the Rift Valley just outside Nakuru, is a 2,490-m- (8,167-ft-) high extinct volcano. Its last eruption is thought to have occurred around 7,000 BC.

## Tectonic Activity

*The earth's crust and lithosphere were pulled apart by violent subterranean forces which forced down chunks of rock below parallel fault lines, and forced up molten rock in volcanic eruptions. The result was cliffs and mountains rimming the valley floor, which over time gradually sank into a low flat plain studded with craters, small scarps and lakes.*

**Lake Magadi** is a saline lake which produces a dense sodium carbonate brine that can, in places, be up to 40 m (130 ft) thick. Several geothermal hot springs feed the lake.

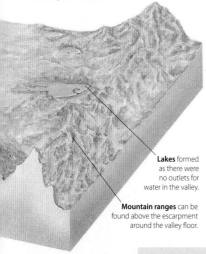

**Lakes** formed as there were no outlets for water in the valley.

**Mountain ranges** can be found above the escarpment around the valley floor.

**Central Island**, a dramatic extinct volcano created by the Rift Valley, rises from the middle of picturesque Lake Turkana. It has three distinct vents, two of which have formed lakes.

## Kenya's Rift Valley

The Rift Valley neatly divides Kenya down its length from the Ethiopian border in the north to the Tanzania border in the south. The valley is characterized by uninhabitable desert in the north, fertile farmland in the middle and flat arid plains to the south. The valley floor is at its lowest near Lake Turkana where there is virtually no distinction between the Great Rift and the surrounding desert, but as it heads south, the valley walls form sheer inward-facing escarpments rising to a height of 600–900 m (2,000–3,000 ft). A number of active and semi-active volcanoes are evidence of volcanic activity in the valley.

**Mount Longonot**, a 2,890-m (9,466-ft) dormant volcano near Naivasha, is lined with spectacular fissures and lava canyons.

The arid landscape of the northern deserts

The farmlands of the Southern Rift Valley

The plains of the southern savannahs

# Indigenous Peoples of Kenya

Kenya has more than 40 major ethnic groups, with several smaller tribes assimilated within them. These tribes range in size from more than seven million Kikuyu people to fewer than 500 Elmolo. All remain firmly rooted in tribal tradition. They can be broadly divided into three linguistic groups – the Bantu, Nilotic and Cushite. Most arrived in this region in tribal migrations from other parts of Africa from AD 1000. The main groups are the Kikuyu, Kalenjin, Meru, Luhya, Luo, Kisii, Kamba, Maasai, Samburu and Turkana. Since the colonial years, some have imbibed the conveniences of the West while other remote tribes remain untouched by the modern world.

A vibrant canvas depicting the indigenous people of Kenya

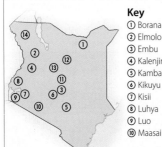

## Key

① Borana
② Elmolo
③ Embu
④ Kalenjin
⑤ Kamba
⑥ Kikuyu
⑦ Kisii
⑧ Luhya
⑨ Luo
⑩ Maasai
⑪ Meru
⑫ Rendille
⑬ Samburu
⑭ Turkana

## Distribution of Ethnic Groups

Thousands of years of migration and displacement caused by colonial land reallocation means that most ethnic groups are centred around specific regions of Kenya. The livelihoods of these groups depend on their environments. Generally, the tribal groups living in the fertile highlands tend to be farmers, while those living on the drier, flat plains of the north tend to be pastoralists.

## Borana

A subgroup of Ethiopia's Oromo people, the Borana *(see p341)* arrived from southern Ethiopia in the early 20th century and settled in the region around Marsabit and Isiolo in Northern Kenya. For this nomadic herding group, life revolves around their livestock. Houses of interwoven branches thatched with grass are built by the women, and villages move as much as 100 km (60 miles) a year to follow fresh pasture and rain. However, conflict with the Rendille and other groups in the region over meagre resources for their cattle has caused the Borana to retreat to safer areas near the towns. Many of their settlements have been abandoned and only armed herdsmen and warriors now accompany their livestock in the wilderness of Kenya's extreme north.

Young Borana in striking attire

Elmolo men building a dried weed hut

## Elmolo

A Cushitic people closely related to the Rendille, Kenya's smallest ethnic group lives on the shores of Lake Turkana at Loiyangalani. The Elmolo *(see p340)* are one of the last hunter-gatherer peoples still in existence, although, through intermarriage, their population has largely been absorbed into the Turkana and Samburu groups. Their livelihoods are largely based on fishing, using nets cast from simple log canoes. Traditionally, villages were made up of clusters of rounded huts built from dried lake weed, but these are gradually being replaced by concrete structures.

## Embu

Traditionally, the Embu occupied the southeastern lower slopes of Mount Kenya around the town of Embu. They are believed to have migrated from the Congo Basin during the 16th century and may have reached as far as the coast, but it is possible that a conflict with the Arab slave traders forced them to retreat to the interior. The family unit is very central to the Embu, and the importance of having daughters suggests that the society was originally matriarchal. They are predominantly agriculturists and well known as bee-keepers.

Embu couple in their colourful clothing

## Kalenjin

Kalenjin woman outside her thatched mud hut

Comprising a group of people formerly called the Nandi by the British, the Kalenjin include the Kipsigis, Nandi, Marakwet, Tugen, Keiyo, Pokot, Terik and Sabaot, all of whom speak mostly the same language but in different dialects. While they were formerly known individually, the Kalenjin groups united in response to colonialism to advocate their interests to the British government. The Kalenjin live in small communities of settled farmers mainly clustered on the western edge of the Rift Valley and make up about 12 per cent of Kenya's population. They have been dubbed the running tribe as, since the mid-1960s, the majority of successful Kenyan runners have been Kalenjin (see p297).

## Kamba

This indigenous group generally inhabits the largely semiarid hills north of the Nairobi–Mombasa Highway, between Nairobi and Mount Kenya and eastwards towards Tsavo East National Park. The Kamba were involved in the Omani slave and ivory trade as middlemen in the 18th century due to their proximity to the coast. Today, they are known for their wood carving skills, and for eking out an agricultural living from their relatively unfertile lands.

Young Kamba women working their land

## Kikuyu

Kikuyu woman with an elaborate headdress

Believed to have arrived in the area around Mount Kenya during the Bantu migrations between the 14th and 16th centuries, the Kikuyu (see pp314–15) are the largest of Kenya's ethnic groups and make up over 20 per cent of the total population. According to Kikuyu legend, their founder Gikuyu was told by their god Ngai to build a house on the slopes of Kirinyaga (Mountain of Brightness), the Kikuyu name for Mount Kenya.

The Kikuyu were the first among the tribes to join the political system. They formed the Kikuyu Association in 1920 and played an active role in Kenya's struggle for independence. Kenya's first president, Jomo Kenyatta, was a Kikuyu.

## Kisii

Based around the town of the same name in Western Kenya, the Kisii (also known as the Gusii) are a Bantu group which originally migrated from the region that is now the Democratic Republic of the Congo. They ended up in a geographical location unique among Bantu groups in that they were surrounded on all sides by Nilotic-speaking communities. As a result they developed an almost warlike culture to defend themselves against cattle-raiding neighbours, and to this day, they have a reputation for being resilient and

Women crafting intricate soapstone figures

very industrious. The region is one of the most economically active in Kenya, blessed with rolling tea, coffee and banana plantations, and the Kisii are well known for fashioning soapstone into outstanding craft items, which are popular as souvenirs with visitors to Kenya.

Luhya woman at the village market

## Luhya

The second-largest indigenous group after the Kikuyu, the Luhya make up 17 per cent of Kenya's population. Luhya society is structured around an extremely complex system of clans and subclans. They come from the west between Lake Victoria, Mount Elgon and the Ugandan border, which is one of the most densely populated regions of Kenya. Traditionally agriculturalists, today the Luhya produce a number of cash crops such as tea, cassava and maize. They are also known for their thatching and weaving skills. One of the best-known Luhya customs, bullfighting, still thrives today.

## Luo

Kenya's third-largest ethnic group, the Luo, constitute about 14 per cent of its population. They inhabit the far west around the shores of Lake Victoria and are traditionally agriculturists and fishermen. The elders control family compounds. Unlike other tribal groups in Kenya, the Luo were not dispossessed of their land on a large scale during colonial times, and eventually adopted the English language and British-style dress and education. Along with the Kikuyu, with whom they shared major political power in the early years of Kenyan independence, the Luo continue to hold positions of power and political influence in the country.

Luo men in their fishing boats

A Maasai warrior dance

## Maasai

Mostly inhabiting southern Kenya and northern Tanzania, the pastoral Maasai *(see pp258–9)* make up about 2 per cent of Kenya's population and are traditional nomadic herdsmen, although this is getting increasingly difficult in modern times. Their herds dominate all aspects of their lives as they believe that back in time when the earth and sky split, the rain god gave them all the cattle for safekeeping. They have successfully conserved their ethnic identity and continue to wear striking body decorations. Women are famous for their beaded jewellery while men typically wear a red checked *shuka* (robe). A Maasai homestead is a *manyatta (see pp260–61)*, a group of low huts made of bent branches daubed with dried mud.

## Meru

Accounting for 5 per cent of the total tribal population of Kenya, the Meru comprise eight subgroups of people who migrated to the northeast side of Mount Kenya around the 14th century. Originally governed together by a council of elected elders, the Meru were perhaps the only democratic society in precolonial Africa. Their complicated mythology shows many similarities to the story of the birth of Christ, leading to the theory that they may have been a lost tribe of Israel. Today, they occupy some of the country's richest farmland and grow several cash crops.

A Meru drummer tapping a rhythm on his log drum

## Rendille

A Rendille elder with his camel

A pastoralist nomadic people, the Rendille live in small communities in the harsh rocky terrain of northeast Kenya around the Kaisut Desert. Camels are central to most aspects of their lives, and are relied on for many of the Rendille's daily needs, such as milk, food, trade and transport. Traditionally, the Rendille lived in semipermanent villages that were moved several times a year. The area they inhabit is one of the country's most unforgiving regions and drought and overgrazing have turned settlements into wastelands, forcing many Rendille to abandon their nomadic way of life in favour of more permanent settlements. Despite linguistic differences, they maintain kinship and economic cooperation with their Samburu neighbours to the southwest.

## Samburu

Closely related to the Maasai and with an almost identical language, the Samburu *(see p351)* inhabit the northern foothills of Mount Kenya in the 21,000-sq-km (8,000-sq-mile) Samburu district. They are seminomadic pastoralists whose mainstay is rearing cows, sheep, goats and camels. Like the Maasai, they have retained their traditional dress and wear striking bright robes, colourful multibeaded necklaces, bracelets and earrings.

Samburu girls wearing bead necklaces

## Turkana

A group dance performed on social occasions

Another pastoralist group, the Turkana *(see p341)* live a harsh existence around Lake Turkana in arid and hostile Northern Kenya. Their livelihood comes chiefly from raising cattle, camels and goats, and fishing in the lake. Of all Kenya's peoples, they are the most isolated and least affected by the modern world. Turkana women often wear plate-like bead necklaces or an aluminium or brass neck ring, while the men cover their hair with mud and ostrich feathers. Men also carry tiny *ekicholongs* (wooden stools) that are used as simple chairs to sit on the hot sand and also double as headrests while sleeping.

# Traditional Dress

There are myriad ethnic groups in Kenya, many of whom adopted Western clothing during the colonial era. Some, however, retained their ethnic attire. Most notably, these include the Maasai and Samburu, whose bright and colourful robes, beaded jewellery and body decoration leave a lasting impression on any visit to the country. In recent years, there has been some effort to introduce a national dress in order to identify the Kenyan people. For example, some government ministers have swapped their plain grey suits for more traditional African tailored outfits.

A tailor at work over bales of floral printed *kitenge* cloth

## Dress

*On top of their everyday clothing, most Kenyans carry an additional piece or two of cloth, which can be worn in many different ways. These are sold across the country, and open markets especially have colourful reams of cloth hanging from stalls. The two most popular streets in Kenya for cloth shops are both called Biashara Street, one in Nairobi and the other in Mombasa.*

The **bui-bui**, worn by Swahili Muslim women, is a long black cloak with matching headdress and veil that covers the body from head to foot.

**The cloth** is brightly coloured and decorated with a variety of patterns.

**The kanga's border**, called *pindo*, has a different design from the cloth's centre (*mji*).

**The *kanga***, usually worn by women, is a length of cloth that is either tied around the chest or waist or used like a headscarf or baby's sling. The hem is sometimes printed with Swahili proverbs, which can be messages of caution, love, reassurance or just acts of self-expression.

**A *shuka*** is a red piece of cloth or, in more modern times, a red blanket, worn by Maasai men, wrapped around the waist and then thrown over one shoulder.

**Kikoys, the traditional garb of Swahili men**, are made from a fringed piece of woven cotton, usually in pastel shades and stripes. New ones are washed in the sea to preserve their colours.

**The *kitenge*** is a multicoloured cotton fabric with a wax-resist print, worn in a similar way to the *kanga*. The various colours, patterns, writings and symbols on the cloth represent a variety of moods, feelings, cultures and traditions.

## Adornment

*Many of Kenya's ethnic groups incorporate body or hair adornment in their dress. The combination of beaded jewellery, body paint, intricate hair braiding and decorated clothing can be visually very striking. Some items are also worn to signify certain stages in life.*

**Beaded necklaces** are a prominent part of a Samburu girl's attire. Given by admirers, these necklaces are accumulated till they form a collar that can support the chin, and only then is a girl deemed old enough to marry. Once married, women carry a metal cross on their headbands.

**The jewellery of the Elmolo and Turkana peoples** around Lake Turkana is made of beads and also incorporates items from the lake, such as fish bones and teeth. Unmarried girls wear soft goatskin aprons covered with pieces of ostrich egg.

**Elaborate hair braiding** is seen among Samburu warriors, who place great significance on physical appearance. They also use ochre body paint to embellish their skin.

**Ostrich feather headdresses** are often worn in ceremonies by Maasai *moran* – warriors who have not yet killed a lion.

**Akalas** are rugged sandals worn by the Maasai to protect their feet from thorns. Also called "thousand milers", they are made from old car tyres but are surprisingly comfortable.

## Beads

Beading symbolizes beauty, age, marriage and social status. It dates back to around 1850, when Arab traders imported tiny glass beads to the East African coast. There are some 40 varieties of beadwork and the most common colours are red (the preferred colour of the Maasai), blue (for the sky), white (for milk) and green (for fresh grass). Beads are also used to demonstrate feelings. Girls often give armbands as a sign of love to warriors, and brides wear large disclike necklaces to present their beauty to their new husband. A boy who is to be initiated receives a beaded pendant known as *surutia* from his mother. After the initiation he returns this to her, and she wears it proudly for the rest of her life as a sign of her son's status.

Beaded necklaces worn by Maasai

**Large brass-hoop earrings** are worn by Pokot women to signify they are married. Pokot men arrange their hair into a bun and cover it with blue clay.

# Religion in Kenya

Most of the tribes in Kenya worshipped a supreme being known by various names but often referred to as Ngai, who was revered for bringing rain. These traditional religions declined when Christian missionaries arrived in the 19th century. Today, about 80 per cent of Kenya's population is Christian, predominantly Anglican or Roman Catholic and, increasingly, Pentecostal. Along the Swahili coast, much of the population follows Islam, as does most of Kenya's Asian community. There is also a small number who follow Hinduism and Sikhism.

Ethiopian painting in a local church, Kalacha

### Christianity

The first missionary to arrive in Kenya was Johann Ludwig Krapf in 1846. The East African coast was still under the administration of the Zanzibar Sultanate and Sultan Seyyid Sa'id permitted Krapf to establish a mission station in Mombasa in 1846. The interior was opened up to Christian missionaries with the building of the Uganda Railway from Mombasa to Kampala at the turn of the 20th century. By the 1920–30s churches had been built across the country, and by the 1950s the Bible had been translated into the Luo and Swahili languages.

**German missionary Johann Ludwig Krapf** is credited with setting up the Kenya Anglican Church. He compiled the first Kiswahili dictionary and translated sections of the Bible into this language.

**The Minor Basilica Holy Family Cathedral**, built in 1960, is Nairobi's largest church and the seat of the Archbishop of Nairobi. A modern building with large multipane stained-glass windows, the cathedral houses one main altar and eight chapels, and can seat up to 4,000 people. Mass is celebrated every day.

**Pentecostal churches** have been drawing crowds for evangelical events, especially in Nairobi. The trend is attracting preachers from the USA, who are joining the local clergy in preaching redemption to growing congregations.

### Islam

Islam is practised, by and large, by the Swahili people on the coast, as well as by the Somali people in the northeast of Kenya and Asian immigrants in the cities. It was introduced on the coast in the 8th century by Arab traders and it is believed that many black Africans converted to Islam in order to avoid being sold as slaves.

**Mosques** are prolific in the old trading towns along the coast such as Lamu, which has as many as 40 mosques in just a small grid of streets.

**The Maulidi Festival**, held on Lamu Island each year, celebrates Prophet Mohammed's birthday and is a festival of solemn prayer. There are also colourful processions and other events, such as donkey and swimming races, held on this occasion.

## Traditional Religion

Before the arrival of Christianity, most traditional religions celebrated one god, who was the creator of earth and brought rain, which in turn provided grass, plants, animals and prosperity. People would both pray for good rain and make sacrifices to the god to appease him during drought, famine, disease and death. He, and sometimes she, was manifested in the sun, moon, thunder and lightning, stars, mountains and in trees, especially the wild fig tree, under which sacrifices were made. Another common belief is in spirit beings, who are believed to reside in powerful places, with soothsayers and witch doctors often acting as intermediaries.

**The Kikuyu god**, also referred to as Ngai, is said to rest on Mount Kenya when he visits earth. Traditionally, the Kikuyu build their houses with their front doors facing the mountain and the dead are buried with their heads pointing towards the revered peak.

**Cattle** are central to the existence of the Maasai. Legend has it that the earth and sky separated and their god Ngai entrusted all the cattle to the Maasai people to look after. Any pursuit other than a pastoral one is considered insulting to Ngai and demeaning to the Maasai.

## Other Religions

Hinduism is only practised by a small minority in Kenya. The religion was introduced when the British brought indentured labour from India to build the Uganda Railway in the late 19th and early 20th centuries. Today, there are Hindu temples in all the major cities and many Sikh gurdwaras built and run by the Ramgarhia Sikh community of Kenya. Both Mombasa and Nairobi also have ornate Jain temples.

**The Sikh gurdwara** at Makindu was built in 1926 by Sikh railway workers. Set in a peaceful patch of woodland about 160 km (100 miles) south of Nairobi on the Nairobi–Mombasa Highway, it still serves as a rest house for both pilgrims and occasional visitors to this popular site.

**The Shri Swaminarayan Mandir** was built in Nairobi in 1999 using 350 tonnes (385 tons) of yellow stone mined near Rajasthan in India and shipped to Kenya. It has an impressive interior of intricately carved wood.

**Mombasa's Jain temple**, completed in 1963, was the first to be built outside India. The temple's dome is topped by a spire of gold and its doors are made of solid silver. Its interior is decorated with sculptures and figures of Jain deities.

# Music and Dance

Kenya's music was originally centred around chanting, drumming and dance, and it played a large role in such ceremonies as initiations and weddings. With the onset of Christianity, these musical traditions were largely replaced by gospel music. The 1950s saw the arrival of the electric guitar, and with it new genres of music and dance. These include Benga music, which has strong elements of social and political criticism, and Congolese pop music, with its distinctive rumba rhythm. Many groups from the Democratic Republic of the Congo made Nairobi their home, and their influence remains a key feature of Kenya's dance music. Today, Kenya's youth enjoy the same current music trends as their contemporaries around the world.

Popular Kenyan group, Gospel Fathers, at Kikwetu Musical Festival

### Dance in Kenya

*Most Kenyans enjoy dancing at ceremonies and church services. Young Kenyans prefer nightclubs, which are popular in Nairobi and Mombasa. Many hotels along the coast and in the national parks arrange traditional and contemporary dance and acrobatic performances by local troupes.*

**Acrobats** are very popular in Kenya, performing as roadside buskers and entertainers in hotels. Many travel as part of international professional troupes.

**The Sarakasi Trust** is the largest performing arts organization in East Africa. It teaches a range of disciplines including acrobatics, cabaret, salsa, drumming and traditional and contemporary dance styles.

**Deep rhythmic chanting** and vertical leaps in the air are part of the *Engilakinoto*, a Maasai ceremony that conventionally followed a successful lion hunt.

## Traditional instruments

*Kenya's wide variety of traditional instruments are made from a number of materials including wood, animal hide, horn and reed.*

**A nyatiti** is an eight-stringed instrument with a curved arm that is plucked. It is similar to a medieval lyre.

**A siwa** is a large curved, ornately carved flute capped with a bull's horn. It is used in Lamu during local festivities and events. Two *siwas* in Lamu Museum, one of brass and one of ivory, date from the 17th century and are thought to be the oldest musical instruments in East Africa.

**Drums** are mostly large and round with taut cow- or goat-hide skins. They can be played while seated or standing. On the coast, smaller drums are held under the arm and are rapped with a curved stick.

## Music in Kenya

*Modern Kenyan music is the fusion of a number of different styles, including ethnic folk music, lively pop music from Central Africa, as well as eastern and Arabian sounds from the coast. Kenyans enjoy live music and there is no shortage of venues for large concerts in Nairobi and Mombasa.*

**Benga music** originated in Nairobi and is a mix of Luo folk music and modern instruments. It is characterized by vocals, bass rhythms, clear guitar riffs and percussion.

**The Kisima Music Awards**, held annually in Nairobi, are East Africa's equivalent of the Grammys. The awards night attracts thousands and is broadcast across Africa on television.

**Joseph Kamaru** is one of Kenya's most successful gospel singers. His earlier music made skilful use of Kikuyu proverbs and was often politically charged.

**The African Children's Choir**, comprising young orphaned children aged between 7 and 12, is assembled each year for a world tour of over 50 cities.

**Gospel music** has risen in popularity since the mid-90s. It is sung by large choirs and features African rhythms and melodies and European harmonic influences.

**Taarab** is a style of music on the coast that combines poetic Kiswahili lyrics and Arabian rhythms using percussion instruments and vocals. Modern *taarab* is similar to Bollywood movie music.

### Unbeatable

Kenya's 2002 election victory by Mwai Kibaki's National Rainbow Coalition (NARC) was largely driven by a single song. "Unbwogable", sung by the hip-hop duo Gidi Gidi Maji Maji, means unbeatable

**Gidi Gidi at Festival Mundail in Holland**

in Luo and was adopted by NARC as the party's campaign anthem. Written in three languages – Luo, English and Kiswahili – the song has lyrics that call for people to rise up and demand change.

**Soukous music** originated in the Democratic Republic of the Congo. In Kenya, it is called Lingala. The music has upbeat danceable rhythms, and is usually accompanied by female dancers.

# Arts and Crafts

Kenya's earliest art is found in caves and was made by ancient nomads. However, painting and other types of visual art were largely introduced by the colonialists. Body art and adornment are important among some of Kenya's people and emphasize social status as well as stages of initiation and rites of passage. The art of carving has been practised in Kenya for centuries and sculptors use indigenous wood, stone and metal to produce both functional and decorative items.

A display of handicrafts at a souvenir shop, Nairobi

### Carving

*Many carved items such as pots, neck pillows (wooden headrests), walking sticks and chests are used by Kenyans in everyday life. The Kamba people, who have long been known as skilled woodworkers, produce carved animals and masks, which are immensely popular. Carving on the coast is centred on the island of Lamu, where the local people have been influenced by Arab craftsmen to create a unique hybrid of styles.*

**Tribal masks** were originally used to ward off evil spirits and scare away enemies. Today, many are produced as decorative wall hangings.

**Lamu's doors** are intricately patterned with carvings. In the Swahili tradition, the greater the wealth and social standing of the inhabitant of the house, the more elaborate the front door. Some date to the late 18th century and are inscribed with Koranic verses.

**Makonde ebony carvings** are black and brown or wholly black. With its origins in Tanzania, this contemporary art specializes in abstract and elongated human figures. A tree of life depicts an entire family in one striking single pose.

### Stone and Clay

*Soapstone, or Kisii stone, was originally carved into vessels as it holds water well. Today, it is fashioned into a wide variety of souvenirs. The quarrying, carving and polishing of the stone are all done by hand. Western Kenya's red earth provides clay to make pots, which are usually made by women using centuries-old methods of shaping, decorating and firing in charcoal ovens.*

**Clay pots** are used for carrying water, storing millet and cereals, as cooking utensils and even for keeping bees.

**Soapstone decorative boxes** are sculpted by the Gusii (or Kisii) people. Designs are created by dyeing the stone with ink, paint, or shoe polish, then sealing the colour with beeswax and finally incising the surface in patterns, which allow the natural lighter colour of the stone to come through.

## Textiles and Weaving

*Textiles produced in Kenya are usually worn as traditional dress (see p32). Women wear two-piece sets of kangas as a wraparound skirt and shawl or scarf, while men on the coast wear cotton kikoys. Weaving, done by women, is most often used to make baskets, but palm leaves, dyed in shades of purple, are also woven into narrow strips and sewn together to make attractive sleeping mats, as well as place mats and coasters.*

**Woven baskets**, once made from fibres of baobab and wild fig trees, and nowadays from sisal, were traditionally carried by Kikuyu women behind their heads with the strap across their forehead.

**Batik**, an Indonesian-Malay word for the wax-resist dyeing of fabric, is characterized by deep rich colours and fine crinkly lines, which are the result of breaks in the layers of wax applied to the cloth. This technique arrived on the African coast during the Indian Ocean trade period.

## Visual Art

*Painting on walls using natural pigments existed for centuries, as witnessed in the many rock paintings found in caves and archaeological sites all over Kenya. The development of painting on canvas, however, only began when foreign artists and missionaries arrived during the colonial era and influenced Kenyan artists to use this medium.*

**Gakunju Kaigwa's** sculpture, *Wings of Love* (1998), draws its inspiration from traditional and contemporary life in Kenya. The acclaimed artist makes detailed sculptures of people and animals.

**Jimmy Ogonga's** most famous sculpture, *Dancing with the Enemy* (2000), was created using jacaranda wood. As well as sculpture, Ogonga's art includes painting, film, printmaking and photography.

**Peter Beard's collages** of Kenya often feature elephants, crocodiles and rhinos. An avant-garde American photographer, he was left an archive of photographs and journals by Karen Blixen *(see p173)*; many feature in his collages.

### Joy Adamson's Art

One of several portraits of Kenya's ethnic people, by Joy Adamson

One of colonial Kenya's best-known names, Joy Adamson became famous for her memoir on hand-rearing a lioness named Elsa. Few people know she was also an accomplished self-taught artist and produced many paintings that document much of Kenya's flora. She was commissioned by the government to paint over 600 portraits of Kenya's tribes in their traditional dress. These now hang in Nairobi's State House and the National Museum *(see pp162–3)* and remain an important testament to Kenya's rich cultural history.

# Kenyan Literature

In Kenya, the oldest way of passing on stories from one generation to the next is through the narration of (often moralistic) tales. Written literature, in Kenyan languages as well as English, began in the early 20th century when missionaries, and later colonialists, introduced formal education. Many of the white settlers became world-renowned authors, and much has been written about the events and characters of the colonial days. *Out of Africa* by Isak Dinesen – the pseudonym of Karen Blixen – is probably the best known such book about Kenya. Independence in the 1960s unleashed a wave of unrestricted Kenyan writing and today Kenya has literary associations and home-grown book awards that encourage contemporary writing.

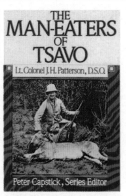

The Man-Eaters of Tsavo featuring author J H Patterson on the cover

## African Writing

Swahili prose and poetry date back to the early 18th century. The oldest known document in the language is "Utenzi wa Tambuka" (Story of Tambuka), an epic poem penned in a royal palace on Pate Island in 1728. It is about the Byzantine, Arab and Ottoman wars across Europe and Arabia from 628 to 1453. By the middle of the 19th century, the first Kiswahili dictionary had been compiled and Bible translated.

The first published writings by Kenyan authors were born out of the experience of colonialism and the struggle for independence. One of Kenya's best-known authors from this time, Ngũgĩ wa Thiong'o, is also the first East

Ngũgĩ wa Thiong'o's epic work *Wizard of the Crow*

African author to have a novel published. His book, *Weep Not Child,* was published in 1964 and deals with how the lives of Kenya's Kikuyu people changed after independence. In the late 1970s, Ngũgĩ was imprisoned for a year because of his politically outspoken play-writing, of which the Moi government disapproved. In 2006, he published *Murogi wa Kagogo* (Wizard of the Crow), an epic novel written in the Kikuyu language about 20th-century dictatorship in developing countries. Six volumes long, it is the biggest book ever written in an African language.

Former Kenyan Culture Minister and United Nations Ambassador, Grace Ogot, has written several novels and short stories, many of which are set against the scenic backdrop of Lake Victoria and the traditions of the Luo people. Meja Mwangi, assistant director on the movie *Out of Africa*, is another prolific writer who is best known for his gritty urban tale, *Going Down River Road* (1976).

## Colonial Literature

With the arrival of the hunters and explorers in the mid-19th century, and later the white settlers, several books about their fearless escapades in the fledgling colony of Kenya were published. *The Man-Eaters of Tsavo* (see p185) is J H Patterson's account of his battle with a pair of maneless lions who were responsible for the deaths of a number of construction workers on the Uganda Railway (see p303) in 1898. In 1935, well-known American author Ernest Hemingway published *Green Hills of Africa*, based on a hunting safari he took in 1933 in the Chyulu and Tsavo regions, as well as at Lake Manyara in Tanzania. *Out of Africa* (1937) by Danish author Karen Blixen (see p173) depicts her life on a coffee farm from 1917 to 1931 and her relationship with the aristocratic big-game hunter Denys Finch Hatton. Blixen's book is as much a story of Kenya's wildlife and scenic beauty as it is of her emotional journey adapting to an isolated life.

Beryl Markham, a champion horse trainer, aviator and celebrated beauty, recounts her record-breaking solo flight across the Atlantic in *West with the Night* (1942). Elspeth Huxley's *Flame Trees of Thika* (1959), and the sequel *The Mottled Lizard* (1962), portray her life as a coffee grower's

Writer Ernest Hemingway

daughter in the early part of the 20th century on a farm that she describes as "a bit of El Dorado my father had been fortunate enough to buy in the bar of the Norfolk Hotel".

The colonial literary legacy was explored after Kenya's independence in James Fox's *White Mischief* (1980), which deals with Lord Erroll's murder in 1941 and the Happy Valley set of white settlers *(see p323)*, and *The In-Between World of Vikram Lall* by M G Vassanji, winner of the 2003 Giller Prize, which explores the lives of Indian settlers in Kenya *(see p54)*. Errol Trzebinski's *The Lives of Beryl Markham* (1994) and *The Life and Death of Lord Erroll* (2000) depict the same period.

## Contemporary Books

Former Italian socialite Kuki Gallmann's *I Dreamed of Africa* (1991) is a vivid account of her life on a ranch on Laikipia Plateau and her subsequent work in conservation. *My Kenya Days* (1994) provides a record of the adventurer Wilfred Thesiger's 30 years in Kenya from 1960, during which time he was an honorary game warden in the northern frontier. John Le Carré's novel

The Italian author Kuki Gallmann, who wrote *I Dreamed of Africa*

*The Constant Gardener* (2001) revolves around a British diplomat in Nairobi whose wife is murdered in Northern Kenya while investigating a drugs trial scandal. Bill Bryson's *African Diary* (2002) is an account of his travels around Kenya at the invitation of CARE International, the charity dedicated to working with local communities to eradicate poverty around the world.

## Wildlife Stories

*Born Free* (1960) is the story of Joy and George Adamson's *(see p337)* successful efforts at rehabilitating Elsa, an orphaned lion cub, into the wild. At the time, it brought a great deal of international attention and focus to conservation issues in Africa.

Other books from Joy and George followed, describing their crucial work with big cats in Kenya. Daphne Sheldrick *(see p165)* has written several books on her conservation work with elephants in Kenya. Her most recent, *An African Love Story: Love, Life and Elephants* (2013), is Daphne's memoir about falling in love with Tsavo and its warden, David Sheldrick, and the couple devoting their lives to saving elephant orphans. Richard Leakey's *Wildlife Wars: My Battle to Save Kenya's Elephants* (2001) is an account of his extra-ordinary, almost warlike, battle with poachers during the late 1980s when he was head of Kenya Wildlife Services (KWS).

Elsa being fed from a bottle by George and Joy Adamson

## Screen Adaptations

Many epic stories set in Kenya have been played out on the big screen and film-makers have fallen in love with Kenya's intriguing colonial history, landscapes and animals. Films adapted from books include *Born Free* (1966), one of the greatest animal stories ever told; *Out of Africa* (1985), starring Meryl Streep and Robert Redford; and *I Dreamed of Africa* (2000), with Kim Basinger in the leading role. Also based on a book is *The Constant Gardener* (2005), starring Ralph Fiennes and Rachel Weisz. Some of it was filmed in Nairobi's Kibera slum as well as in dramatic locations in Northern Kenya. *To Walk With Lions* (1999) follows George Adamson's later life with his lions at Kora National Park and stars Richard Harris as the formidable man. The German-language film *Nowhere in Africa* (2001) is about a Jewish refugee family that escaped Germany for a new life on a Kenyan farm in the 1930s; it won the Oscar for Best Foreign Language Film. *The Flame Trees of Thika* and *Shadow on the Sun*, which is about Beryl Markham, have both been aired as television series.

Poster for the film *Out of Africa* by Sydney Pollack

# KENYA THROUGH THE YEAR

Although Kenya is located on the equator, its seasons follow the southern hemisphere's pattern, with spring beginning in September, summer in December, autumn in March and winter in June. Reflecting this natural order is the country's yearly cycle of festivals and events which showcase both local and national cultures as well as the region's many natural wonders. Owing to the fact that a good part of the population is Christian or Muslim, Christian holidays are observed throughout Kenya, while Islamic festivals are celebrated along the coast and in the northeast. The country also hosts several annual sporting and adventure activities that international visitors can participate in and combine with a safari or beach holiday.

Muslim man offering prayers on Eid-ul-Fitr

**Lamu Cultural Festival** (mid-Nov), Lamu. A 3-day event focusing on Swahili culture, with food, music, races, crafts and a bridal ceremony. Most activities take place at the waterfront or Lamu Fort.

## Summer

The short rains begin at the end of November when brief afternoon thunderstorms are followed by bright sunshine. Christmas is a big celebration at this time of year. It is also high season on the coast when holiday-makers from Europe take winter breaks.

## Spring

The dry spring months from September to November offer good game viewing. The grass is short and wildlife congregates around rivers and waterholes. The skies remain clear for Nairobi's spectacular film festival and several other outdoor events.

### September

**Africa Concours d'Elegance** (last week), Nairobi. Translating as "a gathering of elegance", this popular vintage car and motorcycle fair is held at Nairobi's Ngong Racecourse. Many of the vehicles on display were used in the colonial years, going as far back as 1910.

**Eid-ul-Fitr** (variable), across Kenya. This Islamic festival falls at the end of the lunar month of Ramadan, when Muslims fast by day and feast by night. Festivities are accompanied by traditional Swahili *taarab* music and dancing (see p37).

### October

**Diwali** (Oct–Nov), across Kenya. This five-day "festival of light" is celebrated by Hindus and Sikhs and coincides with the Hindu New Year. The event marks new beginnings and the triumph of good over evil and light over darkness. Fireworks are the main attraction of gatherings and street parades. Candles are also lit, sweets eaten and gifts exchanged.

### November

**Kitale Agricultural Show** (early Nov), Kitale. This farming show takes place in a rich agricultural district. Livestock competitions, produce stands, demonstrations and engaging musical entertainment make for a lively excursion.

## December

**Christmas Fair** (first weekend Dec), Nairobi. This craft fair at Ngong Racecourse sells home-made items from all over Kenya. The entrance fees go to charity.

Painted statuettes at the Christmas Fair

**Islamic New Year** (variable), across Kenya. The first day of Muharram, the first month in the Islamic calendar, is observed quietly with prayers.

**Eid-ul-Haj** (variable), across Kenya. The Islamic festival of the annual pilgrimage, or *haj*, to Mecca, this is held over 3 days of feasting in all Muslim communities.

**Independence Day** (12 Dec), across Kenya. A public holiday, also known as *Jamhuri Day*, which means "republic" in Kiswahili, it is celebrated with friends and family over elaborate feasts and cultural events.

## January

**New Year's Day Dhow Race**
*(1st Jan)*, Lamu. Only eight captains are invited to race, so winning is a great honour. Race day is one of skill and showmanship and celebrations last well into the night.

## Autumn

March to May is the period of the long rains. Vegetation flourishes, providing a surplus of food for the grazers. Animals look their best, but roads become impassable in the wet and it is not usually the best time to go on either a safari or a beach holiday.

## February

**Kijani Kenya Music Festival**
*(Feb–Aug)*, across Kenya. Run by a non-profit organization, this event features international performing artistes, including those from opera and ballet, to raise money for conservation, education and health projects.
**Maulidi or Milad-un-Nabii Festival** *(variable)*, Lamu. The Islamic celebration of Prophet Mohammed's birth is a 4-day event that draws Muslims from all over East Africa. It combines solemn prayer with popular entertainment such as donkey and dhow races, *bao* (a traditional board game) contests and performances of Swahili music and dance. Visitors are welcome but should show respect for local custom.

Muslim men and boys playing the drums at Maulidi, Lamu waterfront

## March

**Barclays Kenya Open** *(early Mar)*, Nairobi. Part of the European PGA Tour, the annual golf tournament is held on the beautiful course at Muthaiga Golf Club. Kenya has over 40 golf courses, making it a great golfing destination.
**KCB Safari Rally** *(variable)*, Rift Valley. One of the world's oldest and toughest rallies that dates back to 1953, this covers 725 km (450 miles) of open and dirt roads over three exciting days, drawing drivers from around the world.

## Winter

The winter months are dry and not overwhelmingly hot, a good time for outdoor activities. A good number of international visitors arrive specifically to run the Lewa (Safaricom) Marathon. July and August are cool with dry, clear skies, and are therefore considered good months to climb Mount Kenya.

## June

**Cricket season** *(Jun–Feb)*, across Kenya. The long cricket season is dominated by league cricket. The Premier League, played on grass wickets, is considered the most prestigious.
**Lewa (Safaricom) Marathon** *(late Jun)*, Lewa Wildlife Conservancy. This is a charity race held in aid of wildlife organizations. The event attracts more than 1,200 runners, both local and international, for the full and half marathon *(see p394)*. It is paced out on dirt roads and is the only marathon in the world to go through an area inhabited by wildlife.
**Rhino Charge** *(usually Jun)*, Laikipia Plateau. A gruelling 4WD off-road endurance event through rugged terrain of dense bush, ditches and boulders. The winner of the Rhino Charge is the team that manages to complete the course with the least distance covered, or as close to the path "as the crow flies".

## August

**International Camel Derby** *(Aug/Sep)*, Maralal. Held over a weekend, this comprises a short amateur race, where camels and riders are assisted by a handler who runs alongside, and a more serious 42-km (26-mile) professional race. Anyone can participate, and for those who have never ridden a camel before it can be a hilarious experience.

Stranded 4WD being heaved back to firmer terrain, Rhino Charge event

# The Climate of Kenya

Kenya lies on the equator, so daytime temperatures in most parts of the country are consistently warm all year round. It only really gets cool in winter months in the Central Highlands, and Mount Kenya is perennially snowcapped. The long rainy season usually lasts from March to May, and the short rainy season runs over November and December. While Kenyan safaris are available throughout the year, game viewing is best in the dry winter months from June to August and the warm months of September and October. Early morning game drives can get chilly. On the coast, temperatures soar from mid-December to mid-February.

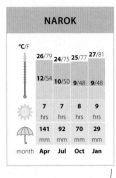

**NAROK**

| °C/F | Apr | Jul | Oct | Jan |
|---|---|---|---|---|
| | 26/79 | 24/75 | 25/77 | 27/81 |
| | 12/54 | 10/50 | 9/48 | 9/48 |
| ☀ | 7 hrs | 7 hrs | 8 hrs | 9 hrs |
| ☂ | 141 mm | 92 mm | 70 mm | 29 mm |
| month | Apr | Jul | Oct | Jan |

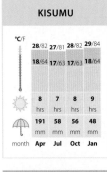

**KISUMU**

| °C/F | Apr | Jul | Oct | Jan |
|---|---|---|---|---|
| | 28/82 | 27/81 | 28/82 | 29/84 |
| | 18/64 | 17/63 | 17/63 | 18/64 |
| ☀ | 8 hrs | 7 hrs | 8 hrs | 9 hrs |
| ☂ | 191 mm | 58 mm | 56 mm | 48 mm |
| month | Apr | Jul | Oct | Jan |

**The northwest** is hot, arid and windy. Total annual rainfall is less than 200 mm (8 inches) and it may not rain for years.

Lokitaung

**Western Kenya** receives rain all year round and is Kenya's most productive agricultural region.

**NAIROBI**

| °C/F | Apr | Jul | Oct | Jan |
|---|---|---|---|---|
| | 24/75 | 21/70 | 24/75 | 25/77 |
| | 14/57 | 11/52 | 13/55 | 12/54 |
| ☀ | 7 hrs | 4 hrs | 7 hrs | 9 hrs |
| ☂ | 211 mm | 15 mm | 53 mm | 38 mm |
| month | Apr | Jul | Oct | Jan |

Average monthly maximum temperature
Average monthly minimum temperature
Average daily hours of sunshine
Average monthly rainfall

Kapenguria

Mara

Kabarnet

Nany

Kisumu    Nakuru    Ny

Narok    Nairobi

Kajiado

**The Southeastern Savannahs** average 33–38° C (91–100° F) during the daytime.

Namang

**Key**

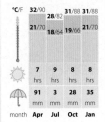

- Equatorial desert: Hot and dry with little rainfall.
- Arid: Hot and arid with dry summer.
- Arid desert: Hot and dry with little or no rainfall.
- Equatorial monsoonal: Hot and humid during the monsoons.
- Equatorial: Hot and humid throughout the year.
- Warm temperate: Dry and warm summer.
- Temperate: Cool dry winter and warm summer.

**NAMANGA**

| °C/F | Apr | Jul | Oct | Jan |
|---|---|---|---|---|
| | 32/90 | 28/82 | 31/88 | 31/88 |
| | 21/70 | 18/64 | 19/66 | 21/70 |
| ☀ | 7 hrs | 9 hrs | 8 hrs | 8 hrs |
| ☂ | 91 mm | 3 mm | 28 mm | 35 mm |
| month | Apr | Jul | Oct | Jan |

## MARSABIT

| °C/F | | | | |
|---|---|---|---|---|
| | **35**/95 | **33**/91 | **35**/95 | **36**/97 |
| | **24**/75 | **23**/73 | **25**/77 | **22**/72 |
| ☀ | 9 hrs | 9 hrs | 10 hrs | 10 hrs |
| ☂ | 48 mm | 19 mm | 9 mm | 8 mm |
| month | **Apr** | **Jul** | **Oct** | **Jan** |

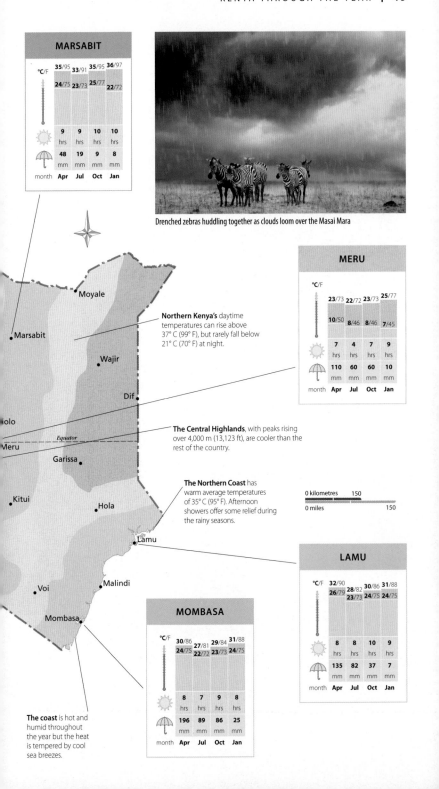

Drenched zebras huddling together as clouds loom over the Masai Mara

## MERU

| °C/F | | | | |
|---|---|---|---|---|
| | **23**/73 | **22**/72 | **23**/73 | **25**/77 |
| | **10**/50 | **8**/46 | **8**/46 | **7**/45 |
| ☀ | 7 hrs | 4 hrs | 7 hrs | 9 hrs |
| ☂ | 110 mm | 60 mm | 60 mm | 10 mm |
| month | **Apr** | **Jul** | **Oct** | **Jan** |

**Northern Kenya's** daytime temperatures can rise above 37° C (99° F), but rarely fall below 21° C (70° F) at night.

**The Central Highlands**, with peaks rising over 4,000 m (13,123 ft), are cooler than the rest of the country.

**The Northern Coast** has warm average temperatures of 35° C (95° F). Afternoon showers offer some relief during the rainy seasons.

Moyale

Marsabit

Wajir

Dif

iolo

*Equator*

Meru

Garissa

Kitui

Hola

Lamu

Voi

Malindi

Mombasa

| 0 kilometres | 150 | |
|---|---|---|
| 0 miles | | 150 |

## LAMU

| °C/F | | | | |
|---|---|---|---|---|
| | **32**/90 | **28**/82 | **30**/86 | **31**/88 |
| | **26**/79 | **23**/73 | **24**/75 | **24**/75 |
| ☀ | 8 hrs | 8 hrs | 10 hrs | 9 hrs |
| ☂ | 135 mm | 82 mm | 37 mm | 7 mm |
| month | **Apr** | **Jul** | **Oct** | **Jan** |

## MOMBASA

| °C/F | | | | |
|---|---|---|---|---|
| | **30**/86 | **27**/81 | **29**/84 | **31**/88 |
| | **24**/75 | **22**/72 | **23**/73 | **24**/75 |
| ☀ | 8 hrs | 7 hrs | 9 hrs | 8 hrs |
| ☂ | 196 mm | 89 mm | 86 mm | 25 mm |
| month | **Apr** | **Jul** | **Oct** | **Jan** |

**The coast** is hot and humid throughout the year but the heat is tempered by cool sea breezes.

# THE HISTORY OF KENYA

Kenya's history dates back to the emergence of mankind, as evidenced by hominid fossils from 6 million years ago. Arabs and Persians reached the coast in the first millennium, while European explorers arrived in the early 19th century, mapping the way for British colonialism and the era of the white settlers in the first half of the 20th century. Charismatic leader Jomo Kenyatta negotiated independence in 1963, and Kenya remains a cosmopolitan and culturally rich nation today.

Archaeological remains from the Tugen Hills and Lake Turkana region suggest that early ape-like species lived in what is now Kenya about 4 to 6 million years ago. From evidence unearthed in the early 20th century, it was thought that these developed, about 1.4 to 2.8 million years ago, into the tool-making hominid *Homo habilis*. This species, until recently, was thought to have evolved into the more advanced *Homo erectus* that evolved into modern man. However, it is now suspected that *Homo habilis* did not precede *Homo erectus* after all but came to an evolutionary dead end. In 2001, near Lake Turkana, Maeve Leakey found the complete skull of *Homo erectus* within walking distance of the upper jaw of a *Homo habilis*. Both must have lived in the region at the same time, and are likely to have evolved from another, older common ancestor – a missing link that has not yet been found. By 10,000 BC, it is thought that early man had mastered making stone tools, discovered the use of fire, developed a basic language and

formed communities organized around hunting and gathering.

From 2,000 BC, Cushitic-speaking pastoral nomads from Ethiopia who herded cattle and experimented with agriculture were the first of many migratory peoples to arrive in Kenya. They initially settled around Lake Turkana but later moved south, attracted by the high rainfall and good grazing in the highlands and Rift Valley. The Yaaku or Eastern Cushites followed 1,000 years later and again occupied much of central Kenya. Bantu-speaking groups from Central Africa and Nilotic-speaking groups from Southern Sudan followed between 500 BC and AD 500. Over time, the original hunter-gatherers became part of these new communities.

While the interior was marked by frequent tribal migrations, the coast was greatly influenced by Arabs, Egyptians and Persians, who originally came to the East African coast to trade. From AD 750, the first Arab seafarers arrived and introduced Islam to the coastal communities.

| | | | **750 AD** Arabs introduce Islam to the coast |
|---|---|---|---|
| **6,000,000 BC** Families of apes begin evolving into the earliest ancestors of humans | **10,000 BC** Hunter-gatherers forage for food and hunt live animals | **600 BC** Egyptians explore the coast | **500 BC** Bantu and Nilote migrations start |

| 6,000,000 BC | 2,000,000 BC | 5,000 BC | AD 1 | AD 750 |
|---|---|---|---|---|

| | | | **AD 100–200** Coastal |
|---|---|---|---|
| **2,000,000 BC** Hominids begin making stone tools | *Hand axe* | **2,000 BC** Cushitic-speaking people arrive from Ethiopia | people live in village communities and forge iron |

◄ A 19th-century illustration by artist Baraldi Severino of the Sultan of Malindi with his royal entourage, in 1498

# The Cradle of Mankind

East Africa has long been considered the "Cradle of Mankind", with archaeological evidence still being uncovered in the region. Discoveries at the Olduvai Gorge in Tanzania, Lake Turkana in Kenya, Hadar in Ethiopia and the Kagera river in Uganda support Charles Darwin's theory that humankind evolved from apes. One species of yet unknown ape eventually evolved into *Homo sapiens* and it is generally believed that it was here that man stood upright. To prove Darwin's hypothesis, Mary and Louis Leakey began pioneering extensive excavations from the 1930s that established many facts about early life in the region.

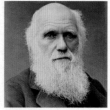

**Charles Darwin**, in his seminal book *On the Origin of Species,* introduced the theories of evolution and natural selection.

## Kenyan sites

*Fossils found around Lake Turkana and Koobi Fora suggest that humans first evolved in Kenya. Other archaeological finds around Lake Victoria and the Rift Valley have provided much of the key evidence for human evolutionary studies.*

**The Millennium Man** (*Orrorin tugenensis*), about 6.5 million years old, was found in 2000 in the Tugen Hills. Some scholars suggest this could be the earliest known upright hominid.

**Stone axes** were discovered by Louis Leakey in 1928 at the Kariandusi Prehistoric Site near Nakuru.

**A 930,000-year-old fossilized skull** of a hominid was excavated by anthropologist Richard Potts at Olorgasailie. Its species, however, is unknown.

**Discoveries** on the eastern shore of Lake Turkana also unearthed a significant yield of animal fossils.

## Kenya's Dinosaurs

Lake Turkana's ample fossil evidence indicates that the lake's shores were once teeming with wildlife, including prehistoric elephants and three-toed ancestors of the horse. The first scientific dinosaur expedition, undertaken in 2004, collected over 200 fossils dating to the Mesozoic era more than 200 million years ago. This provided the first concrete evidence that dinosaurs inhabited what is now Kenya before humans evolved in the region.

Elephant's fossil bones, Lake Turkana

**Turkana Boy** was discovered by Richard Leakey's team near Lake Turkana in 1984. At 1.6 million years old these are believed to be the most complete *Homo erectus* remains found to date.

## East African Sites

*East Africa's most important archaeological site, Olduvai Gorge has yielded many fossils. The gorge was first visited by the Leakeys in 1931, when they found stone tools here. Other sites include Hadar in Ethiopia and Laetoli in Tanzania.*

**Nutcracker Man** *(Paranthropus boisei)*, the Leakeys' first big find, in 1959, in the Olduvai Gorge, was so named due to its large molars. An early hominid, the fossil is 1.75 million years old.

An impressive collection of **Plio-Pleistocene hominids** was discovered by Richard Leakey at Koobi Fora, starting in 1968.

**The Laetoli footprints**, about 3.6 million years old, were discovered in 1978 by Mary Leakey. Preserved in volcanic ash in the Olduvai Gorge, this is the earliest evidence of hominids walking upright.

**Handyman**, dating back 1.4 million years, was discovered in the Olduvai Gorge in 1960. Bone fragments suggested that it was a new species, *Homo habilis*, an evolved hominid capable of carving stone tools.

**Lucy**, a female hominid dating 2.8 million years, was found in Ethiopia in 1974. The team, led by American paleoanthropologist Donald Johanson, established that it was a new species, *Australopithecus afarensis*.

## Hominid Fossil Sites

1. Kariandusi, Kenya *(see p276)*
2. Koobi Fora, Kenya
3. Lake Turkana, Kenya *(see pp354–5)*
4. Olorgasailie, Kenya *(see p174)*
5. Tugen Hills, Kenya *(see p292)*
6. Hadar, Ethiopia
7. Engaruka, Tanzania
8. Laetoli, Tanzania
9. Olduvai Gorge, Tanzania
10. Kagera river, Uganda

## Human Evolution

***Orrorin tugenensis***, who lived between 6.1 and 5.8 million years ago, is thought to be the second-oldest known hominid ancestor that is possibly related to modern human beings.

***Paranthropus boisei***, an early hominid, lived from 2.6 to about 1.2 million years ago. It is the largest of the *Paranthropus* species.

***Australopithecus afarensis***, who lived between 3.9 and 2.9 million years ago, is thought to be ancestral to both the *Australopithecus* and *Homo* genera.

***Australopithecus africanus***, who lived between 2 and 3 million years ago, split into two lines, *Australopithecus robustus* and *Homo habilis*.

***Homo habilis***, the first of the genus *Homo*, and the least similar to humans, evolved 2.5–2 million years ago, when it diverged from the *Australopithecines*.

***Homo rudolfensis*** lived around 1.9–1.6 million years ago. It is not confirmed whether another *habilis* or a separate species, *Homo georgicus*, evolved between *Homo habilis* and *Homo erectus*.

***Homo erectus*** evolved 1.8 million–70,000 years ago and was the first hominid to walk upright.

***Homo antecessor*** lived from 1.2 million–50,000 years ago.

***Homo heidelbergensis*** lived about 800,000–300,000 years ago.

***Homo rhodesiensis***, first discovered in 1921, is believed to have lived around 300,000–125,000 years ago.

***Homo neanderthalensis*** is thought to have existed around 250,000–30,000 years ago.

***Homo sapiens***, or modern man, is thought to have evolved around 250,000 years ago.

## Swahili Civilization

It was the monsoon winds that blow along the East African coast from the northeast from December to March and from the southeast from April to November that brought the first sailors to East Africa on ocean-going dhows. While traders from many different nations visited the coast, it was the Arabs who stayed, and from the 8th century they established a string of powerful commercial settlements. These were founded on trade that was carried across the Indian Ocean to as far away as China. Leopard skins, tortoise shells, ivory, rhinoceros horns, gold and slaves were exported from Africa in exchange for metal tools, utensils, swords and daggers. When commodities were not traded, early currencies of beads and cowrie shells were used. Over time, contact between the Arabs and indigenous Bantu cultures on the coast created the inimitable Swahili culture, in which the

**Chinese porcelain found at Gedi Ruins**

characteristics of both were assimilated, and which was marked by its own unique language and a devotion to Islam. Over the next few centuries Swahili civilization flourished, and by the 15th century Mombasa, Malindi, Pate and Lamu in Kenya, and Zanzibar, Pemba and Kilwa in modern-day Tanzania had developed into prosperous ports with grand houses and several prolific mosques.

## The Portuguese Conquest

The Arabs continued to dominate the coast until they were challenged by the arrival of the Portuguese. Explorer Vasco da Gama, who had been ordered by Portuguese King John to round the Cape of Africa and find the sea route to India, landed at Malindi in 1498. In the years that followed, more fleets of Portuguese ships arrived, and by 1510, most of the Swahili cities on the coastline south of Mogadishu (in present-day Somalia) had been ransacked. By 1512, Malindi had become the northern headquarters of the Portuguese on the East African coast. Later, in 1593, this was moved to Mombasa, when the Portuguese built Fort Jesus as a garrison, and its ramparts and battlements confirmed their dominance over the coast. Throughout the 17th century, the Arabs attempted to re-establish control over their outposts. Envious of the Portuguese possessions in East Africa, the Sultan of Muscat in Oman, Seif bin Sultan, incited the local Arabs to fight the Portuguese in a series of confrontations. The Portuguese downfall

Pate Ruins, a predominant 15th-century Swahili settlement along the coast

**800** The first rag and coral structures built in the early coastal trading centres

**1000** Cattle-raising and possibly cereal-growing are introduced

*Gedi Ruins*

**800**

**1000**

**1200**

**900** Islamic Arabs occupy Mombasa and other seaports

**1200** Swahili culture and language become dominant along the coast

**1200–1300** The palace and mosque built at Gedi

A 19th-century lithograph showing Vasco da Gama's exploration of the coast in the 15th century

finally came in 1698 after a 33-month siege of Fort Jesus. The subsequent Portuguese expulsion from Kilwa and Pemba in 1699 virtually ended their rule in East Africa north of Mozambique, and by 1720 the last remaining Portuguese garrison had left the coast for good.

## Omani Rule

After the Arab victory at Fort Jesus in 1698, the coast fell under the jurisdiction of Muscat but there was a series of conflicts between the local Arabs and the Omanis until the Swahili settlements were finally unified under the rule of Omani Sultan Seyyid Sa'id from 1806 to 1856. He was in control of a profitable slave trade, and moved the capital of his sultanate from Muscat to Zanzibar in 1832. For the first time the Arabs were venturing into the interior of East Africa to capture slaves, who were sold through the slave market in Zanzibar. However, by the early 1800s,

Omani dagger, 17th century

the anti-slave lobby in Europe was gathering momentum, and in 1822 Seyyid Sa'id signed the Moresby Treaty, which deemed it illegal to sell slaves to subjects of Christian countries including Britain and the US. In 1840, the British established a consulate at the sultan's court in Zanzibar in order to monitor the treaty. This casual negotiation marked the beginning of European influence in East Africa. In 1845, Seyyid Sa'id reluctantly signed the Hamerton Treaty, which forbade all slave trading by sea, and after years of pressure, slavery was banned altogether in 1873. Meanwhile, missionaries arrived to lend their support for the abolition of slavery, and to chart the interior at the same time. In 1846, Johann Ludwig Krapf and Johannes Rebmann, two German missionaries, were the first Europeans to venture into the interior of what is now Kenya. Rebmann was the first white man to lay eyes on Kilimanjaro in 1848, and Krapf the first to see the twin peaks of Mount Kenya in 1849.

**1500** First Portuguese attack on the coastal cities

*Fort Jesus*

**1806–56** Rule of Sultan Seyyid Sa'id; Seyyid moves his capital from Muscat in Oman to Zanzibar

**1830s** Omani Arabs consolidate control of coast

**1846** Christian missionaries reach Kenya's heartland to speak out against slavery

400     1600     1800

**1498** Vasco da Gama arrives in Malindi

**1593** Fort Jesus built by the Portuguese in Mombasa

**1698** Arab victory in the siege of Fort Jesus

**1720** Portuguese withdraw from the coast

**1849** Johann Ludwig Krapf is the first white man to see Mount Kenya

Hand-coloured engraving by S Hollyer of explorer John H Speke with Lake Victoria in the background

## Exploration of the Interior

By the mid-19th century, British explorers had ventured inland and the likes of David Livingstone, H M Stanley and Richard Burton mapped much of the East African interior. In 1858, John Hanning Speke discovered the source of the River Nile on what is today the Ugandan side of Lake Victoria. These expeditions revealed a wealth of resources. In 1883, Britain's Royal Geographical Society dispatched Joseph Thomson, a Scottish geologist and naturalist, to the region and with the exception of the northern deserts, he charted almost all of what is today Kenya. His adventurous journey was documented in the 1884 book *Through Masailand*. He travelled from Kilimanjaro across country to Lake Naivasha, then continued up the Rift Valley, climbed the Aberdares, which he named after the then president of the Royal Geographical

Count Samuel Teleki von Szek

Society, and passed Mount Kenya, Lake Baringo and Mount Elgon before returning to the coast via Lake Victoria and the western plains. In 1885, the Austro-Hungarian Count Samuel Teleki de Szek and Austrian naval officer and explorer Ludwig von Höhnel reached Lake Turkana, which they named Lake Rudolph after Austria's crown prince. In the 1890s, Americans Arthur Donaldson Smith and William Astor Chanler surveyed the Tana river and northeastern bush. The land that was to be Kenya was thus mapped out.

## The Scramble for Africa

The reports sent back to Europe by these early explorers stoked imperial interests, and Africa was seen as ripe with potential and there for the taking. The large continent seemingly had plentiful natural and mineral resources such as gum, palm oil and copper that could be utilized in Europe as it entered the grimy years of the industrial revolution, while it was simultaneously seen as a market for manufactured goods made in Europe's factories. During the carve up of Africa, often dubbed the Scramble for Africa, the European powers laid claim to almost all African territories, and most of these claims were settled at the Berlin Conference of 1884. France claimed the majority of western Africa, Belgium obtained the Congo region, Portugal got Mozambique and Angola, and Britain and Germany received the bulk of southern and eastern Africa. Africans were not invited to attend the conference and did not get sovereignty over their land.

---

**1858** John Hanning Speke discovers the source of the River Nile

*An English ship enforcing the abolition of the slave trade*

**1873** Slavery deemed illegal in East Africa

**1850**

**1860**

**1870**

**1854** Krapf produces a rough map of the interior showing an inland sea – Lake Victoria

*Johann Ludwig Krapf*

**1862** Ahmed Fumoluti al-Nabahani declares himself Sultan of Witu, which briefly becomes an independent state, "Swahililand"

**1869** Opening of the Suez Canal increases British accessibility to East Africa

## Britain's Share

In London, gunboat diplomacy was avoided when Britain and Germany agreed to share their eastern African territory as far inland as the Great Lakes. The Germans got mainland Tanzania, and the British got the concession for Kenya and Uganda. Britain offered the tiny island of Heligoland in the North Sea, in return for the British protectorate over Zanzibar. Surprisingly, Germany agreed, but much later benefited from the deal as Heligoland served as an invaluable naval base for the Germans during both world wars. On the coast, the Sultan of Zanzibar, through treaties leasing his territories in exchange for an annual fee, relinquished power to the British.

Officials of the Imperial British East Africa Company signing a treaty with the Kikuyu people

## East African Protectorate

In Mombasa, in 1887, Britain set up the Imperial British East Africa Company, which administered the new East African Protectorate. The company produced its own money and treaty documents, on which were the seal of the British crown. Between 1888 and 1892, through territorial agreements with local chiefs in exchange for British authority, the East Africa Company established outposts throughout the country and cut a 500-km- (310-mile-) long dirt road inland from Mombasa to a swampy, flat area called Ewaso Nyarobi (Place of Cold Water), which later became Nairobi. With the colony growing, administration of the protectorate was transferred from the company to the Foreign Office in 1895, and the British opened up the interior further when work on the Uganda Railway from Mombasa commenced in 1896.

A 19th-century lithograph depicting Mombasa coast captured by British cruisers in 1875

**1884** European nations lay claim over African territories

**1883** Joseph Thomson is the first European to travel to Maasai country

**1887** The British negotiate a concession of the Zanzibar sultan's territory for a 50-year period

**1889–90** The Imperial British East Africa Company employs army officer Fredrick Lugard to survey a new route from Mombasa to Uganda

1890

**1895** The British government takes over present-day Kenya

**1897** The Imperial British East Africa Company negotiates treaties with local chiefs

1880

1900

*British lay claim over Africa*

Lions attacking railway workers' camps in 1898, a 19th-century illustration by W R Stott

### The Uganda Railway

As Britain's endeavours grew in the interior, the only way to supply the outposts was to build a railway from the coast to Uganda. To help build the railway, the British imported skilled labourers from India, many of whom stayed on in East Africa to form the region's large Asian community. The railway, dubbed the Iron Snake by Africans, was called the Lunatic Line *(see p303)* by a cautious parliament back in Britain because of its tremendous cost, £5 million, and the implausibility of its success. Work began in 1896, and 845 km (525 miles), 43 stations and 1,200 bridges later, the railway arrived in Port Florence (now Kisumu) at Lake Victoria in 1901, which at that time was part of Uganda. Not only was it an amazing feat in the history of railway construction but also a long and hazardous task during which every conceivable problem had arisen. Crossing the Rift Valley escarpments was a major technical problem and work was held up at Tsavo for almost a year by two man-eating lions that killed scores of railway

workers. Termites feasted on sleepers, sleeping sickness caused by tsetse flies decimated herds of oxen used to haul material and many workers fell ill or died from malaria. Nevertheless, the railway was hailed as a success and opened up the region to the rest of the world.

### Growth of a Colony

By 1899 the railway had reached the foot of the Kenyan highlands where a camp and depot were established in readiness for the challenge presented ahead by the technically difficult Rift Valley. The site was also chosen because of its network of rivers and for its elevation, as at 1,661 m (5,450 ft) temperatures were too low for the malaria mosquito to survive. The railway's administrative offices were moved here from Mombasa and homes built for the staff, which in turn attracted an influx of Asian merchants to supply goods and services to the railway workforce. Nairobi was born, and by 1905 it had become the seat of the British East Africa

The last peg of the Uganda Railway from Mombasa being driven in at Port Florence

| | | | |
|---|---|---|---|
| **1898** Construction of the Uganda Railway is delayed in Tsavo; two lions kill 135 railway workers | | **1903** Lord Delamere is one of the first of tens of thousands of white settlers that arrive in Kenya up until the 1950s | **1907** A Legislative Council is established with Lord Delamere as one of the settler members |
| | **1899** Railway reaches the foot of the Kenyan highlands | | |

**1895**    **1900**    **1905**    **1910**

| | | |
|---|---|---|
| **1901** Railway arrives in Kisumu at Lake Victoria | **1902** The border between Kenya and Uganda is adjusted; Kisumu is now in Kenya | **1905** Nairobi becomes the capital of the British East Africa Protectorate |

Nairobi, 1900s

Protectorate. In 1920, Kenya, named after the territory's highest mountain, was declared a crown colony run by a governor and a Legislative Council, with Nairobi as its capital. Consequently, all ethnic groups were subject to colonial rules and lost their political independence.

## White Settlers

The railway laid down the infrastructure that opened up the fertile interior. The combination of a pleasant climate and good-quality land made the Central Highlands an ideal environment for dairy farming and to grow tea, coffee, tobacco and other cash crops. A call went out to all corners of the British Empire for people to settle in Kenya and so the era of the White Highlands began. One of the first to arrive was British peer Lord Delamere, who acquired large tracts of land in the Rift Valley and was followed by adventurous farmers, mostly from his home territory of Lancashire, who also staked their claims. By 1912 the population of white settlers stood at 3,000 and by the 1930s more than 30,000 of them lived in Kenya. By then a third of the colonial government's revenue was generated from duties on settlers' produce and their goods imported into Kenya. Perhaps the most famous of the settlers were author Karen Blixen, of *Out of Africa* fame, and the Happy Valley set *(see p323)*, a group of British aristocrats who led decadent lifestyles in Kenya during the 1930s, and became embroiled in the mysterious murder of Lord Erroll in 1941.

Karen Blixen, the famed coffee planter and writer, with her Scottish hounds, near Nairobi

## Land Acquisition

New legislation on land tenure favoured the white settlers and they were granted prime agricultural land, while the Africans were herded into native reserves and formally dispossessed of their land, with the Maasai and Kikuyu suffering the greatest losses. The resentment by Africans of colonial rule grew deeper with every acre lost, and so the struggle for independence began. From the early 1920s, increasing numbers of Kenyans, led by the Kikuyu, formed political groups whose primary focus was the return of their land. The first of these was the East African Association founded in Nairobi in 1921 by Harry Thuku, which campaigned to end the *kipande* (identity card) system. However, this was short-lived – Thuku was arrested for his political activity in 1922, and in the demonstrations that followed 25 Africans were shot dead by both police and white civilians. This was the first challenge to the colonial regime.

Kikuyu farmers working on colonial fields

**1915** African males told to carry identity cards when they leave their native reserves

**1918** After World War I, farms are sold to white war veterans for nominal prices

**1921** The East African Association is founded in Nairobi by Harry Thuku

World War I British troops

**1915**

**1920**

**1925**

**1914** During World War I, a quarter of the 200,000 Africans recruited by the British die in battle

**1920** Kenya is declared a crown colony administered by a British governor

**1922** Thuku is arrested, then exiled without charge or trial to the Northern Frontier Province

Kikuyu tribe members held in a camp by the British government during the Mau Mau Rebellion

## Organized Resistance

The East African Association changed its name in 1924 to the Kikuyu Central Association (KCA), and former Nairobi water meter reader Jomo Kenyatta became its secretary in 1927. After failing to get Nairobi's Legislative Council to listen to the grievances of the African people about land issues, he sailed to Britain in 1929 to present the case to the colonial offices of parliament. He returned to London again in 1931, where he remained in exile, campaigning for the Kenyan people until 1946.

Although Britain made a small attempt to appease African protest by appointing the first black Kenyan to the Legislative Council in 1944, they were not prepared for the thousands of soldiers who returned to Kenya after World War II. These war veterans were empowered by new influences they had encountered overseas and angry that they had given their lives and labour on behalf of the British in yet another World War. Yet, even by 1945, their rights in Kenya had not improved. Political and ethnic factions mushroomed and the time was ripe for Kenyatta to return from exile in order to give

a common voice to these concerns under the banner of the new Kenya African Union (KAU). The land issue was paramount – by 1948, 1.25 million Kikuyu were restricted to 5,200 sq km (2,000 sq miles), while 30,000 settlers occupied 31,000 sq km (12,000 sq miles). By 1953, almost half of all Kikuyu had no land claims at all. Thousands migrated into the cities in search of work, and Nairobi's population doubled between 1938 and 1952. The results were worsening poverty and unemployment.

## Mau Mau Rebellion

Many Africans began to think that freedom from colonial rule could not be achieved by peaceful means. From 1947, various ethnic

Rebels renouncing their ties to the Mau Mau by licking the blood of a goat off sticks held by a shaman

**1927** Kenyatta becomes secretary of the Kikuyu Central Association

**1931** Kenyatta goes to England where he remains in exile until 1946

Jomo Kenyatta, England, 1937

**1945** In WW II Britain uses Kenya as a base for operations in Ethiopia

| 1925 | 1930 | 1935 | 1940 | 1945 |

Ernest Hemingway in Kenya

**1933** American writer Ernest Hemingway visits Kenya and writes some of his most famous works

**1944** Kenya African Union (KAU) formed

**1947** Kenyatta becomes KAU leader

groups joined forces under the Kikuyu-dominated Mau Mau banner and swore oaths that they were ready to fight and die for their rights. The violent Mau Mau Rebellion began in earnest in 1952. White settlers and thousands of Africans who collaborated with the white farmers or sympathized with the government were attacked by Mau Mau gangs. In late 1952, Jomo Kenyatta and six of his colleagues were arrested and sentenced to 7 years imprisonment for allegedly inciting the Mau Mau. A state of emergency was declared in 1952 and troops were brought in to suppress the violence. By the end of 1954, the British had herded 77,000 Kikuyu into concentration camps. The loss of life among the white settlers was perhaps about 100 people; the main victims were some 2,000 other Kikuyu who refused to support the cause and were killed as collaborators, and the Mau Mau themselves, who lost 11,000 people. The crisis neared its end in 1957, when most of the leading Mau Mau leaders were captured in Nyeri. The state of emergency was lifted in 1959, though pockets of fighters remained in the forests until 1963.

Jomo Kenyatta being sworn in as Kenya's first president

## Independence

Despite its victory over the Mau Mau, Britain was now reluctant to hang on to an unstable colony. It began to concede political power and allow Kenyans self-government, and in 1957, 25 African, 15 Asian and 5 Arab members were elected to the Legislative Council. The ban on indigenous people growing coffee was lifted, which led to a dramatic rise in the income of small farmers over the next 10 years. By 1959, freehold land titles in large numbers were issued to Africans, mostly on land of white settlers who had left during the Mau Mau Rebellion, and a campaign was underway to employ landless people. By 1960, Kenya's first African political parties had been formed and were taking part in the developing political process. While still in prison, Kenyatta was elected president of the new Kenya African National Union (KANU), a successor to KAU, which was formed by Tom Mboya and Oginga Odinga. Kenyatta was released in 1961 and went to Lancaster House in London for talks, and the path to full independence was opened. In elections in May 1963 KANU won the majority of seats and at midnight on 12 December 1963, Kenya became independent. In 1964, Kenyatta became president of the new republic and Kenya joined the Commonwealth.

Jomo Kenyatta along with Tom Mboya and Oginga Odinga on a motorcade, Nairobi, 1964 elections

Kenyatta being taken for trial at Kapenguria

**1952** Kenyatta imprisoned for 7 years; Mau Mau Rebellion begins

**1961** Kenyatta assumes presidency of KANU

**1963** Kenya becomes independent; Kenyatta becomes the prime minister

| 1950 | 1955 | 1960 | 1965 |

**1955** Africans allowed to form political parties

**1960** Kenya African National Union formed

**1964** Republic of Kenya formed; Kenyatta becomes president and Odinga vice president

Members of the newly elected government

## The Kenyatta Years

Charismatic and pragmatic, Jomo Kenyatta ruled even-handedly, and in his inaugural address he invited all Kenyans to work at nation-building. To diffuse any lingering tribal tensions, he chose his first cabinet from across the ethnic divide to balance all interests in the new government, and he managed to convince the white settlers of his faith in an undivided multiracial Kenya. The first years of the new republic were dominated by restructuring and rebuilding, and the British government funded a programme of land purchases that resettled landless Africans on farms – a scheme that continued for some years at the cost of millions of pounds. Kenyatta's term featured rapidly improving infrastructure and unprecedented growth in the economy. In the 1970s, Nairobi saw an upsurge of high-rise buildings as foreign investment moved in. The Nairobi–Mombasa Highway was rebuilt, the international airport in Nairobi was extended, the national airline was established, new schools and hospitals were built and large increases in tea and coffee production oiled the country's economy. However, having suffered from ill health since the previous year, the greatly admired Kenyatta died in 1978 and was succeeded by his vice president, Daniel arap Moi.

Kenyan currency depicting President Daniel arap Moi

## The Moi Years

Despite having success in improving infrastructure and social welfare, Moi, unlike his predecessor, led an autocratic, authoritarian and repressive government. He stayed in power for 24 years with little tolerance of any form of opposition. After swiftly crushing an attempted coup in 1982 he went on to expel critics from his government and detain opposition leaders. In 1987, he changed the constitution to extend his presidential powers. By the 1990s, Kenya was floundering economically, there were outbreaks of ethnic violence in the Rift Valley, which left thousands of Kikuyu and Luo dead, and the nation's troubles were compounded by evidence of widespread corruption. The late 1990s saw frequent demonstrations for democracy and change, which were more often than not suppressed violently by the authorities.

By the 2002 elections, people were ready for change and looked towards the

Kenyatta, Mboya and Kibaki rejoicing over their party's victory in elections

| | | | | |
|---|---|---|---|---|
| **1974** Kenyatta re-elected | **1978** Kenyatta dies in office and is succeeded as president by Daniel arap Moi | **1982** Kenya is declared a one-party state by the National Assembly | | **1992** Moi is re-elected in multiparty elections; foreign observers report that KANU manipulated the election |
| **1970** | **1975** | **1980** | **1985** | **1990** |

*Women mourning at Kenyatta's funeral*

**1982** Army suppresses air-force coup attempt

**1991** Multiparty political system is reintroduced

opposition. The National Alliance of Rainbow Coalition (NARC), a coalition of 15 individual parties that had joined forces won in a landslide victory, and Moi's former vice president Mwai Kibaki was elected president by a large majority.

Kenyan President Mwai Kibaki and opposition leader Raila Odinga after signing a power-sharing deal

## The Kibaki Years

Initially, Kenya was awash with optimism and the new government had some early successes. However, the popularity of Kibaki's government was short-lived, as it failed to end endemic corruption and revive the country's stalled economy. Elections were held at the end of 2007 and Kibaki's main contender was Raila Odinga, son of Kenyatta's first vice president Oginga Odinga, of the Orange Democratic Movement (ODM). However, disputed election results, which initially had Odinga as the legitimate winner and then Kibaki as the leader, led to a violent reaction across the country and several hundred deaths. International mediators stepped in and by mid-2008 a power agreement was made placing Kibaki as president and Odinga as prime minister.

On 4 August 2010 Kenyans voted overwhelmingly "yes" in a referendum over the adoption of a long-awaited new constitution to improve good governance and accountability.

## Uhuru Kenyatta

The son of Jomo Kenyatta has played a leading part in politics since he was nominated to parliament in 2001. Moi quickly promoted him as his successor, and Uhuru was KANU's candidate in the 2002 presidential election, but lost to opposition candidate Kibaki by a large margin. In 2008, he became deputy prime minister as part of the coalition government, and was then elected president in the 2013 election, defeating Odinga with a narrow majority.

### Jomo Kenyatta

Kenyatta meeting his supporters post exile

Widely regarded as the founder of modern Kenya, or Baba wa Taifa, which means "father of the nation", Kenyatta was born Kamau wa Ngengi in 1889 in the village of Gatundu. In the 1920s, Kenyatta adopted this new name, Kiswahili for "the light of Kenya". He studied economics in Moscow and anthropology in London in the 1930s, and lobbied for Kikuyu land rights during his long exile from Kenya between 1931 and 1946. Although not without criticism, he presided over the bloody transition to independence, and for 15 years held his country's fractious ethnic groups together and earned respect for his humanity and statesmanship throughout the world. He also oversaw Kenya's admission into the United Nations. In later years, up until his death in 1978, he was affectionately known as *mzee* (old man).

| 1995 | 2000 | 2005 | 2010 | 2015 | 2020 |
|---|---|---|---|---|---|

**1997** Moi wins a further term in widely criticized elections

**2001** Ethnic violence culminates in clashes in Nairobi's Kibera slum

**2004** Wangari Maathai wins the Nobel Peace Prize

**2008** Violent clashes across Kenya; Kibaki and Odinga sign power agreement

**2010** Kenyans vote in favour of a new constitution, gaining a bill of rights

*Wangari Maathai*

**1998** Bomb explodes at US Embassy in Nairobi, killing 218 people and injuring thousands

**2002** Mwai Kibaki wins a landslide victory over KANU rival Uhuru Kenyatta

**2003** Government introduces free primary education

**2009** 10 million Kenyans face food shortage after drought in Northern Kenya

**2013** Jomo Kenyatta's son, Uhuru Kenyatta, is declared president in peaceful elections

Two lions gazing over the Mara plains ▶

# WILD KENYA

# THE SAFARI EXPERIENCE

Some are inspired by the liberating sense of space associated with Kenya's endless plains. Others are overwhelmed by the quality of time-stood-still that seems to inhabit this dusty wilderness. Above all, one cannot help but be captivated by the assortment of wonderful creatures that walk and breathe in this most untrammelled and ancient of landscapes.

Kenya prides itself on being the original home of the safari, a term that is derived from a Swahili word meaning journey, and that came to be associated with trophy-hunting expeditions popularized by the likes of Karen Blixen, Hemingway and Finch-Hatton. Sadly, these earliest gun-toting safaris contributed greatly to the demise of East Africa's wildlife, so that by the end of the colonial era a large percentage of the once free-ranging herds were concentrated in state-run wildlife and forest reserves – precursors to the network of national parks and reserves that forms the cornerstone of Kenya's safari industry today.

Dwindling wildlife numbers, increased conservation awareness and the new influx of visitors brought about by the jet age meant that by the end of the 1960s, the hunting safari was largely a thing of the past. Visitors to Kenya arrived not with guns and bullets but with cameras,

ushering in the era of the photographic safari. Today, the core components of a safari, that is, the landscapes and wildlife, remain little changed since the 1970s. The industry, however, has diversified greatly, so that accommodation might range from rudimentary camping or tin-roof huts to 100-room monolithic hotels and eco-friendly tented camps that exude safari chic.

A legacy of the colonial hunting fraternity is the term used to describe the quarry it considered most dangerous – the Big Five, comprising the lion, leopard, elephant, rhino and buffalo. Sighting them is regarded a virtual rite of passage on safari, and Kenya certainly excels when it comes to this goal. However, be it antelopes locking horns or a dung beetle rolling a ball or widowbirds displaying their plumage, the African bush is a place of limitless adventure and wonder.

Camping in the wilderness, Chyulu Hills National Park

◀ Vehicle travelling along a game track in the Masai Mara National Reserve

# SAFARI ACTIVITIES

The most popular activity on safari are daytime game drives, although in some cases it is also possible to explore the bush by boat or balloon, or on foot, usually in the company of a ranger or guide. Whatever the activity, a typical day on safari – unlike most other holidays – will start early. The African bush is at its most scintillating in the hour or two immediately after sunrise, and the earliest possible start is recommended. This is when secretive nocturnal predators such as leopard or serval are most likely to be encountered, while more conspicuous species such as lion and spotted hyena tend to be most active before the heat of the day kicks in. Other advantages of an early start are the cooler temperatures, the higher level of avian activity and the often sumptuous photographic light.

## Game Drives

A typical day on safari is structured around a 3- to 5-hour game drive in the morning and a shorter afternoon drive, returning to camp in between for a leisurely lunch and siesta or splash in the pool. Visitors who want to explore further afield, or need to travel between lodges, will find a full-day drive more appropriate. For those who want a really early start, or who plan to stay out all day, most lodges will provide a packed breakfast on request.

Driver-guides in Kenya can be highly variable in skill. Many have worked as urban drivers or mechanics before moving into the lucrative tourism industry. This technical background can be reassuring when an engine starts grumbling in the middle of the bush, but it also means that a high proportion of driver-guides have little interest in wildlife or affinity for the bush. Higher tips ensure more active participation from the driver-guides, but the onus is on the individual safarigoer when it comes to emphasizing any specific interests or dislikes to the driver-guide, and a proactive role is encouraged when it comes to wildlife spotting, route planning, bird identification and deciding on places for photographic stops.

## On Foot

There is no more exciting way of seeing wildlife than on foot. Sensibly, however, Kenya Wildlife Service (KWS) has made it illegal for visitors to leave their vehicles in national parks that harbour dangerous wildlife, unless they are at a lodge, rest camp, entrance gate or other desig-nated spot. By contrast, many private reserves and concessions encourage guests to join a guided game walk, which makes for a far more invigorating experience than a game drive, capable of transforming an otherwise relatively mundane sighting into something positively inspirational. Exploring the bush on foot exposes a wealth of sensory stimuli – sounds, smells and physical textures – that tend to be lost

Raised wooden walkway at the Safari Walk, Nairobi National Park

within the confines of a vehicle. Walking with an articulate and knowledgeable guide can greatly enhance one's appreci-ation of the intricacies and minutiae of the bush, whether it is the traditional medical uses of trees, the opportunity to identify otherwise inconspicuous birds and butterflies, the gigantic spider webs that hang from the branches or a series of S-shaped ripples left by an undulating snake on sandy soil. Several Kenyan parks also offer the opportunity to walk unguided among large wildlife. In conventional game-viewing terms, the pick of these is undoubtedly Hell's Gate National Park (see pp274–5), which has a spectacular setting and supports high densities of impala, zebra, buffalo, giraffe and gazelle, and even the odd large predator. Kakamega Forest National Reserve (see pp298–301), Saiwa Swamp National Park (see p294–5) and Mount Kenya National Park (see pp326–7) are

Minibuses with pop-up roofs on a game drive, Amboseli National Park

also very pedestrian-friendly, and even the larger and more popular reserves have a few sites that are explorable on foot – Tsavo West National Park's Mzima Springs area *(see p191)*, for instance, or Amboseli National Park's Observation Hill *(see p198)*.

While most animals are fairly indifferent to the attire and actions of safarigoers in vehicles, they are less relaxed with pedestrians. Persistent chatter is therefore a strict no-no, and it is a good idea to wear neutral colours and avoid wearing strong perfume or aftershave. Trousers, socks and solid shoes will provide good protection against bites and thorns, while a hat and sunblock will help protect against direct sunlight. As it is more difficult to approach wildlife closely on foot than in a vehicle, binoculars are more useful than a camera.

## Balloons and Boats

Although not widely available in Kenya, balloon and boat safaris both present a unique perspective on the bush. The most popular site for balloon trips is the Masai Mara National Reserve *(see pp266–9)*, where they can be arranged – for a hefty price – at most lodges. All balloon excursions leave before dawn, often accompanied by spectacular sunrises, and the sensation of drifting above the

A pod of hippo swimming close to a motorboat on Lake Baringo

open plains and the immense herds they support is truly breathtaking. It is usually all over within an hour of sunrise, when a lavish bush breakfast is provided complete with champagne and, with luck, a few lions or elephants looking on.

Kenya does not have any bona fide boat safaris, but the Rift Valley lakes of Naivasha *(see pp270–73)* and Baringo *(see pp284–7)* offer boat trips that are fantastic for bird-watching.

## After Dark

Most national parks under the jurisdiction of the KWS limit game drives to daylight hours, a rule that is enforced rigidly at busy lodges on main tourist circuits. However, several small and more isolated bush camps, especially in private reserves such as the Laikipia Plateau *(see pp322–5)*, or in concessions adjacent to national parks, offer night drives – generally late afternoon drives that continue for an hour or two after sunset – an opportunity that no wildlife enthusiast will want to pass up. Come dusk, many familiar safari favourites bed down for the night, leaving the stage open for a cast of more elusive creatures, ranging from twitchy-nosed elephant shrews and bug-eyed bushbabies, both frequently picked up in the spotlight, to the singular and seldom seen termite-guzzling aardvark. Carnivores are usually most active after dark, and night drives offer a good chance of seeing leopards, along with smaller hunters such as civets, genets and servals.

Even for those who return to their lodge before dusk, the African bush can take on a thrillingly mysterious quality by night. It is worth spending a little time simply soaking this up from the lodge balcony or somewhere else, away from the lights and crowds. Especially near water, the night air comes alive with a white noise of cicadas and frogs, punctuated by the occasional eerie yelp of a hyena or low grunts of rival lions, providing a compelling backdrop to a night sky of mesmerizing clarity. This is the best time to look out for flashing fireflies, geckos and chameleons – the last go white after dark, a spectral pigmentation that makes them easy to spot – and such spectacular nocturnal birds as Verreaux's eagle-owl and the pennant-winged nightjar.

Lions playing under a setting full moon, the Masai Mara National Reserve

# LOCATING WILDLIFE

For those raised on wildlife documentaries, where obliging menageries enact one thrilling natural drama after the other, it is easy to embark on a safari with unrealistic expectations. In reality, many game drives entail long periods of bumping around seeing little but the odd grazing antelope or perching bird, punctuated by an occasional encounter as sudden as it is thrilling – a herd of elephants trumpeting from deep in the bush, or lions devouring a fresh kill, or a cheetah stalking the plains in search of an unsuspecting gazelle. While luck arguably plays the decisive role in what one might see on any given day, perseverance and skill are also key factors, and safaigoers who play an active role in locating wildlife are more likely to strike the jackpot than those who leave wildlife spotting to their driver-guide.

### How and Where to Spot Game

During the heat of the day, most animals prefer to stand or lie in the shade. In open country, always scan the grass below isolated trees. In denser vegetation, try to look into the thickets rather than at the openings between them. In open-topped vehicles, standing passengers who stick their heads out of the roof will stay more alert than those who sit, and the added height creates a better vantage point for seeing more distant animals.

### Waterbodies

Rivers, reservoirs and lakes are reliable wildlife magnets. Most animals need to drink every day, and watering points attract a steady trickle of thirsty elephant, zebra, giraffe, buffalo and other ungulates from mid-morning onwards, especially in arid climates and during dry

Wading through vegetation in a marsh, Amboseli National Park

seasons. Generally, steep and densely vegetated riverbanks attract fewer transient drinkers than large open reservoirs, but it is surprising how much wildlife emerges after a few minutes of observation at an apparently deserted waterside. A troop of monkeys might leap through the canopy, a crocodile erupt to the surface, a bushbuck or kudu creep quietly from the riverine tangle, or a kingfisher flash past in a blaze of colour.

### Behavioural Clues

The behaviour of one animal can alert safaigoers to the presence of another. For instance, vultures characteristically circle or roost in large numbers in the vicinity of a recent kill and attendant carnivores and scavengers. When a troop of baboons or vervet monkeys takes to the trees in noisy agitation, odds are there is a leopard or lion prowling nearby, while similarly jumpy guinea fowls or exaggeratedly alert antelope might well be responding to the same stimulus. It is common for small birds to become very agitated and vocal when a predatory snake, owl or goshawk is close to their nest. However, the most frequent indirect evidence of an interesting sighting requires no specialist bush knowledge to interpret – a huddle of safari vans in an area usually means that wildlife has been spotted there.

A pair of young giraffes drinking at a shallow waterhole while the adult keeps watch

## Faecal Spoor

Even where wildlife appears to be uncommon, the savannah will be littered with spoor. Among the most conspicuous of these are faeces, which include the heavy steaming pats deposited by elephants and rhinos, the elongated scats of lions and jackals, the calcium-rich white droppings of bone-chomping hyenas and the tidy piles of raisin-sized pellets that mark the territorial boundaries of most of the small antelope species.

## Animal Tracks

Sand roads through reserves often host a veritable logbook of animal prints. Most commonly, these will be antelope hoof marks, which consist of two teardrop-shaped segments shaped like an inverted elongated heart. Antelope prints are usually proportionate in size to the creature that made them, ranging from 13–15 cm (5–6 inches) long for an eland to about 2.5 cm (1 inch) for a duiker. Identification can often be narrowed down by looking at habitat and abundance – a solitary trail of medium-sized prints in riparian forest would most likely be a bushbuck, while a muddle of medium-sized prints in light woodland might be an impala herd. A buffalo print is larger and more rounded than any antelope's, while a giraffe print is squarer and up to 20 cm (8 inches) long. The print of a zebra is very horse-like, a hippo's resembles a four-pronged fig leaf, a rhino's is like a compressed head with cauliflower ears, while the plain oval half-a-metre- (2-ft-) long print of an elephant is recognizable by size alone.

Carnivore prints tend to resemble an inverted heart, topped by a quartet of oblong or circular toe marks. In the early morning, especially, a freshly laid trail will often lead a good tracker to the actual animal. It helps narrow down possibilities to look at size and whether claw marks are

**Lion footprint in soft sand**

visible above the toes, as is the case with all dogs and hyenas, but not in cats except for the cheetah. A clawless 10-cm (4-inch) print is almost certainly a lion's, while a similar print with claw marks would be a spotted hyena's.

## In the Camp

After a long day on the dusty road, most safarigoers return to camp ready for a quick nap, or settle down at the poolside bar with a chilled drink. However, lodges and camps often offer a prime opportunity to see smaller creatures such as lizards, squirrels, hyraxes and frogs. Many also offer great bird-watching, especially in the cooler hours of the day, when fruiting trees and flowering shrubs often attract a range of colourful birds that are unlikely to be noticed from a fast-moving vehicle.

Many lodges are built alongside rivers, lakes or artificial watering points that attract a steady trickle of transient wildlife. These watering points can be particularly rewarding if they are spotlit at night, when scavenging hyenas and smaller predators visit openly or surreptitiously. The notion of the lodge as a hide is taken to its logical conclusion in Taita Hills and at the so-called "tree hotels" of Kenya's Central Highlands – Treetops, The Ark and Serena Mountain Lodge (see pp370–71), where game drives are rendered almost redundant by the rich variety of wildlife that comes to drink throughout the day and night.

A red-bellied coastal squirrel feeding off a table at Shimba Hills Lodge

## Urban Habitats

Urban Kenya may not hold much promise for seeing the likes of elephant or lion, but it can be very rewarding for smaller creatures. Downtown Nairobi, for instance, is a prime site for the ungainly marabou stork, while leafier suburbs are still inhabited by leopards and monkeys, as well as colourful turacos and hornbills and elusive giant chameleons. By night, almost every urban wall below an altitude of around 1,500 m (4,921 ft) is likely to host a few bug-eyed geckos, and the eerie nocturnal call of the bushbaby is often heard reverberating through the suburbs. Nairobi National Park (see pp166–9) is famed for its improbable juxtaposition of giraffes, gazelles and even big cats against a heat-hazed backdrop of shimmering skyscrapers. With a little forethought and initiative, any enforced urban stopover will present visitors with the opportunity for some low-key wildlife watching.

A zebra crossing at the Trans-Africa Highway, Nairobi

# CONSERVATION

Like much of Africa, Kenya has suffered immense loss of natural habitat and a strong decline in wildlife population since the beginning of the 20th century. The plight of flagship animals such as the African wild dog and black rhino serves to underscore the deep vulnerability of the country's wildlife. Equally true, however, is that East Africa's national parks and reserves are among the last places on this planet where people can witness something akin to the volume and variety of mammals that roamed the planet in prehistoric times. Conservation is a major issue in Kenya, but ultimately for the uplifting reason that, by comparison to almost anywhere else on earth, there are still so many wild places and creatures left to conserve.

Eucalyptus and tea plantations encroaching on the countryside

## Habitat Loss

The core environmental issue in Kenya is the competition between wildlife and human population that has increased tenfold since the early colonial era. The most significant manifestation of this rising ecological pressure has been the widespread loss of habitat. Indigenous forests rich in biodiversity have been hacked down, making way for sterile pine and eucalyptus plantations or subsistence farms, while large tracts of savannah and other grassland have been replaced with cash crop monocultures. This situation is now more or less contained within most protected areas. Elsewhere, however, the ongoing destruction of biodiversity-sustaining microhabitats such as forest patches and small wetlands – whether directly or as a result of extensive environmental pollution or colonization by invasive plants of exotic origin – remains a cause for immediate concern.

## Hunting and Poaching

The immense wildlife herds that formerly coexisted with people in East Africa have suffered extensively from direct persecution over the past century, from the European hunters in the colonial era, from the commercial poaching industry that peaked in the 1980s and, at more sustainable levels, from local people. However, since 1990, the prevailing trend among populations of Kenya's large mammals has been positive. Most national wildlife parks and reserves depleted by the poaching wars of the 1980s have experienced significant population growth in many species. In spite of this encouraging trend, lion or cheetah are sometimes hunted by protective pastoralists if they threaten their herds in land bordering Kenya's reserves, and the current wave of rhino poaching is a scourge in Kenya as it is across Africa.

## Protected Areas

The bulk of Kenya's protected areas are state-owned and fall under the auspices of either the Kenya Wildlife Service (KWS) or the Kenya Forest Department (KFD). KWS manages all national parks, marine parks and national reserves (in some cases, on behalf of the district authority), while KFD is responsible for forest reserves. Many of today's key protected areas were initially set aside during the colonial era. This imposed strongly on local communities, who were forcibly relocated to sites outside the park boundary and forbidden from taking their livestock to traditional

Attending on cheetahs at the KWS headquarters in Nairobi

The endangered African wild dog, a rare sight in Kenya's parks

grazing grounds. Furthermore, hunting – whether for food or to protect crops – had abruptly been rebranded as poaching and criminalized.

KWS has taken a different approach in protecting the country's wildlife by involving the local people in the conservation process and encouraging the creation of ecotourism projects that bring direct benefits to communities living in buffer zones, particularly in the vicinity of national parks such as Tsavo (see pp186–91) and Amboseli (see pp198–201). Another important development has been the creation of private reserves, particularly on Laikipia Plateau (see pp322–5), whose agglomeration of small reserves is probably the world's most important stronghold for the black rhino, and also harbours other rarities such as Grevy's zebra, reticulated giraffe and African wild dog.

## Tourism

A healthy and flourishing tourism industry is probably integral to the long-term survival of Kenya's diverse wildlife. Not only does it generate direct revenue in the form of entrance fees to parks and reserves and private wildlife concessions, it also creates a wide range of relatively well-paid conservation- and tourist-related employment for the people of Kenya. Furthermore, it serves as a strong deterrent to commercial poachers, who cannot easily go about their clandestine business in areas regularly visited by tourists. For all that, there is much that visitors can do to minimize their impact on protected areas (see pp76–7).

## Endangered Species

While much of Kenya's wildlife survives in abundant numbers and in some cases thrives in areas that are well-protected, there are some species that are rated as Critically Endangered (CR), Endangered (EN) or Vulnerable (VU) in the IUCN Red List of threatened animals. The eight critically endangered mammals in Kenya are the black rhino, hirola antelope, Tana river red colobus monkey, Cosens's gerbil and four types of shrew. There are 13 mammal species on the endangered list including Grevy's zebra, African wild dog and Aders' duiker, while the 30 or so vulnerable species include elephant, cheetah and lion.

## CITES

The Convention on International Trade in Endangered Species of Wild Fauna and Flora (CITES) is an international agreement blocking trade in specimens or products of plant and animal species that threaten their survival. Signed in 1963, it currently accords protection to 30,000 species and products, ranging from rhino horns to various dried herbs. Many species present in Kenya have been listed by CITES, but its biggest coup in the Kenyan context was the ban on ivory trade implemented in 1990 and considered the key moment in the reversal of the extinction-threatening slaughter of elephants by poachers.

### IUCN Red List

Established in 1963, the International Union for Conservation of Nature (IUCN) Red List of Threatened Species uses a set of precise criteria to evaluate the extinction risk of more than 61,000 species and subspecies of flora and fauna. Every animal or plant taxon evaluated is assigned one of the following categories
- Extinct (EX) – No individuals known to survive.
- Extinct in the Wild (EW) – Survives only in captivity or as an introduced population outside its natural range.
- Critically Endangered (CR) – Extremely high risk of extinction in the wild.
- Endangered (EN) – Very high risk of extinction.
- Vulnerable (VU) – High risk of extinction.
- Near Threatened (NT) – Close to qualifying for or is likely to qualify for a threatened category in the near future.
- Least Concern (LC) – No significant risk of extinction.
- Data Deficient (DD) – Insufficient information available for assessment.
- Not Evaluated (NE).

A rare encounter between a black rhino with a white rhino near Lake Nakuru

# WILDLIFE THROUGH THE YEAR

The natural world does not adhere to the rigid calendars that dictate such human events as festivals and public holidays. All the same, it does follow a clear annual cycle, one that will inevitably display slight variations from any given year to the next, but that is also marked by several reasonably predictable events. Pivotal to all this is the length and duration of the wet seasons. These show a marked regional variation, but usually consist of the short rains from late October into December and the more substantial long rains, which last from late February to late May or early June, generally peaking over April. The short dry spell between the short and long rains usually has little effect on wildlife. However, the main dry season, from June to October, is the toughest time of year for most species.

## Rainy Season (Nov–May)

The arrival of the first rains signals a period of renewal comparable to spring in colder climates. The bush is rejuvenated by the fresh growth of buds, leaves and grass, and the availability of food and water is high. Consequently, this time of year is associated with heightened insect activity, calving and nesting and the arrival of migrant birds from the northern hemisphere.

Spotted hyenas keeping watch over their cubs at the den

**Cuckoos call** *(Nov–Mar)*. There is some regional and species-specific variation, but the wet season is when birds are most likely to perform display flights or spend long periods advertising their presence to potential mates with repetitive calls. No sounds so typify the East African bush during this period as the persistent "it-will-rain" call of the red-chested cuckoo and the overwrought "dee-dee-dee-diederick" sound of Diederick's cuckoo, both of which are heard everywhere but are seldom seen.

**Denning season** *(Nov–Mar)*. Most dogs and hyenas rear their pups in dens, which are often excavated below termite hills or from old aardvark holes. There is some seasonal and regional variation, but jackals and bat-eared foxes in particular tend to give birth at the start of the rains and to stick close to their dens for the next 2 to 3 months, often offering great opportunities for close-up sightings.

**Breeding season for birds** *(Nov–May)*. Although it varies greatly from one species to the next, courtship and breeding activity usually starts with the onset of the rains. This is most visible in the many birds who shed their "ugly duckling" camouflage plumage and emerge in full breeding colours. This phenomenon is especially striking among the bright-yellow masked weavers and dazzling red bishops, as well as the temporarily long-tailed widows and whydahs.

**Wildlife disperses into bush** *(Nov–May)*. During the rainy season, the bush is scattered with temporary pools. The area around these pools provides fresh fodder, allowing ungulates and other grazers to disperse over a wide region. The dispersal also allows overgrazed land close to more permanent waterbodies to recover in time for the next dry season.

**Insect activity peaks** *(Nov–May)*. Insects are most active during the rainy season, whether it is the fireflies that light up forest fringes at night, or the myriad

A masked weaver arriving with building material for his nest

colourful butterflies that flit between flowers and faeces to feed. A striking event, often following an afternoon rainstorm, is the irruption of flying ants that frequently attract flocks of hungry raptors, in particular steppe and tawny eagles, black kites and buzzards.

**Calving season** *(Dec–Feb)*. The window between the short and long rains is the main calving season for wildebeest, plains zebra, gazelle and many other ungulates, particularly in the south. In the Serengeti-Mara system, migrating grazers calve on the Tanzanian side of the border, as do resident populations in Amboseli, Tsavo and the Masai Mara.

**Passage migrants leave** *(Mar–Apr)*. As the rainy season draws to a close and the northern winter thaws, the millions of migrant birds that overwintered in Africa embark on the long flight to Europe. This can result in exceptional aggregations of certain species – especially swallows – as they pass through Kenya en route from southern Africa, and unexpected species being spotted in the oddest places. By late April, all the migrant birds will usually have departed.

## Dry Season (Jun–Oct)

Depleted water and food sources in the dry season make it a period when survival rather than reproduction is crucial in the natural world. Ironically, this

A flock of great white pelicans landing on Lake Nakuru

is also the best time to see large mammals, as visibility is improved by the lack of vegetation and animals congregate close to water sources.

**Secondary gazelle calving season** *(Jun–Aug)*. Although many gazelles calve at the same time as the plains zebra, some calve later on, notably Thomson's in June and July and Grant's in July and August.

**Marsh terrapins aestivate** *(Jun–Sep)*. Within a month of the last rain, the muddy pools that dot the bush start to dry up. Nomadic marsh terrapins that inhabit such pools will either wander away in search of permanent water or aestivate – that is, bury themselves deep in the cracking mud and shut down most life systems until the next rains, when they re-emerge undaunted.

**Wildebeest migration** *(Jul–Oct)*. The wildebeest usually cross

into the Masai Mara from the Serengeti in late July or August, and spend the next 3 months grazing the plains bare before they return southwards in October *(see pp128–9)*.

**Wildlife congregates near water** *(Aug–Oct)*. The dry season really kicks in over this period. Drinking water tends to be restricted to perennial rivers and lakes, which attract high densities of animals. This phenomenon often results in superb game viewing, particularly in Samburu-Buffalo Springs and Amboseli, where the wildlife concentrations can be mind-boggling.

**Bushfire season** *(Aug–Oct)*. The dry season may offer great game viewing but it also brings plenty of hardship to wildlife (and subsistence farmers), not least in the form of the destructive wildfires that frequently sweep across vast tracts of bush, killing smaller or slower-moving animals such as tortoises and snakes, and attracting birds such as storks and raptors that feed on the fleeing insects. Most African trees are fire-resistant, so the bush recovers quickly, and the fresh shoots that emerge from the burnt grass offer juicy pickings to many grazers.

**Passage migrants arrive** *(Oct–Nov)*. The first rains at the end of the dry season coincide with the arrival of millions of migrant birds from the Palaearctic, some of which continue on to southern Africa while others settle in Kenya for the duration of the northern winter. Raptors, waders, warblers and water-fowl are among the better represented groups.

Wildebeest crossing Mara river during the annual cross-border migration

# PRACTICAL INFORMATION

The incredible diversity found in Kenya's national parks and reserves, both in terms of landscape and wildlife, makes for a memorable safari experience. In some respects, booking a safari in Kenya could hardly be more straightforward. The first thing to be decided is the safari destination, and there are plenty of reputable tour operators, both in-country and abroad, that can offer expert guidance. Following that, budget and personal taste will be key factors in determining what kind of safari – fly-in or road, lodges or campsites – seems most suitable. However, it is important to consider all available options carefully before booking, and the following pages are a guide to that process, from planning and booking to packing and preparation; they also highlight various key aspects of getting the most from the safari once it starts.

## Choosing an Itinerary

The most suitable itinerary depends greatly on how long visitors want to spend on safari, what they hope to see and whether they fly or drive between different reserves. The Masai Mara (see pp266–9) is the best starting point for first-time safarigoers in search of the Big Five. By road, it is often combined with the Rift Valley lakes and the tree hotels (see pp320–21) of the Central Highlands, but by air it could as easily be twinned with Amboseli National Park (see pp198–201). Samburu-Buffalo Springs (see pp346–9) is good for repeat safarigoers, Meru (see pp334–7) is the best for untrammelled wilderness and Laikipia Plateau (see pp322–5) is great for walking and night drives. It is advisable to prepare an itinerary in liaison with a reputable tour operator (see pp396–7) with a strong specialist knowledge of Kenya.

## When to Go

Kenya's top wildlife attraction is the Serengeti-Mara migration (see pp128–9), when wildebeest arrive in Masai Mara from late July onwards and cross back into Tanzania before November. If catching this event is the top priority, then any time from August to mid-October is reliable. This is peak tourist season, however, and the parks are less overrun with visitors at other times of year. Of the other seasonal parks, Amboseli is at its best at the end of the dry season between October and early November, while wildlife numbers in Samburu-Buffalo Springs tend to be lower during good rainy seasons. Bird-watching is best from November to March, when resident species are boosted by Palaearctic migrants. There is no truly bad time to go on safari, but the risk of game drives being washed out and vehicles getting bogged down in mud is highest at the peak of the long rains (March and April).

## Types of Safari

There are a number of things to consider when deciding what type of safari to book. These include whether to fly or drive between reserves, whether to travel as part of a group or in a private party and whether to stay in simple campsites, large mid-range lodges or smaller and more upmarket bush camps. To some extent, these decisions come down to choosing between a cheap option and an expensive one – a group driving safari with budget campsites will cost a fraction of a private fly-in safari

Driving through vast herds of wildebeest on the plains of the Masai Mara National Reserve

Camping in the wilderness of Amboseli's stark savannah

using exclusive bush camps. Apart from budget, the decision is purely a matter of personal taste. Flying between reserves reduces transit time and places fewer geographic restrictions on the itinerary. However, it creates a greater distance between travellers and the countryside and people of Kenya. Joining a group safari also has its pros and cons – if the group gels well, it can be great fun and the congenial atmosphere will enhance the experience. However, a private safari allows for a greater degree of autonomy, especially for those with special interests.

In some respects, budget camping safaris, though cheap, offer the most hands-on safari experience, especially at night, when campers are separated from the African night by nothing but a flimsy canvas sheet. A more popular option is a lodge-based safari, with two broad accommodation types being available – the large "hotel in the bush" lodge operated by several chains, and the more intimate bush camp offering standing tents or stand-alone chalets. Larger lodges are often the more reassuring option for nervous safari novices, offering secure accommodation, decent restaurant food and a high degree of comfort, but their institutionalized atmosphere tends to neutralize the wilderness, isolating guests from the immense African night sky and sounds. Bush camps tend to be smaller, with anything from 6 to 20 units, and blend into the surrounding

wilderness in a more authentic manner than the larger lodges. Many bush camps are genuinely luxurious, with chic decor, catering almost entirely to fly-in guests, for whom they provide all activities using experienced in-house guides. If the price tag is within range, there is no better way to experience Africa in the wild.

Bookings can either be made through a local ground operator or a tour agency at home. In most cases, a domestic tour operator will possess greater in-depth knowledge of the terrain and can offer more competitive rates. The advantages of using an international agent are that planning an itinerary is easier, the agency will often get a better flight package than an independent traveller would and there is generally less room

A stamped entrance ticket to Meru National Park

for any complications regarding payment and insurance.

Prices are usually inclusive of accommodation, camping gear, services of a vehicle and driver-guide, all meals, park fees and other activities. Drinks and tips are extra. Check what is included in advance.

## Entrance Fees

All parks and reserves charge significant entrance fees, ranging from US$80 per person for 24 hours at the more popular reserves such as Amboseli and the Masai Mara to US$20 per person for 24 hours at more obscure ones. A low vehicle entrance fee is charged where appropriate. At most parks, fees can be paid in US dollars or Kenyan shillings, but others, such as Amboseli, the Aberdares, Tsavo East and West, Nairobi and Lake Nakuru, now operate a Safari Card system, where visitors can add credit to the card and use them instead of cash. These cards function like debit cards that have to be topped up with sufficient cash to cover park fees. In practice, fees are built into safari quotes by the operator, but self-drive safari-goers will need to familiarize themselves with current fees and the Safari Card system.

Kifaru House's rural façade blending into the surroundings, Lewa Downs

## What to Wear

The ideal clothing for safari is loose-fitting, lightweight and made of natural fabrics. Pale garments are less likely to attract tsetse flies but they tend to show more dirt, while bright colours can be intrusive when tracking wildlife on foot. The quantity required depends on the duration and type of safari – more changes will be necessary on budget camping safaris than at small, exclusive lodges where anything put in the laundry basket is returned clean within 24 hours. Many Kenyan reserves are at high altitudes, and nights can be cooler than might be expected of tropical Africa, so it is sensible to pack sweatshirts and a windbreaker. After dark, closed shoes, socks and trousers offer the best protection against mosquito bites. Vehicle-based safaris do not call for specialized footwear, but decent shoes are essential for walking safaris and mountain ascents.

**A backpacker carrying essentials**

## Photographing Wildlife

Daytime game drives usually offer better photographic opportunities than other activities, because the vehicle doubles as a hide and as a stabilizing device for the camera. Ideally, the camera should be supported with a beanbag or even some bunched-up clothing placed firmly on the roof or window edge, and the driver asked to switch off the car and keep as still as possible – the vibration of a running engine or any other slight movement while the shutter is open will almost certainly result in a blurred image. In an open-topped vehicle, the elevation of the roof will often provide the best photographic vantage point for distant animals and perched birds, but where the subject is at ground level close to the vehicle, a more pleasing result will usually be obtained by shooting from the car window.

Some drivers are skilled at lining up vehicles for photography, others rather less so, and it will almost always help if the photographer provides some guidance. Put simply, the best result is likely to be obtained by approaching wildlife along a line that places the vehicle directly between the animal and the sun, while avoiding placing any distracting vegetation between subject and lens. The most appropriate manner of approach is a matter of judgement – come in too fast and direct, and the animal might be startled away, but an exaggeratedly slow or stop-start approach is likely to make the animal think that it is being stalked.

## Photographic Gear

The two most important considerations in obtaining high-quality wildlife photographs are lens magnification and support sufficient to prevent camera shake while using a long lens. An SLR camera is preferable to a "point and shoot", and the lowest magnification lens that can realistically be used is 200 mm, though 300 mm or even 500 mm is preferable. Zoom lenses of 70–300 mm are cheaper than fixed lenses, and allow for greater flexibility when it comes to composition. However, they tend to lack sharpness and are less useful in low-light conditions – flaws that are exacerbated by the use of a 1.4x or 2x converter.

Photographers with limited experience in the field of wildlife often underestimate the importance of camera support equipment. Tripods, monopods and window clamps can all be used for support, but the most flexible and stable option for shooting out of a vehicle window or roof is a beanbag. This is easy to make at home, and the addition of a zip will allow it to be carried empty on flights and filled with suitable

Photographers taking pictures of flocks of pink flamingoes on the shoreline of a Rift Valley lake

Hikers with a local guide en route to Sheldrick Falls, Shimba Hills

## Other Items to Pack

Some useful and essential items to take on a trip include sunblock, a hat and sunglasses, a penknife, a torch and an alarm clock. A day pack is useful to carry binoculars and field guides, and it is advisable to pack all the toiletries that might be required. Contact-lens users with sensitive eyes might want to carry a pair of glasses for dusty safari conditions. Mosquitoes are present in most reserves and parks, so it is vital to carry a supply of prophylactic drugs.

material, such as beans, rice and corn, at the start of the safari.

It is important to use a camera bag that insulates expensive equipment against the insidious dust associated with most game reserves. Camera users should make sure they have all the batteries, plugs, connecters and storage devices they will need, as well as a universal adapter. Almost all safari accommodation has facilities for recharging cameras, although smaller tented camps or those in very remote areas may rely on electricity generators which are switched on for only a few hours per day.

### Binoculars

Essential for any kind of safari, binoculars help obtain better views of distant wildlife, and are invaluable when it comes to spotting and identifying bird species. The minimal requirement is 8x magnification, but for the steady of hand 10x, 12x or 16x is better. Full-size 8x40 and 10x50 models have a wider field of vision and better colour definition than their compact 8x25 or 10x30 counterparts. However, the latter are more portable, steadier to hold and inexpensive. Obscure brands tend to suffer from poor focusing, distortion and unsatisfactory colour rendition, and gimmicks such as universal focus or zoom are best avoided when selecting a pair.

### Field Guides

Kenya Wildlife Services (KWS) produce some maps for the more popular parks, which are available from their headquarters at the main gate of Nairobi National Park as well as the individual park gates. They list the main animals that safarigoers are likely to see, and for self-drivers, the maps show the numbered junctions which correspond to junction numbers on sign posts within the park. A wide selection of more detailed field guides covers the flora and fauna of Africa as a whole and Kenya more specifically. There are some that will be of use to accompany a general safari, and these generally highlight the mammals and birds typical of Kenya. Bird-watching is naturally a highlight so a specific book on Kenya's birds, and their behaviour and habitat, is recommended for those with a keen interest. There is a good choice available in bookshops in Nairobi and lodge gift shops, but this cannot be guaranteed and it is advisable to purchase the books required before arrival in Kenya

The field guide on the following pages (see pp100–149) will help visitors in putting a name to most mammals and some of the more conspicuous of Kenya's reptiles, amphibians and birds.

## Children on Safari

Taking children on safari can be a mixed blessing. Most children are thrilled at the sight of any wildlife, and early exposure to the wildernesses of Africa is a memory that will endure for a lifetime. Equally, Kenya's game reserves can be strenuous for younger children, who may quickly become tired and irritable on long uneventful drives. In general, older children will take better to the whole safari regime, and many private lodges do not allow younger children for safety reasons or even out of consideration to other guests. It will be a gamble to take children along and the safest way to ensure that the trip remains pleasant and within control is to book a private safari, so that game drives can be curtailed as and when boredom sets in, ensuring that the needs of younger children are catered to and other safarigoers remain undisturbed.

Children experiencing wildlife at close quarters, Masai Mara

## Disabled Travellers

Kenya offers few facilities for disabled travellers, and safaris present a number of additional problems, from the difficulties associated with getting in and out of light aircraft or tall 4WDs to rough roads and lack of wheelchair ramps or other special arrangements at most camps and lodges. On the other hand, Kenyan culture is generally far more accommodating to the elderly and disabled, and the staff at most camps will go out of their way to surmount any logistical obstacles. It is possible for disabled travellers who liaise with a reputable tour operator, and are clear about what they can and cannot do up front, to have a perfectly satisfactory safari in Kenya.

## Health

The biggest health risk on safari, as elsewhere in Kenya, is malaria *(see pp404–5)*. The tropical sun can induce dehydration or sunstroke on foot safaris or in open-topped vehicles, so it is best to keep a hat handy, use sunblock and drink plenty of water. Bilharzia, commonly known as snail fever, is borne by freshwater snails and can be contracted while swimming in lakes or rivers in game reserves, although the more overt threat presented by crocodiles should be enough of a discouragement in itself.

Apart from mosquitoes, the most dangerous biting creatures are snakes, but these

Appropriately dressed hikers on a foot safari with a forest ranger

tend to be secretive, and unprovoked attacks are a rarity. The risk of being bitten by a snake, spider or scorpion is greatly reduced by wearing closed shoes and trousers. The most annoying diurnal biters are the harmless tsetse flies and horseflies. After walking in grassy places, skin should be closely checked for ticks, which are easy to remove within an hour or two, but can be difficult to dislodge once firmly attached. Certain tick species can cause tick-bite fever, a debilitating but easily cured disease.

## Safety Around Wild Animals

In many Kenyan parks and reserves, wildlife is habituated to people and vehicles, but this is not the same thing as

domestication. The lions that laze around obliviously in front of a cluster of safari vehicles will almost certainly respond differently were one of the passengers to disembark. Most likely, they would run away, but it is also possible that they would attack. Similarly, large herbivores such as elephant, hippo, rhino and buffalo might all bulldoze pedestrians under certain circumstances. Such attacks are rare, but they most often stem from a combination of bad judgement and even worse luck, so it is worth keeping in mind a few general rules. Wildlife should not be approached on foot, except in the company of a reliable guide, and visitors should not get between a hippo and water. Food, especially meat or fruit, should not be left in the same tent where people will sleep. If large predators are encountered while on foot, safarigoers should be aware that there is no more certain way of triggering the instinct to give chase than to run away.

## Blending In

Appropriate clothing is important on foot safaris but rather less so in vehicles, as animals generally pay little attention to individual passengers. Pungent perfumes or other strong artificial smells may disturb wildlife or fellow passengers and smoking should be avoided. Far more intrusive – to wildlife and to vehicles in the vicinity – are those whose response to any interesting sighting is to exclaim loudly. Although it has no effect on wildlife, driving around slowly at 20–30 kmph (12–19 mph) makes for a far more involving experience than speeding about in air-conditioned isolation.

## Environmental Impact

The long list of rules that governs the national parks and reserves in Kenya might seem excessive or restrictive to first-time safarigoers, but most of these rules have been designed

A curious lioness mauling a camera, Masai Mara National Reserve

Bushfire ravaging the moorland at Mount Elgon National Park

to ensure the safety of wildlife and visitors, and to minimize the environmental impact of tourism. Littering, for instance, is not only unsightly but potentially dangerous to inquisitive wildlife. Discarded matches or cigarette butts are among the most common causes of uncontrolled bushfires. Also forbidden in most reserves is off-road driving, which can cause considerable damage to fragile ecosystems, and hooting or yelling at animals to attract their attention. Likewise, speed limits are in place to prevent accidents on the often unpredictable road surfaces, as well as collisions with unsuspecting wildlife. Feeding wildlife can also have several negative effects, particularly with respect to baboons and monkeys, which quickly learn to associate humans with food and often become dangerous once they do, leading to them being shot. Collecting plants or buying animals is also expressly forbidden, as is the sale or purchase of products of animals or plants specified on the CITES list *(see p69)*.

On an organized safari, the driver-guides can be expected to take the lead when it comes to sensitive behaviour towards the environment, wildlife and other safarigoers. They will be aware of park rules and of the kind of behaviour that might disturb animals, and can be expected to make their clients conscious of these where necessary. When stopping for a sighting, the driver-guide should switch off the engine, mute the volume on the radio and keep conversation to a hushed minimum so as not to disturb the wildlife or people in other vehicles. Occasionally, however, a driver-guide might contravene park rules – for instance by following a hunting predator off-road, thereby disturbing the hunt, or by provoking an elephant into a mock charge, or driving dangerously fast – in which case the client might want to intervene.

## Staff Relations

Building a good relationship with the driver-guide and other staff, such as a cook on a camping safari, is vital to the success of a safari. Safarigoers should be proactive and make sure that the driver is aware of any special requirements and interests, and feels like his clients are active participants in wildlife spotting and identification. Most drivers are quite poorly paid and appreciate it when clients cover the cost of a meal or drink. They survive mainly on tips, so be generous. There are no hard-and-fast tipping rules, but most safari companies will advise clients as to what constitutes an average or good tip for a driver-guide. It goes without saying that when it comes to sorting out minor frictions or disagreements, humour will usually get better long-term results than anger.

## Special Interests

Although most first-time visitors to Kenya opt for a general interest safari, a variety of more specialized options are available, ranging from dedicated ornithological tours to camel-back adventures in the remote northern deserts of the country *(see pp396–7)*.

Ranger interacting with tourists at the Sweetwaters Chimpanzee Sanctuary

# Safari Parks at a Glance

Kenya's astounding wealth of reserves and national parks often dazzles first-time visitors. In reality, however, the safari industry focuses on a handful of more popular reserves, of which Amboseli, Tsavo, Laikipia, Nairobi and the Masai Mara are obvious starting points, ideally broken up with a night at one of the Aberdare tree hotels. For repeat visits, Samburu, Buffalo Springs and Shaba National Reserves stand out for hosting large mammals that are practically endemic to Kenya, while for one of the most thrillingly untrammelled safari experiences in Africa, Meru is an ideal getaway. Saiwa Swamp and Hell's Gate offer the chance to break the regular game drive regimen with walking or cycling, while Lake Nakuru and Kakamega are essential stops for keen bird-watchers.

**Lake Nakuru National Park**
*(see pp280–83)*, set on the Rift Valley's floor, is popular for its soda lake that supports millions of flamingoes and pelicans.

**Masai Mara National Reserve** *(see pp266–9)* is everybody's favourite safari destination in Kenya. Renowned for the spectacular annual migration of the wildebeest, this popular game reserve also hosts a high density of lion, cheetah, spotted hyena and other carnivores.

0 km          100
0 miles          100

Lokichoggio • Lokitaung

*Lake Turkana*

Kalokol •

*Turkwel*

Lodwar •

*Suam*

Kitale • *Saiwa Swamp National Park*          Maralal •

Kakamega • *Kakamega Forest National Reserve*          *Laikipia* Isi Plateau
*Nzoia*          Nanyuki • M

*Ruma National Park*     Nakuru     *Aberdare National Park*  Na Nyer
• Homa Bay

*Mara*     Narok •     Naivasha •

Nairo

*Nairobi National Park*

**Hell's Gate National Park** *(see pp274–5)* is one of the few sanctuaries in Kenya that offers game viewing on foot.          Namanga

**Amboseli National Park** *(see pp198–201)* is home to some of East Africa's most impressive giant-tusked elephants. This national park is most beautiful at sunset, with spectacular views of Mount Kilimanjaro, which looms dramatically on the southern horizon.

**Samburu-Buffalo Springs-Shaba National Reserves**
*(see pp346–50)* are contiguous and semiarid. Their
austere plains protect a host of dry country species such
as the brilliant cobalt-chested vulturine guinea fowl.
The Ewaso Nyiro river flows through the three reserves,
which offer good leopard sightings.

**Tsavo East and West national parks**
*(see pp186–91)* are home to more than 10,000
elephants, whose trademark red colouration
is caused by bathing in red dust. The two
national parks are also the best places in
Kenya to see the endangered black rhino.

**Meru National Park** *(see pp334–7)*, Kenya's most
underrated major park, is an off-the-beaten-track gem. Its
lush plains are run through by dozens of palm-lined
streams and it is inhabited by large herds of reticulated
giraffe, elephant and buffalo.

Mandera

Moyale

Laga Bor

Laga Boglal

Wajir

Ewaso Nyiro

Laga Dera

Tana

Garissa

Hola

Tiva

avo

Malindi

Voi    Galana

*Taita Hills
Wildlife Sanctuary*

Mombasa

Tsavo East and West
national parks

**Shimba Hills National Reserve**
*(see pp220–23)*,
an underestimated coastal
reserve, is the last Kenyan refuge
for the handsome sable
antelope. It also has the scenic
Sheldrick Falls.

| ■ Safari Destination | What to See | When to Go |
|---|---|---|
|  **Aberdare National Park** Protecting the Aberdare range, this park is home to a wide variety of forest animals. The upper slopes, covered in open heath and bamboo forest and studded with pretty waterfalls, are well worth visiting *(see pp320–21)*. | All the Big Five. The world's largest wild population of the elusive and endangered mountain bongo. Genet, bushbuck, bushpig, black-and-white colobus, blue monkey. | Treetops and The Ark are accessible all year round. During peak rainy seasons (Nov–Dec and Mar–May), exploration is difficult as the dirt tracks to the upper slopes become impassable. |
| **Amboseli National Park** The snowcapped peak of Kilimanjaro dominates the skyline of this small park. Amboseli's dusty savannah and lush swampland are known for their large tuskers, the birdlife and seasonal concentrations of grazers *(see pp198–201)*.  | Elephant, lion, cheetah, spotted hyena, plains zebra, wildebeest, gazelle, giraffe, hippo, waterbirds, a wide variety of birds. | Wildlife densities peak near the end of the rains. Migrant waterfowl numbers are highest over Nov–Mar. The park is best visited outside tourist seasons (Mar–May; Oct–Nov). |
|  **Hell's Gate National Park** Centred upon the dramatic Hell's Gate gorge, this is the only savannah reserve in Kenya where walking and cycling are freely permitted. The plains hold impressive concentrations of grazers and birds *(see pp274–5)*. | Lion, cheetah, elephant, giraffe, buffalo, zebra, wildebeest, gazelle, hartebeest, cliff-dwelling raptors such as Verreaux's eagle and Lammergeyer. | Wildlife concentration is highest in the dry season (Jun–Oct) while bird diversity is greatest in summer (Nov–Mar). An early start is advisable to avoid sunstroke and/or dehydration. |
| **Kakamega Forest National Reserve** A celebrated bird-watching site, this reserve – the country's last substantial tract of western rainforest – also harbours primates such as the nocturnal sloth-like potto *(see pp298–301)*.  | Black-and-white colobus, red-tailed, De Brazza's and blue monkeys, hammer-headed fruit bat, 300-plus bird species including the great blue turaco, 400-plus butterfly species. | All year round. Walking conditions are pleasant in the dry months (Jun–Oct). Birds are easiest to locate during the mating season (Jun–Oct), when butterflies are also most conspicuous. |
|  **Laikipia Plateau** The patchwork of conservancies and ranchland on this plateau includes several of Kenya's most exclusive reserves, including Lewa Wildlife Conservancy, Ol Pejeta and Solio Game Reserve. Lodges offer guided walks and night drives *(see pp322–5)*. | Black and white rhinos, lion, cheetah, Grevy's zebra, greater kudu, reticulated giraffe, Lelwel hartebeest, elephant, chimpanzee (introduced to Ol Pejeta). | Throughout the year, though roads can be more challenging and wildlife is more dispersed during the long rains (Mar–May). |
| **Lake Nakuru National Park** This small park in the heart of the Rift Valley is known for the waterfowl that congregate on its lake. The park's road circuit is easily covered in half a day, and offers the best chance of seeing white rhino in Kenya *(see pp280–83)*.  | Black and white rhinos, buffalo, lion, leopard, waterbuck, giraffe, olive baboon, 400-plus bird species including large flocks of flamingoes and great white pelican. | Throughout the year, although the number and variety of water-associated birds is most impressive in Nov–Mar when resident species are supplemented by Eurasian migrants. |
| **Masai Mara National Reserve** Kenya's famous wildlife destination is a northerly extension of the Serengeti in Tanzania. Its annual wildebeest cross-border migration is one of National Geographic's seven wonders of the modern world *(see pp266–9)*.  | Black and white rhinos, elephant, lion, Maasai giraffe, buffalo, gerenuk, gazelle, lesser kudu, Beisa oryx, hippo. | The wildebeest migration typically crosses in from Tanzania in July and returns in October. Exact timings vary from year to year, but big herds can reliably be seen over Aug–Sep. |
| **Meru National Park** Located in the lush eastern rainshadow of Mount Kenya, Meru is the most underrated of Kenya's major parks. Game viewing can be superb, however, and it is one of those rare havens from tourist traffic *(see pp334–7)*. | Elephant, lion, cheetah, spotted hyena, plains zebra, wildebeest, gazelle, giraffe, hippo, waterbirds. | Throughout the year. Game viewing peaks near the end of the dry season (Jul–Nov), when the grass is low and wildlife congregates along the park's many perennial streams. |

| Accommodation | Practical Information |
|---|---|
|  **Treetops Lodge**<br><br>The only two lodges are The Ark and Treetops *(see p321)*, both of which offer game viewing. Both operate as annexes of hotels outside the park, with guests being bussed in and out in groups. Three small self-catering camps are operated by KWS, and camping is permitted at a few cleared sites. | 160 km (100 miles) NW of Nairobi; 20 km (12 miles) W of Nyeri.<br>**Tel** 020 2046271. **Open** 6am–7pm daily. 🚗 Safari Card. 🏨 🐾 ⛰️<br>**w** **kws.org** |
| The park has at least 10 lodges, ranging from large hotels run by the Serena *(see p365)* chain to luxury tented camps such as Satao and Tortilis on Maasai concessions bordering the park. KWS runs two self-catering guesthouses. Many campsites lie right outside the park managed by Maasai communities.  **Satao Elerai Camp** | 230 km (142 miles) S of Nairobi via Namanga. **Tel** 020 8029705. 🚗<br>**Open** 6am–7pm daily. 🚗 Safari Card.<br>🐾 ⛰️ **w** **kws.org** |
|  **Elsamere, Lake Naivasha**<br><br>Camping is permitted at several sites but otherwise there is no accommodation within the park. However, it is easily visited as a day trip from any one of the dozens of lodges that surround Lake Naivasha, which lies immediately north of the park. | 100 km (62 miles) NW of Nairobi; 3 km (2 miles) S of Lake Naivasha. **Tel** 020 2433037. 🚗 🚌 to within walking distance of entrance gate.<br>**Open** 6am–6pm daily. 🏨 🐾 🐾 ⛰️<br>**w** **kws.org** |
| The closest conventional hotel is in Kakamega town. Within the forest, cosy guesthouse accommodation with meals is available at Rondo Retreat *(see p369)* and there are several affordable self-catering and camping options.  **Rondo Retreat** | 15 km (9 miles) E of Kakamega town.<br>**Tel** 020 2418419. 🚗 🚌<br>**Open** 6am–7pm daily. 🏨 🐾 🐾<br>⛰️ **w** **kws.org** |
|  **Borana Lodge, Laikipia**<br><br>Dozens of private lodges *(see p370)* are dotted around the plateau. Most of them are small exclusive bush or tented camps offering all-inclusive fly-in packages from Nairobi. Many local tribal concessions offer more basic camping facilities aimed at self-drive visitors. | 10 km (6 miles) W of Nanyuki airport.<br>🚗 **Open** varies between conservancies, but typically 6am–6pm daily.<br>🐾 🏨 🐾 🛏️ ⛰️<br>**w** **laikipia.org** |
| There are only three proper lodges in the park, of which the best is Lion Hill Game Lodge *(see p368)*, run by the Sarova hotel chain. Also within the park are several self-catering units and campsites managed by KWS. A wide selection of hotels and guesthouses can be found in the adjacent town of Nakuru. **Sarova Lion Hill Lodge** | Outskirts of Nakuru town; 145 km (90 miles) NW of Nairobi.<br>**Tel** 020 2671685. 🚌 to Nakuru town.<br>**Open** 6am–7pm daily. 🚗 Safari Card.<br>🐾 ⛰️ **w** **kws.org** |
|  **Kicheche Camp**<br><br>Dozens of lodges are scattered in and around the reserve, ranging from chain hotels to exclusive bush lodges. For general game viewing, the best lodges are those situated northwest of the Talek and Mara rivers. Several campsites also operate in and around the park. | 265 km (165 miles) SW of Nairobi via Narok. 🚗 **Open** 6:30am–7pm daily. 🐾 🐾 ⛰️ **w** **maratriangle.org** |
| Only small upmarket bush lodges operate within the park, notably Elsa's Kopje and Rhino River Camp *(see p370)*. KWS also has a few self-catering cottages and there are several campsites. Guesthouse accommodation is available at Maua en route from Meru town.  **Elsa's Kopje** | 75 km (47 miles) E of Meru town.<br>**Tel** 061 2303094. 🚗 **Open** 6am–7pm daily. 🐾 🐾 ⛰️ **w** **kws.org** |

| ■ **Safari Destination** | **What to See** | **When to Go** |
|---|---|---|
|  **Nairobi National Park** The source of numerous publicity shots of wildlife strutting in front of Nairobi's skyscrapers, this remarkable periurban reserve – unfenced except on the city-facing side – protects a wide range of savannah dwellers (*see pp166–9*). | Lion, leopard, black rhino, buffalo, ostrich, gazelle, eland, giraffe, warthog, wildebeest, zebra, secretary bird. | Game viewing is good all year round. The local zebra and wildebeest migration across Athi Plains makes Jul–Aug particularly worthwhile. Eurasian migrants are seen over Nov–Mar. |
| **Ruma National Park** Located in the Lake Victoria basin, Ruma protects Kenya's last viable population of roan antelope. The park is also an interesting goal for self-drive safarigoers seeking an off-the-beaten-track experience (*see p309*).  | Roan antelope, leopard, spotted hyena, buffalo, oribi, Rothschild's giraffe, Jackson's hartebeest, a wide selection of birds including the globally threatened blue swallow. | Most of the wildlife is resident all year through, but the park's black cotton soil can make for treacherous driving conditions in the rainy season, which peaks from Mar to May. |
|  **Saiwa Swamp National Park** One of Western Kenya's gems, this tiny, pedestrian-friendly park protects a 3-sq-km (1-sq-mile) large wetland. Its riparian forest harbours a selection of monkeys and birds normally associated with nearby Uganda (*see pp294–5*). | Sitatunga, leopard, giant forest squirrel, spotted-neck otter, De Brazza's monkey, black-and-white colobus, bushbuck, over 300 bird species including double-toothed barbet. | Game viewing is excellent throughout the year, though a stormy afternoon drenching is likely between March and May. |
| **Samburu-Buffalo Springs-Shaba National Reserves** This trio of near-contiguous reserves lies in semiarid country north of Mount Kenya. It gives safarigoers the chance to experience the region's unique dry-country wildlife (*see pp346–51*).  | Leopard, elephant, lion, reticulated giraffe, Grevy's zebra, gerenuk, lesser kudu, Beisa oryx, Somali bee-eater, vulturine guinea fowl, golden-bellied starling. | Wildlife is present all year through, but concentrations are highest towards the end of the dry season (Jun–Oct) when the Ewaso Nyiro river is the only reliable water source. |
|  **Shimba Hills National Reserve** The closest safari destination to Diani and Mombasa, Shimba Hills lies on a lushly forested ridge offering spectacular views to the coast. Its grasslands are home to Kenya's only population of the sable antelope (*see pp220–23*). | Sable antelope, elephant, oribi, bushbuck, buffalo, red-bellied coast squirrel, greater bushbaby, localized coastal forest birds such as the green-headed oriole. | Most of the wildlife is resident, but visibility can be poor and roads are rather muddy during the long rains of Mar–May. |
| **Taita Hills Wildlife Sanctuary** This small private sanctuary bordering Tsavo West is best known for its superb Salt Lick Game Lodge, which allows visitors close-up encounters with elephant. Other wildlife can be seen on diurnal and night game drives (*see p192*).  | Elephant, buffalo, lion, leopard, topi, impala, giraffe, zebra, more than 300 bird species with the ghoulish marabou stork being especially noticeable. | All year round. Elephant concentrations are especially impressive at the end of the dry season (Aug–Nov), when several hundred might swing past the waterhole in one night. |
| **Tsavo East National Park** Kenya's largest national park retains a wild atmosphere with its rugged terrain and the palm-fringed Galana, Kenya's second-longest river. Its proximity to the coast makes it a popular trip from Malindi (*see pp188–9*). | Elephant, buffalo, hirola, lion, cheetah, fringe-eared oryx, gerenuk, gazelle, hippo, crocodile and dry-country birds such as the golden pipit and golden-bellied starling. | Less strongly seasonal than most parks. The Galana and Voi rivers attract large herds of wildlife in the dry season (Jun–Oct), as do waterholes below Voi Safari Lodge and Mudanda Rock. |
| **Tsavo West National Park** Slightly smaller than its eastern namesake, Tsavo West is fascinating for geological features such as Shetani Lava Flow and Mzima Springs, which relate to the same volcanic activity that created Kilimanjaro (*see pp190–91*).  | Black rhino, hippo, elephant, buffalo, giraffe, lion, cheetah, lesser kudu, impala, yellow baboon, Kirk's dik-dik. | Game is most visible in the dry seasons, with the best months being Jan, Feb and Aug–Oct. For bird-watchers, the Ngulia area receives immense numbers of passage migrants in Oct–Nov. |

| Accommodation | Practical Information |
|---|---|

**Giraffe Manor**

Nairobi National Park has only one tented camp within its boundaries. It is, however, easily visited as a day-trip out of Nairobi, with the hotels situated in Langata or other locales south of the city centre being particularly convenient.

Main gate is less than 10 km (6 miles) SW of the city centre alongside KWS HQ on Langata Rd. **Tel** 020 2423423. 🛩 to Nairobi. 🚐 to Nairobi. 🚍 to entrance gate. **Open** 6am–7pm daily. 🖼 Safari Card. 🚲 💻 🏠 📶 **kws.org**

---

A three-bedroom self-catering guesthouse is operated by KWS, as is the campsite. The closest hotels that offer proper lodging are in the city of Kisumu, which lies on the Lake Victoria shore, while more basic accommodation is available in the nearby town of Homa Bay.

**A hotel in Kisumu**

425 km (264 miles) W of Nairobi; 24 km (15 miles) S of Homa Bay. **Tel** 020 3529119. **Open** 6am–7pm daily. 🖼 🚲 🏕 📶 **kws.org**

---

**Tree Top House**

KWS operates a shaded campsite and a treehouse offering basic self-catering accommodation. Simple hotel accommodation is available at nearby Kitale.

22 km (14 km) N of Kitale. **Tel** 020 29826. 🚐 to Kitale. 🚍 to within walking distance of the entrance gate. **Open** 6am–7pm daily. 🖼 🚲 🏕 📶 **kws.org**

---

At least a dozen lodges (see p371) are scattered around the three reserves, ranging from large chain hotels to a handful of remote and exclusive tented camps. There are also several public campsites within the park, and basic guesthouses in Isiolo.

**A Samburu safari lodge**

340 km (211 miles) N of Nairobi; 40 km (25 miles) N of Isiolo. 🚐 **Open** 6:30am–6:30pm daily. 🖼 🚲 🏕

---

**Shimba Hills Lodge**

An excellent and scenically located "tree hotel" (see p366) is situated within the park although most people visit from the coastal resorts on day trips that usually include lunch there. Self-catering *bandas* and campsites are operated by KWS.

55 km (34 miles) SW of Mombasa via Likoni Ferry; entrance gate at Kwale village. **Tel** 0704 467855. 🚍 to Kwale. **Open** 6am–7pm daily. 🖼 💳 🚲 🚲 🏕 📶 **laikipia.org**

---

Two private lodges, Taita Hills Game Lodge and Salt Lick Game Lodge (see p365), operate within the reserve, jointly managed by the Sarova chain. Sarova Salt Lick Game Lodge, in particular, is most popular as one of the best locations anywhere in Kenya for viewing the magnificent African elephant.

**Taita Hills Game Lodge**

Entrance gate is 38 km (24 miles) SW of Voi along Taveta Rd. **Tel** 043 2030540 (lodges). 🚍 **Open** access to lodges is 24-hr. 🖼 💳 🚲 🏠 🚲 📶 **sarovahotels.com**

---

**Galdessa Camp**

The park supports a varied selection of lodges, ranging from exclusive tented camps to larger, blander monolithic hotels. There is plenty of inexpensive accommodation in Voi town, and a few campsites to choose from within the park itself.

Voi Gate is 157 km (98 miles) NW of Mombasa; 232 km (144 miles) SE of Nairobi. **Tel** 020 2384417. 🚐 to Voi. **Open** 6am–7pm daily. 🖼 Safari Card. 🚲 🏕 📶 **kws.org**

---

A variety of lodges includes several exclusive tented camps and a few larger hotel-like lodges. A selection of self-catering *bandas* and campsites are operated by KWS. Like Tsavo East, many people visit on overnight safaris from the coastal resorts.

**Voyager Camp**

Voi Gate is 157 km (98 miles) NW of Mombasa; 232 km (144 miles) SE of Nairobi. **Tel** 043 30049. 🚐 🚍 to Mtito Andei. 🖼 Safari Card. 🚲 🏕 📶 **kws.org**

# HABITATS

Kenya boasts a wide spectrum of habitats. There is a barren lava desert in the extreme north, the lush tropical rainforest of Kakamega near the border with Uganda and permanent glaciers on equatorial Mount Kenya. The coast is lined with palm-shaded beaches, the mountaintops are swathed in cool forests and windswept moors while the Rift Valley is studded with beautiful lakes.

If any one habitat can be said to be characteristic of Kenya, it is the loosely defined complex of grassland and scattered trees known to ecologists as the savannah. Moister in the southwest, drier in the north and east, savannah is the predominant habitat of popular game sanctuaries such as Amboseli, Masai Mara, Samburu-Buffalo Springs and Tsavo, and it provides a stage to Africa's most varied cast of safari favourites, from lion and zebra to elephant and gazelle.

There are some animals, such as the water-loving hippo and fruit-eating parrots, that have very specific habitat requirements. But even more habitat-tolerant creatures display clear ecological preferences. The versatile but secretive leopard, for example, is most common in rocky or bushed areas that offer it plenty of cover, while the thirsty elephant will range widely and relatively indiscriminately for food, but always within daily walking range of drinking water.

Visitors who are keen to see the broadest variety of wildlife should be especially conscious of the significance of microhabitats. Many of Kenya's savannah reserves, for instance, are bisected by belts of lush riverine woodland that support colobus monkeys, turacos and other forest creatures. Likewise, isolated hills and cliffs often support a distinct specialist fauna whose more visible components include gaudy agama lizards, soaring black eagles and scurrying families of rock hyrax. On a smaller scale, creatures as different as dwarf mongoose, tawny eagle, aardvark, hartebeest, red-and-yellow barbet and cheetah all make regular use of termite hills, or are attracted to their edible contents.

Other habitats have a more cyclic or ephemeral nature, for instance the seasonal leafy canopies of coastal forests, or the temporary roadside ponds that provide breeding grounds to frogs and terrapins during the rains.

The pristine palm-lined stretch of Tiwi Beach near Mombasa

◄ Animals at a drinking place in Tsavo West National Park

# Habitats at a Glance

Habitat types are determined by a miscellany of climatic, vegetational, geological and other criteria, of which the most important in Kenya are rainfall and altitude. Broadly speaking, altitude and precipitation are highest in the southwest quarter of the country, which includes the central and western highlands, much of the Southern Rift Valley, the Lake Victoria basin and the Masai Mara. This relatively small part of the country displays the greatest variation in habitat, ranging from moist savannah and highland meadows to rainforest, vast freshwater lakes, Afro-montane moorland and glacial peaks. Rainfall is quite high along the coast, but otherwise the eastern and northern three-quarters of the country is lower-lying and drier, and supports a relatively uniform cover of dry bush and desert habitats.

**Afro-montane habitats**
*(see pp94–5)*, comprising high altitude vegetation, are seen on the upper slopes of Mount Kenya, Mount Elgon and the Aberdares.

**Kenya's varied wetlands** *(see pp96–7)* range from the immense freshwater sprawl of Lake Victoria to smaller aquatic gems such as Lakes Naivasha and Baringo. Rivers such as the Ewaso Nyiro, Tana and Galana feed isolated ribbons of riparian forest through the semiarid plains of the east and north.

0 km      100

0 miles      100

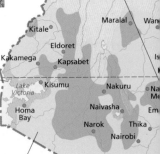

Lokitaung
Ileret
Lake Turkana
Lodwar
Loiyan
Turkwel
Bara
Maralal          Wan
Kitale
Eldoret
Kakamega    Kapsabet          Is
Lake Victoria   Kisumu        Nakuru    Na
Homa Bay             Naivasha   Em
Narok      Thika
Nairobi
Nama

**Savannah and woodland**
*(see pp88–9)* cover much of the Rift Valley and areas to its south. This includes the lush hills of the Masai Mara, the Lake Victoria basin and the drier thorn scrub of Amboseli and Tsavo. In terms of game viewing, this is the most important habitat in the country.

**Key**

- ☐ Arid and semiarid
- ☐ Savannah and woodland
- ☐ Forest
- ☐ Wetlands
- ☐ Afro-montane
- ☐ Intertidal

**Arid and semiarid plains**
*(see pp90–91)* form over half of Kenya's surface, covering much of the country's interior. Arid and semiarid habitats support a mere fraction of Kenya's human population.

## Niche Habitats

Within larger ecosystems exist many microhabitats. A clear example of this is a termite hill, which not only supports its insect creators, but provides shelter to small reptiles, food to aardvarks and barbets and a vantage point for prowling cheetah. Isolated koppies support a unique set of creatures, from klipspringers to agama lizards, while ephemeral puddles might be temporary home to terrapins and waders.

Klipspringers are found in rocky koppies

Seasonal wetlands attract waterbirds

Termite hills house aardvarks

**The intertidal zone** *(see pp98–9)* broadly consists of the stretch of sand and shallow seawater between the upper and lower tide marks. The mangroves seen in this habitat follow some rivers a short distance inland.

Moyale

Marsabit

Tarbaj

Wajir

*Loga Bogal*

*Laga Bor*

Dif

Mado Gashi

*Ewaso Nyiro*

*Equator*

*Tana*

Garissa

Hola

Mutomo

Garsen    Lamu

*Athi*    *Tsavo*

*Galana*

Voi    Malindi

Watamu

Kilifi

Kwale    Mombasa

**Closed canopy forest** *(see pp92–3)* comprises a tiny proportion of Kenya's surface area, but is known for its rich biodiversity. This habitat is particularly attractive to bird-watchers as it hosts many rare species.

# Savannah Habitats

In its broadest definition, the term savannah can be applied to any wooded habitat with an open canopy. The classic savannah landscapes of East Africa consist of a grassy understorey studded with fire-resistant deciduous trees. This open woodland is often interspersed with lush riparian trees along rivers. Savannah is widely thought to be the climax vegetation type in areas such as the Mara, but some ecologists theorize that it is the product of centuries of burning by pastoralists, who do so to stimulate fresh growth for their cattle. This is Kenya's most important habitat in terms of wildlife, although it is less florally diverse than true forest.

A herd of elephants emerging from a wooded area, Masai Mara National Reserve

**Sycamore Fig**
Found in riparian woodlands, this tall evergreen tree has a thick buttressed trunk and wide shady canopy. When in fruit, it attracts a steady stream of monkeys and frugivorous birds.

**Thicker woodland** is often associated with underground water.

**Wag-n-bietjie** or wait-a-bit acacia is named for its large thorns that entangle themselves in clothing.

**Open grassland** often intergrades with more wooded savannah habitats.

**Wildebeest and Zebras**
The open plains support immense herds of mixed grazers, a term used to describe herbivores that feed mainly on grass as opposed to leaves, fruits or roots.

Fireball lily

---

## What Flora to See

### Grassland

**Red oat grass** *(Themeda trianda)* is a coarse grass that dominates tall grass plains.

**Wire grass** *(Pennisetum schimperi)* is a weedlike plant avoided by most grazers.

**Wild cucumber** *(Cucumis spp)* looks like the common vegetable but is inedible.

**Sodom apple** *(Solanum incanium)* is a small flowering plant with large yellow fruit. It is closely related to tomatoes, aubergines (eggplants) and potatoes.

**Umbrella thorn** *(Acacia tortilis)* grows in isolation from other trees and is a favoured food of giraffes.

**Fireball lily** *(Scadoxus multiforus)* has dazzling red flowers that bloom after the rains.

**Euphorbia** *(Euphorbia candelabrum)* grows up to 10 m (33 ft) in height. Its stem and leaves exude a white sap that is toxic to most animals, but not to rhinos.

### Whistling Thorn
Named for the low whistling sound created by wind passing through the ant galls around its twinned thorns, the whistling thorn is a small tree associated with thick woodland.

## Typical Wildlife

**Black rhino** *(see pp124–5)*
**Cheetah** *(see pp108–9)*
**Coke's hartebeest** *(see p135)*
**Flap-necked chameleon**
   *(see p93)*
**Four-toed elephant shrew**
**Golden orb spider**
**Impala** *(see p134)*
**Leopard tortoise** *(see p140)*
**Lion** *(see pp106–7)*
**Maasai giraffe** *(see pp130–31)*
**Rock python** *(see p139)*
**Spotted hyena** *(see p113)*
**Superb starling** *(see p149)*
**Thomson's gazelle**
   *(see p137)*
**Vervet monkey** *(see p117)*

**Umbrella thorns** are medium to tall trees named for their flat shady canopy.

### Bateleur Eagle
This unique raptor of the savannah is a snake-eagle with black feathering and a red face mask.

**Red oat grass**, which gives the plains a golden red hue in low light, provides good feeding for grazers.

### Euphorbia candelabrum
A distinctive tall succulent, this species of euphorbia often grows on the aerated soil of disused termitaria.

Wild date palm

## Thicker Woodland

**Whistling thorn acacia** *(Acacia drepanolobium)* is a short tree that frequently grows in dense clusters.

**Wag-n-bietjie** *(Acacia brevispica)* grows up to 5 m (16 ft) in height, providing shade for grazers.

## Riparian Woodland

**Sausage tree** *(Kigelia agrucana)* is named for its seedpods, which grow to 50 cm (20 inches) in length. These are used as gourds by the Maasai.

**Sycamore fig** *(Ficus sycamoros)*, a spectacular riparian tree, grows up to 20 m (66 ft) in height.

Sausage tree pod

**Wild date palm** *(Phoenix reclinata)* is a beautiful tree with loose wide leaves and a large oval fruit favoured by monkeys. It grows next to rivers and swamps.

# Arid and Semiarid Habitats

Much of the Kenyan interior, especially in the north and east, comprises arid and semiarid habitats. Arid plains typically have a short rainy season, when the grey scrubland comes to brief verdant life, but some parts of the north are dry almost all year round. Arid habitats are locally variable, ranging from red earth plains in the east and around the northern base of Mount Kenya to black stony plains that barely support any life. The unsuitability of such areas to human settlement means that many large tracts are protected in reserves such as Tsavo.

Guided walk on a crescent dune, North Horr, Northern Kenya

**African Baobab**
Often referred to locally as the upside-down tree, the baobab has bare skyward-pointing branches that look like upturned roots.

**Gerenuk**
Endemic to arid parts of East Africa, the peculiar gerenuk uses its elongated neck to browse goat-like on high leaves *(see p136)*.

**The milk bush** is named for its toxic white latex.

## What Flora to See

Penwiper plant

### Succulents

**Euphorbia** *(Euphorbia candelabrum)*, with its candelabra-like leaf formation, is often associated with slopes in the more arid parts of Kenya.

**Desert rose** *(Adenium spp)*, also known as the impala lily, is indigenous to East Africa. It is also seen in Northern Kenya, where it is often planted to brighten lodge gardens.

**Milk bush** *(Euphorbia tirucalli)* is a medium-sized flowering succulent with large yellow fruit.

**Turkana aloe** *(Aloe turkanensis)*, like *Aloe vera*, is one of several aloe species that are used in the making of organic soaps, perfumes and similar products.

**Penwiper plant** *(Kalanchoe marmorata)* is named for its purple blotched leaves, which look a little

like blotting paper. The erect white flowers grow up to 10 cm (4 inches) in length.

**Vulturine Guinea fowl**
This large game bird with a brilliant cobalt chest is one of the most characteristic birds of the semiarid north, being especially common in Samburu-Buffalo Springs.

### Typical Wildlife

**Aardvark** *(see p126)*
**Bat-eared fox** *(see p112)*
**Desert toad**
**Dwarf mongoose** *(see p115)*
**Egyptian vulture**
**Grevy's zebra** *(see p121)*
**Lesser kudu** *(see p132)*
**Red spitting cobra** *(see p139)*
**Red-and-yellow barbet**
  *(see p149)*
**Red-headed agama**
  *(see p138)*
**Reticulated giraffe**
  *(see pp130–31)*
**Somali ostrich** *(see p145)*
**Spring hare**
**Striped hyena** *(see p113)*
**Unstriped ground squirrel**

**Desert Rose**
This striking dry-country succulent is shrub-sized with brilliant pink-red flowers.

**Tamarind and red pod terminalia** are tall leafy trees associated with watercourses and slopes in the semiarid north.

**The false umbrella thorn** has a flat-topped shape similar to that of the "true" umbrella thorn.

**The Turkana aloe**, like other aloes, has spiked succulent leaves and orange inflorescences.

### Vascular Trees and Shrubs

**Kenya hyacinth** *(Sanseviera parva)*, with its long loose leaves, is also known as mother-in-law's tongue.

**African myrrh** *(Commiphora africana)* is a large thorny shrub that produces a fragrant resin.

**Red pod terminalia** *(Terminalia brownii)* is burnt by women of the Borana tribe as a hair perfume.

**African baobab** *(Adansonia digitata)* has a bulbous trunk used to store water during periods of drought.

**False umbrella thorn** *(Acacia reficiens)* is one of many shade-giving acacia species associated with the arid regions of Kenya.

**Three-thorned acacia** *(Acacia senegal)* is the

Three-thorned acacia

source of gum arabic, a popular food additive.

**Tamarind** *(Tamarindus indica)* is a tall leafy tree whose fruit is popular with primates and elephants.

Tamarind pods

# Forest Habitats

Ecologists generally differentiate forest from woodland by the presence of a closed canopy in the former. This distinction is clearly manifested in the inability of sunlight to significantly penetrate the forest interior. The most biodiverse of terrestrial habitats, these tropical forests account for a relatively small part of Kenya's surface area, but harbour a disproportionately high species count and endemism level. There are low-lying and relatively dry coastal forests such as Arabuko Sokoke, sweaty tropical lowland forests around Kakamega and moist Afro-montane forests on the slopes of Mount Kenya, often connected by belts of riparian woodland.

Forest floor covered with moist litter and shade-loving plants

**Strangler Fig**
This parasitic tree starts life as an epiphyte and gradually extends its roots to the forest floor to envelop the host tree, while its branches grow upward to reach above the canopy.

**African mahogany** is one of the tallest forest trees, standing up to 45 m (148 ft) high.

**Ferns**, among the most diverse forest plants, are often seen along streams.

## What Flora to See

Ripe figs, favoured by parrots

### Canopy Trees

**African mahogany** (*Khaya spp*), with its wide, buttressed trunk, is often felled for hardwood timber.

**Strangler figs** (*Ficus spp*), when mature, can be distinguished by the tall, hollow cylinder left inside the trunk after the host tree dies.

**Croton** (*Croton megalocarpus*) is a common upper-canopy forest tree in

lowland and montane forests, reaching a height of 40 m (131 ft).

**Red stinkwood** (*Prunus africana*), popular as timber, exudes a pungent almond-like smell when freshly cut.

**Figs** (*Ficus spp*) are common forest trees whose fruits – which are actually modified flowers – attract fruit bats, monkeys and a variety of birds in season.

**Large-leaved saucer-berry** (*Cordia abyssinica*) has saucer-shaped

flowers and large berries that attract many birds. It often grows along forest streams.

**Black-and-white Colobus**
Forests are the favoured habitat of many monkey species, including the striking black-and-white colobus, which occurs in coastal, Afromontane and tropical lowland forests (see p116).

## Typical Wildlife

African green pigeon
Black-and-white casqued
  hornbill
Blue monkey (see p116)
Bushbabies (see p117)
Bushbuck (see p133)
Duikers (see p136)
Gaboon viper Leopard
  (see pp110–111)
Millipedes
Paradise flycatcher (see p149)
Red-bellied coastal squirrel
Rhinoceros beetle
Tree frogs (see p138)
Tree hyrax
Yellow-rumped elephant
  shrew

**White stinkwood** (Celtis africana) has a grey trunk and grows up to 25 m (82 ft) high in forests.

**African rosewood** (Hagenia abyssinica) is common in high altitude forests.

**Flap-necked Chameleon**
The second-most important centre of chameleon speciation in the world, East Africa's forests host several endemic species, including the flap-necked chameleon.

**Bird's-nest ferns** (Asplenium spp) are epiphytes that grow on trunks.

**Orchids**, whether terrestrial or epiphytic, are the most spectacular flowering plants in the forest.

Tree ferns

## Epiphytic and Understorey Plants

**Epiphytic orchids** (Orchidaceae) are stunning, seasonally flowering plants that grow on the trunks of larger trees.

**Tree ferns** (Cyathea spp) are splendid prehistoric-looking trees with long fronded leaves and trunks that typically reach up to 3 m (10 ft) in height.

**Dragon trees** (Dracaena spp), familiar as pot plants, are spectacular leafy shrubs associated with the forest subcanopy.

**African violets** (Saintpaulia spp), though unrelated to true violets, are popular shade-loving pot plants that originate from the understorey Eastern Arc forests of Tanzania and southeast Kenya.

African violets

# Afro-montane Habitats

Kenya's mountains include several of Africa's tallest peaks, notably Mount Kenya, the Aberdares and Mount Elgon. The unique vegetation associated with them is divided into several altitudinal zones, starting with lower montane forest on slopes below 2,000–3,000 m (6,560–9,840 ft), then rising through bamboo forest, hagenia shrubland and open heath to the Afro-alpine moorland below the snow line. Each mountain effectively forms an evolutionary "island" of Afro-montane habitats, and while the broad floral composition and altitudinal zones are similar throughout, the level of endemism on individual mountains is very high.

Bare slopes and harsh climate above the rocky snow line of Mount Kenya

**Sharpe's Longclaw**
Endemic to the high grasslands of central Kenya, this pipit-like bird was listed by IUCN as endangered in 2000.

**Tussock grass** *(Festuca pilgeri)* and mosses *(Bryophyta spp)* are prolific on wet slopes and rocks of the Afro-alpine zone.

**The giant lobelia** is a spectacular high-altitude plant that grows up to 6 m (20 ft) in height.

**The giant groundsel** is one of several otherworldly examples of gigantism among Afro-alpine flora.

## What Flora to See

### Bamboo and Hagenia Zones

Bamboo forest, the Aberdares

**Bamboo** *(Arundinaria alpina)* is a form of grass that grows to spectacular heights on East Africa's mountains.

**Old Man's Beard** *(Usnea spp)* is a grey-green lichen that hangs from tree branches. Most species are edible and several are used as traditional medicines or as a source of vitamin C.

**African juniper** *(Juniperus procera)* is an aromatic conifer seen on the northern slopes of Mount Kenya.

**East African rosewood** *(Hagenia abyssinica)* grows up to 20 m (66 ft) in height and dominates wooded parts of the hagenia zone.

**Giant St John's wort** *(Hypericum revolutum)* is a dense shrub that dominates more open sections of the hagenia zone.

**Podo** *(Podocarpus milanjianus)* is a spectacular timber tree that grows up to 46 m (150 ft) in height.

**Afro-montane Forest**
Generally dank and chilly, montane Afro-forests have trees draped in the wispy lichen known as Old Man's Beard.

## Typical Wildlife

Alpine-meadow lizard
Alpine-meadow skink
Black-and-white colobus (see p116)
Black-fronted duiker
Eland (see p132)
Giant forest hog (see p127)
Jackson's chameleon
Klipspringer (see p136)
Mount Kenya bush viper
Mount Kenya hornless chameleon
Scaly francolin
Scarce swift
Scarlet-tufted malachite
Tree hyrax
Verreaux's eagle

**The snow line**, the upper limit for flora, is under retreat on most Kenyan mountains.

**Mountain Bongo**
This beautiful, large antelope is thought to number some 100 in the wild (see p133).

Giant lobelia

**The giant thistle** is endemic to Mount Kenya and the Aberdares.

**Pink everlastings** (Helichrysum spp) have pretty flowers that follow the sun's movements.

**The large painted lady** (Gladiolus carneus) is a tall gladiolus with large pink-red flowers.

### Heath Zone

**Red-hot poker** (Kniphofia thomsonii) is found along montane streams. This reed-like shrub is named for its long orange flowers.

**African sage** (Artemisia afra) is a clumped shrub with fern-like leaves and several medicinal uses.

Giant Roundsel

Red-hot poker

**East African sugarbush** (Protea kilimanjaro) has furry leaves and large cup-like flowers.

### Afro-Alpine Zone

**Giant lobelia** is represented by two species on Mount Kenya, namely Lobelia telekii and L. keniensis.

**Giant groundsel** (Senecio keniodendron) can survive at high altitudes due to spongy areas between the leaf cells where water freezes without harming the plant.

**Giant thistle** (Carduus keniensis) is recognized by its orange flowers and bristly leaves.

# Wetland Habitats

The term wetlands embraces all freshwater and most saline aquatic habitats other than open sea. It includes rivers and lagoons, but is most often used in reference to marshlands and lakes, habitats that are of great significance to the survival of aquatic life, as well as to the majority of terrestrial creatures that depend on them for drinking water. Kenya is well endowed with lakes, ranging from the inland seas of Victoria and Turkana to the more confined Baringo and Nakuru, while the rivers form life-sustaining ribbons of green through drier habitats.

Riparian thickets surrounding the meandering Mara river

**Raffia palm** often grows tall on the edge of rivers and lakes.

**Otters**
These secretive aquatic carnivores feed on tilapia and other fish in most of Kenya's larger rivers and lakes.

**Wild date palm** grows in riverside clumps with multiple curved stems.

**Papyrus** is a 2–3 m (6–10 ft) high plant that forms dense clumps in shallow water.

**Water hyacinth** *(Eichhornia crassipes)* is an invasive species that has colonized parts of Lake Victoria.

**White water lilies** are found in still freshwater habitats.

**African Jacana**
This pretty orange, blue, black and white bird has splayed claws that enable it to walk on floating plants.

## What Flora to See

Nile cabbage

### Reed-like Fringing Vegetation

**Common reed** *(Phragmites australis)* is used as a site for nests – and also as nest-building material – by many weavers, bishops and allied bird species.

**Papyrus** *(Cyperus papyrus)*, also known as paper reed, is a giant sedge that was used to make paper by the ancient Egyptians.

**Sedges** *(Cyperus spp)* are tall grass-like plants associated with the margins of East African lakes.

### Floating Vegetation

**White water lily** *(Nymphaea nouchali)* can be distinguished from the invasive hyacinth by its white rather than blue flower.

**Nile cabbage** *(Pistia stratiotes)*, a floating perennial with tint flowers and

thick foot-long leaves, is common on parts of Lake Victoria.

**Blue-green algae** *(Spirulina platensis)*, a microscopic resident of saline inland waters, is the main diet of flamingoes at Lake Nakuru.

**Hippopotamus**
The most iconic of Africa's wetland mammals, hippos can be very vociferous at night. Mainly associated with freshwater habitats, they also occasionally venture into saline waters.

**Typical Wildlife**

**African fish eagle** *(see p144)*
**Cape clawless otter**
  *(see p114)*
**Dragonflies**
**Elephant** *(see pp118–19)*
**Frogs** *(see p138)*
**Hippopotamus** *(see pp120–21)*
**Marsh mongoose** *(see p115)*
**Marsh terrapin** *(see p141)*
**Nile monitor** *(see p139)*
**Pied kingfisher** *(see p149)*
**Pond skaters**
**Sitatunga** *(see p133)*
**Waterbuck** *(see p135)*
**Whirligig beetle**
**Yellow-billed stork**

**The fever tree**, a yellow-barked acacia, grows by marshes and lakes.

**The waterberry** *(Syzygium guineense)* stands up to 15-m (49-ft) tall and has edible leaves and fruits.

**The common reed** is the dominant plant in Kenya's wetland habitats.

**The bulrush**, *(Typha spp)* is a common invasive species in the wetlands.

**Tilapia**
This varied group of cichlid fish is associated with most freshwater and some saline habitats in Kenya.

**Waterside Trees**

**Toothbrush tree** *(Salvadora persica)* is a small riverine tree with fibrous wood, which is traditionally used as a toothbrush in many African cultures.

**Fever tree** *(Acacia xanthophloea)*, with its jaundiced bark and preference for low swampy habitats, is so named because early

Fever trees

colonial settlers thought it propagated malaria.

**Wild date palm** *(Phoenix reclinata)* is a small palm with large, fleshy, yellow, clustered fruits.

**African Olive** *(Olea capensis)*, common in riverine forests, is also known as ironwood due to its hard, fine-grained wood, which is **Wild dates** used to make high-quality furniture.

**Raffia palm** *(Themeda trianda)* is the favoured nesting site of Kenya's palm-nut vulture, which feeds on its fruit.

# Intertidal Habitats

This zoologically rich habitat consists of the narrow stretch of tidal water that divides the beachfront and fringing vegetation from offshore coral reefs. It is popular with visitors who come to swim in the warm surf, which is protected by the reefs at high tide. At low tide, the beaches drain of water, leaving behind sand and rock pools frequented by small fish, marine invertebrates and wading birds. This zone supports a limited flora, although one niche habitat included within its confines are the mangroves that run along coastal creeks and other inlets.

The palm-lined beach at low tide, Kipungani village, Lamu

**Mangroves**
The intertidal flats, estuaries and creeks of the Kenyan coastline support prolific mangrove ecosystems, comprising a select group of plants whose roots can absorb water and oxygen in saline conditions.

**Seaweed**, essentially a spread of multicellular algae, can float in water and occasionally infests the beaches of Kenya.

**Mangrove roots** often protrude from the mudflats at low tide to absorb oxygen directly from the air.

## What Fauna to See

### Mangroves

**Mangrove kingfisher** (*Halcyon senegaloidesis*) is a brilliant blue bird associated almost exclusively with mangroves.

**Hermit crabs** (*Paguroidea*) are colonial decapods that live in "borrowed" shells. Despite their name, they are not closely related to true crabs and several species are terrestrial.

**Mudskippers** (*Oxudercinae*) are amphibious fish whose unique adaptation to intertidal habitats means they are very active on exposed mangrove mudflats.

### Tidal Pools

**Sea urchins** (*Echinoidea*) are the marine equivalent of hedgehogs. These small spiky invertebrates are often seen clinging to rocks in tidal pools.

Sea urchin

**Starfish** (*Asteroidea*) are radially symmetrical predators with extraordinary regenerative powers.

**Crabs**, with their thick exoskeleton and sharp pincers, are common in rock pools and on most beaches.

**Giant Coconut Crab**
The largest terrestrial arthropod in the world, the giant coconut crab weighs in at 4 kg (9 lb) and can crack open a coconut with its strong pincers.

## Typical wildlife

Bottlenose dolphins
Devil firefish
Dugong
**Green turtle** (see p141)
Hammerhead shark
Humpback whale
Jellyfish
**Leatherback turtle** (see p141)
Moray eel
Octopus
Sperm whale
Squids
Stingrays
Swordfish
Whale shark

**Casuarinas** (*Casuarina cunninghamiana*) are tall, conifer-like trees that were introduced to Kenya and are now invasive along the coast.

**The coconut palm** (*Cocos nucifera*), though non-indigenous to Kenya, is well adapted to the saline coastal sands and is widely cultivated for fruit, fronds and wood.

**Offshore Coral Reefs**
Hundreds of fish species and an even greater diversity of invertebrates make their home in coral reefs off the Kenyan coast.

**Marlins**
Often known as spearfish, these fish have spiked snouts and powerful torsos that enable them to glide through the water at up to 80 kmph (50 mph).

Mussels

**Portuguese man-of-war** (*Physalia physalis*) is also known as bluebottle. This is a floating jellyfish-like invertebrate whose sting is excruciatingly painful and very occasionally fatal.

**Mussels** (*Mytilidae*) and other shelled bivalve molluscs frequently cling to the sides of permanent rock pools.

**Reefs**

**Clownfish** (*Amphiprion spp*) are dazzling yellow, orange and black reef fish that live symbiotically with sea anemones.

**Parrot fish** (*Scaridae*) are pastel-hued pink and blue fish. They are so named for their parrot-like "beaks" formed by their teeth.

A pair of clownfish

**Blue-streaked cleaner wrasse** (*Labroides dimidatus*) is a fish that feeds on the parasites of other fish.

**Moorish idol** (*Zanclus cornutus*) is a stunning yellow, black and blue fish with a vertically compressed body and long trailing dorsal fin.

# FIELD GUIDE

Kenya's superb network of national parks and other protected areas harbours a quite extraordinary diversity of wildlife. This is one of Africa's premier destinations for the Big Five as well as a number of other favourites, ranging from the greyhound-like cheetah to several elegant antelope species. Yet these mammalian icons represent a mere fraction of what Kenya has to offer – with over 500 reptile and amphibian species and an astonishing checklist of birds.

Most safaris to Kenya focus on the southern parks bordering Tanzania, namely Amboseli, Masai Mara and Tsavo East and West National Parks, as well as the splendid string of lakes that runs along the floor of the Rift Valley. This vast southern wilderness, home to the enigmatic Maasai pastoralists, seems almost to have been designed to fulfil the expectations of first-time visitors to Africa. The game viewing here can include groups of tusk-heavy elephants gathering at a waterhole in the red plains of Tsavo; the thousands of braying wildebeest that swarm across the Mara river every July; zebras rolling in the ultra-fine dust of Amboseli below the snowcapped peaks of Kilimanjaro; or the white rhinos that graze earnestly on the floodplain of Lake Nakuru in sight of millions of bright pink-flamingoes.

If southern Kenya stands as one of Africa's great conventional safari destinations, the rest of the country is rich in less celebrated but equally fantastic wildlife-viewing opportunities. The semiarid plains of the north, protected in Samburu-Buffalo Springs, are host to numerous dry-country rarities, ranging from the quirky gerenuk antelope and majestic oryx to the near-endemic reticulated giraffe and Grevy's zebra. The forests of the coastal belt form part of one of the world's greatest biodiversity hotspots, home to several endemic birds and monkeys. The central and western forests, such as the Aberdares and Kakamega, show unexpected zoological affinities with the rainforest of Central Africa in the form of bongos, giant forest hogs and numerous colourful forest birds.

Lake Nakuru with its vast flocks of pelicans and flamingoes

◀ Zebras swim across the Mara river watched by a hippo, Masai Mara National Reserve

# Endemic Animals

By definition, endemic animals are peculiar to a single, generally restricted range, and are especially vulnerable to localized habitat destruction and hunting. Kenya's most important centre of endemism is the eastern coast, whose forests harbour at least four large mammal and half a dozen bird species found nowhere else in the world. Also important are the forested Central Highlands and isolated massifs such as the Taita Hills and Mount Marsabit.

**Field Guide Key**

- 🅾 Diurnal
- 🅲 Nocturnal
- 🔺 Savannah
- 🔺 Arid and Semiarid
- 🔺 Forest
- 🔺 Afro-montane
- 🔺 Wetland
- 🔺 Intertidal

## Tana River Red Colobus
*Species: Procolobus rufomitratus*
*Best Seen: Tana River Primate Reserve*

🅾🔺      CR

The only Kenyan representative of a group of rainforest monkeys associated with West and Central Africa, the Tana river red colobus has a distinct ginger cap and fringe, a long tail and a grey-brown coat. Isolated from other red colobus populations by several hundred kilometres, it is restricted to marshy forested habitats about 75 km (47 miles) upstream of the mouth of the Tana river, where recent estimates suggest that the total population is no more than 800.

The ash-grey mangabey with orange-red chest and belly

## Tana River Mangabey
*Species: Cercocebus galeritus*
*Best Seen: Tana River Primate Reserve*

🅾🔺      EN

Sharing its range with the Tana river red colobus, the eponymous mangabey is the only Kenyan representative of a family of large arboreal Cercopithecid monkeys associated with low-altitude rainforest in Central and West Africa. Endemic to riparian woodland along a 60-km (37-mile) stretch of the Tana river, it was listed as one of the world's 25 most endangered primate taxa in 2000, but a subsequent survey showed that the population stands at 2,070 individuals, an increase of 18 per cent since 1974.

The medium-sized, long-limbed Tana river red colobus

## Clarke's Weaver
*Species: Ploceus golandi*
*Best Seen: Arabuko Sokoke FR*

🅾🔺      EN

The most localized of many dozens of weaver species found in Kenya, Clarke's weaver is endemic to the Arabuko-Sokoke Forest and immediate surrounds, where it is almost exclusively associated with brachystegia woodland. It is often seen in large flocks that mingle with helmet-shrikes. The global population is estimated to be fewer than 1,000.

This chameleon species varies from black to bright green

## Jackson's Three-Horned Chameleon
*Species: Chamaeleo jacksonI*
*Best Seen: Nairobi NP, Aberdare NP, Mount Kenya*

🅾🔺      NE

Common in the forest suburbia of Nairobi, this striking 0.3-m- (1-ft-) long chameleon is named for the trio of impressive horns that grow on its snout. With the exception of one racially discrete population on Tanzania's Mount Meru, it is endemic to the Central Highlands of Kenya, where it spends most of its time in the trees.

Clarke's weaver, mostly yellow with an all-black head

**IUCN status** CR: Critically Endangered; EN: Endangered; VU: Vulnerable; LC: Least Concern; NE: Not Evaluated

## Hirola

*Species:* **Beatragus hunteri**
*Best Seen:* **Tsavo East NP, Arawale Hirola Reserve**

 CR

Also known as Hunter's hartebeest, the hirola is similar in appearance to other hartebeests, but is much smaller, has impala-like horns and distinctive white "spectacles". It is naturally confined to an area of dry grassland in southern Somalia and the Northern Coast of Kenya, but is now almost certainly extinct outside Kenya, where its population plummeted to fewer than 1,000 in the late 1990s as a result of drought and competition with livestock. This decline led to the creation of the 530-sq-km (205-sq-mile) Arawale Hirola Reserve, about 100 km (62 miles) northwest of Lamu. Two herds introduced to Tsavo East have adapted well to its semiarid habitat, and small herds are occasionally seen on the plains south of Voi and Aruba Dam.

The white spectacle-like marks identify the hirola

## Taita Thrush

*Species:* **Turdus helleri**
*Best Seen:* **Taita Hills**

CR

Confined to three fragmented pockets of cloud forest covering a total area of less than 4 sq km (2 sq miles), this handsome black, red and white thrush is endemic to Taita Hills. The total population was estimated at 1,350 in 1997, but it has probably declined in the interim due to further habitat loss and fragmentation. Within its restricted range, the Taita thrush is a shy skulking bird associated with leaf litter, and its song is yet to be identified.

Taita thrush, with distinctive red beak and eye-ring

A long nose and yellow rump distinguish this shrew

## Golden-Rumped Elephant Shrew

*Species:* **Rhynchocyon chrysopygus**
*Best Seen:* **Arabuko Sokoke FR, Gedi Ruins**

EN

The golden-rumped elephant shrew is the largest and most vulnerable member of the ancient African order Macroscelidea, consisting of roughly 15 species of peculiar rodent-sized creatures – known as elephant-shrews or sangis – that hop around like miniature kangaroos and possess absurdly elongated and perpetually twitchy noses. Confined to the coastal Arabuko Sokoke National Park and its immediate vicinity, the golden-rumped elephant shrew is one of the few diurnal members of the order. It is often glimpsed from footpaths through the Gedi Ruins, which border Arabuko Sokoke. Comparable in size to a rabbit, it weighs 500 g (18 oz) and is dark russet-brown in colour but with a bright yellow-gold rump and throat. It feeds on the forest floor with its sensitive nose, scratching noisily through the leaf litter to locate its prey of crickets, millipedes and other medium to large insects.

Hinde's babbler, with scaly feathering and red eyes

## Hinde's Babbler

*Species:* **Turdoides hindei**
*Best Seen:* **Mwea NR**

VU

Endemic to the eastern slopes of the Central Highlands, Hinde's babbler is a black, brown and white bird distinguished from other members of the babbler family by its bold red eyes. A major quarry for bird-watchers in Kenya, it has a limited distribution and some estimates place the population at 1,500, which means it is unlikely to be seen unless actively sought.

**For key to Field Guide icons** *see p102*

# Cats

Secretive and solitary, the cats of the family Felidae are the most stealthy and efficient killers among carnivores. Also the most strictly carnivorous, they feed exclusively on other warm-blooded creatures, from sparrows and mice to buffalo and giraffe. Although they differ greatly in colouration and size, all cats have a similar body plan to their familiar domestic counterpart, with an elongated body, long tail, small head, sensitive whiskers, prominent canines and keen bifocal vision. Much wild felid behaviour will be familiar to the average cat owner.

## Family

Kenya's seven felid species, traditionally split between three genera, are *Felis*, small- to medium-size cats; *Panthera*, big cats distinguished by a larynx modification enabling them to roar; and *Acinonyx*, the cheetah, the only felid with non-retractable claws.

## African Wild Cat

*Species: Felis silvestris*
*Best Seen: Masai Mara GR, Tsavo NP, Samburu-Buffalo Springs NR*

 LC

The smallest African felid, and the most elusive of those associated with savannah habitats, the African wild cat is closely related to its much rarer European counterpart. DNA evidence suggests that it is the sole wild ancestor of the domestic cat, which was first domesticated in North Africa some 10,000 years ago. Very similar in appearance to a domestic tabby but with markedly longer legs, it is a versatile hunter of rodents, birds and insects. It has a high habitat tolerance, which means that it is the most widely distributed of all African predators, being absent only from rainforest interiors and true deserts. Although seldom seen, it remains very common away from human habitation. Its genetic integrity, however, is under increasing threat as a result of interbreeding with the feral domestic cats that are occasionally seen in East Africa's game reserves.

The African wild cat, progenitor of the domestic cat

**Small rounded ears** are the most obvious physical difference between the golden cat and caracal.

## Golden Cat

*Species: Felis aurata*
*Best Seen: Aberdare NP, Arabuko Sokoke FR, Mount Kenya*

 NT

The rainforest counterpart to the caracal, the golden cat is similar in general appearance and overall build, but richer in colour, with black spotting on the belly, light striping on the tail and non-tufted and relatively small ears. Essentially a species of the Congolese rainforest, its range extends to suitable habitats in East Africa, where it is uncommon and very secretive. It has been sighted in Western Kenya and in the Arabuko Sokoke Forest. Among the least studied of the African carnivores, the golden cat is extremely unlikely to be observed, even in the few localities where it is known to be present.

The golden cat, named for its lustrous tawny-gold coat

**IUCN status** NT: Near Threatened; LC: Least Concern

## Caracal

*Species:* **Felis caracal**
*Best Seen:* **Masai Mara GR, Tsavo NP, Buffalo Springs NR**

🅲 🌱 🌿                                        LC

The largest and most powerful of Africa's "small cats", the caracal bears a strong resemblance to the Eurasian lynx, and the two were long thought to be conspecific. However, genetic studies suggest that the caracal is more closely allied to the serval and golden cat than to any non-African species. A male can be 1 m (3 ft) in length from head to tail and weigh up to 20 kg (44 lb); females are usually a lot smaller. The caracal has a fairly uniform tan coat with light spotting sometimes distinguishable on the paler belly, and long tufted ears whose dark colouration is referred to in Turkish as *karakulak* (black ear) from which the cat gets its name. It is exceptionally sharp of hearing, even by felid standards, thanks to this tufting and some 20 muscles that control ear direction. A versatile hunter, it is particularly skilled at hunting birds in flight, and its agility and preference for rocky habitats means that it presents the greatest threat to hyraxes after Verreaux's eagle. Like other small cats, the caracal is a solitary nocturnal hunter, seldom observed by day or night. For all that, it is widespread in Kenya, and probably very common, generally favouring more arid and rocky habitats than the serval.

Caracal, the cat most strongly associated with dry habitats

The serval is the smallest of Africa's spotted cats

## Serval

*Species:* **Felis serval**
*Best Seen:* **Masai Mara GR, Meru NP, Aberdare NP**

🅲 🌱 🌿                                        LC

Superficially similar to the larger cheetah, the serval is a sleek spotted cat associated with rank grassland and other non-forested habitats offering good access to water. It can be distinguished from the cheetah by its proportionately shorter tail (about one-third of its body length), and the most common colour morph has streaky as opposed to circular black-on-gold spots, although speckled and melanistic morphs are also seen in some areas. It has the longest legs in relation to body size of any felid, and very large ears – adaptations that help it locate prey in its preferred habitat of tall grassland. It feeds mainly on small mammals and birds, which it pounces upon with a spectacular high spring, delivering the fatal blow by striking the victim swift and hard with one of its powerful claws. The serval will also occasionally catch fish and pounce on frogs. Diurnal serval sightings are not commonplace, but it is the most readily seen of the smaller felids, especially during the first 30 minutes after sunrise.

**For key to Field Guide icons** *see p102*

# Lion

The largest terrestrial predator in Africa, the lion is the most sociable and least secretive of the world's 36 cat species. It is unusual among felids in that it seldom takes to the trees, and that an adult male sports a regal blond or black mane. For most people, the charismatic "king of the jungle" is the ultimate African safari icon, so much so that it is often easy to forget that lions once ranged widely across Eurasia. Though common and conspicuous in several Kenyan reserves, lions are in decline elsewhere, with Africa's lion population having seen a 75 per cent decline since 1990.

**Lions are remarkably indolent** creatures, spending up to 20 hours a day at rest. Though seldom active in the heat of the day, they often cover long distances at night.

## Family and Breeding

The most sociable of cats, the lion lives in prides of five to ten animals, including an adult male, a few adult females, and their offspring. Larger prides are seen in the Serengeti-Mara ecosystem, where they are presided over by two or more adult male siblings. Prides are active in defending their territories, which typically cover 20–200 sq km (8–77 sq miles). Takeover battles are often fought to the death, and if successful, result in the usurper killing all existing cubs, thereby encouraging the females back into oestrus sooner. Lions undergo an extraordinary mating ritual. A male and female pair off, mating briefly but violently at gradually increasing intervals of 12–25 minutes for up to 3 days, after which they return to their pride.

**Females in a pride give birth more or less simultaneously** and rear their cubs cooperatively. Large prides consist of up to half a dozen lionesses and their offspring. Females usually stay with their birth pride, but young males are forced out by the dominant male when they reach sexual maturity.

## What You Might See

The first lion sighting often results in disappointment, as the animals loll disinterestedly in the shade. Observe them for a while, however, and one is bound to see exciting interactions. It is always worth staying with an isolated female and male pair, as they may well start mating; and if a lioness is lying low in the grass, looking intently into the distance, odds are she is part of a hunt.

**Rivalry between adult males** can be intense and fights are often to the death.

**Grooming and social licking** are an important part of the daily ritual in any lion pride.

**IUCN status** VU: Vulnerable

## Feeding

Hunting is normally a team effort undertaken by females, who rely on stealth more than speed. A common strategy is for one or two lionesses to herd their prey in the direction of other pride members lying hidden in tall grass. Males seldom take part in a hunt but are quick to exercise their feeding rights once a kill is made. Favoured prey includes antelope, and large prides can even bring down a giraffe or a buffalo.

A large male lion takes first pickings on a fresh giraffe kill

## Communication and Voice

Adult lions are most active around dusk and dawn, but cubs interact throughout the day, playing and mock fighting for hours on end. Subordinate individuals frequently stop to greet or groom dominant pride members, especially when they reunite after a period apart. The most common call, made by females as well as males, is a series of far-carrying moaning grunts that first increase in volume, then fade away. As dominant males often move separately from the main pride (regrouping after a kill), this characteristic sound of the African night has the dual purpose of advertising the caller's presence to the pride and warning rivals off its territory.

A cub displays submissiveness to one of the adult males in the pride

## KEY FACTS

### Panthera Leo

Kiswahili: **Simba**

 **Size** Shoulder height: 100–130 cm (40–51 inches); Weight: up to 280 kg (617 lb).

**Lifespan** 12–15 years in the wild.
**Population in Kenya** 2,000–3,000.
**Conservation Status** VU.
**Gestation Period** 105–112 days.
**Reproduction** Females reach sexual maturity at three years and give birth to litters of two to six cubs every 18 months.

 **Habitat** All habitats, except desert and rainforest. Most often in savannah.

 **Top Places to See** Masai Mara National Reserve (see pp266–9), Nairobi NP (see pp166–9), Tsavo NP (see pp186–91).

**Sighting Tips**
Look out for resting prides during the day – it is worth returning at dawn or dusk to catch them in action.

**Friends and Foes**
Contrary to belief, lions feeding on a carcass are as likely to have stolen it from a hyena as to have killed it themselves.

 **Facts and Trivia**
Traditionally, the only form of hunting permitted by the Maasai is the Olamayio lion hunt, a form of group hunting held as an initiation ritual.

**The main diet** of lions in Kenya comprises ungulates such as zebra, buffalo and antelope.

**Cubs** spend a large part of their day mock fighting and playing with each other, or with adults.

**A mating bout** often lasts for less than a minute and is accompanied by growling and hissing.

# Cheetah

The world's fastest runner, the cheetah can reach 115 kmph (71 mph) in short bursts, accelerating from a standstill in four seconds. It is anatomically distinct from true big cats, with a greyhound-like build, disproportionately small head and unique semi-retractable claws catering to its specialist pursuit of sprinting. Once widespread in Asia, Arabia and Africa, it has suffered a massive range retraction in recent times, and is now practically endemic to sub-Saharan Africa.

**The king cheetah**, a rare mutant, has a striped coat. Prone to unusual colour morphs, cheetahs have included all-black and all-white individuals, as well as those with unspotted golden coats or tawny or blue-grey spots on a creamy coat.

## Family and Breeding

Though not as sociable as lions, cheetahs are less solitary than most cats. The highly territorial adult male is generally solitary, although coalitions of two to three brothers are often seen. Females are solitary except when rearing cubs, and related females often have overlapping territories. The cheetah follows a protracted courtship ritual, which leads to the female coming into oestrus after 1–2 weeks. Mortal fights between competing males are common during this period. Litters consist of four to five cubs, born blind and hidden away for the first few months of their life. Even so, the cub mortality rate is high, partly due to the harsh habitat, and partly because the mother is unable to ward off predators. The surviving cubs stay with the mother for about 18 months, and are unique among felids in that they need to be taught how to hunt.

**Cubs often stay together** after they are abandoned by their mother, honing their hunting skills as a pack before they eventually separate to fend for themselves.

## What You Might See

Almost always associated with open country, cheetahs have a more restless temperament than other large predators. They are most often seen trotting through the grass with a distinct air of determination, breaking step only to climb on a tree trunk or termite mound that presents itself as a lookout post. They are also more likely to be seen hunting in daylight than other cats.

**Cheetahs regularly sharpen their claws,** which are only partly retractable.

**The black "tear marks"** that run down a cheetah's face help differentiate it from a leopard.

**IUCN status** VU: Vulnerable

## Feeding

Where most feline predators combine hunting with scavenging, cheetahs feed solely on fresh meat. A diurnal and crepuscular hunter, the cheetah usually creeps to within 15–31 m (50–100 ft) of its prey before opening chase at immense speed, eventually knocking down its victim and suffocating it with its mouth. High tourist concentrations can adversely affect a cheetah's hunting habits – safari vehicles often alert prey to its presence – although some individuals have turned the tables by using parked vehicles as cover to stalk gazelles and other prey.

Devouring a freshly killed gazelle, while keeping an eye out for predators

### Communication and Voice

The cheetah differs from true big cats such as the leopard and lion in several respects, one of which is that the cheetah lacks the ability to roar. The most common vocalization, often made by a mother looking for her cubs, is a peculiar high-pitched twitter called yipping, which sounds more like a small bird or bat than a large carnivore. In common with other cats, a cheetah will purr when content or when it meets a familiar individual, and will growl, hiss and yelp when threatened or annoyed.

Cheetahs communicate with a wide repertoire of sounds such as growling, hissing and spitting

## KEY FACTS

### Acinonyx Jubatus
*Kiswahili:* **Duma**

**Size** Shoulder height: 80 cm (31 inches); Weight: 41–60 kg (90–130 lb).

**Lifespan** 6–12 years in the wild.
**Population in Kenya** Below 1,000.
**Conservation Status** VU.
**Gestation period** 3 months.
**Reproduction** Females reach sexual maturity at around two years and give birth to up to five cubs a year thereafter.

**Habitat** Thinly vegetated plains and open or broken grassland.

**Top Places to See**
Masai Mara GR (see pp266–9), Tsavo NP (see pp186–91), Nairobi NP (see pp166–9), Ol Pejeta (see p324).

**Sighting Tips**
If a cheetah on the hunt is sighted, maintain some distance – guides often drive too close and chase off the intended prey.

**Friends and Foes**
Easily intimidated, a cheetah will wolf down a kill before it can be chased off by scavengers, consuming up to 10 kg (22 lb) in 15 minutes.

**Facts and Trivia**
Striped cheetahs were thought to be a local superstition until 1926, when British zoologist R I Pocock was shown the pelt of one.

**Cheetah cubs** are very playful but also wary, and will often flee into a burrow when disturbed.

**A short high-speed chase**, generally over open grassland, is the hallmark of the cheetah's hunting strategy.

**Cheetahs often ascend trunks** or termite mounds to scan the area for rivals and prey.

# Leopard

Paradoxically the most abundant and the most elusive of Africa's large predators, the leopard is distinguishable by its rosette-patterned coat, powerfully pugilistic physique and preference for dense cover. This determinedly nocturnal cat is the supreme solitary hunter, capable of creeping to within a few feet of its prey before it pounces. Despite widespread persecution, the global leopard population remains in good shape, comprising an estimated 500,000 individuals ranging across sub-Saharan Africa, the Middle East and tropical Asia.

**The melanistic leopard**, popularly known as a panther, is less proportionately common in Africa than in Asia. The exception is in highland areas, notably Aberdare National Park, where melanistic individuals are regularly reported.

## Family and Breeding

The leopard is among the most solitary and territorial of cats. Adults live alone in well-marked territories that are never shared with individuals of the same sex, although males and females frequently have partial territorial overlap. Even so, a chance meeting between two individuals is usually accompanied by real or feigned aggression. Far smaller than males, female leopards come into oestrus every 6–7 weeks. At this time, males from bordering or overlapping territories will often fight to the death for coupling rights. Mating itself is an ill-tempered and abruptly executed affair, and the male has no involvement in rearing the cubs. Females give birth to litters of two to three cubs in a sheltered cave or thicket, and keep a close watch over them for the next 10–14 days, when the cubs' eyes open. Infant mortality is high; it is unusual for more than one cub to survive to adulthood. Cubs can fend for themselves at around one year, but usually stay close to their mother for another 6–12 months before becoming fully independent.

**Leopard cubs** typically have greyer pelts than the adults. Leopards are famously solitary, and two individuals keeping peaceful company will almost certainly be a female and her cub.

## What You Might See

For most safarigoers, the leopard is the most ardently sought of the Big Five. It is most likely to be seen resting up in a tree, in which case it is often worth waiting to see whether there is a kill secured nearby, or if it decides to descend to the ground. Even more thrilling is to catch a leopard on the move, showing off its sleek yet pugilistic build to the full.

**A creature of shadow**, cover and darkness, the leopard is most active after dark.

**Sharpened claws** are essential components in this cat's hunting and defensive arsenal.

**IUCN status** LC: Least Concern

## Feeding

The leopard is an adaptable and opportunistic hunter, feeding on anything from medium-sized antelope to hares, birds, baboons, hyraxes and insects. It depends almost entirely on stealth, stalking silently through thick vegetation before emerging at the last possible moment to pounce and strangle its prey with its powerful jaws. In rainforests and other habitats where lions are absent, the leopard is typically the apex predator, and adults tend to be notably heavier than their savannah counterparts. A leopard will frequently carry a large kill high into the canopy, where it is safely out of the reach of less arboreal scavengers such as lion, hyena and jackal.

Leopard dragging prey, often three times its weight, into the canopy

## Communication and Voice

As might be expected of such a potentially fearsome creature known for its ability to survive in close, near-spectral proximity to humans, the leopard is not given to extensive vocalization. Males in particular advertise their presence with a repetitive rasping cough that sounds not unlike wood being sawed. Purring has also been recorded, probably to indicate contentment when feeding. Territorial clashes between males are accompanied by snarling and hissing. However, the most remarkable feature of the leopard remains the capacity for furtiveness that ensures that the species still persists, although barely detected, in peri-urban areas such as Karen Forest on the outskirts of Nairobi.

Display of affection between leopards, seldom observed in unrelated adults

### KEY FACTS

## Panthera Pardus
*Kiswahili:* **Chui**

 **Size** Shoulder height: 70–80 cm (28–32 inches); Weight: up to 90 kg (198 lb).

**Lifespan** 20-plus years.
**Population in Kenya** Unknown – probably several thousand.
**Conservation Status** LC.
**Gestation period** 3–4 months.
**Reproduction** Females reach sexual maturity at two to four years, when they come into oestrus.

 **Habitat** Shows high habitat tolerance and might occur anywhere.

 **Top Places to See** Samburu-Buffalo Springs NR *(see pp346–9)*, Masai Mara GR *(see pp266–9)*, Laikipia Plateau *(see pp322–5)*,

**Sighting Tips** Leopards often take refuge in the branches of tall trees, where they may be detected by a tail flickering below the canopy.

**Friends and Foes** Leopards are the only large cats that regularly prey on baboons, which therefore react hysterically to the cat, issuing a distinctive panicked alarm call.

 **Facts and Trivia** The leopard's name reflects an ancient belief that it is a hybrid between a lion *(leo)* and a panther *(pardos)*.

**The leopard is compulsively clean** and spends much of the day grooming itself.

**Although highly adaptable,** leopards favour habitats that offer them plenty of camouflage.

**Leopards frequently spend their day** lying quietly in the branches of the upper canopy.

# Dogs and Hyenas

Cats aside, the two major families of large carnivore in Kenya, Canidae (dogs) and Hyaenidae (hyenas), are exciting to see in the wild. Indeed, spotted hyenas are probably the most socially complex of the region's carnivores, and it is riveting to watch clan members meet and greet at a den. Jackals, foxes and wild dogs are also at their most confiding and inquisitive while denning, offering plenty of opportunity to watch the pups at play.

### Family

Dogs and hyenas, though similar in appearance, split evolutionarily about 45 million years ago – the suborder Feliformia includes cats, mongooses and hyenas; Caniformia includes seals, bears, otters, pandas and dogs.

Young jackals often play in a puppy-like manner

## Black-Backed Jackal

*Species: Canis mesomelas*
*Best Seen: Masai Mara GR, Tsavo NP*

 LC

The most common of three closely related small dog species in East Africa, the black-backed jackal lives in pairs rather than packs. It is most active at dusk and dawn, and its shrill yelping is a characteristic sound of the African night. It has a shoulder height of 40 cm (16 inches), and an ochre coat offset by a prominent silver-flecked black saddle. An opportunistic feeder, it subsists on small mammals, birds and carrion, and is often seen lurking near lion kills.

The least distinctively marked of the three jackal species

## Golden Jackal

*Species: Canis aureus*
*Best Seen: Masai Mara GR, Samburu-Buffalo Springs NR*

 LC

Also known as the common jackal, this northern hemisphere species is the only jackal whose range extends north of the Sahara – where it was revered by ancient Egyptians as the jackal god Anubis – and into Eurasia. The golden jackal is widely but thinly distributed throughout Kenya, with the Serengeti-Mara ecosystem forming the southern extreme of its global range. More or less uniform in colour, it is more diurnal in habit than the black-backed jackal, and equally vocal.

## Side-Striped Jackal

*Species: Canis adustus*
*Best Seen: Masai Mara GR, Tsavo NP*

 LC

Associated with brachystegia woodland rather than acacia woodland, the unobtrusive side-striped jackal is more strictly nocturnal and less vocal than the other two jackal species. It is similar in general colouration to the black-backed jackal, but with an indistinct pale stripe along the flanks. An adaptable omnivore seen singly or in pairs, it supplements a diet based on meat with fruit, grain and carrion.

A white-tipped tail identifies the side-striped jackal

## Bat-Eared Fox

*Species: Otocyon megalotis*
*Best Seen: Masai Mara GR, Amboseli NP, Tsavo NP, Samburu-Buffalo Springs NR*

 LC

Easily distinguished from any jackal by its uniform silver-grey coat, huge ears and black eye-mask, this small canid is not a true fox. A number of peculiarities – up to 50 sharp teeth, for instance – have led to it being placed in its own genus. Exclusively insectivorous, it tends to be nocturnal during the hot months and diurnal in the cooler ones. Pairs and small family groups can be seen throughout the year.

The large ears help detect subterranean insect activity

**IUCN status** EN: Endangered; NT: Near Threatened; LC: Least Concern

The blotchy brown coat of the spotted hyena

## Spotted Hyena

*Species: Crocuta crocuta*
*Best Seen: Masai Mara GR, Aberdare NP, Tsavo NP,*
*Samburu-Buffalo Springs NR, Amboseli NP*

 LC

Africa's second-largest predator stands 1 m (3 ft)
high at the shoulder, and weighs about 70 kg
(154 lb), with females being larger than males.
The most common and conspicuous large
predator in many reserves, it is most often seen
at dusk and dawn. Though highly vocal at night,
its famous "laugh" is less commonly heard than a
haunted whoooo-whoop that ranks as perhaps the
definitive sound of the African night. The hyena has
a complex social structure, living in wide-ranging
clans of five to 25 animals that follow a strict
matriarchal hierarchy and perform an elaborate
ritual when two members meet. Powerfully built, it
has a characteristic sloping back, bone-crushingly
powerful jaws and a dog-like face and snout.
Routinely portrayed as a giggling coward whose
livelihood depends on scavenging from the noble
big cats, it is actually an adept hunter, capable of
killing an animal as large as a wildebeest.

The aardwolf is jackal-sized but hyena-shaped

## Aardwolf

*Species: Proteles cristatus*
*Best Seen: Tsavo East NP, Samburu-Buffalo Springs NR,*
*Masai Mara GR*

 LC

A lightly built and strictly nocturnal Hyaenid,
the aardwolf (literally, earth wolf) weighs
10 kg (22 lb) and is often confused with jackals,
from which it differs in appearance by having a
soft creamy striped coat and prominent dorsal
mane. It is exclusively insectivorous, feeding
almost entirely on two specific termite genera,
and its distribution, generally in drier areas,
is linked strongly to the presence of suitable
nests, into which it burrows nose-first to feed.

## African Wild Dog

*Species: Lycaon pictus*
*Best Seen: Laikipia Plateau, Masai Mara GR*

 EN

Africa's largest canid, also known as the
hunting or painted dog, is small in comparison
to a Eurasian wolf, and is distinguished from
similar species in the region by its black, brown
and cream coat. It typically lives in packs of
five to 50 animals that hunt cooperatively,
literally tearing apart prey on the run. Once so
common that it was treated as vermin, it has
suffered enormous losses in recent decades,
partially through direct persecution and partially
through the packs' susceptibility to infectious
diseases spread by domestic and feral dogs.
It is now Africa's second-most endangered large
carnivore, with a total wild population of around
5,000, of which 5 per cent is centred in Kenya.
Once common in the Serengeti-Mara ecosystem,
the species is now extremely rare, although
recent sightings of this legendarily nomadic
creature are cause for hope that it may yet
recolonize the area.

African wild-dog packs may include up to 50 animals

## Striped Hyena

*Species: Hyaena hyaena*
*Best Seen: Masai Mara GR, Tsavo NP, Samburu-Buffalo*
*Springs NR*

 NT

Essentially a northern hemisphere species, this
was the hyena known to ancient Mediterranean
civilizations, who believed it to be hermaphroditic
and capable of changing sex at will. Much smaller
than the spotted hyena, it has a pale brown or
grey coat with black streaks, and a luxuriant dorsal
mane. It occurs alongside the spotted hyena in
dry parts of East Africa, but is thinly distributed,
shy and seldom observed.

Striped hyena, less sociable than its spotted namesake

**For key to Field Guide icons** see p102

# Small Carnivores

Kenya supports a wide diversity of small carnivorous mammals, some very conspicuous and easily observed, others highly secretive and elusive. Falling firmly into the first category are the mongooses of the family Herpestidae, several species of which are likely to be seen in the course of any safari. The nocturnal viverrids and mustelids are generally less likely to be seen, although genets often become very tame in lodges where they are regularly fed.

## Family

Genets and civets belong to the most ancient of carnivore families, Viverridae, which is confined to Africa and Asia. Mustelidae, by contrast, is the most diverse carnivore family, represented by 55 species and 24 genera worldwide.

### Cape Clawless Otter
*Species: Aonyx capensis*

 LC

Arguably the largest of "small" carnivores, weighing as much as 35 kg (77 lb) in some cases, the Cape clawless otter is a dark brown piscivore with a bold white collar. While seen in any suitable wetland habitat, it is most common in waters where it can evade crocodiles.

### Spotted-Necked Otter
*Species: Lutra maculicollis*

 LC

Seldom weighing more than 6 kg (13 lb), the spotted-necked otter appears all brown from a distance, but has a lightly spotted throat. Absent from alkaline or saline aquatic habitats, or those with poor visibility, it is most likely to be seen on Lake Victoria's shores.

### Honey Badger
*Species: Mellivora capensis*

LC

The honey badger, or ratel, has a fearless temperament and pugilistic build, with a black body bisected by an off-white stripe down its back, a deceptively puppyish face and heavy bear-like claws. An opportunistic feeder, its diet includes snakes, scorpions and the soft parts of tortoises.

### African Civet
*Species: Civettictis civetta*

LC

Larger and heftier-looking than the related genets, the African civet is a long-haired omnivore with a black, white and gold coat. It feeds on small animals, including certain snakes, but will also eat fruits and roots. It is seen on night drives, pacing deliberately with its nose to the ground as if following a scent.

### Common Genet
*Species: Genetta genetta*

LC

Also known as the small-spotted genet, this is the most familiar member of a genus of cat-like predators represented by some eight species in sub-Saharan Africa, to which it is endemic. It regularly visits lodges at night, especially in Samburu-Buffalo Springs, but is seldom seen otherwise.

### Blotched Genet
*Species: Genetta tigrina*

 LC

Similar in appearance to the common genet but with a black-tipped tail instead of a white-tipped one, the blotched or large-spotted genet has a slender low-slung torso, spotted black on gold coat and a long striped tail. It is a frequent nocturnal visitor at The Ark in the Aberdares.

**IUCN status** LC: Least Concern

## Predator and Prey

Small carnivores are often undiscerning feeders, snaffling up anything from insects to small rodents and birds, as well as fruit and carrion. The honey badger is famed for its symbiotic relationship with the greater honeyguide, a bird which leads it to beehives and feeds on the scraps as the hive is torn apart. The Herpestidae mongooses are known to prey on snakes, but this behaviour is more common in Asia than in Africa, where they prey on small animals that are less well equipped to bite back.

The banded mongoose feasting on egg

### Banded Mongoose
*Species: Mungos mungo*
 LC

The most common of several mongoose species in Kenya, the banded mongoose is a slender cat-sized carnivore whose dark brown coat bears a dozen or so faint black stripes along the back. Highly sociable and diurnally active, it is typically seen in family bands of ten to 20 members.

### Dwarf Mongoose
*Species: Helogale parvula*
 LC

The diminutive and highly social dwarf mongoose has a shoulder height of 7 cm (2.8 inches). It is a light brown predator often seen in the vicinity of the termite mounds and hollowed dead branches that it uses as a home. Family members can sometimes be seen interacting near the den.

### Slender Mongoose
*Species: Herpestes sanguineus*
 LC

A widespread species, the slender mongoose divides its time between foraging terrestrially and arboreally. Though quite variable in shade, it is almost always uniform grey or brown in colour with an elongated body and tail, the latter with a diagnostic black tip.

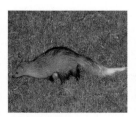

### White-Tailed Mongoose
*Species: Ichneumia albicauda*
 LC

About the size of a badger with a bushy white tail, this is the largest African mongoose. One of the most strictly nocturnal and solitary species, it is often observed by spotlight on night drives, and is also a regular visitor to "tree hotels" in the Central Highlands.

### Marsh Mongoose
*Species: Atilax paludinosus*
 LC

This large grizzled brown mongoose tends to be solitary and is mainly, though not exclusively, nocturnal. Most numerous in papyrus swamps and other moist habitats, it feeds on aquatic creatures such as molluscs and lungfish, obtained by filtering mud through its slender fingers.

### Striped Weasel
*Species: Poecilogale albincha*
 LC

A widespread but uncommon resident of open grassland, the striped weasel is mostly black below and white on top, with an all-white tail. With its very short legs and almost cylindrical body shape, it could almost be mistaken for a snake at first glance. It preys almost exclusively on small rodents.

**For key to Field Guide icons** *see p102*

# Primates

Intelligent, hyperactive and graceful, monkeys are among the most entertaining of creatures. Most Kenyan species are Cercopithecids, an adaptable family of omnivores that fill many ecological niches from swamp forests to semi arid plains. This group includes the vervet and baboon, the most commonly seen primates on safari. By contrast, the leaf-eating colobus monkeys are strongly arboreal and live in forests within 12 degrees of the equator.

### Family

Aside from bushbabies, Kenya's primates are all Old World monkeys (family Cercopithecidae), split between the subfamilies Colobinae (colobuses) and Cercopithecinae (cheek-pouched monkeys).

The blue monkey, identifiable by its white throat

## Blue Monkey

*Species: Cercopithecus mitis*
*Best Seen: Aberdare NP, Mount Kenya, Arabuko Sokoke FR*

 LC

The most widespread of African forest primates, the blue monkey shows a high level of racial variability, and is also known as diademed, white-throated, Sykes and samango monkey. Seen mainly in forest margins, it lives in troops of up to ten animals that willingly travel riparian corridors through savannah habitats. The races in Kenya typically have a grizzled blue-grey coat, a rustier hue on the back and a white throat extending along the chest or collar.

## Black-and-White Colobus

*Species: Colobus guereza*
*Best Seen: Aberdare NP, Mount Kenya, Kakamega Forest NR*

LC

The most beautiful of Kenya's primates, this colobus is almost exclusively arboreal and can cover up to 31 m (100 ft) in one leap. Larger than other forest monkeys, it weighs up to 12 kg (26 lb), feeds solely on leaves and is associated with highland and mid-altitude forests. It is typically seen in troops of three to ten adults with a couple of albino-white babies in tow.

A striking albino-white colobus baby with its mother

The red-tailed monkey, usually seen high in the canopy

## Red-Tailed Monkey

*Species: Cercopithecus ascanius*
*Best Seen: Kakamega Forest NR and other forested areas in the Uganda border area*

LC

This lightly built and strongly arboreal monkey is named for its coppery-red tail, but is more easily recognized by the striking heart-shaped white blob on its nose. It is more omnivorous than most monkeys and unusually unsocial, living singly or in pairs that frequently feed alongside other monkey species.

## De Brazza's Monkey

*Species: Cercopithecus neglectus*
*Best Seen: Saiwa Swamp NP*

LC

Associated with swampy forested habitats, De Brazza's monkey is confined in East Africa to a handful of localities near the Kenya–Uganda border, and is only seen in Saiwa Swamp National Park *(see pp294–5)*. A spectacular thickset and dark grey-brown guenon, it has a reddish-brown patch around its eyes, a white band across its brow, and is rendered unmistakeable by its white moustache and beard.

The swamp-loving De Brazza's monkey

The sociable vervet spends long stretches grooming

## Vervet Monkey

*Species: Chlorocebus aethiops*
*Best Seen: Masai Mara GR, Lake Naivasha, Meru NP*

LC

Delightful or mischievous, depending on its level of familiarity with people, the vervet monkey is one of the true characters of the African savannah. It lives in troops of 30–75 animals that are constantly engaged in entertaining interaction, whether fighting, grooming, carrying their young on their chest, clambering around branches, or raiding a lodge's lunch buffet. It is thought to be the world's most numerous primate species (apart from humans) and is mainly terrestrial, although it seldom strays too far from trees. Smaller and lankier than any baboon, it has a grizzled light-olive or grey coat offset by a black face, white ruff and pale belly, though this rather dull colouration is balanced in the male by a gaudy blue scrotum. It is highly intelligent, boasting an array of alarm calls that has been likened to a rudimentary language.

## Olive And Yellow Baboons

*Species: Papio anubis and p. cynocephalus*
*Best Seen: Masai Mara GR, Lake Nakuru NP, Tsavo NP*

LC

Weighing up to 45 kg (99 lb), the baboon is the largest primate in Kenya, and is recognized by its inverted U-shaped tail and dog-like head. Two species with marginally overlapping ranges occur in Kenya: the bulkier and darker olive baboon of the west, and the lankier yellow species of the east. Like the equally sociable vervet, the baboon is behaviourally fascinating, living in large, perpetually squabbling, and sex-obsessed matriarchal troops, with the dominance-seeking males moving between troops. Adaptable omnivores, baboons steer clear of people but can become very aggressive around campsites and lodges that they associate with food. In such circumstances, they should be treated with caution.

Though mainly terrestrial, baboons feel safest near trees

The patas has a streamlined runner's build

## Patas Monkey

*Species: Erythrocebus patas*
*Best Seen: Laikipia Plateau, Samburu-Buffalo Springs NR*

LC

The dry-country equivalent of the vervet, the patas monkey is thinly distributed in Kenya in the semiarid plains and mountains northwest of Mount Kenya. It is the spindliest of African monkeys, longer limbed and more russet in colouration than the vervet or baboon, and can attain a speed of 48 kmph (30 mph), making it the world's fastest-running primate.

## Bushbabies

*Family: Galagonidae*
*Best Seen: Aberdare NP, Laikipia Plateau, Shimba Hills NR*

LC

Closely related to the lemurs of Madagascar, bushbabies are endearing creatures with wide round eyes and agile bodies that enable them to leap from tree to tree. Several species are recognized, but most are difficult to distinguish except by call, and are only likely to be seen if sought with a spotlight.

The large eyes are an adaptation to a nocturnal lifestyle

**For key to Field Guide icons** *see p102*

# African Bush Elephant

The world's largest land animal, the African elephant is one of the most enduringly exciting creatures encountered on safari, not only for its imposing bulk, but also for its complex social behaviour. Elephants are notable for two unique adaptations – a long trunk that combines immense strength with the sensitivity to isolate and tear out a single blade of grass, and outsized tusks that grow throughout its life, sometimes reaching lengths in excess of 3 m (10 ft).

**Bloody combat** between male elephants is unusual, since breeding rights are generally established within the community through mock fights which involve trunk locking and tusk clashing.

## Family and Breeding

Elephants are intensely sociable creatures. Females and youngsters move around in close-knit matriarchal clans. Females typically come into oestrus between one and 5 years after giving birth. Once impregnated, they give birth about 22 months later. Unlike their female kin, males are generally booted out of their birth group in their early teens, after which they roam around singly or form bachelor herds, often tailing the larger breeding herds with which they share a territory. Males periodically come into musth, a sexually related condition characterized by a fifty-fold increase in testosterone levels; such elephants are unpredictable and best treated with caution by other elephants and humans alike.

**Adult females maintain a vigilant watch** over their young until they are old enough to deter predators. A female gives birth to a 100-kg (220-lb) calf every 5 to 10 years. Each calf thus represents a major genetic investment for the matriarchal herd, and is raised communally. Matriarchal herds comprise up to four generations of sisters, daughters and granddaughters, dominated by the oldest female.

## What You Might See

Elephants are interactive and great entertainers. Their tusks are versatile tools, used to dig for salt or water, tear bark, and are even used in defence. The trunk is employed to place food in the mouth, to suck up water and is wielded threateningly in displays of dominance. When an elephant raises its trunk in your direction, trumpeting and stamping its feet, it is best to retreat.

**Ears flap continuously** in hot weather to cool circulating blood below the thin skin.

**Faced with a potential threat**, a herd "periscopes" – moves its trunks around to investigate.

**IUCN status** NT: Near Threatened

## Feeding

A versatile feeder, the African elephant is a mixed grazer-browser that spends up to 15 hours daily chomping some 200 kg (440 lb) of vegetable matter. It

The trunk, used to manoeuvre food into the mouth

drinks up to 200 litres (53 gallons) daily, arriving at a waterhole a few hours after sunrise and often lingering on until late afternoon to play in the water or spray itself. Herds range widely in search of food, but concentrated populations in protected areas often cause serious environmental degradation by uprooting trees.

## Communication and Voice

Elephant herds interact physically the whole time, but it was long thought that their aural communication was limited to the occasional bout of irate trumpeting. Only in 1987 did researchers in Amboseli National Park discover that the elephant's main means of communication in fact consists of subsonic rumblings, well below or at the very edge of human perception, that can travel through the earth for several miles. These are picked up by the skin on the trunk and feet, allowing dispersed herds to coordinate their movements over a vast area. Elephants also have an exceptional sense of smell and good eyesight.

Elephants use their feet to sense the distant subsonic rumblings of a peer

## KEY FACTS

### Loxodonta Africana
*Kiswahili:* **Ndovu**

 **Size** Shoulder height: 2.5–4 m (8.2–13 ft); Weight: up to 6,300 kg (13,890 lb).

**Lifespan** 65 years.
**Population in Kenya** 38,000.
**Conservation Status** NT.
**Gestation Period** 22 months.
**Reproduction** Typically, females first conceive in their early teens and give birth at 5-yearly intervals until their late 50s.

 **Habitat** All habitats except the northern deserts.

 **Top Places to See** Amboseli NP *(see pp198–201)*, Tsavo NP *(see pp186–91)*, Masai Mara GR *(see pp266–9)*.

**Sighting Tips**
A trail of steaming football-sized dung and vegetation destruction are signs that elephants have passed by.

**Friends and Foes**
The elephant's droppings are festive material for dung beetles, which feed almost exclusively on faecal matter.

 **Facts and Trivia**
The legend of elephant graveyards has a factual basis. Old elephants whose last set of teeth has worn down gather in marshes to feed on waterlogged vegetation until even that gets difficult and they die of starvation.

**Tusks and trunk** are both used to dig for subterranean water in riverbeds during the dry season.

**The trunk** is regularly used to tear juicy branches from the canopy and dislodge ripe fruit.

**Elephants spray themselves** with water or dust to help cool down.

The white rhino can easily be identified by its square mouth

## White Rhinoceros

*Species:* **Ceratotherium simum**
*Best Seen:* **Lake Nakuru, Laikipia Plateau, Meru NP**

 NT

Bulkier than the black rhino, the white rhino is held to be the world's heaviest non-marine mammal after the elephant, weighing up to 3,600 kg (7,937 lb). Misleadingly named, it has smooth grey skin – the misnomer "white" derives from the Dutch word *weit* (wide) and refers to the square lips it uses to crop grass so efficiently. Prehistoric Saharan rock art and skeletal remains indicate that the white rhino once occurred throughout Africa, but its historical range comprises two geographically and racially discrete populations, neither of which occurs naturally in Kenya. The southern race, saved from the brink of extinction in the early 20th century, now numbers some 20,000 animals in the wild, all descended from a bottleneck population of fewer than 30 individuals in South Africa's Imfolozi Game Reserve. The northern race, however, is now the rarest and most endangered of all living rhino taxa.

## Common Hippopotamus

*Species:* **Hippopotamus amphibius**
*Best Seen:* **Lake Naivasha, Masai Mara GR, Nairobi NP**

 VU

The most characteristic resident of Africa's rivers and freshwater lakes is the common hippo, whose purple-grey hairless hide, pink undersides and cheeks, barrel-like torso and stumpy legs render it unmistakeable. Ears, eyes and nostrils are placed high on the skull, allowing it to spend most of its time submerged in the shallows. It feeds terrestrially, however, emerging between dusk and dawn to crop grass with its wide mouth, often ranging far from water in the process. The hippo is highly gregarious, living in pods of up to 30 members, and very territorial, with fights for dominance between males often resulting in serious injury or death. Contrary to appearance, the hippo is highly mobile on land and can easily attain a speed of above 32 kmph (20 mph). It can be very dangerous to humans, as it typically heads straight to the safety of the water when disturbed, mowing down anything in its path. The fantastic communal grunting of the hippo, a characteristic sound of waterside lodges, can be heard by day as well as after dark.

Hippos are poor swimmers, tending to stick to shallow water

**IUCN status** EN: Endangered; VU: Vulnerable; NT: Near Threatened; LC: Least Concern

The striping on a plains zebra reaches right under the belly

## Plains Zebra

*Species: Equus quagga*
*Best Seen: Amboseli NP, Masai Mara GR, Meru NP*

 LC

Placed in the same genus as their domestic counterparts, zebras resemble a striped hybrid between a horse and an ass, with each individual possessing a stripe pattern as unique as a human fingerprint. The most common of the two Kenyan species is the plains zebra, or Burchell's zebra, a grazer whose natural distribution ranges from Ethiopia to South Africa. The plains zebra is often seen in large ephemeral herds, but its core social unit is an aggressively defended non-territorial herd comprising one stallion, up to five mares and their respective foals. The purpose of the zebra's stripes is often cited as camouflage, breaking up the animal's outline in long grass, but this fails to explain their benefit in arid habitats. It is more likely that the striping is visually confusing to predators when the herd scatters.

The stripe pattern seen on Grevy's zebra is dense and narrow

## Grevy's Zebra

*Species: Equus grevyi*
*Best Seen: Samburu-Buffalo Springs NR, Laikipia Plateau, Sibiloi NP*

 EN

This magnificent dry-country equivalent to the plains zebra is the world's largest wild equid, standing 1.5-m (5-ft) tall at the shoulder and weighing up to 430 kg (948 lb). It is distinguished by its narrower striping, white belly and bear-like round ears. Grevy's zebra move in smaller herds than the plains zebra and a stallion generally enjoys exclusive mating rights with any female passing through its territory. Once widespread in the Horn of Africa, it is now practically endemic to Northern Kenya, whose estimated population of 1,500–2,000 is concentrated in Lewa Downs and Samburu-Buffalo Springs National Reserve.

# African Buffalo

Africa's only wild ox, the African buffalo is similar in appearance to the Indian water buffalo and closely related to domestic cattle. Powerfully built, with a bulk of up to 800 kg (1,764 lb) and heavy splayed horns, it is famed for its unpredictable temperament. Indeed, the "great white hunters" who coined the term Big Five regarded this ox as the most dangerous of foes. Buffalo are the most numerous of the Big Five, with a continent-wide population estimated at over 1 million, and are highly conspicuous on most Kenyan safaris.

**Affectionately known as Daga Boys** after a local African word meaning mud, elderly male buffaloes tend to live singly or in small bachelor herds and have a reputation for grumpiness, as well as for being quicker to charge than individuals in breeding herds.

## Family and Breeding

The African buffalo is highly gregarious and non-territorial, generally moving in mixed-sex herds of ten to 50 animals, with one dominant male and a hierarchical structure binding the adult females and non-dominant males. Females come into oestrus at the start of the rainy season and give birth to a single calf, or more occasionally twins, almost exactly a year later. Tensions between males run high during the mating season, with dominant bulls trying to pull rank and subordinate males fighting to challenge their breeding rights. The imposing bulk of an adult buffalo ensures that it has few natural enemies, and a strongly bonded herd will cooperate to chase away predators. Nevertheless, buffaloes are regularly preyed upon by larger lion prides in national parks such as Masai Mara National Reserve, with the lion occasionally coming off second best.

**Aggregations of more than 1,000 buffalo** can still be seen during the rainy season in some parts of Kenya, especially the Masai Mara and Tsavo East National Park.

## What You Might See

Buffaloes are less visibly interactive than certain other sociable animals. When a vehicle approaches a buffalo herd, the mass response will often be to stare down the vehicle or even to close in on it. While this can be quite intimidating, it signals curiosity – and chronic myopia – more than anything sinister. Buffaloes often support hitchhiking birds – cattle egrets, oxpeckers and starlings.

**Rival males** often lock horns during the mating season, but serious injuries are rare.

**Buffaloes take to a wallow** during the day more so than even rhinos and elephants.

### Feeding

Buffalo herds gathering at a waterhole to drink and wallow

Primarily a grazer, the African buffalo requires a significant proportion of grass in its diet, although it can supplement this by browsing on low trees and shrubs. Large herds are common in most grassland habitats, while forests support smaller herds. The buffalo feeds throughout the day, but will readily adopt a nocturnal feeding pattern in areas where it is repeatedly disturbed. It must drink at least once every 24 hours – and also enjoys wallowing – so herds seldom stray more than 10–15 km (6–9 miles) away from a reliable water source.

### Communication and Voice

The African buffalo is generally far quieter than its mooing domestic counterpart when it comes to day-to-day communication. However, upon sighting a predator, it makes an explosive snorting alarm call that swiftly mobilizes the rest of the herd into defensive mode. A threatened animal may also grunt aggressively. The buffalo has an acute sense of smell and exceptional hearing, but poor eyesight, for which reason a herd may often stand and stare myopically at a perceived intruder.

Buffalo herds tend to walk in a single file when covering long distances

## KEY FACTS

### Syncerus Caffer
*Kiswahili:* **Nyati or Mbogo**

 **Size** Shoulder height: 1.2–1.7 m (4-6 ft); Weight: up to 500–800 kg (1,102–1,764 lb).

**Lifespan** 20–25 years.
**Population in Kenya** 80,000.
**Conservation Status** LC.
**Gestation period** 22 months.
**Reproduction** Females mature at the age of four to five years and give birth to a single calf at the start of the rainy season.

 **Habitat** Mostly non-arid environments.

 **Top Places to See**
Tsavo East NP *(see pp188–9)*, Masai Mara GR *(see pp266–9)*, Samburu-Buffalo Springs-Shaba NR *(see pp346–50)*.

**Sighting Tips**
Buffaloes are present in many habitats where hiking is permitted, such as in the forested zones of Mount Kenya and Hell's Gate NP.

**Friends and Foes**
Cattle egrets flock around herds of buffalo to feed on insects that are disturbed by the mammals' movements.

 **Facts and Trivia**
The Maasai taboo on eating wild animals recognizes two exceptions, buffalo and eland. This ancient belief reflects the close kinship between domestic cattle, eland and buffalo.

**A courting male buffalo** will rest his head on the female's rump as a prelude to mating.

**Female calves** stay with their birth herd, but males may be forced out upon reaching sexual maturity.

**The large packs of lion** in the Masai Mara routinely try to prey on buffalo, with mixed success.

# Black Rhinoceros

With its armoured grey hide, massive bulk, fearsome horns and irascible disposition, the black rhino is one of the most ancient surviving branches of the ungulate line. It stands on the brink of extinction, with its continental population having plummeted from 100,000 to 2,500 over 20 years prior to the early 1990s. The situation has improved slightly since then, but the black rhino remains among the most critically endangered of African animals. Kenya, supporting more than 20 per cent of the global total, is now possibly the best place to see it.

**The rhino and oxpecker** were long thought to have had a symbiotic relationship, with oxpeckers cleansing the rhino's skin of ticks and other pests. It is now known that oxpeckers also suck blood from cuts and wounds in their host's hide.

**The bond between mother and calf** is generally strong and lasts for 3–4 years. During the first 12 months, the calf is vulnerable to predation from lions and hyenas, and is protected aggressively by its mother. The female will eventually terminate the relationship once another calf is imminent.

## Family and Breeding

Adult black rhinos are essentially solitary, though not especially territorial. Both sexes are aggressive towards unfamiliar individuals but equable towards rhinos with neighbouring or overlapping territories, sometimes even pairing off temporarily. The bond between a mother and calf, however, is more enduring. Courtship between black rhinos is a protracted affair. The female scrapes her territorial dung piles vigorously, and the first male to pick up the scent trails behind her trying to cover it up with his own faeces. Prior to mating, the pair often indulge in noisy mock-sparring. Once the male is accepted, the two stay together for days or even weeks. A single calf weighing up to 50 kg (110 lb) is born 15 months later, and is fully mobile within 3 days.

## What You Might See

Black rhinos are reclusive animals, and most safarigoers consider themselves lucky to see one in the wild. The solitary nature of these beasts means that most sightings involve no interaction. Visitors may occasionally locate a mother and calf, or a few adults assembled at a wallow. Black rhinos have a proclivity to charge when disturbed, so it is necessary to stay alert.

**An adult male defecates** at a communal dung post, signalling his passing to other rhinos.

**Rhinos enjoy wallowing in mud**, whose colour often alters their own appearance.

**IUCN status** CR: Critically Endangered

## Feeding

The black rhino is a dedicated browser, utilizing leaves, branches and fruits of at least 200 plant species. This behaviour is indirectly accountable for the misleading names of black and white rhinos – the original Dutch name *weit* (wide), later mistranslated to "white", was an allusion to the square grass-cropping mouth of the white rhino *(see p120)*; the black rhino received its name by default. The black rhino feeds most busily in the early morning and late afternoon, ideally retiring to a wallow or waterhole at midday, though it can go almost a week without drinking water if need be.

Plucking twigs with its prehensile upper lip

## Communication and Voice

Vocalizations, though complex and varied, are seldom observed during a casual rhino encounter. When two individuals meet, they may growl or trumpet to signal aggression, but will more likely snort in amicable greeting. Rhinos give a high-pitched alarm call when moderately threatened, and emit a loud pig-like squeal when seriously alarmed. Indirect communication between neighbours includes the sharing of common dung heaps at waterholes and feeding places, which allows every individual to know which other rhinos have passed by recently. In contrast to its acute sense of smell, the black rhino has poor sight, with a focal range of less than 10 m (33 ft).

The awesome sight of two adult males locking horns in combat

## KEY FACTS

### Diceros Bicornis

*Kiswahili:* **Faru**

 **Size** Shoulder height: 1.4–1.8 m (4.6–5.9 ft); Weight: up to 1,400 kg (3,086 lb).

**Lifespan** 40–45 years.
**Population in Kenya** less than 650.
**Conservation Status** CR.
**Gestation Period** 15 months.
**Reproduction** Typically females mature sexually at five years and give birth to a calf every three to four years.

 **Habitat** Well-wooded and open savannah.

 **Top Places to See** Tsavo West NP *(see pp190–91)*, Lake Nakuru NP *(see pp280–83)*, Meru NP *(see pp334–7)*. Masai Mara GR *(see pp266–9)*.

**Sighting Tips**
Rhinos are fond of rolling in mud wallows, which are therefore good places to spot these elusive animals.

**Friends and Foes**
The black rhino is the third-largest animal in Africa and a full-grown adult has little to fear from predators, but it is sometimes chased away by peeved elephants.

 **Facts and Trivia**
The primary cause of the modern decline in Africa's rhino population is the mistaken belief that its horn has medicinal properties.

**Rhinos are solitary creatures** and seldom interact with each other or with different species.

**A rhino might charge** at the slightest provocation, and can quickly accelerate to a terrifying 55 kmph (34 mph).

**Rhinos return daily** to favoured rubbing posts, gradually polishing the top smooth.

# Small Mammals

Kenya is best known for its rich megafauna, but the country also supports a fascinating variety of smaller and more obscure mammals. These range from diverse and highly conspicuous orders such as the rodents and bats, which keen observers are likely to encounter on a daily basis, to the more quirky and elusive giant forest hog, aardvark and pangolin, all of which come close to topping the wish list of seasoned safarigoers.

### Family

Many of these animals are evolutionary one-offs. For instance, the aardvark is the only living member of the order Tubulidentata. By contrast, pigs belong to the same order as giraffes, camels and antelopes.

The pangolin with its thick armour-plated scaling

## Pangolin

Family: *Manidae*
Best Seen: *Widespread but seldom seen*

Most Species : NT

Also known as scaly anteaters, pangolins are unobtrusive nocturnal insectivores whose name derives from the Malay *penguling*, a reference to their habit of curling into a tight ball when disturbed. The savannah-dwelling ground pangolin is the more widespread of the two Kenyan species, while the 35 kg (77 lb) giant pangolin is confined to the forests of the west. Both animals are rarely seen in the wild.

Aardvarks use clawed feet to dig into termite mounds

## Aardvark

Species: *Orycteropus afer*
Best Seen: *Laikipia Plateau, Masai Mara GR, Tsavo NP*

LC

One of the most peculiar of African mammals, the aardvark – a Dutch name meaning earth pig – weighs up to 80 kg (176 lb). It is a shy, strictly nocturnal insectivore with pinkish skin, a heavy tail not unlike a kangaroo's and long upright ears. It uses an elongated snout and long retractable sticky tongue to snaffle up as many as 50,000 termites in one night.

## Hyrax

Order: *Hyracoidea*
Best Seen: *Hell's Gate NP, Masai Mara GR, Tsavo NP*

LC

Endemic to Africa, hyraxes are dwarfish relicts of a once-prolific near-ungulate order more closely related to elephants than any other living creature. The widespread rock hyrax *Procavia capensis*, a conspicuous resident of rocky outcrops and mountains, lives in territorial family groups of up to 20 individuals. The forest-loving tree hyrax *Dendrohyrax arboreus* is seldom seen, but often heard emitting a terrifying banshee wail that rips through the night air.

Hyraxes spend long periods basking in the sun

## Porcupine

Family: *Hystricidae*
Best Seen: *Widespread but seldom seen*

Both species : LC

The largest African rodent, weighing up to 27 kg (60 lb), the porcupine is represented in Kenya by two almost indistinguishable and seldom seen species, both coated in long black and white quills that occasionally betray the animal's presence by rattling as it walks.

The long quills of the porcupine are modified hair

**IUCN status** NT: Near Threatened; LC: Least Concern

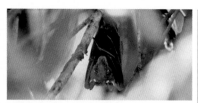

Fruit bats generally roost in colonies in trees

# Bats

*Order: Chiroptera*
*Best Seen: Kakamega Forest NR*

Most Species : Variable

Chiroptera (bats) is the second-most successful mammalian order, with 1,000-plus species globally. Although widely feared, no African bat sucks blood, and they play a vital ecological role in controlling flying insect populations. Small insect-eating bats are often seen hawking at dusk throughout Kenya, but larger fruit bats tend to prefer wooded habitats. The largest African mainland species, the hammer-headed fruit bat *Hypsignathus monstrosus*, is distinguished by the distended head sac it uses to broadcast a far-carrying booming mating call through the western Kenyan rainforests.

The tusks of the warthog are the largest in any swine

# Warthog

*Species: Phacochoerus africanus*
*Best Seen: Masai Mara GR, Lake Nakuru NP, Tsavo NP*

LC

The most common and conspicuous of Kenya's wild pigs, the warthog is a long-legged slender-bodied swine that stands 80 cm (32 inches) high at the shoulder and weighs up to 150 kg (331 lb) in exceptional cases. It has an almost hairless grey coat, a long dorsal mane, upward-curving tusks and a trio of callus-like "warts" on its face. Family groups, a regular sight in many savannah reserves, are often seen trotting briskly away with long, thin tails stiffly erect. The warthog is an unfussy omnivore whose favoured food consists of roots and bulbs. It defends itself against predators by reversing into a burrow with tusks facing out aggressively. The remote northeast of Kenya is home to the desert warthog *Phacochoerus aethiopicus*, a similar-looking species, which is IUCN red-listed as Least Concern, and is most likely to be seen in the vicinity of Marsabit and Turkana.

# Bushpig

*Species: Potamochoerus larvatus*
*Best Seen: Aberdare NP, Mount Kenya*

LC

Larger, more hirsute and shorter-legged than the warthog, the bushpig is the other widespread Kenyan swine. It is less conspicuous as a result of its strictly nocturnal habits, its secretive nature and a preference for dense riverine and forested vegetation. The bushpig has small tusks but can be quite aggressive when cornered. It displays a high degree of colour variation, ranging from grey-brown to chestnut. Sightings are almost guaranteed when staying overnight at a tree hotel in Aberdare National Park or Mount Kenya.

The bushpig, with its pale grey dorsal crest

# Giant Forest Hog

*Species: Hylochoerus meinertzhageni*
*Best Seen: Aberdare NP, Mount Kenya*

LC

Measuring up to 2 m (6 ft) in length and weighing around 250 kg (551 lb), the giant forest hog is the world's largest swine, and the only one that can be described as magnificent. Bizarrely, despite its monstrous proportions, this mighty porker eluded Western science until 1904, when a specimen was shot in the Congo rainforest. Dark grey-brown in general colouration, this hog is a very hairy creature, with a naked face, wide snout and fairly large tusks, and normally moves in pairs or small family parties. A nocturnal and strictly vegetarian animal, it is typically associated with western lowland rainforests, but the eastern race occurs in montane forests in Kenya. Unlikely to be seen elsewhere, it is a regular nocturnal visitor to Serena Mountain Lodge *(see p370)* on Mount Kenya.

Unable to root like most pigs, this hog digs with its tusks

# The Wildebeest Migration

One of the world's greatest natural spectacles, the annual migration of up to two and a half million ungulates through the Serengeti-Mara extends over approximately 40,000 sq km (15,500 sq miles) of wilderness in southern Kenya and northern Tanzania, making it Africa's largest intact migratory ecosystem. The cycle breaks up into three distinct periods of migratory motion – the march between the southern and western Serengeti, the northward trek across the Grumeti and Mara rivers towards the Masai Mara, and the return leg to south-eastern Serengeti's short grass. These are punctuated by two periods of dispersal – into the Masai Mara (August–October) and the southeastern Serengeti (December–April).

Wildebeest herds stretch across the plains below a hot-air balloon

## Migrating Herds

Moving in a deafeningly braying column that can reach up to 40 km (25 miles) in length, the cross-border migration covers over 800 km (500 miles) annually, following a fairly predictable annual cycle dictated by local rainfall patterns. Numerically, the migration is dominated by up to two million wildebeest, but fellow travellers include plains zebra, Thomson's gazelle, Grant's gazelle, topi, Coke's hartebeest and eland.

**The arrival of the short rains (October–November)** is the signal for the migration to head south from the Masai Mara to the plains of the southeastern Serengeti and western Ngorongoro Conservation Area. It is here that the wildebeest calve over January and February, replenishing the population.

**The westward migration begins** as the long rains draw to a close, usually in May. The dispersed wildebeest march northwest into the Serengeti's Western Corridor, amassing along the south banks of the Grumeti river (May–June), sometimes coming almost to the shores of Lake Victoria.

**At the start of the northward trek to the Masai Mara**, the wildebeest must cross the deep and wide Grumeti river, a tense but spectacular event that takes place in early June. Many animals drown in the crossing, or are taken by the massive crocodiles that lurk in the river's muddy waters.

## The Migratory Route

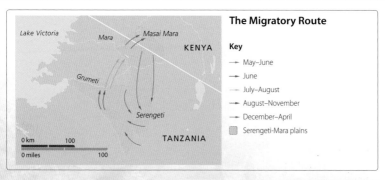

Lake Victoria

Mara

Masai Mara

KENYA

Grumeti

Serengeti

TANZANIA

0 km 100
0 miles 100

**Key**

→ May–June
→ June
→ July–August
→ August–November
→ December–April
▨ Serengeti-Mara plains

**The Masai Mara is carpeted with wildebeest** for the 2 to 3 months that divide the treacherous northward and southward crossings of the Mara river. About half of the two million migratory beasts are dispersed across the reserve's green plains, while the remainder spread out into the remote northwest of the Serengeti.

**Many thousands of zebra, gazelle and antelope** join the wildebeest in the Serengeti-Mara migration. These large herds of ungulates are followed by an entourage of well-fed predators, most conspicuously lion and spotted hyena.

**The crossing of the Mara river into Kenya** claims the lives of several hundred animals annually. The first herds to cross run the greatest risk of being devoured. For this reason, tens of thousands of animals will congregate by the river, often waiting for a week or two before the first brave individual takes the plunge. The rest of the herd follows in its wake.

# Giraffe

The world's heaviest ruminant and the tallest land mammal, the giraffe is instantly recognizable by its elongated neck and attractively patterned coat. It is common in most Kenyan national parks and reserves. Three distinct regional races are represented, with the common Maasai giraffe of the south and east being replaced by the handsome, more endangered reticulated giraffe further north, and Rothschild's giraffe in the west.

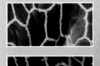

**Distinct coat patterns** distinguish the three races of giraffe found in Kenya. The reticulated giraffe *(top)* has chestnut-coloured polygonal spots with bright white outlines, the Maasai giraffe *(bottom)* has ragged spots on a coat of yellow-fawn, and the Rothschild's giraffe is intermediate.

## Family and Breeding

Giraffes typically move in groups of ten to 15 animals, although aggregations of up to 50 are common in certain areas. Herds are impermanent, with individuals often leaving or joining at will, and may be all male, all female or mixed in composition. Males are significantly larger in size than females, and homosexual coupling is more frequent than heterosexual coupling. The social structure is polygynous, and a male might have several female partners, guarding them against approaches from other bulls during oestrus. Females normally have one calf, more occasionally twins, and give birth standing, allowing the newborn to drop up to 2 m (7 ft) to the ground. The calf gets up on its feet immediately and might start suckling within 30 minutes.

**Giraffes are usually seen in loose herds** that might consist of anything from five to 20 individuals, though ten to 15 is most normal in Kenya. In addition to bachelor herds and their all-female counterpart, crèche herds consisting solely of sub-adults are sometimes encountered.

## What You Might See

Giraffes are one of the iconic sights of the Kenyan savannah, and it is fascinating to watch their feeding habits, splay-legged drinking stance and extraordinary running gait – rather clumsy yet oddly graceful. Although they are herd animals, physical interaction is relatively infrequent, so it is always worth sticking with a pair of necking males to see how the situation will develop.

**The long neck of the giraffe** forces it to splay its legs wide and even bend at the knees when it drinks.

**A running giraffe** can move at speeds of up to 55 kmph (34 mph).

## Feeding

The giraffe is a highly specialized canopy feeder, browsing on high-grade leaf foliage at heights of up to 6 m (20 ft), although it will occasionally eat grass too. At least 100 different tree species are utilized, but the various acacias are strongly favoured. The combination of a long neck and versatile tongue allows a giraffe to reach leaves that no other species can. It mostly feeds in the early morning and late afternoon, retiring into the shade to chew the cud during the hottest hours of the day.

Browsing on acacia leaves, savannah grassland

## Communication and Voice

Giraffes are often thought to be mute, but do occasionally bleat, bellow or emit a high-pitched whistle and make a snorting alarm call when threatened. It is now thought that most of their communication occurs at low frequencies that are inaudible to the human ear. Males often engage in a behaviour called necking – intertwining their necks and heads and occasionally dealing out heavy blows. This has various functions, ranging from combat to a prelude to homosexual mounting.

A display of affection between adult giraffes

## KEY FACTS

### Giraffa Camelopardalis
*Kiswahili:* **Twiga**

**Size** Shoulder height: 3–4 m (10–13 ft); Weight: up to 2,000 kg (4,400 lb).

**Lifespan** 25 years.
**Population in Kenya** At least 10,000.
**Conservation Status** LC.
**Gestation Period** 15–16 months.
**Reproduction** Females reach sexual maturity at three to four years of age and give birth every two years.

**Habitat** Open savannah and woodland.

**Top Places to See**
Masai Mara GR *(see pp266–9)*, Amboseli NP *(see pp198–201)*, Lake Nakuru NP *(see pp280–83)*, Meru NP *(see pp334–7)*, Samburu-Buffalo Springs NR *(see pp346–9)*.

**Sighting Tips**
It is worth waiting to watch a giraffe that is heading towards water – the sight of it bending over to drink is truly astonishing.

**Friends and Foes**
Giraffes seldom eat from the whistling thorn acacia because the *Crematogaster* ant nests at the base of the thorns and inflicts a nasty bite on browsers.

**Facts and Trivia**
The myth that a giraffe will die if it lies down probably derives from its limited sleep requirements of about 30 minutes a day.

**Giraffes do lie down** – contrary to myth – but only where they can see predators from afar.

**Giraffes are not averse to mingling** with zebras, antelope and other ungulates.

**Necking between males**, a dramatic sight, is often a sign of aggression in giraffes.

# Spiral-horned Antelopes

Endemic to Africa, spiral-horned antelopes of the tribe Tragelaphini are medium to large bovids with dark grey- or chestnut-brown coats, white spots or vertical stripes on their flanks and pronounced dewlaps or spinal crests. Six species are present in Kenya, and most display considerable sexual dimorphism, with the male generally sporting magnificent twisted or spiralled horns and being larger and darker than the hornless females.

## Family

The Tragelaphines are less closely related to other antelope than to buffaloes and cows. This genetic affinity is most apparent in the eland, which looks like a cross between a kudu and a domestic cow.

## Common Eland

*Species: Tragelaphus oryx*
*Best Seen: Masai Mara GR, Samburu-Buffalo Springs NR, Laikipia Plateau*

 LC

Also known as the Cape eland, Africa's largest antelope has a maximum shoulder height of 1.8 m (6 ft) and can weigh almost 950 kg (2,094 lb). The most overtly cow-like of the spiral-horned antelopes, it is light tan in colour, with faint white vertical stripes, small unisex horns and a hefty dewlap. It moves in groups of about ten animals, but larger parties are also seen. The eland was revered by the hunter-gatherers who once inhabited East Africa and often depicted the animal on the rock paintings they left behind.

The eland has relatively short, straight horns

**The male greater kudu** has the only horns that go into a full double spiral.

An adult male kudu sporting horns and a fringe of hair on its throat

## Greater Kudu

*Species: Tragelaphus strepsiceros*
*Best Seen: Lake Bogoria, Laikipia Plateau*

 LC

The most magnificent of African antelopes, the greater kudu is second in stature only to the eland. It stands up to 1.5 m (5 ft) high and has a greyish coat with up to 10 vertical white stripes on each side. Males have massive double-spiralled horns. Small family parties are seen in dense woodland along dry-country watercourses. An accomplished jumper, it can clear fences twice its shoulder height. The kudu was hammered by rinderpest in the late 19th century in East Africa, and remains localized.

## Lesser Kudu

*Species: Tragelaphus imberbis*
*Best Seen: Samburu-Buffalo Springs NR, Tsavo West NP, Meru NP*

 NT

An East African dry-country endemic whose range is centred on Kenya and southern Ethiopia, the lesser kudu is a predominantly nocturnal inhabitant of semiarid thornbush, where it is often seen in the denser vegetation following watercourses. As its name suggests, it looks very much like a miniature of the greater kudu, and the two often occur alongside each other. The lesser kudu's grey coat is typically marked by at least 11 vertical white stripes as well as a pair of white throat patches, and the male's horns are far less impressive. Thinly distributed, it might be seen in any dry-country reserve, but will most often flee before it can be observed closely.

The lesser kudu is very shy and skittish

**IUCN status** NT: Near Threatened; LC: Least Concern

A lone bushbuck grazing in a forest clearing

## Bushbuck

*Species: Tragelaphus scriptus*
*Best Seen: Shimba Hills NR, Masai Mara GR, Aberdare NP*

 LC

The closest thing in East Africa to a Bambi lookalike, the bushbuck is a widespread medium-sized antelope of forest and riparian woodland. It is likely to be present in such habitats in any ecosystem, even outside of protected areas. It is very attractive, with a coat that is regionally variable. The male is usually dark brown or chestnut in colour and has relatively small horns, while the more petite female is generally pale red-brown. Both sexes have similar white throat patches to the lesser kudu, and a variable combination of white spots and sometimes stripes on the coat. The bushbuck usually moves singly or in pairs, and although it is common in suitable habitats, it tends to be rather furtive.

## Sitatunga

*Species: Tragelaphus spekeii*
*Best Seen: Saiwa Swamp NP, Kingwal Swamp*

 LC

The semiaquatic sitatunga is a widespread but infrequently observed inhabitant of swampy habitats from Botswana to Sudan. It is similar in appearance to a bushbuck, but the male in particular is significantly larger and more shaggy coated, with more prominent striping and duller overall colouration. Most often seen singly, more occasionally in pairs, it communicates with loud barking cries that often carry long distances at night. It feeds primarily on rush, sedge and other typical marsh vegetation, with its head held low and legs spreadeagled. Its most obvious adaptation to a semiaquatic lifestyle is the uniquely splayed hooves that allow it to move easily through swamps and marshes, but make it look rather clumsy on dry land. It can swim well, too, but generally only takes to water to avoid predators.

The sitatunga, associated with waterside vegetation

## Mountain Bongo

*Species: Tragelaphus eurycerus*
*Best Seen: Aberdare NP*

 LC

A subspecies of the more widespread and common forest bongo of West and Central Africa, the mountain bongo (*T. e. isaaci*) is a massive heavy-set antelope whose deep chestnut coat is marked with a dozen bold white vertical stripes. Weighing up to 400 kg (882 lb), it is bulkier even than the greater kudu and has short but heavy black horns with prominent ivory tips. This bongo has been regarded as an effective Kenyan endemic since 1914, when the last Ugandan specimen was shot on Mount Elgon. Its wild population is now estimated at 100 inhabitants in isolated montane forest pockets in the Aberdares and Mau Escarpment. A few dozen individuals bred at the Mount Kenya Safari Club on the northwest footslopes are in the process of being reintroduced to Mount Kenya National Park.

The forest-dwelling mountain bongo, primarily a browser

**For key to Field Guide icons** *see p102*

# Large Antelopes

Antelopes are a constant of Africa's wild places, thriving in every habitat from rainforest to semidesert. Although they range in size from the diminutive duikers to the horse-like roan antelope, most members of this group are medium sized, as typified by the gazelles and impala that move in ubiquitous herds through the open savannah. Highly photogenic and socially fascinating, it is arguably the antelope that defines the safari experience.

### Family

Antelope are not related to deer. Indeed, deer form a separate family, whose most distinguishing feature is the growth of bony seasonal antlers, unlike the antelope's permanent non-bony horns.

The impala, a fast runner and prodigious jumper

## Impala

*Species: Aepyceros melampus*
*Best Seen: Tsavo NP, Masai Mara GR, Lake Nakuru NP*

LC

A relative of the wildebeest, this elegantly proportioned antelope has a chestnut coat with black-and-white stripes on the rump and tail. Males have magnificent black annulated horns. Impalas are usually seen in herds of over 100, dominated numerically by females and young. They are agile jumpers, and herds often jump in all directions to confuse predators.

## Sable Antelope

*Species: Hippotragus niger*
*Best Seen: Shimba Hills NR*

LC

Among the largest and most handsome of antelopes, the male sable has a jet-black coat offset by a white face, underbelly and rump. Its splendid decurved horns reach up to 1.4 m (4.6 ft) in length. The female is less striking, with a chestnut-brown coat and shorter horns. Common in certain other parts of Africa, the sable is confined to a single protected area in Kenya, whose population of around 120 animals is quite conspicuous on game drives.

The handsome sable antelope, Shimba Hills

Roan antelope, often seen in densely wooded savannah

## Roan Antelope

*Species: Hippotragus equinus*
*Best Seen: Ruma NP*

LC

Similar in proportions to the sable, the roan has short decurved horns, a fawn-grey coat with a pale belly and a light mane. Although common elsewhere in Africa, it is rare in Kenya, where a few herds of five to ten animals survive near Lake Victoria. There is currently talk of reintroducing it to the Masai Mara.

## Common Oryx

*Species: Oryx gazella*
*Best Seen: Samburu-Buffalo Springs NR, Tsavo NP, Laikipia Plateau*

LC

This dry-country antelope has a shoulder height of 1.2 m (4 ft) and striking horns that sweep straight back from the skull at the same angle as the forehead and muzzle. Seen in nomadic herds of up to ten animals, it can go without water for almost as long as a camel, obtaining all its needs from the plants it eats.

The ash-grey oryx with bold black face markings

**IUCN status** LC: Least Concern

Blue wildebeest at the Mara river during the migration

## Blue Wildebeest

*Species: Connochaetes taurinus*
*Best Seen: Masai Mara GR, Amboseli NP, Tsavo NP*

LC

The blue wildebeest is common in southern hemisphere grassland habitats, such as the Serengeti-Mara, but is totally absent north of the equator. It is highly gregarious, with up to two million animals undergoing a spectacular annual migration *(see pp128–9)*. The wildebeest's dark grey-brown coat precludes confusion with other antelope, but it could be mistaken for a buffalo at a distance, although its slighter build and shaggy beard are diagnostic.

The topi's dark coat distinguishes it from the hartebeest

## Topi

*Species: Damaliscus lunatus*
*Best Seen: Masai Mara GR, Tsavo NP, Ruma NP*

LC

Known as the tsessebe or tiang elsewhere in its range, the topi comes across as a darker and glossier variation of the Coke's hartebeest, with which it shares similar habits and a habitat preference for open grassland. It is dark brown in general colouration, with some black on the flanks and snout, and striking yellow lower legs. Widespread but thinly and patchily distributed, small herds are especially common in the Masai Mara ecosystem. They are one of the fastest antelopes in Africa.

## Waterbuck

*Species: Kobus ellipsiprymnus*
*Best Seen: Lake Nakuru, Masai Mara GR, Crescent Island*

LC

The waterbuck is the largest, most distinctive member of the kob family, and is recognized by its shaggy grey-brown to chestnut coat, the male's large lyre-shaped horns, and its bold white rump markings. As its name suggests, the waterbuck is seen in the vicinity of standing water, with herds of up to ten individuals lorded over by an aggressive dominant male. Two races are known: the Defassa waterbuck of the Rift Valley and Western Kenya is more chestnut and has a full white rump, while the eastern race has a white U on its rump.

Male waterbucks lock horns in aggressive combat

## Coke's Hartebeest

*Species: Alcelaphus buselaphus*
*Best Seen: Masai Mara GR, Samburu-Buffalo Springs NR, Amboseli NP*

LC

One of the more conspicuous large antelopes in Kenya's grasslands, Coke's hartebeest – also called the kongoni – is similar in height to the related blue wildebeest, with large shoulders, a backward sloping back, slender torso, pale yellow-brown coat, smallish unisex horns and a narrow heart-shaped face alluded to in its Dutch name. Males frequently climb on termite hills to scan, as a display of territorial dominance. Usually seen in parties of up to eight animals, Coke's hartebeest *(A. b. cokei)* is replaced by the stubbier horned Jackson's hartebeest *(A. b. jacksoni)* in the far north.

The slender hartebeest, set apart by its narrow face

**For key to Field Guide icons** *see p102*

### Common Duiker
*Species: Sylvicapra grimmia*
*Best Seen: Masai Mara GR, Tsavo NP, Amboseli NP*

 LC

The least typical but most widespread and conspicuous of Africa's 18 duiker species, the common or grey duiker is a variably coloured resident of wooded savannah habitats that may be seen almost anywhere in Kenya apart from forest interiors and deserts. Most often seen in pairs, it could be confused with steenbok, but it is generally greyer. The duiker has a unique identifier in the form of a black tuft of hair that divides its horns.

### Blue Duiker
*Species: Philantomba monticola*
*Best Seen: Arabuko Sokoke FR, Tana River Primate Reserve*

 LC

A widespread but shy resident of coastal forests, the blue duiker is the smallest Kenyan antelope, with a height of about 35 cm (14 inches) and a weight of 5 kg (11 lb). It is one of a group of hunch-backed forest-dwellers that rank as perhaps the least well understood and most elusive of East African antelopes. Seldom seen, it can be distinguished by its white undertail, which it flicks regularly.

### Harvey's Red Duiker
*Species: Cephalophus Harveyi*
*Best Seen: Aberdare NP, Mount Kenya, Shimba Hills NR*

 LC

The 46-cm (18-inch) tall Harvey's red duiker is among the more widespread of a cluster of red duiker species, most of which are deep chestnut with a white tail and black snout patch. The duiker most likely to be observed in Kenya, it is usually seen in forest clearings. It is replaced by Peter's red duiker in Western Kenya and by the critically endangered Ader's duiker in Arabuko Sokoke.

### Suni
*Species: Neotragus moschatus*
*Best Seen: Arabuko Sokoke NP, Tana River Primate Reserve*

 LC

The suni is a small antelope of coastal forests and thickets whose posture, colouration and habits make it easy to confuse with a duiker. It has a more freckled coat than any duiker, however, and on close inspection it can also be distinguished by its backward sweeping horns, large and almost rabbit-like ears, pro-nounced facial glands, and habit of flicking its black-and-white tail from side to side, rather than up and down.

### Gerenuk
*Species: Litocranius walleri*
*Best Seen: Samburu-Buffalo Springs NR, Meru NP, Tsavo NP*

 NT

As reflected in its Swahili name *swala twiga* (gazelle giraffe), the gerenuk is distinguished from the otherwise similar gazelle and impala by its strikingly long neck. It makes the most of this feature when it feeds, standing goat-like on its hind legs with its neck at full stretch to nibble at leaves that other antelope cannot reach. Endemic to East Africa, it lives in small family herds and is strongly associated with dry acacia thornbush.

### Klipspringer
*Species: Oreotragus oreotragus*
*Best Seen: Lake Nakuru NP, Mount Kenya, Tsavo West NP*

 LC

A relict of an ancient antelope lineage, the klipspringer (rock jumper) boasts several unusual adaptations to its mountainous habitat. Binocular vision enables it to gauge jumping distances accurately, it has a unique ability to walk on hoof tips, and its hollow fur insulates at high altitude. Pairs bond for life, and both sexes have a grizzled grey-brown coat, short forward-curving horns and an arched back.

**IUCN status** NT: Near Threatened; LC: Least Concern

## Thomson's Gazelle

*Species: Eudorcas thomsonii*
*Best Seen: Masai Mara GR, Amboseli NP, Nairobi NP*

LC

One of the most familiar East African antelopes, Thomson's gazelle, or "Tommy", has a tan-brown coat with white belly, bold black horizontal patch on the flank and small horns. Swift and graceful, it usually occurs in small herds in open grassland habitats, often alongside other grazers such as the wildebeest and zebra. Endemic to East Africa, its range is centred on the Serengeti-Mara ecosystem.

## Grant's Gazelle

*Species: Nanger granti*
*Best Seen: Samburu-Buffalo Springs NR, Masai Mara GR, Tsavo NP*

LC

Although it occurs alongside the Tommy, Grant's gazelle can easily be distinguished by its much larger size and lack of a black side stripe. It also has larger horns, which reach extraordinary dimensions in the racially discrete northern population in Samburu-Buffalo Springs. It lives in smaller herds than Thomson's gazelle and is less numerous where their ranges overlap, although it is far more widespread.

## Reedbuck

*Genus: Redunca*
*Best Seen: Aberdare NP, Masai Mara GR, Lake Nakuru NP*

LC

Two species of reedbuck occur in Kenya, both pale, lightly built and rather skittish grassland-dwellers with white underbellies and small horns. The Bohor reedbuck is a lowland and mid-altitude species with short forward-curving horns, while the chunkier and greyer mountain reedbuck is almost exclusively associated with grassy and rocky mountain slopes. Both species are common in their habitats, and are seen in pairs or trios.

## Oribi

*Species: Ourebia ourebi*
*Best Seen: Ruma Hills NP, Masai Mara GR, Shimba Hills NR*

LC

A patchily distributed small- to medium-sized antelope, the oribi has a shoulder height of around 50 cm (20 inches) and small straight unisex horns. It has a sandy coat with a white belly and can be recognized by the diagnostic round black glandular patch below its ears. Typically seen in pairs or small herds in tall open grass, it tends to draw attention to itself with a trademark sneezing alarm call before rapidly fleeing.

## Steenbok

*Species: Raphicerus campestris*
*Best Seen: Masai Mara GR, Tsavo NP, Amboseli NP*

LC

Somewhat resembling a scaled-down version of the oribi, the steenbok is a small antelope with tan upperparts, white underbelly and short straight horns. It tends to prefer thicker vegetation than the oribi, however, and its smaller size means it is more likely to be mistaken for a duiker. The name steenbok is Afrikaans for stone buck and refers not to the animal's habitat, but to its habit of "freezing" when disturbed.

## Dik-Dik

*Genus: Madoqua*
*Best Seen: Samburu-Buffalo Springs NR, Meru NP, Tsavo NP*

LC

Two species of this group of small, pretty antelopes are present in Kenya – Kirk's in the south and Guenther's in the north. Their ranges overlap in Samburu-Buffalo Springs, where a degree of hybridization may occur. Usually seen in pairs, the two species are difficult to tell apart by sight, but either is readily distinguishable from other antelopes by their grey-brown coat, white eye circles and twitchy, elongated nose.

**For key to Field Guide icons** *see p102*

# Amphibians and Reptiles

Amphibians and reptiles tend to get a lot of bad press, and not entirely without reason, considering that the Nile crocodile kills dozens of villagers annually and several snake species can inflict lethal bites. However, most reptiles are harmless to people and of great ecological value. These cold-blooded creatures maintain their body heat using external sources, for instance by basking in the sun. They are therefore prolific in warm climates and tend to be poorly represented at high altitudes.

## Family

DNA and fossil evidence indicate that crocodiles are more closely related to birds than to lizards or snakes. As such, the class Reptilia is an artificial construct, one that would only gain scientific validity were it to include birds.

## African Bullfrog
*Species: Pyxicephalus Adspersus*
 LC

Among the most common and vocal of Kenya's 100-odd species of frog, which are mostly nocturnal, the African bullfrog is also the largest and can weigh up to 1 kg (2 lb). After the rains, safarigoers are frequently treated to an evening medley of guttural croaks and ethereal whistles.

## Tree Frogs
*Family: Hyperoliidae*
 Variable

Africa's most diverse frog family, found in moist woodland habitats, tree frogs are small and brightly coloured, with long broad-tipped toes used to climb trees and reeds. A common species is the bubbling kassina, whose popping chorus is among the most wondrous of African sounds.

## Skinks
*Family: Scincidae*
 Variable

Represented in Kenya by about two dozen species, skinks are small fleet-footed lizards with slender bodies, long tails and dark scaling. Among the more visible species are the variable, striped and rainbow skinks of the genus Mabuya, most of which are associated with rocks.

## Geckoes
*Family: Gekkonidae*
NE

The most diverse African lizard family, geckoes have lidless bug-eyes suited to nocturnal hunting and adhesive toes that allow them to run upside-down on smooth surfaces. Most familiar is the common house gecko, a translucent white lizard that can be seen in most safari lodges.

## Chameleons
*Family: Chamaeleonidae*
NE

Kenya has about a dozen chameleon species, including four endemics. These charismatic lizards are known for their colour changes (influenced by mood rather than background), independently swivelling eyes and long sticky tongues that uncoil to lunge at insect prey.

## Agamas
*Family: Agamidae*
NE

Agamas are medium to large lizards with bright plastic-looking scales – blue, purple, red or orange, depending on the species. The flattened head is generally differently coloured from the torso. Particularly spectacular are the male red-headed agamas that are often observed basking on rocks.

**IUCN status** VU: Vulnerable; LC: Least Concern; NE: Not Evaluated

### Harmless Snakes

Of the 200 snake species recorded in East Africa, all but 45 are entirely harmless. Among the more common of these benign slitherers, snakes of the genus *Philothamnus* are generally bright-green with large dark eyes, and are often seen near water. The widespread rhombic egg-eater, sometimes mistaken for the venomous puff adder owing to its cryptic mottled skin, can dislocate its jaws to swallow an egg whole, regurgitating the crushed shell in a neat little package.

Rhombic egg-eater, a non-venomous snake

### African Rock Python
*Species: Python Sebae*
◯ C 🌿 👣 🐾 🌙  NE

Africa's largest snake, this python can reach lengths of 6 m (20 ft), and may be seen on safari. It is non-venomous, wrapping its body around its prey, swallowing it whole and slumbering for weeks or months while the digestive juices do their work.

### Mambas
*Genus: Dendroaspis*
◯ 🌿 👣 🌙  NE

Mambas are fast-moving and widely feared snakes that generally attack only when cornered. The 4 m (12 ft) black mamba, Africa's largest venomous snake, has a distinctive coffin-shaped head. The eastern green mamba is smaller and shyer. Bites are rare but the venom is fatal.

### Cobras
*Genus: Naja*
◯ C 🌿 👣 🐾  NE

Cobras are long snakes – up to 3 m (10 ft) – whose trademark hoods open in warning when they raise their head to strike or spit venom into the target's eye. Bites can be fatal. Spitting, though it can result in temporary blindness, causes little long-term damage if the venom is diluted with water.

### Boomslang
*Species: Dispholidus Typus*
◯ 🌿 🐾  NE

As its Afrikaans name suggests, the boomslang (tree snake) is almost exclusively arboreal. It is generally green in colour, but may also be brown or olive. Theoretically the most toxic of Kenyan snakes, it is back-fanged and passive, and, aside from snake handlers, it has never inflicted a fatal bite.

### Adders and Vipers
*Family: Viperidae*
◯ C 🌿 👣 🐾 ⛰  Variable

The sluggish disposition of the puff adder means that it is more frequently disturbed than other snakes. A thickset and cryptically marked species, it is outranked in size and beauty by the Gaboon viper, whose geometric gold, black and brown scaling blends perfectly with its habitat.

### Monitors
*Family: Varanidae*
◯ 🌿 👣 🌙  NE

Africa's largest lizard, the Nile monitor can grow to be 3 m (10 ft) long, and is often seen along river margins, while the closely related savannah monitor is marginally smaller in size. Both species feed on meat and carrion, and though not normally dangerous, can inflict a nasty bite if cornered.

**For key to Field Guide icons** *see p102*

## Nile crocodile

*Species:* **Crocodylus niloticus**
*Best Seen:* **Masai Mara GR, Tsavo East NP,
Lake Turkana**

LC

Crocodiles have lurked in the lakes and rivers of Africa for at least 150 million years, and are the nearest thing alive to a relict of the Jurassic Era, being more closely related to dinosaurs than to any living creature. Kenya is home to the Nile crocodile, which is Africa's bulkiest and longest-lived predator, growing to a maximum recorded length of 8 m (26 ft), weighing up to 1,000 kg (2,205 lb) and boasting a lifespan similar to that of humans. It occurs naturally in non-montane freshwater habitats, basking open-mouthed on the sandbanks before it slips, sinister and silent, into the water on the approach of a boat. Lake Turkana harbours the world's densest population of Nile crocodile, with up to 15,000 individuals breeding on its islands. A female lays up to 100 hard-shelled eggs in a small hole, covers them to protect them from predators, then returns 3 months later to carry the hatchlings to the water, where she leaves them to fend for themselves. The Nile crocodile feeds mainly on fish, but occasionally drags a mammal as large as a lion into the water; in fact, mammals form the main prey of crocodiles in the Mara river, as seen to grisly effect during the wildebeest migration (*see pp128–9*).

**The hide of dark, heavy scales** is valued by commercial poachers to make handbags, shoes and other leather goods.

**A crocodile can stay submerged** in water without drawing breath for 45–60 minutes.

**A Nile crocodile has about 80 teeth** which are shed and replaced twice annually.

Crocodiles make for a primeval sight as they bask on a bank

Like other reptiles, the leopard tortoise has scaled skin

## Tortoises

*Family:* **Testudinidae**
*Best Seen:* **Masai Mara GR, Tsavo NP,
Samburu-Buffalo Springs NR**

Most Species: Variable

The term tortoise is used to describe any terrestrial chelonian, an order of shelled reptiles that also includes freshwater terrapins and marine turtles. The most visible species on safari is the leopard tortoise, which is Kenya's largest terrestrial chelonian, occasionally weighing as much as 40 kg (88 lb). It can be recognized by the tall domed gold-and-black mottled shell after which it is named. Often seen making its way slowly along game reserve roads, the leopard tortoise has a lifespan of 50 years and few natural enemies, but its lack of mobility makes it susceptible to fast-spreading bush fires. It is also frequently hunted by local people. Kenya also has two hinged tortoise species, which are smaller and have a hinged shell, and the peculiar flat-shelled pancake tortoise, which is placed in its own genus and spends much of its time tucked away in rock fissures or below boulders.

**IUCN status** CR: Critically Endangered; EN: Endangered; LC: Least Concern

**The long muscular tail** is used to propel and steer through the water.

## Terrapins

*Family: Pelomedusidae*
*Best Seen: Meru NP, Nairobi NP, Lake Turkana*

 Most Species: LC

Kenya is home to five freshwater terrapin species, including the endemic Lake Turkana hinged terrapin. The region's terrapins are generally flatter and a plainer brown than its tortoises, and are usually seen in or close to water, sunning on partially submerged rocks or dead logs, or peering out from roadside puddles. Probably the most common species is the marsh terrapin, which inhabits waterholes, puddles and other stagnant waterbodies in savannah habitats, but often wanders considerable distances on land in rainy weather. It aestivates during the dry season, burying itself deep in mud only to re-emerge after the first rains – hence the local legend that terrapins drop from the sky during storms.

Hinged terrapins basking in the sun

Hawksbill turtle swimming gracefully through the reefs

## Marine Turtles

*Family: Chelonioidea*
*Best Seen: Watamu, Kisite-Mpunguti Marine Park, Malindi*

 Most Species: CR or EN

Five of the world's seven turtle species occur along the East African coast, and all are much larger than any indigenous tortoises or terrapins. The green turtle, named for the colour of its fat, breeds along the beaches of Kenya, as does the scarcer hawksbill. An individual turtle lays several hundred eggs in the sand every season. After 2 months of incubation in the sand, the hatchlings make their way towards the sea, whose temperature will affect the sex of the hatchlings – the cooler it is, the higher the proportion of males. In the late 19th century, marine turtles remained common to abundant throughout their natural habitat, with some populations numbering well into the millions. Today, as a result of poaching and pollution, all but one of the world's seven species are on the IUCN Red List, and the hawksbill and leatherback are both listed as Critically Endangered.

**For key to Field Guide icons** *see p102*

# Birds

With a national checklist of 1,136 species, Kenya has the second most varied avifauna in Africa. Birds are a prolific feature of the landscape, especially in Kakamega Forest, the Rift Valley lakes and reserves such as the Masai Mara, where enthusiasts may easily see up to 120 species in a day. Avian diversity is greatest from September to April, when migrants arrive and resident species shed their drab plumage to emerge in brilliant breeding colours.

## Family

A growing body of genetic and fossil evidence suggests that birds are most properly placed with crocodiles as the only living members of the Archosauria, a group that also includes the extinct dinosaurs.

The marabou, with its unique fleshy neck pouch

## Marabou Stork

*Species: Leptoptilos crumeniferus*
*Relatives: saddle-billed stork, yellow-billed stork, open-billed stork*

 LC

A fabulously ungainly omnivore that stands 1.5 m (5 ft) tall, the marabou is identified by its scabrous bald head and inflatable flesh-coloured neck pouch. The most common and habitat-tolerant of eight resident stork species, it may be seen near water, alongside vultures at a kill or even in urban environments, particularly in the vicinity of rubbish dumps.

## Hadeda ibis

*Species: Bostrychia hagedash*
*Relatives: sacred ibis, glossy ibis, African spoonbill*

 LC

A characteristic bird of suburban lawns, hotel gardens and grassy wetlands, the hadeda is best known for its harsh onomatopoeic cackle, most often emitted on take-off or in flight. Like other ibises, it is a robustly built bird that spends the day using its long decurved bill to probe the soil in search of snails and other invertebrates. Also common is the black-and-white sacred ibis, which was revered and frequently mummified in ancient Egypt, but is extinct there today.

Hadeda ibis, known for its raucous "ha-ha-hadeda" call

## African darter

*Species: Anhinga rufa*
*Relatives: white-breasted cormorant, long-tailed cormorant, African finfoot*

 LC

Frequently seen perching on bare branches overhanging rivers and lakes, the African darter or snakebird looks like a distended cormorant, with a kinked serpentine neck almost as long as its torso and striking russet patches that glow off-gold in the right light. The gregarious, boldly marked white-breasted cormorant and the more solitary long-tailed cormorant are also common.

The African darter's snake-like neck is distinctive when fully stretched

Egyptian goose, seen in large lakes and open water

## Egyptian goose

*Species: Alopochen aegyptiacus*
*Relatives: spur-winged goose, yellow-billed duck, white-faced whistling duck*

 LC

East Africa's lakes support 14 resident species of waterfowl, of which the largest is the spur-winged goose, but the most conspicuous is the ubiquitous Egyptian goose – a large rufous-brown bird that is very assertive and perpetually honking. Waterfowl populations tend to be densest during the European winter, when the residents are joined by ten migrant species.

**IUCN status** LC: Least Concern

Pelicans often roost communally on lakeshores

## Great white pelican

*Species:* **Pelecanus onocrotalus**
*Relatives:* **pink-backed pelican**

 LC

Easily recognized by their bulk, enormous wingspan and larder-like bills, Kenya's two pelican species are its largest water-associated birds. Most common is the great white pelican, an almost all-white bird with a large yellow pouch hanging from its long bill and black underwings that are clearly visible in flight. The smaller and more sparsely distributed pink-backed pelican has a pink-grey back and dark grey flight feathers. Both species can be seen bobbing along the surface of Rift Valley lakes such as Nakuru, often forming synchronized flotillas of around six to 12 individuals.

## Greater Flamingo

*Species:* **Phoenicopterus roseus**
*Relatives:* **lesser flamingo**

 LC

Represented by two species in Kenya, both of which are abundant on the soda lakes of the Rift Valley, flamingoes are pink-tinged birds that feed on algae and microscopic fauna, which are sifted through filters in their unique down-turned bills. They are very sensitive to water levels and chemical composition, and will easily relocate. The greater flamingo is the larger of the two species found in Kenya, but is usually outnumbered by the lesser flamingo, which is much pinker, especially on the bill.

Flamingoes, the most gregarious of waterbirds

Goliaths have the largest wingspan of any African heron

## Goliath Heron

*Species:* **Ardea goliath**
*Relatives:* **black-headed heron, great white egret, cattle egret**

 LC

The herons and egrets of the Ardeidae family are among the most distinctive waterbirds in Kenya. Most are tall and long-necked, and use their elongated sharp bills to spear fish, frogs and other prey. The star of the group is the goliath heron, which stands up to 1.5 m (5 ft) tall and is common on Lake Baringo. The familiar Eurasian grey heron, black-headed heron and cattle egret are, however, more common.

## Grey Crowned Crane

*Species:* **Balearica regulorum**
*Relatives:* **black-crowned crane**

LC

The 1-m- (3.2-ft-) high crowned crane is a beautiful grey, white and chestnut bird with a bristly golden crown and red neck wattle. Pairs and small parties are often seen in Masai Mara and Western Kenya. Its courtship dance is a riveting, albeit rather comic display that involves plenty of agitated flapping and whack movements. It has a distinctive and boomingly nasal two-note call, usually issued in flight.

A grey crowned crane has an elaborate courtship dance

**For key to Field Guide icons** *see p102*

The lappet-faced vulture is usually seen singly or in pairs

## Lappet-Faced Vulture

Species: *Torgos tracheliotos*
Relatives: *white-backed vulture, hooded vulture, palm-nut vulture*

 VU

Africa's largest raptor is a truly impressive bird, with a bald pink head, a massive blue-and-ivory bill and heavy black wings that spread open like a cape reinforcing its menacing demeanour. It often shares kills with other carrion-eating vulture species, squabbling and squawking over the spoils. Capable of soaring on thermals for hours on end, this vulture ranks among the world's most powerful fliers, and its vision is practically unmatched in the animal kingdom. It is also unexpectedly fastidious, and will spend hours preening itself after feeding.

Augur buzzard, seen in Central Highlands and Rift Valley

## Augur Buzzard

Species: *Buteo augur*
Relatives: *yellow-billed kite, chanting goshawk, harrier hawk*

LC

Among the most common raptors in Kenya, this buzzard is a handsome, medium to large bird with a black back, a variable (black, white or intermediate) breast and a bright orange-red tail. Like other buzzards, it has long broad wings, a relatively short tail and stocky build that makes it look rather like an eagle when it perches. It is probably outnumbered by the duller migrant steppe buzzard in March and October, when migrants flying between Europe and southern Africa pass through Kenya.

**IUCN status** VU: Vulnerable; LC: Least Concern

## African Fish Eagle

Species: *Hakliaeetus vocifer*
Relatives: *martial eagle, bateleur, Verreaux's eagle*

 LC

Among the most evocative sounds of the bush is the far-carrying call of the African fish eagle, a high, piercing banshee wail delivered in duet, with both birds throwing back their heads dramatically. This strongly monogamous eagle is visually distinctive and striking, with black-and-white feathering against a rich chestnut belly and hooked yellow bill. It is a conspicuous resident of rivers and lakes, perching high in the branches of tall fringing trees, or soaring above the water for long periods, sweeping down occasionally to scoop a fish into its talons. It might be confused with two other water-associated raptors, the palm-nut vulture and osprey.

African fish eagles perch openly in the vicinity of water

## Verreaux's Eagle-Owl

Species: *Bubo lacteus*
Relatives: *barn owl, spotted eagle-owl, scops owl*

LC

Also known as the giant eagle-owl, Africa's largest nocturnal bird is most often seen near the large acacia trees in which it likes to breed. It is identified by its black eyes with pinkish eyelids that it closes during diurnal rest, and distinguished from the similarly proportioned Pel's fishing owl by its grey-brown feathering, crested ears and bold black facial disk marks. Usually unobtrusive, it is sometimes heard hooting at night. As with other owls, it is feared as a harbinger of death in many East African cultures.

Verreaux's eagle-owls stand more than 60 cm (2 ft) tall

The secretary bird, the world's most atypical raptor

## Secretary Bird

*Species:* **Sagittarius serpentarius**
*Relatives:* **no close relatives, affinities uncertain**

LC

A bizarre grassland bird with long skinny legs, a slender grey torso, long black tail and bare red face mask, the 1.5-m- (5-ft-) tall secretary bird may have been named for its flaccid black crest, which recalls the quills used by Victorian secretaries. It is also claimed that "secretary" is a corruption of the Arabic saqr-et-tair (hunting bird). The monotypic family to which it belongs is thought to be ancestral to all modern eagles, buzzards and vultures. A terrestrial hunter, it feeds on snakes and lizards, which it stamps to death in a flailing dance ritual. It roosts in trees, but otherwise flies only when disturbed.

The flightless ostrich is associated with open landscapes

## Common Ostrich

*Species:* **Struthio camelus**
*Relatives:* **Somali ostrich**

LC

At a height of 2 m (7 ft) and weighing more than 100 kg (220 lb), ostriches are the world's largest birds. Two species are recognized, and their ranges overlap in Kenya. The pink-legged common ostrich is a familiar resident of protected grassland areas in the south and the blue-legged Somali ostrich is more thinly distributed in the semiarid north. In both species, the larger male has a handsome black-and-white plumage, while the female is smaller and duller. They are farmed in certain areas for their feathers, eggs and low-cholesterol meat.

## Southern Ground Hornbill

*Species:* **Bucorvus cafer**
*Relatives:* **black-and-white casqued hornbill, Abyssinian ground hornbill, silvery-cheeked hornbill**

LC

Ground hornbills are rather fantastic turkey look-alikes, with black feathers, white underwings, large casqued bills, conspicuous throat and eye wattles and long fluttering eyelashes. They are typically seen marching along in small family parties in open habitats, probing the ground for the large insects that form their main diet. Despite their terrestrial habits, they are strong fliers. Their low booming call is most often heard shortly after dusk. The southern ground hornbill, whose wattles are red, is replaced in the far northwest by the Abyssinian ground hornbill, a slightly larger species with blue eye wattles and a blue or red neck wattle.

The southern ground hornbill with large red wattles

## Kori Bustard

*Species:* **Ardeotis kori**
*Relatives:* **Denham's bustard, black-bellied bustard, Hartlaub's bustard**

LC

Loosely related to cranes but more sturdily built, bustards are medium to large ground birds associated with open habitats. The most conspicuous species is the kori bustard, the world's heaviest flying bird, weighing up to 12.5 kg (27.6 lb) and standing about 1.3 m (4.3 ft) tall. Usually rather measured and stately in demeanour, it performs a manic courtship dance, raising and fanning its tail and flapping its wings up and down in apparent agitation.

The large size of the kori bustard renders it unique

For key to Field Guide icons *see p102*

## Helmeted Guinea fowl

*Species: Numida meleagris*
*Relatives: yellow-necked spurfowl,*
*coqui francolin*

 LC

Endemic to Africa, guinea fowls are large, gregarious ground birds with spotted white-on-grey feathers and blue heads. The helmeted guinea fowl, the most common of three Kenyan species, is regularly seen scurrying along dirt roads. The star of the family, however, is the vulturine guinea fowl, a dry-country bird with a brilliant cobalt chest draped in lacy black-and-white feathers.

## Hamerkop

*Species: Scopus umbretta*
*Relatives: no close relatives,*
*affinities uncertain*

 LC

Belonging to a monospecific family, the hamerkop is a rusty brown, rook-sized bird whose long, flattened bill and angular crest combine to create its hammer-headed appearance. This odd bird's massive and amorphous nest is normally constructed untidily over several months in a tree fork close to the water, and is made of litter, branches, mud and other natural and artificial objects.

## African Jacana

*Species: Actophilornis africanus*
*Relatives: blacksmith plover, pied*
*avocet, crowned plover*

 LC

Also known as the lily-trotter, the African jacana is one of East Africa's most characteristic waterbirds, usually associated with lily pads and other floating vegetation on which it is able to walk thanks to its exceptionally far-spreading toes. A totally unmistakeable and very attractive bird, it has a rich chestnut torso and wings, white neck, black cap and blue bill and frontal shield.

## Northern Red-Billed Hornbill

*Species: Tockus erythrorhynchus*
*Relatives: African grey, Von der*
*Decken's, yellow-billed hornbills*

 LC

Typical savannah hornbills of this genus are large birds with heavy decurved bills, often seen in lodge gardens. The northern red-billed hornbill is one of the more common species. Most nest in holes in tree trunks: the female plasters the entrance to seal herself in for the incubation period, while the male feeds her through a slit until the eggs hatch.

## African Grey Parrot

*Species: Psittacus erithacus*
*Relatives: orange-bellied parrot,*
*Fischer's lovebird, Narina trogon*

 NT

African parrots tend to be elusive in the wild, calling attention to themselves with a series of explosive screeches, then flapping out of view with their characteristically direct flight. Particularly vociferous, the African grey parrot is a familiar red-rumped bird whose Kenyan range is limited to the vicinity of Kakamega Forest, though it is often kept caged at coastal resorts.

## African Hoopoe

*Species: Upapa africana*
*Relatives: green woodhoopoe, forest*
*woodhoopoe, common scimitar-bill*

 LC

The African hoopoe is a handsome orange, black and white bird whose crest is very striking when held erect. Seen singly or in pairs, it is most common in park-like habitats and hotel gardens, where it feeds on the lawn, poking around for insects with its long, curved bill. Its closest relatives are woodhoopoes, glossy-black birds with long tails and decurved bills.

**IUCN status** NT: Near Threatened; LC: Least Concern

### Hartlaub's Turaco

Species: *Tauraco hartlaubii*
Relatives: *great blue turaco, bare-faced go-away bird, Ross's turaco*

                    LC

Endemic to Africa, turacos and go-away birds are large vocal frugivores with elongated bodies, long tails and prominent crests. The lovely Hartlaub's turaco of the Central Highlands forests has a green back, blue wings, red underwings and white face patches. The go-away birds, named for their explosive onomatopoeic call, are common in savannah habitats.

### Lilac-Breasted Roller

Species: *Coracius caudata*
Relatives: *broad-billed roller, Eurasian roller, Abyssinian roller*

                    LC

One of the most popular and recognizable safari birds, the lilac-breasted roller is a robust jay-like bird with a lilac chest, sky-blue underparts and gold back. It is often seen perching on an acacia branch, then swooping down to hawk on its prey. Four similar-looking rollers occur in Kenya's savannahs, all of whom indulge in the agile aerial displays to which their name refers.

### Long-Tailed Widowbird

Species: *Euplectes progne*
Relatives: *Jackson's widowbird, red bishop, golden bishop*

                    LC

Related to the smaller weavers, this is a black bird with red and white shoulder markings and an extraordinary long droopy tail that gives it a total length of up to 80 cm (31.5 inches) during the breeding season. It is often seen flying low and ponderous over reedy marshes and grassland, where it occurs alongside several other attractive but less dramatic widows and bishops.

### Carmine Bee-Eater

Species: *Merops nubicus*
Relatives: *little bee-eater, white-throated bee-eater, blue-headed bee-eater*

                    LC

A vivid red bird with turquoise head markings, the carmine bee-eater is the most stunning member of a family of dashing colourful insectivores whose sleek profile is determined by an upright stance, long wings and tail and long decurved bills. Bee-eaters are easy to observe, perching openly on bare branches, sporadically darting off to catch an insect.

### Fork-Tailed Drongo

Species: *Discrurus adsimilis*
Relatives: *square-tailed drongo*

                    LC

A characteristic savannah and woodland passerine, the fork-tailed drongo is an all-black insectivore that tends to hawk its prey from an open perch below the canopy. It is a bold and assertive character, and emits a wide array of indignant nasal calls. It is sometimes confused with black cuckoos, male black cuckoo-shrikes and black flycatchers, but none of the above have a comparably deep fork in their tail.

### White-Browed Coucal

Species: *Centropus superciliosus*
Relatives: *red-chested cuckoo, yellowbill, Diederick's cuckoo*

                    LC

The white-browed coucal is a large, clumsy bird seen in rank grassland, marsh and lake margins. It has a white eye-strip and streaked underparts. It is most visible before rainstorms, which it tends to predict with a dove-like bubbling that gives it the name of rainbird. The coucal is related to cuckoos, which are common but secretive in African habitats.

**For key to Field Guide icons** *see p102*

### African Firefinch

*Species: Lagonosticta rubricata*
*Relatives: common waxbill, pin-tailed wydah, purple grenadier*

 LC

Bright red with light spotting on the flanks, this ubiquitous but unobtrusive gem frequents gardens and lodge grounds. It is one of several colourful seedeaters in the family Estrildidae, most of which are smaller than a sparrow and have conical bills whose waxen sheen gives it the common name of waxbill. They are parasitized by the related colourful wydahs.

### Common Bulbul

*Species: Pycnonotus barbatus*
*Relatives: spotted nicator, rufous chatterer, mountain greenbul*

 LC

Among the first birds likely to be seen in Kenya, this cheerful and habitat-tolerant small bird is a common resident of gardens and lodge grounds in the Central Highlands and elsewhere. A restless but confiding character with a bright tuneful song, it is most common in the canopy of forest margins, and is also known as the yellow-vented bulbul after its most conspicuous field character.

### Malachite Sunbird

*Species: Nectarinia famosa*
*Relatives: golden-winged sunbird, Hunter's sunbird*

 LC

Sunbirds are small restless nectar-eaters with long decurved bills. Most species are sexually dimorphic, with the rather dowdy females being smaller and less conspicuous than the iridescent males. The malachite sunbird, long-tailed and dazzling metallic green in colour, is arguably the most beautiful of these, and is associated with aloes and other flowering shrubs.

### Masked weaver

*Species: Ploceus intermedius*
*Relatives: red-billed quelea, golden weaver, white-headed buffalo-weaver*

 LC

The *Ploceus* weavers are surely the most characteristic of African bird genera, and the masked weaver is among the more common species in Kenya. The dexterous male builds intricate ball-shaped nests at the end of a thin hanging branch, which is stripped of leaves as protection against snakes. Once completed, the nest is inspected by the female, who deconstructs it ruthlessly if she deems it unsatisfactory.

### African Pied Wagtail

*Species: Motacilla aguimp*
*Relatives: yellow wagtail, golden pipit, yellow-throated longclaw*

 LC

Frequently observed walking along the edge of rivers, lakes and swimming pools, the African pied wagtail is named for its bold black and white markings and incessantly bobbing tail. It is Kenya's most common resident wagtail, but is outnumbered in some areas by the yellow wagtail, one of three migrant species, during the northern winter. The colourful longclaws and duller pipits are closely related.

### Speckled Mousebird

*Species: Colius striatus*
*Relatives: blue-naped mousebird, white-headed mousebird*

 LC

This scruffy frugivore is the most widespread member of the order Coliidae, which is endemic to Africa, and consists of half a dozen long-tailed and prominently crested species. Generally seen in flocks of around five to eight birds, the name mousebird refers to their habit of shuffling nimbly along branches, though it might equally apply to their grey-brown colouration. Four species occur in Kenya.

**IUCN status** LC: Least Concern

## Olive Thrush

*Species:* **Turdus olivaceous**
*Relatives:* **Cape robin-chat, common rock thrush, stonechat**

 LC

The Turdidae is a diverse family of medium-to-small insectivores, represented by about 50 species and 20 genera in Kenya. Among the most recognisable is the olive thrush, which is often seen hopping around hotel lawns. The family also includes robin-chats, a group of orange, blue, black and white birds that are also common in gardens, but tend to prefer thicker cover.

## African Paradise Flycatcher

*Species:* **Terpsiphone viridis**
*Relatives:* **silverbird, chin spot batis, common wattle-eye**

 LC

This hyperactive leaf-gleaning flycatcher tolerates most habitats other than true desert, and might be seen anywhere, although local abundance is affected by complex seasonal intra-African movements. Usually bluish with an orange tail, it also has black-and-white and intermediate morphs. The male's tail can be up to three times the body length.

## Pied Kingfisher

*Species:* **Ceryle rudis**
*Relatives:* **malachite kingfisher, giant kingfisher**

 LC

Probably the most numerous and visible of Kenya's water-associated kingfishers, this black-and-white bird has a unique hunting method that involves hovering above open water then diving down sharply to spear a fish with its dagger-like bill. Other water-associated species range from the gem-like, finch-sized malachite kingfisher to the crow-sized giant kingfisher.

## Red-and-Yellow Barbet

*Species:* **Trachyphonus erythro-cephalus**
*Relatives:* **double-toothed barbet, red-fronted tinkerbird, cardinal woodpecker**

 LC

One of the most striking birds in dry-savannah habitats is the red-and-yellow barbet, pairs of which frequently perch conspicuously to perform a comic and very loud duet. Seldom seen but very vocal, tinkerbirds are sparrow-sized barbets that tend to perch high in the forest canopy, tirelessly repeating a piping one-note call for hours on end.

## Superb Starling

*Species:* **Lamprotornis superbus**
*Relatives:* **red-winged starling, violet-backed starling, red-billed oxpecker**

LC

Common and colourful, with a glossy green back and rufous belly separated by a narrow white line, the superb starling is mainly a savannah bird. It is the most visible of several beautiful Kenyan starlings, including the plum-coloured violet-backed starling of riverine woodland and thornbush, the cliff-dwelling red-winged starling and the utterly breathtaking golden-breasted starling, a dry-country special.

## Tropical Boubou

*Species:* **Laniarius aethiopicus**
*Relatives:* **long-tailed shrike, black-headed gonolek**

LC

Boubous are handsome but furtive shrike-like birds who betray their presence with tightly synchronized duets that involve the male singing a short series of loud antiphonal notes and the female replying with a harsh click or chirr sound. The black-and-white tropical boubou, often known as the bellbird in reference to its ringing call, is common in the Central Highlands, but is replaced by the slate-coloured boubou in savannah habitats.

**For key to Field Guide icons** *see p102*

# KENYA
# AREA BY AREA

# Kenya at a Glance

Kenya's diverse terrain and topography afford it a magnificent array of landscapes. On the coast, white sandy beaches are backed by dense forests, and intriguing alleyways and mosques in the ancient towns reveal the coast's history. The Southeastern Savannah's burnt grasslands host East Africa's big game. Further inland, Nairobi has plenty of urban attractions, good shopping and nightlife. Volcanoes and lakes dot the Rift Valley, and above it lie Western Kenya's fertile hills and escarpments. To the south the Masai Mara, part of Africa's greatest ecosystems, supports a wealth of wildlife. The Central Highlands feature dense forests and moorland. By contrast, the north is empty, with stony sun-baked deserts.

**Mount Kenya** *(see pp326–9)* straddles the equator and is Africa's second tallest mountain. The ring road around it offers sweeping views of its peaks towering over the forest.

**Kakamega Forest National Reserve** *(see pp298–301)*, north of Kisumu, is Kenya's last remaining patch of indigenous rainforest that once spread over most of Central Africa. Its pathways wind beneath a rich canopy of trees full of monkeys, birds and clouds of butterflies.

Lokichoggio    Lokitaung

*Lake Turkana*

Kalokol

Lodwar

*Turkwel*

*Suam*

**WESTERN KENYA**
*(See pp288–311)*   Mara

Kakamega

*Nzoia*

Nakuru

Homa Bay    Naivas

**SOUTHERN RIFT VALLEY AND MASAI MARA**
*(See pp256–287)*   Na

**NAIRO**
*(See pp154–*

Nam

**Masai Mara** *(see pp266–9)* is Kenya's best-known reserve. Its highlight is the annual migration of the wildebeest that cut across the savannah tracking rain and new pastures, with predators in hot pursuit.

| 0 km | 150 |
|------|-----|
| 0 miles | 150 |

**The Karen Blixen Museum** *(see p172)* is dedicated to the celebrated author of *Out of Africa*. The period house, located in Nairobi, gives a fascinating insight into the lives of Kenya's early aristocratic white settlers when the city was in its infancy.

◀ The magnificent view from the eastern escarpment of the Great Rift Valley at Poro near Maralal

## Key

- ▭ Highway
- ▭ Major road
- ▭ Minor road
- — Railway

Zebras at Nairobi NP, with the Nairobi skyline in the background

### Getting Around

The city centre is compact enough to be explored on foot. However, visitors need to be cautious while walking around Downtown Nairobi. Taxis, found on just about every street corner, are relatively inexpensive and should always be used after dark. Any tour operator can arrange a day tour of Nairobi National Park combined with the attractions to the immediate southwest of the city. Visitors with private cars can also find these sights as they are clearly signposted off Langata Road.

0 metres 500
0 yards 500

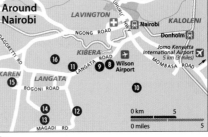

## Around Nairobi

0 km 5
0 miles 5

## Key

▨ Area of the main map

**For keys to symbols** *see back flap*

# Street-by-Street: Downtown Nairobi

Nairobi began life as a swampy railway camp, but after more than a century of development its compact downtown area now comprises imposing skyscrapers, colonial buildings and Asian-style architecture with shops set back under long, covered walkways. As the capital of Kenya, it houses government buildings, banks and large hotels, including the modern Hilton Hotel and the historic Fairmont The Norfolk. The centre is a commercial hive and it is not unusual to see an executive in a suit walk down the same street as a Maasai warrior in full regalia. Neatly bisected by the Uhuru Highway, the centre's main thoroughfares are the Kenyatta and Moi avenues. Purple blooms of jacaranda trees colour the streets in December.

**Locator Map**
*See Street Finder maps 1, 2*

**Jamia Mosque**
Kenya's leading mosque and one of its most impressive religious structures, the Jamia Mosque has a pillared façade, imposing twin minarets and gleaming silver domes.

**Kenyatta Avenue** runs through the heart of the city and is a hub of commercial activity.

**❶ ★ City Market**
With a huge range of good-quality art, curios and tribal artifacts from all over Africa, this market is very popular with visitors to Kenya. It also has food stalls which offer authentic African cuisine.

KENYATT

KAUNDA ST

UHURU HIGHWAY

| 0 metres | 200 |
| 0 yards | 200 |

**The Minor Basilica Holy Family Cathedral**, built in 1960, is the seat of the Archbishop of Nairobi. It is also the city's largest church, with a seating capacity for 4,000 people.

**Key**

— Suggested route

*For hotels and restaurants see p364 and pp376–7*

**Kenyatta International Conference Centre**
Built in 1974, this 30-storey towering building has hosted many important international conferences.

### Stanley Hotel

Now a modern tower block, the Stanley first opened its doors in 1902 as a boarding house on Victoria Street before moving to the present location in 1909. The site of Nairobi's first stock exchange, the hotel was very popular with visitors in the 1960s for its legendary Thorn Tree Café, where travellers would pin messages and letters for fellow travellers to the trunk of an acacia tree. The hotel has hosted famous stars such as Gregory Peck, Clark Gable and Grace Kelly.

The grand façade of the iconic Stanley Hotel, Nairobi

**2 National Archives**
Housed in the former Bank of India building, the archives hold an excellent collection of tribal and contemporary art, documents and reference material.

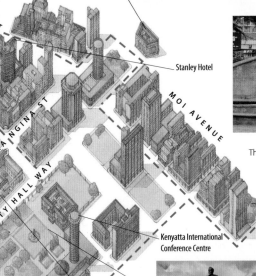

Stanley Hotel

MOI AVENUE

MANGINA ST

CITY HALL WAY

HARAMBEE AVE

Kenyatta International Conference Centre

City Hall

**3 ★ August 7th Memorial Park**
The site of the 1998 US Embassy bomb attack that killed 218 people and left thousands injured, this tranquil park has a black granite memorial commemorating the victims of that fateful day.

**Parliament House** is the seat of Kenya's government. It is housed in a 1950s building with an impressive clock tower.

**★ City Square**
Dominated by the statue of Jomo Kenyatta, Kenya's first president, this paved 705-sq-m (7,585-sq-ft) courtyard has ornamental fountains, gardens and flag poles and is flanked by the City Hall and law courts.

# ❶ City Market

**City Map** 1 B3. Koinange St. 🚌
**Open** 8am–6pm Mon–Sat.
**Closed** public holidays. ♿

Housed in an aged Art Deco building and spread over two levels, Nairobi City Market is crammed full of compact and colourful stalls. Fruit and vegetables are stacked high in mounds and flower sellers arrange their blooms in giant buckets, while outside, around the edge of the market, shops sell fresh meat, fish and seafood and dairy products. There are a number of inexpensive crafts and curios for sale such as batiks, Kisii soapstone, sisal mats and baskets, the famous Kenyan *kiondo* bags and wood carvings – the herds of wooden giraffes standing to attention are particularly eye-catching. Prices are negotiable and there is an opportunity for a bout of good-natured haggling with the local traders. For fabrics, including cheap *kikoys*, *kangas* and Maasai blankets, visitors should cross Koinange Street to Biashara Street, to the northeast of the market, where there are many Asian shops specializing in textiles.

# ❷ National Archives

**City Map** 2 D3. Corner of Moi and Luthuli Aves. **Tel** 020 2228959. 🚌
**Open** 8:15am–4:15pm Mon–Fri, 8:15am–1pm Sat. **Closed** public holidays. ♿

With its impressive columned façade, Kenya's National Archives is housed in the former

Plaque bearing the names of people killed at the US Embassy bomb attack

Bank of India building, which was built in 1906 and is one of Nairobi's oldest stone buildings. The ground floor has a lobby and gallery that display historical photographs of Nairobi, paintings and handicrafts. Among the displayed items are some superb pieces from the private collection of Joseph Murumbi, avid art collector and former vice president of Kenya. These include Persian carpets, Indian furniture and a number of drums and other tribal artifacts gathered from across Africa. When Murumbi died in 1990, it was discovered that he had collected some 50,000 books. Along with his art collection, approximately 8,000 rare pre-1900 books were bequeathed to the National Archives.

The first floor of the building has reading rooms that house a vast number of documents relating to the country's history since its colonial days. Also in this area are collections of photographs of former presidents Jomo Kenyatta and Daniel arap Moi during their terms in office and on travels abroad.

The distinctly colonial edifice housing the National Archives

# ❸ August 7th Memorial Park

**City Map** 2 D4. Corner of Moi and Haile Selassie Aves. **Tel** 020 341062. 🚌 **Open** 9am–6pm Mon–Sat, 1–6pm Sun. ♿ 🌐 memorialparkkenya.org

On 7 August 1998, a terrorist bomb attack on Nairobi's US Embassy resulted in the death of 218 people and seriously injured thousands more. The explosives, loaded on to the back of a truck, were intended to be driven into the embassy's basement car park. However, security guards stopped the truck at the gates, at which point the terrorists detonated the bomb. The explosion ripped through the building and killed many on the street. Simultaneously, a terrorist strike was unleashed upon the US Embassy in Dar es Salaam, Tanzania, killing 11 people. The Memorial Gardens were opened on the site on 7 August 2001. It is a quiet area with benches, a statue made of debris from the attack and a granite wall bearing a plaque of the names of those who died here. An information centre displays photographs of that tragic day.

# ❹ Railway Museum

**City Map** 1 C5. Station Rd. 🚆 up to Station Rd. A dirt track directly ahead of it leads to the museum. **Tel** 020 2215211. **Open** 8:15am–5pm daily. ♿

Anyone with an interest in Kenya's history will thoroughly enjoy the informative Railway Museum. Here, the full and fascinating story of the building of the Uganda Railway, dubbed the Lunatic Line *(see p303)*, unfolds through a series of displays of old memorabilia, photographs and original rolling stock. Here, a poster of early colonial administrator, Sir Charles Eliot, is inscribed with his memorable quote, "It is not an uncommon thing for a [railway] line to open a country, but this line literally created a country". Another exhibit of interest is the railway coach christened Kima Killer. It was from this coach that, in 1900, a lion dragged out and killed railway superintendent Charles Henry Ryall at Kima Station. Crockery and silverware used by Queen Elizabeth II on the Royal Train in 1959 are also on display. Smaller items include brass lanterns, beautiful clocks, old-fashioned telephone heads and typewriters used in trains and ships. Just outside the building are several restored locomotives and carriages built between 1923 and 1955 that visitors can clamber over. These include one that the former US President Theodore Roosevelt rode to take pot shots at unsuspecting wildlife during a hunting safari in 1909, and the steam train used in the film *Out of Africa* (1985).

The old Kenya Railways logo

## ❺ Nairobi National Museum

*See pp162–3.*

## ❻ Nairobi Arboretum

Arboretum Rd, off State House Rd. 🚌 ℹ️ Tree Centre, 020 2725471. **Open** sunrise–sunset. ♿ 🌐 **naturkenya.org**

With a network of walking and jogging trails and shady picnic sites, the 80-acre (32-ha) Nairobi Arboretum is home to over 350 species of trees. Rimmed by high-rise buildings, it has been regenerated in the last few years and is now transformed into a green and vibrant public space popular with families and courting couples. Originally open grassland scattered with a few hardy acacia trees, the arboretum began life in 1907 as a trial area to see if exotic and fast growing softwood trees, which were needed to fuel wood-burning steam trains, could survive in Nairobi's climate. Many species from Australia and the Americas did survive and went on to become commercially valuable in Kenya. In the 1930s, indigenous trees were introduced to the arboretum and today there is a sizable collection of the country's 800 or so species. All trees are clearly labelled, mentioning the year in which they were planted as well as their commercial use. In the case of exotic trees, the country of origin is also given.

Picnickers under a bougainvillea at the City Park

## ❼ City Park

Main entrance on Limuru Rd. 🚌 **Open** sunrise–sunset. ♿ 🚻

Laid out in 1904 as Nairobi's first recreational area, the 300-acre (121-ha) City Park has magnificently landscaped gardens with flowerbeds, trees and shrubs, a sunken garden with ponds full of fish, a canal and a nursery. The Boscawen Collection here houses rare and unusual plants, including orchids. The adjacent war cemetery has 97 graves from both world wars, while a maze and an early-20th-century bandstand bear testament to the colonial days. Thick patches of indigenous forest in the park harbour birds such as the hadeda ibis and black-and-white hornbill, as well as Sykes and vervet monkey and clouds of butterflies. The open-air restaurant adds to the park's popularity with picnickers.

A steam locomotive on display at Nairobi's Railway Museum

# ❺ Nairobi National Museum

Established in 1910, the Nairobi National Museum presents an overview of Kenya's culture and natural history. It was greatly expanded in the 1950s and in 2008 reopened after a 2-year modernization. The museum documents much of Kenya's ethnology, plus the country's flora and fauna. It also has an impressive prehistory section, which also includes displays of fossils uncovered by the Leakeys. Outside in the well-forested grounds are a number of attractions, including a glass mosaic garden and a snake park that houses most of the reptilian species found in Kenya. A walk along the well-tended paths offers views of the Nairobi river at the bottom of Museum Hill. The museum has craft shops and a café.

Spiral stairwell with a suspended column of old Nairobi photographs

**Ahmed the Elephant**
In the courtyard stands a replica of Ahmed, the famous tusker who was put under armed protection in the 1970s to demonstrate Kenya's commitment to eradicating poaching.

Asian African Heritage gallery

**★ Tower of Gourds**
This impressive tower is the central feature of the Hall of Kenya. Assembled from about 42 ethnic groups, the gourds symbolize the diversity of cultures in Kenya. Gourds are traditionally used as drinking vessels and for storage.

## Gallery Guide

*The ground-floor galleries include the Hall of Kenya, with displays relating to the ethnic groups, a collection of East African birds and a hall dedicated to the history of evolutionary finds in Kenya. Upstairs are displays of artifacts, ancient rock art and two galleries of photographs.*

**Mother and Child**
Among the many statues scattered around the grounds is this piece sculpted by Francis Nagenda from trachyte, a volcanic rock.

**Great Hall of Mammals**
On the central podium is a selection of some key large mammals, along with the skeleton of Ahmed the elephant complete with extra-long tusks. There are also displays on the evolutionary history and characteristics of several animals.

**Key**

- 🔲 The Hall of Kenya
- 🔲 Great Hall of Mammals
- 🔲 Cradle of Humankind
- 🔲 History of Nairobi National Museum
- 🔲 Birds of East Africa
- ⬛ History of Kenya
- 🔲 Cycles of Life
- 🔲 Ecology Gallery
- 🔲 Asian African Heritage
- 🔲 Temporary Exhibitions
- 🔲 Non-exhibition space

First floor

★ **Cradle of Humankind**
This gallery showcases human evolution. The central display shows a reconstruction of early humans who lived millions of years ago, including *Homo erectus*.

**Statue of Louis Leakey**
The History of Nairobi National Museum gallery contains a larger-than-life bronze of Kenya's famous archaeologist who was the museum's honorary curator from 1941 to 1961 before he opened his Centre for Prehistory and Paleontology in the same grounds.

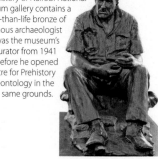

Ground floor

Snake Park

**Snake Park**
Started in 1959 to facilitate research on reptiles, the snake park was opened to the public in 1961. The park houses many snake species found in Kenya, including cobras, puff adders, mambas and large African rock pythons.

## ⑧ Uhuru Gardens

Langata Rd, just after the turn-off for Wilson Airport. 🚌 **Open** 8am–6pm daily. ♿

Located to the west of Uhuru Highway, the Uhuru Gardens are home to two monuments dedicated to Kenya's struggle for independence. Built in 1983 and marking 20 years of the country's independence, the soaring obelisk-like 24-m (79-ft) granite-and-marble **Uhuru Monument** is built on the site where the end of British rule was declared at midnight on 12 December 1963 and Jomo Kenyatta became Kenya's first president. At its base are a pair of clasped hands, a dove of peace and a statue depicting a group of freedom fighters raising the new Kenya flag.

Across the car park, a more abstract granite-and-black marble structure built in 1988 also commemorates Kenya's independence. The gardens themselves are bare and unremarkable but provide an open space for Nairobi residents to picnic at weekends. The large mugumo (fig) tree in the grounds is significant too because it was planted on the spot where the British Union Jack flag was lowered and Kenya's national flag was first hoisted on 12 December 1963.

Roasting meat on Maasai swords at Carnivore Restaurant

## ⑨ Carnivore Restaurant

Off Langata Rd, behind Uhuru Monument. **Tel** 020 6005933. 📞 **Open** noon–2:30pm daily, 7pm–10:30pm daily. ♿ 🅿 🅦 **tamarind.co.ke**

Acclaimed as one of the best restaurants in East Africa, Carnivore is most famous for serving a set menu of a variety of excellent roast meat. Its signature dish *nyama choma*, Kiswahili for barbecued meat, is roasted on traditional Maasai swords over a huge charcoal pit. A typical meal begins with soup, before waiters set down hot cast-iron plates, salads, sauces and relishes. Each table has a small white flag and as long as it is upright, the waiters carve sizzling slices of meat off

*Uhuru Monument in Uhuru Gardens*

the Maasai swords on to the plates. Leg of lamb and pork, rump and sirloin steak, spare ribs, sausages, chicken wings, and game meat such as ostrich and crocodile are all served. The meal is only over when diners lower the flag. Another Carnivore speciality is *dawa*, Kiswahili for medicine, and is made by stirring lime, sugar and vodka into crushed ice.

The adjacent **Simba Saloon** offers lighter meals, and from Wednesday to Sunday hosts a popular nightclub. In the car park to the left of Carnivore's main entrance, the upmarket gallery **African Heritage** sells quality crafts, textiles and traditional beaded jewellery.

## ⑩ Nairobi National Park

*See pp166–9.*

Sculpture of freedom fighters raising the Kenyan flag, Uhuru Monument, Uhuru Gardens

## ⓫ Bomas of Kenya

Forest Edge Rd, 10 km (6 miles) SW of Nairobi, off Langata Rd. **Tel** 020 8068400. 🚍 **Open** 2:30–4pm Mon–Fri, 3:30–5:15pm Sat–Sun and public holidays. 🔲 🔳 🔲 🔲
🔲 **bomasofkenya.co.ke**

Established in 1971 by the government specifically to preserve Kenya's fast diminishing traditional culture, the Bomas of Kenya showcases the country's major tribal groups. In 11 mock-up villages of *bomas* (homesteads), guides explain the traditional way of life, including craft-making, family structure and cooking and social living arrangements.

Among the highlights here are the colourful dance performances, acrobatics and storytelling, which are presented every afternoon. The massive circular amphitheatre has a central stage where Kenya's only resident dance company, the Harambee Dancers, perform a selection of the 30 or so Kenyan tribal dances in their repertoire. Many of the dances presented here are no longer commonly performed in Kenya. The centre offers a comprehensive introduction to traditional dancing styles, such as the mesmeric Kalenjin and Maasai warrior dances, with perhaps the most striking being the Samburu warriors leaping

Dancers in traditional regalia enacting a hunting scene, Bomas of Kenya

vertically into the air with twirling spears in a bid to win the hearts of their maidens.

## ⓬ David Sheldrick Wildlife Trust

Bogan Gate, Nairobi National Park, Magadi Rd. **Tel** 020 2301396. 🚗 access only by a private vehicle or on a guided tour. **Open** 11am–noon daily. 🔲 🔳 🔲 **sheldrick wildlifetrust.org**

A non-profit conservation trust established after the death of David Sheldrick in 1977, Daphne Sheldrick's unique elephant orphanage on the edge of Nairobi National Park (*see pp166–9*) provides an important refuge for lost,

orphaned or abandoned baby elephants. The trust's patient and attentive keepers, who are experts on hand-rearing baby elephants and duplicate a natural mother's role of nurturing, teach the orphans how to suckle and bathe and use their trunks and ears.

Every morning visitors can watch the baby elephants at play, while a keeper tells the story of each individual and explains the process of bringing up the babies until they are self-sufficient and old enough to be rereleased into the wild in Tsavo National Park, as the closer Nairobi National Park is too small to sustain them. It is an endearing sight to watch the young elephants trot after their keepers, chasing each other, splashing in the waterhole and being fed from giant milk bottles. On occasion, the trust also cares for orphaned rhino.

Daphne with one of the elephants

### The Sheldricks

David Sheldrick was the founder warden of Tsavo National Park, when it was established in 1948. He remained the park's warden for 28 years and developed its infrastructure of over 2,000 km (1,250 miles) of roads for game viewing, dams, causeways, boreholes and windmills to provide water for the animals. He also embarked on a long and pioneering study on the behaviour of elephants and was the first person to hand-rear these animals. Since his death in 1977, his wife Daphne has continued to raise and rerelease animals into the wild. She was the first person to perfect the milk formula for elephants dependant on infant milk – essential for their survival, as a calf under 2 years old can die within 24 hours without milk. The trust has released over 70 elephants into Tsavo National Park, while Daphne continues to promote wildlife conservation worldwide through books, articles, lectures and television appearances.

Baby elephant wallowing in mud, David Sheldrick Wildlife Trust

# ⑩ Nairobi National Park

Established in 1946, the 117-sq-km (45-sq-mile) Nairobi National Park lies within sight of Nairobi's suburbs, and animals can sometimes be seen stalking through the grass against a backdrop of city skyscrapers. Characterized by open grassy plains studded with acacia, Kenya's first national park is home to over 80 game and 400 bird species. Larger animals include buffalo, the big cats and antelope. On the southern boundary is the Athi river, home to hippo and crocodile. The park is best known for its large population of black rhino who were moved here from remote parts of the country to protect them from poaching. The notable exception is elephant as the park is too small to sustain them, but baby elephants can be seen at the David Sheldrick Wildlife Trust on the edge of the park.

**Kenya Wildlife Service HQ**
Located at the park entrance, the headquarters offers information on Kenya's national parks and loads the Safari Cards that provide access to parks and reserves.

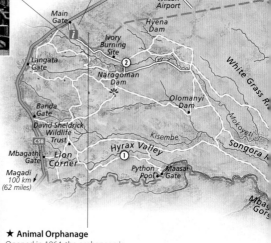

0 km    2
0 miles    2

Nairobi
5 km
(3 miles)

Wilson Airport

Main Gate

Hyena Dam

Ivory Burning Site

Langata Gate

② Narogoman Dam

Olomanyi Dam

White Grass R...

Banda Gate

David Sheldrick Wildlife Trust

C58

Kisembe

Mokoyeti

Songora R...

Mbagathi Gate

Lion Corner

Hyrax Valley ①

Magadi
100 km ⚡
(62 miles)

Python Pool

Maasai Gate

Mba...
Gor...

★ **Safari Walk**
A boardwalk takes visitors through a patch of indigenous forest with around 150 species of local trees, home to white rhino, giraffe and unusual animals such as the albino zebra and bongo antelope.

★ **Animal Orphanage**
Opened in 1964, the orphanage is a refuge for injured animals from all over Kenya. The animals are either released back into the wild or transferred to the Safari Walk.

## KEY

① **Hyrax Valley**, an area of open plains, is good for spotting grassland game such as giraffe, impala and buffalo.

② **Narogoman Dam**, an artificial dam and the largest in the park, has a rich variety of birdlife.

③ **Kitengela Corridor**

**Black Rhinos**
Nairobi National Park is one of Kenya's most successful rhino sanctuaries in terms of breeding. Rhinos are relocated from here to former habitats where they once occurred naturally.

**Athi Plains and Kitengela Corridor**
This region is where wildebeest and zebra follow the annual migration in and out of the park to the dispersal area on the southern boundary in March and July, and again in November and January.

## Getting Around

There is a well-maintained network of dirt roads and adequate signage to picnic sites and waterholes. Visitors with private transport should allow half a day to explore the park. Alternatively, Nairobi's tour operators offer half-day guided excursions into the park. No walking is allowed except at the nature trail at the Hippo Pool. The Safari Walk and Animal Orphanage are at the main entrance of the park and can be visited separately.

### VISITORS' CHECKLIST

**Practical Information**
**Road Map** C5. 5 km (3 miles) SW of Nairobi on Langata Rd.
020 6000800 (Kenya Wildlife Service HQ). **Open** 6am–6pm daily. Safari Card. local tour operators offer half-day tours. kws.org
Safari Walk: **Open** 8am–6pm daily. Animal Orphanage: **Open** 8am–6pm daily; feeding time 2.30pm daily.

**Transport**

### Key

— Major road

— Minor road

::: Unpaved motorable road

— Railway

—•– Park boundary

Jomo Kenyatta International Airport
5 km (3 miles)

*Embakasi Plain*

*Middle Ridge*

*Sosian*

③

*Athi Plains*

A104

*Leopard Cliff*

*Athi*

*Hippo Pool*

*Athi Basin Dam*

*Boma Valley*

*Athi*

Mombasa
450 km (280 miles)

Namanga
135 km (84 miles)

★ **Athi River Track**
Located in the south of the park, the track leads past some good distractions such as picnic sites, viewpoints over escarpments and cliffs, artificial dams and a walking trail at the Hippo Pool.

**Baboon Escarpment**
An impressive viewpoint on the southern border of the park, Baboon Escarpment looks down over dense vegetation and cliffs. It is home to the comical rodent-like rock hyrax and, of course, the ever-inquisitive baboon.

For keys to symbols *see back flap*

# Exploring Nairobi National Park

The open grassy plains of the national park, dotted with acacia trees and man-made dams, offer rewarding game viewing only a 15-minute drive from Nairobi's city centre. There is an extensive network of gravel roads, and apart from a few steep ones in the hilly south, most are navigable in an ordinary car. A map can be bought at the Main Gate with detailed numbered points that match road junctions in the park. Staff at this gate provide information on where to locate the park's wildlife, especially lion and cheetah, which are monitored closely. It takes 3–4 hours for visitors to see most of the park, its picnic sites and the nature trail at the Hippo Pool on the Athi river.

Rhino sculpture at the entrance to Nairobi National Park

## Main Gate

Off Langata Rd. **Open** 6am–6pm daily.
🚻 ♿ 🅿 📷

While there are several gates into the park, Main Gate, located just beyond Wilson Airport, is the most suitable point of access. The headquarters of Kenya Wildlife Service (KWS) and the office of the Safety and Communication Centre *(see p406)* are both located in a cluster of buildings here. Visitors will also find a park information centre in this complex, along with such facilities as a car park, cafés, the Ranger's restaurant and a shop that sells gifts and maps of the park. Two of the park's most popular attractions, the Safari Walk and the Animal Orphanage, are situated near Main Gate. To the left of the gate is the office where travellers pay for and top up their Safari Card *(see p73)*.

The **Conservation Heroes Monument** in the car park lists all the names of KWS employees who have lost their lives working for KWS since it was formed in 1990. Some died in accidents when relocating animals and others in armed battles with poachers. Poaching was at its critical high in 1990, and since then, all KWS employees have been armed.

## 🦓 Safari Walk

Main Gate. **Tel** 020 6000800.
**Open** 8am–6pm daily. 🚻 ♿ ♿
🅦 kws.org

Opened in 2006 and funded by the European Union, this is a fantastic walk through 40 acres (16 ha) of forest that is home to some 150 indigenous species of flora, which in turn attract plenty of birds. The walk starts on a paved path and rises into the forest on a wheelchair-friendly boardwalk that eventually winds its way to overlook a waterhole. Visitors can hire a guide at the gate, or make their own way around by reading the notice boards that not only describe the animals but also provide information about human-animal conflict in the wild.

Animals inhabit spacious grassy mounds that are separated by moats and single electric fencing. Despite this, the atmosphere is anything but zoo-like. Residents include the big cats, buffalo, monkey, pygmy hippo, rhino, plains zebra, hyena, ostrich, unusual albino zebras and the rare bongo antelope. Lions can be seen behind a glass barrier at grass level in a sunken hide, while leopards can be viewed from above, at tree level. At the cheetah enclosure, visitors are permitted to enter and pat the cat and take photographs. At the beginning of the walk is a time capsule earmarked to be opened in 2050. Inside are messages from local people about what improvements they would like to see for the welfare of wildlife in Kenya.

## 🐾 Animal Orphanage

Main Gate. **Tel** 020 6000800.
**Open** 8am–6pm daily; feeding time 2:30pm daily. 🚻 📷 ♿
🅦 kws.org

With spacious enclosures, the Animal Orphanage provides a refuge for sick and orphaned animals. Some of these animals are brought here from the country's various national parks for cure and care, while others, such as baby cheetahs that were captured to become pets, have been rescued from poachers by KWS staff. Whenever possible, animals are reintroduced into the wild. When this is not possible, the orphanage becomes their home for the rest of their lives. Informative boards narrate the story of each individual animal,

Viewing platform above the leopard pen at the Safari Walk

The Athi river wending its way through the spectacular gorge between Leopard Cliffs, Nairobi National Park

and when there are cubs resident, visitors are permitted into the enclosures for a close-up photograph. Although the orphanage was established in 1964, the enclosures are regularly added to and improved upon, including the one for a leopard that has been built around a tree.

The distinctly bovine eland, Africa's largest antelope, on the Athi Plains

### Athi Plains

While the western, northern and eastern sides of Nairobi National Park are fenced to keep wildlife out of Nairobi's residential areas and off the Nairobi–Mombasa Highway, the southern boundary is unfenced and provides access to the Athi Plains. Owned by group ranches and private land owners, this dispersal area covers approximately 1,000 sq km (385 sq miles) and is an essential component of the park's ecosystem, particularly because it serves as a natural open corridor for migrating wildlife. Many herbivores migrate to the Athi Plains during the rainy season that starts in November. They move back to the park's permanent waterholes during

the dry season from July to August. Large populations of giraffe, zebra, wildebeest, eland and Thomson's gazelle can be seen grazing across the seemingly endless plains. A number of birds, including the strutting secretary bird, crested crane and ostrich, are also plentiful during this time.

### Athi River and Hippo Pool

One of the most magnificent areas of the park is along its southwestern boundary, which has steep valleys created by streams joining the Athi river. The Athi enters the park in the southeastern corner, and forms a natural boundary along the

park's southern edge. Hyraxes are plentiful on the rocks and the sure-sighted may even spot a klipspringer or mountain reedbuck. The Athi's park side is favoured by zebra. A stretch on the river's southern boundary known as the Hippo Pool is a popular picnic spot. There is a ranger post here, allowing people to leave their vehicles. An armed warden will accompany visitors on the short, shady walk through a riverine forest well populated with vervet monkey. Pigeons, barbets and starlings feed on the fig trees here, while the acacia trees are a favourite roost for white-backed and Ruppell's griffon vultures.

### Ivory Burning Site

On 18 July 1989, 12 tonnes (13 tons) of confiscated ivory, thought to be worth 60 million KSh, were burnt on a site just inside Nairobi National Park in an attempt to stop the mass slaughter of African elephants by poachers. The fire was lit by President Moi and the event was televised across the world in a plea to end the trade in ivory. It subsequently contributed to the worldwide ban on ivory trading imposed by the Convention on International Trade in Endangered Species of Wild Fauna and Flora (CITES). At independence, there were an estimated 170,000 elephants in Kenya, but by 1989, they numbered only 16,000 and some 1,000 elephants a month were being killed by poachers. In 1990, KWS declared war on the poachers and imposed a shoot-to-kill policy. Elephant numbers improved dramatically and the population today is put at around 38,000.

Memorial built at the ivory burning site

Nairobi in late afternoon sunlight with Uhuru Park in the foreground ▶

## ⑬ Nairobi Mamba Village

North Langata Rd, Karen. **Tel** 0771 297472. 🚌 to Karen. **Open** 9am–5:30pm daily; feeding time 4:30pm Sun. 🐊 🍴 ♿ 🚻 📷 📷
🌐 **nairobimamba.com**

A popular family getaway, Nairobi Mamba Village is laid out around a man-made lake with manicured gardens that are dotted with interesting sculptures and picnic sites. The restaurant here offers a lunchtime buffet on the lawn and transforms into a disco at night. Visitors interested in semiprecious stones will find it worthwhile to stop in at the **Mamba Art Gallery**.

In keeping with its name – *mamba* meaning crocodile in Kiswahili – the resort is home to around 60 Nile crocodile. While motionless for most of the day, these reptiles come alive at feeding time when attendants toss meat chunks into their eager jaws. A footpath leads to the other side of the lake where a spacious pen houses some ostriches that can be handfed. The lake also attracts several waterfowl species. Boats and fishing rods are available for hire here.

## ⑭ AFEW Giraffe Centre

Koitobus Rd, Karen. **Tel** 020 8070804. 🚌 to Karen. **Open** 9am–5:30pm daily. 🐊 🍴 📷 📷 🌐 **giraffecenter.org**

Established in 1983 to protect Rothschild's giraffe, the African Fund for Endangered Wildlife (AFEW) Giraffe Centre is one of Nairobi's most popular

Rothschild's giraffes at the viewing platform, AFEW Giraffe Centre

The colonial Karen Blixen Museum amid its beautifully maintained gardens

excursions. At the time it was set up, there were only 130 Rothschild's giraffe left in the wild in Western Kenya and their habitat was constantly shrinking due to heavy cultivation. Funds were raised to move three of the wild herds to Lake Nakuru National Park *(see pp280–83)*, Mwea National Reserve *(see p333)* and Ruma National Park *(see p309)*, while a dozen or so animals were established at the AFEW Giraffe Centre.

A particular favourite with children is the circular viewing platform built on stilts, which allows them to feed pellets to the giraffe at eyeball height. The platform also has a lovely view of the nearby **Giraffe Manor** *(see p364)*, a luxury hotel which has giraffe stalking across its lawns. Guides are available to walk visitors through the centre. Across the road from the main entrance is a small patch of forest with a nature trail.

Old tractor, Karen Blixen Museum

## ⑮ Karen Blixen Museum

Karen Rd, Karen. **Tel** 020 8002139. 🚌 to Karen. **Open** 9:30am–6pm daily. 🐊 🍴 ♿ 📷 📷
🌐 **museums.or.ke**

Danish-born Karen Blixen is best known for her book *Out of Africa*, which she wrote under the pseudonym Isak Dinesen *(see p40)*. This autobiographical work recounts her days on a coffee farm in Kenya where she lived from 1914 to 1932. Located in Nairobi's suburb of Karen, her farmhouse with its wide verandas and red-tiled roof has been converted into a museum. It features original furnishings and props from the movie *Out of Africa (see p41)* as well as photographs relating to Blixen's life. Guides are on hand to take visitors around the clutch of rooms, which give an insight into the privileged lives of Kenya's white settlers. Outside, there are a few antique farming implements on display. The house is surrounded by a tranquil garden that provides splendid views of Blixen's beloved Ngong Hills. The museum shop sells handicrafts, postcards, books, including *Out of Africa*, as well as souvenirs. The **Karen Blixen Coffee Garden** restaurant *(see p376)* is further along Karen Road adjacent to another former settler's house.

Serene grasslands carpeting gently undulating slopes, Ngong Hills

## ⓰ Ngong Forest Sanctuary

Kibera Rd, off Ngong Rd, 6 km (4 miles) SW of Nairobi. **Tel** 020 2113358. Open 8am–6pm daily. ngongforest.org

The 5-sq-km (2-sq-mile) Ngong Forest Sanctuary serves as an important green lung for Nairobi. A lush tract of indigenous forest covered by a network of paths, streams and dams, the reserve is home to several butterfly species and some small, shy mammals such as duikers. Some 120 species of birds have been identified here, including a variety of shrikes, cuckoos and waxbills.

Lush and dense vegetation, Ngong Forest Sanctuary

## ⓱ Ngong Hills

**Road Map** C5. Ngong village, 8 km (5 miles) from Ngong Rd and Langata Rd Junction. to Ngong. Open sunrise–sunset.

Located on the southwestern edge of Nairobi, the hills take their name from the Maasai word *ngong* (knuckles), which refers to the hills' four-peaked ridge. From Nairobi they seem to be of an unassuming height, but on the western side they drop to the Rift Valley floor some 1,200 m (3,950 ft) below, which is scattered with small Maasai settlements. The rolling grassy slopes are good for walks, but security can be an issue, so always hike in a group. A trail runs along the top of the hills and on a clear day Mount Longonot can be seen in the north, while Kilimanjaro may be spotted on the southern horizon. The eastern slopes overlooking Nairobi National Park hold the grave of Denys Finch Hatton – believed to be the lover of Karen Blixen – which is marked by an obelisk and a small garden.

## ⓲ Karura Forest

**Road Map** C5. Main entrance off Limuru Road, Muthaiga. to Belgian Embassy on Limuru Rd. **Tel** 0722 891654. Open 6am–6pm. friendsofkarura.org

Covering just over 10 sq km (4 sq miles), Karura Forest is the largest of the gazetted forests within Nairobi's city limits. It straddles the suburbs of Muthaiga and Gigiri and is adjacent to the United Nations offices. It was saved from destruction in the late 1990s by the actions of the late conservationist and Nobel Prize winner, Professor Wangari Maathai, when it was earmarked for housing and other development. It features a waterfall, tracts of bamboo stands and marshland, some intriguing Mau Mau caves, and is dissected by four tributaries of the Nairobi River. Visitors can explore on 50 km (31 miles) of nature trails, and it is popular with mountain bikers, joggers and dog-walkers. More than 200 species of birds have been recorded – a bird list can be picked up at the entrance – and include the African crowned eagle, crested crane, silvery-cheeked hornbill, Hartlaub's turaco, and numerous doves, owls and weavers.

### Karen Blixen

"I had a farm in Africa at the foot of the Ngong Hills", is Karen Blixen's immortal opening line to her famous autobiography *Out of Africa*. Born in Denmark in 1885, she went to the British colony of Kenya in 1914 with her husband Baron Bror von Blixen-Finecke to farm coffee. However, the couple divorced in 1925 and Karen was left to

Karen Blixen at her farm in Kenya

run the financially troubled farm on her own. She began a long affair with English aristocrat and safari hunter Denys Finch Hatton. In 1931, Hatton died when his Gypsy Moth crashed in Tsavo. A distraught Blixen returned to Denmark where her writing career began in earnest – *Out of Africa* was published in 1937. Beautifully written with evocative descriptions of the people, animals and landscape, *Out of Africa* is not so much a story of Blixen's life in Kenya as it is of her love of Africa. Much of the eponymous and much-acclaimed 1985 movie was filmed at her former home. She remained in Demark until her death in 1962.

## ⓳ Athi River

**Road Map** C5. 25 km (16 miles) SE of Nairobi on the A109. ⛰ 140,000. 🚌 Maasai Ostrich Resort: Namanga Road from Athi River, turn off 10 km (6 miles) from Kitengela. **Tel** 050 2502128. 📱 **Open** 7am–6pm daily. 🍴 📷 🛍 🏨 🛏 🌐 **maasaiostrich.com**

The town of Athi River is a sprawling urban centre to the southeast of Nairobi on the Nairobi–Mombasa Highway. The town gets its name from the Athi river, which flows through it after crossing the Athi Plains to the south of Nairobi National Park *(see pp166–9)*. Beyond the town the river is met by the Nairobi river and goes northeast to Thika, where it forms the Fourteen Falls *(see p318)*. The river turns southeast from this point and flows through the Tsavo East National Park *(see pp186–9)* as the Galana river.

The notable attraction in the area is **Maasai Ostrich Resort**, which is set in 200 acres (81 ha) of rolling grassland on the Athi Plains. Visitors to the farm will see both juvenile and adult ostriches, and ostrich rides are offered. A shop here sells painted eggshells and ostrich leather products, such as handbags and wallets. Popular for weekend day trips from Nairobi, the farm also has a garden restaurant that serves *nyama choma*, which includes grilled ostrich meat. Its resort has 45 spacious cottages with facilities such as a swimming pool, sauna and tennis court.

The terraced slopes and verdant countryside around Machakos

## ⓴ Machakos

**Road Map** C5. 70 km (43 miles) SE of Nairobi. ⛰ 150,000. 🚌

Ringed by the pleasant, green Ukambani Hills, Machakos is a simple country town to the south of Nairobi. This region is home to the Akamba people who, long before the arrival of the Europeans, were great traders, organizing caravans to take ivory to Arab merchants in Mombasa in exchange for copper, bracelets, beads, rolls of cloth and salt. These goods were brought back to Akamba trading posts in the interior. Today the Akamba are well known as talented woodcarvers and many of the wooden figurines, animals and masks that are seen in the tourist shops and markets in Nairobi and on the coast have come from this region.

The original name of the town was Masaku, after a local chief, but the British found it difficult to pronounce and it ended up as Machakos. It was Britain's first upcountry administrative centre and it remained so for a decade, until the administration moved to Nairobi in 1899.

Today, subsistence farming sustains the region, and terraced fields cover every hill. Its tree-lined streets give Machakos a rustic charm. The only structure of note here is the square, concrete clock tower at the town centre erected in honour of a visit by Princess Margaret in 1956. Worth a look is the vibrant open-air market, where local farmers come to sell fruit and vegetables grown in the fertile climate.

## ㉑ Olorgasailie Prehistoric Site

**Road Map** B5. 64 km (40 miles) S of Nairobi. **Tel** 020 8164134. 🚌 **Open** 8am–6pm daily. 🍴 📷 🛏 🏕 🌐 **museums.or.ke**

Archaeologists first began exploring the Stone Age Olorgasailie Prehistoric Site on Magadi Road in 1919. It was further excavated by Mary and Louis Leakey *(see p353)* in the 1940s, and there are still digs here today. Located within the basin of an ancient lake that drained perhaps over one million years ago due to tectonic activity, the site is rich in fossils thanks

Skull from Olorgasailie

Visitors inspect the hominid dig site from the boardwalk at Olorgasailie

to heavy falls of alkaline ash from surrounding volcanoes, including Mount Suswa and Mount Longonot. It is thought that the lake attracted a number of animals, which were followed by early hunters, who fashioned the stone tools discovered at the archaeological sites.

Olorgasailie also has a museum with a wooden boardwalk over the fossils and displays of the finds. These include numerous hand axes and cleavers made by *Homo erectus* around half-a-million years ago, as well as fossils of elephants, hippos and baboons. Excursions to the actual sites can be arranged at the museum. Basic accommodation is available in *bandas* (huts). Camping is also an option, but it can get intolerably hot here.

## ㉒ Lake Magadi

**Road Map** B5. End of the C58, 110 km (68 miles) S of Nairobi.

Nestled in a low-lying basin on the floor of the Rift Valley near the border with Tanzania and covering 104 sq km (40 sq miles), Lake Magadi is located in one of the hottest and driest places in Kenya. From a distance, it shimmers in the heat haze and is surrounded by sparse, open bushland where Maasai may be seen herding their livestock. Several hot springs, mostly to the south of the lake, feed it with a constant supply of alkaline soda – *magadi* being the Maasai word for soda – which in turn attracts a number of wading birds including storks and flamingoes. After the rainy season, the pinkish lake fills with dense sodium carbonate brine, but this evaporates quickly in the sun, leaving behind a vast expanse of white salt that can be 15–30 m (50–100 ft) deep in places.

Located on the eastern shore of the lake is a factory that produces soda ash from the salt. It is, in fact, the second-largest producer of soda in the world, and the small settlement

Alkaline Lake Magadi, with the extinct Shompole volcano rising behind it

of Magadi has grown around it. A causeway over the lake leads to the Nguruman Escarpment area to the west, but people crossing over it need to wear sunglasses as the reflections off the soda surface can be blinding.

## ㉓ Nguruman Escarpment

**Road Map** B5. 140 km (87 miles) S of Nairobi. 4WD.

Beyond Lake Magadi, the 2,300-m (7,550-ft) high Nguruman Escarpment rises dramatically above the floor of the Rift Valley and forms its western wall. From the escarpment, stupendous views can be had back over the lake and over the Ewaso Nyiro River Valley, which becomes the Engare Ngiro Swamp before it reaches Lake Natron in Tanzania. Wild and remote, the area has no roads, but tracks are negotiable by 4WD. This is good trekking country and a number of tour operators *(see p397)* can organize treks with Maasai guides. The Ewaso Nyiro river, shaded by wild fig trees, is an especially scenic place to walk and paddle in.

Yellow-billed stork at Lake Magadi

On nearing the escarpment's foothills from Lake Magadi's valley, the vegetation changes dramatically, from open arid bushland to flourishing groves of mango and pawpaw trees. These attract numerous birds such as African pied wagtails, as well as vervet and black-and-white colobus monkeys. The escarpment is topped by the **Loita Hills**, which level out to the Masai Mara National Reserve *(see pp266–9)* to the east across the Loita Plains, a favourite habitat for large herds of wildebeest and buffalo.

The cascading Olasurr Falls, in the remote Loita Hills

# NAIROBI STREET FINDER

Map references given in this guide for entertainment venues, shopping areas and other attractions in Nairobi refer to the Street Finder map on the following pages. Map references are also provided for leading Nairobi hotels *(see p364)* and restaurants *(see pp376–7)*. The first figure in the map reference indicates which Street Finder map to turn to and the letter and the number

which follow refer to the grid reference on the map. The map below shows central Nairobi and around, as well as the main highways to the suburbs. Symbols used for sights and other useful information are displayed in the key. The index on the opposite page lists most of the important streets and avenues located in central Nairobi.

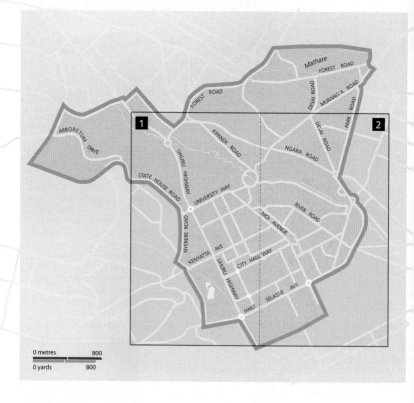

**Key**

Major sight

Place of interest

Other building

🚉 Railway station

🚌 Bus station

ℹ️ Visitor information

🚓 Police station

✡️ Synagogue

🕌 Mosque

⛪ Church

🛕 Gurdwara

**Scale of Maps 1–2**

View of Nairobi from Kenyatta International Conference Centre

alone after the shops have closed or on Sundays. After nightfall, hire a taxi and steer clear of deserted areas.

Areas to avoid are isolated spots near Uhuru Highway and Uhuru Park and the streets near River Road to the east of Moi Avenue, which are frequented by petty thieves jostling the passengers off the *matatus* and buses. Koinange Street is perfectly fine for walks in the daytime, but transforms into Nairobi's red-light district late at night.

When withdrawing cash from an ATM, use ones inside banks, shopping malls or petrol stations rather than on the street.

Carjacking and traffic light robberies can occur, so exercise caution if driving at night. Traffic can be congested, but roads are well signposted and traffic police are generally present.

## Streetwise in Nairobi

Nairobi's city centre is a neat grid arranged in square blocks of streets and buildings. Close-circuit television cameras on street corners, a visible police presence and private security guards at business premises mean that security is fairly good. As with any large city, street crime does occasionally occur, but can be avoided if common sense precautions are taken.

Visitors need to be vigilant in crowded areas. Do not carry valuables and avoid walking

# Street Finder Index

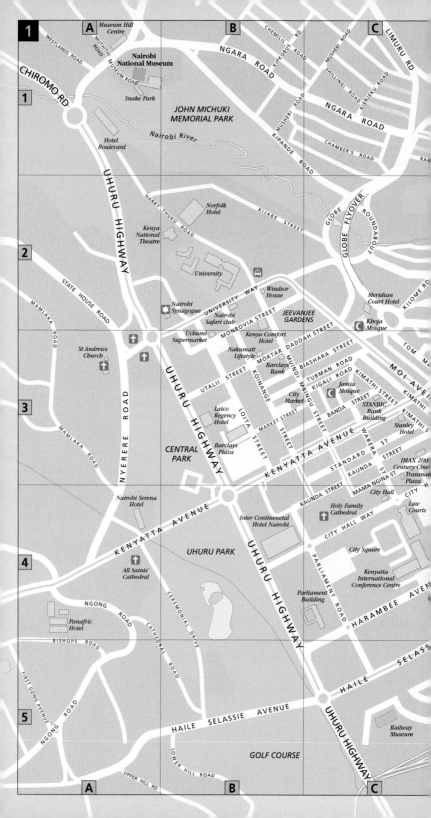

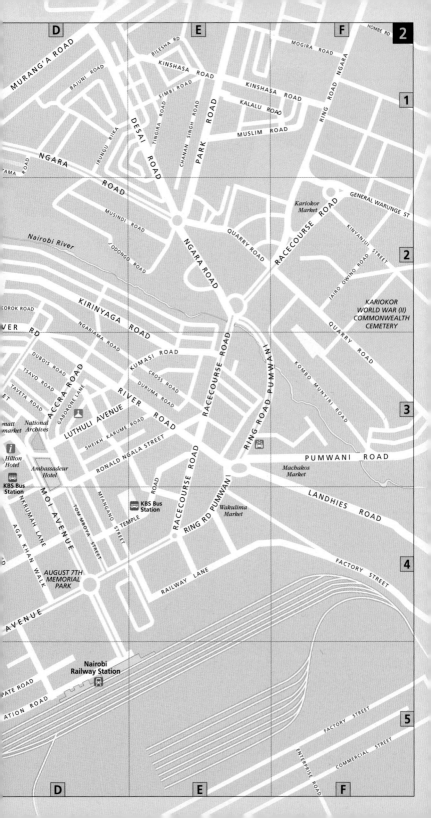

# SOUTHEASTERN SAVANNAHS

Studded with rocky outcrops, flat-topped acacias and spectral baobabs, the semiarid plains that slope eastwards from Nairobi support exceptional concentrations of wildlife. There are jewel-like crater lakes and broken lava flows so fresh that they remain bare of vegetation, while towering above it all, the majestic snowcapped outline of volcanic Kilimanjaro dominates the southern skyline.

Owing to the region's inherent aridity, settlements are few and far between, and tend to be somewhat insubstantial. With the exception of the fertile Taita Hills, the area is poorly suited to cultivation, although hardy sisal plantations cover large tracts of land bordering Tsavo. Most of the Southeastern Savannahs is given over to low-density pastoralism or is protected in national parks and private reserves.

Nevertheless, the region supports a rich mosaic of rural cultures. Oloitokitok and Namanga are important bases for the pastoralist Maasai. The Akamba, famed for their honey and wood carvings, inhabit the area between Tsavo and Nairobi, while industrious Taita farmers cultivate terraced smallholdings near Wundanyi.

Much of the area is hot and dry, but the open plains are interspersed with some striking manifestations of geologically recent volcanic activity. For added drama,

there is Kilimanjaro, the world's tallest freestanding mountain. The great mountain is an important watershed, feeding most of the surface and underground streams and rivers that run through the region's main reserves to join the mighty Galana river.

Wildlife is the key attraction for visitors to this vast wilderness. All of the Big Five are well represented, along with other safari favourites such as zebra, giraffe and the larger antelopes. The contiguous Tsavo East and West National Parks collectively form the country's largest protected area, and are flanked by several smaller private reserves. Further west, Amboseli, Kenya's busiest national park, is famed for its giant tuskers. The plains, bisected inland of Mombasa by one of East Africa's most celebrated colonial legacies, the Lunatic Line railway, were also the site of pivotal battles between British and German troops during World War I.

Giraffes on the vast plains of Amboseli with the mighty Kilimanjaro in the backdrop

◄ African elephant (*Loxodonta Africana*) feeding in swamps, Amboseli National Park

# Exploring the Southeastern Savannahs

The region's major reserves, Tsavo and Amboseli, are best visited on an organized safari. Tsavo East, thanks to its proximity to Malindi, is a popular destination for those who want to punctuate their beach holiday with a day or overnight safari. Sites that are more accessible to independent travellers include the lovely Lake Chala, embedded in an extinct caldera outside Taveta, and the lush and little-explored Taita Hills, while the starker Chyulu Hills National Park offers some excellent but relatively demanding hiking in an area rich with game. Located at the base of Taita Hills, Taita Hills Wildlife Sanctuary offers close-up sightings of elephant and buffalo.

**Key**

░ Area illustrated

Elephants drinking at Salt Lick Game Lodge, Taita Hills Wildlife Sanctuary

*For hotels and restaurants see pp365–6 and p378*

## Key

— Major road

=== Minor road

== Untarred major road

== Untarred minor road

-- 4WD track

⌒ Major railway

— Minor railway

▬ International border

△ Peak

Safari 4WD on a red dirt road in Tsavo West National Park

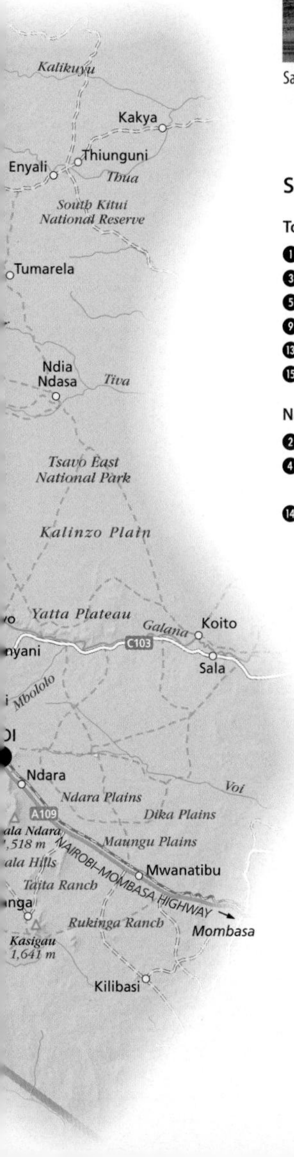

## Sights at a Glance

### Towns

❶ Makindu

❸ Mtito Andei

❺ Voi

❾ Taveta

⓭ Oloitokitok

⓯ Namanga

### National Parks

❷ Chyulu Hills National Park

❹ *Tsavo East and West National Parks pp186–91*

⓮ *Amboseli National Park pp198–201*

### Wildlife Sanctuaries

❼ Taita Hills Wildlife Sanctuary

❽ Lumo Community Wildlife Sanctuary

### Areas of Natural Beauty

❻ Taita Hills

⓫ Lake Jipe

⓬ Lake Chala

### Historical Buildings

❿ Grogan's Castle

0 km      25

0 miles      25

*Map labels:*

Kalikuyu

Kakya

Enyali   Thiunguni

Tbua

South Kitui National Reserve

Tumarela

Ndia Ndasa   Tiva

Tsavo East National Park

Kalinzo Plain

Yatta Plateau   Galana   Koito

nyani   Sala

Mbololo

Ndara

Ndara Plains

Dika Plains

ala Ndara ,518 m

Maungu Plains

ala Hills

Taita Ranch

Mwanatibu

NAIROBI-MOMBASA HIGHWAY

nga

Rukinga Ranch   Mombasa

Kasigau 1,641 m

Kilibasi

## Getting Around

The overwhelming majority of people who visit the Southeastern Savannahs do so on an organized road or fly-in safari, taking in one or more of the major national parks and private reserves in various combinations. The most important main road in the region connects the country's two largest towns, Nairobi and Mombasa, and is flanked by Tsavo East and West National Parks. This highway consists of just one lane in either direction for most of its length of 490 km (304 miles). There are frequent public buses between the two cities, and the passenger trains that run three times a week along the parallel railway line are another, albeit slower, option. Adequate surfaced or dirt roads connect the Nairobi–Mombasa Highway to Taveta, Wundanyi and Namanga, but other roads in the region tend to be rough, frequently potholed and therefore slow going.

**For keys to symbols** *see back flap*

Façade of the Sikh temple at Makindu

# ❶ Makindu

**Road Map** C6. 165 km (103 miles) SE of Nairobi. 🚗 2,500. 🏠 🚌
w sikhyouthmakindu.com

Located on the Nairobi–Mombasa Highway, the small town of Makindu was founded during the construction of the Lunatic Line *(see p303)* to Uganda. On a clear day, there are views of Mount Kilimanjaro across the border in Tanzania, to the southeast. If travelling from Nairobi to Mombasa, Makindu is the first place that has distinctive baobab trees that can be seen from the road.

It is home to the most revered and possibly the oldest Sikh temple in the East African interior. Set in peaceful flowering gardens on the north side of the highway, the main temple building dates to 1926, but its tin-roofed predecessor, built by Sikh railway workers in 1902, still stands alongside it. A huge entrance gate is visible from the main road with a 50-m- (164-ft-) high *Nishan Sahib* (Sikh flag). Makindu is an important pilgrimage site for Nairobi-based followers of Guru Nanak Dev, the founder of Sikhism. However, visitors of all religious affiliations are accorded a warm welcome. A 24-hour facility offers accommodation and food to travellers for a donation.

# ❷ Chyulu Hills National Park

**Road Map** C6. 22 km (14 miles) S of Makindu via Kibwezi. **Tel** 020 2153433. 🚕 4WD. **Open** 6am–7pm daily. 🅿 🛖 w kws.org

Extending over 741 sq km (286 sq miles), this finger-shaped park was gazetted in 1983 to protect the Chyulu Hills, a vital catchment area that runs around 80 km (50 miles) north-west of a shared boundary with Tsavo West National Park *(see pp190–91)*. One of the world's youngest mountain ranges, Chyulu formed as recently as 500 years ago, and its jagged black rocks and ashen lava flows pay testament to the violence of its volcanic origin. The park supports a selection of wildlife that is similar to neighbouring Tsavo West's, and includes populations of elephant, buffalo, giraffe, zebra and eland. However, their natural densities are relatively low and the animals tend to be shy. The old lava flows are sparsely vegetated, but a spine of forested land along the upper slopes harbours 37 species of flowering orchid.

The **Kisula Caves** lie 15 km (9 miles) from the entrance gate, along a rough track that can be explored in a 4WD. Also of interest is the 13-km- (8-mile-) long **Leviathan Cave**, the world's largest known lava tube when it was discovered in 1975, although it has since been relegated to second place by Hawaii's Kazumura Cave. A limited infrastructure makes this national park most suitable for adventurous hikers, who can explore the untrammelled slopes in the company of an armed ranger.

Volcanic hills rising dramatically beyond Chyulu Hills National Park

## ❸ Mtito Andei

**Road Map** D6. 75 km (47 miles) SE of Makindu. 🏠 4,700. 🚉 🚌

Flanking the main highway, halfway between Mombasa and Nairobi, Mtito Andei (Forest of Vultures) is an important truck stop and is well equipped with filling stations, shops and eateries. It is also of interest as it is the location of the first park gates if coming from the Nairobi direction to both Tsavo West and Tsavo East National Parks.

## ❹ Tsavo East and West National Parks

*See pp186–91.*

Rows of sisal at a plantation, a familiar sight around Voi

## ❺ Voi

**Road Map** D6. 80 km (50 miles) SE of Mtito Andei. 🏠 20,000. 🚉 🚌

By far the largest town on the Nairobi–Mombasa Highway, Voi is named after its reputed founder, Kivoi, a 17th-century chief of the Akamba tribe. The town emerged as an important centre of local commerce and sisal agriculture after the railway was built linking it to Mombasa in 1898. Voi also stands at the junction of the main road to the Taita Hills and the border town of Taveta. However, few visitors stop here unless they are en route to Tsavo East National Park (*see pp188–9*) and the Voi Gate, which lies just 7 km (4 miles) from the town centre. Good lodges can be found near the park's entrance, while the town is well-equipped with filling stations, shops, restaurants and ATMs.

The verdant slopes and scrubland of the Taita Hills

## ❻ Taita Hills

**Road Map** D6. 50 km (31 miles) W of Voi. 🚗 4WD.

Not to be confused with the eponymous wildlife sanctuary that lies in its shadow, Taita Hills is the most northerly of the Eastern Arc Mountains, a series of Precambrian massifs rich in endemic life. Home to the local Taita people, the hills' fertile slopes are covered in lush tropical cultivation and montane forests. The highest point in the range is the 2,208-m (7,244-ft) **Vuria**, recognizable from afar by its numerous satellite towers and aerials.

The main attraction of Taita for bird-watchers is the lovely Taita thrush (*Turdus helleri*), a montane forest endemic, whose total population is estimated at 1,350 individuals. The thrush's range is now confined to three forest patches, of which the most accessible is **Ngangao**, 13 km (8 miles) from Wundanyi via **Maghambinyi**. Also endemic to Taita are the Taita apalis (*Apalis fascigularis*) and Taita violet (*Saintpaulia teitensis*).

Near the gateway town of Wundanyi is a site called **Ngomenyi** (Cave of Skulls), just 2 km (1 mile) along the Mbale Road, but difficult to find without local guidance. The exhumed skulls of ancestral chiefs are displayed on a small overhanging rock. Also on this road is **Shimoto Rock**, from where suspected witches were thrown to their death in precolonial times. **Mbale** itself is the site of a pretty church founded in 1906 by Father Maynard, known locally as *mlete* (tall man).

Historical photograph of the man-eating lion from Tsavo

### Man-eaters of Tsavo

In March 1898, construction of the railway bridge across the Tsavo river was brought to a virtual standstill by a pair of man-eating lions who devoured at least 28 Indian labourers – and possibly as many as 140 – before they were shot dead that December, by hunter, author and army man J H Patterson (*see p40*). The maneless lions are almost certainly the most dedicated man-eaters on record, and their legend has lived on in books and movies such as *Bwana Devil* (1952) and *The Ghost and the Darkness* (1996). It is now thought that their taste for human flesh was acquired as a result of their scavenging improperly buried bodies of malaria victims associated with the railway. Patterson kept the lions' skins as floor rugs until the 1920s, when he sold them to the Chicago Field Museum in the USA, where they remain on display to this day.

# ❹ Tsavo East and West National Parks

Kenya's largest, second oldest and arguably wildest national park, Tsavo was gazetted in 1948 to protect a 21,812-sq-km (8,420-sq-mile) tract of savannah that remained largely unsettled as a result of limited water resources. An untrammelled wilderness larger than Wales, it was subsequently split into Tsavo East and West, which are administered separately. The smaller Tsavo West protects a hilly volcanic landscape overlooked by Kilimanjaro, while Tsavo East comprises open semiarid plains stretching 200 km (124 miles) north of the Nairobi–Mombasa Highway. Together, they support Kenya's largest elephant population and plenty of lions as well, although the latter tend to lack the long manes of their Masai Mara counterparts. Cheetah, gerenuk, oryx and hirola are more common in Tsavo East, while black rhino and lesser kudu are more likely to be seen in Tsavo West.

**Key**

Tsavo East and West National Parks

★ **Shetani Lava Flow**
This solidified lava flow, perhaps the bleakest of the many volcanic features that scar the hills and plains of Tsavo West, was deposited some 200 years ago. The cataclysmic event is still recalled in local folklore.

★ **Mzima Springs**
A short trail through the lush forest that encloses freshwater pools fed by Mzima Springs is one of the few places in Tsavo West where visitors can walk unguided and see large mammals.

## Getting Around

Tsavo East and West are separated by the Nairobi–Mombasa Highway. Several entrance gates to both parks lie along this road, including the widely used Voi Gate (to Tsavo East) and Mtito Andei Gate (to Tsavo East and Tsavo West). Despite their vast size and the presence of lodges and camps, these parks carry a low tourist volume and the most popular areas for game drives are the developed Kilaguni-Ngulia area of Tsavo West and the Voi river route through Tsavo East.

**Lake Jipe**
Located on the border with Tanzania, whose North Pare Mountains provide its scenic backdrop, the shallow Lake Jipe is renowned for bird-watching and at times it also attracts plenty of elephants.

*For hotels and restaurants see pp365–6 and p378*

**Galana River**
Fed by tributaries that originate in Kilimanjaro and the Central Highlands, Kenya's second longest river is the most important perennial water source in Tsavo East, and its palm-lined banks support hippo, buffalo and lesser kudu.

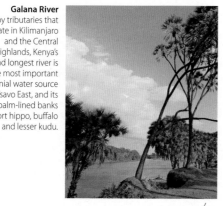

**Key**

═══ Major road

══ Minor road

::: Unpaved major road

::: Unpaved motorable road

— Railway

–·– Park boundary

▬▬ International boundary

★ **Mudanda Rock**
This heavily striated quartzite formation, which towers in magnificent isolation above a small waterhole, stands a few miles east of the Nairobi–Mombasa Highway between the Mtito Andei and Voi gates. It can be accessed from Tsavo Gate by a good dirt road.

**Golden-breasted Starling**
The semiarid thorn scrub of Tsavo East is brightened up by several colourful birds more often seen in Northern Kenya, including the golden-breasted starling and golden pipit.

### KEY

① Chaimu Crater

② **Ngulia Rhino Sanctuary** is the last stronghold for Tsavo West's critically endangered rhino.

③ **Lugard Falls** is a set of rapids named after Lord Frederick Lugard, a colonial administrator who passed through the area en route to Uganda in 1890.

**For keys to symbols** see back flap

# Exploring Tsavo East National Park

Even without its westerly neighbour, Tsavo East National Park stands out as the largest of Kenya's national parks, covering 13,747 sq km (5,307 sq miles) of semiarid scrubland cut into two unequal parts by the perennial flow of the palm-fringed Galana river. The northern two-thirds of Tsavo East is rarely toured by casual visitors, which means that the park looks larger on a map than it feels on the ground. Even so, it is a vast tract of African wilderness, notable for its overwhelming sense of space, but also for the wildlife that concentrates seasonally along the Galana and Voi rivers, both of which are serviced by a network of good game-viewing roads. The main points of access are the Voi Gate when coming from the Nairobi–Mombasa Highway, the Mtito Andei or Manyani Gates when arriving from Nairobi or Tsavo West National Park and the Sala Gate when driving from Malindi.

The striking black-flecked yellow-throated francolin seen in Tsavo

### 🏨 Voi Safari Lodge

10 km (6 miles) N of Voi, 4 km (2 miles) by road from Voi Entrance Gate.
**Tel** 0733 333400. 🚗 🏊
🌐 safari-hotels.com

The clifftop Voi Safari Lodge, situated less than a 10-minute drive from Voi Gate, makes for an excellent first stop in the park, with its commanding position above the scrubby flatlands that run towards the distant Galana river. Below the lodge, a muddy waterhole frequently attracts thousand-strong buffalo herds, while a slow scan of the interminable plains almost invariably reveals herds of elephants grazing below shady trees or making their way to drink at the waterhole. Visitors can watch the wildlife action

over a drink at the bar or follow a well-marked footpath down to a small hide for close-up photographs of antelope, baboon and storks alongside the waterhole. The grounds of the lodge support rich and varied birdlife, with Alpine swift and red-winged starling being particularly conspicuous, along with the colourful red-headed agama lizards and oddball hyraxes that scurry across the rocks.

Sign, Voi Entrance Gate

### 🦁 Voi River Route

The park's most accessible and reliable game-viewing circuit follows the Voi river east from

Voi Gate to **Aruba Dam**. Impala, zebra and gazelle are common in this area, and it is a good place to look for the localized gerenuk and Besia oryx, as well as striking dry-country birds such as golden pipit, vulturine guinea fowl, golden-breasted starling and Somali ostrich. The trademark maneless lions of Tsavo East are often seen lounging below trees in the vicinity of Aruba Dam, while cheetahs inhabit the open country around the entrance gate. The dam, constructed in 1951 to create a near-permanent water source in this otherwise arid locale, has an attractive setting below low hills. It generally supports a wide selection of waterbirds and wildlife, except when it dries up in years of severe drought. The lush **Kanderi**

Voi Safari Lodge, overlooking the sweeping savannah grassland

The Galana river meandering through Tsavo East National Park

**Swamp**, which lies south of the main game-viewing road between Voi Road and Aruba, is another near-perennial source of water.

### 🦅 Galana River

Running through the heart of Tsavo East before it flows into the Indian Ocean a short distance north of Malindi, this 390-km (242-mile) river, also known as the Sabaki, is the second longest in Kenya. Its 70,000-sq-km (27,000-sq-mile) catchment area runs from the foothills of Kilimanjaro to the Athi Plains outside Nairobi. Two popular tented camps lie on the river's southern banks, which are lined with doum palms and lush riverine vegetation. The most significant landmark along the Galana is the misleadingly named **Lugard Falls**, a series of white-water rapids running

across a potholed bed of black dolomite striated with quartzite. A short distance downriver, there is a viewpoint over a pool where hippos and crocodiles are almost always in residence. A public game-viewing road follows the southern bank of the Galana as far east as Sala Gate, through an area of dense scrubland inhabited by large numbers of elephants and buffaloes. The area to the north of the Galana has reopened after being closed since the 1980s, when it was overrun with poachers.

### 🦅 Mudanda Rock

10 km (6 miles) S of Manyani Gate. Often compared to a scaled-down version of Australia's famous Ayer's Rock, Mudanda Rock, a 2-km- (1-mile-) long inselberg, rears impressively from the surrounding plains,

offering excellent views across to the distant Galana river. The name Mudanda (Strips of Drying Meat) refers to the near vertical quartzite striations that run through the rock like multicoloured veins. The crest of Mudanda Rock, which can be reached from a clearly sign-posted car park via a set of concrete stairs, overlooks a small natural waterhole where large numbers of elephant and other animals, including buffaloes, frequently gather to drink and wallow. The area is also known for its dense leopard population, but these elusive cats are seldom seen in daylight hours.

A visitor climbing down the steep incline of Mudanda Rock

### Poaching in Tsavo

As recently as the 1970s, Tsavo supported an estimated 6,000 black rhinoceros, the largest concentration anywhere on the continent. At its peak, the park also provided refuge to over 20,000 elephants, an unsustainable density of around one individual per square kilometre that prompted intensive debate about the implementation of a culling programme. However, this debate was rendered moot by Somali poachers who started crossing into the area in the early 1970s. Initially, their main quarry was Tsavo's prodigious elephant population, with ivory fetching around US$300 per kilogram on the open market. Soon, however, the rhinoceros also became a target, and, by the mid-1980s, had been poached to virtual extinction, while elephant were being lost at a rate of several thousand individuals annually. Fortunately, the trend was reversed in the early 1990s. Key turning points included the CITES (see p69) ban on international ivory sale and the unification of the country's disparate conservation bodies into the Kenya Wildlife Service (KWS) under Richard Leakey (see p353). As a result, the elephant population is now above the 12,000 mark and rhinoceros are also slowly recovering, up from a mere three confirmed individuals in 1986 to over 120 today. Seeing these species coated in Tsavo's red dust is one of the highlights of visiting the park.

Elephants ambling across Tsavo East National Park

# Exploring Tsavo West National Park

Although Tsavo West sprawls over an impressive 7,065 sq km (2,728 sq miles), the main tourist circuit is relatively compact, focusing on the volcanic landscapes to the north of the Tsavo river. The dense bush means that wildlife is less easily spotted than in some other national parks, and predator sightings are rather hit and miss. Among the more commonly seen large mammals are zebra, elephant, buffalo, impala and giraffe. The Ngulia Rhino Sanctuary within Tsavo West is one of the more reliable places in Kenya to look for black rhinoceros, and the park is also good for the skittish lesser kudu. This area is accessible from the Nairobi–Mombasa Highway via Mtito Andei Gate and the more southerly Tsavo Gate, while visitors coming from Amboseli can use the Chyulu gate.

Entrance gate, Ngulia Rhino Sanctuary

### 🦏 Shetani Lava Flow

3 km (2 miles) NW of Chyulu Gate.
A relict of the most recent major volcanic eruption in the Tsavo area, Shetani is a solidified stream of magma that erupted from the southern end of the Chyulu Hills *(see p184)* about 200 years ago. According to local oral tradition, many people and animals were buried alive by the fast flowing stream of fiery lava, accounting for its

Swahili name of Shetani, which means devil. The site is strewn with jagged tar-coloured rocks that look like they might have been deposited recently thanks to the sparse vegetation. The site can be explored on foot in the company of an armed ranger, although the treacherous caves that undercut some of the rocks probably pose a far greater threat than any wildlife, so it is best to tread very carefully.

### 🦏 Ngulia Rhino Sanctuary

25 km (16 miles) by road from Tsavo Gate, close to Ngulia airstrip.
**Open** 4–6pm daily.

In the 1960s the combined Tsavo parks had the largest population of black rhino in Africa (between 6,000 and 9,000) and they were a common sight. By 1981, however, Tsavo's rhino had been poached to the brink of extinction and only 100 animals remained. As a result, most of Tsavo West's surviving rhino were moved to the 62-sq-km (24-sq-mile) Ngulia Rhino Sanctuary, which was established in the northeast of the park in 1986. It is surrounded by electric fencing and has a dedicated KWS anti-poaching unit that provides round-the-clock protection to these rare creatures.

The sanctuary is only open to guided safaris from the lodges for a couple of hours each day. It is serviced by a limited road network and five waterholes and the chances of seeing rhino are fairly high in such a concentrated area. However, under the present threat of renewed poaching, the KWS are undertaking a different tactic to foil poachers – by moving rhino out of the sanctuary and dispersing them in greater areas of the park. While it seems at odds with the reason for establishing the sanctuary in the first place, this approach is simply a way to hide the actual whereabouts of each individual animal, making it harder for poachers to find them.

Solidified expanse of lava at the foot of the Chyulu Hills

Mzima Springs, surrounded by a canopy of trees inhabited by birds

### 🐾 Mzima Springs
48 km (30 miles) SW of the Mtito Andei Gate.

A freshwater oasis in the heart of Tsavo West's dry savannah, Mzima Springs is a fascinating geological phenomenon. Fed by water that drains from the slopes of Kilimanjaro and Chyulu into a network of subterranean streams that flow above the non-porous Precambrian bedrock, the spring surfaces some 50 km (31 miles) east of its source. Having undergone a process of natural filtration via the porous volcanic rocks of the Chyulu Hills, this sparkling water emerges into a series of crystal clear pools at a daily rate of more than 200 million litres (53 million gal), some 10 per cent of which is diverted along an artificial pipeline to form the main source of water for Mombasa and its environs.

A unique feature of the largest pool is an underwater observation chamber built at the end of a small wooden pier in 1969 to offer spectacular subsurface views of hippos in their aquatic milieu. Not surprisingly, the hippos have since retreated to a more private location at the other end of the pool, but a swirl of fish is visible through the windows, with giant carp-like golden mudsuckers being especially common.

A walking trail through the lush palm and fever-tree thickets that surround Mzima might take anything from 15 minutes to an hour, depending on how often the walkers stop. The birdlife here can be excellent. The liquid song of the pretty black-headed oriole reverberates through the canopy, while more secretive woodland species include the African paradise flycatcher and Narina trogon. Fish eagles and African darters perch on overhanging branches, while pied kingfishers hover above the surface ready to feast on their favoured prey of small fish. Hippos and crocodiles are resident, antelope such as eland and lesser kudu

frequently come down to drink from the pools, while bushbuck and duikers haunt the forest undergrowth.

### 🐾 Chaimu Crater
5 km (3 miles) E of Kilaguni Lodge.

This volcanic hill rises in stark isolation from a setting of solidified lava flows, forming an almost perfect conical pyramid whose coal black ashy slopes support a meagre cover of yellow grass on one side, and are totally denuded on the other. The natural equivalent of a giant slagheap, the honeycombed hill can be climbed via a steep, soft and shadeless path to the rim, which offers fantastic views over the surrounding plains. The hot, dusty ascent is best taken in the relative cool of the early morning, keeping an eye open for snakes and resting mammals.

The conical Chaimu Crater rising above its ashy slopes

### Ngulia Bird-Ringing Project

Situated along one of the world's busiest avian migration routes, the Ngulia Hills have acquired something close to legendary status among ornithologists for the large number of birds attracted to Ngulia Safari Lodge (see p365) during the peak migration months of October and November. Millions of Eurasian migrants pass this way annually, representing several dozen species. For this reason, Ngulia is the site of Africa's foremost bird-ringing project, which has ringed more than 300,000 individual birds since 1969. More than 100 migrant and resident species have been ringed, with the most prolific being marsh warbler, river warbler, red-backed shrike, sprosser and common whitethroat.

Marsh warbler, distinguished by its yellowish buff breast

A view of Taita Hills from the *bandas* of Sarova Salt Lick Game Lodge

## ❼ Taita Hills Wildlife Sanctuary

**Road Map** D7. 37 km (23 miles) SW of Voi along the Taveta road. 🚌 buses run past the entrance gate but not into the reserve. 🚕 4WD. 🏨 🍴 🏪 🏦 🐾

Established in 1972, Taita Hills Wildlife Sanctuary is a private reserve extending over approximately 110 sq km (43 sq miles) of thorny savannah set below the craggy volcanic peaks of Taita Hills *(see p185)*. The sanctuary shares an unfenced border with Tsavo West National Park *(see pp190–91)*, allowing wildlife free movement in and out of the national park, but an electric fence runs along the northern boundary to prevent elephant and buffalo from damaging crops in the neighbouring villages.

More than 50 mammal and 300 bird species have been recorded at the sanctuary. However, populations tend to fluctuate according to season, with elephant and buffalo in particular being densest towards the end of the dry season (June to November). Resident within the reserve are three lion prides as well as small populations of leopard and cheetah.

The main attraction of the wildlife sanctuary is a stilted construction – **Sarova Salt Lick Game Lodge** *(see p365)*, whose Germanic architecture is said to resemble bunkers, in recognition of the World War I

battles fought in the vicinity. The lodge offers fine views over a waterhole, which attracts a steady stream of thirsty wildlife – elephant gather here in their hundreds on busy nights. Sarova Hotels also runs the other lodge in the sanctuary – the Sarova Taita Hills Game Lodge – which is an attractive stone building covered in ivy.

Visitors in their own vehicles can drive around the well-maintained network of internal roads, and overnight lodge guests can go on guided game drives, where giraffe and Coke's hartebeest are among the more common ungulates. Owing to the sanctuary's small size, the night drives offered by the lodges are a good chance of spotting nocturnal species such as hyena, leopard, honey badger, genet and white-tailed mongoose.

## ❽ Lumo Community Wildlife Sanctuary

**Road Map** D6. 50 km (31 miles) W of Voi along the Taveta road. **Tel** 020 268580. 🚌 🚕 4WD. **Open** 6am–6pm daily. 🏨 🍴 🏪 🏦 🌐 **lumoconservancy.com**

Formed in 1993, when the tribal lands of the Lualenyi, Mramba and Oza communities were united, this 450-sq-km (174-sq-mile) sanctuary bordering Tsavo West supports the Big Five, except rhino. It is named after the Lumo people, a Taita clan of these plains. Visitors with private transport can explore the reserve on their own, but most stay at **Lions Bluff Lodge** *(see p365)*, an eco-lodge that offers guided day and night drives and walks through the tangled scrub.

Entrance to the Lumo Community Wildlife Sanctuary

# ❾ Taveta

**Road Map** C6. 110 km (68 miles) W of Voi. 🚹 15,000. 🚌 ⛴ Wed & Sat.

Named after the Bantu-speaking Taveta people of the area, this modest border town comes to life on the bi-weekly market days, when villagers from both Kenya and Tanzania arrive to trade fresh produce and imported goods at the large market. The town's facilities include basic hotels, restaurants and banks, but it is of interest primarily as a base to explore the Chala and Jipe lakes. The **Taveta Military Cemetery** houses the graves of 123 soldiers from the World War I campaign against what was then German East Africa. It is believed to be one of the few wartime cemeteries where British and German soldiers were laid to rest side by side.

Placid Lake Jipe, with the Pare Mountains rising from its furthest shores

The graves of World War I soldiers, Taveta Military Cemetery

# ❿ Grogan's Castle

**Road Map** C6. 20 km (12 miles) S of Taveta along the Lake Jipe road. **Tel** 0737 066444. 🚌 🚕 4WD. 🌐 **groganscastle.com**

Perched imperiously on a tall volcanic plug that looms above the dirt road to Lake Jipe, this unusual building was constructed during the 1930s as the home of Ewart Grogan, a Scottish settler and former employee of African imperialist, Cecil John Rhodes. Grogan is best known for his pioneering journey on foot from the Cape to Cairo between 1898 and 1900 when he was surveying Rhodes's vision of building a railway and telegraph line, the length of Africa (which was never achieved). He was only 25 when he set off and carried the Union Jack throughout his journey, which he presented to Queen Victoria on his arrival in England. He was forced to face several dangers in the form of wild animals such as hippos, lions and crocodiles, and sometimes even cannibals, en route to Cairo.

In later life and as a prosperous man, Grogan bought land around Taveta to grow sisal (a plant from which rope is made). His castle was built on a spot from where he could survey the vast expanse of his plantations. Combining Swahili-style arches and courtyards with contemporary 1930s European flourishes, the whitewashed building resembled a monastery. The windows offered grand views across the plains of Tsavo to Lake Jipe, the Pare Mountains and Kilimanjaro. With the exception of cement and glass, he constructed his castle entirely from materials found on his property, such as clay for roof tiles and sisal poles for beams. The engine that drives the electrical generator was built in 1898 and it is still powering Grogan's Castle today. The building has been converted into a hotel after standing in a semi-derelict state for more than 40 years. It has five comfortable rooms and a dining room where guests share meals around Grogan's original dining table.

# ⓫ Lake Jipe

**Road Map** C7. 25 km (16 miles) S of Taveta. 🚌 **Open** 6am–7pm daily. 🛶 🏕 The northern shore lies outside Tsavo West and can be explored on foot without paying park entrance fees. 🌐 **kws.org**

Located partially within the southern sector of Tsavo West, Lake Jipe is a shallow, papyrus-lined freshwater body set within a natural sump that runs along the border with Tanzania for 10 km (6 miles). It is a magnificent spot, with the Pare Mountains rising above the Tanzanian shore and Kilimanjaro, the lake's main source of water, hulking over the northern skyline. Wildlife is usually visible, especially during the dry season, when elephants come to drink and bathe at the lake. Hippos and crocodiles are plentiful, and the reedy shore harbours local birds such as African water rail and pygmy goose. Local fishermen can be persuaded to take visitors out onto the lake for a fee.

The presence of an endemic fish, *Tilapia jipe*, suggests a long history of isolation from other wetlands. There are indications that the lake is becoming shallower and choked with papyrus, probably due to an increase in silt washed down from Kilimanjaro as a consequence of deforestation and associated erosion.

Lake Chala, confined by the steep walls of a crater

## ⑫ Lake Chala

**Road Map** C6. 8 km (5 miles) N of
Taveta. ⛟

Straddling the Kenyan border
near the southern footslopes
of Kilimanjaro, this spectacular
circular lake has a diameter of
3 km (2 miles). Despite that, it
remains practically invisible until
the tall rim of the volcanic crater
in which it is nestled is reached.
The lake's still and calm waters
are hemmed in by sheer cliffs
draped in tropical greenery, and
can be reached via a rather
steep path on the eastern rim.
From the rocky shore, translucent waters plunge almost
vertically to undetermined
depths. The lake supports an
abundance of waterbirds and a
species of endemic cichlid fish,
named *Oreochromis hunteri*.
There is no accommodation on
the Kenyan side, but on the
Tanzanian side there is a tented
lodge and campsite, which are
accessed by crossing the nearby
Taveta border crossing.

## ⑬ Oloitokitok

**Road Map** C6. 100 km (60 miles) N of
Taveta. ⛰ 5,000. ⛟ Tue & Sat.

Also known as Loitokitok, this
small and little-visited border
town has the distinction of
being the closest place to
Kilimanjaro anywhere in Kenya.
Set at a warm, dusty elevation
of 1,700 m (5,580 ft), it feels
more like the plains than the
mountains. Weather permitting,
the town centre and surrounding country roads offer stunning
views of the snowcapped

Uhuru Peak, little more than
20 km (12 miles) distant as the
crow flies. The poor state of
roads on this side of the border
means that Oloitokitok probably
has closer economic links with
Tanzania than the rest of Kenya.
Indeed, if it were not for visa
and other border complications,
it would be far quicker to drive
here from Taveta *(see p193)*
along the partially surfaced road
through Marangu in Tanzania.

Equipped with one bank, a
filling station and a plethora of
budget lodgings and eateries,
this unassuming town is an
important trading centre for the
local Maasai, who come from
surrounding villages on both
sides of the border on the
twice-weekly market days. It
offers a splendid opportunity to
interact with these fascinating
people. Local touts might be
willing to set up Kilimanjaro
climbs from Oloitokitok, but

the legality of these is highly
questionable given that the
upper slopes of the mountain
all lie within Tanzania.

## ⑭ Amboseli National Park

*See pp198–201.*

## ⑮ Namanga

**Road Map** C6. 170 km (106 miles) S of
Nairobi. ⛰ 10,000. ⛟ 🚌 daily.

Set in the heart of Maasailand,
Namanga will be passed
through by visitors driving down
to Amboseli National Park from
the capital, and it is also probably
Kenya's busiest border town,
situated on the surfaced road
between Nairobi and Tanzania's
"safari capital" of Arusha. Tourism
is pivotal to the local economy,
and the road to the border post
is lined with stalls and street
vendors selling everything
from beaded Maasai jewellery
to chilled soft drinks.

The hectic border-town
atmosphere notwithstanding,
Namanga has a pretty riverside
location below the striking Ol
Doinyo Orok (Black Mountain),
and offers impressive views of
Mount Meru and Kilimanjaro.
With a restaurant set in lush
riverside gardens, the colonial
**Namanga River Hotel** is the
best place for a break before
embarking on the insanely
rutted road to Amboseli.

Row of street stalls in the border town of Namanga

# Kilimanjaro

The 5,891-m (19,330-ft) Kilimanjaro is not only the highest mountain in Africa, but also the world's tallest freestanding mountain, rising about 5 km (3 miles) above the dusty plains below. Its upper slopes stand within Tanzania, but for non-climbers the best views are obtained from Kenya's Southeastern Savannahs, with Amboseli being the most popular vantage point. Among the most breathtaking sights on the continent, the snowcapped peak is often hidden in clouds, which usually clear around dusk and dawn. The origin of its name is obscure – *kilima* is Kiswahili for "little mountain," but *njaro* could derive from the Chagga word for "trade caravan", or from the Maasai *ngare* meaning water, or the name of a Swahili demon of cold. Others claim it is a distortion of *kilema kyaro* (impossible journey), the initial Chagga response to European queries about ascending the peak.

**Known as Ol Doinyo Naibor** (White Mountain) to the Maasai, Kilimanjaro was believed to be protected by evil spirits that froze anybody who tried to ascend it.

**Dubbed the Roof of Africa**, the 5,891-m (19,330-ft) Uhuru Peak is the highest point on the continent.

Mawenzi

Kibo

## Kilimanjaro Range

*Volcanic in origin, Kilimanjaro is a relatively young mountain, having first erupted about one million years ago as a result of the same tectonic activity that formed the Great Rift Valley (see pp26–7). It has not displayed any serious volcanic activity in the last 150,000 to 200,000 years, and is considered dormant.*

**The ice cap and glaciers** that cover Kilimanjaro have retreated drastically as a result of global warming since the first recorded ascent by Hans Meyer and Ludwig Purtscheller in 1889.

**Mawenzi Peak** rises to 5,149 m (16,893 ft). Chagga legend has it that Mawenzi and Kibo are sisters. One day, in a fit of anger, Kibo beat her junior Mawenzi over the head, leading to her jagged shape today.

**Kilimanjaro's montane forest** lies between 1,800 m (5,906 ft) and 3,000 m (9,843 ft) and displays high biodiversity, including black-and-white colobus monkey, the endangered Abbott's duiker and 40 Afro-montane forest birds.

Common zebras with a backdrop of Mount Kilimanjaro, Amboseli National Park ▶

# ⓮ Amboseli National Park

Amboseli is a land of giants. Practically unscathed by ivory poaching in the 1980s, it still harbours some of the region's oldest and bulkiest elephants, sporting tusks whose dimensions have been consigned to history elsewhere in the area. Towering above the park is the jagged dome of Kilimanjaro, the highest point in Africa and the tallest freestanding mountain in the world. An ever-mutating patchwork of dusty plains and marshland, this wildlife-rich park is not a self-contained ecological unit but the unfenced and watery core of a more expansive semiarid ecosystem protected in buffer reserves on land owned by the Maasai. A game reserve since 1899, Amboseli was made a national park in 1974.

**Key**

  Amboseli National Park

**★ Lake Amboseli**
Dominating the western third of the park, Lake Amboseli is most often a dust bowl, going years on end without holding significant quantities of water. However, when it does fill up, it attracts large volumes of game.

**Observation Hill**
One of the few places in Amboseli where visitors are permitted to leave their vehicle, the isolated volcanic plug, known to the local Maasai as *Noomotio*, offers superb views of the surrounding plains and marshland and the wildlife that thrives here.

**Enkongo Narok Swamp**
Fed by subterranean springs that rise on Kilimanjaro, this vast and ever-changing morass of marsh and open water is an important feeding and drinking point for large mammals in the dry season.

0 kilometres   3
0 miles        3

*For hotels and restaurants see pp365–6 and p378*

★ **Kilimanjaro from the Amboseli Plains**
Eulogized by authors such as Ernest Hemingway and Robert Ruark, the inspirational sight of Kilimanjaro's snowcapped peak towering some 5 km (3 miles) above the Amboseli plains provides a superb backdrop for the park's prodigious wildlife.

### VISITORS' CHECKLIST

**Practical Information**
Road Map C6. 230 km
(142 miles) S of Nairobi via
Namanga. ℹ 020 8029705.
**Open** 6am–7pm daily.
🏞 🏊 ⛰ 🌐 kws.org

**Transport**
✈

### Key

=== Minor road

≡≡≡ Unpaved motorable road

– – Park boundary

▲ Peak

**Ol Tukai**
The site of the park's headquarters and two lodges, Ol Tukai lies at the very heart of the national park. The shady yellow fever trees that cover the area provide a sharp contrast to the surrounding plains and marshes, and harbour plenty of monkeys and woodland birds.

★ **Ol Okenya Swamp**
Elephants are often very common in the vicinity of Ol Okenya Swamp, which lies a few minutes' drive from the Ol Tukai park headquarters. When not feeding by the shore, they are generally seen semi-submerged and foraging in the water itself.

### Getting Around

The somewhat rutted main road through the park runs southeast from Meshanani Gate to Kimana Gate, passing through Ol Tukai about halfway through. Meshanani Gate is the main point of access coming from Nairobi, via Namanga on the Tanzania border (*see p194*). The Kimana Gate leads to the tarred C102 road to Emali, on the Nairobi–Mombasa road. This provides an alternative route between Nairobi and Amboseli on safaris that also include the Tsavo West National Park. Game-viewing circuits are compact, so the best time to explore is shortly after sunrise or before sunset, when the clouds that typically hover on the southern horizon dissipate to reveal Kilimanjaro.

**For keys to symbols** *see back flap*

# Exploring Amboseli National Park

Like most major national parks, Amboseli is not accessible by public transport but is reached through an organized safari or self-drive visit. Standalone fly-in and drive-in safaris operate out of Nairobi, 230 km (140 miles) away, but poor road conditions between Namanga town and Meshanani Gate make it a bumpy 4-hour drive. The park extends over a relatively compact 150 sq miles (390 sq km), and a full day is adequate to explore its main road circuits, with 2–3 days being the recommended minimum duration for a safari. The park is often included in more wide-ranging safari itineraries such as to Tsavo West National Park.

Blue wildebeest at Lake Kioko, with Observation Hill in the background

### 🏵 Ol Tukai

Set in the heart of Amboseli National Park, this oasis of greenery consists of a ground-water forest of yellow fever trees that contrasts strikingly with the surrounding plains and shallow marshes. Visible from miles away, Ol Tukai is the site of the park's headquarters and one of its oldest lodges, **Ol Tukai Lodge** (see p365). The site is a popular starting point for game drives as well as a good place to break up drives with a leg stretch and cold drink. The fauna here differs from that in the rest of the national park, with monkeys, especially baboons and woodland birds being particularly conspicuous.

### 🏵 Observation Hill

10 km (6 miles) W of Ol Tukai.
This isolated rocky outcrop is situated along a road that skirts the marshy northern verge of **Lake Kioko** – almost certainly a corruption of the Swahili word *kiboko* (hippo). The short but steep footpath to the hill's crest leads to a shelter offering a grandstand view of the surrounding plains and marshes, most spectacular at dawn and dusk, when Kilimanjaro provides an eye-catching backdrop. Elephants can be seen at the lake during the day, and grazers kick up dust as they march across the open savannah, sometimes in thousands. Observation Hill is known as Noomotio meaning "a rocky depression that holds

water", in the local Maa tongue, probably in reference to its black porous rock, a product of the same Pleistocene volcanic activity that created Kilimanjaro.

### 🏵 Amboseli Plains

Kilimanjaro does not merely provide Amboseli with a splendid backdrop. The extinct volcanic mountain is arguably the defining influence on the park's ecology and landscape. The very name Amboseli derives from the Maasai *empusel*, a reference to the insinuating layer of grey saline volcanic ash that was deposited by Kilimanjaro during its volatile infancy. The plains support an abundance of large herbivores, with wildebeest, Burchell's zebra and Grant's and Thomson's gazelles most characteristic of the open areas, while impala and Maasai giraffe browse amid stands of *Acacia tortilis*.

Predators are scarce, having been hunted down in protest by the Maasai who were evicted from the park when it was gazetted. However, numbers are said to be on the rise, and there is a fair chance of seeing wildlife such as lion, cheetah, spotted hyena and jackal. The open plains also support a variety of birdlife including the secretary bird, yellow-necked spurfowl and the localized Pangani longclaw, while the woodland has Von der Decken's hornbill, white-bellied go-away bird, red-and-yellow barbet and steel-blue wydah.

Maasai herders in their colourful robes, on the stark plains of Amboseli

Elephants wading through swathes of swamp vegetation, Amboseli National Park

### 🐘 Ol Okenya and Enkongo Narok Swamps

Visitors arriving at Amboseli during the dry season are bound to wonder at the large numbers of game living in Amboseli's desert-like conditions. This phenomenon was first noticed in 1883 by Scottish geologist and explorer Joseph Thomson on his long dusty trek through Maasailand. The reason lies with Kilimanjaro, whose molten snow and spring water vanish below ground on its upper slopes, forming a network of subterranean streams that re-emerge at the base of the mountain to feed Amboseli's ceaselessly mutating network of lakes and marshland.

By far the most important swamps are Ol Okenya, which lies to the east of Ol Tukai, and the much larger Enkongo Narok Swamp, to the west. These perennial wetlands provide a reliable source of drinking water to the immense herds of grazers that congregate on Amboseli towards the end of the dry season (August to October/ November), only to disperse widely outside its borders as soon as it rains. Likewise, the elephants that converge on the marshes by day often wander outside the park to graze at night.

The marshes of Amboseli are one of its principal attractions. Towards the end of the rains, game viewing can be truly fantastic, the highlight of which is the elephant population that can be seen wading deep into the marsh to forage on the soft vegetation, while mud-stained buffalo look on from the reedy fringes. Bird-watchers are well catered for, with some 50 water-associated species likely to be recorded by enthusiasts, ranging from the long-toed lapwings and greater jacanas that mince through the vegetated shallows of the swamps, to the pelicans, cranes and herons that stand and feed on the edge of the waters.

### 🐘 Lake Amboseli

Maps of the park show Lake Amboseli as a vast blue tract covering much of the park's western third. In reality, this immense pan has only filled with water on a few occasions in the past century. More often, it is a barren expanse of cracked clay, swept across by swirling armies of dust devils and the occasional herd of wildebeest or zebra.

Swamps in Amboseli National Park

### Amboseli Elephant Research Project

Founded by Cynthia Moss in 1972, the Amboseli Elephant Research Project is the world's longest running study of a wild elephant population. Now known as the Amboseli Trust for Elephants, the project has compiled more than 40 years' worth of births, deaths and kinship within a community of 50 elephant families totalling more than 1,300 individuals. Today, much of what is known about

Elephants crossing a road within proximity of a safari van

elephants is owing to the trust, whose work has been accorded recognition through many fascinating documentaries. Due to their efforts, the local elephant population was spared the attention of poachers who were so active in East Africa in the 1980s. As a result, they have little fear of vehicles, making this park one of the finest places in Africa to view elephants at close quarters.

# SOUTHERN COAST

The sultry south coast of Kenya is lined by a seemingly endless succession of white sandy beaches lapped by the warm blue waters of the Indian Ocean. At its heart lies the historic port of Mombasa, the country's second-largest city. Kenya is widely regarded as the quintessential land of the safari, but the south coast ensures that it also holds its own as a world-class beach destination.

About 2,000 years ago, the Bantu-speaking ancestors of the coastal Swahili arrived on the southern shores of Kenya. By around AD 1000, they had a well-established maritime trade network with Arabia and Asia, which led to the settlement of many Shirazi Arabs and their integration into the Swahili community through intermarriage. This is reflected in the large stone cities constructed at ports such as Mombasa, which was founded at least 800 years ago, and in the growth of Islam as the main religion. Immediately inland lies the territory of the "nine tribes" of the Mijikenda, whose ancestors migrated southwards from the Somali border region in the 17th century.

Although a sequence of foreign incursions has left its mark on the south coast – beginning with the Portuguese in the early 16th century, Omani Arabs in the 19th and, more recently, the British – the mood remains predominantly Swahili.

Fishing, subsistence agriculture and other traditional occupations drive this region's rural economy, but Mombasa, serviced by the country's deepest seaport, remains an important centre of international trade and commerce. In recent years, tourism has had a strong impact on the coastal economy, particularly on the holiday resorts closest to Mombasa.

Along with dozens of beach resorts, the south coast of Kenya is studded with enigmatic jungle-bound ruins and time-warped fishing villages that evoke millennia of maritime trade with Arabia. The area is steeped in history, with atmospheric old towns and remnants of Portuguese architecture. Wildlife enthusiasts will be drawn to the offshore reefs protected along the coast's five marine reserves, and to the opportunity of elephant and buffalo sightings in the forested environs of Shimba Hills National Reserve.

Omani House built in the late 18th century, Fort Jesus, Mombasa

◀ Nyali beach, one of the loveliest around Mombasa

# The Portuguese at the Coast

Portuguese explorers first sailed south along the Atlantic coastline of Africa in search of a maritime route to the source of the Indian spice trade in 1420. Only in 1488, however, did Bartolomeu Dias round the Cape of Good Hope, followed a decade later by Vasco da Gama, who crossed the Indian Ocean to finally reach India in 1498. Within a decade, the East African coastline was effectively under Portuguese control, leading to the collapse of a centuries-old economy based on the gold and ivory trade with ships from Arabia and Asia. For two centuries Portugal remained the dominant force, but under increasing pressure from other European powers and the Sultanate of Oman it finally left Kenya in 1728.

The formidable seaward bastion of Fort Jesus, Mombasa

### Alliance with Malindi

*Vasco da Gama, following a hostile reception from the Sultan of Mombasa, was eagerly entertained by his archrival at Malindi in 1498. This alliance persisted throughout the Portuguese era, when the court at Malindi relocated to Mombasa to enjoy the protection of Fort Jesus.*

**Vasco da Gama Cross** stands sentinel on the Malindi waterfront. This tall cross, made of stone, was erected by Vasco da Gama in 1499 for navigational purposes and as a gesture of appreciation for the Sultan of Malindi.

### Da Gama's Route Around Africa

Vasco da Gama set sail from Lisbon with a fleet of four ships in July 1497. Following a route pioneered by Dias a decade earlier around the Cape of Good Hope, he headed into the – from a European perspective – *mare incognita* of the Indian Ocean. Da Gama rounded the Cape in December and sailed north to Mombasa and Malindi, before crossing the Indian Ocean to arrive at the Indian port of Calicut on 20 May 1498.

Lisbon

Goa

Calicut

Malindi
Mombasa

INDIAN
OCEAN

ATLANTIC
OCEAN

Maputo

St Helena
Bay

0 km        2000
0 miles      2000

## The Portuguese Conquest

*Sailing from Lisbon in March 1505, Dom Francisco de Almeida's 22-ship armada was decisive to the Portuguese conquest of the Swahili coast. With over 1,000 soldiers at his disposal, Almeida razed or captured a succession of prominent ports, including Mombasa, Kilwa, Zanzibar and Mozambique Island.*

**Drawings on the walls of Fort Jesus** by Portuguese soldiers, dated to 1639 or earlier, illustrate the conquest of the East African coast by this heavily armed power. The Omani navy's 33-month siege, from 1696 to 1698, ended Portugal's long tenure over Fort Jesus.

**An extravagant bronze throne and the royal entourage** display the prosperity of Malindi at the time of Vasco da Gama's arrival.

**Dom Francisco de Almeida** was the architect of the Portuguese conquest of East Africa. In 1505, assisted by Portugal's ally, the Sultan of Malindi, he plundered and torched Mombasa, killing more than 1,500 islanders.

**The Sultan of Malindi** offered Vasco da Gama the services of a Swahili or Arabian sailor to help him navigate his way to India across the Indian Ocean.

## The Portuguese Legacy

*Although it endured for two centuries, the Portuguese occupation left a limited mark on coastal cultures north of Mozambique. A few Portuguese words have been incorporated into the Kiswahili language, some ruins still stand, but the most enduring legacy is the introduction of crops that revolutionized local agricultural output.*

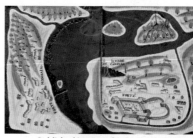

**Published in 1646, this Portuguese map** of Mombasa Island shows Fort Jesus during the Portuguese years guarding the Mombasa harbour and a wall protecting the rest of the town.

**Corn**, locally known as maize, was one of the New World crops introduced to Africa by the Portuguese. It now forms the basis of *ugali*, the local staple in most parts of East Africa.

**Porcelain**, made in China, was carried by Portuguese ships from the 16th century onwards to East Africa and Europe, where it was first manufactured successfully as recently as 1708.

# Exploring the Southern Coast

The urban highlight of this region is undoubtedly Mombasa's Old Town, which spreads northwards from the imposing walls of historic Fort Jesus. Also of historical interest are the ruined medieval Swahili towns of Jumba la Mtwana and Mnarani and the more southerly Shimoni Caves. More contemporary sites include Haller Park and Bombolulu Cultural Centre, which lie just north of Mombasa. Wildlife enthusiasts can visit the Shimba Hills and adjacent Mwaluganje Conservancy, as well as the offshore reefs that run the length of the coast around Mombasa and offer some of the world's most scintillating snorkelling and diving.

The crumbling doorway of a mosque at Mnarani, near Kilifi

## Sights at a Glance

### Villages and Towns
1 Mombasa pp208–213
8 Gazi
9 Msambweni
10 Shirazi
11 Shimoni
21 Mtwapa
23 Takaungu
24 Kilifi
25 Mnarani

### National Reserves
6 Shimba Hills National Reserve pp220–23
17 Mombasa Marine Reserve

### Wildlife Sanctuaries and Marine Reserves
5 Kaya Kinondo
7 Mwaluganje Conservancy
13 Kisite-Mpunguti Marine Park
18 Haller Park

### Archaeological Sites
22 Jumba la Mtwana

### Historical Buildings
2 Rabai Museum
14 Kongowea Junction
15 Bombolulu Workshops and Cultural Centre

### Beaches and Islands
3 Tiwi Beach
4 Diani Beach
12 Wasini Island
16 Nyali Beach
19 Kenyatta Beach
20 Bamburi and Shanzu Beaches

Holiday-makers relaxing at Diani Beach

For hotels and restaurants see pp366–7 and pp378–9

## Key

— Major road

═ Minor road

- - Untarred major road

= = Untarred minor road

- - 4WD track

⌁ Major railway

▬ International border

A lesson in sea-kayaking at Nyali Beach

Malindi ↑

Shambweni

Dida
*Rare*

uswani

Roka

Sokoke

Ganze

Tezo

Mtondia

C115

ozoyunt

🎵🅲 **24** 🅰 **KILIFI**

**MNARANI** **25**  *Kilifi Creek*

Mkongoni

🚉 **23** **TAKAUNGU**

ngo

Shauri
Moyo

Kibaoni

i C107

B8

Kurvitu

ama

Vipingo

Kaloleni

C111

🏛 **AI MUSEUM**

Mtwapa

eras

Shimo
La Tewa

Nyali

🛫

Likoni

**1** 🏖🚉 **MOMBASA**

Ngombeni

*See inset*

A14

🚉 **TIWI BEACH**

nda

🚉 **IANI BEACH**

**YA KINONDO**

*sland*

*INDIAN OCEAN*

0 km          15

0 miles          15

**MTWAPA**
**21**

🅲 **JUMBA LA**
**22** **MTWANA**

**BAMBURI AND**
**SHANZU BEACHES**
**20** 🏖🚉

**BOMBOLULU**
**WORKSHOPS AND**
**CULTURAL CENTRE**

**HALLER**
**PARK**
🚉 **18**
B8

**KENYATTA**
**BEACH**

**15**

**19** 🚉

🛫
A109

**14**

**KONGOWEA**
**JUNCTION**

🚉 **16**

**17**

**MOMBASA MARINE RESERVE**

*INDIAN*
*OCEAN*

Mombasa

Likoni 🏖

**NYALI**
**BEACH**

*Shelly*
*Beach*

A14

Ngombeni

0 km          5

0 miles          5

## Getting Around

Most visitors to the coast land at Moi International Airport, which lies on the mainland about 10 km (6 miles) west of the Mombasa city centre. For those who have not arranged a hotel transfer, taxis are available for charters to the city centre or any of the beach resorts to the north or south – the latter involving a short crossing on the Likoni Ferry. Good surfaced roads connect most resorts and points of interest along the coast south to Shimoni and north to Kilifi, and public transport is plentiful, as are charter taxis.

**For keys to symbols** *see back flap*

# ① Mombasa

Kenya's second-largest city and most important port occupies a small offshore island linked to the mainland by bridges to the north and west, and the Likoni Ferry to the south. The town was a prosperous trade centre for the best part of a millennium; today, local tourism is centred on the beaches north and south of the island, and many visitors spend a week or more here without setting foot in the city proper. One reason is that Mombasa's considerable vintage is not reflected in the plethora of old buildings and ruins one might expect. Noteworthy exceptions are Fort Jesus and Old Town, the destinations of most day tours from the beach resorts.

The colonial façade of the Municipal Council office, Treasury Square

### 🏛 Treasury Square

Nkrumah Rd.

Surrounded by stately colonial buildings, including the historic **City Hall** and several inter-national banks, Treasury Square has long lain at the financial and administrative heart of Mombasa. Today, complete with neat flowerbeds, tall trees, a few park benches and an intermittently functional fountain, the square provides an attractive enclave of tropical greenery in the otherwise built-up city centre. It is also the site of a monument com-memorating Allidina Visram, an Indian merchant who established a trade network into the East African interior prior to his death in 1916.

### 🏛 Old Law Courts

Nkrumah Rd, adjacent to Fort Jesus. **Open** 8am–6pm daily.

Situated between Treasury Square and Fort Jesus (see pp212–13), the Old Law Courts, which opened in 1902, is one of the city's most impressive colonial edifices. The building now houses a museum dedicated to Swahili culture and local history, as well as occasional art exhibitions.

### 🏛 ACK Mombasa Memorial Cathedral

Nkrumah Rd and Cathedral Rd. **Tel** 041 2230502. **Open** 7am–6pm daily. 🔲 ackmombasa cathedral.com

The oldest cathedral in Mombasa could be mistaken for a mosque, thanks to its tall domed roof, arched entrances and other Moorish architectural elements. A plaque close to the main door commemorates 150 years of Anglicanism in Mombasa, dating from the arrival of J L Krapf (see p34) in 1844.

## Central Mombasa

① Treasury Square
② Old Law Courts
③ ACK Mombasa Memorial Cathedral
④ Jain Temple
⑤ MacKinnon Market
⑥ Shri Swaminarayan Temple
⑦ Uhuru Gardens and Giant Tusks

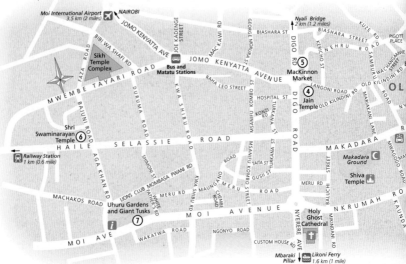

The bustle outside MacKinnon Market

### 🏛 Jain Temple

Langoni Rd, off Digo Rd.
**Open** 10am–12.30pm daily.

Consecrated in 1963, the Jain Temple in Mombasa is the oldest outside India. The temple's fantastic interior is decorated with statues of deities and paintings from floor to ceiling. Founded in India in the 6th century BC, Jainism places great emphasis on reincarnation, *karma* and the attainment of a state of salvation referred to as *moksha*. In keeping with the Jain belief that all life is sacred, the courtyard is home to a large flock of plump feral pigeons, and all shoes and leather clothing must be removed before entering the temple.

**Key**

🟦 Street by street area:
see pp210–11

### 🏪 MacKinnon Market and Biashara Street

Digo Rd, along the western fringe of the Old Town. **Open** 7am–3pm daily.

Mombasa's oldest municipal market is named after Sir William MacKinnon, the Scotsman who founded the Imperial British East Africa Company by royal charter in 1888. Not at all touristy, the lively, bustling covered market is dedicated mainly to fruit and vegetable stalls and an amazing variety of tropical produce. Outside, a confusion of other stalls spills out on to the surrounding streets and alleys, selling everything from electrical goods to clothing.

A block to the north, Biashara (Commerce) Street is the centre of the local textile retail industry, although these days the shops selling unremarkable imported fabrics far outnumber those that specialize in *kitenge* (woven sarongs) and other local cloths.

### 🏛 Shri Swaminarayan Temple

Haile Selassie Rd. **Tel** 041 2223339.
🌐 scsstmsa.org

One of the oldest and most striking Hindu temples in East Africa, this three-storey edifice near the railway station is reminiscent of a gigantic brightly decorated wedding cake. The interior is, if anything, even more ornately decorated, with numerous idols and religious scenes carved or painted on the walls. Non-Hindu visitors are warmly welcomed and will often be given a free guided tour, although a donation might be expected.

### 🌳 Uhuru Gardens and Giant Tusks

Moi Ave.

Mombasa's best-known landmark is a quartet of giant artificial tusks constructed to commemorate the coronation of Queen Elizabeth II in 1953. Situated on Moi Avenue, where they coincidentally form an "M" shape, the tusks are not worth going out of the way to see, but can be combined with a visit to the adjacent Uhuru Gardens, whose centrepiece is a fountain and pool decorated with a large, multicoloured and rather outdated political map of Africa.

Two of the four sculpted giant tusks, Mombasa's leading landmark

### 🏛 Mbaraki Pillar

Mbaraki Rd.

This 7-m- (23-ft-) tall pillar tomb is situated on the industrial south of Mombasa Island, a 5-minute walk west of Likoni Ferry. If, as some authorities believe, the pillar was erected in the 14th century, it must be the most substantial surviving relic of medieval Mombasa yet identified. However, local legend has it that the coral-rag pillar marks the burial spot of a 17th-century Mijikenda chief from the facing mainland.

**For keys to symbols** *see back flap*

# Street-by-Street: Old Town

The compact maze of narrow Old Town alleys lends itself to casual exploration. Most of its buildings date from 1870 to 1930, and the architecture combines British colonial influences with more ornate Indian flourishes. This historic area possesses a tangible sense of community, and while it may be less overtly Swahili than old Lamu, many of its predominantly Islamic residents can trace family roots back to the 19th century. Today, the Old Town carries an aura of rejuvenation, due to the efforts of conservationists and to the tourist boom that prompted the reinvention of many old houses as boutiques, galleries or craft shops.

An atmospheric Old Town house by the Mbarak Hinawy Road

**The Bohra Mosque,** originally dating to 1901, was replaced in the 1980s by a replica of a famous mosque in Yemen.

**Leven Steps**
Built by Lieutenant James Emery in 1824, when Mombasa was briefly a British protectorate, these steps offer a good view across the old dhow harbour to the Krapf Memorial.

**The White House** was built by an Indian trader. Occupied by the ladies of the Church Missionary Society in the 1890s, it became Kenya's first American Consulate in 1915.

| 0 metres | 100 |
| 0 yards | 100 |

**Basheikh Mosque**
Claimed locally to have been founded in the 13th century, Basheikh Mosque is probably Mombasa's oldest, and is topped by a plain but appealingly tall and curvaceous whitewashed minaret.

**★ Ndia Kuu Road**
Originally known as Main Road, Ndia Kuu is flanked by 19th-century homesteads notable for their fretwork balconies and wooden Zanzibari doors, many still recognizable from Victorian-era photographs.

### Government Square
The administrative and commercial hub of Mombasa in the 1890s, this concrete square on Mbarak Hinawy Road is surrounded by period buildings such as the original post office, the Old Customs House and the fish market.

### The Old Post Office
was built in 1899 so that the Indian railway workers could send their money home.

**Mandhry Mosque**

**MBARAK HINAWY ROAD**

**KUU ROAD**

**NKRUMAH ROAD**

### Old Police Station and Mombasa Club
The open square in front of Fort Jesus is lined with early colonial buildings, including the original 1898 police station, which now houses Ali's Curio Market, and the Mombasa Club, a members-only club since it opened in 1897.

Mombasa Club

**Key**
— Suggested route

Treasury Square

### ★ Fort Jesus
The most important historic landmark in Mombasa, Fort Jesus resisted and succumbed to many lengthy sieges over the three centuries following its construction by the Portuguese in 1593 (see pp212–13).

# Mombasa: Fort Jesus

Standing sentinel over Mombasa harbour, Fort Jesus was built for the Portuguese by an Italian architect in 1593. Expanded and renovated several times since, it was the Swahili coast's most strategic building for three centuries. The fort changed hands more than a dozen times, usually with considerable violence. The most protracted battle in its history, a 33-month siege by the Omani navy from 1696 to 1698, claimed at least 6,000 lives. The fort's significance diminished during the colonial era, when it served as military barracks and then a prison. It is now the region's most popular museum.

The arched entrance gate to Fort Jesus, dating back to the 16th century

**★ Omani House**
An Omani trader built this house circa 1800 on the gun platform where the Portuguese made their last stand in 1698 before the fort's captain was shot and beheaded.

**★ Site Museum**
The site museum displays an impressive collection of artifacts unearthed during excavations of the fort, ranging from Chinese porcelain to Arabic earthenware. There are also displays about Swahili and Mijikenda culture.

### KEY

① **The cistern**, excavated in 1603 by the Portuguese to collect rainwater from the church roof via a system of covered drains, was in use until 1790.

② **The fort** was built on a coral ridge at the harbour entrance.

**Seaward Bastion**
Fort Jesus is most imposing from the seaward side. The tall walls are made of 3-m- (10-ft-) thick blocks of coral stone, and rise a full 16 m (52 ft) from the coral base to the fortified turrets.

**Views**
The seaward side of Fort Jesus offers lovely views over the palm-lined harbour, while the other walls look over the town of Mombasa.

**VISITORS' CHECKLIST**

**Practical Information**
Nkrumah Rd. **Tel** 041 2225934.
**Open** 8am–6pm daily.
**w** museums.or.ke

**Transport**

**★ Portuguese Graffiti**
A Portuguese sailor painted this vivid panel with ships, human figures, fish and other animals around 1639.

②

**Bastion of San Matheus**
Depicted in plans dating to 1610, this seaward bastion was named after San Matheus (St Matthew).

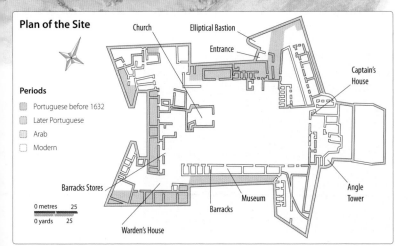

**Plan of the Site**

Church

Elliptical Bastion

Entrance

Captain's House

**Periods**

Portuguese before 1632

Later Portuguese

Arab

Modern

Barracks Stores

Museum

Barracks

Angle Tower

Warden's House

0 metres 25

0 yards 25

## ❷ Rabai Museum

**Road Map** E7. 30 km (19 miles) NW of Mombasa. 🚌 **Open** 8am–6pm daily. 🐾 🚻 ♿ ✝ 7:30am (English), 9:30am (Kiswahili) Sun. 🌐 **museums.co.ke**

Perched on an escarpment inland of Mombasa, Rabai Museum is a national monument and is the site of the earliest Christian mission in the East African interior, established in 1846 by Dr J L Krapf. The original church, built in 1848, is now the museum dedicated to this founding father of the Anglican Church of Kenya. Krapf also compiled the first Kiswahili dictionary and grammar, and was the first European visitor to Mount Kenya (*see p326–9*).

**St Paul's Church**, constructed in 1887, is still in active use, and contains several artifacts imported by Krapf and his colleague Johan Rebmann, including a church bell and a piano. Krapf and Rebmann's houses are still standing and the mission staff will show visitors around. Behind them is a cemetery where several early missionaries and their children are buried.

## ❸ Tiwi Beach

**Road Map** E7. 20 km (12 miles) S of Mombasa. 🚌 🚗 ⚠

One of the most alluring beaches near Mombasa, Tiwi Beach is great for snorkelling and hundreds of rock pools are

The palm-fringed expanse of Diani Beach

exposed when the tide goes out. It is studded with low-key accommodations including Twiga Lodge, a legendary backpacker's haunt since the 1970s. About 20 km (12 miles) to its north is **Likoni Ferry**, the only traffic conduit on Mombasa Island that is used by all vehicles heading from Mombasa city centre or Moi International Airport to the south coast. The ferry started operating in 1937, and takes only a few minutes to cross Kilindini Harbour, the main channel of Mombasa's port. Passengers and bicycles are transported free of charge.

## ❹ Diani Beach

**Road Map** E7. 13 km (8 miles) S of Tiwi Beach via Ukunda Junction. 🚌 🚗 🖥 🏨 🚗 ⚠ 🌐 **dianibeach.com**

The focal point of Kenya's seaside destinations, Diani Beach is a 20-km- (13-mile)-long, idyllic stretch of palm-fringed white sand, with dozens of resort hotels offering all-inclusive deals in the mid-range to upmarket bracket. Although these have numerous facilities, most have been built to blend sensitively into the landscape. The surfaced road linking the resorts has shops and malls offering all manner of products and services, such as tour operators, diving shops, restaurants, craft markets and launderettes. A variety of activities are on offer, including short safaris to Tsavo East National Park (*see pp188–9*), Shimba Hills National Reserve (*see pp220–23*) and Taita Hills (*see p185*), and water sports, such as diving, snorkelling, wind-surfing, kitesurfing, trips on glass-bottom boats and game fishing.

The landward side of Diani Road supports patches of native forest, with Sykes and vervet monkeys as well as forest birds such as the raucous trumpeter hornbill. It also hosts an estimated 500 Angola colobus monkeys, about 10 per cent of the East African population. Founded in 1997 after several monkeys were killed by speed-ing cars, the NGO **Colobus Conservation** erected "colobridges" of wire and plastic casing at strategic points, allowing the monkeys to cross the road aerially. The Colobus Cottage is an information centre and home to a habituated troop of colobus monkeys. One-hour guided primate walks are offered.

**Colobus Conservation**
Diani Beach, 6 km (4 miles) S of Ukunda Junction. **Tel** 0711 479453. **Open** 8am–5pm Mon–Sat. 🐾 🚻 🖥 🌐 **colobusconservation.org**

Disembarking from Likoni Ferry at Mombasa Island

# Snorkelling and Diving

The warm equatorial waters of the Indian Ocean support a rich and diverse marine fauna, and make Kenya's coast one of the world's premier diving and snorkelling destinations. For snorkellers, the main attractions are the offshore reefs that run the length of the coast, allowing even complete novices access to a kaleidoscopic world of multihued coral formations and reef fish. More experienced divers combine exploration of the reefs with forays into the open sea, where the deeper waters host a wonderful cast of turtles, squid, dolphins, sharks, dugongs, rays and billfish. Underwater excursions can be arranged on the spot through the beach resorts. Among the prime sites are the Malindi Marine National Park, the Watamu Marine National Reserve and the Kisite-Mpunguti Marine Park at Wasini, south of Diani Beach.

## Underwater Sports

*Kenya's offshore barrier reefs are among the most rewarding sites for first-time divers and snorkellers. For those with diving experience or the desire to take a full course of several days, there are exciting deep-sea and wreck dives on offer.*

**Wreck diving**, available at Diani, Bamburi and Watamu, is a popular alternative to visiting natural reefs. The artificial habitat is a good place to spot large fish, such as grouper, barracuda and cornetfish.

**The attraction of reef diving** is that larger marine creatures, such as rays, sharks, turtles and the eagerly sought whale shark, might be seen alongside the guaranteed array of brightly coloured reef fish.

**The best site for snorkelling** in Kenya is Watamu, where the coral outcrops are protected within calm clear waters hemmed in by the main barrier reef.

## Marine Life

*Thousands of vertebrate and invertebrate species inhabit the offshore coral reefs of Kenya, occurring in a dazzling variety of shapes and colours, ranging from whales and seahorses to squids and rays.*

**The bottle-nosed dolphin** is one of several marine mammals resident in the warm waters of Kenya.

**The whale shark**, the world's largest living fish, is harmless to divers, being a plankton feeder.

**The clown triggerfish**, measuring up to 50 cm (20 inches), is among the largest and most distinctive of the numerous bright-hued fish that inhabit the reefs.

**The blue ribbon eel**, although not electric, is an aggressive species and can inflict a nasty bite if provoked.

Mural painted by Portuguese sailors at Fort Jesus, a fortress city set above Mombasa harbour ▶

Cattle grazing on the grassy fringes of the sacred Kinondo forest

## ❺ Kaya Kinondo

**Road Map** E7. 13 km (8 miles) S of Diani Beach. **Tel** 0722 446916. 📧
**Open** 8am–5pm Mon–Sat. **Closed** on the Digo holiday of Chipalata, which falls every fourth day, the most sacred sites cannot be visited; call in advance to check. 🔆 📷 📹 forbidden at a few specific sacred spots. **W** kaya-kinondo-kenya.com

The coastal belt south of Mombasa (see pp208–15) is dotted with 38 *kayas*, patches of indigenous forests, considered sacred by the Mijikenda people, a group of nine Bantu-speaking tribes. Gazetted as national monuments, these ancient forests were also inscribed as a UNESCO World Heritage Site in 2008. Traditionally, outsiders were not permitted to enter a *kaya*. However, that changed in 2001 with the opening of the 74-acre (30-ha) Kaya Kinondo as a community-based ecotourism project initiated by the local Digo tribe, a subgroup of the Mijikenda.

Sign, Kaya Kinondo Sacred Forest

Once inhabited by the Mijikenda, most *kayas* today are maintained as ceremonial shrines, where ancestral spirits can be worshipped and medicinal plants collected. The Mijikenda place strict taboos on non-medicinal use of vegetation and hunting in their *kayas*, which account for more than 10 per cent of Kenya's coastal forest, offering refuge to several rare plant and bird species. Kaya Kinondo alone harbours at least 187 plant, 45 butterfly and 48 bird species, including the endangered spotted ground thrush and charismatic black-and-white casqued hornbill. Angola colobus and other monkeys are found here. The forest is also home to Ader's duiker and Zanj elephant shrews.

A guide is mandatory to enter the forest. A half-day visit is arranged from the resorts, which includes a guided walk, followed by a visit to a tribal medicine man and the school in Kinondo village.

## ❻ Shimba Hills National Reserve

*See pp220–23.*

## ❼ Mwaluganje Conservancy

**Road Map** E7. 45 km (28 miles) SW of Mombasa. **Open** 6am–6pm daily. 🔆 📷 **W** kws.org

This 36-sq-km (14-sq-mile) northern extension of Shimba Hills operates as a community project, with its proceeds going to the 200 Mijikenda families who volunteered the land as a sanctuary in 1995. Although it protects rolling terrain similar to Shimba, its lushly vegetated hills are more densely studded with baobabs and cycads, and are bisected by the Manalo river.

Elephants are the main attraction. The estimated population of 100 is composed mainly of bulls, as family herds tend to prefer the thicker forests of Shimba. The odds of an elephant sighting are far less here than in Shimba proper, but other large mammals such as buffalo, zebra, waterbuck, warthog and sable antelope are fairly common. The conservancy is usually visited as part of a day trip to Shimba Hills, although there are plans by KWS to set up a lodge and campsite here.

## ❽ Gazi

**Road Map** E7. 20 km (12 miles) S of Diani via Ukunda. 🏕 1,000. 📧

Historically, the sleepy fishing village of Gazi was known as the headquarters of Mbaruk

Low-lying area around Manalo river dominated by baobab trees, Mwaluganje Conservancy

bin Rashid, a notorious slave trader who claimed descent from the Mazrui dynasty ousted by the Omani capture of Fort Jesus *(see pp212–13)* in 1828. A strong opponent of British colonization, Mbaruk masterminded the Mazrui Rebellion of 1895, an ill-fated enterprise that led to his eventual defeat and death in exile in neighbouring German East Africa.

A compelling reason to visit this historic village is the **Gazi Women's Mangrove Boardwalk**, a community project opened in 2006 to protect the mangroves that line Gazi Bay. Six different species of mangrove can be seen from the 300-m (984-ft) boardwalk. Wildlife includes mudskipper crabs, the dazzling kingfisher and various marine birds.

**Gazi Women's Mangrove Boardwalk**
**Open** daylight hours. 🚗
📷 **w** mangrove actionproject.org

## ⑨ Msambweni

**Road Map** E7. 26.5 km (16 miles) S of Diani via Ukunda. 🚠 11,000. 🚌 🚉

Just 6.5 km (4 miles) south of Gazi, the beach at the fishing village of Msambweni is one of Kenya's quieter, unspoiled beaches. It can be reached by following a coral track from the main road through coastal coconut plantations. With rocky outcrops and low clifftops, the beach itself is not as wide as others on the south coast, and often has a steeper gradient into the ocean, but there are some secluded accommodations including the **Msambweni Beach House** *(see p366)* . Fishermen sell their catch from baskets, and fruit sellers on bicycles offer freshly picked mangoes, paw-paws, limes and coconuts. The reef offshore here is the most southerly point of the continuous fringing reef that stretches from Msambweni to Malindi in the north, and the snorkelling is superb.

Outer walls of a ruined medieval mosque amid thick foliage, Shirazi

## ⑩ Shirazi

**Road Map** E7. 12 km (7 miles) S of Msambweni. 🚌 🚉 🚲

This tiny fishing village, also known as Kifunzi, which means Little Funzi, is named after its close-knit Shirazi people. The community traces its ancestry to the city of Shiraz in Iran, which is the birthplace of many of the medieval traders who settled on the Swahili coast. The only relic of this ancient link is a venerable coral-rag mosque lying in partial ruins on the north side of the village, which was thought to have been

Detail, ruined medieval mosque

abandoned at the beginning of the 20th century. All of the tracks from the main coast road through the sugar plantations lead to Shirazi where there is a scattering of houses as well as a small harbour among the mangroves.

Offshore, **Funzi Island** is a wonderful tropical beach accessible by boat at high water or by wading across when the tide is out from the village of Bodo, just to the southwest of Shirazi. Situated on the island in glorious isolation, **The Funzi Keys** *(see p366)* is an idyllic beach lodge built in an inspired Swahili style that offers various activities such as snorkelling and scuba diving.

### Palm Trees and their Traditional Uses

So ubiquitous is the coconut palm, *Cocos nucifera*, in Kenya that it may come as a surprise to learn that it is exotic to East Africa, having arrived there from Asia or South America several centuries ago. Since then, it has become one of the region's most diversely used plants. The young coconuts provide a refreshing alternative to bottled soft drinks, while the flesh of older coconuts is a popular snack, a source of cooking oil and an essential ingredient in Swahili cuisine. The fibrous husk that encloses the nut is twined to make rope or matting, or dried for fire fuel. Palm

*Makuti*-roofed *bandas*, made from palm fronds

fronds can be made into a disposable shopping basket with just a few deft strokes of the hand, and they are also used to create the *makuti* thatching characteristic of the roofs along the coast. Finally, the sap and flower are brewed together to make palm wine, a popular drink in coastal parts of Kenya.

# ❻ Shimba Hills National Reserve

Gazetted as a state forest in 1903 and upgraded to national reserve status 65 years later, Shimba Hills runs along the table escarpment that rises sharply from the coastal flats about 20 km (12 miles) inland of the popular Diani and Tiwi beaches. Extending over a scenic 300 sq km (116 sq miles), the reserve is dominated by rolling green grasslands, but it also supports part of Kenya's second-largest coastal forest after Arabuko Sokoke Forest Reserve. Shimba is best known as the last Kenyan stronghold of the sable antelope, hosting an estimated population of 200 of these magnificent creatures, while other large mammals include giraffe, leopard, zebra, warthog, several monkey species and substantial populations of elephant and buffalo.

**Key**

▨ Shimba Hills National Reserve

★ **Sable Antelope**
Shimba Hills is the last Kenyan refuge for the handsome sable antelope, small herds of which are frequently seen in the open grassland in the northern part of the reserve.

0 kilometres 2

0 miles 2

**Shimba Forest**
Shimba and various contiguous forest reserves support Kenya's second-largest coastal forest, although this habitat is interspersed with moist undulating grassland.

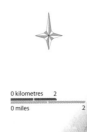

Makadara
Forest

① Pengo Hill
450 m

Kidongo
Gate

## Getting Around

Less than an hour's drive from Diani or Mombasa, Shimba Hills is most often visited on an all-inclusive package. Day and overnight trips can be arranged at short notice through any coastal tour operator. The village of Kwale at the park entrance is connected to Diani and Mombasa by a good road and public transport. Private transport is not required for the guided walk offered by the Shimba Hills Forest Guides Association (SHIFOGA) but it is necessary for entering the park itself.

### KEY

① **Pengo Hill** is the highest point in the reserve.

② **Makadara Forest** is the best place in the reserve to see the forest's birdlife.

**Crested Guinea fowl**
Shimba is home to a number of forest birds including the crested guinea fowl, which differs from the more familiar helmeted guinea fowl in having a shaggy black hairdo.

★ **Shimba Hills Lodge**
The closest thing to
Treetops *(see p321)* near
the coast, this lodge offers
its overnight visitors plenty
of game viewing of wildlife,
ranging from gargantuan
elephants to cute
bushbabies.

## VISITORS' CHECKLIST

**Practical Information**
**Road Map** E7. 55 km (34 miles)
S of Mombasa via the Likoni Ferry.
📱 0704 467855.
**Open** 6am–7pm daily. 🚫 📷
📝 ♿ ⛺ 🌐 kws.org

**Transport**
🚌 to Kwale.

### Key
=== Minor road
≡≡≡ Unpaved motorable road
– – Park boundary

Kwale
*Warden's
Office*

C106

*Shimba
Hills Lodge*  Kwale Gate

*Kivunoni
Gate*

*Ronyo Mwagandi*

*Elephant
Lookout*

**Kwale Gate**
The main access point to the national reserve,
Kwale Gate lies at the northern edge of the
park to the south of Kwale village.

★ **Giriama Viewpoint**
Perched on the escarpment that runs
along the eastern boundary of
Shimba, Giriama Viewpoint is one of
several spots that offer magnificent
views around Diani on a clear day.

**Sheldrick Falls**
This pretty waterfall is worth seeing in its
own right, but the walk to it is also notable
for the opportunity to glimpse elephant,
buffalo and other forest creatures, as well
as for the view back towards the beaches.

*For keys to symbols see back flap*

# Exploring Shimba Hills National Reserve

A wonderfully peaceful bush retreat, Shimba Hills tends to be viewed as an extension of the coastal tourist trade rather than as part of any safari circuit. The climate, though far from chilly, is noticeably cooler than the coast below, and thoroughly refreshing. So too, coming from the human overload of the popular resort beaches, is a sense of being in a relatively untrammelled vista of African bush. Day or overnight trips offer the opportunity to see sable antelope, elephant, buffalo and forest specialists such as Angola colobus, Sykes monkey, blue duiker, suni, bushbuck and the exquisite red-bellied coast squirrel. A wealth of rare plants includes primeval cycads, flame lilies, terrestrial and epiphytic orchids and an endemic evergreen tree *Diospyros shimbaensis*. More than 250 butterfly and 200 bird species have been recorded here, several of them localized forest dwellers.

Dark timber façade of the atmospheric Shimba Hills Lodge

### 🏠 Shimba Hills Forest Guides Association (SHIFOGA)

Edge of Kwale village, towards park entrance gate. **Tel** 0724 227224. **Open** 6am–6pm daily. 🚫 🎫 🚲 🛶 🏍 **w** shifogaecotours.com

Established in 2004, Shimba Forest Guides Association (SHIFOGA) is a community project on the outskirts of Kwale, operating a guided nature trail through a patch of secondary forest donated to the association for that purpose by Kenya Wildlife Service (KWS) and the Forestry Department. The guided walk takes around 45 minutes – although dedicated bird-watchers might need longer – and runs through a patch of forest where a troop of Sykes monkeys comes to feed on most days. The best time to look for monkeys is after 10am, but birds are more active earlier in the day, and include the colourful Fischer's turaco and loudly duetting tropical boubou. The project provides employment to several villagers, who can also be hired as guides on game drives into the park. SHIFOGA also runs the simple Golini Resort, which is 3 km (1.2 miles) from Kwale on the coast. It has two rooms, three *bandas*, a campsite, and cold drinks and basic meals are available. Kwale is serviced by sporadic public transport from Mombasa and Diani.

### 🏕 Shimba Hills Lodge

2 km (1 mile) from Shimba Gate. **Tel** 020 4452095. 🚲 🛶 **w** aberdaresafarihotels.co.ke

One of the most underrated lodges in the country, Shimba Hills Lodge – a rambling, overgrown treehouse – is under the same management as the world-famous Treetops Lodge in the Aberdares *(see pp320–21)*. The lodge feels like an extension of the luxuriant jungle that surrounds it, and the waterhole below its dining area regularly attracts groups of elephants and other big game. The lodge offers one of Africa's best "small game" experiences, with red-bellied coast squirrels clambering around its wooden frames by day, while the night shift is taken by a multitude of bug-eyed greater bushbabies.

An elevated walkway through the forest offers the opportunity to watch troops of Sykes and Angola colobus monkeys swing between the trees, and provides good views into a canopy inhabited by green barbets, Fischer's turacos, forest batises, palm-nut vultures, olive sunbirds and dark-backed weavers. Overnight visitors will find that a deafening chorus of insects and frogs gives the forest an almost physical presence. Even day visitors will find it worthwhile to stop by for lunch or a drink.

Elephants drinking at a waterhole, Shimba Hills National Reserve

Hiking to Sheldrick Falls across the forested slopes of Shimba Hills

### 🐾 Giriama and Ocean Viewpoints

Situated 2 km (1 mile) apart from each other on the crest of a ridge overlooking Diani Beach, Giriama and Ocean viewpoints offer superb views over verdant hills to the distant Indian Ocean, although conditions are often rather hazy. There is a shelter and a small information display at Ocean Viewpoint.

### 🐾 Makadara Forest and Pengo Hill

About 10 km (6 miles) south of the main gate, the game-viewing road passes through Makadara Forest. This is regarded as the top site in the park for forest birds, which are most easily seen from a cleared picnic site where visitors are allowed to step out of their vehicles. The main attraction here is the green-headed oriole, a vociferous and pretty coastal forest endemic at the very north of its restricted range. The area supports various other birds, including the Narina trogon, brown-breasted barbet, trumpeter hornbill and four-coloured bush-shrike. At the forest's southern end, the road climbs to Pengo Hill, the highest point in the reserve at 450 m (1,476 ft). On a clear day, it offers views all the way to the Taita Hills and Kilimanjaro.

### 🐾 Sheldrick Falls

📷 by arrangement.

On the same ridge as Giriama Viewpoint, but further south,

**Elephant Lookout** is the starting point for the 2 km (1 mile) descent to Sheldrick Falls, a 45-minute round hike that must be accompanied by a mandatory armed ranger; arrange at the lodge or the main gate. The lookout is a good place from which to spot elephants.

The hike to Sheldrick Falls passes through forested and occasionally steep slopes where Sykes monkey, buffalo and elephant are observed with some regularity, particularly during the early hours of the day. The trail also provides superb views towards the ocean. The waterfall plunges 21 m (69 ft) over a rock shelf into a cool forest-fringed pool where swimming and picnicking are permitted. The falls are named after the late David Sheldrick, the founder-warden of Tsavo East National Park *(see pp188–9)*, and husband of the celebrated elephant researcher, Daphne Sheldrick.

### 🏠 Grassland Game Drives

Shimba has a well-maintained, well-signposted network of game-viewing roads, centred on the grassland south of the main gate. The major road network can easily be covered in 2–3 hours, with vehicles generally being thin on the ground. The most productive time to do the drive is early morning or late afternoon. Wildlife might literally be seen anywhere, but the muddy wallow between markers 4D and 4E often hosts a herd of contented buffalo, and the surrounding slopes are good for the indigenous herds of sable antelope. Elephant are best seen on the forest margins, as are the striking bushbuck. The grassland has a limited variety of birds, but the red-necked spurfowl, yellow-throated longclaw and black-bellied bustard are worth looking out for.

Heavy clouds and hazy weather at Giriama Viewpoint

## ⓫ Shimoni

**Road Map** E7. 80 km (50 miles) S of
Mombasa. 👥 2,400. 🚌

Only 10 km (6 miles) from the
Tanzanian border as the crow
flies, the attractive fishing village
of Shimoni served as the
headquarters of the Imperial
British East Africa Company
before Kenya was formally
colonized in the late 19th
century. Shimoni is dotted
with relics from that period,
including a ruinous former
District Commissioner's
residence and the grave of
Captain F E Lawrence, a victim
of the 1895 Mazrui Rebellion.
On the outskirts of Shimoni is a
coral forest that supports troops
of Sykes and vervet monkeys
and the rare Angola colobus.
Another interesting natural
feature are the hundreds of little
swifts that breed on the jetty.

Shimoni translates as "place
of the hole" in Kiswahili, in
reference to the eponymous
**Shimoni Caves**, which
reputedly extend inland for up
to 20 km (12 miles) and are held
sacred by local Digo people.
During the slave trading era, this
gloomy coral and limestone
labyrinth was used to incar-
cerate captives from the interior
before they could be shipped
for sale at the Zanzibar slave
market. The beachfront
entrance through which the
slaves were led is now silted
up, but the caves can be
entered via a staircase located
above the caves. A guide
will point out where chains
and hooks are embedded

District Commissioner's house made from coral stone, Shimoni

into the walls, as well as the
natural well of semi-saline water
from which the slaves were
forced to drink.

Several operators run day trips
from Diani to Shimoni and
Wasini, and the small village is
often overrun with tourists
around 9–10am.

**Shimoni Caves**
**Open** 8:30am–6pm daily. 🅿️ 📷
🌐 shimonimuseum.org

## ⓬ Wasini Island

**Road Map** E7. 1 km (half a mile) SE of
Shimoni. **Tel** 0722 205155. 🅿️ 🚌 📷
🍴 🏨 🌐 wasini.com

Separated from Shimoni by a
narrow channel, this 5-sq-km
(2-sq-mile) island is named for
the Chinese – called *wa-cini* in
Kiswahili – who used to visit it
regularly to trade porcelain for
mangrove poles and other local
products. Located on the
baobab-studded landward
shore, the main village is surrounded by old walls and graves,
including a pillar tomb inset
with Ming porcelain. Wasini is

one of the four islands that lie
within the Kisite-Mpunguti
Marine Park, and a visit here is
the most popular day trip on
the south coast. The normal drill
is to take a dhow ride, do some
snorkelling and eat lunch at the
legendary seafood restaurant
**Charlie Claw's** *(see p379)*.

Wasini's other star attraction is
a boardwalk that runs through
its Coral Garden, a stark landscape
of coral outcrops interspersed
with sand flats and mangroves
where mudskippers and hermit
crabs scuttle past. Late afternoon
visitors might well be rewarded
with sightings of the spectacular
coconut crab, the world's largest
terrestrial crustacean.

## ⓭ Kisite-Mpunguti Marine Park

**Road Map** E7. HQ opposite Shimoni
Jetty. 🚌 organized day trips from
Diani or locally hired boats from
Shimoni. **Tel** 040 52027. **Open**
6am–7pm daily. 🅿️ 📷 🌐 kws.org

Protecting 40 sq km (16 sq miles)
of open sea and four small
islands surrounded by coral
reefs, Kisite-Mpunguti was
gazetted in 1973 to control over-
fishing and trophy collection
around Kisite Island, a waterless
coral outcrop 8 km (5 miles)
from Shimoni. The area harbours
some of Kenya's richest marine
life, including five species of
dolphin. It can be reached easily
by motor boat or dhow from
Shimoni for snorkelling and
diving, which is especially
good by the Mpunguti ya Juu,
Mpunguti ya Chini and Liwe la
Jahazi coral islets. The Shimoni
headquarters has a short nature
trail through a forest patch.

Exposed coral and mangroves at low tide, Coral Garden, Wasini

# The 19th-century Slave Trade

Two main factors lay behind the 19th-century boom in the slave trade out of East Africa. One was the reduction in the transatlantic traffic out of West Africa, following the abolition of the slave trade there. The other was the takeover of the Swahili coast in 1828 by Omani settlers. By 1840, they were exporting over 40,000 slaves annually. The effects on the interior were devastating. A few tribes became powerful by serving as porters and organizing slave raids. Others had their villages ransacked for able-bodied men and women, and the young and old killed or left to die. This terrible flow of human booty was stemmed in 1873, when a naval blockade allowed Scottish explorer John Kirk to persuade Sultan Barghash of Zanzibar to outlaw the slave trade in exchange for British protection.

**Omani Arabs**, who colonized the East African coast in the 1830s, were the driving force behind the 19th-century slave trade.

**David Livingstone**, the famous explorer, was one of slavery's most outspoken critics. His funeral became the catalyst for the blockade that led to the abolition of Zanzibar's slave trade.

## Slave Raids in East Africa

*Thousands of East Africans were sold into slavery during the 19th century. Perhaps twice as many died of disease or exhaustion on the long march to the coast, and nobody knows how many old, young and infirm Africans died as a result of murderous slave raids.*

**Slaves** were captured in the interior and sold to Omani traders at coastal villages before being shipped to the Great Slave Market at Zanzibar.

**Fresh captives were herded into a stockade** by one of the local tribes, who collaborated with the Omani Arabs, terrorizing parts of the interior with their brutal slave raids.

**Shimoni Caves** were an important holding dungeon for slaves en route to Zanzibar, where an estimated 50,000 African captives were sold annually at the Great Slave Market.

**William Wilberforce**, British politician and philanthropist, was the most influential figure in the abolition of slavery in the British Empire and the curtailment of the slave trade out of Africa.

The main building at Bombolulu Workshops and Cultural Centre

## ⓴ Kongowea Junction

**Road Map** B6. Immediately NE of Nyali Bridge, off Mombasa Island.

Located on the mainland off Mombasa Island is Kongowea Junction, formerly known as Freretown (pronounced Freetown) after Sir Bartle Frere, who played a major role in negotiating the abolition of the slave trade with the Sultan of Zanzibar in the 1870s. Between 1874 and 1888, around 1,400 freed slaves were settled in Freretown to form a thriving self-reliant Christian community under the leadership of William Salter Peel, the first Anglican Bishop of East Africa.

South of the junction is **Freretown Bell**, which once warned the community of imminent danger, and gave the area the nickname Kengeleni (Place of the Bell). This town was formally disbanded in the 1920s, but many local residents trace their ancestry to the freed slaves who built the attractive **Emmanuel Anglican Church** by the Freretown Bell in 1889.

About 3 km (2 miles) south of the bell is the **Krapf Memorial**, a 6-m- (20-ft-) tall stone cross commemorating the works of German missionary Dr J L Krapf (see p214), who lived in Kenya between 1844 and 1881. Below the memorial, a low stone wall encloses the graves of his wife and child.

Spanning the west end of the old harbour, the 400-m- (1,300-ft-) long Nyali Bridge is the only road conduit between Mombasa Island and the

coast further north. Built in the early 1980s, it replaced what was then the world's longest pontoon bridge.

## ⓵ Bombolulu Workshops and Cultural Centre

**Road Map** B6. 4 km (1 mile) N of Mombasa via Nyali Bridge. **Tel** 020 2399716. 🚌 **Open** 8am–5pm Mon–Sat, 10am–3pm Sun. 🅿 🍴 📷 🛒 📷 🛒 **w** apdkbombolulu.org

Founded by the Association of the Physically Disabled of Kenya (APDK) in 1969, the Bombolulu Workshops and Cultural Centre is a highly regarded crafts centre, manufacturing a wide selection of good-quality leatherwork, basketry, wood carvings and jewellery, which is sold both on site and further afield. Visitors are encouraged to visit the five workshops, each of which specializes in a different craft. The cultural centre consists of rural homesteads from all over Kenya, and puts on traditional

dance performances several times a day. Set in grounds that were formerly part of a botanical garden, the leafy complex also houses a restaurant serving traditional Swahili lunches and a craft shop. The centre generates employment for more than 100 disabled people.

## ⓶ Nyali Beach

**Road Map** B6. 7 km (2 miles) N of Mombasa. 🚌 🍴 🏧 🏨 🛒

One of the loveliest beaches around Mombasa, Nyali is lined with prestigious hotels and resorts including the pioneering Nyali International Beach Hotel & Spa, which kick-started the Mombasa beach tourism industry when it opened in 1946. Running down to the beach, the **Nyali Golf & Country Club**, founded in 1956, is one of the finest in Kenya, although conditions can be tricky when the oceanic winds are up. Its perfectly formed greens are flanked by flamboyant flame trees, and the fairways are famous for their resident troops of vervet monkeys.

Directly opposite the Nyali golf course, and easily recognized by the gigantic sculpted crocodile that guards the entrance, **Mamba Village** claims to be the largest crocodile farm in Kenya. The centre also has a snake park, spider house, botanical garden, horse-riding facilities and aquarium. The restaurant specializes in crocodile meat and houses one of the most popular discos in Kenya, with a capacity of 5,000 people.

Beachgoers walking past colourful sailboats at Nyali Beach

Racing to the ocean across Kenyatta Beach

**Nyali Golf & Country Club**
Links Rd. **Tel** 0726 414477.

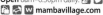 **Mamba Village**
Links Rd. **Tel** 020 3549303.
**Open** 8am–6:30pm daily.
**mambavillage.com**

## ⑰ Mombasa Marine Reserve

**Road Map** B6. Off the coast of
Mombasa. **Tel** 041 2312744.
**kws.org**

The developed coastline north
of Mombasa is protected in the
200-sq-km (77-sq-mile) stretch
of the Mombasa Marine Reserve,
including the eponymous
10-sq-km (4-sq-mile) national
park. The reserve is often used
for water sports, which are
organized at the resorts. The
offshore coral gardens support
a wealth of reef fish and invertebrates, and are excellent for
diving and snorkelling.

## ⑱ Haller Park

**Road Map** B6. 7 km (4 miles) N of
Nyali Bridge. **Tel** 041 2101000.
**Open** 8am–5pm daily. Giraffes are fed
at 3pm, crocodiles at 4:30pm and
hippos at 4:45pm.

Formerly known as Bamburi
Nature Trails, Haller Park is a small
private reserve, named after the
Swiss agronomist Rene Haller,
who engineered its exemplary
ecological transformation from
barren limestone quarry 30 years
ago to verdant nature sanctuary
today. The highlight of this idyllic

little park is a relaxed nature trail
that takes around 90 minutes,
passing enclosures inhabited by
hippo, Rothschild's giraffe,
crocodile, buffalo, bushbuck,
suni antelope, vervet monkey
and other introduced wildlife.

The woodland and streams
naturally support a diverse
assortment of birdlife, including
the conspicuous African fish
eagle, pied kingfisher and white-
browed robin-chat. Other
attractions include a thatched
butterfly pavilion, a reptile park
housing numerous snakes and
crocodiles, a good restaurant and
a shop selling locally made curios.

## ⑲ Kenyatta Beach

**Road Map** B6. 7 km (4 miles) N of
Nyali, off the main Mtwapa Rd
opposite Haller Park.

Named after Jomo Kenyatta,
Kenya's first president, Kenyatta

Beach is the only public beach
on the coast north of Mombasa,
and it tends to be a lot busier
with Kenyans than with tourists,
especially at the weekend. Swimming is pleasant at high tide,
and this is a good place to
arrange excursions in glass-
bottomed boats to Mombasa
Marine National Reserve. Low
tide is the ideal time to explore
rock pools and coral outcrops.
The main attraction at the north
end bordering Bamburi Beach is
**Aquadrom Yul's**, an open-air
restaurant, beach bar and water-
sports centre which offers banana
boat rides, jet-skiing and wake-
boarding. Yul's is also famous for
its home-made Italian ice cream.

**Aquadrom Yul's**

Off Mombasa–Malindi road, turn-off
before Bamburi Beach Hotel. **Tel** 041
5485950. **Open** 9am–11pm daily;
water sports 8:30am–6pm daily.
**aquadrom-yuls.com**

Frog trail, one of many paths winding through the woodlands of Haller Park

Pristine palm-fringed white-sand beach at Bamburi

## ⓩ Bamburi and Shanzu Beaches

**Road Map** B6. 10 km (6 miles) N of Nyali Bridge. 🚌 🏊 🖥 🏨 🌊
Note: beach access is through the upmarket resorts; visitors are required to dress appropriately to use resort facilities.

Running northward from Kenyatta Beach to Mtwapa Creek, Bamburi and Shanzu beaches form a near-continuous 10-km (6-mile) stretch of classic Indian Ocean coastline – white sand, swaying palms and turquoise-blue water hemmed in by offshore reefs. Around a dozen upmarket beach hotels serve the area and offer a range of seaside activities, from swimming and sunbathing to snork-elling, windsurfing and scuba diving. Other facilities in the area include a scattering of restaurants and banks. A short distance inland is **Shanzu Workshop**, a Girl Guide affiliated NGO founded in 1992 to train and educate disabled young women to find employment or generate an income. Tailoring, leatherwork and jewellery design are among the various trades taught here. An on-site gift shop stocks a fabulous selection of clothes, bags and other items made from colourful *kikoy* fabrics (see p387).

Souvenir, Shanzu Workshop

### 🏠 Shanzu Workshop

20 km (12 miles) N of Nyali Bridge; 2 km (1 mile) E of Mtwapa Rd along the road to the Serena Beach Hotel & Spa. **Tel** 0733 994007. **Open** 8am–5pm Mon–Sat. 🖷 🚻
🌐 shanzu.kbo.co.ke

## ㉑ Mtwapa

**Road Map** B6. 20 km (12 miles) N of Mombasa. 🚹 70,000. 🚌

Set above the mangrove-lined north shore of Mtwapa Creek, this small but rapidly expanding town has a lively yachting, restaurant and nightlife scene that attracts Mombasa residents at weekends. The creek is an Indian Ocean inlet, perfect for waterskiing and game fishing.

There is no shortage of affordable hotels and eateries to choose from, but Mtwapa's chief tourist attraction is dining by the creek shore. **La Marina** has a romantic setting on the north shore of the creek and, as well as lunch or candlelit dinner, offers the option of dhow cruises with on-board entertainment. **The Moorings** floating restaurant (see p379), further along the creek, offers great seafood at more modest prices.

About 8 km (5 miles) north of Mtwapa, a turn-off leads to Kikambala Beach. Backed by palms and clutches of coastal forest, this reef-protected

The Moorings floating restaurant

expanse of powder-white sand is a lot less busy than other beaches north of Mombasa and there are only a couple of resorts. However it's very flat, so the sea goes out a long way and swimming is only feasible at high tide. Beyond Kikambala the coast road north goes through vast sisal estates towards Kilifi.

## ㉒ Jumba la Mtwana

**Road Map** B6. 4 km (3 miles) along a side road running E of Mtwapa. **Open** 8am–6pm daily. 🅿 📷
🌐 museums.or.ke

The most impressive Shirazi ruin along the Kenyan coast south of Gedi (see pp242–3), Jumba la Mtwana has a beautiful beachfront location a short distance north of the mouth of Mtwapa Creek. Cooled by constant sea breezes and blessed with an ample supply of fresh water, this ruin was probably once a substantial settlement. The site is now rather overgrown, with gigantic fig and baobab trees erupting from the old coral-rag walls. Excavated by British archaeologist James Kirkman in 1972, the site was cleared and gazetted as a national monument 10 years later. Among the buildings that remain in a recognizable state are four houses, an inscribed tomb and three mosques, of which the **Mosque by the Sea** is interesting for its arched doorways and well-preserved mihrab.

The enigmatic aura that permeates the ruins is reflected in its absence from all historical records. Based on Chinese porcelain unearthed by Kirkman, the town is thought to have been founded circa 1350 and abandoned a century later, for reasons that remain unclear. Its original name is unknown, and the modern appellation Jumba la Mtwana is obscure in origin. Although it is translated as "mansion of the slave", no link with the slave trade *(see p225)* has been established.

## ❷❸ Takaungu

**Road Map** E7. 6 km (4 miles) from Kibaoni on the Mtwapa–Kilifi Rd. ⛰️ 1,500. 🚌 🎿 important pilgrimage site during Maulidi (variable).

This sleepy and little-visited fishing village, set on a low cliff above the south bank of Kivukoni Creek, may come across as the consummate coastal backwater, but it has quite a historical pedigree. One of the region's oldest slave trade centres, it is where the ruling Mazrui family of Mombasa re-established itself after Fort Jesus was captured by the Omanis in 1828. In 1844, the missionary J H Krapf visited this "hospitable village" before settling on Rabai *(see p214)* further inland as the site of his first mission. Scattered relics of the village's 19th-century incarnation include a deep coral-rag well, the crumbling slave market and an old mosque overgrown with strangler figs. A 10-minute walk from the town centre, the beach consists of a steep incline flanked by tall coral outcrops. Utterly idyllic by day, it is claimed to be haunted by the ghosts of slaves after dark.

Tomb detail with Arabic inscriptions, Mnarani Ruins

## ❷❹ Kilifi

**Road Map** E7. 50 km (31 miles) N of Mombasa. ⛰️ 123,000. 🚌

Kilifi is the largest town between Mombasa and Malindi. It was established in the 1930s when cashews were grown in the region, and then rapidly expanded from the 1980s thanks to tourism. Most of the commercial activity is concentrated on the north side of Kilifi Creek, where there is the daily market, banks and shops. The long Bofa Beach runs northwards from the town centre, while the much more compact Kilifi Beach is tucked inside the south side of the creek. Kilifi Creek itself is known as one of the safest natural harbours on the East African coast, and the **Kilifi Boatyard**, about 1 km (half a mile) inland on the south side of the creek,

has long served as a focal point for the country's yachting community. Day visitors are welcome and the seafood is excellent in the beach bar and restaurant, which have fine views.

**Kilifi Boatyard**
**Tel** 020 3509505. **Open** 7:30am– 6:30pm daily. 🌐 **kilifiboats.com**

## ❷❺ Mnarani

**Road Map** E7. 200 m (656 ft) W of the main Mtwapa–Kilifi Rd, on the south bank of Kilifi Creek. Mnarani National Monument: **Open** 9:30am–6pm daily. 🎿 📷 🌐 **museums.or.ke**

From the 13th to 16th centuries, Mnarani was the most important settlement on Kilifi Creek. Its ruins, set on a cliff above the south bank, are protected as **Mnarani National Monument** and can be reached via a steep flight of 104 concrete steps. Mnarani means "place of the pillar" in reference to an engraved 13th-century pillar tomb that marks the grave of a sultan. First excavated in the 1950s, two well-preserved mosques adorn the site; one is inscribed in an Arabic script yet to be translated. The ruins also include one of the deepest wells found along the Southern Coast. An impressive natural feature at Mnarani is an 800-year-old baobab that is credibly claimed to be the largest in Kenya.

Mosque by the Sea, one of the few remaining mosques in Kenya from the 15th century, Jumba la Mtwana

# NORTHERN COAST

Running from the picturesque Kilifi Creek to the remote Somali border, Kenya's Northern Coast is a stretch of palm-lined beaches and atmospheric ruins, and with some exceptions, is refreshingly unspoiled by urbanisation. The area is profoundly Swahili in character. Life in this coastal haven unfolds at a reassuringly slow pace and visitors are made to feel at home by the local hospitality.

Interred within the humid depths of the Northern Coast's forests are the crumbling mosques and palace walls of the Gedi Ruins, Kenya's very own lost city. Abandoned in the 16th century, these medieval relics of a once-wealthy trading port, whose name has been lost in the mists of time, stand witness to the 2,000-year-old Swahili coastal culture. A far less enduring, though still notable, presence on the Northern Coast came in the form of the Portuguese empire. Vasco da Gama stopped off at Malindi in 1498 on his way to India, paving the way for the Portuguese invasion of 1505. Following their loss of Fort Jesus at Mombasa, in 1729, the Portuguese abandoned the area entirely in favour of present-day Mozambique.

More recently, popular holiday resort destinations have developed at Malindi and Watamu, which lie along a lovely stretch of Indian Ocean coastline notable for its fantastic coral outcrops.

Sun-worshippers are catered for by a seemingly endless succession of bone-white beaches scattered with great beach resorts that offer a broadly comparable experience to the south coast, while the offshore reefs offer superlative diving and snorkelling. The open sea off Watamu has also retained its charm as a game fishing destination, first popularized by the American author Ernest Hemingway. Despite its development as a resort destination, this region still holds on to traditional Islamic values.

Culturally, the undoubted travel highlight of the Northern Coast is the Lamu Archipelago, which boasts superb sightseeing opportunities and some beautiful beaches. This is where the various strands of the Swahili coast, past and present, intertwine to form a satisfying whole, epitomized by the lovely laid-back authenticity that permeates the alleys of Lamu town, a UNESCO World Heritage Site.

Traditional sailing dhows lining the picturesque Lamu waterfront

◀ A garden with coral walls and views of the Indian Ocean at Watamu, Kilifi County

# The Swahili Coast

The name Swahili derives from the Arabic *sawahil* – meaning edge or coast – and Islam has been the predominant religion here for many centuries. The Swahili language, or Kiswahili, by contrast, forms part of the indigenous Bantu linguistic group, but has a liberal peppering of Arabic words. It is difficult to say when these exotic and indigenous elements first fused into a distinct Afro-Islamic culture, but as early as the 12th century, the coast was studded with stone-walled city-states recognizably Swahili in character. Many such cities, including Mombasa and Malindi, survive to the present day.

The commanding Lamu Fort, built in the mid-19th century

**The Swahili settlement of Mombasa** dates back at least 800 years, but the multistorey buildings that line the narrow alleys of the present-day Old Town mostly date to the 19th century.

**Arches**, one of several Arabic features associated with Swahili architecture, are amply used.

## Architectural Influence

*Swahili harbour towns such as Lamu show a clear Arabic influence in architectural style. The whitewashed coral-rag buildings typically span two or three storeys, and line a maze of narrow alleys to form a compact high-rise settlement.*

**The pillar tomb**, an architectural innovation associated with the Swahili coast, has no counterparts in any other Islamic culture. This may well be an adaptation of the fields of more overtly phallic stelae erected in parts of Ethiopia.

**Zanzibari doors**, made of heavy wood, are often seen in old Mombasa and Lamu. The spikes served as protection against war elephants – a practice that originated in medieval India, where tuskers were used to ram down doors.

**The medieval ruins** on Pate Island date to when the Swahili coast was a hub of international trade. Gold transported to the coast via the Zambezi Valley was sold at the now ruined city of Kilwa.

## Swahili Culture

*A strong unifying factor in Swahili culture is Islam, which first took hold in the region in the 10th century or earlier. Many other aspects of Swahili culture demonstrate a strong Arabic influence, ranging from the traditional dress and forms of body adornment to the spicy cuisine.*

**Maulidi** is one of the most important events in the Islamic calendar of the Swahili. It is celebrated most ardently in Lamu where men move in procession along the waterfront.

**Most Swahili men** wear ornamental amulets containing Koranic verses around their necks as protection against evil spirits known as *jinns* or *djinns* in Arabic and Kiswahili.

**Lamu town**, declared a World Heritage Site by UNESCO in 2001, has a number of old houses with ornately carved timbered doors.

**Swahili cuisine** reflects the cosmopolitan history of the coast, with Indian and Arabic spices complimented by the trademark Swahili ingredient of grated coconut flesh or coconut milk.

The *bui-bui*, an all-black veiled dress, is the most common female attire in more conservative Swahili settlements.

**Taarab music** fuses Swahili lyrics with Arabic-style melodies. An evolving art form, it combines traditional instruments such as the lute-like *udi*, *darbuk* drums and zither-like *gannon* with the likes of guitar and violin.

**Henna painting**, traditionally reserved for special occasions, is now accepted as day-to-day adornment of the hands and feet.

### Swahili Proverbs

Kiswahili is rich in proverbs, many of which are inscribed on the *kanga* cloths worn by women, and inform contemporary Swahili rap music. Popular sayings include *Haraka haraka haina baraka* (Hurrying brings no blessing) and *Baraka zitasimama tukimsahau mama* (Blessings will stop if we forget Mother).

Vibrant *kanga* fabric with printed Swahili proverbs

# Exploring the Northern Coast

The most popular bases for exploration are Watamu and Malindi, both of which cater to the all-inclusive beach package market. The most worthwhile day trip in the area is Gedi Ruins near Arabuko Sokoke Forest Reserve, off the main road to Watamu. This site is particularly recommended to keen walkers and bird-watchers, who can visit it in conjunction with Mida Creek. The more remote, but equally rewarding, Tana River Primate Reserve and scenic Hell's Kitchen near Marafa are difficult to reach without an experienced local guide. To the north lies the Lamu Archipelago. Visitors will require at least four days to soak up the time-warped atmospheric Lamu town, including a full-day dhow trip to the Manda Toto reefs and the medieval Takwa Ruins.

The fantastic rock formations at Hell's Kitchen north of Malindi

Aerial view of the palm-fringed Old Town, Lamu

## Sights at a Glance

### Towns and Islands

1 Watamu
5 Malindi pp244–5
8 Lamu Archipelago pp248–54

### National Parks and Reserves

2 Malindi Marine National Park
3 Arabuko Sokoke Forest Reserve and Gedi Ruins pp238–43
7 Tana River Primate Reserve

### Areas of Natural Beauty

4 Mida Creek
6 Hell's Kitchen

## Key

— Major road

=== Minor road

= = Untarred major road

= = Untarred minor road

-- 4WD track

▬ International border

The remnants of the Great Mosque, Gedi Ruins

0 kilometres 25

0 miles 25

### Getting Around

A good surfaced road and plenty of public transport connects Mombasa to Malindi and Watamu, and offers ready access to sites such as Arabuko Sokoke Forest Reserve, Gedi Ruins and Mida Creek. All roads are clearly sign-posted. The drive from Mombasa, the closest international airport to Malindi, takes less than two hours, but can be longer on public transport. Malindi Airport, a 20-minute drive from Watamu, has regular flights from Mombasa and Nairobi. The journey by road from Malindi to Lamu takes about four hours. The last part is a 40-minute ferry ride from Mokowe on the mainland to Lamu town. Visitors can fly from Malindi, Mombasa or Nairobi too.

The pristine Vasco da Gama Cross standing sentinel over the Malindi coast

**For keys to symbols** *see back flap*

The eye-catching coral outcrops at Turtle Bay

# ❶ Watamu

**Road Map** E6. 55 km (34 miles)
N of Kilifi. 🚗 2,000. 🚌 🚌
**W** watamu.net

Blessed with one of the most inspiring coastal settings in East Africa, the Swahili fishing village of Watamu lies at the northern end of Turtle Bay. The bay's 7 km (4 miles) of sandy beach overlooks shallow turquoise waters interrupted by a succession of fantastically ragged coral outcrops that explode from the water like giant surrealist mushrooms. The village itself is something of an oddity, with its combination of Swahili traditionalism and overt commercialism. It is, however, a pleasant place, and visitors are rarely hassled. The focus is inevitably the beach, which is a gem, whether as a place to pull up a deckchair and relax below the swaying palms or to snorkel and dive among the kaleidoscopic array of reef fish that inhabit the magnificent offshore coral gardens. Another of Watamu's assets is its proximity to the Arabuko Sokoke Forest Reserve and Gedi Ruins *(see pp238–43)*, which lie within a 10-km (6-mile) radius.

Located outside Watamu, the **Bio-Ken Snake Farm** houses the largest collection of snakes in East Africa, most of them acquired through the free "remove a snake" service it offers to locals. Almost all of the region's venomous species are on display here, including various cobras, vipers and all three mambas, and are regularly milked for antivenin for regional distribution. It is a fascinating

place, and the staff show a clear commitment to eradicating ignorance about these often reviled but ecologically important reptiles. It is necessary to call ahead to find out about day outings to look for snakes in the wild and any upcoming evening talks at one of the nearby resorts.

🐍 **Bio-Ken Snake Farm**
5 km (3 miles) N of Watamu. **Tel** 042 2332303. **Open** 10am–noon, 2–5pm daily. 🚫 📷 ♿ **W** bio-ken.com

# ❷ Malindi Marine National Park

**Road Map** E6. Casuarina Point, 5 km (3 miles) S of Malindi. 🚌 **Tel** 020 2335684. **Open** 6am–6pm daily. 🚫 📷 **W** kws.org

Africa's oldest marine park was gazetted in 1979 to protect a 213-sq-km (82-sq-mile) expanse of coastline, offshore reefs and open water running from Mida Creek at Watamu to the north of Malindi. Within its boundaries, it encompasses the smaller **Watamu Marine National Reserve**, which has a 30-km

Coral reef exposed at low tide, Watamu Marine National Reserve

(17-mile) coastline with a fringing reef along its entirety. It offers some of the best diving opportunities in Kenya, with over 300 recorded species of reef fish and a variety of marine invertebrates and birds. It is a breeding site for hawksbill, olive ridley and green and leatherback turtles.

🐢 **Watamu Marine National Reserve**
6 km (4 miles) SW of Watamu. 🚌
**Tel** 020 2335459. **Open** 6am–6pm daily. 🚫 📷 **W** kws.org

# ❸ Arabuko Sokoke Forest Reserve and Gedi Ruins

*See pp238–43.*

# ❹ Mida Creek

**Road Map** E6. 6 km (4 miles) S of Watamu Junction. 🚌 **Open** sunrise–sunset. 🚫 📷

The 6-km- (4-mile-) long Mida Creek, located at the southern end of the Watamu peninsula, is renowned for its coastal birdlife. Recent counts of over 6,000 waders have been made along its sandy shore. It is a significant wintering site for Palearctic migrants, such as the eagerly sought crab plover. Besides this, some 70 other aquatic species have been recorded, with the likes of greater sand-plover, lesser sand-plover, mangrove kingfisher, grey plover, greater flamingo and dimorphic egret among the more commonly seen residents and visitors.

The offshore **Whale Island** hosts thousands of breeding pairs of roseate and sooty terns between June and October, while the dense coastal scrub around the creek hosts several interesting non-aquatic birds, ranging from the carmine bee-eater to the Sokoke pipit and chestnut-fronted helmet-shrike.

A local community group constructed a 260-m (853-ft) suspended wooden boardwalk through the surrounding mangroves to a hide overlooking the sand flats.

Spectacular rock formations at Marafa Depression, popularly known as Hell's Kitchen

The community project is run by enthusiastic local guides. The quality of birding from the boardwalk and hide depends strongly on tidal factors and is best during an incoming tide when birds are busy feeding. The creek's calm waters are ideal for most aquatic activities, which can be arranged through any hotel in Watamu.

## ❺ Malindi

*See pp244–5.*

## ❻ Hell's Kitchen

**Road Map** E6. 35 km (22 miles) NW of Malindi. ▣ **Open** 6am–6pm daily.
🅿 📷

Reminiscent, in a scaled-down way, of the Grand Canyon in the USA, Hell's Kitchen is the popular name for Marafa Depression, a valley of spectacularly eroded sandstone pillars, known as demoiselles, that stand up to 30 m (98 ft) tall. According to local folklore, Marafa was formerly inhabited by a Giriama tribe so wealthy that its people washed their bodies with milk rather than water. The gods punished this ostentatious behaviour by brewing up a mighty overnight storm that caused the area to sink and all its human inhabitants and livestock to be washed into the Sabaki river.

Impressive at any time of day, the valley is stunning in the early morning, when the soft light makes the layered columns look like they have been sprinkled with pink icing sugar. Now

managed as a community project, the gorge is overlooked by a fenced car park and can be reached via a footpath that runs about 3 km (2 miles) through its base.

## ❼ Tana River Primate Reserve

**Road Map** E5. 50 km (31 miles) N of Garsen, on Malindi–Garissa Rd.
**Tel** 046 2035. ▣ **Open** 6am–7pm daily. 🅿 📷 ⓦ **kws.org**

This far-flung and little-visited reserve runs for about 35 km (22 miles) along the forested course of the Tana, Kenya's largest river. The area was gazetted in 1976 to protect the last remaining habitat of the Tana river red colobus and Tana mangabey, a pair of endemic monkeys that show a strong affiliation to Congolese species, suggesting that the forests were linked in the Miocene Era. Neither monkey is thought to number more than 1,000 individuals in the wild, and both

are critically endangered, though they are quite easily seen within the confines of the reserve.

In addition to being of great interest to primate enthusiasts, this area supports a native population of the endangered hirola antelope, and a variety of avifauna, including Pel's fishing owl, Fischer's turaco, east coast akalat and brown-breasted barbet. It is also the only known habitat of the Tana river cistocola – not seen in the wild since the 1970s – and the elusive white-winged apalis, feared by some biologists to be extinct.

Difficult to reach by public transport, this remote reserve is very pedestrian-friendly. Organized overnight tours based at the upmarket **Delta Dunes** *(see p367)*, can be booked in Malindi.

The Tana river delta, which sprawls southward from the reserve, is an important breeding site for birds, but large areas of it are rendered inaccessible by marshy conditions.

The muddy Tana river delta meets the Indian Ocean

# ❸ Arabuko Sokoke Forest Reserve and Gedi Ruins

Extending over 420 sq km (162 sq miles) northwest of the main coastal road between Kilifi and Watamu, Arabuko Sokoke Forest Reserve protects the largest remaining tract of coastal forest in East Africa. The area is well known as a stronghold for six globally threatened birds, among a recorded 230, while at least four of its 260 recorded butterfly species occur nowhere else in the world. A popular goal for day trips here is the ruined city of Gedi just outside the park's boundaries. This is the most extensive and atmospheric of the many medieval ruins along the Kenyan coast, and a walking trail to the old city walls is a good introduction to the forest itself.

**★ Forest Paths**
Guided walks through Arabuko Sokoke's network of paths offer hikers the opportunity to see plenty of forest wildlife.

**Whistling Duck Pond**
Covered in beautiful blue water lilies, this small forest-ringed pond on the Nyati Trail is named for the white-faced whistling duck, one of several waterfowl sometimes seen here. Although seldom seen, the buffalo and elephant that drink here in the dry season often leave conspicuous spoor.

**Key**

━━━ Major road

══ Minor road

= = = Unpaved motorable road

– – Trail

■ ■ Park boundary

0 km — 5
0 miles — 5

Lake J
Bird Sar

Arabuko Sokoke
Forest Reserve

Dida

Rare

Sokoke   Tezo

C115

Mtordja

Kilifi

Kilifi
Creek

Mombasa
50 km
(31 miles)

**★ Sokoke Scops Owl**
Arabuko Sokoke Forest is renowned among ornithologists for its selection of rare and endemic coastal birds, including the endemic Sokoke scops owl and five other globally threatened birds.

### ★ Gedi Ruins
The best-known archaeological attraction in the vicinity of Arabuko Sokoke, the ruined city of Gedi is an impressive relic of one of the most important Islamic medieval trade centres along the Swahili coast of Kenya.

**Giriama Dancers**
The Giriama people of the Arabuko Sokoke area are not traditionally Islamic, and many adhere to animist beliefs. Living on the outskirts of Gedi Ruins, they can be seen performing dances in their traditional attire.

**Kipepeo Butterfly Project**
This community-based eco-project, founded in 1993, encourages local subsistence farmers to breed the pupae of some of the 250 butterfly species found in Arabuko Sokoke for export.

**Watamu**, with its stunning bays and coral cliffs, is a popular stopover for beach-lovers.

**Colourful Tree Frogs**
The forest pools and trees of this national park are home to a wide variety of reptiles and amphibians, including several species of tree frog. These are most easily tracked after dark by their distinctive and repetitive calls.

## Getting Around
One of Kenya's most important protected areas in terms of global biodiversity, the forest is best explored on foot, following a network of well-maintained tracks that emanate from the forest headquarters alongside the main Mombasa–Malindi Highway. Guides are mandatory. The forest can be explored as a day trip from Malindi or Watamu, or from the campsite at the headquarters. The self-guided trail around the old city walls of Gedi also provides a good introduction to the reserve.

# Exploring Arabuko Sokoke Forest Reserve

The forest reserve is accessible by public transport and can be explored on foot, although a vehicle, ideally a 4WD, will allow visitors to cover far more ground and to go deeper into the forest. All visitors must report to the main gate, on the north side of the Mombasa–Malindi Highway about 2 km (1 mile) west of the junction for Watamu, the closest base for visits. Park fees are collected at the gate, where local guides are also available – the latter highly recommended but not mandatory. A network of walking trails runs northeast from the main gate, though the route through Mida Gate to Whistling Duck Pond and Nyati Viewpoint is preferable by vehicle. Bird-watchers might deviate to Komani track and Dakacha to see the rare Sokoke scops owl and Clarke's weaver.

A 4WD manoeuvres through a narrow dirt track, Nyati Trail

### 🐾 Nyati Trail

The 14-km (9-mile) motorable track running from Mida Gate to **Nyati Viewpoint** probably offers the best introduction to Arabuko Sokoke Forest Reserve's main habitats. Those without a vehicle will find that the first 8 km (5 miles) are a flat stretch and can easily be undertaken as a return walk, turning back at **Whistling Duck Pond**.

The first part of the track passes through a lovely patch of mixed evergreen forest, notable botanically for the prehistoric-looking cycad *Encephalartos hildebrandtii*. The spiky fronds of this fern-like shrub are often stripped bare by the forest's furtive population of around 120 elephants – elusive and seldom seen creatures, whose distinctive large pats are often splattered along the road. Vehicle-bound bird-watchers can step out to walk part of this stretch, looking out for east coast akalat, forest batis,

blue-mantled flycatcher and various greenbuls – some difficult to locate without a recording of the bird's calls, which a guide can provide.

After about 4 km (2 miles), the mixed forest gives way to deciduous *Brachystegia* woodland, which sheds its leaves between January and March, and supports an interesting assortment of epiphytic creepers, orchids and lichens. The open canopy here is probably the

reserve's most worthwhile bird habitat, supporting busy mixed flocks whose numbers include the Sokoke pipit, chestnut-fronted helmet-shrike, little yellow flycatcher, Amani sunbird and occasionally Clarke's weaver.

Whistling Duck Pond, a pretty lily-covered expanse enclosed by tall forest, often hosts a selection of waterfowl, and forms an important drinking hole for buffalo and elephant in the dry season. The track then passes through dense *Cynometra* woodland, where wildlife is scarcer, although this is the preferred habitat of Sokoke scops owl and Ader's duiker, and buffalo and elephant spoor are also much in evidence. About 5 km (3 miles) after the pond, the track ascends a low ridge to Nyati Viewpoint, which offers sweeping views across the woodland canopy to the coastline between Malindi and Mida Creek.

### 🐾 Arabuko Swamp and Treehouse

Running along the eastern boundary about 5 km (3 miles) from the Mombasa–Malindi Highway, Arabuko Swamp is the park's largest wetland, hemmed in by tall forests in the west and open cultivated land in the east. A varied selection of herons and other waterbirds is present, and a 2-km (1-mile) walking trail leads around the south shore to a fabulous treehouse, a viewing platform perched atop a colossal baobab. En route, visitors pass through a mixed woodland that hosts a similar selection of bird species to the first stretch of the Nyati Trail,

Lilies on Whistling Duck Pond, a favourite haunt of the white-faced duck

The dense expanse of forest canopy, Arabuko Sokoke Forest Reserve

along with Sykes and vervet monkeys, though other large mammals are scarce due to encroaching cultivation.

### Komani Track

This rough track runs for about 5 km (3 miles) west of Arabuko Swamp to a patch of *Cynometra* thicket where, ideally around 6:30pm, the guides from the Visitor Centre can reliably locate the Sokoke scops owl. This endangered small owl, which comes in grey and russet morphs, was first described in 1965 and was thought to be endemic to Arabuko Sokoke until an individual was netted in Tanzania's East Usambara in 1992. The owl rests up in holes in trees by day, and is very unlikely to be seen unless spotted by somebody very familiar with its nesting sites. The presence of this nocturnal insectivore is documented or suspected in a few other small Kenyan forests, but Arabuko Sokoke remains its main stronghold, supporting up to 80 per cent of the estimated global population of 2,000–3,000.

### Dakacha

An obvious extension to any ornithological visit to the forest, the Dakacha area lies a short distance outside the park's northern boundary, and is the most reliable site for Clarke's weaver, arguably the most alluring of the many rare birds associated with Arabuko Sokoke. With a global population

estimated at around 2,000, this bright-yellow Kenyan coastal forest endemic is listed as endangered by the world conservation union IUCN, and its numbers remain in slow decline as a result of habitat destruction. Although the weaver is regularly recorded in *Brachystegia* woodland within Arabuko Sokoke from August to November, it is less common at other times and vanishes almost entirely over the breeding season (April–July). It is thought that the weaver's main breeding site is around Dakacha, where it is quite easily seen through-out the year, provided that visitors are accompanied by a knowledgeable local guide.

### Kipepeo Butterfly Project

Outside entrance gate to Gedi Ruins. **Tel** 042 32380. **Open** 8am–5pm daily.
kipepeo.org

This community-based eco-project was founded in 1993 to discourage local subsistence farmers from chopping down indigenous trees used as breeding sites by the 260 butterfly species associated with Arabuko Sokoke. Today, pupae are bred by more than 800 individual farmers for export to the USA, Europe and South Africa, where they are hatched for live greenhouse exhibits. As an offshoot, the project now also supports a community mushroom farming enterprise

A butterfly with speckled wings

and breeds silkworms, while a beekeeping enterprise produces honey sold locally to various beach resorts and marketed more widely under the Kipepeo label. It is an admirable and educational set-up, but visitors may feel a bit disappointed, for most often the only butterflies present are the ones still cocooned in their pupae.

A butterfly catcher working for Kipepeo Butterfly Project

### Giriama Dancers

The Giriama are among the most traditional of the Mijikenda tribes, and this amiable troupe, based immediately outside Gedi Ruins, will perform their traditional dances on request. Propelled by a trio of drummers and a panel of corrugated iron that plays a similar percussive role to a tambourine, the performance involves about a dozen male and female dancers, and can last anything from 10 minutes to an hour. They can also be seen performing at the coastal hotels.

# Exploring Gedi Ruins

Of all the archaeological sites on the coast, Gedi is the most impressive, both for its brooding enigmatic atmosphere and its well-preserved Swahili architecture. Its name, from the Oromaic Gede (Precious), alludes to the abundant water of its deep stone wells. It is believed to have been founded in the 12th century, but some excavations have traced its origins to two centuries earlier. At its peak, Gedi spread over 49 acres (20 ha) with a population of 3,000 people and eight mosques. Yet, its existence goes undocumented in any surviving Swahili, Arabic or Portuguese source. Archaeological evidence suggests that it was abandoned by the end of the 17th century after the domination of the Indian Ocean trade by the Portuguese.

**★ Pillar Tomb**
One of the several Islamic pillar tombs of the Swahili coast, this tomb has a phallic form that is disputed locally, and may have been inspired by tombstones from Ethiopia or Madagascar.

**Audience Court**
Located on the north side of the palace, this court was most probably used by the sultan to address his subjects at ceremonial events and in times of crisis.

**★ Great Mosque**
Built in the mid-15th century, when Gedi was at its economic prime, this was the largest of the city's eight mosques, with six doors and a thick roof that was supported by 18 pillars. A 15-m- (50-ft-) deep well stands outside.

Great Mosque

## KEY

① **The Women's Court** is where marital guidance was given.

② **The Reception Court** was reached through a fine arched doorway that still stands today.

③ **Stone wells**, some still usable today, provided fresh water to the people of Gedi.

## Getting Around

The best starting point is the museum, which offers a good introduction to Gedi. From here, a footpath leads through the original town centre, passing the Dated Tomb, the Great Mosque, the Tree Platform and the Palace. Another path runs through the forest to the inner and outer city walls, passing many crumbling structures en route and offering the chance to spot the peculiar golden-rumped elephant shrew and a variety of secretive forest creatures. Watch out for the vicious safari ants underfoot.

### Sykes' Monkeys

Small troops of Sykes' monkey are often seen clambering along the old walls in the late afternoon, while bird activity peaks in the early morning.

## VISITORS' CHECKLIST

**Practical Information**
**Road Map** E6. 1 km (half a mile) N of Watamu alongside Gedi Village. ℹ 042 32065.
**Open** 9:30am–6pm daily. ♿ 📷 ♿ 🏠 📷 🌐 **museums.or.ke**

**Transport**
🚌

### Tree Platform

Built in the canopy of a massive baobab, this bird-watching platform also offers a great aerial view over the ruined city.

②

③

### ★ Palace

Dating to the 15th century, the palace covers 900 sq m (9,700 sq ft) and was used by three generations of sultans. It features a large court and an annexe for the sultans' many wives.

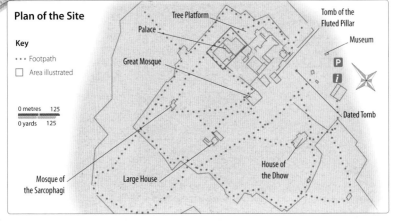

## Plan of the Site

**Key**

••• Footpath
☐ Area illustrated

0 metres 125
0 yards 125

Tree Platform
Palace
Tomb of the Fluted Pillar
Museum
Great Mosque
P
ℹ
Dated Tomb
Mosque of the Sarcophagi
Large House
House of the Dhow

# ❺ Malindi

Kenya's second-largest coastal settlement, Malindi is one of the oldest ports along the Swahili coast. The town enjoyed its greatest era of prosperity in the early 16th century, when it entered into alliance with Portugal against Mombasa, but the modern town is essentially a 19th-century entity, one that has since prospered as the country's leading urban beach resort. The town centre boasts a rather limited selection of historical landmarks, but it is well endowed with tourist facilities. A string of resort hotels running south of town caters to beach-goers and water-sport enthusiasts. Malindi is well placed for day trips to Gedi, Arabuko Sokoke and Hell's Kitchen, and for short safaris to Tsavo East National Park.

Uhuru Gardens, a pleasant retreat in the heart of Malindi

## 🏛 Uhuru Gardens

Cnr Tsavo and Mama Ngina Rds.
Named Uhuru, which means freedom, shortly after independence, this small park-like enclave of shady trees is a good place for visitors to get their bearings before embarking on further exploration of Malindi. A couple of good craft shops run along the west side of the park. The fabulously run-down balconied double-storey building to the east of the park was built in 1890 as a combined residence and workplace for Malindi's first British district officer, J Bell Smith. Designated a national monument a century later, the building still functions as a District Office today.

The modest concrete construction in front of the office is the **Henry the Navigator Monument**, erected by Portugal in 1960 to commemorate the voyages of global exploration initiated by that 16th-century monarch.

Friday Mosque on the seafront, the town's principal mosque

## 🏛 Friday Mosque and Pillar Tombs

Mama Ngina Rd.
Situated to the south of Uhuru Gardens, the old town of Malindi suffers in comparison to its counterpart in Lamu or even Mombasa, in large part thanks to the destructive fires that have swept through it at several points in its history. Indeed, the only Islamic monument of historical significance is the pair of pillar tombs that stand in front of the large seafront Friday Mosque. The larger tomb stands about 5 m (16 ft) high and dates to the 15th century, but the smaller may be more recent. The tombs can only be reached by entering a side door into the mosque compound and treading carefully and respectfully through the rows of rectangular graves outlined by coral stones.

## 🏛 Malindi Tourist Market

Lamu Rd. **Open** 8am–7pm daily.
Located opposite the Friday Mosque, this conglomeration of at least 50 stalls sells curios and crafts from all over Kenya, ranging from locally made batiks and paintings to beaded jewellery and sandstone carvings from Western Kenya. Inconvenience levels are low, and bargaining is undertaken with typically laid-back good humour. Open daily, many stalls only kick into action later in the day.

## 🏛 Malindi Museum

Mama Ngina Rd. **Tel** 042 31479. **Open** 9:30am–6pm daily. includes same-day entry to the Portuguese Chapel and Vasco da Gama Cross. **museums.or.ke**
Webb Memorial Library: **Open** 9:30am–5pm Mon–Fri.

This museum opened in 2004 in the House of Columns, a three-storey waterfront building that began life as the trading store of Adulhusein Gulamhusein some time before 1891. The building served as a hospital for several decades until 1952, and was later the local headquarters of the Department of Wildlife. It was acquired by the National Museums of Kenya in 1999 and restored in 2004.

The bell-shaped Vasco da Gama Cross at the northern end of Malindi

Displays on the ground floor include a stuffed 77-kg (170-lb) coelacanth, a remarkable fish regarded by anatomists to be a living fossil. The highlight on the first floor is a collection of rare *vigango* (wooden burial totems) carved by the Gohu society of the coastal Giriama tribe, and believed to represent a link between the living and the dead. The top floor is given over to the **Webb Memorial Library**, which includes many out-of-print volumes dedicated to the history and culture of East Africa.

### Portuguese Chapel
Mama Ngina Rd. **Open** 8am–6pm daily.

There is an appealing simplicity to this small thatched coral-rag building, which has overlooked the waterfront since before 1542, the year in which St Francis Xavier visited Malindi. In a ruinous state for much of the 17th and 18th centuries, the chapel was restored in the early 1890s. Most of the graves surrounding the chapel are unmarked – some may be Portuguese – although it is known that J Bell Smith was buried here in 1894.

## VISITORS' CHECKLIST

**Practical Information**
**Road Map** E6. 115 km (71 miles)
N of Mombasa. 205,000.
at the Malindi Museum.

**Transport**

### Vasco da Gama Cross
Casuarina Rd. **Open** 8am–6pm daily.

One of the oldest surviving European monuments in equatorial Africa, this large limestone *padrao* (cross) was erected by the Portuguese navigator Vasco da Gama in 1499 to commemorate his historical landing at Malindi. It originally stood outside the Sultan of Malindi's palace, but its overt Christian connotations were considered offensive by local Muslims, and as a compromise it was relocated to its present out-of-town site in the 16th century. Visible from the town centre, the cross, which is a 10-minute walk past the Portuguese Chapel, has a splendid location on a windswept coral outcrop overlooking the bay and tidal flats that are inhabited by flocks of small waders.

## Malindi

1. Uhuru Gardens
2. Friday Mosque and Pillar Tombs
3. Malindi Tourist Market
4. Malindi Museum
5. Portuguese Chapel
6. Vasco da Gama Cross

For keys to symbols *see back flap*

# ⓭ Lamu Archipelago

The least conventional resort destination on the Kenyan coast, the Lamu Archipelago consists of a trio of large offshore islands – Pate, Manda and Lamu – and smaller islets nestled in a sheltered bay midway between the Tana river-mouth and Somali border. Soporific, steeped in Swahili tradition, the islands boast their fair share of idyllic beaches, but their main attractions are cultural and historical. The focal point is Lamu town, whose distinct architecture and a sense of cultural integrity make it unique among comparably sized settlements along the Swahili coast, resulting in its inscription as a UNESCO World Heritage Site in 2001. Visitors are advised not to travel to coastal areas north of Pate and Kiwaiyu due to unrest in Somalia.

Swahili women in their traditional black *bui buis*

**Key**

⎯ Major road

= Minor road

≡≡≡ Unpaved motorable road

– – Trail

0 kilometres    5

0 miles    5

**★ Nabahani Ruins**
The Lamu Archipelago, in particular Manda and Pate islands, is dotted with Islamic ruins dating to the prime of the medieval maritime trade along the Swahili coast.

**Lamu Waterfront**
The attractive waterfront is lined by 19th-century houses and shops, most of which are in the traditional Swahili style, spanning two or three storeys and with whitewashed coral-rag walls.

*Malindi 210 km (130 miles)* — Hindi

*Manda Bay*

Mtangawa

Mokowe

Matondoni

Ras Kilindini

Mwana Mariyamu

*Manda Island*

Lamu

Lamu Island

Shela

Kitau

Kipungani

*Lamu Bay*

Kilwe

**KEY**

① **Lamu Island** is the main sightseeing focus of the archipelago.

② **Faza** lies surrounded by the ruins of several mosques, including the beautiful Mbwarashally mosque built in the 18th century.

③ **Kiwaiyu Island** is the smallest and most remote in the archipelago.

**★ Shela Beach**
This attractive beach is the most popular recreational beach on Lamu Island, stretching along miles of semi-deserted coastline.

◀ Striking orange colour of Hell's Kitchen at sunset

### Manda Toto Island
The best snorkelling destination within day-trip distance of Lamu town, Manda Toto is often visited in conjunction with Manda, the larger island that houses the Takwa Ruins.

Ndau Bay
Kiwaiyu Island
Kiwaiyu
Uvondo Island
Ndau Island
Channel
Kiwaiyu Bay
Tundwa
Kisingitini
Bajumwali
Pate Island
Sylph Channel
🄽
isingati Island

### ★ Dhow Trips
The most pleasant way of getting between Lamu, Manda, Pate and the smaller islands is by the traditional dhows that have sailed along the Swahili coast for centuries.

## Getting Around

The first destination of most visitors to the archipelago, Lamu town, which has plenty of hotels and eateries, can easily be explored on foot (aside from donkeys, no practical alternative exists). Shela is within reasonable walking distance of Lamu, but other sites on the main island are only accessible by donkey or dhow. Motorized dhows run daily between Lamu town and Pate Island, requiring that at least one night be spent on Pate. Those with limited time can charter private dhows to visit either Manda or Pate, usually as a day trip.

### Siyu
The largest structure on Pate Island, Siyu Fort was built in the mid-19th century to protect what was then one of the most important sultanates on the Swahili coast from Omani occupation. The town diminished greatly in importance since it was absorbed into the Omani Sultanate of Zanzibar in 1863.

**For keys to symbols** *see back flap*

# Exploring Lamu and Manda Islands

Most visitors to the archipelago base themselves in Lamu town, which is serviced by scheduled flights from Nairobi, Mombasa and Malindi. All flights land at the airstrip on Manda Island, from where motorized dhows ferry visitors across the channel to Lamu itself. It is worth dedicating at least one full day to the old town of Lamu, which is easily explored on foot. It is also possible to walk or catch a dhow ferry to nearby Shela without making prior arrangements. Other excursions are best organized a day in advance through a hotel or local guide. The most popular day option is the snorkelling trip to Manda Toto and the Takwa Ruins by motorized dhow, followed by the donkey excursion to Matondoni.

The minaret of the Friday Mosque towering over Shela town

## Lamu Island

Separated from the tiny mainland port of Mokowe by a 3-km- (2-mile-) wide channel, Lamu Island takes its name from the eponymous town on its eastern shore. The Lamu archipelago's largest settlement, **Lamu** *(see pp252–3)* seems at once an anachronism and oddly cosmopolitan in mood, having adapted to tourism without sacrificing too much of the time-warped atmosphere on which its charm relies.

A 30–45-minute walk from Lamu town, and connected to it by regular passenger dhows, **Shela** overlooks the archipelago's most accessible and popular beach. A fabulous arc of bone-white sand, Shela Beach runs for more than 10 km (6 miles) in the other direction to town. Swimming here is generally safe, even though it is one of the few Kenyan beaches to lack a protective reef. However, it is inadvisable to wander alone along the beach too far out of

view as occasional muggings are reported. The main focus of beachfront tourist activity is the upmarket **Peponi Hotel** *(see p367)* at the east end of Shela, which has been in the same family for 40 years. There are also a couple of other restaurants dotted along the sandy shore.

Shela village itself is a far more venerable settlement than its modest proportions might seem to indicate. Founded around 400 years ago by refugees from the ruined city of **Takwa** on Manda Island, it is the site of two important mosques. Most striking is the whitewashed **Friday Mosque**, whose conical minaret, built in 1829, towers to a height of 18 m (59 ft) above the surrounding houses, and has an internal spiral stairwell of 58 steps. Separated from this tall edifice by a sand dune, the disused **Wa Deule Mosque** has an intricately carved mihrab dated to 1848.

A popular day trip from Lamu town, the small village of **Matondoni** is most easily reached on donkeyback, following a flat path across the island's dry interior to the mainland-facing shore. The village's cluster of brick and thatch huts bears little resemblance to the archipelago's more ostentatious settlements, but it is an important centre of dhow building, and the local residents are willing to demonstrate this and other traditional crafts to visitors. On the whole, a visit to Matondoni is one of the instances where the journey is more memorable

The scenic and tranquil waters of Shela Beach

The unusual pillar tomb at the Friday Mosque, Takwa Ruins

than the destination, with the added bonus of observing interesting birdlife in the form of colourful rollers and bee-eaters that hawk from the low coastal shrub.

**Kipungani**, a village with a population of 300 people, lies on the far southwestern shore of Lamu Island, overlooking the mangrove-lined channel that divides the island from the mainland. The main attraction here is **Kipungani Explorer** *(see p367)*, which ranks among the most wonderfully remote upmarket beach retreats anywhere in Kenya. Its clients are generally ferried direct by motorized dhow from the airstrip on Manda Island or from Lamu town. There would be nothing preventing independent travellers from heading to Kipungani by donkey or dhow, but tourist facilities are limited.

Passenger dhow in Lamu town

**Shela**
3 km (2 miles) SE of Lamu town.

**Matondoni**
7 km (4 miles) W of Lamu town.

**Kipungani**
10 km (6 miles) SW of Lamu town.

**Manda Island**
2 km (1 mile) E of Lamu.
Separated from Lamu town by a mile-wide channel, Manda, the smallest of the archipelago's three main islands, is the site of Lamu's only airstrip. The island is

otherwise practically uninhabited due to the absence of potable water. It was not so 500 years ago, however, when the Swahili trading centre of Takwa stood on the narrowest part of the island, a site that was probably chosen for defensive reasons, as the surrounding shallow water would have made it difficult for a hostile ship to approach in safety. It is thought that the city was abandoned in the early 17th century, due to the increased salinity of the water supply and ongoing fighting with the rival port of Pate *(see p254)*. The substantial **Takwa Ruins** can still be visited on the far side of the island to Lamu, about 5 km (3 miles) from the airstrip, and include a striking Friday Mosque with a large pillar tomb rising from its wall. The tomb is probably that of an important

sheikh, and it remains the site of a biannual pilgrimage from Shela, many of whose inhabitants claim descent from the 17th-century Takwa refugees.

**Manda Toto**, literally "child of Manda", is a small uninhabited coral island that juts out from the channel dividing Manda from the mainland. Surrounded by reefs, it is easily the best snorkelling site in the Lamu area, with a plethora of colourful reef fish likely to be seen alongside more occasional visitors such as the immense whale shark, schools of dolphin and marine turtles.

An important nesting site for marine birds, the island is most easily visited by dhow together with the Takwa Ruins as part of a day package from Lamu town.

**Takwa Ruins**
**Open** 9:30am–6pm daily.
**W** museums.or.ke

A secluded beach at Manda Toto, off the northeast coast of Manda

# Lamu: Old Town

If any one place represents a clear continuum between the Swahili coast past and present, it is Lamu, whose old town has changed little since the 18th century, and whose profusion of traditional architecture makes it the best-preserved of East Africa's old Swahili towns. Lamu homesteads typically rise to two or three storeys, featuring shaded inner courtyards and verandas, elaborately carved wooden doors and high plastered ceilings supported by poles of mangrove timber. The town is a compact labyrinth of alleyways and whitewashed buildings that lends itself to pedestrian exploration. The maze of alleys can be disorientating, but the predictable terrain, sloping towards the waterfront, makes it impossible to be lost for very long.

**Riyadha Mosque**
Built by the Yemenite settler Sharif Habib Salih in 1900, this is the most prestigious mosque in Lamu and an important pilgrimage site during the Maulidi festival.

Riyadha Mosque

① German Post Office Museum

②

**★ Lamu Fort**
Built between 1813 and 1821 with the assistance of Sultan Seyyid Sa'id of Oman, this imposing two-storey stone structure now doubles as a community centre and a museum and gallery.

0 metres       50
0 yards        50

### KEY

① **The German Post Office Museum** was established in 1888 to service the German Protectorate at Witu.

② **Pwani Mosque**, founded circa 1370, is the oldest of Lamu's 23 mosques, although nothing of the original building remains now.

**Harambee Avenue**
This avenue ran along the seafront prior to the mid-19th century. It is now the busiest thoroughfare through Lamu, and is lined with small shops, boutiques, cafés and restaurants.

**Swahili House Museum**
This restored 18th-century house, centred around a typical Lamu courtyard, is furnished in period style, with ornate hardwood furniture and four-poster beds.

**Lamu Donkey Sanctuary**
The sanctuary was set up by the International Donkey Protection Trust to treat the island's working donkeys.

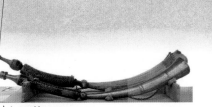

★ **Lamu Museum**
Built in 1891 as a residence for colonial governors, Lamu Museum houses a selection of traditional Swahili musical instruments, notably two ancient Siwa horns. It also has displays on the historical evolution of Lamu town, and non-Swahili coastal cultures such as the pastoralist Orma and Pokomo.

★ **Lamu Waterfront**
The 2-km- (1-mile-) long waterfront took its present shape in the mid-19th century as a result of land infill. It is very pleasant to stroll along it or relax at one of the laid-back restaurants and watch the traditional dhows sail past.

# Exploring Pate Island

The other principal island in the Lamu Archipelago, Pate, is notable for its three small towns that are as time-warped and absorbing as any in East Africa. Travelling to this island from Lamu can be a challenging experience as it remains resolutely off the beaten track. While there is a regular motorized ferry to Pate, the Mkanda Channel between the islands is accessible only during high tide. It takes between two and three hours to reach Mtangwanda, from where it is about an hour's walk to Pate town. It takes an additional five hours by ferry to arrive at Faza. No formal accommodation exists on the island, although it is relatively straightforward to arrange to stay in a local homestead.

The imposing Siyu Fort sitting dramatically on the waterfront

## Pate Island

**Road Map** F5. 32 km (20 miles) NE of Lamu. 🚌 Siyu Fort: **Open** 8am–6pm daily. 🚫 📷 💳 🌐 **museums.or.ke**

East Africa's oddest urban anachronism, Pate town was founded in the 9th century by Omani refugees and peaked in influence during the 12th to 15th centuries under the Nabahani dynasty. The "modern" town centre, which rises phoenix-like from the more expansive ruins of its medieval precursor, took shape in the 18th century, when Pate enjoyed a second golden age as a prosperous centre of Swahili arts and crafts. Today, Pate has the disorientating labyrinthine quality of a traditional city centre. However, when viewed from the rooftops of its characteristic three-storey stone buildings, it becomes clear that this urban enclave consists of no more than 100 houses, isolated on one side by thick mangroves, and on

the rest by tall palms rising from the crumbling walls of the Nabahani Ruins.

About 8 km (5 miles) north of Pate town, the modern town of **Siyu** is less architecturally impressive than Pate, but has a welcoming atmosphere. Little more than a century ago Siyu was described as "the pulse of the whole district" by Fredrick Holmwood, Vice Consul of Zanzibar. Only 50 years before that it was a renowned centre of Islamic scholarship, whose population of 20,000 remained aloof from regional political machinations until the Omani occupation of 1847, and only succumbed to Omani rule in 1863.

The outskirts of the town are dotted with ancient walls and imposing tombs, but the most notable building is the partially ruined **Siyu Fort**, constructed in the mid-19th century to safeguard the town from Omani attacks. Further afield, about a 45-minute walk from the town, are the sprawling but elusive

**Shanga Ruins**, containing more than 100 homesteads and 300 tombs dating from the 11th century. These are best visited with a local guide.

Located on the northern shore of Pate Island, **Faza** is its largest town and dates to medieval times. The island boasts relatively few antiquities, having been razed to the ground during a military attack by Pate in the 15th century and again by a 650-strong Portuguese army from Goa a century later. The site was briefly settled by the Portuguese, who built a church here, though no trace of it remains today. The town was revived as a Swahili trade centre in the 18th century, when the Shala Fatani Mosque, now an architecturally intriguing ruin, was built.

Faza has been haunted by periodic fire outbreaks. In 1990 a fire nearly destroyed the settlement, and again in 2009 another disastrous fire destroyed more than 430 houses and all but reduced the town to rubble. Most of the mud and thatched dwellings have now been rebuilt. Despite its physical state, Faza is important as the district headquarter for Pate Island and some of the mainland. It has a bank, post office, school, police station and several shops. A hospital with a theatre has removed the need for the 4-hour boat trip to Lamu in emergencies. It is possible to walk to neighbouring villages on the northeast tip of the island from Faza, including Kisingitini which is the main fishing port on Pate.

*Makuti-*roofed houses flanked by palm trees, Siyu

# Dhows of the Swahili Coast

There are few sights more characteristic of East Africa's Swahili coast than that of a traditional fishing dhow sailing past the shore, white sail billowing in the wind, as it might have done at any time in the past thousand or so years of trade with Arabia. It may come as a surprise to learn that the term dhow – applied by Europeans to practically any traditional East African seafaring vessel – is neither Arabic in origin, nor is it used in Kiswahili to describe a specific type of boat. More likely, dhow is a corruption of *não*, a Portuguese term that covers any small local seafaring vessel, possibly via the Swahili *kidau*, a particular type of small boat.

**Most large dhows** are now powered with motors in addition to or instead of sails.

**The sail**, when not in use, is rolled up to rest at a 90-degree angle to the mast.

### Sailing Vessels

*Dhows range in size from small fishing craft to large ocean-going vessels. The international nature of coastal trade is reflected in their names –* dengiya, *for instance, is thought to be the root of the English word dinghy, while the* jahazi's *alternative name of* jalbut *derives from the English "jolly boat" or Indian "gallevat".*

**The *jahazi*,** the largest traditional sailing vessel to remain in wide use in East Africa, has changed little in design since medieval times. It measures up to 20 m (66 ft) and is used to carry cargo or up to 100 passengers across long tracts of open water.

**The *mashua*,** smaller than a *jahazi* but similar in appearance, design and purpose, measures up to 10 m (33 ft) from bow to stern. It typically has a capacity of 25 passengers and is used for offshore fishing expeditions, as well as for long-distance transport between ports.

**The dugout-like *mtumbwi*,** used to fish in protected waters, is the most rudimentary boat used on the Swahili coast. It is made from a hollowed tree trunk, a design replicating the very first boats crafted by humans.

**The *ngalawa*** consists of a long dugout supported by two narrow outriggers, a design that is sufficiently stable to be propelled by a sail in calm conditions. Unsuitable for the open sea, it is mainly used by local fishermen in protected waters.

# SOUTHERN RIFT VALLEY AND MASAI MARA

The classic African savannah of the Southern Rift Valley and Masai Mara forms the heart of Kenya's popular safari industry. Superb Big Five viewing is practically guaranteed in the Masai Mara, home to the country's densest wildlife populations, while the Southern Rift Valley also offers plentiful wildlife viewing in a setting of blackened volcanic outcrops, severe basalt cliffs and sparkling lakes.

Widely regarded to be the cradle of mankind, the East African Rift – part of an immense tectonic chasm that stretches from the Red Sea to the Zambezi river – is scattered with a wealth of paleontological sites associated with our earliest hominid ancestors. These ancient soils have supported human habitation for millions of years, most recently by the pastoral Maasai, who migrated into the area in the 18th century, and whose ferocity in battle ensured it was one of the last parts of East Africa to be explored by Europeans.

Staunchly traditionalist, the Maasai today adhere to pastoralist ways. Elsewhere, much of the Southern Rift Valley is given over to large-scale agriculture, while smaller pockets of land are protected in a network of national reserves. Urbanization levels are low and towns are mostly very small, the only obvious exception being Nakuru, the country's fourth-largest city.

The main attractions of this dramatic stretch of the Rift are its natural assets. The Rift Valley floor supports a quintet of beautiful lakes, ranging from freshwater Naivasha and Baringo, with their profusion of fish, hippo and birds, to alkaline Bogoria and Nakuru, whose hyper-saline waters host up to two million flamingoes. For wildlife, the Masai Mara, most rewarding over August–October when migrant wildebeest swarm across its hills, offers peerless big-cat sightings, while Lake Nakuru National Park is a stronghold for flamingoes and the endangered rhino.

A hot-spring fountain at Loburu, on the shore of Lake Bogoria

◄ Hot-air balloon carrying tourists over the Masai Mara at dawn

# The Maasai

The archetypal East African pastoralists, the Maasai migrated from the Sudanese Nile to the Kenya–Tanzania border area in the 18th century. A reputation as fearsome warriors ensured that the Maasai were avoided by the slave caravans and European explorers who penetrated the interior in the 19th century. European settlement brought disaster in the form of a rinderpest epidemic that killed most of the Maasai's cattle and caused large tracts of their territory to be made into game reserves and settler farms. The central unit of Maasai society is the age-set, which changes every 15 years or so following the initiation of a new generation of *ilmoran* (warriors).

Maasai woman adorned with colourful beaded jewellery

**The calabash** is made from the pod of a sausage tree.

**Multicoloured jewellery** offsets the bright shawls worn by the Maasai people.

**The spiralled horn of a greater kudu**, an antelope that is now rare in Kenya, is used to summon the next generation of *ilmoran* to the Eunoto ceremony that marks their coming of age as warriors.

## Maasai Groups

*Social interaction between neighbouring families and distant relations is integral to Maasai culture, since their communities – like those of other pastoralists – tend to be more dispersed than their agricultural cousins. During key events such as Eunoto, families belonging to the same clan will travel long distances to be present at the initiation of an* ilmoran, *carrying a range of gifts for the celebrations.*

**A Shuka** is the red robe worn by Maasai men.

**Family wealth** is measured in terms of children and cattle – a herd of 50 cattle is respectable, the more offspring the better, and a man with plenty of one but not the other is considered poor. This means that even inherently wealthy families live on the poverty line – most have several children and converting a household's cattle to cash would demean its standing.

**Every teenage boy** must undergo initiation by circumcision before being accepted as an *ilmoran*. This ritual is performed without anaesthetic. Should the initiate cry out, his post-circumcision ceremony is cancelled and he will be rejected by his peers for several years before being forgiven.

**Bleeding the cattle** is a tradition practised by the Maasai. Blood, drained painlessly and harmlessly from a nick in the cow's jugular vein, is mixed with milk and fermented in a calabash for several days before being drunk. This is the main diet of the Maasai who feed almost exclusively off their cattle, shunning wildlife, vegetable matter or fish.

**Sticks** are used as defence against animals and for ritual stick fights.

**Beef** is seldom eaten by the Maasai, as a living cow is more valuable to them than a dead one. However, a cow will be slaughtered, grilled and eaten – with immense relish – on special occasions.

**Ochre dye** is used to redden the hair of the Maasai.

**Maasai dancing** resembles pogoing and an individual's skill is measured by how high the dancer is able to jump.

**Slipper-like shoes** are made of leather, or sometimes rubber from old car tyres.

**Maasai warriors** are easily recognizable, with their toga-like red *shuka*, ochre hair styled in a manner that has been compared to a Roman helmet, earlobes cut away from the main part of the ear, and trademark wooden poles or spears.

### Ol Doinyo L'Engai

The Maasai believe in a single deity called Engai, but it possesses a dualistic nature, characterized as the benevolent Engai Narok (Black God) and vengeful Engai Nanyokie (Red God). This deity is said to live on the Tanzanian shore of Lake Natron in the crater of Ol Doinyo L'Engai (Mountain of God), a volcano that most recently erupted in 2008.

The Ol Doinyo volcano spewing red-hot lava

# The Maasai Manyatta

The Maasai customarily live in family compounds known as *manyattas*. A single *manyatta* will normally be inhabited by a nuclear family, which can amount to many dozens of people. As Maasai society is polygamous, an elder can take as many wives as he can afford and father as many children as possible. Conventionally, a Maasai man of the active *ilmoran* (warrior) age-set is forbidden from marrying or from starting his own *manyatta* until the next *ilmoran* generation is initiated, when he and his peers – typically in their early to mid-30s – become junior elders, the group responsible for political and legislative decisions. Women, by contrast, are usually married off in their teenage years, leading to a large age discrepancy between a man and his wives.

Children peeking from the doorway of a traditionally constructed hut

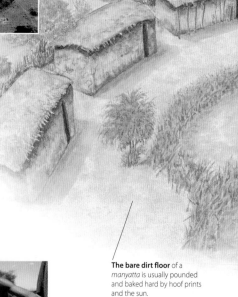

The **manyatta** is often set amid acacia trees.

The **manyatta** is normally designed to form a circular pattern for defence purposes. Huts are arranged around the perimeter to guard the livestock pens in the centre.

## The Manyatta Layout

*The* manyatta *typically consists of a protective outer fence made of spiked branches or euphorbia trees. Within this lies an outer circle of huts, one of which is reserved for the man of the family and one apiece for each of his wives and their younger offspring. The stock pens form the inner circle, affording maximum protection to the precious cattle and goats.*

The **bare dirt floor** of a *manyatta* is usually pounded and baked hard by hoof prints and the sun.

**Making fire** is part of the immense bush craft of the Maasai. Rural *manyattas* still depend less on shop-bought gadgets than on traditional techniques such as the impressive feat of starting a fire simply by rubbing two sticks together furiously until they spark.

**Traditional Maasai huts**, with some regional variations, are typically made by first creating a frame of strong sticks. The huts are then plastered with smooth mud or mud mixed with grass. The low flat ceilings are usually made with thatch, although these too may be regularly strengthened with the mud mixture.

**The thatched roof** of a Maasai hut is usually low and flat.

**A single entrance** is guarded by *ilmoran* at night to prevent cattle rustling and predation by lions.

**Cooking** is done by the women in a chimney-free hut that is easily recognized by its smoky smell. The classic Maasai diet is strongly centred on protein derived from cows and other livestock and is usually supplemented by *ugali* (maize porridge) and other local staples.

**Stock pens**, like the outer walls, are made with acacia and other thorny branches.

**Tending livestock** is a job for boys that have yet to become *ilmoran*. Younger children look after goats and sheep, while teenagers are given the far greater responsibility of cattle-herding. Even today, many Maasai households prefer their children to tend livestock than to attend school.

**Cattle are milked usually by the women**, either in the early morning before the cattle are taken out to graze for the day or in late afternoon after they are brought back. Milk and cattle blood form an important part of the Maasai diet, but it is regarded as insulting to the cattle to consume milk and meat – the living and the dead – on the same day.

# Exploring Southern Rift Valley and Masai Mara

Apart from the great draw of the wildlife-rich Masai Mara National Reserve, this region is most popular for its lakes, in particular Naivasha and Nakuru. The former has superb birdlife and offers the exciting opportunity to hike or cycle unguided through the spectacular plains at Hell's Gate, while the latter is famous for its large flocks of flamingoes and the near certainty of close-up encounters with rhinos. Lakes Bogoria and Baringo are equally popular for their relaxed atmosphere and varied birdlife. Located near the scenic Naivasha Road, Mount Longonot National Park is pedestrian-friendly and offers a unique perspective on the region's turbulent geological past. Further north, excavated sites at Hyrax Hill and Kariandusi offer a glimpse of hominid history.

A tusker on the eastern plains of the Masai Mara

Flamingoes feeding beside an erupting geyser, Lake Bogoria

## Getting Around

The main road through the Southern Rift Valley is the A104, which connects Nairobi to Nakuru via Naivasha. It is well served by buses and *matatus*, but the little-used railway service has been discontinued. From Nakuru, the B4 is a good surfaced road running north to Baringo, with sufficient public transport. The B3/C12 to Masai Mara via Narok runs south from the A104. Given that it is one of the busiest tourist routes in the country, this road is appallingly corrugated in parts, and flying is a better option. Public transport to Masai Mara extends along the B3 up to Narok, from where private transport is required to complete the last leg of the journey.

*For hotels and restaurants see pp367–9 and p380*

One of the towering cliffs of Hell's Gate National Park

0 km    20

0 miles    20

## Sights at a Glance

### Towns

**1** Narok
**6** Naivasha
**12** Nakuru

### Parks and Reserves

**2** *Masai Mara National Reserve
pp266–9*
**5** Mount Longonot National Park
**8** *Hell's Gate National Park
pp274–5*
**9** Kigio Wildlife Conservancy
**15** *Lake Nakuru National Park
pp280–83*

### Areas of Natural Beauty

**3** Mau Escarpment
**4** The Naivasha Road
**7** *Lake Naivasha pp270–73*
**11** Lake Elmenteita
**14** Menengai Crater
**16** *Lakes Bogoria and Baringo
pp284–7*

### Archaeological Sites

**10** Kariandusi Prehistoric Site
**13** Hyrax Hill Prehistoric Site

**For keys to symbols** *see back flap*

### Key

— Major road
== Minor road
≡≡ Untarred major road
== Untarred minor road
-- 4WD track
— Major railway
— Minor railway
▬ International border
△ Peak

# ❶ Narok

**Road Map** B5. 140 km (87 miles) W of Nairobi along the B3.  40,000.

This small but fast-growing district capital is the last town of substance along the main road from Nairobi to Masai Mara National Reserve. It is named after the Enkare Narok River (meaning "black water") that flows through the town. The population of this area is mostly transient as most inhabitants are the nomadic Maasai. The Narok County Council, not the KWS, administers the Masai Mara and it is the council that levies entrance fees and employs wardens and rangers in the reserve. A popular refuelling and refreshment stop, Narok offers good facilities, including the last bank and ATM. On the Mara side of town, the Kenol Filling Station, where most tour groups stop for a few minutes, has well-stocked curio and grocery shops and an efficient garden restaurant.

Narok's most prominent, indeed only, attraction for visitors is the **Narok Museum**. Housed in a former community centre on Narok's eastern outskirts, it has several displays relating to Kenya's Maa-speaking people, which include the Maasai, Samburu and Njemps. These include some exceptional ethnographic portraits painted by Joy Adamson in the early 1950s, along with a gallery of more recent photographs taken with disposable cameras by Maasai women to depict day-to-day events in the *manyattas* (*see pp260–61*).

🏛 **Narok Museum**
Signposted at entrance to Narok coming from Nairobi. **Tel** 020 2014533. **Open** 9am–6pm daily.
**museums.or.ke**

# ❷ Masai Mara National Reserve

*See pp266–9.*

Tracts of farmland and forest at the western edge of Mau Escarpment

# ❸ Mau Escarpment

**Road Map** B4.

Rising to an altitude of 3,100 m (10,170 ft), this rather inaccessible mountain range runs for more than 100 km (60 miles) along the western Rift Valley Escarpment north of Narok. Seldom visited, the Mau Escarpment is one of East Africa's greatest ecological treasure houses. Its crest supports the region's largest existing block of montane forest, extending over 900 sq km (348 sq miles), and is home to the only remaining wild population of mountain bongo outside Aberdare National Park (*see pp320–21*). Other rare or localized forest dwellers include the yellow-backed duiker, golden cat, giant forest hog, black-and-white colobus and a primate known as the potto. About 173 montane bird species have been recorded, several with very localized distributions.

With its heavy rainfall, the Mau Escarpment is an important watershed, feeding dozens of streams and rivers that eventually empty into Lakes Victoria, Nakuru and Natron. Five forest reserves have been gazetted and a sixth earmarked for the future. Mau is a stronghold for Kenya's oldest ethnic group, the Okiek, who have traditionally practised a sustainable hunter-gatherer lifestyle within these forests. Since colonial times, however, their presence has been perceived to be at odds with conservation, leading to several controversial, and so far only partially successful, attempts to evict them from the forests their ancestors inhabited for millennia.

# ❹ The Naivasha Road

**Road Map** C5.

The main road from Nairobi to Naivasha (the A104) and Nakuru is one of the busiest in Kenya. The scenic 90-km (56-mile) drive normally takes about 90 minutes. The largest town on the way is **Limuru**, birthplace of Kikuyu novelist Ngũgĩ wa Thiong'o (*see p40*), and site of the country's largest shoe factory. This breezy highland town lies off the main road, and the principal draw here is a large swampy reservoir to the right of the road. The reservoir is a rewarding place for those who are interested in waders and other waterbirds.

The spectacular descent into the Rift Valley starts a few kilometres past Limuru, and it is de rigueur to stop at one of several viewpoints offering

A diorama of Maasai life at Narok Museum

The vast northern slopes of Mount Longonot rising dramatically from the Rift Valley floor

fabulous panoramic views over a stretch of the valley floor dominated by the dormant volcanoes **Longonot** and **Suswa**. Several curio stalls along the route offer a wide range of items, white sheepskins being the local speciality.

## ❺ Mount Longonot National Park

**Road Map** C5. 60 km (37 miles) NW of Nairobi, entrance at Longonot village on the old Naivasha Rd. 🚌 **Open** 6am–6pm daily (though it is inadvisable to attempt the ascent after 2pm). 🅿️ 📷 🅦 kws.org

This 52-sq-km (20-sq-mile) park protects the majestic Mount Longonot, a dormant volcano that rises sharply from the Rift Valley floor southeast of Lake Naivasha to an altitude of 2,776 m (9,108 ft). Dominating the landscape for miles around, Longonot last erupted in the 1860s, and until recently its floor was alive with steam vents, although this evidence of subterranean activity appears to have declined of late. Longonot derives from the Maasai name Olo Nong'ot, meaning "mountain of many spurs", a reference to the dozens of deep ravines incised into the ashy soil of the starkly vegetated slopes.

For visitors who are fairly fit, Mount Longonot is ideal for a wonderful day hike, although the lack of cover makes it advisable to leave in the early morning to avoid overexposure to the sun. The ascent from the park entrance gate to the crater rim takes about 90 minutes, and is best undertaken in the company of a ranger. En route, there is good chance of encountering gazelle, zebra, giraffe and other wildlife. Almost perfectly circular, the caldera is fully intact and the view over its 3-km- (2-mile-) wide forest floor is spectacular, as are the views across the Rift Valley to Naivasha. It is possible to hike the full circumference of the crater rim in 3 to 4 hours, and adventurous travellers have also been known to descend into the crater, although the path down is rather treacherous and the buffalo that inhabit the floor have a reputation for aggression.

## ❻ Naivasha

**Road Map** B4. 90 km (56 miles) NW of Nairobi on the new Naivasha Rd. 🏔️ 182,000. 🚀 🚉 🚌 🅰️ daily. 🎪 Naivasha Horticultural Fair (Sep).

The sprawling market town of Naivasha is most often visited en route from Nairobi to Lake Naivasha (see pp270–73), which is a short drive to the southwest of the town. Naivasha is well-equipped with several filling stations, banks and ATMs, a few reasonably stocked supermarkets, an excellent daily market and the long-serving **La Belle Inn** (see p380), which is at least one highly agreeable spot for an alfresco drink or snack.

Since the late 1980s, the area around Naivasha has flourished as the centre of Kenya's horticulture and floriculture industry for the European export market. The favourable climate, nutrient-rich soil and the ready supply of water for irrigation, are ideal for production of flowers and crops such as green beans and peas. Greenhouses line the lakeshore, and there are more than 55 farms that employ over 30,000 workers. Kenya is the largest supplier of flowers to supermarkets across Europe, and exporting flowers is the country's biggest foreign exchange earner after tourism. Flowers grown include roses, carnations chrysanthemums, and lilies.

The colourful façade of a streetside shop, Naivasha town

# ❷ Masai Mara National Reserve

The 1,510-sq-km (583-sq-mile) Masai Mara National Reserve is Kenya's most celebrated wildlife reserve, and arguably its best. Gazetted in 1968, it is dominated by open grassland, but as implied by the Maasai name Mara, meaning spotted, it is interspersed with rocky hills, acacia woodland and riparian forest. The Mara is rewarding not just for predators such as leopard and cheetah, but spotted hyena, bat-eared fox and black-backed jackal as well. Elephant and buffalo are common, and a number of black rhinos still survive. Other ungulates include impala, eland and reedbuck. A checklist of 450-plus birds includes raptors and ground birds such as ostrich and ground hornbill.

**★ Wildebeest Migration**
The legendary wildebeest migration, which streams across the Mara river from the Serengeti Plains in Tanzania, forms one of the world's greatest wildlife spectacles.

**Cheetahs in the Mara Triangle**
A healthy population of more than 50 cheetah families stalk the reserve's open plains, and regular sightings are to be had in the Mara Triangle.

Oloololo Gate

Musiara Gate

Musiara Swamp

E175

Mara

Esoit Oloololo Escarpment

Olpunyata Swamp

Paradise Plain

Rhino

Lookout Hill

Emarti 1,654 m

E1481

Talek

Burrunga

Ol Keja Ro

E176

Mara

Hippo Pools

TANZAN

**★ Balloon Safaris**
A highlight of any visit to the Masai Mara is an early morning balloon safari, which offers the opportunity to have a bird's-eye view over the plains and their wildlife in the haunting dawn light. Flights are usually rounded off with an alfresco champagne breakfast.

0 kilometres    5

0 miles         5

*For hotels and restaurants see pp367–9 and p380*

**★ Lion Sightings**
An estimated 400 to 500 lions have territories within the Masai Mara and the average pride size is about 20 individuals. This is one of the highest densities anywhere in Africa and good sightings are practically guaranteed daily, especially in the open plains.

## VISITORS' CHECKLIST

**Practical Information**
**Road Map** B5. Sekenani Gate is 265 km (165 miles) SW of Nairobi. **Open** 6:30am–7pm daily. 🚗 🛫
🦁 🏕 🌐 maratriangle.org

### Key

= = Minor road

::::: Unpaved motorable road

– – Park boundary

–·– International boundary

△ Peak

## KEY

① **The South Mara Bridge** connects the eastern and western sectors of the reserve.

② **Eastern Plains** now have all-weather roads with a new route from Talek to Sekenani Gate.

**Hippo Pools**
The Mara river and its various tributaries support several permanent hippo pools, where pods of these engaging beasts can be seen lazing around in the muddy water.

## Getting Around

The road from Nairobi to the Masai Mara makes heavy demands on drivers unused to the local conditions, so it is easiest to visit on an organized fly-in or drive-in safari. Those who prefer the self-drive safari should note that there is only one bridge across the Mara river within the reserve, and one each across the Mara and Talek outside the northern boundary. Seeing the Mara on public transport is not possible. Game viewing is exceptional through the year, but it peaks over August to October during the wildebeest migration.

**Ngama Hills**
Standing out like a beacon from an otherwise rather flat landscape, the Ngama Hills are a useful landmark for those navigating themselves around the unsignposted dirt tracks of the Mara.

**For keys to symbols** *see back flap*

# Exploring the Masai Mara National Reserve

The reserve can be divided into three distinct parts. The eastern sector runs southeast from the Mara and Talek rivers to the Ngama Hills, the central sector lies cupped between these two rivers north of their confluence, and the western sector is flanked by Oloololo Escarpment and the Mara river. The east carries the heaviest traffic, which can detract from the wilderness atmosphere. Bear in mind that game drives are generally confined to the same sector as the lodge or campsite. Visitors with more than 3 nights at their disposal could divide their time between lodges in different sectors. It is easiest to visit the Masai Mara on an organized safari from Nairobi, but self-drive safaris are also an option. However, internal roads are rough and signposts non-existent.

Lionesses keeping watch over their cubs at the Masai Mara National Reserve

### 🦁 Ngama Hills and the Eastern Plains

Accounting for about half of the reserve, the eastern sector of Masai Mara is the closest to Nairobi and the most visited. Dozens of campsites and lodges are set within its boundaries or lie immediately outside them. The most prominent geographical landmark, the quartzite Ngama Hills, tower above the main Sekenani Entrance Gate and are visible from all corners. The smaller Ol Opelagonya and Ololoitikoshi hills both lie in the far southeast towards Ololaimutiek Gate. The rock-strewn grassland of these hills does not support the wildlife volumes associated with the plains below, but its dense thicket patches are a favoured haunt of the reserve's last few dozen remaining black rhino, while the margins harbour buffalo, dik-dik and impala.

The flatter plains that run from the base of the Ngama Hills to the banks of the Mara river form the classic East African landscape of short grassland interspersed with a parsimonious scattering of acacia and other trees. The main roads through this part of the reserve are somewhat rutted and the relatively heavy traffic seems to be a deterrent to wildlife, so it is generally more productive to stick to the maze of regularly intersecting tracks that run between them. Lion and cheetah are common in this area, along with topi, gazelle, eland, ostrich and kori bustard. The park supports a much higher elephant density than expected in such open terrain. On self-drive visits, the distinctive eastern outline of the towering Ngama Hills and the more distant Oloololo Escarpment help visitors maintain their bearings. Other landmarks include the long-serving **Keekerok Lodge** *(see p368)*, which is the launch site for early morning balloon trips. Further south, the seasonal Sand river more or less follows the Tanzanian border west towards its confluence with the Mara. Practically at the border, the South Mara Bridge is the only crossing point between the reserve's eastern and western sectors, and overlooks a hippo pool that is a popular picnic spot.

### 🦁 Mara and Talek Rivers

The Mara river and its tributary the Talek are the only perennial waterways to flow through the Masai Mara National Reserve. Dotted with dozens of deep hippo pools, the Mara river supports a varied aquatic wildlife that includes hippo, crocodile and otter, along with riverine birds such as hamerkop and African darter. The lush ribbon of riparian forest that follows both rivers for much of their length is densely populated with leopard, vervet monkey and bushbuck, as well as a selection of birds that is strikingly different from those in the rest of the park. This includes the brilliantly coloured Schalow's and Ross's turacos and the melodic white-browed robin-chat.

Giant herds of wildebeest staggering across the swift Mara river

Mixed herd of wildebeest and zebra at a waterhole near the eye-catching Oloololo Escarpment

One of the most spectacular events in the Serengeti-Mara migration is the wildebeest crossing of the Mara river. This might happen several times during the migrant wildebeest's 3-month Masai Mara tenure. There are eight major crossing points, of which the four most regularly used lie along a 5-km (3-mile) stretch of the Mara upriver of its confluence with the Talek and overlooked by the **Mara Serena Safari Lodge** (see p368). Often, wildebeest will congregate in their thousands on the banks for days before one impatient individual takes the plunge, triggering a lemming-like stampede that provides rich pickings to the waiting crocodiles. An estimated 3,000 wildebeests perish annually while crossing the Mara, but numbers are readily replenished by the average of 400,000 calves born in the Serengeti every January to February.

### Central Plains

Located in the heart of the reserve and serviced by a handful of upmarket camps, the untrammelled plains of the central Masai Mara – flanked by the Mara river to the west and the Talek to the south – offer exceptionally reliable game viewing, particularly when it comes to big cats. Dominated by a long succession of thick-maned males, the legendary "marsh lion" pride hangs around the grassy verges of **Musiara Swamp** and Governor's Camp, and is habituated to vehicles.

The open grassland around **Paradise Plain** is arguably the best place in Kenya to look for cheetah, while several generations of habituated leopard inhabit the vicinity of **Leopard Gorge**, a short drive outside the reserve from the Musiara Gate. By contrast, the prominent **Rhino Ridge** overlooking Paradise Plain seldom lives up to its name.

Crisscrossed by motorable tracks, the short grass plains north of Rhino Ridge are densely excavated with aardvark holes that now serve as dens to spotted hyena, bat-eared fox and black-backed jackal. Two localized birds associated with this part of the park are Denham's bustard and the lovely rufus-bellied heron that inhabits Musiara Swamp. The central plains are spectacular from August to October when zebra and wildebeest congregate there in their tens of thousands. The best place to view large numbers of hippo and wildebeest – and with luck the occasional river crossing – is **Lookout Hill**, located opposite Serena Lodge.

### Mara Triangle

This most westerly sector of the Masai Mara is also the oldest, having first been gazetted as a 510-sq-km (197-sq-mile) game reserve in the late 1940s. It is the most scenically dramatic part of the reserve, set below the 400-m- (1,312-ft-) tall **Oloololo Escarpment** and studded with isolated granite hills known as koppies. The open grassland supports dense seasonal concentrations of migrant zebra and wildebeest.

The Mara Triangle is good for spotting big cats and other members of the Big Five, although rhino are not very common. Roan antelope and African wild dog were once widespread here, but have not been seen since the late 1980s, although plans are afoot to reintroduce the former from Ruma National Park (see p309), their only extant haunt in Kenya. The Oloololo Escarpment along the western boundary is a good place to spot the dainty klipspringer antelope, the rock hyrax and spectacular Verreaux's eagle.

Cheetah, not so elusive in the Masai Mara National Reserve

# ❼ Lake Naivasha

A popular first stop out of Nairobi, this near-circular and shallow freshwater lake has a beautiful Rift Valley setting, with the distinctive volcanic outline of Mount Longonot rising to the south. The name Naivasha is a corruption of the Maasai *enaiposha* (restless water), in possible reference to the rough waves that often sweep its surface in the afternoon. The Gilgil and Malewa rivers flow into Naivasha's swampy northern shore, but there is no known outlet and the water most probably stays fresh due to a subterranean outlet that emerges at Lake Magadi. First documented by Scottish geologist Joseph Thomson in 1884, the lake typically extends over 130 sq km (50 sq miles) but has experienced several inexplicable fluctuations in level, almost drying out in the late 1940s.

The African fish eagle, a vocal lakeshore resident

**★ Green Crater Lake**
Nestled at the base of a lush volcanic crater, this small, beautiful lake forms the centrepiece of a private wildlife sanctuary whose attractions include colobus monkeys, giraffes and flamingoes.

**Oserengoni Wildlife Sanctuary**
This private sanctuary offers the best game viewing around Naivasha, with naturally occurring populations of leopard, cheetah, plains zebra and various grazers, as well as introduced herds of white rhino and Grevy's zebra.

**★ Elsamere**
This former home of Joy Adamson is now a centre dedicated to the preservation of the lake's ecology, and also offers insights into Adamson's life.

**Key**

=== Minor road

··· Unpaved motorable road

▪ ▪ Park boundary

0 kilometres    2

0 miles    2

*For hotels and restaurants see pp367–9 and p380*

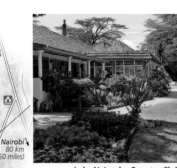

**Crescent Island Game Park**
Originally the rim of an extinct volcanic crater, as can be clearly seen from the air, Crescent Island encloses the deepest part of Lake Naivasha and supports a variety of wildlife, including waterbuck and giraffe.

## VISITORS' CHECKLIST

**Practical Information**
**Road Map** B4. 4 km (2 miles) SE of Naivasha town then SW on the Moi South Lake Rd.

**Transport**

**Lake Naivasha Country Club**
Now a hotel, the club was a popular party venue in the colonial era for the decadent Happy Valley set (see p323).

## Getting Around

The lake is encircled by the Moi South and North Lake roads. The southern road is surfaced for most of its length and serviced by regular public transport. The unsurfaced northern road is erratic in quality, and little traffic runs beyond the entrance to Crater Lake Game Sanctuary. Bicycles are available for rent from the many lakeside camps and are a good way to explore the lake's environs, particularly around Hell's Gate. Weather permitting, boat rides offer a chance to spot birdlife. Visitors are advised not to do the 5-km (3-mile) walk from Kongoni to Crater Lake Game Sanctuary alone.

**★ Bird-watching**
Renowned as one of Kenya's ornithological high points, Lake Naivasha supports around 500 bird species, with large flotillas of the handsome great white pelican being particularly conspicuous.

# Exploring Lake Naivasha

Lake Naivasha is easily reached from Nairobi, although travellers using public transport need to change vehicles in Naivasha town. It is a popular stop on tours to the Masai Mara and an excellent base for freshly landed independent travellers, with enough activities to keep them occupied for several days. Access to the lake is along the surfaced Moi South Lake Road, which runs southwest out of Naivasha town along the southern shore for about 30 km (19 miles) before veering northward as far as Kongoni Junction, where it becomes the Moi North Lake Road. This northern road is unsurfaced and erratic in quality, with little traffic, especially after the entrance gate to Crater Lake Game Sanctuary.

A loose herd of wildebeest grazing on the plains of Crescent Island

## 🦓 Southeastern Shore

Fringed by lush papyrus beds and a fever tree forest giving way to drier plains dotted with euphorbia and acacia scrub, the southeastern shore is the closest part of the lake to Naivasha town. The shore is well developed for tourism, with a number of upmarket hotels, self-catering complexes and campsites. Some of the finest bird-watching in Kenya is along this stretch, and most hotels welcome day visitors. Of particular interest is the stately **Lake Naivasha Country Club** (see p368), which opened in 1937 as a staging post for the flying boat service from the UK to South Africa, and stands in massive lakeshore grounds inhabited by hundreds of bird species, monkeys and hippo. This is a good place to call in for afternoon tea. The club also has

a swimming pool, which is open to club members and casual customers. Visitors may easily see some 30 species of water-associated birds in the space of 10 minutes here. The **Elmenteita Weavers**, stocks a wide selection of beautiful handcrafted tapestries, carpets, clothing and much else besides.

### 🏠 Elmenteita Weavers

8 km (5 miles) SW of Naivasha town on Moi South Lake Road. **Tel** 050 2023011. **Open** 9am–5pm daily. 🏠

### 🏞 Crescent Island Game Park

9 km (6 miles) SW of Naivasha town on Moi South Lake Rd. **Tel** 050 2021030. 🚤 🛥 boat trips are offered by all hotels along the lake's southwestern shore. 🌐 **crescentisland.co**

Shaped rather like a leaping dolphin, Crescent Island Game Park consists of the western rim of an extinct volcanic

caldera whose floor is submerged within Naivasha to form the deepest point of the lake at around 20 m (66 ft). A popular half-day outing, the island is connected to the mainland by a marshy causeway that dries up completely when the lake is low. As there are no predatory animals, visitors are permitted to walk freely among the abundant wildlife, which includes giraffe, zebra, water-buck, Thomson's and Grant's gazelle and buffalo, as well as a profusion of waterbirds.

### 🏛 Elsamere

25 km (14 miles) S of Naivasha town on Moi South Lake Rd. **Tel** 0722 648123. **Open** 9am–6pm daily. 🚤 🛥 ♿ 🖊 🏠 🍽 🌐 **elsamere.com**

The home of Joy Adamson (see p337) from 1966 until she was murdered in Shaba National Reserve in 1980, Elsamere lies on the south-western shore of Naivasha, in pretty landscaped gardens surrounded by a fever tree forest. The house is maintained as a museum with its original furnishings intact. The walls are hung with Adamson's paintings of local tribespeople, and several of her personal possessions are on display, along with a selection of first editions of her books in various languages. Visitors with an hour or two to spare can watch a detailed video dedicated to her life and works. The best time to visit Elsamere is from 2pm when

Tour boats moored at a camp on the Lake Naivasha shore

a lavish afternoon tea is served on the lawns. Homely accommodation is also available.

More than 200 bird species have been recorded in the immediate vicinity, and a troop of the lovely black-and-white colobus monkey passes through the garden frequently, while hippo regularly graze the lawn at night. All proceeds go towards a Field Study Centre established in 1989 to increase ecological awareness among locals.

### Lake Oloiden

27 km (17 miles) SW of Naivasha town on Moi South Lake Rd.
Tel 0702 993131.
oloidencamp.com

Past Elsamere, the Moi South Lake Road passes through a wilder landscape of towering forests of fever trees and spiky euphorbia sloping down towards the alkaline shores of Lake Oloiden. Formerly part of Lake Naivasha, Oloiden is now separated from its southwest shore by a stretch of elevated land. There is plenty of wildlife to be seen from the road here. Giraffe are particularly common, gliding serenely through the trees, as well as zebra, waterbuck and impala. The lovely Oloiden Camp here has grassy tent pitches next to the lakeshore and non-campers can pull in for a drink or a simple meal at the rustic thatched bar overlooking the serene lake.

The emerald waters of Green Crater Lake, Crater Lake Game Sanctuary

### Oserengoni Wildlife Sanctuary

30 km (19 miles) SW of Naivasha town on Moi South Lake Rd.
Tel 050 2020792.
oserengoniwildlife.com

Bordering the road to the west of Lake Naivasha, shadowed by the Mau Escarpment *(see p264)*, is the Oserengoni Wildlife Sanctuary, a 100-sq-km (40-sq-mile) private sanctuary established in 1996 on a former dairy and beef farm and serviced by exclusive accommodation units, including the excellent **Chui Lodge** *(see p368)*.

As a connecting game corridor between Hell's Gate National Park and Lake Naivasha, Oserengoni supports a wide range of wildlife, including leopard, topi, cheetah, buffalo, greater kudu, spotted hyena and various smaller antelope, along with small herds of Grevy's zebra and Beisa oryx introduced from Northern Kenya and a herd of white rhino introduced from Mount Kenya. Some 300 bird species include the largest known population of the endangered grey-crested helmet-shrike. Game drives in open vehicles and exciting bush walks are conducted by well-informed guides. Day visitors are not permitted in the sanctuary.

### Crater Lake Game Sanctuary

5 km (3 miles) NE of Oserengoni on Moi South Lake Rd. Tel 050 2020613.
craterlakecamp.com

A short distance northeast of Oserengoni, this 50-sq-km

(20-sq-mile) fenced sanctuary is one of the underrated gems of the Rift Valley region in Kenya. The reserve's centrepiece is a small but spectacular crater lake whose water is shaded green by a dense concentration of the algae *Spirulina* which, with a pH of 11.5, is too alkaline to support fish or any other subaquatic fauna. Local Maasai call the lake Songasoi (Sterile Bull) in reference to its lifelessness, but they also recognize the algae-rich water as having curative properties for cattle with worms and other intestinal problems.

Overlooked by the wonderful **Crater Lake Tented Camp** *(see p368)*, where day visitors are welcome, the forested crater floor supports a rich assortment of birdlife. Lesser flamingo feed on the lake's algae, with the largest aggregations being present over June–August. Troops of black-and-white colobus monkey are seen from the camp daily, along with vervet monkey, eland, waterbuck and bushbuck. Leopard and spotted hyena are resident in the crater but are seldom observed. An outstanding choice of activities includes guided game walks, bird walks around the crater rim, horseback excursions and game drives by day and night. The property was formerly part of the Ndabibi Estate that belonged to Lady Diana Delamere of *White Mischief* fame, and it contains the hilltop grave where she was buried in 1987.

Luxuriant pastures and forest at the Mau Escarpment

# ❺ Hell's Gate National Park

This most overtly volcanic of Kenyan landscapes is protected within a 68-sq-km (26-sq-mile) national park whose name refers to a dramatic steep-sided valley carved by a former outlet of Lake Naivasha. The region's past geological instability is testified to by ancient lava plugs, steam vents and dormant volcanoes, but it is most popular with visitors for the chance to walk or cycle among big game. Hell's Gate was once famed as a breeding site for the lammergeyer, an endangered cliff-nesting vulture that is now an irregular visitor; however, Egyptian vultures and augur buzzards are often seen soaring above the cliffs. Other cliff-associated wildlife includes rock hyrax, klipspringer and Chanler's mountain reedbuck.

River running through the bottom of Hell's Gate Gorge

**★ Main Cliffs**
The facing pair of 120-m-(394-ft-) tall basaltic cliffs for which Hell's Gate is named are most beautiful in the late afternoon and early morning, when they are burnished by the golden sunlight.

Ol Karia Gate

Ol Koria Geothermal Power Station

Hobley's Volcano

Elkarian Forest

Maib Picn Site

Narasha Gate

Ranger's Post

Oloorkarian Maasai Centre

Ol Njorowa

**★ Cycling Tours**
Hell's Gate is one of the few places in Kenya where it is permitted to cycle or walk unguided through herds of big game – Thomson's gazelle, Grant's gazelle, buffalo, wildebeest, giraffe, impala and eland are all likely to be spotted.

0 kilometres          2

0 miles               2

**Central Tower**
Towering conspicuously above the picnic site at Maiben, the imposing volcanic plug referred to as Central Tower has the more memorable and enigmatic Maasai name of Ol Basta (The Horse). As with other cliffs in the park, it forms a breeding site for several species of raptor.

★ **Fischer's Tower**
The park's most famous landmark is the jagged 25-m- (82-ft-) tall volcanic plug that stands sentinel over Elsa's Gate. A Maasai tradition, reminiscent of the Biblical story of Job, claims the formation to be a petrified bride who defied tradition by looking back at her home before her wedding.

## VISITORS' CHECKLIST

**Practical Information**
Road Map B5. Elsa's Gate is 20 km (12 miles) SW of Naivasha town on Moi South Lake Rd. 
*i* 050 50407 (Park Head-quarters). **Open** 6am–6pm daily.
kws.org
Note: bicycles can be hired from Elsa's Gate Junction.

**Transport**
to within walking distance of entrance gate.

Airstrip
10 km
(6 miles)

Naivasha
20 km (12 miles)

Elsa's Gate

Twiga Loop

Buffalo Circuit

**Key**

=== Unpaved motorable road

— — Park boundary

**Grazing Zebra**
The plains zebra is one of the more conspicuous mammals in Hell's Gate. However, buffalo, giraffe, leopard, cheetah and spotted hyena are also resident, as are baboons and rock hyraxes.

**Obsidian Cave**
Set in a narrow valley at the end of Twiga Loop, Obsidian Cave is named after a type of black igneous rock commonly found in the Rift Valley. This glassy rock, used by early man to create cutting tools, is associated with lava flows that cooled too quickly for crystallization.

## Getting Around

The most rewarding route entails following the 12-km (8-mile) road through the flat valley floor between Elsa's Gate and Maiben, returning the same way. It is a 3-hour walk or 1-hour cycling trip in either direction. A dawn start is recommended for the best game viewing and to avoid over-exposure to the midday sun. It is essential to take along a hat, sunscreen and plenty of drinking water. From Maiben, a 2-km (1-mile) walking trail leads into the lower gorge, which is riddled with steam vents. Cultural tours are available at Oloorkarian Maasai Centre. Visitors with a vehicle could continue west from Maiben to the little-visited Ol Koria Geothermal Power Station, and explore the eastern Twiga Loop.

**For keys to symbols** *see back flap*

## ❾ Kigio Wildlife Conservancy

**Road Map** B4. 20 km (12 miles) NW of Naivasha. **Tel** 020 7606015. 🦁 📷 🚐 🌐 **kigio.com**

Formerly a cattle ranch, this small fenced wildlife conservancy lies alongside the Malewa river a few kilometres before it empties into Lake Naivasha. Its cover of tangled acacia scrub interspersed with open grassland supports a wide variety of naturally occurring and introduced wildlife such as zebra, waterbuck warthog and eland. A herd of eight endangered Rothschild's giraffes, translocated from Lake Nakuru in 2003, has since bred and now number about 30. The conservancy is served by two lodges including the **Malewa Wildlife Lodge** (see p367), which fronts onto the Malewa river. The absence of dangerous wildlife means that guided walks are offered along with the usual day and night game drives.

## ❿ Kariandusi Prehistoric Site

**Road Map** B4. 30 km (18 miles) NW of Naivasha. 🚐 **Open** 9:30am–6pm daily. 🦁 📷 🏔 🌐 **museums.or.ke**

Excavated by Louis Leakey (see p353) from 1928 to 1931, Kariandusi was inhabited by Stone Age people between one million and 700,000 years ago, when it probably stood alongside the shore of a vast lake that encompassed the present-day Lakes Naivasha, Elmenteita and Nakuru. Hundreds of bolas, Acheulean hand-axes and several other stone artifacts have been unearthed at the site, which may have served as a workshop for the production of tools. Most of the tools are made from lava rocks sourced in situ, but cutting tools were fashioned from sharp-edged obsidian glass transported from nearby Mount Eburu.

A guided tour of the site takes around half an hour, and requires a fair degree of mobility. The small site museum is also worth a visit. Alongside a

Secluded Lake Elmenteita, one of the Rift Valley's soda lakes

tour of Kariandusi, it is possible to visit a diatomite quarry. Diatomite is a soft silica-based rock composed of a layer of diatoms, microscopic shelled algae that were deposited on the floor of the extinct lake and then compressed to form a chalky strata of crumbly white rock. It is mined for use as a water filter and insecticide.

Stone axe, Kariandusi Prehistoric Site

## ⓫ Lake Elmenteita

**Road Map** B4. 3 km (2 miles) E of Kariandusi on the opposite side of the Naivasha–Nakuru Rd. **Tel** 0711 235039. 🚐 📷 🚐 🌐 **soysambu conservancy.org**

The smallest of Kenya's Rift Valley lakes, the 18-sq-km (7-sq-mile) Elmenteita lies within the privately owned Delamere Estate. Part of the estate is made up of the **Soysambu Conservancy**, which covers 198 sq km (76 sq miles) of lightly wooded hills and three-quarters of the lake's shoreline. This area is home to more than

15,000 heads of hoofed game, including the Rothschild's giraffe and 450 species of birds, and the lake's shallows often host a large concentration of both lesser and greater flamingos. Elmenteita is the only breeding ground in East Africa for great white pelican, which nest on rocky islands in the lake.

The conservancy is accessible if you are staying at one of the small camps or lodges on the eastern shoreline. However, from the main Nakuru Road there are adequate viewpoints over Elmenteita, as well as to the striking volcanic outcrops that the Maasai refer to as **Elngirigata Ol Morani** (Sleeping Warrior), and the colonials nicknamed "Delamere's Nose", after the British aristocrat who founded the estate in 1906.

## ⓬ Nakuru

**Road Map** B4. 70 km (44 miles) NW of Naivasha. 👥 310,000. 🚖 🚌 🚐

Few visitors spend any time in Kenya's fourth-largest city, preferring instead to head straight to the adjacent Lake Nakuru National Park (see pp280–83). However, Nakuru is a pleasant town, and quite attractive in November when its jacaranda-lined avenues bloom purple below a mountainous horizon. It has good facilities, including a number of banks, ATMs, Internet cafés, restaurants, hotels and shops. There is also a very lively daily market in front of the railway station. Students

A diatomite mine cut into the hillside below Kariandusi Prehistoric Site

An early morning view across Menengai Crater near Nakuru

of colonial architecture will find rich pickings in this town around the junction of Moi and Kenyatta avenues. They should also make an effort to seek entry into the members-only **Rift Valley Sport Club**. Built in 1907 on Club Road, this place still has an Edwardian smoking-room atmosphere. Aside from the national park, the town is also a good base for visits to Hyrax Hill and Menengai Crater.

### ⑬ Hyrax Hill Prehistoric Site

**Road Map** B4. 4 km (3 miles) E of Nakuru, clearly signposted. **Tel** 051 2217175. **Open** 9:30am–6pm daily. **museums.or.ke**

Named after the rock hyraxes that once thrived here, this important Neolithic site on the outskirts of Nakuru was discovered by paleontologist Louis Leakey in 1926 and excavated by his wife Mary Leakey starting in 1937. It was inhabited between 5,000 and 2,000 years ago and has thrown up some of the region's oldest Iron Age artifacts, including metal tools and iron bracelets, along with cutting instruments fashioned from glass-like obsidian rock. A more recent occupation, within the last millennium, is represented by the hollowed floors of the Sirikwa tribe's cattle pens. More difficult to date are the 13 *bao* games that have been cut into rocks on the site. *Bao* is a highly complex game that involves

shifting small pebbles between indentations on a wooden board or, in this case, a rock. It has been played throughout Africa for millennia, so these carved examples could as easily be 100 years old as they might be several thousand.

A Neolithic burial mound on the site contains 19 decapitated male skeletons, probably the remains of warriors who were killed in battle and given a ceremonial burial. A small site **museum** displays various artifacts from this and other Rift Valley sites.

### ⑭ Menengai Crater

**Road Map** B4. The rim is 8 km (5 miles) from Nakuru town centre along Menengai Drive and Crater Climb.

The gently sloping mountain on Nakuru's northern horizon is Menengai, a massive shield volcano that rises to an altitude

of 2,278 m (7,474 ft) from the Rift Valley floor. The spectacular nested caldera at its summit is one of the largest in the world, with an average diameter of 8 km (5 miles); it is nearly 500 m (1,640 ft) deep in places. The rim is accessible by a rough dirt road out of Nakuru, which offers superb views across the crater and back towards Lake Nakuru. The presence of fumaroles, cinder cones and steam vents on the crater floor indicate that the volcano is dormant rather than extinct, although geological evidence suggests that it has not erupted within the last 6,000 years, and the relict lava flows on its flanks support a fair cover of vegetation.

The origin of the Maasai name Menengai is disputed. It can be translated as "bottomless pit" or as "place of corpses", since the crater was the site of a violent confrontation between two Maasai clans in the 1850s. More likely, in common with its Kikuyu name Kirima kia Ngoma (Devil's Mountain), Menengai means "place of demons", in reference to the evil spirits associated with the steam vents that rise from the crater floor. Either way, locals treat the crater with suspicion, and narrate numerous stories of people taking suicidal plunges from the rim, wandering lost for days around the floor or being killed by Menengai's malevolent spirits.

Visitors considering walking to the crater are advised to hike in a group as muggings have been reported.

The museum at Hyrax Hill Prehistoric Site, near Nakuru

Flamingoes flying over Lake Nakuru, Lake Nakuru National Park ▶

# ⑮ Lake Nakuru National Park

Small in size but rich in biodiversity, Lake Nakuru was gazetted as a national park in 1968. It is best known for its birdlife, with more than 500 species listed. The avian highlights are the millions of flamingo that gather along its shore and the pelican that cluster on the southern floodplain. Nakuru is a stronghold for both of Africa's endangered rhino species, and there is probably no better place in East Africa to observe the white rhino. While flamingo and rhino top most visitors' wish list, Nakuru offers excellent bird-watching and game viewing, with all the Big Five present, alongside giraffe, waterbuck, gazelle and baboon.

White pelican at the mouth of the Enderit river

### ★ Rhino Sightings

In the 1990s several black and white rhinos were translocated from other areas of Kenya as well as from South Africa and the park was fenced. Populations have flourished and this is one of the most reliable places in East Africa to see them.

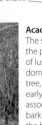

### Acacia Forest

The southern part of the park supports a cover of lush acacia woodland dominated by the fever tree, so named because early European settlers associated its jaundiced bark with malaria. This is the best place to look for black rhino, lion, leopard and woodland birds.

| 0 km | 3 |
| 0 miles | 3 |

### ★ Baboon Cliff

The superb Rift Valley scenery of this park is capped by the spectacular Baboon Cliff, which offers panoramic views over the lake and its hinterland.

Map labels:
Eldoret 150 km (93 miles)
NAKURU
B4
Bah Sp.
Main Gate
Warden's House
Park HQ
Njoro
Baboon Cliff
Lake Na
Pelican Point
Ac Fo
Enasoit Hill
Zakalia Gate
Naishi HQ
Makalia Falls

*For hotels and restaurants see pp367–9 and p380*

### Rothschild's Giraffe

Lake Nakuru is an important stronghold for Rothschild's giraffe, a rare western race that has thrived since its introduction to the park in the 1980s. The Nakuru population of this giraffe is the second-largest in the world after Murchison Falls National Park in Uganda, and the largest in Kenya.

### VISITORS' CHECKLIST

**Practical Information**
Road Map B4. 5 km (3 miles) from the city centre along Flamingo Rd on the outskirts of Nakuru town. *i* 0727 995498 (Main Gate). **Open** 6am–7pm daily. KWS Safari Cards are only available at the Main Gate at the edge of Nakuru town, not at Lanet or Enderit gates. **kws.org**

**Transport**
to Nakuru town.

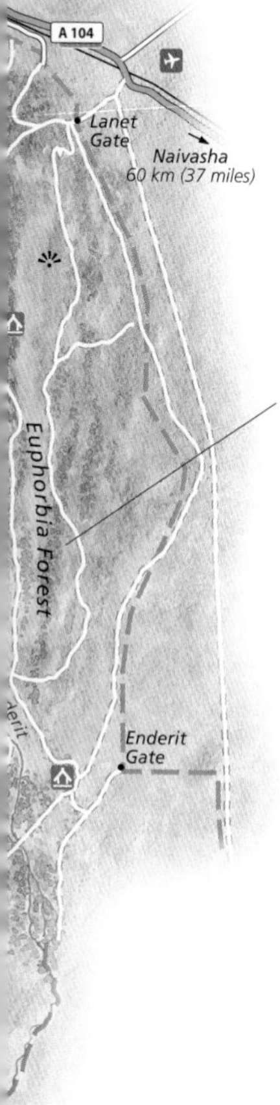

### Euphorbia Forest

The Rift Valley escarpment rising to the southeast of Lake Nakuru supports Kenya's largest concentration of the cactus-like euphorbia, a striking tree-sized succulent whose thick sap is poisonous to most animals.

## Getting Around

Lake Nakuru is among the most easily explored of Kenya's national parks. The main entrance gate lies in the north of the park within walking distance of Nakuru town centre. The park's proximity to the town and the good state of its compact circuit of dirt roads means that many travellers visit this park as a half-day trip by taxi, which is sufficient to view the lake and its flamingoes. However, it is better to stay overnight in the park and explore it over several game drives, which greatly improves the odds of seeing scarcer species such as the black rhino, lion and leopard.

### ★ Flamingoes on Lake Nakuru

The flocks of up to two million flamingoes that aggregate periodically on Lake Nakuru were proclaimed "the most fabulous bird spectacle in the world" by renowned American ornithologist Roger Tory Peterson.

### Key

— Major road
= Minor road
::: Unpaved motorable road
— Railway
−· Park boundary
△ Peak

**For keys to symbols** *see back flap*

# Exploring Lake Nakuru National Park

Most people visit Lake Nakuru on an organized safari, often en route between the Masai Mara and Samburu-Buffalo Springs. While the most productive area for a game drive is the open floodplain south of the lake, visitors with more time can also explore the relatively untrammelled southern half of the park. Most roads in the park, although unsurfaced, are in good condition and a 4WD is not required except after exceptional rains. Of Kenya's major wildlife-viewing destinations, Lake Nakuru is the most accessible due to its proximity to Nakuru town, which is easily reached from Nairobi or elsewhere by bus or *matatu*. Once there, it is easy to arrange game drives into the park with taxis or any of several tour operators dotted around the town. As with other reserves in Kenya, walking is forbidden within the park.

Salt encrusted on the shores of Lake Nakuru

### 🐾 Lake Nakuru

The focal point of the national park is Lake Nakuru itself, whose shallow turquoise-green waters are highly alkaline and support dense concentrations of the algae *Spirulina platensis*. Enclosed by mountains and hills, the lake is fed by three major rivers – the Makalia, Njoro and Enderit. This inflow is supplemented by a series of springs that rise along the shore, treated water from the town sewage works and possibly also some untreated urban effluent. Despite no known outlet, Nakuru's relatively small catchment area has made it the most fluctuation-prone of the Rift Valley lakes, varying in area from 5 to 62 sq km (2 to 24 sq miles). To some extent this follows an annual pattern, with large areas of soda-encrusted flats usually being exposed during the dry seasons (July–October and January–February). However, longer cycles may also come into play; indeed, in the 1990s it was feared that Lake Nakuru might dry up altogether,

but water levels have been consistently higher since the El Niño flooding of 1998.

The most conspicuous feature of Lake Nakuru is the immense concentration of lesser flamingo that thrive in its shallows, consuming algae at an estimated rate of 250 tonnes per hectare (110 tons per acre) of surface area annually. The total flamingo count varies from year to year and season to season, but it frequently stands at about two million, with lesser flamingo outnumbering greater flamingo a hundredfold. During the 1990s, the recession of the lake's waters caused a flamingo exodus to Bogoria, Elmenteita and elsewhere, but numbers have seldom dropped below 500,000 in recent years. This avian migration is utterly mesmerizing to behold, especially when a flock of several hundred birds rises above the general squawk and chatter to reveal, in flight, a harmony of bright-pink, black-fringed under-wings. Surprisingly, Nakuru is only a feeding ground for this multitude of flamingoes, which breed at Lake Natron in Tanzania, leading to a slight dip in numbers at the Kenyan lakes over October and November.

The alkaline waters of Nakuru do not naturally support any fish, and its ecology has changed significantly following the introduction of an alkali-tolerant tilapia from Lake Magadi in 1953. The tilapia has thrived in this new environment, leading to an influx of piscivorous birds such as the pelicans that congregate at the mouth of Enderit river.

### 🐾 The Lakeshore Circuit

The park's most popular game drive involves looping along the well-maintained dirt road that encircles Lake Nakuru in its entirety, a distance of around 35 km (22 miles) that takes in several contrasting habitats. Heading clockwise from the Main Gate in the north, the road passes through a patch of dense riparian yellow fever forest that offers restricted views of the lake, but is often good for baboon and

Mother and baby white rhino in Lake Nakuru National Park

Pelicans flying over Lake Nakuru with a flock of flamingoes in the background

waterbuck, and is also a popular haunt for the ever-secretive leopard. After about 5 km (3 miles), a short side road to the right leads to a marshy reed-fringed stretch of shore known as **Hippo Point**. Despite the name, hippo are uncommon here, but buffalo often wallow in the mud, and visitors can easily spot some water-associated birds, ranging from the jewel-like malachite kingfisher to the African spoonbill.

The road following the eastern lakeshore is too densely wooded to offer many clear views over the lake, but it is superb buffalo country, and the immense euphorbia forest that runs up the rocky slopes south of **Sarova Lion Hill Game Lodge** (see p368) is very striking. At the first main junction, visitors should keep to the right, crossing the Enderit river at Muya's causeway – a great spot for ducks, teals, plovers and sandpipers – before emerging on the open grassland that extends along the lake's southern floodplain. This is a great area for white rhino – on a busy day, visitors may see as many as three or four pairs – along with antelope, zebra and other grazers. A rough 2-km (1-mile) track through the grass northeast to the Enderit river-mouth reveals large flocks of lesser and greater

African spoonbill

flamingo, along with great white pelican, yellow-billed stork and various waders.

The western shore supports a mixture of woodland and grassland habitats, and wildlife is usually plentiful. Another must-do hike along this road is the short but steep ascent to **Baboon Cliff**, which offers a superb view over the lake and surrounding mountains. It is also from here that the full scale of the flamingo phenomenon is most apparent, with the individual birds blending into a solid shimmering pink band that separates the green-blue alkaline water from its bleached rim.

### 🐾 Southern Savannah
The southern half of the park sees far less tourist traffic than the north, particularly in the early morning when visitors may drive for hours without seeing another vehicle. The area can be explored reasonably thoroughly over the space of one lengthy game drive. The flattish terrain here supports a park-like mix of open grassland and acacia woodland, the latter dominated by the lovely fever tree, suggesting a very high water table throughout. The thick woodland of the south is the favoured haunt of the critically endangered black rhino, but in comparison to white rhino, these secretive creatures are very seldom seen.

One landmark worth aiming for is **Enasoit Hill**, a thickly vegetated volcanic plug that rises in splendid isolation from grassland north of the park's Naishi sub-headquarters. This is the best area for lions, which are often found hidden away in the tall grass or lazing on one of the rocky perches at the hill's base. Between this outcrop and the sub-headquarters is a holding pen for rhinos – usually empty, but occasionally used to hold a sick or soon-to-be translocated individual. About 3 km (2 miles) further south on the park boundary, a gushing waterfall is formed by the Makalia river as it plunges over a 10-m- (33-ft-) high cliff. The lush woodland here is ideal for birds and monkeys, and is the most likely site in the park for spotting a leopard, in the early morning or late afternoon.

Makalia Falls cascading down the cliff, southern end of Lake Nakuru

# ⑯ Lakes Bogoria and Baringo

The hot and low-lying Rift Valley north of Nakuru provides a rewarding scenic and ecological taster for the arid badlands that run towards the Ethiopian border. This climatic austerity is, however, alleviated by a pair of beautiful but very different lakes – southerly Lake Bogoria, a saline sump whose alkaline algae-rich waters support high densities of flamingo, and freshwater Lake Baringo, with its prolific crocodile and hippo. The area is a favourite with ornithological tours for its wealth of waterbirds and dry-country specials at the southern limit of their range. It is also of considerable scenic interest – it was after his 1892 visit to the forbidding Baringo cliffs that the Scots geologist John Gregory coined the name Rift Valley.

The red-and-yellow barbet, common around Lake Baringo

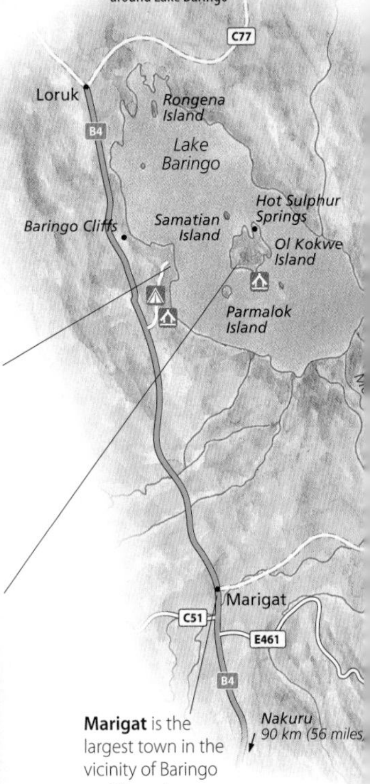
C77
Loruk
B4
Rongena Island
Lake Baringo
Hot Sulphur Springs
Baringo Cliffs
Samatian Island
Ol Kokwe Island
Parmalok Island
Marigat
C51
E461
B4
Nakuru 90 km (56 miles)

**Kampi Ya Samaki**
Kampi ya Samaki is a small but rapidly growing village on the western shore of Lake Baringo. It boasts several small guesthouses and restaurants, and forms a good base for boat trips.

**Marigat** is the largest town in the vicinity of Baringo and Bogoria.

**★ Boat Trips**
Crossing by boat to Ol Kokwe – the largest island on Baringo and site of the popular Island Camp – offers a good opportunity to see some of the numerous waterbirds and other creatures that thrive in this freshwater habitat.

**Hippo Sightings**
The largest resident of Lake Baringo, the hippo can be seen – and heard – grazing nocturnally on the lawns of the lakeshore hotels and campsites.

*For hotels and restaurants see pp367–9 and p380*

### Greater Kudu
Recognizable by its long spiralled horns, the greater kudu can be seen on the shallow shores of Lake Bogoria. This handsome antelope is uncommon elsewhere in Kenya.

### VISITORS' CHECKLIST

**Practical Information**
**Road Map** B3–4. Lake Bogoria National Reserve is 111 km (69 miles) N of Nakuru; Lake Baringo is 116 km (72 miles) N of Nakuru via Marigat.
**Open** 7am–7pm daily for Lake Bogoria National Reserve; 24 hrs for Baringo.

**Transport**
🚌

### Key

━━ Major road
━━ Minor road
═ ═ ═ Unpaved motorable road
━ ▪ Park boundary

*Maralal 90 km (18 miles)*

### Njemps Fisherman
The lakeshore Njemps people of Baringo are close linguistic affiliates of the Maasai but subsist very differently. Their main food is fish caught from light balsa dugout canoes.

### ★ Flamingoes on Lake Bogoria
Rich in algae, Lake Bogoria almost always supports large flocks of flamingoes, where they sometimes even outnumber those at Lake Nakuru when conditions are suitable.

```
0 km        5
0 miles     5
```

### Getting Around
Access is along the B4, the road that runs northwards from Nakuru to Kampi Ya Samaki on the shore of Lake Baringo, passing en route through Marigat, the junction town for Lake Bogoria. The road is surfaced for most of its length but a couple of washed-away bridges en route can create impassable obstacles after heavy rain. Normally, however, both lakes are accessible in any saloon car with reasonable clearance. There is also plenty of public transport to Kampi Ya Samaki and Marigat, though not to Bogoria itself.

### ★ Loburu Hot Springs
The boiling geysers that erupt from the western shore of Bogoria are a reminder of the high level of recent tectonic activity that shaped this stretch of the Kenyan Rift Valley.

*For keys to symbols see back flap*

# Exploring Lakes Bogoria and Baringo

Bogoria peaked as a tourist destination in the mid-1990s, when it took over from Lake Nakuru as the most popular feeding site for the Rift Valley's million-strong flocks of flamingo. Today, flock-size varies greatly on both lakes as the birds move en masse from one lake to the other. There is no transport to the lake itself, but the occasional *matatu* runs to the village of Loboi at the main entrance gate, and it is permitted to walk or cycle unguided from there as far as Loburu Hot Springs. A 4WD is needed to explore deeper into the park. Baringo has regular minibus connections from Nakuru to the lakeside village of Kampi ya Samaki, and is a regular fixture on organized safaris, especially with ornithologists. Once there, the shore and cliffs can be explored on foot, and boat trips to the lake's islands can be arranged through a hotel.

Jets of sulphuric steam erupt from the geysers at Loburu Hot Springs

## 🏞 Lake Bogoria National Reserve

This 107-sq-km (42-sq-mile) national reserve protects Lake Bogoria, which lies in a basin-like trench at the base of the sheer 600-m- (1,968-ft-) high cliffs of the eastern Laikipia Escarpment, along with a band of dry acacia woodland around its circumference. Bogoria was formerly known as Lake Hannington, after the Scottish bishop who first documented its existence in 1885, prior to being killed by the King of Buganda. The reserve was created in 1973, and was included in the Ramsar List of Wetlands of International Importance in 2000.

Extending over 34 sq km (13 sq miles), Lake Bogoria is fed by the Sandai and Emsos rivers, together with at least 200 hot springs spread across three main sites. The water is highly saline and alkaline, thanks to the rapid rate of evaporation and lack of any known outlet, and cannot support fish, crocodiles or hippos. However, it is rich in the *Spirulina* algae fed upon by flocks of lesser flamingo, which are almost always present in large numbers, regularly topping the million mark in the 1990s. The handsome fish eagle is also common around the lakeshore, where – in lieu of fishing – it has acquired the unusual habit of preying and feeding on flamingoes and other large wading birds.

The national reserve protects 18 geysers, the largest such concentration in Africa. The most impressive of these are to be found on the western lakeshore at **Loburu Hot Springs**, where a trio of geysers bursts from below the earth in a haze of sulphuric steam to form an ever-mutating series of multihued pools and streams that drain into the lake. It is a thrilling, primeval sight, but one best approached with caution, as the edges of the streams and pools are prone to crumbling, and the seething water has claimed more than one fatality.

Despite its protection in a national reserve, the dense semiarid acacia scrub surrounding the lake clearly suffers from overgrazing, and livestock is more conspicuous than wildlife. With luck, however, the road between the entrance gate and springs should throw up the odd impala, dik-dik or warthog. More alluring is one of Kenya's few remaining populations of greater kudu, a shy but magnificently horned antelope that is most numerous along the eastern shore of the lake, but might also be glimpsed along the northwest shore, especially towards dusk.

Flamingoes flock in large numbers to feed in the shallows of Lake Bogoria

The Island Camp's landing point on Ol Kokwe Island

### 🐾 Lake Baringo

Like Bogoria, Lake Baringo is fed by a combination of river water and hot springs, has no surface outlet and experiences high rates of evaporation, but it differs in that its water is fresh rather than saline. First described by the explorer Joseph Thomson in 1883, the lake extends over some 130 to 170 sq km (50 to 66 sq miles), depending on the water level, which is less prone to fluctuation than others in the Rift Valley. Baringo is home to the Njemps people, who number fewer than 20,000 and speak the same language as the Maasai and Samburu, but specialize in fishing rather than pastoralism. The Njemps fish in Baringo using small flimsy-looking boats made from balsa sticks grown on the eastern shore.

Njemps fishing boat made of saplings

Situated about halfway up the western shore, the centre of activity on Baringo is the small but rapidly expanding Njemps village of **Kampi ya Samaki**, which translates, somewhat prosaically, as "fishing camp". It is a scruffy little place, but well equipped with budget lodgings and eateries, and the excellent and long-serving **Lake Baringo Club** and **Robert's Camp** *(see p367)* lie along the lakeshore immediately to its south.

Lake Baringo is not afforded official protection, but it supports a varied aquatic fauna, most strikingly the outsized crocodiles, gigantic monitor lizards and grunting hippos that are easily seen from the western shore around Kampi ya Samaki. The avian checklist for Baringo and its immediate vicinity stands well above 500, and includes a wide selection of water-associated birds along with dry-country species normally associated with sites further north. An abundance of fish includes one endemic species of tilapia, which is claimed locally to keep the lake's substantial crocodile population too well fed for them to trouble people, although this is an assertion visitors are advised not to put to the test. It is well worth taking a boat out on to the lake to visit some of the islands, of which the largest is **Ol Kokwe**, the peak of an extinct volcano whose slopes are still dotted with hot springs. En route, the boatmen take visitors past papyrus beds teeming with hippos, crocodiles and birds. Usually, they will also lure some of the lake's prodigious fish eagles by throwing fish into the lake for the bird to swoop down and catch as it hits the surface – a thrilling sight and a great opportunity to photograph, although one has to be quick to catch it. A rocky outcrop off Ol Kokwe's shores, known locally as Gibraltar, once hosted a breeding colony of 20 pairs of goliath heron, but while this impressively bulky bird is still common around the lake, breeding has been sporadic in recent years.

### 🐾 Baringo Cliffs

Set back about 2 km (1 mile) west of the lakeshore, this tall basaltic escarpment is easily ascended on foot by following the tar road back from Kampi ya Samaki to the junction with the B4. The view from the top is immense, taking in Baringo in its entirety, as well as the soaring cliffs behind it and the 1,477-m- (4,850-ft-) high peak of volcanic **Mount Korosi** on the northern lakeshore. Seen here are the dik-dik, klipspringer and rock hyrax. A local guide might well be able to locate a few scorpions and snakes. The walk through the gorge below the cliffs is worth a couple of hours, offering a good chance of sighting the spectacular Verreaux's eagle, along with dry-country specials such as the localized Hemprich's and Jackson's hornbill, white-crested turaco and bristle-crowned starling.

Semiarid and scrub vegetation covers the cliffs near Lake Baringo

# WESTERN KENYA

With its mild climate and fertile land, Western Kenya offers a scenery of terraced farmland, bright-green tea plantations, verdant forests and lovely hills with panoramic views. The region also has Kenya's share of Lake Victoria, Africa's largest lake, as well as Kakamega Forest, the only tropical rainforest in East Africa, and Mount Elgon, the country's second-tallest mountain.

Ripe for agricultural use, the hills that rise above the western arm of the Rift Valley have been home to the Luo, Gusii and Luhya peoples for centuries. Today, it is the most densely populated rural region of Kenya. In 1901, the railway reached Port Florence (now Kisumu), and since then the town has developed as a port serving the communities around Lake Victoria and is now the country's third-largest city. Fast-growing Eldoret with its textile mills and other industries is also increasingly becoming an important regional centre for economic activity and is a major service centre for transport along the busy Nairobi–Kampala Road.

With many hours of sunshine and frequent rain, farming is the mainstay of Western Kenya. Fruits, vegetables and flowers are grown commercially for export to the rest of the country and beyond. Tea was introduced from India during the colonial period and the southern hillsides are blanketed in plantations. Other cash crops include sorghum, maize, wheat, sugarcane and cassava. The entire region is dotted with small, agriculture-orientated service towns and industries, such as paper mills and sugar-processing plants.

Western Kenya receives few visitors and as such accommodation and facilities are more basic here than in other parts of the country. Nevertheless, a loop through Western Kenya's tranquil forests, gentle hills and patchwork of fields gives real insight into the country's rural way of life. Attractions here include a couple of interesting museums depicting the lives of the local people and archaeological finds in the area, plus forested parks and reserves that harbour birds, monkeys and butterflies. Around Lake Victoria, there are small fishing villages where local canoes can be hired to explore the papyrus reedbeds to see hippos and birds.

Koitobos Peak, the summit of Mount Elgon, Mount Elgon National Park

◄ People walk through a large-scale tea estate at Nandi Hills, Kapsabet District

# Exploring Western Kenya

Some 50 km (31 miles) northwest of Nakuru, the centre of Kenya's tea industry lies in the undulating hills around Kericho and Kisii in the Rift Valley. To the north of this area are Kisumu, the lakeside capital of the region, and Kakamega Forest National Reserve, which harbours a beautiful canopy of giant trees and tangled vines full of birds and small mammals. Further north are Kitale, the springboard town to hiking in the Cherangani Hills, Mount Elgon National Park, where the extinct volcano straddles the border with Uganda, and Saiwa Swamp National Park, which protects the rare sitatunga antelope. Also popular are drives through the panoramic Tugen Hills and Kerio Valley and, more to the west, through Kapsabet and Nandi Hills.

## Sights at a Glance

### Towns and Cities

- ❷ Kabarnet
- ❹ Eldoret
- ❺ Kitale
- ❽ Kapenguria
- ⓫ Kakamega
- ⓭ *Kisumu pp302–303*
- ⓯ Kendu Bay and Simbi Nyaima
- ⓰ Homa Bay
- ㉑ Kisii
- ㉒ Tabaka
- ㉓ Kericho

### Areas of Natural Beauty

- ❸ Kingwal Swamp
- ❾ Cherangani Hills
- ❿ Kapsabet and Nandi Hills
- ㉔ Chagaik Dam and Arboretum

### Tours

- ❶ *Tugen Hills and Kerio Valley Drive p292*

### National Parks and Reserves

- ❻ Mount Elgon National Park
- ❼ Saiwa Swamp National Park
- ⓬ *Kakamega Forest National Reserve pp298–301*
- ⓳ Ruma National Park

### Lakes and Islands

- ⓮ *Lake Victoria pp306–307*
- ⓱ Mfangano Island
- ⓲ Rusinga Island

### Archaeological Sites and Museums

- ⓴ Thimlich Ohinga

The tropical rainforest at Kakamega Forest National Reserve

*For hotels and restaurants see pp369–70 and p381*

Sitatunga antelope in Saiwa Swamp National Park

## Key

— Major road

=== Minor road

═ ═ Untarred major road

= = Untarred minor road

− − 4WD track

— Scenic route

⚋⚋ Major railway

— Minor railway

▦▦ International border

⤬ Pass

△ Peak

### Getting Around

Daily scheduled domestic flights operate between Nairobi and Kisumu and Eldoret, while charter companies can also touch down on the airstrips at Kakamega and Kitale. The network of roads is extensive and most roads linking the towns are tarred and in fairly good condition. Local *matatus* run between the settlements along the main roads, and long-distance buses from Nairobi and Nakuru serve the principal towns. Few tour operators run scheduled tours to the region, but tailor-made trips can be arranged.

**For keys to symbols** *see back flap*

# ❶ Tugen Hills and Kerio Valley Drive

Heading into Western Kenya, the Nakuru to Eldoret route offers panoramic views of the Rift Valley. The steep hills and escarpments are dotted with neat terraced smallholdings, dense pine, cedar and giant gum forests, and cascading waterfalls. Near Marigat, the road climbs through the rolling Tugen Hills to Kabarnet on a series of switchbacks. It then drops dizzyingly 1,000 m (3,280 ft) into the dramatic Kerio Valley, also dubbed Kenya's Grand Canyon. Across the Kerio river, the road zigzags up to Elgeyo Escarpment offering sweeping views of the valley, and flattens out through pine plantations to Eldoret.

### Tips for Drivers

**Starting point:** The C51 begins at Marigat, near Lake Baringo.
**Length:** 119 km (74 miles) from Marigat to Eldoret.
**Road conditions:** The C51 is in good condition, but the detour to Lake Kamnarok requires a 4WD.

### Key

━━ Major road
═══ Minor road
── Railway
▬ ▬ Park boundary

### ⑥ Kerio View
This popular bar and restaurant is an ideal lunch stop and its wide glass frontage offers a splendid broad view of Kerio Valley and the Tugen Hills.

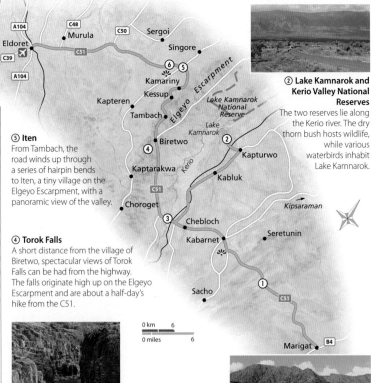

### ② Lake Kamnarok and Kerio Valley National Reserves
The two reserves lie along the Kerio river. The dry thorn bush hosts wildlife, while various waterbirds inhabit Lake Kamnarok.

### ⑤ Iten
From Tambach, the road winds up through a series of hairpin bends to Iten, a tiny village on the Elgeyo Escarpment, with a panoramic view of the valley.

### ④ Torok Falls
A short distance from the village of Biretwo, spectacular views of Torok Falls can be had from the highway. The falls originate high up on the Elgeyo Escarpment and are about a half-day's hike from the C51.

0 km    6
0 miles    6

### ③ Chebloch Gorge
The Kerio river plunges through a narrow fissure of rock into the steep-sided Chebloch Gorge beyond the point where the C51 crosses the river.

### ① Tugen Hills
The hills run north to south for about 100 km (65 miles). A viewpoint after the Kabarnet road's last hairpin bend offers stunning views of Lake Baringo.

*Map labels:* A104, C48, Murula, C50, Sergoi, Eldoret, C51, Singore, C39, A104, ⑥, ⑤, Kamariny, Elgeyo Escarpment, Kapteren, Kessup, Lake Kamnarok National Reserve, Tambach, Lake Kamnarok, ④, Biretwo, Kaptarakwa, Kerio, ②, Kapturwo, Choroget, Kabluk, C51, ③, Chebloch, Kipsaraman, Kabarnet, Seretunin, Sacho, ①, C51, Marigat, B4

The colonial façade of the Kabarnet Museum

## ❷ Kabarnet

**Road Map** B4. 94 km (58 miles) N of Nakuru. 18,000.

The little town of Kabarnet sits on the eastern tree-clad edge of the plunging Kerio Valley. Despite its scenic location, it is little more than a tiny administrative centre for the Baringo district, with a bank, a clutch of shops and a petrol station. Its claim to fame is that it is the hometown of former president Daniel arap Moi.

Set in lush botanical gardens with labelled trees and shrubs, **Kabarnet Museum** is worth stopping for. Housed in what used to be the District Commissioner's residence, the small museum's four galleries have displays highlighting the culture of the local Samburu, Keiyo, Pokot, Marakwet and Nandi peoples, and exhibits on the area's colonial history. The museum also provides information about nearby Lake Baringo (see pp284–7).

🏛 **Kabarnet Museum**
Hospital Rd. **Tel** 053 21221.
**Open** 9am–6pm daily. 📷 🎟
W **museums.or.ke**

## ❸ Kingwal Swamp

**Road Map** B4. 24 km (16 miles) S of Eldoret.

Between Kapsabet and Eldoret the road skims the eastern edge of an unprotected wetland area, the Kingwal Swamp, that is home to a variety of wildlife. Hemmed in by farms and cereal fields, the swamp stretches across some 40 hectares (100 acres) of valley floor and is a refuge for the

second-largest population in Kenya of the extremely rare semiaquatic sitatunga antelope (see p133). Kenya's largest population of sitatunga is found in Saiwa Swamp National Park (see pp298–9). Visitors can spot these beautiful animals late in the evening or early in the morning when they emerge to graze. The middle of Kingwal Swamp is dense with beautiful papyrus and is also a good site for bird-watching. Swamp-adapted Syzygium (myrtle) trees have been planted on the fringes of the swamp to limit encroachment of agriculture. However, large areas of former swampland have already been planted with Eucalyptus trees to drain the land for agriculture, which is leading to a loss of habitat.

## ❹ Eldoret

**Road Map** B4. 53 km (33 miles) W of Kabarnet on the C51. 290,000. ✈ 🚌 Uganda Hwy.

The most prosperous urban centre in Western Kenya and the country's fifth-largest town, Eldoret straddles the Kenya–

Uganda Highway. The town has an unusual history. It was originally founded in 1908 by a group of Voortrekers from South Africa, emigrants who belonged to the farming community of the Cape Colony. This particular group had sailed to Mombasa and then trekked inland. The place where they settled was dubbed "64" as it was 64 miles from the newly built Uganda Railway railhead at Kibigori. In 1910, it was renamed Eldoret after the Maasai eldore (stony river), a reference to the nearby Sosiani river.

Eldoret has gained importance as a busy service centre for goods trucks heading to Kampala and beyond, with many factories and plants scattered around town for light industries as diverse as textiles, tanning, woollen mills and mushroom cultivation. The town is also the collection and distribution point for much of the fresh produce grown in Western Kenya and the ornamental flowers and exotic vegetables that are exported from Eldoret International Airport. **Moi University** and its training hospital are also located here, giving the town a fairly youthful feel. Like other Western Kenyan towns, Eldoret has produced many successful Kenyan athletes.

There are few attractions in Eldoret, and the architecture of multistorey breeze block buildings is unremarkable, but the town centre boasts prolific banks, shops, petrol stations, trading stores and other facilities.

A busy street in the town centre, Eldoret

Farmland near Kitale resplendent with sunflowers

## ❺ Kitale

**Road Map** A3. 69 km (43 miles) NW of Eldoret. 🚗 105,000. 🚉 🚌

Founded in 1920 by white settlers and expanded when the railway arrived here in 1925, Kitale is an agricultural town surrounded by a patchwork of burnt-orange fields and acres of greenhouses that are used to grow flowers, which are exported to Europe. With a clutch of supermarkets and banks, it is the last sizable settlement before the A1 highway heads into the remote north.

Set in a patch of indigenous riverine tropical forest, the **Kitale Museum** is well worth a visit. The museum has natural history and ethnographical displays, including replicas of traditional homesteads of the Bukusu, Luo, Turkana, Maasai and Elgon peoples. The museum sells locally made handicrafts. There is also an agroforestry centre, set up to educate local farmers, and a snake park. An interesting nature trail leads to a number of picnic spots in the forest, which is home to the rare De Brazza's monkey, and which offers a good chance of spotting black-and-white colobus monkeys and a number of birds.

Antelope,
Kitale Museum

### 🏛 Kitale Museum

1 km (half a mile) SE of the bus station on Main St. **Tel** 054 30996.
**Open** 9am–6pm daily. 🅿 📷
🌐 museums.or.ke

## ❻ Mount Elgon National Park

**Road Map** A3. 11 km (7 miles) NW of Kitale. **Tel** 054 31456. 🚗 🏕 ⛰
🌐 kws.org

With a huge intact caldera and distinctive flat top, Mount Elgon straddles the Kenya–Uganda border. Despite its 4,321-m- (14,177-ft-) high Wagagai peak being located in Uganda, it is recognized as Kenya's second tallest mountain. From Kenya, it can be visited in the 169-sq-km (65-sq-mile) Mount Elgon National Park, a wild and intact wilderness with breathtaking scenery of cliffs, caves, waterfalls, gorges and impressive peaks. The park's vegetation varies with altitude and the lower slopes feature thick-canopied forests of giant Elgon teak and cedar trees, while higher altitudes support bamboo zones, tussock grasslands, heath moorlands

Entrance to Kitum Cave surrounded by forest, Mount Elgon National Park

and unusual vegetation such as the giant lobelia. The park provides habitat to elephant, buffalo, leopard, several species of monkeys, giant forest hog, various types of antelope and over 240 species of birds. There are several 4WD vehicle circuits and three self-guided nature trails to Kitum Cave, Makingeni Cave and the Elephant Bluff.

The 4,155-m- (13,632-ft-) high Koitobos peak, the highest on the Kenyan side, can be hiked in about 3 hours from the road's end at Koroborte (3,580 m/ 11,745 ft), which is about a 3-hour drive from Chorlim Gate. No special climbing gear is required, except warm clothes, and the park can arrange a guide. To summit Wagagai and the caldera, the mountain must be tackled from the Ugandan side.

## ❼ Saiwa Swamp National Park

**Road Map** B3. 22 km (14 miles) NE of Kitale. **Tel** 054 29826. **Open** 6:30am– 6pm daily. 🅿 ⛰ 🌐 kws.org

Located to the north of Kitale and below the Cherangani Hills, the tiny 3-sq-km (1-sq-mile) Saiwa Swamp National Park is the smallest in Kenya. It was established to protect the rare semiaquatic sitatunga antelope, distinguished by its long, splayed hooves, which are well adapted for walking through the muddy, vegetated swamp fed by the Saiwa river. The park features riverine forest and patches of grassland dotted with acacia trees, and is also home to De Brazza's and black-and-white colobus monkeys, otter, bushbuck and grey duiker. Only accessible on foot, the park has well-maintained trails, plus four observation towers and a basic campsite at the gate.

## ❽ Kapenguria

**Road Map** B3. 40 km (25 miles) N of Kitale. 🚌 🚐 13,000.

Lying in an area of steep hills and grazing lands, Kapenguria is a small town of red dusty streets, squat buildings with corrugated tin roofs and little infrastructure. The road from Kitale is tarred and in good condition, but beyond Kapenguria it drops down a steep escarpment with sharp bends and potholes. A 4WD is essential to head anywhere further north.

The town rose to fame during Kenya's struggle for independence, when, in 1952, the colonial authorities arrested six leading Kenyan nationalists here, including Jomo Kenyatta (see p56). They became known as the Kapenguria Six and were tried and imprisoned in Kapenguria for being involved in the Mau Mau Rebellion (see pp56–7). They were finally released in 1961 and Kenyatta became president of newly independent Kenya in 1963. Today, the one-storey prison they were held in is the small **Kapenguria Museum**. Displays

The verdant slopes of the Cherangani Hills

include photographs, documents and books relating to the era and visitors can also look at Kenyatta's small cell. There is a very good display of photographs of the Pokot people, who farm millet and sorghum on the Cherangani foothills, and are shown in their traditional dress. There is also a mock-up of a Pokot homestead outside the museum.

🏛 **Kapenguria Museum**
Near Kapenguria district offices.
**Open** 9am–6pm daily. 🅿
🌐 **museums.or.ke**

## ❾ Cherangani Hills

**Road Map** B3. 90 km (56 miles) NE of Kitale.

To the north of Kapenguria, the dramatic and lofty peaks of the Cherangani Hills form a natural barrier between the fertile western highlands and the stony deserts in Northern Kenya. The

highest point is the 3,517-m (11,539-ft) Nagen Peak in the north of the range, which is the fourth-highest mountain in Kenya. The hills are riddled with small villages, dirt tracks and streams. Most of the slopes are undemanding at high altitude, and the verdant hills offer perfect walking country for self-sufficient and adventurous hikers.

Wild, closed-canopy forest, tracts of bamboo, alpine meadows and heath-covered moorland can be found on the higher slopes. The birdlife here is rich and varied and lammergeyers are often seen drifting on the thermals.

There are numerous tracks into the hills, some of them accessible by vehicle, but most are rough and tortuously steep, including the paved A1 highway that runs north through the region. Visitors can book a guided tour with a safari company specializing in treks in this region.

A diorama depicting the Pokot way of life, Kapenguria Museum

### Salt Mining Elephants of Mount Elgon

Elephants mining for salt in Mount Elgon National Park

Mount Elgon National Park features a series of four caves – Kitum, Makingeni, Chepnyalil and Ngwarisha. The caves are best known for their frequent night visitors: convoys of elephants that come to mine and lick the caves for salt – they use their tusks to gouge out the rich deposits. With its steep slopes and heavy rainfall, much of Elgon's salts have been leached away. The cave walls are the most concentrated salt source in the area and by bringing their calves to the caves, the elephants pass the salt mining technique on to the next generation.

The lush slopes of Nandi Hills near Kapsabet, carpeted by tea plantations

## ⑩ Kapsabet and Nandi Hills

**Road Map** B4. 48 km (30 miles) SW of Eldoret. 🚖 🚌

A small regional settlement, Kapsabet is a one-street town of mud homes and a row of concrete traders' buildings. The region is famed for producing some of Kenya's most successful long-distance runners, and in the 1930s, it was here that former president Daniel arap Moi went to junior school.

Just to the west is **South Nandi Forest**, a patch of canopy forest that was once contiguous with Kakamega Forest National Reserve (see pp298–301). South Nandi and Kakamega are still no more than a few miles apart at their closest points.

At the tiny settlement of Nandi Hills, to the south of Kapsabet, the old British Nandi Bears Golf Club is one of the most scenic in the country and hosts several annual golf tournaments. It has a colonial clubhouse dating from 1928 and wide fairways that provide sweeping views over the hills.

The Nandi Hills are famous as the site where Nandi warriors clashed with British colonial forces over the building of the Lunatic Line (see p303). The altitude range of 1,800–2,500 m (5,900–8,200 ft), a cool and wet climate and rich volcanic soil create the ideal environment for growing tea. Verdant plantations blanket the upper slopes while sugarcane grows on the valley floors.

## ⑪ Kakamega

**Road Map** A4. 106 km (66 miles) SW of Eldoret. 🚹 100,000. 🚖 🚌

The medium-sized town of Kakamega lies in green fertile country and serves as a springboard to the nearby Kakamega Forest National Reserve. In the 1930s, the town briefly attracted a mini-gold rush of prospectors, but not enough gold was found to sustain a mining industry. About 3 km (2 miles) south, on the Kakamega–Kisumu Road, is the **Weeping Stone of Shinyalu**. A large granite boulder resting on top of a pillar of rocks that rises to a height of 8 m (26 ft), it resembles a solemn head falling on weary shoulders. From the top a constant stream of spring water flows down the sides and the stone is stained from many years of "weeping".

Kakamega is the heartland of the Luhya people (see p30) who are known for their traditional bullfighting. Spurred on by horn-blowing, excited supporters, the two bulls lock horns and fight until one turns and runs. The victorious bull's owner wins money, and a good deal of local gambling rests on the outcome.

### Nandi Bear

Nandi and Tugen legends speak of the Nandi Bear – a large, hairy carnivorous animal that can walk upright, with high shoulders and a sloping back. It is believed to attack livestock during the night and only eats the heads of its victims. There were many reputed sightings of the "bear" during the 1800s–1900s. Early colonial settlers also claimed to have encountered the beast, giving further credence to the myth. In reality, the hyena is the most likely candidate for the Nandi Bear's true identity. Although hyenas are scavengers by nature, they are known to occasionally attack animals. However, local people would have recognized the hyena, and their descriptions of the bear do not match the physical attributes of a hyena. Perhaps the Nandi Bear could be a type of undiscovered giant hyena that has still not been identified or even a prehistoric survivor – the myth lives on.

The giant Weeping Stone of Shinyalu, just south of Kakamega

# The Runners of Western Kenya

Kenya has more world-record holders and Olympic medallists in athletics than any other country. Over the last 40 years, Kenyans, especially the Kalenjin of Western Kenya, have become the world's most successful long- and middle-distance runners in various international track events. Many highly successful long-distance runners have been born in or near Kapsabet, including Bernard Lagat, Peter Rono, Martin Lei and Nancy Langat. Their achievements have been so extraordinary that they have fascinated sports physiologists and sociologists around the world.

### Setting the Pace

*Running exceedingly long distances at high altitudes, a diet rich in carbohydrates as well as conducive landscape and climate are believed to be among the reasons behind the powerful presence of Kenyan athletes in world track and field events.*

**Runners in training** can be seen pounding along the dirt roads or climbing the hills in the tea plantations of Western Kenya. Former Kenyan athletes have opened several high-altitude training camps that also attract international athletes.

**Pamela Jelimo and Janeth Busienei**, both from villages around Kapsabet, clinched the gold and silver medals respectively in the women's 800 metres at the Beijing 2008 Olympics.

**Kenya's Abel Kirul**, from Kapsabet, won the silver in the men's marathon at the 2012 London Olympics. Ugandan Stephen Kiprotich, who trained near Eldoret, won the gold, while Kenyan Kipsang Kiprotich took the bronze.

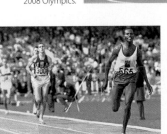

**The history of Kalenjin long-distance running** began at the 1968 Olympics in Mexico City when Kipchoge Keino won the gold medal for the 1,500 metres event. Despite suffering acute stomach pains, Kipchoge won by a 20-m (66-ft) lead, and a Kenyan athletic dynasty was born.

# ⑫ Kakamega Forest National Reserve

The only tropical forest left in Kenya, Kakamega Forest National Reserve is a 230-sq-km (90-sq-mile) swath of beautiful rainforest in the heart of an intensively cultivated agricultural region. The forest once joined the Guineo-Congolan equatorial belt of forest that covered all the land from the Rift Valley to the Atlantic Ocean some 400 years ago. Protected since the 1930s, Kakamega is presently managed by both the Kenya Wildlife Service (KWS) and a community forestry group. The forest features towering ancient hardwood trees, tangled vines and a dense and richly green forest floor of ferns and orchids. It is inhabited by a diverse range of birds, insects, butterflies and small mammals.

A path running through lush vegetation, Kakamega Forest

**★ Buyangu Viewpoint**
A 4-km (2-mile) drive from the forest station, Buyangu Hill gives a bird's-eye view of the forest canopy. On a clear day there are views over the Nandi Hills and Mount Elgon in the north.

## Getting Around

There are two gates to the park – Buyangu in the north and Isecheno in the south. Both offer basic campsites and accommodation. Two dirt roads link the A1 main road to the C39 through the southern part of the forest. The park is best explored on foot and trails vary in length from 1 km (half a mile) to 7 km (4 miles). The Isiukhu Trail connects Isecheno to Isiukhu Falls. Driving is also an option, although roads are rough and the engine noise can scare the wildlife away. Rainfall is heaviest in April and May; January and February are the driest months.

*Kitale 100 km (62 miles)*

Kabili Junction

Buyangu G

A1

Lubao

Kakamega

Isiukhu

Lugu sida

Weeping Stone of Shinyalu

Ilesi

Shibuye    Shinyalu    Isecher Ga

A1

Khayega

Rivendell Gardens

*Kisumu 48 km (30 miles)*

Yala

Kaimosi

C39

**Hammer-headed Fruit Bats**
Resident in Kakamega Forest, these nocturnal animals are the largest bats in Africa, with a wing span just under 1 m (3 ft).

**Key**

━━━ Major road

━━ Minor road

═ ═ ═ Unpaved motorable road

- - - Trail

— ∙ Park boundary

△ Peak

**Kisere Forest Reserve**
Separated from the main reserve, Kisere is a dense area of ancient trees, including the giant Elgon olive, and is home to the exceedingly rare De Brazza's monkey.

## VISITORS' CHECKLIST

**Practical Information**
**Road Map** A4. Buyangu Gate in the northern part of the forest is 2 km (1.2 miles) from Kabili Junction on the main A1 road; the turn-off is 15 km (9 miles) N of Kakamega town. Isecheno Gate in the south is 15 km (9 miles) off the A1 from Kakamega town via Shinyalu village. *i* 056 30603 (KWS HQ). **Open** 6am–7pm daily.

**Transport**
to Kabili Junction.

**★ Isiukhu Falls**
An easy excursion from the Kenya Wildlife Service Forest Station at Buyangu, the Isiukhu Falls are best seen during the rainy season when a torrent of foamy water spills down a rocky escarpment.

**★ Isecheno Forest Station**
A number of labyrinthine jungle trails emanate from this forest station. It offers the services of self-trained guides who take visitors along the trails under the beautiful canopy. The indigenous trees are identified by signs with their local and Latin names.

*WS Forest ation*

*Nanugo*

*Nandi Escarpment*

*Isiukhu Trail*

**Lirhanda Hill**

*Ikuyyiwa*

*Chepsonoi*
*Yala 4 km (3 miles)*

*Kapsabet*
*25 km*
*(16 miles)*

*ibiri Forest tation*

0 km — 3
0 miles — 3

**Gaboon Vipers**
This brown, patterned sluggish snake is among many rare species of reptiles found in Kakamega reserve.

## Forest Birds of Western Kenya

Kakamega Forest Reserve is well known for its diverse birdlife. Over 300 species of birds, including some very rare ones, have been identified in the reserve. These include the grey parrot, great blue turaco, blue-headed bee-eater, chestnut wattle-eye and black-and-white casqued hornbill. Other birds seen in this region include cuckoos, nightjars, owls, kingfishers, tawny eagles and hornbills.

Casqued hornbill    African grey parrot    Blue-headed bee-eater

For keys to symbols *see back flap*

# Exploring Kakamega Forest National Reserve

A superb stretch of virgin tropical forest, Kakamega Forest is easily accessed from Kakamega town along the Kakamega–Eldoret Highway. The southern part of the forest is accessed at Isecheno by a dirt road, which can be slippery when wet, going 15 km (9 miles) east from Kakamega along the A1 via the village of Shinyalu. The reserve has two forest stations – the KWS station at Buyangu in the north of the forest and the Kakamega Environmental Education Programme (KEEP) at Isecheno that administers the southern part of the reserve. Although some of the forest tracks are car-worthy, the best way to explore the beauty of the forest is on foot.

Buyangu viewpoint across Kakamega Forest National Reserve

## 🗙 Buyangu

19 km (12 miles) NE of Kakamega.
🛈 056 30603 (KWS headquarters).
🚗 🅿 🖼 🛖 w kws.org

On the A1, a turn-off to the right signposted Kakamega Forest National Reserve leads a further 2 km (1 mile) to the KWS Forest Station at Buyangu, the northern area of the forest. A number of paths through the cool of the trees begin just beyond the forest station, where it is also possible to hire a guide. The climate is generally drier here than further south, with the result that there is a greater diversity of habitat, which includes areas of scrub, marshland and young and ancient forest. The oldest part of the forest, this area supports diverse birdlife such as great blue turacos and a variety of hornbills as well as black-and-white colobus and red-tailed monkeys. The many colossal trees here bear plaques that invite visitors to guess their girth, and the correct answers are inscribed behind the trees.

A 5-km (3-mile) walk from the KWS Forest Station, the **Buyangu Hill** viewpoint is a

worthwhile excursion. A short scramble to the top leads to a viewpoint offering spectacular panoramic views across the top of Kakamega's canopy of trees and east to the Nandi Escarpment. This is the highest point in the forest, and on a clear day it offers great views of Mount Elgon to the north. At the top is a picnic site with a thatched shade.

Another popular excursion from the forest station is to **Isiukhu Falls**, a 7-km (4-mile) walk following the Isiukhu river. The falls themselves are rather feeble, except after rain, but the walk goes under some lush canopies of foliage.

## 🗙 Isecheno

18 km (11 miles) SE of Kakamega via Shinyalu village. **Tel** 0716 294939.
🛈 forest road from Chepsonoi on the C39. 🚗 🅿 🖼 🛖 w keep-kakamega.or.ke

The southern region of Kakamega Forest, Isecheno is maintained by the community-based Kakamega Environmental Education Programme (KEEP), which operates a forest station here. KEEP is instrumental in protecting the forest and educating the local population about ecological awareness, conservation and tree planting. It provides extensive information about the different animal and plant species found in the forest reserve. A plant nursery here produces seedlings used to patch the unnecessary glades in the forest, and also sells medicinal plants to the local communities.

At the forest station, visitors can hire guides who are know-ledgeable and well versed in the Latin names of the fascinating flora and fauna of the reserve, and who are especially good at pointing out birds in the high trees. For those staying overnight, the station also offers night walks along the many trails, with flashlights to locate nocturnal creatures.

Not far from Isecheno, **Lirhanda Hill** rises steeply over the lush canopy of trees and provides excellent views of the surrounding countryside and forest. The trail to the hill starts near the **Rondo Retreat** guesthouse *(see p369)* on the road towards Chepsonoi. Visitors starting from the forest station will need approximately 2 hours to get there.

The tree nursery at the KEEP headquarters, Isecheno

# Flora and Fauna of Kakamega

Kenya's only vestige of equatorial rainforest, Kakamega harbours an immense biodiversity. This richly tropical environment is home to a variety of small mammals, birds, primates, insects and reptiles, some of which are not seen elsewhere in East Africa. The forest has an estimated 380 species of woody trees, vines, shrubs, ferns, herbs and flowers. Some 360 species of birds have been identified, 36 of which are endemic to the forest. There are over 400 species of butterflies – representing 45 per cent of all recorded butterflies in Kenya – as well as the shiny black goliath beetle, various ants, leaf insects, spiders and dragonflies. Although shy and rarely seen, there are as many as 40 species of snakes as well as numerous lizard and frog species. The wealth of forest mammals includes seven species of primates.

## Flora

*The forest glade is home to ferns and flowering plants such as flame lilies and dracaenas. The deeper forest comprises dense tracts of ancient hard wood trees such as Elgon teak.*

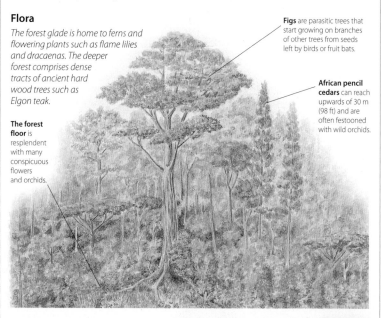

**Figs** are parasitic trees that start growing on branches of other trees from seeds left by birds or fruit bats.

**African pencil cedars** can reach upwards of 30 m (98 ft) and are often festooned with wild orchids.

**The forest floor** is resplendent with many conspicuous flowers and orchids.

## Fauna

*Kakamega's best-known primates are the black-and-white colobus, bushbaby and red-tailed and blue monkeys. Also commonly seen are the duiker, dik-dik, genet, serval, flying squirrels and bats. The forest floor shelters reptiles such as the Gabon viper and monitor lizard.*

**The charaxe**, Africa's fastest flying butterfly, feeds off fallen fruit.

**The red-tailed monkey** stores food in its cheek pouches while it travels through the forest.

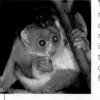

**The potto** is a large nocturnal sloth-like creature unique to rainforests. It sleeps in the canopy during the day and rarely descends to the forest floor.

**The goliath beetle** can grow as big as a man's hand and feeds mainly on tree sap and fruit.

**Nile monitor lizards** can grow up to 2 m (7 ft) in length, and live off the forest's birds and eggs, which they obtain by stealing nests.

# ⑬ Kisumu

The administrative centre for Western Kenya, Kisumu lies on the edge of Lake Victoria, and is Kenya's third-largest city after Nairobi and Mombasa. It began as a railhead known as Port Florence in 1901, and grew into a busy port with connections to other ports in Uganda and Tanzania. Since the 1970s, however, there has been a decline in trade by boat across the lake – road transport being more favoured – and Kisumu is not as prosperous as it once was. One delightful feature of Kisumu is the many thousands of *boda-bodas* (motorbike taxis) that throng the streets. These are fun to ride, but first-timers need to be cautious. Dunga village, just to the south, offers the best views of the lake, its hippo and the rich birdlife.

### 🏛 Kisumu Museum
Nairobi Rd. **Tel** 057 2020332.
**Open** 9:30am–6pm daily. 🅿 📷
🌐 **museums.or.ke**

An interesting regional museum dedicated to the Luo, Luhya, Kipsigis and Nandi peoples, this is set in a pretty patch of greenery. The trees are labelled, and this is a good place to look out for weavers' nests hanging precariously from branches.

The central hall of the museum has a number of traditional artifacts such as jewellery, cooking pots and utensils, fishing baskets, pipes and weapons. There are also stuffed animals and birds, the most impressive of which is a lion pouncing on a wildebeest.

The grounds house a snake house containing a few of Kenya's most poisonous snakes behind glass, such as Gaboon

A graphic display of predator-prey interaction, Kisumu Museum

vipers, cobras and mambas from Kakamega Forest, while the tiny aquarium has a few small fish from Lake Victoria, such as tilapia. There are also several small fenced ponds containing Nile crocodiles, which are fed on Monday afternoons.

### 🏪 Kibuye Market
Jomo Kenyatta Ave.
**Open** 8am–6pm daily.

Kisumu is home to Western Kenya's largest market, which sells just about anything from flip-flops and fish to fresh produce and furniture. Stalls display colourful pyramids of fruits and vegetables, and tilapia fish from the lake, which are split open, salted and dried in the sun. Although a tad chaotic, the market is surprisingly well organized, with similar items being clumped together in the same lanes. Locally produced sisal rope, clay pots and soapstone souvenirs are popular here. The *mitumba* (second-hand clothes) section of the market consists of clothes sent to East Africa from the USA, Europe and the Far East, so visitors will find plenty of familiar brands and some designer labels as well.

### 🕌 Jamia Mosque
Otieno Oyoo Street.

The first Muslims arrived in Kisumu with the railway, mostly as indentured labour from India, and many stayed on to become traders. The Railway Mosque was built by them in 1905, but as Arabian traders arrived from the coast and local Africans converted to Islam, the Railway Mosque was felt to be too small and was replaced by the Jamia Mosque. Built in 1919, this features two elegant minarets,

The centre of Kisumu, one of Kenya's largest cities

Resident impalas at the Impala Sanctuary near Kisumu

three impressive silver domes and a weathervane. The mosque holds 1,000 people during prayer time, and runs a Muslim school as well. Muslim visitors are welcome and non-Muslim males may be allowed in the grounds. For others, there are good views of the green and white building with its striking roof from Otieno Oyoo Street.

### 🏞 Dunga

Dunga, 5 km (3 miles) S of town centre. Dunga is a ramshackle village reached by a ride on a *boda-boda*. It is known for the **Kiboko Bay Resort** *(see p369)*, which has lovely views of the lake.

### 🐾 Impala Sanctuary

Harambee Rd, 2 km (1 mile) S of town centre. **Tel** 057 2501535. **Open** 8am–6pm daily. 🏞 🎟
**W** kws.org

The Impala Sanctuary was created in the 1980s to protect the last population of impala in the area. Today, many of these graceful antelope can be seen in this tiny reserve. Some animals are housed in enclosures. These include spotted hyena, leopard, blue and patas monkeys, grey duiker, hartebeest and ostrich. The reserve has a museum, a nature trail and picnic sites.

### 🏞 Hippo Point

Hippo Point, 3 km (2 miles) S of town centre.

This viewing area on Lake Victoria is a great place to watch sunsets over the lake. Hippos can be seen occasionally.

## The Lunatic Line

In 1901, the railway from Mombasa reached what is now Kisumu; it was then called Port Florence after Florence Preston, the wife of a railway engineer. The railway was called the Lunatic Line at the time of its construction by Liberal British politicians who objected to a railway being built at great expense in what they considered to be the middle of nowhere. The line was later renamed the Uganda Railway, and it went on to become the communications artery for Kenya. It opened up the highlands for agriculture and towns sprang up alongside the tracks. It was dubbed the Lunatic Express in author Charles Miller's popular 1971 book of the same name.

*The Lunatic Express* by Charles Miller

## Kisumu

① Kisumu Museum
② Kibuye Market
③ Jamia Mosque

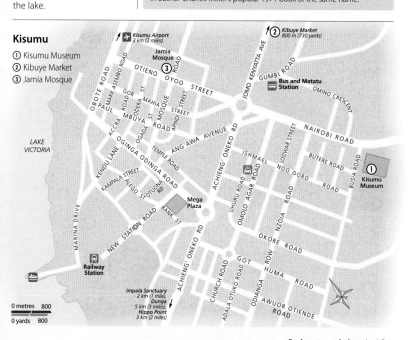

# ⑭ Lake Victoria

Straddling the equator, Africa's largest lake covers 68,800 sq km (26,550 sq miles) and is the second-largest freshwater lake in the world after Lake Superior in North America. The lake has a catchment area of over 184,000 sq km (71,000 sq miles). It was first sighted by Europeans in 1858 when the British explorer John Hanning Speke reached its southern shore and named it after his queen. The lake borders Kenya, Tanzania and Uganda, and supports some 30 million people living in the lakeside communities. In Kenya, fishing for tilapia and Nile perch provides a living for many of the Luo people living on the lakeshore. The lake once had abundant hippo and crocodile but their numbers are now much reduced.

**Locator Map**

★ **Rusinga Island**
Attached to the mainland by a causeway, this peaceful island is home to fishing settlements and the luxurious Rusinga Island Lodge *(see p370)*. It is also the birth and burial place of Tom Mboya, who was tipped to become the president of Kenya before his assassination in 1969.

0 km    15
0 miles   15

## Getting Around

The A1, the main highway that runs west between Kisumu and Kenya's border with Tanzania, is in good condition, but many of the minor roads leading to the lakeshore are in a poor state, so a 4WD is advised. Although there are no formal ferry services on the lake, it is possible to negotiate a ride with local fishermen.

★ **Mfangano Island**
Isolated from the mainland by a short stretch of water that is crossed in a 90-minute boat trip between Mbita Point and Sena, Mfangano Island is noted for its ancient cave paintings, which are believed to be 1,000 to 4,000 years old.

◄ Fishermen returning in their boats on Lake Victoria

★ **Kisumu**
The principal port on the Kenyan shore, Kisumu has wide boulevards and leafy avenues that were laid out during the colonial era. Among the town's few distractions is the interesting Kisumu Museum *(see p302)*.

**Ndere Island National Park**, a 4-sq-km (2-sq-mile) island, protects populations of hippo, monkeys and birds and a small herd of introduced impala.

### VISITORS' CHECKLIST

**Practical Information**
Road Map A4. 2 km (1 mile) W of Kisumu.

**Transport**
🛫 Kisumu. 🚌 from Kisumu, Kisii and Kericho. ⛴ small boats run between the lakeshore villages.

### Key

━━ Major road
━━ Minor road
═ ═ ═ Unpaved motorable road
─── Railway
━ ━ Park boundary
▬▬▬ International boundary
△ Peak

Kakamega
50 km (31 miles)
Kisian
Pau Akuche
Kaloka
Kisumu
Hippo Point
Dunga
Kericho
80 km (50 miles)
Ahero
Winam Gulf
Awach
Osoda Point
Nyakach Bay
Osoda Bay
Papondit
Kendu Bay
Rakwaro
Kusa
Mount Homa 1,753 m
Simbi Nyaima Lake
Gendia
Sondu
Sondu
Huma Lime
Kabondo
Ateta
Nyangweso
Kagan
Oyugis
Ringa
Bonyunyu
Homa Bay
Kisii
25 km (15 miles)

**Dunga**
Located on the eastern lakeshore, Dunga is a small fishing village with boats, nets and fishermen's homes. It is possible here to arrange a trip on the lake in a wooden handcrafted *ssese* canoe.

**Homa Bay**
Located at the base of the volcanic massif Got Asego, this friendly market town serves as a starting point for trips to Ruma National Park *(see p309)*.

### Lake Victoria's Ecological Degradation

Over the past four decades, Lake Victoria has experienced drastic environmental changes. The lake's water levels have been affected by high rates of evaporation and consumption, limited river inflow and silting. In places it is now only some 40 m (130 ft) deep. In the 1950s and 1960s, Nile perch was introduced as a game fish, but massive growth in the populations of this giant predator resulted in many species of the endemic chilid fish becoming extinct. By the end of the 1990s, an additional threat was posed by the water hyacinth that had clogged almost 40 per cent of the lakeshore. This problem is currently being addressed with the introduction of two small weevils of the *Neochetina* genus that have an insatiable appetite for the hyacinth.

Nile perch, driving most local species to extinction

For keys to symbols *see back flap*

The verdant slopes of Mount Homa rising above Homa Bay

### ⓰ Kendu Bay and Simbi Nyaima

**Road Map** A4. 70 km (44 miles) SW of Kisumu. 🚌

A small fishing village of mud houses centred around one main street, Kendu Bay lies on the shores of Lake Victoria. The local Luo people often venture offshore to fish with their fishing nets in tiny wooden canoes.

The lake Simbi Nyaima, literally "the village that sank", is a 45-minute walk west of the village on Homa Bay Road. It is a bright-green patch of algae-filled water in a volcanic crater, with no known inlet or outlet, and with shores that are devoid of vegetation. The local people believe it to be unlucky and it is not fished. Luo legend claims that it was created when the Simbi people were celebrating at the chief's house. A weary old woman turned up looking for shelter and food but was denied these. In vengeance, she induced a flood that sank the village and created a lake. Today, there is a footpath around its rim where greater and lesser flamingoes can be seen feeding off the algae.

### ⓱ Homa Bay

**Road Map** A4. 58 km (36 miles) W of Kisii. 🏚 32,000. 🚌

Located near Lake Victoria, Homa Bay is a ramshackle market town along two main streets, with a covered market and facilities including a bank and post office. Once a bustling port, its shores are now infested with water hyacinth. Above the town rises Mount Homa, a 1,751-m (5,745-ft) massif, known by the Luo as Got Asego (Famous Mountain), which is the highest of many extinct volcanic plugs in the region. Although it is a tough scramble to the top along goat tracks that go through thick thorn bushes, it offers superb views over Lake Victoria, the patchwork of fields and Luo huts. Beyond Homa Bay, the road heads to **Mbita Point**, a small rural community and a collection point for boats to the lake's islands.

### ⓲ Mfangano Island

**Road Map** A4. 8 km (5 miles) offshore. ✈ charter flights. 🚢 from Mbita Point. 🚢

The largest of Lake Victoria's islands in Kenya, Mfangano has a rocky shoreline and rugged terrain covered in fig trees. The island also has a few black-sand beaches. The highest point on Mfangano is the 1,694-m (5,558-ft-) high Mount Kwitutu. Local fishermen and subsistence farmers once got around the island by foot or boat, but a road has now been built circling Mfangano so that the island is now accessible by car and bicycle as well.

An hour or two's walk into the interior from **Sena**, the island's capital, brings visitors to a high bluff with good views over the island's northern coast. An overhang here has cave paintings of white and reddish spirals. The paintings are thought to be 1,000–4,000 years old, and have been traced back to Twa pygmies from the Congo Basin who are believed to have sheltered in this cave. It has been suggested that the white spirals represent the moon and

Prehistoric rock art in a cave near Ukula village on the northern coast of Mfangano Island

The southern stretch of Rusinga Island with Lake Victoria in the distance

the red ones the sun. The Twa may have believed that the paintings could invoke rain.

## ⑱ Rusinga Island

**Road Map** A4. Just offshore of Mbita Point. 🛩 charter flights. 🚌 to Mbita Point. 🚢

Connected to the mainland by a causeway, Rusinga Island has a rocky shoreline and is home to populations of giant monitor lizard, spotted-neck otter, hippo and over 100 species of birds. The best places to spot these are from **Hippo Bay** or the small offshore **Bird Island**, which is a short boat-ride from **Rusinga Island Lodge** *(see p370)*. The goat-grazed interior of the island is, however, rather desolate as many of its trees have been cut down for firewood. There is at present an initiative to restore the greenery of Rusinga and thousands of trees have been planted on the island.

Rusinga is also the final resting place of Tom Mboya, a leading politician during Kenya's fight for independence. His mausoleum, which has a cone-shaped roof, stands behind his grave on family land in the north of the island, approximately 7 km (4 miles) from Mbita on a dirt road.

Rusinga is also rich in fossils and the skull of *Proconsul heseloni*, a 5-million-year-old anthropoid ape, was found here by anthropologist Mary Leakey in 1947.

## ⑲ Ruma National Park

**Road Map** A4. 24 km (15 miles) W of Homa Bay. 🚕 4WD. **Open** 6am–6pm daily. 🏕 🚻 🔥 🚾 **kws.org**

Only accessible by 4WD vehicles, the little-visited 120-sq-km (46-sq-mile) Ruma National Park in the Lambwe Valley lies 10 km (6 miles) east of Lake Victoria. The park was established in 1966 to protect Kenya's last and only population of roan antelope *(see p134)*. More recently, it has been stocked with several introduced animals including Bohor's reedbuck, Jackson's hartebeest, Rothschild's giraffe, zebra and buffalo. Leopard and hyena are also present but remain elusive. The landscape is a mix of grassy savannah on rolling hills, with a few tracts of woodland that attract a number of birds, including the endangered blue swallow that migrates between here and southern Tanzania. The park has three rough gravel tracks for game viewing, but these become impassable in wet weather because of the sticky dark mud known locally as black cotton soil. There is a simple self-catering guesthouse in the park along with two campsites. However, there are no facilities available and visitors to the park need to be totally self-sufficient.

A roan antelope bull in the grasslands of Ruma National Park

### Tom Mboya

Politician Tom Mboya at Embakasi Airport

Tom Mboya was an influential politician during the early years of independent Kenya. In 1957, he became the first African to win a seat on the colonial Legislative Council. His People's Congress Party merged with other political parties in 1960 to form the Kenyan African National Union (KANU), with Mboya as secretary general during the period when independence was negotiated. After independence, he became Minister for Economic Planning and Development. In 1969, Mboya was shot dead on a street in Nairobi at the age of 39. The assassin, who was arrested and hanged, was quoted as saying, "Why don't you go after the big man?" The identity of the "big man" has never been revealed, but the incident sparked speculation that someone in government played a part in Mboya's death, as he was considered a contender for president against Jomo Kenyatta. The inscription on Mboya's mausoleum reads, "Go and fight like this man, Who fought for mankind's cause, Who died because he fought, Whose battles are still unwon."

A banana plantation in the rich soils near Kisii

## ⑳ Thimlich Ohinga

**Road Map** A5. 181 km (112 miles) S of Kisumu. 🚉 from Migori, take the A1 towards Isebania. Turn right after 4 km (3 miles), on to a rough murram road at the junction of Muhoro Bay. Take the first right after the depot for 55 km (35 miles). **Open** 9:30am–6pm daily. 🅿️ 🌐 **museums.or.ke**

Hidden in the bush, the Iron Age site of Thimlich Ohinga is the remains of a 15th-century stone enclosure thought to be built by an early Bantu group whose history has been forgotten. The main enclosure, around 150 m (490 ft) across, has many houses within it along with pens for livestock, a forge for smelting iron and what is believed to have been some form of athletic playing field. The walls are 1–4 m (3–13 ft) high, 1–3 m (3–10 ft) wide and built of loose stones without mortar. Although other groups have lived there since, and the area was still inhabited at the beginning of the 20th century, few alterations have been made to the structures and they are some of the best preserved Iron Age remains in East Africa. Despite its protection as a national monument, however, Thimlich Ohinga is isolated and rarely visited. There are no visitor facilities and travellers require private transport to get here.

## ㉑ Kisii

**Road Map** A4. 120 km (75 miles) S of Kisumu. 🔺 84,000. 🚌 Moi Highway.

Straddling the A1 that runs from Kisumu into Tanzania, Kisii is the main urban and commercial town of the Gusii Highlands. It is a fast-growing rambling market town surrounded by picturesque undulating hills of terraced smallholdings. The region is dissected by rivers flowing west into Lake Victoria, notably the Kuja and Mogusi rivers. The town has a colourful market crammed with burgeoning fruit and vegetable stalls, which serve as a reminder of how fertile this area is with its abundant sunshine and rainfall. Local cash crops include oranges, bananas, maize, beans, millet and potatoes.

The town has a number of Indian and Kikuyu traders, but the population is largely made up of the Gusii people. This group is one of the most rapidly growing populations in Kenya, on average women bear nine children – so the Gusii Highlands is one of the country's most heavily populated rural areas, with some 70–80 per cent of the land under cultivation. Tall commercial buildings, super-markets, petrol stations, banks, dozens of cheap board and lodgings and the sprawling open market can be found on Moi Highway, which runs through the town. This over-crowded, and often muddy, road also serves as one long *matatu* stage with vehicles clustered along the length of it.

## ㉒ Tabaka

**Road Map** A4. 24 km (10 miles) W of Kisii. 🚌 🏨

The settlement of Tabaka is home to Kenya's soapstone quarries and the Gusii community here are renowned for their artistic skill as carvers. Soft pliable stone from these quarries is fashioned into all sorts of items for practical use, such as bowls and plates, or tourist items such as animal

The bustling streets in central Kisii

statues, chess sets and abstract figures. In the village, the carvers sit outside on the white dusty soapstone rubble, where visitors can watch them work with chisels. Some may offer a chisel and a piece of rock to let visitors have a go at carving themselves. People can observe the workers smoothening the soapstone with sandpaper and water and polishing the finished products with wax. The soapstone comes in a variety of colours from pale cream – the softest – to deep red – the hardest. Finished carvings are sold in some half a dozen shops in Tabaka. These items are also exported all over the country and can be found in most tourist markets and shops.

An artisan carving soft soapstone using a simple chisel, Tabaka

## ㉓ Kericho

**Road Map** B4. 107 km (67 miles) NE of Kisii. 36,000.

Thanks to the consistent weather of sunny mornings and rainy afternoons, Kericho is the heart of Western Kenya's tea industry. The origin of the town's name is under some dispute. It could have been named after Ole Kericho, an 18th-century Maasai chief who was killed in the area, or after John Kerich, an early British tea planter. Commercial production of tea was established by the British in the region after World War I. Many of the estates have now been reallocated to small farmers and operate under the

Kenya Union of Small Scale Tea Owners (KUSSTO), although the area is dominated by giant tea plantations owned by international companies such as Brooke Bond. The best place to try a cup of Kenyan tea is on the manicured lawns of the charming colonial **Tea Hotel** *(see p369)*, which also organizes tours of the plantations.

In town, most amenities are spread along the main road, Moi Highway. The layout is very orderly with a town square called Chai Square, a village green and the beautiful stone- and ivy-clad British-built **Holy Trinity Church**, which was constructed in 1952.

## ㉔ Chagaik Dam and Arboretum

**Road Map** B4. 8 km (5 miles) E of Kericho on the B1 towards Nakuru.

Located by the shores of a small lake, which is covered in water lilies and surrounded by clutches of bamboo, the Chagaik Dam and Arboretum is a lovely picnic spot. The arboretum is an easy 5-minute walk from the dam. Hemmed

The picturesque lake at Chagaik Dam, an excellent picnic spot

in by tea plantations, the formal gardens of tropical trees and well-manicured lawns were originally laid out by tea planter Tom Grumbley in the 1940s. Across the lake is a small tangled clutch of sprawling trees and undergrowth that is home to a troop of black-and-white colobus. Bird-watchers should look out for the yellow-spotted barbet, snowy-headed robin-chat, banded and white-chinned prinia and black-billed weaver. Visits to this area can be arranged through the guides at the Tea Hotel in Kericho.

### Kenya's Tea Story

Tea was introduced in Kenya from India in 1903. Now, with more than 1,100 sq km (425 sq miles) of land devoted to its cultivation, Kenya is the world's third-largest producer of tea, with an annual output of 406,760 tonnes (369,000 tons). The country's main plantations are in the highland areas on either side of the Rift Valley, at altitudes of 1,500–2,700 m (4,900–8,850 ft) above sea level. The tea bush is an evergreen grown in tropical climates, so that bushes are harvested throughout the year and tea is picked on a continual cycle of 7–14 days. Only the choicest upper two leaves and a bud are plucked each time. The majority of Kenyan tea is sold through auctions in Mombasa, with Pakistan, the UK and Egypt being the biggest buyers.

Tea plantations dominating the rolling countryside around Kericho

# CENTRAL HIGHLANDS

Blessed with fertile volcanic soils and generous rainfall, and dominated by the imposing jagged peaks of Mount Kenya and the Aberdare Range, the Central Highlands rank among the most densely populated and cultivated areas in Kenya. In addition to being the national breadbasket, the region is also home to the politically and economically influential Kikuyu people.

Although they share a similar ecology, Mount Kenya and the Aberdares represent extremes of antiquity. The latter is among the most ancient ranges in East Africa, dating to before the age of dinosaurs. By contrast, Mount Kenya, Africa's second-highest mountain, is a geological infant, having erupted into existence long after our earliest bipedal ancestors first strode through the region.

The Central Highlands have long been home to agricultural communities such as the Kikuyu, Meru, Embu and Akamba. Heavily settled by European farmers during the colonial era, the highlands lay at the centre of the notorious Happy Valley *(see p323)* scene of the 1930s, while its forests provided shelter to the Mau Mau movement that would strike effectively against colonial rule two decades later. Today, the area is studded with easygoing and well-equipped but generally unremarkable towns, while the sprawling agricultural estates of colonial times have been replaced by a patchwork of low-key *shambas* (smallholdings) planted with papayas, bananas, coffee and other crops.

Forming an elevated grassy saddle between Mount Kenya and the Aberdares, this area supports the bulk of Kenya's remaining highland forest. Protected within national parks, the mountains support a rich diversity of habitats and an impressive volume of wildlife, ranging from large mammals, such as elephants and lions, to colobus monkeys and chameleons. Other key wildlife areas include the underrated Meru National Park, set in the eastern rainshadow of Mount Kenya, and the agglomeration of private reserves sprawling northwards from the Central Highlands across the Laikipia Plateau.

Moorland vegetation against the spectacular backdrop of the Aberdare Range

◄ Typical Afro-alpine vegetation leading up to the Batian and Nelion peaks, Mount Kenya National Park

# The Kikuyu

The Kikuyu are Kenya's most populous ethnic group, comprising 22 per cent of the national population. In common with the other Bantu-speakers of the region, the ancestral Kikuyu migration eastwards from West Africa took place about 2,000 years ago. They finally settled in the fertile highlands north of Nairobi – their present homeland. Oral traditions suggest that they abandoned their original hunter-gatherer lifestyle for agriculture and pastoralism after their arrival. Today, the Kikuyu are prominent both in business and national affairs, and most individuals dress in a Western style and practise Christianity rather than traditional beliefs.

British officials and Kikuyu people signing a land acquisition treaty

### The Kikuyu Way of Life

*The traditional Kikuyu way of life in the Central Highlands is based on agriculture, though pastoralism and hunting are also practised. During the colonial era Europeans who settled on Kikuyu land enforced a feudal system of dependency. In the long term, this close association with the colonists has led to the Kikuyu becoming the most educated and Westernized of Kenya's tribes.*

**The elaborate traditional attire** of Kikuyu women includes beads, animal skin headdresses and white body paint.

**Ostrich feathers** form an impressive part of the traditional Kikuyu headdress.

**Most rural Kikuyu** are subsistence farmers, growing a variety of fruit and grains in small holdings known as *shambas*.

### Kikuyu religion

The Kikuyu traditionally worship a single god known as Ngai (The Provider), though they also place a high premium on ancestor worship. Partly owing to the high missionary presence in the region and partly because they are predisposed to monotheism, the Kikuyu today are predominantly Christian and most individuals actively shun traditional beliefs.

**Residing in the glacial peaks of Mount Kenya** is the Kikuyu god Ngai. Traditionally, Kikuyu homesteads always face the sacred peaks, a custom referred to in the title of former President Jomo Kenyatta's autobiography, *Facing Mount Kenya*.

**About 75 per cent of the Kikuyu** identify themselves as Christians and are regular church-goers. Most practise Protestant faiths.

## Eminent Kikuyus

*The Kikuyu are Kenya's most politically and economically influential community, probably as a result of their traditional homeland's proximity to Nairobi, and a higher than average level of education.*

**Wangari Maathai**, the late well-known environmental activist, became the first African woman to win a Nobel Peace Prize in 2004, for "her contribution to sustainable development, democracy and peace".

**Jomo Kenyatta**, the first president and founding father of independent Kenya, was a few months shy of 70 when he was elected in 1963. He served as president of Kenya until his death in 1978.

**Uhuru Kenyatta**, the son of Jomo Kenyatta, was given the name Uhuru from the Kiswahili term for "freedom" when he was born in October 1961 in anticipation of Kenya's upcoming independence. He has been president of Kenya since 2013.

**Dedan Kimathi** was the commander-in-chief of the Mau Mau Rebellion. When it petered out, Kimathi was captured by the colonial army in Nyeri in October 1956, and was later hanged.

Soldiers patrolling near Nyeri during the Mau Mau uprising, 1955

## The Mau Mau Rebellion

By 1950, settler farms covered some 10,000 sq km (3,850 sq miles) of the Central Highlands, an area six times larger than that allocated to the country's million-plus rural Kikuyu. The resultant sense of displacement led to the formation of Mau Mau, a Kikuyu-dominated guerilla army that hid out in the forests of Mount Kenya and the Aberdares, attacking colonial government targets and settler farms from 1952 to 1956. Repeated attacks on civilian targets led to the Mau Mau being portrayed as bloodthirsty savages by the colonial authorities. However, the number of settlers killed was just a fraction of the 10,000–50,000 Kikuyu civilians who were killed by the authorities or died while they were interred in unsanitary concentration camps. A military failure, the rebellion nevertheless did much to hasten the end of colonial rule, and it was a former Mau Mau leader, Jomo Kenyatta, who led Kenya to independence and served as the country's first president.

# Exploring the Central Highlands

Highland towns offer an agreeable way of experiencing the less touristic side of Kenya. Nyahururu is notable for the spectacular Thomson's Falls, and Nyeri for its association with Lord Baden-Powell of scouting fame. Meru has a worthwhile museum, and Thika offers easy access to Ol Donyo Sabuk National Park. Few organized safaris linger beyond an overnight stop at one of the tree hotels on the slopes of Mount Kenya or the Aberdares. Those seeking an off-the-beaten-track wildlife experience can try Meru National Park or one of the upmarket camps on the Laikipia Plateau. The region's major draw is Mount Kenya, which offers enough hiking opportunities to last weeks.

Wooden exterior of the popular Mountain Lodge near Mount Kenya

Camping on the grassy slopes of Mount Kenya

## Key

— Highway
— Major road
═ Minor road
-- Untarred major road
═ Untarred minor road
== 4WD track
— Minor railway
△ Peak

A herd of Burchell's zebra grazing in Meru National Park

*For hotels and restaurants see pp370–71 and p381*

## Getting Around

The Central Highlands are well suited to independent travel, whether in a private vehicle or using the plentiful public transport between all towns. The surfaced Ring Road around Mount Kenya, linked to Nairobi by a highway through Thika and Karatina, connects Nyeri, Naro Moru, Nanyuki, Meru, Chogoria and Embu, while another surfaced road runs from Nyeri to Nyahururu. There is no public transport to the Laikipia Plateau or Meru National Park, but guests at the tree hotels of Aberdare National Park are shuttled there from Nyeri by the lodge management, and hikes up Mount Kenya can easily be arranged on the spot at Naro Moru, Chogoria and most other towns in the vicinity.

The secluded Thomson's Falls on the outskirts of Nyahururu

## Sights at a Glance

### Towns and Cities

① Thika
④ Nyeri
⑥ Nyahururu
⑨ Naro Moru
⑩ Nanyuki
⑪ Meru
⑬ Embu

### National Parks and Reserves

③ Ol Donyo Sabuk National Park
⑤ *Aberdare National Park pp320–21*
⑧ *Mount Kenya National Park pp326–9*
⑫ *Meru National Park pp334–7*
⑭ Mwea National Reserve

### Areas of Natural Beauty

② Fourteen Falls
⑦ *Laikipia Plateau pp322–5*

**For keys to symbols** *see back flap*

## ❶ Thika

**Road Map** C5. 45 km (28 miles) N of Nairobi. 🚐 140,000. 🚍 🚌

Linked to Nairobi by the eight-lane A2 highway, this bustling and rapidly growing highland town is best known outside Kenya as the setting of Elspeth Huxley's novelistic account of her colonial childhood, *The Flame Trees of Thika* (1959), which was adapted as a television series in the 1980s. Thika is not quite the rustic outpost it was in Edwardian times; today, it practically functions as a satellite of Nairobi. Any flame trees that may have survived are out-numbered by smoking *matatus* and introduced conifers. The council motto "Your Industrial Town" more realistically describes the place, with more than 20 large textile, food-processing and motor vehicle-assembly factories scattered around the periphery comprising its industry.

A more worthwhile stop than Thika is the **Blue Posts Hotel** *(see p371)*, which lies in pretty flowering grounds on the northern outskirts of town. Established in 1908 as a stopover for white settlers who lived and farmed in the highlands, Blue Posts claims to be older than Thika itself, and the ivy-clad period architecture in the hotel ensures that it still exudes a faint aura of the colonial era commemorated by Huxley. Before African touches like *makuti*-thatched roofs were added to the structure, the original bar featured blue pillars,

Mists cover the summit of Ol Donyo Sabuk

which is how it derived its name. The Chania and Thika rivers both flow through the well-wooded grounds of the hotel, tumbling over a pair of attractive waterfalls in the process, and there is plenty of birdlife around too.

## ❷ Fourteen Falls

**Road Map** C5. 25 km (16 miles) SE of Thika on Graissa Rd. 🚐
**Open** 9am–5pm daily. 🏊 🚗 🏕

Managed by the Thika Town Council, this pretty waterfall is formed by the Athi river as it splits into several small streams before tumbling over a wide rock lip close to the base of Ol Donyo Sabuk (Big Mountain). The main drop is not especially high, no more than 10 m (33 ft), and the name is slightly misleading as the water may form a single sheet or be broken up into more than 14 mini-cataracts, depending on the seasonal strength of the flow. A group of local teenagers often hang round the site and in

order to earn some money will dive over the waterfall to the pool below – an activity that is best not encouraged. The site is generally most impressive in April and December when the water level is highest. At any time of year, it is worth looking at the small hippo pool, a 5-minute walk up the river.

## ❸ Ol Donyo Sabuk National Park

**Road Map** C5. 28 km (17 miles) SE of Thika. **Tel** 020 2062503. 🚐 🚾 4WD.
**Open** 8:30am–6pm daily. 🏊 🚗 🚓 🏕 🚾 kws.org

This scenic but little-visited national park protects the isolated 2,145-m (7,050-ft) mountain known to the Maasai as Ol Donyo Sabuk, a name that seems a little ironic given its proximity to the far taller Mount Kenya and Aberdare Range. A 10-km- (6-mile-) long dirt road leads uphill from the entrance gate, passing through forested slopes that are home

The roaring waters of Fourteen Falls, near Thika

to blue monkey, bushbuck, leopard and numerous highland birds. It climbs to the grassy summit, which offers great views on clear days. About 3 km (2 miles) before reaching the top of the mountain, the road passes the grave of Sir William McMillan, a wealthy settler whose immense bulk foiled the tractor that was meant to carry his coffin to the summit and forced the burial to take place en route. The road requires 4WD and may be impassable in rain. Walking is permitted, but given the reputation for irritability of local buffalo, only in the company of an armed ranger.

## ❹ Nyeri

**Road Map** C4. 135 km (84 miles) NW of Nairobi on the road to Nyahururu. 140,000.

This burgeoning town lies between the eastern base of the Aberdare Range and the western slopes of Mount Kenya. Despite its status as a regional administrative capital, Nyeri retains a small-town feel, with a compact centre surrounded on all sides by leafy suburbia and densely planted smallholdings. The town centre has good facilities, including several banks, hotels, eateries and supermarkets. The main focus for visitors is the **Outspan Hotel** *(see p371)*, a smart colonial-era edifice that also serves as the official springboard for overnight forays to the legendary Treetops Lodge in Aberdare National Park *(see pp320–21)*. The hotel is a pleasant place, and visitors can follow a short downhill walking trail to the forest-fringed Chania river or visit the Kikuyu cultural village where there are daily dance performances.

Nyeri has produced several Kenyans of note, including former president Mwai Kibaki, Nobel Peace Prize winner Wangari Maathai and marathon runner Catherine Ndereba. The most famous former resident, however, is Lord Robert Baden-Powell, whose cottage on the grounds of the Outspan is now

Farmers working in the fertile fields near Nyeri

a small museum. He is buried in **St Peter's Cemetery** near the Anglican church. His gravestone bears a circle with a dot in the centre, which is the Scout's trail sign for "Going Home", while the walkway to the cemetery is lined with stones embossed with scout and Girl Guide mottos.

## ❺ Aberdare National Park

*See pp320–21.*

## ❻ Nyahururu

**Road Map** B4. 100 km (60 miles) NW of Nyeri. 37,000.

Nyahururu is perched at an altitude of 2,360 m (7,750 ft) on the edge of the Laikipia Plateau

*(see pp322–5)*. It is otherwise a rather humdrum market town, with adequate amenities but few distinguishing features. The main point of interest is **Thomson's Falls**, which sees the Ewaso Nyiro river plummeting 75 m (246 ft) in one single drop over a volcanic ledge on its course from the Aberdares to Samburu-Buffalo Springs National Reserves *(see pp346–7)*. A footpath leads from the gardens of the distinctly colonial-era **Thomson's Falls Lodge** *(see p371)* to the base of the waterfall, which is named after Scottish explorer Joseph Thomson, who was in this area in 1883. A tract of riparian woodland follows the river below the falls and supports a selection of highland forest birds along with black-and-white colobus monkey.

### Lord Robert Baden-Powell

The Baden-Powells, circa 1910

Born in London on 22 February 1857, Robert Baden-Powell served in the British army in India and Africa between 1876 and 1910, becoming Lieutenant-General and winning several medals for his heroic efforts, most famously in the Siege of Mafeking in the Anglo-Boer War of 1899–1902. He is best known posthumously as the founder of the Boy Scout movement, an event usually dated to the publication of his book *Scouting for Boys* (1908). He retired from the military at the request of King Edward VII in 1910 in order to promote scouting. Two years later, he met his future wife Olave, later in charge of the Girl Guide movement started by Baden-Powell in 1910. He was knighted in 1921. Baden-Powell and Olave moved to Nyeri in 1939, where they lived in a specially commissioned one-bedroom bungalow called Paxtu on the grounds of the Outspan Hotel. He died on 8 January 1941 and was buried in Nyeri, facing Mount Kenya. Olave was buried alongside him in 1977. The joint grave is now a national monument.

# ❺ Aberdare National Park

This 767-sq-km (296-sq-mile) national park protects a 75-km-(47-mile-) long, 4,000-m- (13,100-ft-) tall mountain range that rises from the Rift Valley escarpment above Lake Naivasha to form the western buttress of the Central Highlands. It was named by Joseph Thomson in 1884 after Lord Aberdare, then president of the Royal Geographic Society, but the local Kikuyu call it Nyandurua (Drying Hide) after its similarity to a pegged-out animal skin. The Aberdare bedrock is more ancient than volcanic Mount Kenya, but both mountains are ecologically similar, with forested lower slopes leading to more open vegetation. Rare species among its wildlife include the mountain bongo antelope, golden cat and giant forest hog.

Bamboo forest between the montane and moorland belts

**★ Afro-alpine Moorland**
Set at altitudes of above 3,000 m (9,843 ft), the misty belt of Afro-alpine moorland supports open vegetation scattered with otherworldly giant lobelias, groundsels and heathers.

**Karura Falls**
Seldom visited by tourists, the upper moorland of the Aberdares is dotted with pretty waterfalls, many accessible along rough dirt roads that become mud baths after heavy rain.

Nyahururu
30 km (19 miles)

• Rhino Gate

Shamata Gate

Chebuswa
3,364 m

Engore Ngobit

Ol Doinyo La Satima
4,001 m
②

Table Mountain
3,791 m

Aberdare Range

Maratini Hill
3,698 m

Chania

Naivasha
50 km (31 miles)

Matubio Gate

Nyandarua
3,906 m

Elephant Hill
3,590 m

### KEY

① **Gura Falls** is Kenya's tallest waterfall, plunging 300 m (984 ft) into a deep ravine.

② **Ol Doinyo La Satima**, the highest peak in Aberdare, has a Maasai name meaning "bull-calf mountain".

**Elephant Sightings**
With an estimated 2,000 individuals resident in the park, the African elephant is probably the most conspicuous of the Big Five animals here, although leopard, buffalo and black rhino are also present.

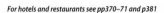

**★ The Ark**
The more modern of Kenya's tree hotels, this attractive wooden edifice has a waterhole that is visited by rhino, elephant and buffalo, with leopard also making sporadic appearances.

**★ Treetops**
Like The Ark, Treetops offers nightly game viewing from its own waterhole. The hotel made headlines in 1952, when it hosted the young Princess Elizabeth on the night that King George VI died and she awoke the uncrowned Queen of England.

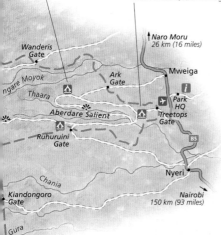

Naro Moru
26 km (16 miles)

Wanderis Gate

ngare Moyok

Thaara

Ark Gate

Mweiga

Aberdare Salient

Park HQ

Treetops Gate

Ruhuruini Gate

Chania

Nyeri

Kiandongoro Gate

Nairobi
150 km (93 miles)

Gura

## Getting Around

The most accessible part of the park is the Aberdare Salient, a mid-altitude eastern extension of the main north-south axis running towards Nyeri via Ruhuruini Gate. The only part of the park serviced by all-weather roads, the Salient is home to the legendary tree hotels – Treetops and The Ark. To the southwest, the other popular gate – Matubio Gate leading towards Naivasha – is located at the higher altitudes of the park where hiking is only permitted in the company of an armed ranger. In addition to spectacular highland scenery, these rarefied altitudes offer the opportunity to encounter park specials such as the melanistic leopard and mountain bongo.

0 km        5
0 miles      5

## The Tree Hotels of Aberdare National Park

The concept of a tree hotel – a game lodge that doubles as a hide – was pioneered in 1934, when a rudimentary treehouse-like structure called Treetops opened on the forested Aberdare Salient. The expanded Treetops and The Ark, a similar hotel, now form a break between the Rift Valley and Samburu-Buffalo Springs. The drill at both lodges is similar – lunch at a base outside the park (Aberdare Country Club for The Ark, Outspan Hotel for Treetops), then a bus ride across for the night to watch animals drink at the waterhole. Treetops, with its association with Queen Elizabeth II, boasts the greater sense of history, but The Ark surpasses it in terms of game viewing.

**Key**
▬▬ Major road
=== Unpaved motorable road
▬ ▪ Park boundary
△ Peak

**For keys to symbols** *see back flap*

# ❼ Laikipia Plateau

Extending over 9,500 sq km (3,670 sq miles) northwards from Mount Kenya, Laikipia is a mid-altitude plateau of semiarid plains punctuated by basalt outcrops, forested slopes and spectacular gorges hemming the Ewaso Nyiro and Ewaso Narok rivers. The plateau was split between ranchland and community land during the colonial era, when the wildlife was frequently persecuted, but decreased profitability of ranching coupled with greater eco-awareness eventually led to most of the plateau being turned into a patchwork of private and community-based wildlife sanctuaries. Collectively, this so-called Ewaso Ecosystem is larger than any protected area in Kenya other than Tsavo. It supports wildlife densities second only to Masai Mara, including about 7,000 elephants, plenty of predators and more than half the country's black rhino.

**★ African Wild Dog**
Laikipia provides sanctuary to the only viable African wild-dog population in the northern hemisphere. There are several large packs with a combined total of around 300 individuals.

**Walking Safaris**
The focal point at most conservancies and lodges in northern Laikipia is walking safaris, which are usually led by local Samburu or Pokot scouts, and provide the thrill of seeing wildlife without the barrier of a vehicle.

## Getting Around

The plateau can be visited by road en route between the Aberdares and Samburu-Buffalo Springs, in which case it is advisable to pick one of the less remote lodges or to charter a flight from Nanyuki. There is no public transport to the plateau, but Solio Ranch and Ol Pejeta are readily accessible from the main road in a private 4WD, and day visitors are welcomed. It is also easy to get to Nanyuki airport on public transport and fly to a lodge from there.

Maralal
35 km (22 miles)

Suguta
Marmar

Churo

Kuti
2,105 m

Ol Ari Nyiro
Conservancy

Ol Keju Losero

C77

Kinamba

Ngelesha
2,273 m    Tandaro

Ol Arabel      Lariak
Forest         Forest

Karandi        Rumuruti

Rumuruti
Forest                    Nabolo
C51   C77                  1,912 m

Marmanet
2,610 m

Nyahururu

Nakuru         B5            C76
50 km     C77
(31 miles)   Ndaragwa            Ngobit
Onge

**★ Ol Pejeta Conservancy and Sweetwaters Chimpanzee Sanctuary**
An observation tower at Ol Pejeta allows visitors to observe Kenya's only chimpanzees – an introduced community of orphaned animals from war-torn Burundi.

*For hotels and restaurants see pp370–71 and p381*

## Happy Valley

*White Mischief*, on the murder of Josslyn Hay, Earl of Erroll

Happy Valley was a hedonist community of aristocrats, farmers and socialites whose promiscuous lifestyle was centred on the Kenyan highlands in the 1930s. Today, it is best remembered for the murder of the 22nd Earl of Erroll, shot dead in his car in 1941. The police initially arrested Sir Henry "Jock" Delves Broughton, whose wife had had a dalliance with the Earl, but he was later acquitted, as immortalized in the movie *White Mischief*. More recent evidence suggests that the Earl was executed by British military intelligence due to his links with the British Fascist movement.

### VISITORS' CHECKLIST

**Practical Information**
**Road Map** C4. 10 km (6 miles) N of Nanyuki airport along main surfaced road to Naro Moru. **Open** varies between conservancies, but typically 6am–6pm daily. no entrance fee for public roads through Laikipia. 🚗 🚲 🖥 🍴 ⛺
 **laikipiatourism.com**

**Transport**
✈ 🚌 to Nanyuki airport.

**Key**

═══ Major road

══ Minor road

= = Unpaved motorable road

- - Trail

—·— Park boundary

△ Peak

**Horseback Safaris**
Reticulated giraffe and other ungulates will often let people on horses approach them far more closely than they would a vehicle or a human pedestrian.

**★ Night Drives**
The private conservancies of Laikipia mostly offer night drives, which come with an excellent chance of seeing nocturnal creatures such as the genet, leopard, aardvark and the bushbaby.

**Solio Game Reserve**
This is Kenya's oldest and most important project for the conservation of rhinos in their natural habitat. Breeding has been so successful that rhinos from Solio have stocked other reserves.

**For keys to symbols** *see back flap*

# Exploring Laikipia Plateau

Laikipia differs from other conservation areas in Kenya in that it consists of dozens of autonomous private conservancies, although it is overseen by the Laikipia Wildlife Forum (LWF), a non-profit organization which was formed in 1992 and includes all stakeholders in Laikipia – some 40 lodges or tented camps, jointly owned by ranch owners and the local land-owning communities as diverse as the Maasai, Kikuyu, Samburu and Pokot. Each is managed as an exclusive and self-contained entity, and the experience offered is strikingly different to any national park. Game drives are almost invariably run by the reserves using their own skilled driver-guides. Also on offer are activities usually forbidden in official parks, such as guided walks and spotlighted night drives.

## 🏠 Ol Pejeta Conservancy and Sweetwaters Chimpanzee Sanctuary

25 km (16 miles) NW of Nanyuki on the C76. **Tel** 020 2033244. **Open** 7am– 7pm for day visitors. 🐾 📷 🌿 🐒 🏔
🌐 olpejetaconservancy.org

Formerly a cattle ranch owned by Lord Delamere, Ol Pejeta extends over 365 sq km (140 sq miles) of semiarid grassland and acacia thornbush flanking the upper reaches of the Ewaso Nyiro river in southern Laikipia. It was first established as a conservancy in 1988, and is now home to all the Big Five and a staggering population of over 10,000 large mammals. It has the highest ratio of animal to area of any park or reserve in Kenya. Lion, leopard, cheetah, buffalo, black rhino, reticulated giraffe and elephant are present, while a varied selection of antelope includes the localized gerenuk and Beisa oryx. More than 500 bird species have also been recorded. In 2009 four of the world's last remaining seven northern white rhinos arrived from a zoo in the Czech Republic. They now live in the endangered species enclosure, along with small populations of Grevy's zebra and Jackson's hartebeest.

The conservancy is known for its high standard of guiding, with night drives and guided walks offered in addition to the usual daytime game drives. Other activities include horse and camel riding and visits to *manyattas (see pp260–61).*

Following the establishment of a chimpanzee sanctuary in 1993, Ol Pejeta supports the country's only population of chimpanzee, a species that does not naturally occur in Kenya *(see p322).* The sanctuary was created to provide a natural refuge for orphaned chimpanzees formerly housed at the Jane Goodall Institute in Burundi prior to the outbreak of civil war. Today, Ol Pejeta supports around 40 chimpanzees, which are split across two communities living in the forest along either side of the Ewaso Nyiro river. As it is a refuge rather than a conservation project, the females are sterilized on arrival to prevent breeding. There are several programmes for day visitors, and accommodation is in six lodges and five campsites.

Logo, Sweetwaters Chimpanzee Sanctuary

Accommodation at the lush Solio Game Ranch

## 🏠 Solio Game Reserve

33 km (21 miles) N of Nyeri along the Nyahururu Rd. 🐾 📷 🐒

This 70-sq-km (27-sq-mile) sanctuary on the Solio Cattle Ranch was founded in 1970, primarily as a breeding centre for rhinos. The first introduced breeding populations of 23 black and 16 white rhino have bred with great success, and more than 100 individuals have been translocated out of Solio to Lake Nakuru *(see pp280–83),* Tsavo West *(see pp190–91),* and Aberdare *(see pp320–21)* National Parks, along with other locations in Laikipia. Today, as well as the rhino, most of the plains species can be seen, including zebra, buffalo, giraffe eland, waterbuck and impala, and two of Kenya's northern species, the Beisa oryx and gerenuk. Lion, cheetah, leopard and spotted hyena are either resident or pass through regularly, and smaller predators such as black-backed jackal, dwarf mongoose and genet are common. The reserve's **Solio Lodge** *(see p370),* offers luxury accommodation and game activities, and other lodges in the region can arrange game drives.

Elephants roaming at Ol Pejeta Conservancy

### 🏠 Lewa Wildlife Conservancy

7 km (4 miles) from the main Nanyuki-
Isiolo Rd along a dirt track; signposted
4 km (2 miles) N of the junction to
Meru. **Tel** 064 31405. 🔲 🖋 🖉 🖉
🌿 🕸 lewa.org

Like so many other sanctuaries
on the Laikipia Plateau, Lewa
was established as a colonial
cattle ranch in the 1920s. A
portion was set aside as a
wildlife sanctuary in 1983, and
the remainder of the 263-sq-km
(102-sq-mile) ranch followed
10 years later. Since then,
the wildlife sanctuary has also
been awarded guardianship of
the contiguous state-owned
**Ngare Ndare Forest Reserve**.

As well as another Laikipia
refuge for both black and white
rhino, Lewa is also one of the
most important strongholds for
the endangered Grevy's zebra,
with an estimated 380 individuals representing some
20 per cent of the global wild
population. It's a good place to
see the very localized sitatunga
antelope, which has thrived
since being translocated from
Saiwa Swamp National Park to a
permanent swamp in Lewa in
the 1980s. Aside from these
specials, Lewa offers good
general game viewing, with
high wildlife densities and is
home to the Big Five and more
than 400 species of birds. Lewa
has a fluctuating population of
100 to 400 elephant which have
traditionally used the conservancy as a dry-season feeding
ground as they migrate between
the ecosystems of Lewa, Ngare
Ndare and Mount Kenya.

The endangered Grevy's zebra, Lewa
Wildlife Conservancy

An alfresco lunch in the bush organized by a lodge on Laikipia

There are five accommodation
options and expertly guided
day and night game drives are
available, along with guided
bush walks. Lewa also houses an
important Acheulean hand-axe
site, where an abundance of
hand tools made from volcanic
rocks have been found, dating
to around 800,000 years ago.
Some of these are on display in
the **Meru Museum** (see p333).
Lewa is run as a non-profit-
making organization, with
proceeds going to conservation,
local community projects and
economic development. The
popular **Lewa (Safaricom)
Marathon** (see p43) takes place
in the conservancy in June.

### 🦌 Northern Laikipia

70 km (43 miles) NW of Nanyuki.
🚙 4WD. 🖉 🌿 Note: not all private
conservancies are open to day visitors.

The northern part of the Laikipia
Plateau is covered with a patchwork of small community and
private conservancies, most of
which offer frontage to the
Ewaso Nyiro river. The bush here
is thicker and scrubbier than in
southern Laikipia, and the area
is more notable for its pristine
atmosphere and wild riverine
scenery than great densities
of game. One animal that is
common here is the stately
greater kudu, a spiral-horned
antelope seldom seen elsewhere
in Kenya. This expanse of
wilderness is most rewardingly
explored on foot, and guided
walks rather than game drives
tend to be the main activity,
with the possibility of coming
across buffalo, elephant and
other members of the Big Five.
The area's rich avian diversity
means that bird-watchers will be
in their element. The premier
properties in this area include
**Loisaba Koija Starbeds** (see
p370), which also offer activities
such as horse riding, bush
walking and camel trekking.

### Sweetwaters Chimpanzee Sanctuary

Denizens of the West African rainforest, chimpanzees do not
naturally occur in Kenya, although it is possible that they inhabited
forested sites such as Kakamega in prehistoric times. However,
the excursion to see the introduced community of orphans from
Burundi is one of the most popular attractions at Ol Pejeta, almost
as exciting as seeing these primates in the wild. Their crescendo
of communal pant-hoot calls
allow chimpanzees within
earshot to identify which
other chimps are also in the
vicinity. Interaction between
them is also fascinating to
observe, and includes plenty
of grooming and displays of
affection as well as regular shows
of dominance. More rarely seen
is their ability to use tools, for
instance to "fish" for termites
in termite mounds.

Chimpanzee searching for
termites, Sweetwaters

# ❾ Mount Kenya National Park

In clear weather, the jagged peaks of Mount Kenya – considered by the Kikuyu, Meru and Akamba to be the abode of their gods – dominate the skyline of the Central Highlands. While its existence was first reported in 1849 by the missionary Ludwig Krapf, the first person to summit was Sir Halford Mackinder in 1899. An extinct volcano, Mount Kenya was most active some 2.5–3 million years ago. Today, it hosts a diverse flora, with forest on the lower slopes, then rising through bamboo forest, montane heath and Afro-alpine moorland to its barren glacial peaks. Its upper slopes are protected in a 715-sq-km (275-sq-mile) national park and the middle slopes in a 2,100-sq-km (810-sq-mile) forest reserve, jointly inscribed as a UNESCO World Heritage Site in 1997.

Blue monkey, a resident of Mount Kenya's forest zone

**The Sirimon Route**, although less often used, offers better game viewing than the alternatives.

Timau 11 km (7 miles)

Sirimon Gate

Mount Kenya Forest Reserve

Global Atmosph Watch Station

Likii

Sirimon Route

Mackinder Valley

Shipton's Cave

Nelion 5,189 m

Burguret Route

Batian 5,199 m

Le Ro 4,9

Austria Hut

Meteorological Station

Naro Moru

Park HQ

Naro Moru Route

Lake Höhnel

Naro Moru Gate 16 km (10 miles)

Park Gate

Höhnel Valley

Nyamindi

Peak Circular Path

Kamweti Route

**Batian and Nelion Peaks**
The name Kenya derives from the Akamba word *Kiinya*, meaning "mountain of the ostrich", a reference to the Batian and Nelion peaks' resemblance to a black-and-white ostrich tail feather.

**★ Serena Mountain Lodge**
This forest-enclosed tree hotel on the southern slopes offers the best wildlife viewing in the vicinity of Mount Kenya.

Embu 45 km (28 miles)

0 kilometres 5

0 miles 5

**★ Abseiling at Lewis Glacier**
The mountain's dozen glaciers, all of which are in recession as a result of global warming, are popular with adventurous climbers.

*For hotels and restaurants see pp370–71 and p381*

★ **Afro-alpine Moorland**
Although less rich in wildlife, the higher altitude Afro-alpine moorland of Mount Kenya supports an unusual cover of low pastel-shaded heathers and grassy tussocks interspersed with giant lobelias, groundsels, aloes and other odd plants.

**VISITORS' CHECKLIST**

**Practical Information**
Road Map C4. 140 km (87 miles) NE of Nairobi. 📱 020 3568763 (Park Headquarters).
**Open** 6am–7pm daily.
🏕️ 🏞️ 🏔️ **W** kws.org

**Transport**
🚐

**Key**

=== Unpaved motorable road

--- Trail

-- Park boundary

△ Peak

**Chogoria Route**
Rated as the most scenic of the main routes up Mount Kenya, Chogoria offers a rather gradual ascent along a track that is still reputedly the highest motorable track in Africa. This track was first explored by car in 1929 to as high as the 4,260-m (14,000-ft) contour.

**Lenana Point**
Lenana is the highest point on Mount Kenya that can be reached without special mountaineering equipment and experience.

**Getting Around**
Although there are several trails leading to Mount Kenya's twin peaks of Batian and Nelion, in practice only three are commonly used. The shortest of these is Naro Moru Route, while the most beautiful is the Chogoria Route. The Sirimon Route passes through wide swathes of moorland, home to a number of rare mammals. Less-used trails include the Meru, Burguret and Kamweti routes. The Timau Route can only be hiked with a special permit. Guides and porters are not usually available at the park gates and need to be hired in the nearest town. The park charges entry fees for the anticipated period of a visitor's stay.

**For keys to symbols** *see back flap*

# Exploring Mount Kenya National Park

Several thousand people climb Mount Kenya annually, although most go no higher than Lenana Point, the highest peak that can be reached without specialist rock-climbing gear. Several routes are available, but whichever is used, the ascent is not to be taken lightly. Subzero temperatures carry a risk of hypothermia, the rapid ascent often induces altitude sickness and occasional blizzards can lead the unwary away from their routes. Hikes must be arranged with a reputable operator and be equipped with a good local guide and adequate mountain gear. The upper slopes of Mount Kenya are inaccessible to non-hikers, but the forest zone can be accessed at several points, most notably from the Serena Mountain Lodge.

### 🌾 Naro Moru Route

The Meteorological Station is 25 km (16 miles) E of Naro Moru town.

The shortest, easiest and most popular path up Mount Kenya approximates the route taken by the British geologists Halford Mackinder and John Gregory in the 1890s, following the Naro Moru river uphill from Naro Moru town to its source on the western base of the glacial peaks. The round hike can be completed in 3 days, using the **Meteorological Station** as a starting point, but allowing an extra day would greatly reduce the risk of altitude-related illness. It is normal to spend the first night at the station, which lies above the forest line, so hikers on this route will only see the forest and its wildlife from behind a car window unless they opt to walk some or all of the way from Naro Moru. From the station, the hike to **Mackinder's Camp** takes

Hiking up the popular Naro Moru Route to Mount Kenya

around 6 hours, passing first through a steep marshy area known as the Vertical Bog before entering the Teleki Valley, which offers superb views to the peaks in clear weather. The valley is studded with giant lobelias and other floral oddities associated with the Afro-alpine zone. Wildlife here includes rock hyraxes, mole-rats and various

birds, although zebra, eland, buffalo and even elephant are seen from time to time. With an early start from the camp, it is possible to ascend Lenana and return to the trailhead at the Meteorological Station in one long day. Those who wish to spend more time in the glacial zone will find that **Austrian Hut** is the highest permanent structure in the mountain, and well positioned for the ascent of Lenana, while the more immediate vicinity is notable for its sparsely vegetated lava formations and views over the **Lewis Glacier**, especially at dusk.

### 🌾 Chogoria Route

66 km (41 miles) S of Meru town.

Widely regarded to be the most beautiful hiking route up Mount Kenya, and the longest of those in regular use, Chogoria was pioneered by the aptly named Edward Carr, who drove a Model-T Ford along it as far as the 4,260-m (14,000-ft) contour in 1929, the same year that mountaineer Eric Shipton undertook the second ascent of the peaks. The ascent starts at the **Chogoria Mission Station**, and most people drive at least some of the way through the extensive forest and bamboo zones using the renovated Carr's Road, still said to be the highest motorable track in Africa. Scenic highlights of the upper slopes include **Hall Tarns** and the Afro-alpine moorland of the **Nithi Valley**, both of which are crossed en route to **Minto's Campsite**, the base for the final climb to Lenana. At least 4 days and ideally 5 or

Chogoria Route, Mount Kenya National Park

Mount Kenya's snowcapped peaks towering above hikers on the Sirimon Route

more should be set aside for this route, descending via the Naro Moru Route to save time.

### 🏔 Sirimon Route

10 km (6 miles) S of the main Timau Road, after a turn-off signposted 16 km (10 miles) NE of Nanyuki.

A very beautiful and rather gradual ascent from the northwest, the little used Sirimon Route offers a relatively unhurried and untrammelled 5-day hike to the peaks, descending via Naro Moru. The northwest slopes receive a significantly lower precipitation than other parts of the mountain, which makes this route particularly attractive during the rainy season. Passing through more extensive moorland than any other route, Sirimon is excellent for Afroalpine flora and is regarded as the best route for encounters with zebra, klipspringer, elephant, eland and other large mammals. Weather permitting, the moorland also offers fine views to the peaks, particularly from the spectacular Mackinder Valley.

### 🏔 Timau, Burguret and Kamweti Routes

These three ascent routes require special permission from KWS, have limited facilities and are seldom used these days. The most alluring is the Timau Route, a leisurely and scenic approach from the northeast that connects with the Sirimon Route at Shipton's Hut, and is best

undertaken over 6 to 7 days. The Burguret Route is a former mule trail that starts in **Gathiuru**, north of Naro Moru, and runs parallel to the North Burguret river for most of its length. This route is of interest for its bamboo forest and for access to caves formerly used as Mau Mau *(see pp56–7)* hideouts. It is most suitable from January to March, before the start of the long rains. The practically unused Kamweti Route is a very long ascent from the south, starting in Kamweti village and passing through extensive montane forest as it follows the Nyamindi river.

The tree hyrax, Mount Kenya

### 🏠 Serena Mountain Lodge

Similar in conception to the iconic tree hotels of Aberdare National Park *(see pp320–21)*, but if anything superior, Serena Mountain Lodge *(see p370)* has

a perfect setting overlooking a small waterhole encircled by tall gallery forest, with Mount Kenya's peaks emerging at dusk to loom above the canopy. Unlike the Aberdare tree hotels, there is no shuttle from outside the park, which makes it possible to spend all day in the lodge and surrounding forest to enjoy the chattering monkeys, colourful birds and cacophonous wail of the silvery-cheeked hornbill. At night, a white noise of insects and frogs is punctuated by the explosive, heart-stopping braying of tree hyraxes from deep in the forest. Elephant and buffalo pass by daily, while rhino, leopard and lion are more occasional. The undoubted mammalian star is the giant forest hog, a hirsute outsized animal more easily seen here than in any other African forest locality.

The rustic ambience of the restaurant at Serena Mountain Lodge

The Gura Falls on the moorlands of the Aberdare Mountains, Kenya Highlands ▶

Plantations are prolific around the countryside near Meru

## ❾ Naro Moru

**Road Map** C4. 30 km (19 miles) N of Nyeri on the A2. 🔼 2,700. ✈ 🚌

This small market town is named after, and lies on the banks of, the Naro Moru river, a chilly tributary of the Ewaso Nyiro that rises in the glacial peaks of Mount Kenya. Naro Moru is the starting point for the most popular hiking route up Mount Kenya, and a good base for the casual exploration of its forested western slopes. However, hotels aside, the town is lacking in most visitor facilities.

The most upmarket base is the **Naro Moru River Lodge** *(see p370)*, which is set in lovely wooded grounds overlooking the bubbling Naru Moru river at an elevation of 1,982 m (6,502 ft). The lodge also has a campsite with a bunk house, especially for budget travellers. Staff at the lodge have been arranging extremely reliable guided hikes in and around the area for a large number of years.

## ❿ Nanyuki

**Road Map** C4. 30 km (19 miles) N of Naro Moru on the A2. 🔼 37,000. ✈ 🚌

Founded in 1907 by English settlers, Nanyuki is the supply centre for ranches and conservancies on Laikipia and the main gateway to the district for travellers visiting by road. The town has a military association dating back to colonial times, and it remains the country's most important air-force base, as well as being the site of a long-serving British army base. The main road attains a moderate degree of architectural distinction by virtue of its colonial-era storefronts, but otherwise it is a typically unassuming highlands town, with more to offer in the way of useful facilities – shops, banks, hotels, restaurants and filling stations – than tourist attractions.

Woven bag from Nanyuki

Wildlife enthusiasts passing through Nanyuki should definitely make the effort to visit the **Mount Kenya Wildlife Conservancy**, which forms part of the prestigious **Fairmont Mount Kenya Safari Club** *(see p370)* but welcomes day visitors. The main attraction here is the world's largest herd of captive-born mountain bongo, an endangered and beautifully marked antelope that is significantly bulkier than its more common lowland West African cousin. Once common in the forests of Mount Kenya, a wild mountain bongo has not been recorded there since 1994, meaning that its natural range is now confined to Aberdare National Park *(see pp320–21)* and the Mau Escarpment. The sanctuary protects various other species associated with Mount Kenya, including the colobus monkey, eland, serval and caracal cat, bushbuck and crowned crane.

🏠 **Mount Kenya Wildlife Conservancy**
Mount Kenya Safari Club, 8 km (5 miles) SE of Nanyuki. **Open** 10am–5pm daily. 🅿 🚻 ♿ 🚫 📷
🌐 animalorphanagekenya.com

## ⓫ Meru

**Road Map** C4. 75 km (47 miles) E of Nanyuki along the A2 and B6. 🔼 240,000. 🚌

The largest town in the Central Highlands and sixth largest in Kenya as a whole, Meru sprawls seemingly interminably along the main road circling the northeast footslopes of Mount Kenya. It receives a higher

Luxurious Mount Kenya Safari Club

rainfall than the towns on the mountain's western slopes, and the surrounding bountiful countryside is densely cultivated, forming an important centre for fruit, timber, coffee, bean and tea production. It is also the most important area in Kenya for growing khat, a popular leafy stimulant known locally as *miraa*. A wonderful selection of fresh produce is sold at the sprawling municipal market, and the town is also well-equipped when it comes to amenities such as banks, ATMs, hotels, restaurants and supermarkets.

The town is named after the local Meru people, Bantu-speaking agriculturists who share strong affinities with the more populous and politically influential Kikuyu. The Meru form the main subject of the **Meru Museum**, which, since 1976, has occupied the town's oldest building, a rehabilitated District Commissioner's office originally built in 1916. The museum has three galleries, of which the most interesting is an outdoor display of medicinal shrubs and herbs traditionally used by Meru healers. Also of interest, 13 km (8 miles) outside the town along the same road as Meru National Park, is the *njuuri* (a traditional high court), which was constructed in 1962 at Ncheke. It is still used occasionally by the council of tribal elders.

**Meru Museum**
Main Rd, opposite Meru Country Hotel. **Tel** 064 32482. **Open** 9am–6pm daily. 🖼 📷 🌐 **museums.or.ke**

The ranger's office at Mwea National Reserve

## ⓬ Meru National Park

*See pp334–7.*

## ⓭ Embu

**Road Map** C4. 140 km (87 miles) S of Meru along the B6. 🚹 43,000. 🚌

Linked to Meru by a madly winding road that clings precipitously to the lushly scenic eastern foothills of Mount Kenya, this moderately proportioned but lively town was founded in 1906 by English settlers. Today, it serves as the administrative headquarters of the Eastern Province and main trading centre of the Bantu-speaking people for which it is named. There is very little to distinguish Embu from other similarly sized towns in the Central Highlands, but it has a relaxed leafy feel, and is rather pretty during October and November when its jacaranda trees start to bloom. The most impressive building in town is the African-themed **Catholic**

Cathedral built in 1986 when Embu was recognized as a diocese separate from Meru.

## ⓮ Mwea National Reserve

**Road Map** C4. 45 km (28 miles) S of Embu along the B7. **Tel** 020 2052727. 🚌 to within 2 km (1 mile) of the entrance gate. **Open** 6am–7pm daily. 🖼 📷 🏕 🌐 **kws.org**

Little known and somewhat out of the way, this 42-sq-km (16-sq-mile) reserve protects the unspoiled rolling woodland that runs north from the Kamburu Reservoir at the confluence of the Tana and Thiba rivers. Although small in area and fenced in its entirety, the reserve harbours a variety of large mammals, such as impala, waterbuck, elephant, buffalo and Grant's gazelle. The rare Rothschild's giraffe has been introduced to Mwea, and this is one of the better places in Kenya to see the localized lesser kudu. Despite its proximity to Mount Kenya, whose peaks are visible on a clear day, the reserve has a dry climate more typical of the lowlands. Hippo, crocodile and a varied selection of waterbirds can be seen at **Hippo Point**, while the riverine forest supports bushbuck, Sykes monkey, Pel's fishing owl and white-crowned night heron, and is the best habitat for the endemic Hinde's babbler. There are several campsites but visitors must be completely self-sufficient.

Cyclists make their way down a quiet street in Embu

# ⑫ Meru National Park

One of East Africa's best-kept wildlife secrets, Meru National Park extends over 870 sq km (335 sq miles) of moist savannah in the eastern rainshadow of Mount Kenya and Nyambeni Hills. It lies at the core of a more extensive ecosystem comprising the contiguous Bisanadi, Mwingi and Rahole National Reserves and Kora National Park. In the early 1980s, this was one of Kenya's star attractions, with up to 40,000 visitors annually, and famous for its high densities of buffalo, elephant, lion and other wildlife. The park became a target for poachers in the late 1980s, and fell off the tourist map following the 1988 slaughter of several white rhinos and the rangers guarding them, and the fatal attack on conservationist George Adamson a year later. The park has been safe since the mid-1990s, and wildlife numbers are on the increase.

Vulturine guinea fowl in the open grassland

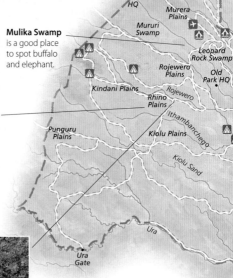

**Mulika Swamp**
is a good place
to spot buffalo
and elephant.

**★ Rhino Sanctuary**
Reintroduced from Lake Nakuru National Park and other protected areas in Kenya, black and white rhinos inhabit the western part of Meru National Park, in a large fenced-off area, and are monitored around the clock by rangers.

**★ Rojewero River**
The largest of several fast-flowing streams that run through the park after rising in Mount Kenya, the Rojewero river is fringed by riparian forest and supports several hippo pools.

**Key**

═ ═ ═ Unpaved motorable road

▬ ▬ Park boundary

**Doum Palms**
A highly conspicuous component of Meru's flora are the tall doum palms whose narrow trunks and branches run in silhouette along the park's many watercourses.

*For hotels and restaurants see pp370–71 and p381*

**Reticulated Giraffe**
Meru National Park is a good place to see Northern Kenyan "specials" such as the stretch-necked gerenuk, the skittish lesser kudu and the magnificent reticulated giraffe.

★ **Elsa's Grave**
This affecting stone memorial, situated in a forest clearing in the south of the park, is something of a pilgrimage site for devotees of conservationist Joy Adamson's bestselling book *Born Free (see p337)*.

0 kilometres  5
0 miles  5

Bisanadi
National
Reserve

Bughwango Swamp

Rojewero

Elsa's Grave

Tana

Mwingi
National Reserve

Adamson's
Falls

Kora
National Park

**Elsa's Kopje**
With its swimming-pool area overlooking a vast plain, the exclusive hilltop Elsa's Kopje *(see p370)* is one of the most scenically located lodges in Kenya.

**Getting Around**
Meru is most easily visited as part of an organized safari, with both fly-in and drive-in options available. There is no access by public transport, but Meru can also be visited in a private 4WD. The internal road network is well maintained and junctions are numbered, both on the ground and on maps, making it easy to navigate. The park's lodges employ specialist guides to take visitors around.

**Tana River**
Although it lies some distance south of the main wildlife-viewing circuit, the Tana river is the largest waterway in Kenya and it is well worth making a diversion there for the scenery and birdlife.

**For keys to symbols** *see back flap*

# Exploring Meru National Park

Although wildlife is quite plentiful, Meru National Park's greatest attraction is undoubtedly its atmosphere of uncrowded wilderness, which ensures that most sightings retain an aura of exclusivity rare in more popular reserves. The Big Five are all present, with elephant and buffalo being particularly conspicuous throughout. A cover of tall grass and dense bush makes predators other than lion difficult to see. An ideal destination for a first game drive is the rhino sanctuary, which comes with a near guarantee of rhino sightings. Elsewhere, wildlife concentrations are mobile and unpredictable, and there is a lot to be said for just exploring the park's mesmerizing patchwork of grassland and riverine forest.

### 🐦 Mulika Swamp

Site of the now defunct Meru Mulika Tourist Lodge, Mulika Swamp lies near Junction 35, a short distance inside the entrance gate. It is particularly worth a diversion in the dry season, when large numbers of animals congregate there to drink. Unlike the narrower streams that cut through the park, the swamp is well suited to elephants seeking a midday splash. It also attracts herds of several hundred buffalo,

**Pied kingfisher**

accompanied by flapping flocks of cattle egrets. Giraffe, zebra and impala are frequent visitors, while Bohor reedbuck and waterbuck are resident in the vicinity. The swamp is home to an abundant birdlife that includes grey and purple heron, blacksmith plover and pied kingfisher.

### 🐦 Riverine Forests

A striking feature of Meru National Park is the series of clear and fast-flowing fresh-water rivers that rise in the **Nyambeni Hills** in the west, cutting through the grassy plains before they converge with the Tana river along the southern boundary. Most of the rivers support a lush ribbon of riparian forest, whose most conspicuous component is tall doum palms, their narrow trunks and branches standing in stark silhouette against the clear blue sky and providing a playground – and refuge from predators – to the park's numerous olive baboons and vervet monkeys.

The largest of these rivers is the **Rojewero**, which flows through the heart of the park before running along the east-ern boundary with the adjacent **Bisanadi National Reserve**, to its confluence with the Tana. An

excellent goal for a game drive is the deep hippo pool and nearby group of rapids reached along a road between Junctions 72 and 75. A family of eight to ten hippo is resident here, and the slope of the bank allows for a safe eye-level view of these bumptious creatures. A short drive further along is a view-point consisting of a wooden boardwalk overlooking a wide stretch of river above a set of rapids. This is a good site for spotting the endemic golden palm weaver and for observing other riverine species such as the elusive African finfoot, eagerly sought Pel's fishing owl and spectacular giant kingfisher.

An African elephant in the riverine forests of Meru National Park

### 🐾 Rhino Sanctuary

In the early 1980s, Meru was renowned for its rhinos. Large numbers of black rhino were resident through the park, while a herd of white rhino introduced from South Africa hung around the park headquarters and campsite. These endangered

Doum palms tower above the vegetation surrounding Mulika Swamp

Open-fronted thatched cottage with its pool, Elsa's Kopje

animals were the biggest victims of the poaching war that took place in the park, and by 1990 it is thought that none remained. However, as part of a KWS initiative to draw tourists back to Meru, some 55 rhino – mostly black but also white – were reintroduced between 2005 and 2007, and several more calves have been born in the reserve since then. In order to prevent them falling victim to poachers, the rhinos are contained within a large fenced sanctuary covering 80 sq km (31 sq miles) running south from the main entrance gate past the Mururi Swamp. The relatively dense rhino population within this small area means that the animals are quite easily spotted, and visitors are likely to run into one on a game drive. As all of them are monitored, they are well habituated to people, so visitors may be able to take photos at close range. Mururi Swamp, set within the fenced sanctuary, is also a favoured haunt of elephant and buffalo.

### 🎦 Eastern Plains and Tana River

Away from the rivers, the eastern plains of Meru support a cover of lush swaying grass and tangled acacia woodland. Wildlife densities tend to be lower than in the west, but reticulated giraffe, gerenuk, impala, zebra and Somali ostrich are likely to be encountered on a regular basis. The area is

dotted with landmarks related to the tenure of George and Joy Adamson. These include **Elsa's grave**, a simple but affecting stone memorial situated in a forest clearing alongside the Ura river south of Junction 87, as well as the grave of Pippa the cheetah near Junction 13. **Elsa's Kopje** (see p370), an upmarket tented camp on an isolated hill near **Mughwango Swamp**, overlooks one of the earliest campsites of the Adamsons. Somewhat more remote, but well worth the effort for those with a few days

Pippa's gravestone at Meru

in the park, is the stretch of the Tana river along the southeastern boundary with **Mwingi National Reserve**.

This is one of the few areas where Kenya's largest river is easily accessible to travellers. Its forested banks support plenty of wildlife and birds. Spectacular rapids run along the black volcanic bedrock close to Junction 96, while **Adamson's Falls** – named after George, who had a camp in the area after his separation from Joy – lie just across the border with **Kora National Park**.

### Joy and George Adamson

Joy and George at Kora National Park

Meru became a safari destination in the 1960s thanks in part to its association with conservationists Joy and George Adamson, whose pioneering success in releasing captive-raised lions into the wild was immortalized in the book Born Free. Mainly known for her work with lions, Joy was also an accomplished artist whose evocative portraits of tribal Kenyans are on display at the National Museum (see pp162–3). Born Friederike Gessner in Austria-Hungary, she moved to Kenya with her first husband to escape World War II. She was nicknamed Joy by her second husband. She married her third husband, India-born George Adamson, then working as a ranger in Northern Kenya, in the early 1940s. The Adamsons acquired Born Free's leonine star Elsa in 1956 and released her into Meru two years later. Subsequent experiments with a cheetah, Pippa, and leopard, Shaba, also met with success. The couple separated in 1970, but still spent Christmas together every year. Tragically, both met violent deaths – Joy was murdered by a former employee in January 1980, and George was shot dead by Somali poachers in August 1989.

# NORTHERN KENYA

Remote, thinly inhabited and practically unknown to outsiders, Northern Kenya is one of Africa's last great wilderness areas. An uncompromising desert landscape of scrubland and rocky plains, it is home to some of East Africa's most traditional pastoralist ethnic groups. This stretch of badlands is broken by one of the largest lakes in the world, Lake Turkana, which runs south from the border with Ethiopia.

Fossil discoveries near Lake Turkana suggest that Northern Kenya has been inhabited by hominids for at least 2.5 million years. Paradoxically, its current occupants are relatively recent arrivals, with ancestral roots in present-day Sudan, Somalia and Ethiopia. Northern Kenya was one of the last parts of Africa to be penetrated by outsiders, remaining terra incognita until 1888, when Count Samuel Teleki, a Hungarian aristocrat, trekked north from Lake Baringo to Turkana. It would be another 7 years before explorer Arthur Donaldson-Smith became the first Westerner to reach Marsabit mountain *(see p352)*. The last of the region's cartographic blanks was filled in 1909, when British colonial administrator Major Chauncey Stigand crossed the Chalbi Desert.

Culturally and economically, there is little about Northern Kenya today that could be described as Westernized. Pastoral societies such as the Samburu,

Turkana and Borana remain staunchly traditionalist, herding cattle, goats or camels for a living, and many people still practise a seminomadic lifestyle. There are few towns of any substance and cultivation is almost non-existent.

Northern Kenya supports several unique mammal and bird species, most of which can be viewed in the popular complex of national reserves near Isiolo. Otherwise, the region boasts few recognized attractions for visitors, with brooding Lake Turkana forming the main goal of most trips further north. For aficionados, however, it is the fantastically empty landscapes en route to the lake, and their stoic pastoralist inhabitants, that impress themselves most firmly on the imagination. Any expedition into these ancient badlands is best viewed as being primarily about the thrillingly unpredictable journey rather than the ultimate destination.

A gathering of camels on the harsh, arid expanse of Chalbi Desert

◀ A Turkana man spear-fishing in the shallow waters of Lake Turkana

# Nomads of the North

Culturally, Northern Kenya is probably the closest thing to "unchanged Africa" that exists on any kind of scale anywhere on the continent. It is inhabited by a thin scattering of livestock-farming communities who shun modernity and cultural homogenization in favour of an uncluttered lifestyle bequeathed by generations of stoic desert-dwelling ancestors. Among the ethnic groups here are the Samburu, Borana, Turkana, Gabbra, Rendille and Elmolo. Each group has its own traditional culture, dress and customs, and these are usually adhered to, although a certain degree of intertribal exchange takes place in settlements such as Loiyangalani, where the Rendille, Samburu and Turkana coexist alongside each other.

Fetching and storing water, a major occupation among desert dwellers

## Nomadic Lifestyle

*By tradition, the ethnic groups of Northern Kenya are nomadic pastoralists. This means that they move regularly from one place to another and depend on livestock (rather than hunting or agriculture) for a living. Prior to the 20th century, the northern nomads had fluid tribal territories, but intertribal boundaries became more entrenched under colonial rule, and remain so today.*

**Camels** are often found in drier areas of the north, replacing cattle that are the popular livestock in most parts of Kenya.

**"Singing" wells**, found around the Marsabit area, are named for the Borana's custom of singing communally as the men hoist up buckets of water from the pool in the well's deep base.

**Traditional dance and music** play important social roles among the northern nomads. In most cultures, dances are accompanied by chanting, clapping and competitive pogoing – pride of place goes to whoever jumps highest.

## The Elmolo People

*The oldest inhabitants of the region, the Elmolo differ from their neighbours in lacking a strong tradition of nomadism. They depend on fishing in Lake Turkana, a diet supplemented by hippo or crocodile.*

**Elmolo women**, like their pastoralist neighbours, are fond of colourful cloths and beadwork jewellery.

**An island near Loiyangalani** is the main centre of the Elmolo, who are said to be Africa's smallest ethnic group, consisting of a mere 300 individuals.

**The domed reed-and-cloth huts**
built by the Gabbra around Kalacha
bear no resemblance to other East
African homesteads, yet show
strong affinities to huts built by
inhabitants of other African deserts
such as the Sahara and Kalahari.

**The Gabbra** display an
ancient Arabic influence
both in their
complicated calendar
(which has allowed them
to maintain a very
precise oral history) and
in their dress of long,
flowing white or
coloured robes.

**The nomadic lifestyle**
makes camels the most
suitable pack animals as
they are capable of carrying
heavy loads despite harsh
desert conditions.

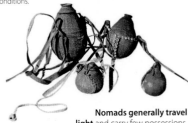

**Nomads generally travel
light** and carry few possessions,
though calabashes – water containers –
are an essential item when they travel
long distances.

## The Borana Nomads

*The Borana or Boran – of which the Gabbra form a
subgroup – are the most widespread and numerous
of East Africa's desert nomads, with a territory that
covers vast swathes of Northern Kenya and southern
Ethiopia. They are closely affiliated to the Oromo of
Ethiopia, and speak a mutually intelligible Cushitic
language that is known as Afaani Boraana.*

## The Turkana People

*Northern Kenya is home to about 250,000
Turkana people. They are Nilotic-speaking
camel-herders whose territory centres around
the lake with which they share a name. Though
pastoralists by tradition, many Turkana people
have now also taken to fishing.*

**The attire of Turkana
women** is particularly
impressive, comprising
striking beaten hides and
beaded jewellery topped
by a dreadlocked Mohican
dyed with henna. Many
women also wear a
goatee-like lower lip plug.

**Turkana houses** are neat and
impermanent structures made
entirely of thatch and wood, often
built by the women of the family.

**Notable for their unique
hairstyle**, Turkana men cover their
heads with mud. They seldom
travel far without a spear and the
dual-purpose stool that also
serves as a headrest when they
sleep outdoors.

# Exploring Northern Kenya

The most regularly visited place in Northern Kenya is the Samburu-Buffalo Springs-Shaba complex of reserves near Isiolo, offering exceptional wildlife viewing. Independent travellers can also explore the extraordinary forests of Marsabit mountain and the Samburu stronghold of Maralal. One of the most exciting and remote trips to be done anywhere in Africa starts from Samburu to Marsabit, veers west through the Chalbi Desert to Loiyangalani on the shores of Turkana, and then north, exploring the islands and lakeshore. This expedition can take over a week, but offers a fuller view of Northern Kenya's extraordinary landscapes and people.

**Key**

▨ Area illustrated

Glittering waters of the vast Lake Turkana

## Key

— Major road

== Minor road

▪▪ Untarred major road

== Untarred minor road

-- 4WD track

⤶ Major railway

— Minor railway

▬ International border

△ Peak

## Sights at a Glance

**Towns**

❶ Isiolo

❹ Maralal

❺ Baragoi

❻ South Horr

❼ Marsabit

❾ Moyale

**National Reserves**

❷ Samburu-Buffalo Springs-Shaba
National Reserves pp346–50

**Areas of Natural Beauty**

❸ Matthews Range

❽ Chalbi Desert

❿ Lake Turkana pp354–7

Camels at Kalacha, an oasis in the stark Chalbi Desert

## Getting Around

Roads are mostly unsurfaced and in poor condition. The Trans-Africa Highway that runs north for 473 km (293 miles) from Archer's Post to Moyale via Marsabit is partially tarred and the rest is under construction. Public transport is very limited. There are occasional buses as far north as Marsabit, and minibuses connect Nyahururu to Maralal. Some Nairobi-based operators run overland truck trips to Turkana, usually of 6 to 12 days in duration depending on the route used. The only practical option is a self-drive expedition or bespoke safari, ideally in convoy as rescue may be a long way off in the case of a breakdown.

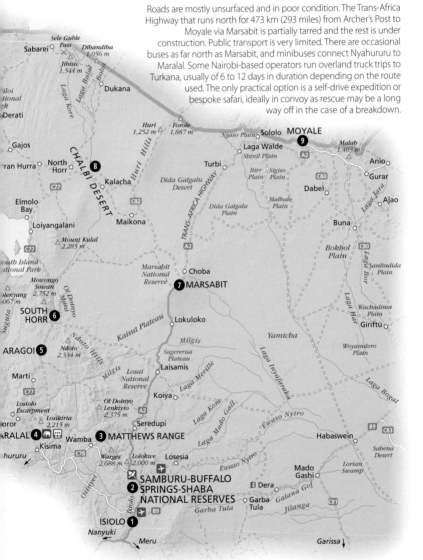

For keys to symbols *see back flap*

# ❶ Isiolo

**Road Map** C4. 80 km (50 miles) N of Nanyuki. 140,000.

As you head northwards from the Central Highlands along the A2 to Isiolo, the transition from grassy upland meadow to low-lying acacia scrub is both abrupt and striking. The main urban gateway to Samburu-Buffalo Springs National Reserves and other places further north, Isiolo has a dusty frontier-town feel, which is still further accentuated by the relatively widespread use of traditional clothing among the people.

Founded at the close of World War I as a resettlement camp for former Somali soldiers, the town retains a strong military presence, with three army training corps and a tank unit being based here.

Culturally, Isiolo is a melting pot, home to numerous Somali, Samburu, Rendille and Borana, as well as many Kikuyu and other Bantu-speaking traders from the highlands. It is predominantly Muslim, with around 15 mosques scattered through the town. There is also a large Catholic church. The main highlight for most visitors is the bustling market, which is a good place to buy the handcrafted bead and metal jewellery characteristic of the region. The market is an important centre for trading in *miraa* (khat) leaves as well as the cattle and other livestock that form the lifeblood of the north's limited economy. Isiolo has several

One of several beautiful mosques in the small town of Isiolo

small hotels and campsites, eateries, banks and filling stations, and its supermarkets provide a last opportunity to stock up on manufactured foodstuffs before hitting the open spaces of the north.

# ❷ Samburu-Buffalo Springs-Shaba National Reserves

*See pp346–50.*

# ❸ Matthews Range

**Road Map** C3. The gateway town of Wamba is 55 km (34 miles) E of Maralal on the Samburu-Buffalo Springs Rd.

Known as Ol Doinyo Lenkiyio by the local Samburu people, the Matthews Range stretches for about 150 km (93 miles) along a north-south axis and rises to

a maximum altitude of 2,688 m (8,819 ft) at **Warges Peak**, near the southern end of the range. The rocky slopes support extensive stands of an endemic species of prehistoric cycad, while the peaks support a cover of dense fragrant juniper forest. A significant portion of the range is now protected by Namunyak Wildlife Conservation Trust, a community-based organization established in 1995 to protect the area's once prodigious number of large mammals and promote ecotourism in a manner that benefits local communities. Several hundred elephant are thought to be resident or to pass through the area seasonally, and other wildlife present includes buffalo, giraffe, Grevy's zebra, eland, lesser kudu and several other species of antelope. The forests are a favourite of leopard but they are seldom seen. The area is also rich in butterflies and birds. For the independent traveller, the best base for exploration is **Wamba**, an overgrown village situated at the range's southern end.

# ❹ Maralal

**Road Map** C3. 125 km (78 miles) N of Nyahururu. 21,000. International Camel Derby (Aug).

The self-styled capital of the Samburu people, Maralal is a lively town whose modern facilities belie the strongly traditional feel of its populace and its spiritual significance in Samburu culture – its name

The densely forested slopes of the Matthews Range

Impalas grazing peacefully in a grove at Maralal Wildlife Sanctuary

literally means "house of god". Another important springboard for travel in the arid north, the town confounds all expectations with its breezy highland setting at an altitude of 1,965 m (6,450 ft) on the northern edge of Laikipia Plateau. The town centre boasts few notable landmarks, the main exception being **Jomo Kenyatta House**, the tin-roofed bungalow where Kenyatta, who would later become Kenya's first president, was detained by the colonial authorities in 1961. Maralal was also home to the author Wilfred Thesiger until 1994. The entertaining and exciting International Camel Derby *(see p43)*, usually held in August, has become a popular social event with both foreign visitors and Kenyans.

The town lies near the unfenced **Maralal Wildlife Sanctuary**, where zebra, eland, baboon, impala, spotted hyena and the occasional leopard can be seen at the waterhole overlooked by Maralal Safari Lodge only 3 km (2 miles) from the town centre.

🏛 **Jomo Kenyatta House**
Maralal. **Open** 9am–6pm daily.
🖼 🎫

## ❺ Baragoi

**Road Map** C3. 150 km (93 miles) N of Maralal on the Turkana Road.
🅿 1,000. 🚌

The small town of Baragoi, founded in the 1930s, is the major trade centre of an eponymous district that supports a thin population of traditional pastoralists – mainly Samburu but also Turkana, Rendille and Somali. The most important feature, on the outskirts of the small town centre, is a daily livestock market that attracts sellers and buyers from all over the district, many of whom walk for days to get there. Aside from camels, cattle and goats, the leisurely market has sections dedicated to fresh produce, and local jewellery and handicrafts.

Coming from Baragoi, after about 80 km (50 miles) the road passes through Poror, from where a 5-km (3-mile) track leads west to the so-called **World's End Viewpoint**. Here, the Losiolo Escarpment plunges more than 2,000 m (6,562 ft) to the base of the Suguta Valley, forming the highest single drop along the Rift Valley Escarpment.

## ❻ South Horr

**Road Map** C2. 40 km (25 miles) N of Baragoi. 🅿 1,000. 🚌

Set in a valley flanked by the northern base of the Ndoto Hills and southern base of **Ol Doinyo Mara** (Speckled Mountain), the pleasant and atypically lush Samburu settlement of South Horr is a logical overnight stop between Maralal and Lake Turkana. The town is named after the perennial river that runs through it – *horr* means river – and supports shady rows of fever trees along with cultivated stands of bananas and papayas.

South Horr is a good place for visitors to familiarize themselves with traditional Samburu ways. The forest-clad Ndoto Hills offer some excellent and undersubscribed walking and birdwatching opportunities. These are best explored from the out-of-town **Desert Rose Lodge** *(see p371)*. The demanding day hike to the 2,682-m- (8,800-ft-) high **Nyiro Peaks** usually offers good wildlife sightings, including buffalo, as well as sterling views north to Lake Turkana.

Explorer and author Wilfred Thesiger in Kenya

### Wilfred Thesiger

From 1980 to 1994, Maralal was home to Sir Wilfred Thesiger, an inveterate traveller and prolific author known for his fascination with people of deserts and other arid environments. The son of a British diplomat, Thesiger was born in Addis Ababa, Ethiopia, in 1910 and returned there 20 years later to attend the coronation of Emperor Haile Selassie. In 1933, he became the first European explorer to return alive from the Danakil area of Ethiopia's Rift Valley (whose Afar residents were known for their custom of killing male intruders), in the process establishing that the mighty Awash river evaporated in the saline lake Abbé on the border with Djibouti. He later travelled extensively in Arabia and North Africa, and published several classic books including *The Danakil Diary*, *The Marsh Arabs* and *My Kenya Days*, the last a fascinating account of his 14-year sojourn in Maralal. Thesiger returned to England in 1994 and died in a home for the elderly in 2003, aged 93.

# ❷ Samburu-Buffalo Springs-Shaba National Reserves

The one part of Northern Kenya that attracts visitors in significant numbers is this trio of ecologically affiliated and unfenced reserves, which collectively protect 440 sq km (170 sq miles) of semiarid savannah flanking the Ewaso Nyiro river. Their ecology is defined by the contrasting habitats of riverine forest along the Ewaso Nyiro and austere acacia scrub and rocky slopes extending outward from it. The reserves probably offer the best chance of sighting leopard in Kenya, and lion, elephant and buffalo are also quite common. The main attraction, however, is a host of dry-country specials absent or rare in most other East African parks. This includes mammals, such as Beisa oryx and gerenuk, and a long list of birds of which the cobalt-chested vulturine guinea fowl is the most spectacular.

**Ol Doinyo Koitogorr**
This pyramidal hill is a conspicuous landmark in Samburu. Game drives on its scrub-covered slopes come with a near guarantee of sighting gerenuk, dik-dik and various dry-country birds.

**★ Ewaso Nyiro River**
Sustaining this complex of dry-country reserves is the Ewaso Nyiro river, a near-perennial river that rises in the Aberdares and provides a vital source of water for elephants and other large mammals.

0 kilometres 5

0 miles

*Samburu National Reserve*

Marsabit 220 km (137 miles)

*Bar Lolgoto*

*Giltaman*

*Six-Mile Circuit*

Ol Doinyo Koitogorr 1,244 m

West Gate

*Ewaso Nyiro*

Uaso Gate

Samburu HQ

*Upper River Circuit*

*Lower River Circuit*

*Isiolo*

*Champagne R.*

**Buffalo Springs National Reserve**

Ranger's Post

Ngare Mar Gate

**★ Buffalo Springs**
Another important perennial water source are the Buffalo Springs, which bubble from below the earth a short drive south of the river and attract a steady stream of thirsty gazelles, giraffes, zebras and other ungulates.

## KEY

① **Archer's Post Gate**, named after the nearby village, is the main entry point to Samburu National Reserve.

② **Joy's Camp** *(see p371)*, an exclusive upmarket lodge, stands on the campsite where Joy Adamson raised a leopard called Penny – the heroine of her last book, *Queen of Sheba*.

★ **Grevy's Zebra**
Larger than the more widespread plains zebra and with a
narrower stripe pattern, the endangered Grevy's zebra is more
or less endemic to Northern Kenya.

## Getting Around

Samburu and Buffalo Springs form a block to the west of the Trans-
Africa Highway, respectively running along the north and south
banks of the Ewaso Nyiro. Most lodges are located along the
north bank, but the two reserves are connected by a
bridge near Samburu Game Lodge. Shaba lies east of
the highway, on the south bank of the river. All three
can be explored from each other, with Samburu-
Buffalo Springs offering the best game viewing
and Shaba the more untrammelled atmosphere.

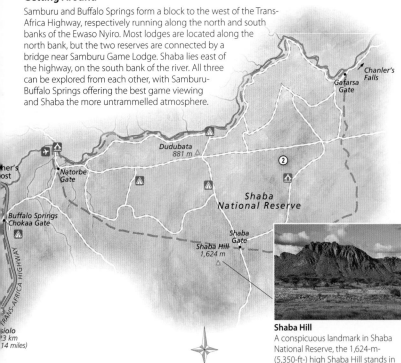

Chanler's
Falls

Gafarsa
Gate

Dudubata
881 m △

②

*Shaba
National Reserve*

Natorbe
Gate

Buffalo Springs
Chokaa Gate

Shaba
Gate

Shaba Hill
1,624 m
△

her's
ost

siolo
23 km
14 miles)

**Shaba Hill**
A conspicuous landmark in Shaba
National Reserve, the 1,624-m-
(5,350-ft-) high Shaba Hill stands in
isolation on the southern boundary.

**Key**

━━ Major road

═══ Unpaved motorable road

■ ■ Park boundary

△ Peak

**Leopard Sightings**
The riverine forest in the eastern half of
Buffalo Springs is renowned for its
excellent leopard sightings due to the
presence of several individuals that have
become habituated to vehicles.

**For keys to symbols** *see back flap*

# Exploring Samburu-Buffalo Springs National Reserves

Originally a single reserve in 1948, Samburu and Buffalo Springs were regazetted as separate entities in 1963. They are separated by the Ewaso Nyiro river and connected by a solitary low bridge in the west, close to the warden's office and Samburu Game Lodge. The bridge may flood occasionally after heavy rain, when the only safe crossing is on the main Trans-Africa Highway south of Archer's Post. Normally, it is easy to cross between the two reserves for game drives, making it possible to explore Samburu-Buffalo Springs in its entirety by using a single lodge as a base. The dirt roads within the park are in good condition, but a 4WD may be essential after the rains, particularly on the loose sandy soils that characterize the eastern plains of Buffalo Springs.

### 🦓 Ewaso Nyiro River

The centrepiece of Samburu-Buffalo Springs is the Ewaso Nyiro river, which rises in the Aberdares and arcs through the Laikipia Plateau (see pp322–5) before eventually emptying into the expansive Lorian Swamp in Kenya's remote northeast. Although it has been known to cease flowing in very dry years, the river is essentially perennial and its name, which means muddy water or brown water, refers to the rich red-brown top soil it carries down from Laikipia. Within the reserves, the river supports a lush ribbon of palm-studded riparian forest that contrasts pleasingly with the surrounding aridity. In the dry season, it forms the most important source of drinking water for miles around, and mammal concentrations in Samburu-Buffalo Springs tend to be far higher at this time than after the rains, when the wildlife

Signpost in Samburu National Reserve

disperses deep into the desert and meets its drinking needs there using temporary pools.

For visitors with limited time, the well-maintained tracks that run parallel to both the north and south banks of the river are undoubtedly the most rewarding focus for game drives. Hippo and crocodile are resident and easily seen, as are a host of water-associated birds such as the African fish eagle, African spoonbill, water thick-knee, yellow-billed stork and chestnut-bellied kingfisher. The riverine vegetation also attracts plenty of elephant and buffalo. Waterbuck, Burchell's zebra and reticulated giraffe are common, and flocks of orange-bellied parrot often attract attention with their lively screeches.

Samburu-Buffalo Springs has a reputation for guaranteed leopard sightings, based largely on the fact that several lodges used to bait these elusive creatures with fresh meat. This practice has now been outlawed on ecological grounds. The individual leopards that used to benefit from it remain habituated to people and vehicles, as do their offspring, and the odds of an extended leopard sighting are better here than in any other part of Kenya. The best place to look for them is in Buffalo Springs, following the network of tracks that run through the riparian forest on the south bank of the river. Good sightings can sometimes be had in Samburu, on the north bank.

Gerenuk in the foothills of Samburu's Ol Doinyo Koitogorr

### 🦓 Ol Doinyo Koitogorr and the Northern Scrubland

North of the river, Samburu National Reserve protects a far more undulating terrain than Shaba or Buffalo Springs. The skyline is dominated by the impressive 1,250-m- (4,100-ft-) high Ol Doinyo Koitogorr. The rocky slopes here support a tangled cover of dry thorn scrub, dominated by stunted acacia trees, their branches laden with untidy nests built by buffalo-weaver and sparrow-weaver colonies. These are interspersed with impressive termite towers that stand taller than a person, and often host colonies of the endearing dwarf mongoose, or provide a stage for brightly coloured pairs of D'Arnaud's or red-and-yellow barbet to perform their striking duets.

Wildlife concentrations are lower away from the river, but the emphasis is on species associated specifically with the badlands of Northern Kenya. The rubber-necked gerenuk is common here, and family parties

The forested banks of the Ewaso Nyiro in Samburu National Reserve

are often seen foraging on acacia canopies. Pairs of the diminutive Günther's dik-dik scurry twitch-nosed along the roadside, and larger antelope such as eland, impala, lesser kudu and Grant's gazelle are also very visible – the last with much larger horns than the more southerly race of the Masai Mara and Serengeti. The area is good for cheetah, too, but some luck is required for a decent lion sighting.

This northern scrubland is especially rewarding for visitors who are on the lookout for dry-country birds. Two of the more eye-catching species are the vulturine guinea fowl and yellow-throated spurfowl, both of which spend much of their time scurrying around on the ground along the margins of the road. Also a common sight are the blue-legged Somali ostrich, the localized Egyptian vulture and the dazzlingly colourful golden pipit and golden-breasted starling. Somewhat more drab, but no less interesting to serious bird-watchers, are such dry-country endemics as the Abyssinian scimitar-bill, black-capped social weaver, white-headed mousebird, Somali bee-eater and bristle-crowned starling.

### 🦌 Buffalo Springs and the Southern Plains

Flatter and more lightly vegetated than its northern counterpart, Buffalo Springs is characterized by thin claylike soils that support a cover of open grassland interspersed with low greyish stands of

Entrance gate to Samburu National Reserve

whistling thorn and isolated flat-topped umbrella thorns. Grevy's zebra, Beisa oryx and Grant's gazelle seem especially drawn to this open environment. It is also good for a number of large ground birds such as the comically eyelid-fluttering ground hornbill, the mincing secretary bird and a variety of bustards, including the kori bustard, a contender for the accolade of the world's heaviest flying creature. The more common predators are present in small numbers, with cheetah and striped hyena being something of a local speciality.

Away from the river, the game-viewing centrepiece is the eponymous springs in the east of the reserve near Buffalo Springs Shimba Lodge. There are in fact three springs, although the largest is hidden behind a nondescript concrete wall from where sprouts a trio of tall palm trees. Another spring is used to feed a warm swimming pool, although swimming is no

Samburu woman at Archer's Post

longer permitted. The third spring has been left as it is, and it forms a major magnet for thirsty wildlife in the dry season, leading to heavy overgrazing in the immediate vicinity. Whatever the season, groups of oryx and reticulated giraffe are almost always present, but buffalo are relatively scarce.

### Archer's Post

Straddling the main road between Samburu-Buffalo Springs and Shaba, Archer's Post is an important trading centre for the Samburu people of the region, whose colourful traditional attire stands in striking contrast to the arid surroundings. The village offers campers a last chance to stock up on basic foodstuffs before they enter the park, and even boasts a couple of basic guesthouses and eateries aimed at safari drivers but occasionally used by intrepid backpackers. While informal interaction with the Samburu is likely for visitors spending time in Archer's Post, the small town is also surrounded by semiformal cultural villages aimed at safarigoers who want to learn more about traditional Samburu ways. Village visits of this sort are the one occasion when photo-graphing the normally camera-shy Samburu is tolerated. These visits generally culminate in an exciting display of singing, ululation and pogo-style dancing – a memorable addition to any safari, and one that ensures some of the money gen-erated by tourism goes straight to grassroots communities.

A group of oryx on the open arid plains of Buffalo Springs

# Exploring Shaba National Reserve

Gazetted as a reserve in 1974, Shaba made headlines in 1980 as the site of the murder of Joy Adamson (see p337), and served as the setting for the American reality show *Survivor: Africa* in 2001. More recently, the reserve attracted global attention when a resident lioness, nicknamed Kamuniak (Blessed One) by local Samburu, adopted a succession of half a dozen oryx calves over a two-year period. Despite being almost as large as Samburu and Buffalo Springs combined, Shaba has rather little wildlife, and tours based at its solitary large lodge tend to conduct most game drives in Buffalo Springs. Tourist traffic is, therefore, very low, and visitors can often drive for hours through the magnificent semiarid scenery without seeing another vehicle.

A herd of impala grazing while the dominant male keeps watch

### 🦓 Ewaso Nyiro River

As with Samburu-Buffalo Springs, the Ewaso Nyiro river is the major geographic feature in Shaba. The river flows eastwards along the park's northern boundary for some 35 km (22 miles) and supports a lush ribbon of riverine forest dominated by doum palms, sycamore figs, fever trees and camel thorns. One of the best access points is the **Sarova Shaba Game Lodge** (see p371) on the western boundary. The verdant grounds of this lodge are fed by freshwater springs that run through a sequence of streams and ponds into the river, so the riverine forest here is especially luxuriant and rattling with monkeys, baboons and birds such as the handsome bristle-crowned starling. Numerous outsized crocodiles and monitor lizards frequent the shady southern banks of the river, and a variety of storks and smaller waders can usually be seen picking their way along the northern banks. Game-viewing roads east of the lodge also offer several views of the river.

### 🏞 Western Game-viewing Circuit

The main game-viewing loop through the western half of Shaba entails following the main track east of the entrance gate for about 3 km (2 miles), then veering northeast along a series of tracks that run parallel to the river for about 16 km (10 miles) before cutting back south again to the main road at **Dudubata Hill**. It is a very scenic drive, with the palm-fringed river often visible, and the sheer basaltic cliffs of **Ol Doinyo Sabache** – site of a rare breeding colony of Rüppell's vulture – rising to an altitude of 1,880 m (6,168 ft) above the northern bank. Several hot springs rise in the area, but otherwise the habitat is very open, consisting of a mosaic of lava-strewn plains, grassland and dry thornbush. A good variety of dry-country mammals are seen here, including Beisa oryx, gerenuk and Grant's gazelle, but population densities are rather low. The birdlife, by contrast, is superb, with a strong emphasis on species associated with very dry habitats, such as coursers, sandgrouse and bustards, as well as the gorgeous rosy-patched shrike and golden-breasted starling and the very localized masked lark. Visitors take at least 3 hours to cover this loop, more if they are serious about birds.

### 🏞 Eastern Game-viewing Circuit

The eastern plains of Shaba are scenically reminiscent of the west, with the river and Ol Doinyo Sabache visible to the north and the 1,624-m- (5,350-ft-) high **Shaba Hill** dominating the southern horizon. However, this area is even more untrammelled, thanks to its relatively remote location. A major landmark is the campsite where Joy Adamson raised the heroine of her last book, a leopard called Penny, and where she was murdered in 1980. Originally adorned with a simple memorial plaque, this is now the site of an exclusive tented lodge called **Joy's Camp** (see p371) overlooking a spring-fed waterhole that attracts a steady stream of buffalo, reticulated giraffe, elephant, Grevy's zebra and lion. The untidy fields of black lava that characterize this harsh landscape are home to the ultra-localized Williams lark.

Further afield, it is possible to make a day trip following the Ewaso Nyiro river for about 32 km (20 miles) beyond the park's eastern boundary to the remote **Chanler's Falls**, named after William Astor Chanler, the American explorer.

The cascading waters of Chanler's Falls, near Shaba National Reserve

# The Samburu People

Samburu National Reserve is named after the Samburu people, close cultural affiliates of the Maasai, with whom they share a common language called Maa. The two tribes migrated together from their original homeland in Ethiopia or Sudan but split near the Turkana area in the 17th century, with the Samburu settling on the fringe of the Central Highlands and northern deserts, and the Maasai continuing southwards. Pastoralists by tradition, the Samburu cling staunchly to the ways of their forefathers. The social system is based around three male age-sets, namely *ilayoik*, uncircumcised boys who tend livestock, *ilmoran*, circumcised warriors who defend the clan, and *ilpayiani*, elders who are responsible for administration and law-making. For the Samburu, the idea of God is strongly associated with large mountains, and elders are customarily buried facing such a location.

**Samburu huts are temporary structures**, constructed to suit the nomadic lifestyle of the Samburu.

**Most Samburu people still dress in traditional attire**, adorning themselves with an elaborate selection of beaded and other jewellery.

## The Samburu Way of Life

*The Samburu people are nomadic pastoralists by custom, moving from one temporary camp to the next in search of water and grazing for their livestock. Their homes reflect this lifestyle, being simple and somewhat impermanent structures of mud, wood and thatch.*

**The men are striking** in their customary dress of red chequered blankets.

**Traditional forms of dancing** are an important part of Samburu life. The dancers employ a pogoing technique very similar to that of the Maasai.

**The main diet of the Samburu**, who seldom hunt and eat meat only on special occasions, is a fermented mix of cow's milk and blood, sometimes sweetened with honey.

**Loibor Kineji**, literally "people of the white goats", is another name for the Samburu.

**The warrior tradition** is still very much part of Samburu culture, and an *ilmoran* is seldom seen without a spear in hand.

## ❼ Marsabit

**Road Map** D2. 300 km (186 miles) N of Isiolo. 🏨 15,000. 🚌

An isolated massif rising to a lofty 1,700 m (5,600 ft) from the surrounding plains, Mount Marsabit is a long-dormant basaltic shield volcano whose slopes support one of the few towns of any substance in the northern deserts. The mountain has an oasis-like quality, and the cool moist highland air for which it is named – Marsabit means "cold place" – provides welcome relief from the parched desert below. Climate and setting aside, Marsabit is much like other towns in this area, although it does support a diverse mix of Somali, Rendille, Samburu, Turkana, Borana, Gabbra and Burji peoples, as well as businesspeople from the Central Highlands and immigrants from neighbouring Ethiopia. Facilities include a bank, petrol stations and general stores.

The lower-lying badlands outside town are protected in the **Marsabit National Park**, which hosts small populations of reticulated giraffe, Grevy's zebra, gerenuk and even lion and cheetah. The area is studded with extinct volcanic craters and Borana "singing" wells. Its game-viewing centrepiece is a beautiful forest-ringed crater lake overlooked by **Marsabit Lodge** (see p371). Elephants pass by the lake daily, and the birdlife is wonderful, with fish eagles and falcons soaring above the waders and storks gathering in the shallows.

The forest-fringed Lake Paradise, Marsabit National Park

*For hotels and restaurants see p371 and p381*

Deeper in the park is **Lake Paradise**, another lovely crater lake, while the **Bongole Crater** graces the mountain's summit.

Marsabit's most famous resident was Ahmed, an elephant whose ground-scraping 3-m- (10-ft-) long tusks earned him 24-hour armed protection by presidential decree until his death in 1974. The tusks are on display at the Nairobi National Museum *(see pp162–3)*. While few Marsabit elephants can match this today, their tusks are notably larger than in most parts of Kenya.

🏞 **Marsabit National Park**
Outskirts of Marsabit town.
**Tel** 069 2102028. **Open** 6am–7pm daily. 🏞 🚗 🛶 🏔 🌐 kws.org

## ❽ Chalbi Desert

**Road Map** C2. 100 km (62 miles) NW of Marsabit.

Traversed by the only motorable track between Marsabit and Turkana, the startling Chalbi Desert is an expanse of flat, cracked, treeless earth inhabited by ostriches that run away in hysterics at the approach of a vehicle, and herds of domestic camel that are only slightly more habituated. It is practically uninhabited, although in wet years the entire desert becomes a shallow water-filled pan attracting thousands of waterbirds. The one permanent settlement is **Kalacha**, a small Gabbra village set around a perennial freshwater spring that has

Painting at the church in Kalacha

The cracked arid landscape of the Chalbi Desert near Kalacha

supported human habitation for centuries. Excavations nearby have revealed ancient skeletons averaging over 2 m (7 ft) in height, supporting local legends that an extinct race of giants dug the deep wells that dot Marsabit and built the massive burial cairns found throughout the region. The village's main attraction is its small church, with walls covered in Ethiopic paintings.

## ❾ Moyale

**Road Map** D1. 250 km (155 miles) NW of Marsabit. 🏨 16,000. 🚌 ⛴

Straddling the Ethiopian border at the end of a long stretch of corrugated road running north from Marsabit, Moyale is not a destination that is easily accessible. Historically, its one claim to fame is that both the Kenyan and Ethiopian sides were taken by Italy in 1940 during World War II and recaptured by Allied Forces a year later. Both sides of town are inhabited by Borana and Somali majorities, but are otherwise quite different in character, with architecture typical of their respective countries. However, the Kenyan side offers visitors from the south an intriguing first taste of Ethiopia's unique cuisine – a fiery red *wat* sauce eaten with *injera*, a vast sour pancake. Those heading across the border will find that the road is surfaced almost all the way to Addis Ababa. The lava desert of **Dida Galgalu** between Marsabit and Moyale is the main stronghold of the endemic Williams lark.

# The Leakey Family

Born in 1903 and 1916 respectively, Louis Leakey and his wife Mary were arguably the leading paleontological figures of the 20th century. They excavated dozens of sites in East Africa, ranging from Acheulean stone tool repositories at Olorgasailie and Kariandusi to the Kondoa rock art of Tanzania. The Leakeys' most ground-breaking discovery, a 1.75 million-year-old Paranthropus skull unearthed at Olduvai Gorge in 1959, provided the first concrete evidence that human evolution stretched past the million-year mark. The family tradition was continued by their son Richard, whose 1970s discoveries at Koobi Fora included the 1.6-million-year-old Turkana Boy and the 2.5-million-year-old Black Skull. Richard retired from paleontology to head up Kenya Wildlife Service in 1989, but his wife Meave and daughter Louise remain active in the field at Koobi Fora.

### Louis and Mary Leakey

*The founders of Kenya's most famous paleontological dynasty, Louis and Mary Leakey have contributed significantly to the study of human evolution, and their work has provided compelling evidence to support Charles Darwin's assertions that human beings evolved in Africa.*

**Jane Goodall's pioneering chimp study**, and Dian Fossey and Birute Galdika's parallel research on gorillas and orangutans respectively, were initiated by Louis Leakey in the belief that ape behaviour would shed light on early human society.

**This partial *Homo habilis* skull** was unearthed in 1972. One of several key hominid fossils from Koobi Fora, it is believed to be 1.9 million years old.

**Richard Leakey**, like his father Louis, made his name in the field of paleontology. He is, however, better known for his work as a conservationist and his outspoken anti-corruption stance during the Moi era.

**The mother and daughter team of Meave and Louise Leakey** unearthed a 3.5-million-year-old skull in the vicinity of Lake Turkana in 2001. This belonged to a previously undescribed hominid *Kenyanthropus platyops* – literally "flat-faced man of Kenya".

**The classic book, *The Making of Mankind*** (1981) is among prolific writer Richard Leakey's popular works on human evolution.

# ❿ Lake Turkana

Immortalized in John Hillaby's classic travel account *Journey to the Jade Sea*, Turkana is the undisputed jewel of Northern Kenya. This 6,400-sq-km (2,450-sq-mile) inland sea is ranked as the largest alkaline lake in the world, and the largest lake of any kind to be set in a desert. The Samburu call it Asso Narok (Black Lake); it was known as Lake Rudolf during the colonial era and was renamed Turkana after the local people post-independence. Primordial yet eerily beautiful, Turkana lies in a barren hinterland of volcanic rock swept by a brutally incessant dry southeaster. Its annual rainfall is below 200 mm (8 inches), so vegetation is sparse and can be viciously spiky to the touch. The lake's three islands are a stopover for migrant birds and a breeding site for crocodile and hippo.

A Turkana woman in bright traditional dress, Elmolo Bay

**North Island**
Formed several million years ago but still riddled with fumaroles and other signs of latent activity, North Island consists of a nested volcano rising to 140 m (459 ft) above the lake surface.

ETHIOPIA

Namuruputh
Todenyang

Lapurr Range
C47
Lapurr
1,295 m

Lokitaung

Lake
Turkana

Kalimapus Hills

Ferguson's
Gulf

Kalokol ● Longe

Namoratunga

Cen
Isla

B4

Eliye
Spring

Lodwar

Turk

A1

Napedet
Hills

Lokir

**Central Island National Park**
The three crater lakes on this island are the main breeding site for Turkana's crocodile population of 15,000–20,000.

0 kilometres    25

0 miles         25

**Fishing on Lake Turkana**
The lake supports a thriving population of tilapia and other fish, as attested to by its Turkana name *Anam Ka'alakol*, literally "sea of abundant fish".

*For hotels and restaurants see p371 and p381*

★ **Sibiloi National Park**
This park protects some wildlife, but is more famous for the paleontological treasures unearthed at sites such as Koobi Fora. It lies at the core of a UNESCO World Heritage Site inscribed in 1997.

**VISITORS' CHECKLIST**

**Practical Information**
Road Map B1. Loiyangalani is 270 km (168 miles) W of Marsabit.
🚩 🛶 🏕 **w** kws.org

**Transport**
✈ from Nairobi to Lodwar. 🚌

## Getting Around

Loiyangalani on the southeastern shore is accessible by organized truck trips from Nairobi. From here, South Island can be visited by boat. The rest of the eastern shore has dirt roads and is accessible only by 4WD. Limited public transport is available to Kalokol on the western shore; from here boat trips to Central Island are easily arranged.

**Key**

— Major road

═ Minor road

⋯ Unpaved motorable road

– – Park boundary

■‧ International boundary

△ Peak

★ **Loiyangalani**
Although it is the largest settlement on the eastern lakeshore, Loiyangalani remains little more than an overgrown village, and most of its residents – Turkana, Samburu and Elmolo – still live in traditional grass huts.

★ **South Island National Park**
Like the other islands in Turkana, South Island is volcanic in origin, as evident by the presence of 16 craters. Oral traditions and the existence of non-vegetated lava flows suggest it probably last erupted in the early 19th century.

## Exploring Lake Turkana

Its serpentine shape determined by the steep contours of the Rift Valley, Lake Turkana once extended southwards as far as modern-day Baringo, and stretched northwards to feed a tributary of the Ethiopian Blue Nile. Today, fed primarily by Ethiopia's Omo river, it no longer has a surface outlet and the alkaline water, though drinkable, is soapy, saline and saturated with algae, which gives it the blue-green shade alluded to in the nickname "Jade Sea". Most driving safaris to Turkana end up at Loiyangalani; although the eastern lakeshore is not serviced by public transport, private vehicles occasionally head up here from Maralal and will offer travellers a seat at a negotiable rate.

Barren South Island and the vast Lake Turkana

### Loiyangalani

270 km (168 miles) W of Marsabit.

Locals refer to Loiyangalani as Turkana City with a mixture of affection and facetiousness. The largest settlement anywhere on Turkana's eastern lakeshore and the main travel gateway of the region, Loiyangalani consists of a few dozen concrete buildings surrounded by a sprawl of about 500 traditional reed huts inhabited by Rendille, Samburu and Turkana pastoralists. It is a truly unique and wonderful place to visit, a distinctly Wild West outpost that owes less to the presence of Lake Turkana than to the freshwater springs that bubble to the surface here. Dress codes and body ornamentations are defiantly traditional, ranging from the striking red robes and colourful beaded jewellery favoured by the Samburu to the henna-dyed Mohican hairstyles and goatee-like lip plugs of the Turkana women.

A popular excursion from Loiyangalani is a half-day boat trip to **Elmolo Bay**, where the last few hundred members of the piscivorous Elmolo people eke out an existence on a small island they share with hippos, crocodiles and waterbirds. By contrast, the glittering quartzite rocks and semiprecious stones hawked around the small town come from **Mount Kulal**, whose main volcanic peak soars 2,293 m (7,500 ft) above the lakeshore immediately east of Loiyangalani. A UNESCO International Biosphere Reserve since 1978, Mount Kulal is a worthwhile climb for well-equipped hikers. The upper slopes offer stunning views across the lake to the opposite wall of the Rift Valley. The mountain is the only known locale for the endemic Kulal white-eye bird.

Yellow-billed stork, South Island

### South Island National Park

16 km (10 miles) SW of Loiyangalani.
kws.org

The largest of three uninhabited volcanic islands that rear up from the deep floors of Lake Turkana, South Island is also sometimes known as Höhnel Island, after Lieutenant Ritter von Höhnel, a member of the 1888 Teleki expedition to Turkana, who apparently witnessed a small eruption off its shore. Ancient lava flows can still be seen at the north end of the island. Local oral tradition talks of fire rising from the peaks, but no evidence of a more recent eruption exists.

Gazetted as a national park in 1983, South Island consists of 16 volcanic craters aligned on a 12-km- (8-mile-) long ridge that rises steeply to around 320 m (1,050 ft) above the lakeshore. The event recorded here by von Höhnel's expedition may have simply been the steaming of sulphur-rich gases. Like Turkana's other islands, South Island supports large numbers of crocodile, but its main zoological interest is as a breeding point for resident and migratory birds. Birds such as the pink-backed pelican, greater flamingo, spur-winged plover, Caspian plover and little stint are seasonally common, while resident species include the African fish eagle, fox kestrel, goliath heron, saddle-billed stork and African skimmer.

Tourist boat on Lake Turkana, Loiyangalani

*For hotels and restaurants see p371 and p381*

### Sibiloi National Park

125 km (78 miles) N of Loiyangalani.
**Tel** 054 21223. **Open** 6am–7pm daily.
kws.org

Gazetted in 1973, the remote 1,570-sq-km (606-sq-mile) Sibiloi National Park extends along the northeast shore of Lake Turkana. Named after the volcanic Mount Sibiloi, the park is best known as the site of **Koobi Fora**, whose rich sedimentary rocks have yielded more than 10,000 vertebrate fossils – including more than 350 specimens of *Australopithecines* and other extinct hominids – since it was first excavated by the Leakeys *(see p353)* in 1968. Specific areas of interest here include a Stone Age burial site marked by the basaltic **Jarigole Pillars**, a 12-million-year-old fossil forest on Sibiloi Mountain overlooking Alia Bay and the in situ excavated skeletons of extinct elephant, tortoise and crocodile species – the latter measuring almost 15 m (49 ft) long.

Sibiloi also protects a rich desert fauna and flora, ranging from the pink-flowered desert rose and sky-scraping euphorbia trees to a variety of dry-country larks, bustards and raptors. The open plains and *Commiphora* woodland harbour Grevy's zebra, lesser kudu and Beisa oryx, along with thinly distributed populations of cheetah, lion, striped hyena and silver-backed jackal.

The jade waters of Lake Turkana provide the perfect scenic counterpoint to the barren terrestrial landscape, as does the Karsa Waterhole, a drinking point for wildlife, and the Hasuma Forest along the seasonal Alia river.

Flamingoes and other waders, Lake Turkana

### North Island

25 km (16 miles) NW of Koobi Fora.

The smallest and least accessible of Turkana's three volcanic islands, North Island is also the only one yet to be accorded national park status. It consists of several nested tuff cones and rises to about 140 m (460 ft) above the surface of the lake. Although the main volcano is thought to be more than 3 million years old, it still displays regular signs of latent activity. Exactly when it last erupted is unknown, but two non-vegetated lava flows run down to the shore, suggesting that it was some time in the last few hundred years, and fumaroles run along the main fault ridge. Crocodiles are common along the shore, and a wide selection of waterbirds is present seasonally.

### Western Turkana

Kalokol is 380 km (235 miles) N of Kitale via Lodwar.

More accessible than the eastern shore for those dependent on public transport, western Turkana is not so wild and remote in character, although reaching the lake itself can be difficult following a drop in water levels and significant retreat of the shore in the 1990s. Access to west Turkana is via Kitale in Western Kenya, and entails passing through the medium-sized town of Lodwar en route to Kalokol, the largest settlement anywhere on the lake, and the only one accessible by public transport. Kalokol no longer lies on the lakeshore, but a jetty about an hour's walk away is the best place to cross to Central Island. The nearby **Ferguson's Gulf** and more distant **Eliye Springs** are more attractive bases for exploring the western shore, but the sandy access roads require a 4WD.

### Central Island National Park

9 km (6 miles) E of Kalokol.
**Open** 6am–7pm daily.
kws.org

Also known as Crocodile Island, Central Island was accorded national park status in 1983 in recognition of its significance as the main breeding site for the lake's estimated 15,000–20,000 Nile crocodiles, the largest population in Africa. The island consists of 15 volcanic craters and cones, of which three contain permanent lakes and one is periodically inundated. Birds are also plentiful, with thousands of lesser flamingo congregating on the lake at times, and the lava-strewn ground, with its sparse cover of spiny grass, is evidently a serpentine paradise, with the venomous puff adder, Egyptian cobra and saw-scaled viper all common.

The Koobi Fora research centre overlooking Lake Turkana

# TRAVELLERS' NEEDS

# WHERE TO STAY

Kenya's accommodation varies from lavish lodges and camps, with impeccable service, gourmet food and swimming pools in the popular tourist areas, to basic board and lodging, consisting of a bare room with a bed and an often erratic water supply, in the small towns. Safari lodges range from large blocks of rooms catering to tour groups to smaller intimate camps made up of temporary tents erected on platforms. Wildlife parks also have campsites, which attend to self-sufficient visitors and campers on organized budget safaris. Alongside some good-value accommodation and a few luxurious beach hideaways ideal for honeymooners, Kenya's sublime coastline also offers all-inclusive resorts to package holiday-makers. Accommodation on Lamu Island is often in old atmospheric Swahili houses decorated with antiques. Nairobi boasts plenty of international hotel chains. Other large towns usually have at least one adequate mid-range hotel, some of which retain the old colonial charm.

Swahili-style seating and a plunge pool, Lamu House *(see p367)*

## Choosing Accommodation

While there is a star grading system in Kenya, the classi-fication is based on facilities provided and not ambience or quality of service. The standard of accommodation is generally reflected in its price. All visitors to the game-viewing parks are going to have a broadly similar experience, but the price of a safari depends on the type of accommodation offered. At the top end are small tented camps, less expensive are the larger safari lodges, while at the budget end are basic campsites. Likewise, all visitors can equally enjoy the beach, whether they prefer to be bussed in from the airport to spend a week in a fully inclusive luxury resort, or rent a cheaper self-catering cottage or house. The latter work out more economical for a family or group. Away from the main tourist areas, most towns have at least one mid-range hotel aimed at local business travellers, which may often be dull but comfortable enough. There are dozens of places offering very basic board and lodgings. Self-sufficient campers with their own or hired vehicles can get around Kenya utilizing campsites in the parks and rural areas, some of which have additional *bandas* (huts).

## Pricing

There is a two-tier pricing system for accommodation in Kenya and visitors or non-residents are required to pay almost double that of Kenyan and regional (Tanzania and Uganda) residents. Most rates for non-residents are published in US dollars but can also be paid in Kenyan shillings – however, it is worth checking that the hotel offers a competitive rate of exchange.

Hotels in cities and towns aimed at business travellers generally keep the same room rates all year round, while in the parks and on the coast rates are seasonal. Low season in Kenya is from April to June when rates drop considerably, in some cases to half, but holidays during this time are hampered by the long rains. High season is mid-December to mid-February when rates are at their highest. Some coastal resorts add an extra surcharge over Christmas and New Year. Out of high season, walk-in rates, especially along the coast, can be lower than published rates, although there is no guarantee of a room. The upmarket establishments accept credit cards, while low-budget accommodation options only accept Kenyan shillings for payment.

## Facilities

Mainstream international hotels in Nairobi, such as the Hilton and InterContinental, and the coastal resorts have the usual facilities such as air conditioning, satellite TV, Internet access, swimming pools, restaurants and bars, and additional recreational facilities. Smaller hotels often have a simple restaurant and bar serving some form of Continental (European) cuisine, while at basic board and lodgings a plate of local food and beer may be on offer. Safari lodges and tented camps are set in commanding positions and the more expensive are very comfortable. Larger ones have restaurants with buffets or set menus, while at camps that only accommodate a few guests, meals are taken at a communal dining table. In remote regions, many hotels rely on solar power and borehole water, but facilities are not compromised by this. Mosquitoes can pose a problem, so ideally a room should have an air conditioner, a fan or a mosquito net and at the very least mosquito netting in the windows. If travelling in a vehicle, visitors must enquire about parking facilities on offer.

## Booking

Reservations made through a European or North American travel agent may be more expensive than contacting the lodge or hotel directly. Most establishments in the tourist regions of Kenya are easily accessible on the Internet, and there are often discounts for booking directly online. In the case of extended safaris using a variety of accommodation, good deals can be done through the tour operators who get accommodation at wholesale prices.

## Children

Kenya is generally a good destination for families, especially on organized tours. While some exclusive safari

Rothschild's giraffes on the lawns of the Giraffe Manor, Nairobi *(see p364)*

lodges do not accept children, others are child-friendly. Beach lodges are mostly family-orientated and offer adjoining rooms or discounts to children under 12 sharing a room with their parents, and often under-fives go free. Some establishments at the beach such as **Bamburi Beach Hotel** and **Leopard Beach Resort & Spa** have children's clubs, which keep little ones entertained. In the parks, the **Heritage Hotels** group offers special children's guides to the parks and organizes bush experiences and engaging activities for children.

## Hotel Groups

Kenya has a vast range of reputable chains such as **Fairmont Hotels**, **Sopa Lodges**, **Serena Hotels**, Heritage Hotels and **Sarova Hotels**, all of which offer international standards in terms of facilities and service. Most hotels in Nairobi have conference and business centres and the bars and restaurants are

focal meeting places for its residents. The five-star Nairobi Serena Hotel *(see p364)* is regarded as the best of the modern hotels, set in lush gardens with fine views of the city's soaring skyline. There are some historical hotels in the city, including the atmospheric Fairmont The Norfolk Hotel *(see p364)*, whose previous guests have included dignitaries such as Winston Churchill and Theodore Roosevelt, or the charming Karen Blixen Coffee Garden and Cottages *(see p364)*. One of the more unusual places to stay is the Giraffe Manor *(see p364)* where it is not uncommon for a giraffe to look through a bedroom window or stick its head through a doorway.

There are some good-value mid-range hotels around the city centre, but furnishings and decor tend to be a little dated and service often slow in the adjoining restaurants and bars. The same can be said for the principal hotels in other towns, which can be bland and old-fashioned, but nevertheless offer the best accommodation outside the more tourist-orientated parks. There are, however, some fine country hotels, such as the Lake Naivasha Country Club *(see p368)*, set in spacious grounds full of giant yellow-wood acacia trees on the lakeshore, and Fairmont Mount Kenya Safari Club *(see p370)*, which oozes plenty of old-world charm and is set in landscaped gardens in the foothills of Mount Kenya.

The lush garden of Sarova Shaba Game Lodge, Shaba National Reserve *(see p371)*

Fairmont The Norfolk Hotel, Nairobi *(see p364)*

## Budget Lodging

Most towns in Kenya have several cheap hotels referred to as board and lodgings. A careful scrutiny of these is needed as they sometimes double up as local bars and brothels and are not wholly clean. Nevertheless, they offer cheap accommodation at under US$20 a night. Visitors must ensure that the door locks, there is a fan that works, water runs from the tap and the bedding is clean. Guests must also enquire about the availability of food and hot water. Nairobi has many of these places, mostly concentrated around River Road, which is not an especially safe area of the city. However, the capital also offers a few good alternatives to budget travellers in the way of campsites and backpacker-style accommodation with dormitories and double rooms.

## Self-Catering Cottages and Homestays

In the national parks, **KWS** (Kenya Wildlife Service) offers a number of accommodation options in guesthouses or *bandas*, which usually cater to four people but can accommodate up to 18. In each, linen and bedding is provided and there are fully equipped self-catering kitchens, though in some cases guests have to bring their own drinking water and firewood. On the coast, houses and cottages are available for hire, and usually provide cooking and eating utensils, but sometimes guests have to bring their own bedding and towels. Some provide personal staff such as a cook or maid. These places tend to be old and simply furnished, but the advantage is that you stay in a peaceful and relatively private location near

the beach but away from the glitzy resorts. They are ideal for families and groups of friends. Homestays on private farms and ranches, usually owned by the descendents of settler families, are becoming popular, especially on the Laikipia Plateau. These accommodate just a handful of people and communal meals are taken with the hosts and other guests. **Langata Link Holiday Homes** offers a wide range of fully equipped homes in Kenya.

## Beach Resorts

Fully self-contained beach resorts line the coast to the south and north of Mombasa. While some are arranged in lines of concrete blocks, others have been designed to blend in with the landscape, with thatched roofs and chalets hidden in the coastal forest. The larger resorts have swimming pools, landscaped gardens with sun-loungers, a choice of bars and restaurants and additional discotheques (some-open air), shops, health and sports facilities and live entertainment. A few are adjoined to a golf course or casino. At short notice, a full range of water-sports can be organized, including snorkelling and scuba diving, and trips on glass-bottomed boats are on offer. There is also the option of going on day trips to Wasini Island or Shimba Hills National Reserve *(see pp220–23)* or overnight trips

The upscale palm-fringed Serena Beach Resort & Spa, Northern Mombasa *(see p366)*

Voi Safari Lodge with a rock-cut swimming pool overlooking the landscape *(see p365)*

to one of the parks, such as Tsavo. Most of the resorts are aimed at package holiday-makers staying for at least one week, with flights and airport transfers included in the cost of their holidays organized via a travel agent. However, resorts also take reservations directly.

## On Safari

Most tour operators *(see pp396–7)* offer a similar safari experience with early morning and late afternoon guided game drives and the opportunity to sleep in the wild. It is vital to consider the options available before planning a safari trip to Kenya *(see pp72–7)*. The cost of a safari depends on the type of accom-modation. For a 3-day safari from Nairobi to the Masai Mara, an expensive option would be to fly directly to an intimate luxury tented camp, a medium-priced one would be to drive or

fly to a large safari lodge, and a budget one would be to drive to and stay at a campsite. Tented camps only take a few guests at a time and provide excellent personalized service. Spacious, permanently erected shade-cloth or thatch tents have an attached bathroom where water is heated by solar power, and there is a central dining and lounge area. Less expensive are larger safari lodges that sleep up to 150 people, have high standards but are more impersonal. These are either in blocks, or individual units grouped around a waterhole or swimming pool, with central restaurants and bars. All parks have campsites and some have pre-erected tents, shared showers, camp beds and toilets and a kitchen hut. More basic campsites will have a long drop toilet, with tour operators providing cooks, camp assistants and equipment

needed. Some of the more established Kenyan tour operators that organize accommodation on safari include **UNIGLOBE Let's Go Travel**, **Cheli & Peacock** and **Kenya One Tours**.

## Recommended Hotels

The many different hotels listed on the following pages have been carefully selected for their excellent facilities, location and atmosphere. A wide variety of accommodation is covered, from historic buildings in towns, to tented camps in the game reserves. For most visitors, a safari is an important part of a visit to Kenya and accommodation in the parks is judged using a differ-ent set of criteria, as they tend to offer an experience as opposed to just a place to stay. Camping is the bottom level, and exclusive tented camps, which usually have standing beds and en-suite facilities, are often the best of this type of accommodation. Towns and cities tend to be visited as a stopover to the bush or the beach. Options here range from functional city hotels to cheap hostels, and historic or traditional hotels that blend into the culture and traditions of the town.

Entries labelled as DK Choice highlight establishments that are exceptional in some way. They may be set in stunning surroundings, offer excellent service, or have beautiful interiors and rooms. Whatever the reason you will have a memorable stay.

## DIRECTORY

### Children

**Bamburi Beach Hotel**
Tel 041 5485611. ⓦ bam
buribeachkenya.com

**Heritage Hotels**
Tel 020 2103445.
ⓦ heritage-eastafrica.
com

**Leopard Beach Resort & Spa**
Tel 020 2049270.
ⓦ leopardbeachresort.
com

### Hotel Groups

**Fairmont Hotels**
Tel 020 2265555.
ⓦ fairmont.com

**Sarova Hotels**
Tel 020 2767000.
ⓦ sarovahotels.com

**Serena Hotels**
Tel 0732 123333.
ⓦ serenahotels.com

**Sopa Lodges**
Tel 020 3750235.
ⓦ sopalodges.com

### Self-catering Cottages and Homestays

**KWS**
Tel 020 6000800.
ⓦ kws.org

**Langata Link Holiday Homes**
Tel 0735 965636.
ⓦ holidayhomes
kenya.com

### On Safari

**Cheli & Peacock**
Tel 0730 127000.
ⓦ chelipeacock.com

**Kenya One Tours**
Tel 020 4453318.
ⓦ kenyaonetours.com

**UNIGLOBE Let's Go Travel**
Tel 020 444715.
ⓦ uniglobelets
gotravel.com

# Where to Stay

## Nairobi

### DK Choice

**DOWNTOWN: Fairmont
The Norfolk Hotel** $$
Historic hotel     Map 1 B2
*Harry Thuku Road*
**Tel** *020 2265555*
W fairmont.com
This colonial hotel from 1904 is a
well-known landmark in Nairobi.
It offers old world charm with
modern facilities. The luxurious
rooms are set around private
tropical gardens. Top-class
restaurants and a wine bar.

**DOWNTOWN: Fairview Hotel** $$
City hotel     Map 1 A5
*Bishops Road*
**Tel** *020 2881419*
W fairviewkenya.com
At this family hotel with
comfortable rooms and large
gardens there are restaurants, a
wine cellar, a pool and a gym.

**DOWNTOWN: Nairobi
Serena Hotel** $$
City hotel     Map 1 A4
*Kenyatta Avenue*
**Tel** *0732 123333*
W serenahotels.com
The individually decorated rooms
have all the mod-cons of a 5-star
hotel. Enjoy the lavish Maisha Spa.

**DOWNTOWN: Sarova
Stanley Hotel** $$
City hotel     Map 1 C3
*Corner of Kenyatta Avenue and
Kimathi Street*
**Tel** *020 2757000*
W sarovahotels.com
Set in an eight-floor tower, this
hotel offers stylish rooms and the
legendary Thorn Tree Café.

**GIGIRI: Tribe Hotel** $$
Boutique hotel
*Limuru Road*
**Tel** *020 7200000*
W tribe-hotel.com
An elegant luxury hotel attached
to the Village Market shopping and
entertainment complex. Facilities
include a gym and a restaurant.

**KAREN: Milimani Backpackers** $
Hostel
*St Helens Lane*
**Tel** *0718 919020*
W milimanibackpackers.com
Friendly option set in a spacious
house and garden offering dormi-
tories, double cabins, beds in
pre-erected tents and a campsite.

**KAREN: Karen Blixen Coffee
Garden and Cottages** $$
Historic cottage
*Karen Road*
**Tel** *020 882138*
W karenblixencoffeegarden.com
A historic option, offering stone
cottages in one of Kenya's oldest
formal gardens. One- or two-
bedroom suites feature fireplaces.

**KAREN: House of Waine** $$$
Boutique hotel
*Crn Masai Lane and Bongani Road*
**Tel** *020 2601455*
W houseofwaine.com
This luxury hotel in large grounds
offers excellent service and
individually decorated rooms, with
fresh flowers and *objets d'arts*.

**KAREN: Ngong House** $$$
Country lodge
*Ndovu Lane*
**Tel** *020 891856*
W ngonghouse.com
Rustic rooms with views of the
Ngong Hills are set in a forest
with great birdlife. Formal
candlelit dinners are a highlight.

**Price Guide**
Prices are for a standard double room
per night (in high season), with breakfast,
tax and service charge included.

| $ | up to $100 |
|---|---|
| $$ | $100 to 350 |
| $$$ | over $350 |

**KAREN: Palacina Residence &
Suites** $$$
Boutique hotel
*Kitale Lane*
**Tel** *0733 777173*
W palacina.com
All the sumptuous rooms here
come with a sitting room, a walk-
in dresser, a balcony, a bathroom,
with Jacuzzi and shower, and
a mini kitchen.

**LANGATA: Wildebeest
Eco Camp** $
Hostel
*Mokoyeti Road West*
**Tel** *0734 770733*
W wildebeestecocamp.com
Options for every budget are
available here, including
dormitories, basic rooms and
deluxe permanent safari tents.
Camping is also permitted.

**LANGATA: Nairobi Tented
Camp** $$
Tented camp
*Nairobi National Park*
**Tel** *0774 136523*
W nairobitentedcamp.com
This is the only accommodation
in Nairobi National Park offering
an overnight safari experience.
The comfortable tents feature
en-suite bathrooms.

### DK Choice

**LANGATA: Giraffe Manor** $$$
Boutique hotel
*Koitobos Road*
**Tel** *020 5020888*
W thesafaricollection.com
This manor house with ten
luxury suites is set in indigenous
forest bordering the AFEW
Giraffe Centre. Giraffes roam the
gardens and are regular visitors
at breakfast when they love to
be fed through the windows.
A formal dinner is served at a
communal table.

**WESTLANDS: Sankara Nairobi** $$
Luxury hotel
*Woodvale Grove, Westlands*
**Tel** *020 4208000*
W sankara.com
Stylish, modern hotel, boasting a
rooftop pool, award-winning spa,
fine dining and a wine bar.

Giraffe feeding at a window of Giraffe Manor, Langata

Porini Amboseli Camp on a reserve bordering Amboseli National Park

# Southeastern Savannahs

**AMBOSELI NATIONAL PARK:
KWS Bandas & Guesthouses** $
Self-catering banda **Road Map** C6
*Several locations inside the park*
**Tel** 020 600800
**w** kws.org
No-frills, self-catering accommodation inside the park. There is no shop or restaurant so all provisions need to be brought in.

**AMBOSELI NATIONAL PARK:
Amboseli Serena Lodge** $$
Safari lodge **Road Map** C6
*Southern area, near road junction 33*
**Tel** 020 2842000
**w** serenahotels.com
The most luxurious of the larger lodges in Amboseli offers Maasai-inspired decor, a swimming pool and excellent buffet meals.

**AMBOSELI NATIONAL PARK:
Amboseli Sopa Lodge** $$
Safari lodge **Road Map** C6
*Outside Kimana Gate*
**Tel** 020 3750235
**w** sopalodges.com
Located on a private Maasai conservancy bordering the park, rooms are in chalets scattered around the lush gardens. There is a Maasai craft market on site.

**AMBOSELI NATIONAL PARK:
Ol Tukai Lodge** $$$
Safari lodge
*Central area, 6 km (4 miles) from Amboseli airstrip*
**Tel** 020 4442475
**w** oltukailodge.com
This lodge has been designed to provide a constant safari experience with views of Kilimanjaro and the plains of Amboseli from every angle. The 80 rooms are spread out among shady acacias.

**AMBOSELI NATIONAL PARK:
Porini Amboseli Camp** $$$
Tented camp **Road Map** C6
*Selenkay Conservancy, 30 km (18 miles) north of Amboseli airstrip*
**Tel** 0774 136523
**w** porini.com
An eco-camp consisting of nine large, tastefully furnished, en-suite standing tents in a vast community reserve bordering Amboseli. Safari activities are included in the rates.

## DK Choice

**AMBOSELI NATIONAL PARK:
Tortilis Camp** $$$
Tented camp **Road Map** C6
*Outside southern boundary, Kitirua*
**Tel** 0730 127000
**w** tortilis.com
This award-winning exclusive camp offers wonderful views of Mount Kilimanjaro from each luxury en-suite standing tent. Coffee and biscuits are delivered to each tent in the morning. The cuisine is of the highest quality, and dinner and afternoon tea are served in a large semi-open thatched *boma*. There is a swimming pool and the lounge area has good views of a watering hole. Rates include safari activities.

**CHYULU HILLS NATIONAL PARK: Ol Donyo Lodge** $$$
Luxury lodge **Road Map** C6
*Western foothills of Chyulu range, 29 km (19 miles) from Mbirikani*
**Tel** 020 6000457
**w** greatplainsconservation.com
Set on the Mbirikani Group Ranch are ten large, deluxe suites with private balcony, roof terrace and plunge pool. Game drives and many other activities are on offer.

## DK Choice

**LUMO COMMUNITY WILDLIFE SANCTUARY:
Lions Bluff Lodge** $$
Safari camp **Road Map** D6
*48 km (30 miles) west of Voi on the Taveta road*
**Tel** 0717 555498
**w** lionsblufflodge.com
Perched on the top of a bluff with remarkable 360-degree views of Lumo's plains below, accommodation is in 12 thatched and canvas *bandas* linked by timber bridges. Alternatively, stay at their Cheetah Campsite, which has excellent facilities and campers can eat at the lodge.

**TAITA HILLS WILDLIFE SANCTUARY: Sarova Salt Lick Game Lodge** $$
Safari lodge **Road Map** D7
*Southern Sanctuary*
**Tel** 0728 608765
**w** sarovahotels.com
This stilted lodge overlooking a waterhole is frequented by a lot of wildlife, especially elephants. Quirky architecture, basic rooms and wonderful hospitality.

**TSAVO EAST NATIONAL PARK:
Voi Safari Lodge** $$
Safari lodge **Road Map** D6
*4 km (2 miles) from Voi Gate*
**Tel** 0733 333400
**w** safari-hotels.com
This place is a bit dated, but the location is outstanding, as it is on a cliff overlooking the park and a waterhole regularly visited by big herds of game.

**TSAVO EAST NATIONAL PARK:
Galdessa** $$$
Tented camp **Road Map** D6
*West of road junction 111*
**Tel** 040 3202217
**w** galdessa.com
Exclusive tented camp with world-class safari decor in a stunning setting on the banks of the Galana river. The remote location guarantees a real bush experience.

**TSAVO EAST NATIONAL PARK:
Satao Camp** $$$
Tented camp **Road Map** D6
*Off road junction 144*
**Tel** 020 2434600
**w** sataocamp.com
This old-style tented camp in a remote corner of the park aims to provide a genuine bush experience. It has comfortable standing tents with private balconies.

**TSAVO EAST NATIONAL PARK:
Voi Wildlife Lodge** $$$
Safari lodge **Road Map** D6
*Immediately outside Voi Gate*
**Tel** 0722 201240
**w** voiwildlifelodge.com
The large lodge overlooking a waterhole is rather bland but offers good facilities. Extensive choice at the buffet meals.

**TSAVO WEST NATIONAL PARK:
Ngulia Safari Lodge** $$
Safari lodge **Road Map** D6
*IOff C103, 40 km (25 miles) from Tsavo Gate*
**Tel** 0733 333400
**w** safari-hotels.com
This older, basic lodge has good facilities and is in a great location perched on the Ndawe Escarpment. Rooms are comfortable and the bar and restaurant overlook a floodlit waterhole.

**For more information on types of hotels** *see pp360–63*

Thatched-roof accommodation at The Funzi Keys resort on Funzi Island

**TSAVO WEST NATIONAL PARK: Kilanguni Serena Safari Lodge** $$
Safari lodge          **Road Map** D6
*West of Mtiti Andei Gate, off road junction 8*
**Tel** *020 2842000*
W serenahotels.com
This modern lodge has spacious rooms with great facilities. The dining area overlooks a busy waterhole. Mount Kilimanjaro can be seen on a clear day.

**TSAVO WEST NATIONAL PARK: Voyager Ziwani** $$$
Tented camp          **Road Map** C6
*Ziwani Gate*
**Tel** *020 4446651*
W heritage-eastafrica.com
Unpretentious camp with comfortable standing tents on the bank of the Sante river. Bush walks and a children's programme on offer.

## Southern Coast

**CHALE ISLAND: The Sands at Chale Island** $$
Resort          **Road Map** E7
*10 km (6 miles) south of Diani*
**Tel** *0733 610455*
W thesandsatchaleisland.com
Romantic, luxury island resort and spa where thatched rooms and suites have Swahili decor. Activities include diving and fishing.

**DIANI BEACH: Diani Marine Diver's Village** $$
Resort          **Road Map** E7
*Diani Beach Road, Ukunda*
**Tel** *0707 629060*
W dianibeachvillas.com
The village has a collection of B&B and self-catering accommodation: villas for families or groups, thatched chalets and a standing tent sleeping four. Five-star PADI dive school on site.

**DIANI BEACH: Leopard Beach Resort & Spa** $$
Resort          **Road Map** E7
*Diani Beach Road, Ukunda*
**Tel** *020 2049270*
W leopardbeachresort.com
Smart and spaciously laid out resort with standard rooms, suites, cottages and luxurious private villas in magnificent tropical gardens. Amenities include bars and restaurants, a spa and gym, swimming pools and a dive centre.

**DIANI BEACH: Papillion Lagoon Reef** $$
Resort          **Road Map** E7
*Diani Beach Road, Ukunda*
**Tel** *040 3202213*
W rexresorts.com
This friendly, all-inclusive resort offers simple cottages and beachfront rooms in landscaped gardens. Activities include scuba diving and deep-sea fishing.

**DIANI BEACH: Pinewood Beach Resort & Spa** $$
Resort          **Road Map** E7
*Galu Beach at the south end of Diani*
**Tel** *020 2080981*
W pinewood-beach.comy
Family-oriented resort on one of Diani's most secluded beaches. Swimming pool, dive centre and excellent dinner buffets.

**DIANI BEACH: The Sands at Nomad** $$
Resort          **Road Map** E7
*Diani Beach Road, Ukunda*
**Tel** *0725 373888*
W thesandsatnomad.com
Medium-sized resort set in a coastal forest on a beautiful beach. Dining options include a restaurant, sushi bar and pizzeria.

**FUNZI ISLAND: The Funzi Keys** $$$
Luxury resort          **Road Map** E7
*South of Msambweni on mainland*
**Tel** *0733 900446*
W thefunzikeys.com
A romantic private island resort that is especially popular with honeymooners. Beautiful rooms feature stone baths, four-poster beds and Jacuzzis.

**KILIFI: Mnarani** $$
Resort          **Road Map** E7
*Malindi Road*
**Tel** *020 8070501*
W mnarani.co.za
This South African-run resort on a cliff overlooking Kilifi Creek offers simple rooms, a good restaurant, bird-watching and boat trips.

**MOMBASA: Pride Inn Hotel** $$
City hotel          **Road Map** A6
*Haile Selassie Avenue*
**Tel** *041 2317895*
W prideinn.co.ke
Bland hotel on Mombasa's busy main road, but with modern and comfortable rooms. Convenient for sightseeing and shopping.

**MSAMBWENI: Msambweni Beach House** $$$
Boutique hotel          **Road Map** E7
*8 km (5 miles) from Msambweni village*
**Tel** *020 3577093*
W msambweni-beach-house.com
Luxurious retreat ideal for honeymooners. The Swahili-style suites and villas are private and spacious. There is a large infinity pool and a secluded baobab-studded beach lies below the clifftop property. The food is exquisite. Excursions to Shimba Hills and various dive sites are offered.

**NORTHERN MOMBASA: Bamburi Beach Hotel** $$
Resort          **Road Map** B6
*Bamburi Beach*
**Tel** *041 5485611*
W bamburibeachkenya.com
All-inclusive resort offering diving, windsurfing and fishing. Rooms are in three-storey blocks.

**NORTHERN MOMBASA: Voyager Beach Resort** $$
Resort          **Road Map** B6
*Nyali Beach*
**Tel** *020 4446651*
W heritage-eastafrica.com
Large, family-friendly, nautically themed resort with a full range of water activities, kids' clubs and evening entertainment. Guests stay in modern cabins.

**NORTHERN MOMBASA: Serena Beach Hotel & Spa** $$$
Resort          **Road Map** B6
*Shanzu Beach*
**Tel** *0732 125000*
W serenahotels.com
Superior spa hotel in Swahili style, with beautiful rooms and several restaurants, as well as a gym.

**SHIMBA HILLS: Shimba Hills Lodge** $$
Tree lodge          **Road Map** E7
*Shimba Hills National Reserve, Kwale*
**Tel** *020 4452095*
W aberdaresafarihotels.co.ke
Rustic wooden, stilted lodge overlooking a waterhole. Small rooms, but the setting is great.

**SHIMONI: Shimoni Reef Lodge** $$
Cottage                    **Road Map** E7
*Shimoni Village*
**Tel** *0736 474005*
W shimonireeflodge.com
Small, friendly lodge with simple
thatched cottages dotted around
the grounds. There is a seawater
pool. Dolphins are often spotted
from the dining terrace.

**TIWI BEACH: Amani Tiwi
Beach resort**            $$
Resort                    **Road Map** E7
*Ukunda*
**Tel** *020 2120192*
W amanitiwibeachresort.com
Large resort with rooms in
thatched blocks set in tropical
gardens. Facilities include a kids'
club, dive school and tennis courts.

# Northern Coast

**LAMU ARCHIPELAGO:
New Lamu Palace Hotel** $$
Traditional hotel    **Road Map** F6
*Waterfront, Lamu town, Lamu Island*
**Tel** *042 4633164*
Air-conditioned small rooms with
four-poster beds in a traditional
Swahili building. Pleasant bar.

**LAMU ARCHIPELAGO:
Peponi Hotel**            $$
Boutique hotel       **Road Map** F6
*Shela Village, Lamu Island*
**Tel** *0722 202082*
W peponi-lamu.com
Small, family-run hotel with sea-
facing rooms. Rooms are bright
and airy and have overhead fans.

**LAMU ARCHIPELAGO:
Kipungani Explorer** $$$
Exclusive resort     **Road Map** F6
*Southern tip of Lamu Island*
**Tel** *020 4446651*
W heritage-eastafrica.com
Spacious chalets in a coconut
plantation with ocean views. Lots
of chill-out areas and a range of
water and cultural activities.

**LAMU ARCHIPELAGO:
Lamu House**              $$$
Boutique hotel       **Road Map** F6
*Waterfront Lamu town, Lamu Island*
**Tel** *0720 604408*
W lamuhouse.com
This stylish hotel consists of two
traditional Swahili houses. Every
room is individually decorated
with antiques and modern art.
There is a plunge pool in the
central courtyard.

**LAMU ARCHIPELAGO:
Manda Bay**               $$$
Exclusive resort     **Road Map** F6
*Manda Island*
**Tel** *020 2115453*
W mandabay.com
Exclusive island lodge offering an
all-inclusive package including
water sports. Accommodation is
in large airy cottages. Dinners are
served on the beach or in a dhow.

## DK Choice

**LAMU ARCHIPELAGO:
The Red Pepper House** $$$
Exclusive resort   **Road Map** F6
*5 minutes north of Lamu town by
motorized boat*
**Tel** *020 2513147*
W theredpepperhouse.com
Sumptuous resort on a private
beach. There are five spacious
villas, each one individually
decorated in a bush-Swahili
style. There is a dhow for private
excursions and the food is
superb, with a good selection
of wines and other drinks. Great
option for honeymooners.

**MALINDI: Driftwood
Beach Club**              $$
Resort                    **Road Map** E6
*Silversands Road*
**Tel** *0721 724489*
W driftwoodclub.com
Family-friendly hotel set right
on a tropical palm-fringed beach.
Rooms are in thatched cottages
or spacious villas.

**MALINDI: Lawford's**   $$
Resort                    **Road Map** E6
*Harambee Road*
**Tel** *042 2121265*
W malindikey.com
One of Kenya's oldest beach
hotels has been renovated, but
still carries the "old England"
atmosphere. Rooms have garden-
facing balconies. There's a spa,
and several pools and restaurants.

**TANA RIVER: Delta Dunes** $$$
Exclusive lodge     **Road Map** E6
*Tana river-mouth, about halfway
between Malindi and Lamu*
**Tel** *0718 139359*
W deltadunes.co.ke
This place has seven beautifully
decorated cottages perched on
sand dunes, with private
verandas and ocean views. Meals
are served in a communal tent.

**WATAMU BEACH: Turtle Bay
Beach Club**              $$
Resort                    **Road Map** E6
*Mida Creek Drive*
**Tel** *042 2332003*
W turtlebay.co.ke
Family-oriented resort. Comfort-
able, air-conditioned rooms, four
restaurants, a big swimming pool
and access to a stretch of beach.

**WATAMU BEACH:
Hemingways**              $$$
Resort                    **Road Map** E6
*Mida Creek Drive*
**Tel** *020 2649399*
W hemingways-watamu.com
This resort has a British feel. It has
its own fleet of boats that attract
many big-game fishermen.

# Southern Rift Valley
and Masai Mara

**KIGIO WILDLIFE CONSERVANCY:
Malewa Wildlife Lodge** $$
Safari camp          **Road Map** B4
*20 km (12 miles) NW of Naivasha*
**Tel** *0702 975923*
W kigio.com
Set within woodland along the
Malewa river, this rustic eco-
lodge has stone cottages and
unique stilted canvas, reed
and thatch river suites. The
emphasis in the restaurant is
on excellent home cooking.

**LAKE BARINGO: Robert's Camp** $
Campsite             **Road Map** B4
*Kampi ya Samaki*
**Tel** *0717 176656*
W robertscamp.com
In addition to camping, basic
cottages, *bandas* and standing
safari tents are offered on a self-
catering or full-board basis.

Spacious suite at Hemingways resort, Watamu Beach

**For more information on types of hotels** *see pp360–63*

Grazers among the stone cottages at Lake Naivasha Sopa Resort, Lake Naivasha

## DK Choice

**LAKE BARINGO:**
**Island Camp** $$$
Tented camp **Road Map** B4
*Ol Kokwe Island*
**Tel** *0724 874661*
🌐 islandcamp.co.ke
Located on its own little island
in the middle of the lake, the
rooms here are in luxury,
thatched standing tents, with
balconies overlooking the lake.
The lush vegetation attracts
a variety of birds. Meals are
served in an open-air thatched
dining area.

**LAKE ELMENTEITA: Sleeping**
**Warrior Lodge** $$$
Safari lodge **Road Map** B4
*Soysambu Conservancy*
**Tel** *0735 408698*
🌐 sleepingwarriorkenya.com
Guests at this lodge, which
stands on a volcanic hill offering
stunning views ,stay in beautifully
designed stone cottages or in a
tented camp. Set menu meals are
offered in the cosy dining room

**LAKE NAIVASHA:**
**Crater Lake Tented Camp** $$
Tented camp **Road Map** B4
*Crater Lake Game Sanctuary*
**Tel** *050 2020613*
🌐 craterlakecamp.com
Overlooking the crater lake, this
lodge has spacious tents under
thatch with big four-poster beds.
All tents have showers.

**LAKE NAIVASHA:**
**Elsamere** $$
Historic hotel **Road Map** B5
*Moi South Lake Road, 22 km*
*(14 miles) from Naivasha*
**Tel** *0722 648123*
🌐 elsamere.com
Elsamere is the former home of
Joy and George Adamson. The
rooms are in simple cottages and
the main building is a museum.
Meals are taken communally in
the dining room.

**LAKE NAIVASHA:**
**Lake Naivasha Country Club** $$
Country hotel **Road Map** B4
*Moi South Lake Road, 8 km (5 miles)*
*from Naivasha*
**Tel** *0703 048200*
🌐 sunafricahotels.com
Lakeshore hotel built in 1937 with
accommodation in stone cottages
dotted around the grounds.
The public areas retain a British
colonial charm, with fireplaces,
bay windows and a billiards room.

**LAKE NAIVASHA:**
**Lake Naivasha Sopa Resort** $$
Country hotel **Road Map** B5
*Moi South Lake Road, 12 km (7 miles)*
*from Naivasha*
**Tel** *020 3750235*
🌐 sopalodges.com
Modern country lakeside resort
offering comfortable stone
cottages dotted on the lawns
frequented by many grazers like
antelopes, warthogs and hippos.

**LAKE NAIVASHA: Chui Lodge** $$$
Safari lodge **Road Map** B5
*Oserengoni Wildlife Sanctuary, Moi*
*South Lake Road*
**Tel** *0722 200596*
🌐 chuisafaricollection.com
This place has eight stunning
cottages with four-poster beds,
marble bathrooms and log fires.

**LAKE NAKURU: Sarova Lion**
**Hill Game Lodge** $$
Safari lodge **Road Map** B4
*East of lake Nakuru*
**Tel** *020 2767000*
🌐 sarovahotels.com
Located on a hill with views of
Lake Nakuru, this place has
modern rooms and a swimming
pool. Massages are available.

**MASAI MARA NATIONAL**
**RESERVE: Keekorok Lodge** $$
Safari lodge **Road Map** B5
*Eastern Mara*
**Tel** *0703 048000*
🌐 sunafricahotels.com
This is the Mara's first safari lodge,
built in 1962. The comfortable

rooms are in stone bungalows,
and a highlight is the elevated
walkway to a dam where resident
hippo and other game are seen.

**MASAI MARA NATIONAL**
**RESERVE: Mara Serena**
**Safari Lodge** $$
Safari lodge **Road Map** B5
*Western Mara*
**Tel** *020 2842000*
🌐 serenahotels.com
This lodge is built on a ridge and
has superb views of the reserve.
The decor is based on the Maasai
*manyatta* (hut).

**MASAI MARA NATIONAL**
**RESERVE: Riverside Camp** $$
Safari lodge **Road Map** B5
*Bordering the Central Mara, outside*
*Talek Gate*
**Tel** *0734 697211*
🌐 riversidecampmara.com
Good-value lodge, owned and
managed by the local Maasai
community. Stay in a *banda* or
standing tent, or camp.

**MASAI MARA NATIONAL**
**RESERVE: Cottar's 1920s**
**Safari Camp** $$$
Tented camp **Road Map** B5
*Southeast Mara*
**Tel** *0733 773378*
🌐 cottars.com
Run by renowned safari guide
Calvin Cottar, this luxury bush
camp with 1920s safari decor
is set on a private concession.

**MASAI MARA NATIONAL**
**RESERVE: Governor's Camp** $$$
Tented camp **Road Map** B5
*Northern Mara*
**Tel** *020 2734000*
🌐 governorscamp.com
At this classic tented camp each
tent has a private veranda
overlooking the game-rich Mara
river or Mara Plains. Great guiding.

**MASAI MARA NATIONAL**
**RESERVE: Kichwa Tembo**
**Tented Camp** $$$
Tented camp **Road Map** B5
*Concession northwest of Oloololo Gate*
**Tel** *020 3745238*
🌐 andbeyond.com
Luxurious camp offering spacious
tents and a swimming pool. The
dining room has panoramic views.

**MASAI MARA NATIONAL**
**RESERVE: Masai Mara**
**Sopa Lodge** $$$
Safari lodge **Road Map** B5
*Eastern Mara*
**Tel** *020 3750235*
🌐 sopalodges.com
Chain lodge, with Maasai-themed
decor, offering rooms in thatched
buildings. Large swimming pool.

**MASAI MARA NATIONAL RESERVE: Porini Lion Camp** $$$
Tented camp          Road Map B5
*Olare Motorogi Conservancy, east of Musiara Gate*
**Tel** *020 7123129*
W porinisafaricamps.com
Classic no-frills tented camp in a private concession. The Maasai guides are highly skilled.

**DK Choice**

**MASAI MARA NATIONAL RESERVE: Rekero Camp** $$$
Tented camp          Road Map B5
*Central Mara, on the West bank of the Talek River*
**Tel** *020 2324904*
W asiliaafrica.com
One of the most luxurious tented camps in the Mara, set in riverine forest along the Talek river. It is well positioned for general game viewing and the wildebeest crossing during the migration. Excellent guides and superb food and service.

**NAKURU: Midland Hotel** $$
City hotel          Road Map B4
*Geoffrey Kamau Highway*
**Tel** *051 2212125*
W midlandhotel.co.ke
This historic hotel offers comfortable rooms in the heart of Nakuru town, and with secure parking.

## Western Kenya

**ELDORET: Naiberi River Campsite and Resort** $
Hostel          Road Map B4
*16 km (10 miles) southeast of Eldoret*
**Tel** *020 3550051*
W naiberi.com
This place offers camping, dormitory beds and rooms. There is a swimming pool overlooking the Naiberi River and a stone cave bar.

**HOMA BAY: Homa Bay Tourist Hotel** $
City hotel          Road Map A4
*Rongo Road along the lakeshore*
**Tel** *059 22722*
The rooms here are simple, but set in gardens with lake views. Boat trips can be arranged.

**KAKAMEGA: Udo's Bandas** $
Self-catering banda Road Map A4
*Kakamega Forest National Reserve*
**Tel** *020 2418419*
W kws.go.ke
Basic two-bed thatched *bandas* with mosquito nets and hurricane lamps. There is a kitchen, but bring all provisions, firewood and bedding. Camping available, too.

**KAKAMEGA: Golf Hotel** $$
City hotel          Road Map A4
*Khasakhala Road*
**Tel** *0728 833974*
W golfhotelkakamega.com
Slightly old-fashioned option, but the rooms are comfortable and all have balconies. Good base for forest excursions. Golf and tennis on offer in the adjacent club.

**DK Choice**

**KAKAMEGA: Rondo Retreat** $$
Lodge          Road Map A4
*Kakamega Forest National Reserve*
**Tel** *056 2030268*
W rondoretreat.com
Christian-run retreat in the heart of the forest. Rooms are in the old 1940s saw-miller's main house and in cottages set in a lush garden. Furnished with both antiques and modern pieces. Hearty meals are taken in the cosy dining room, where a fire is lit in cold weather.

**KERICHO: Tea Hotel** $
Historical hotel          Road Map B34
*Moi Highway*
**Tel** *0714 51082*
W teahotel.co.ke
At this faded colonial hotel, with charming, old-fashioned rooms surrounded by tea plantations, guests can enjoy the pool, tennis court and golf club next door.

**KERIO VALLEY: Kerio View** $
Cottage          Road Map B4
*Elgeyo Escarpment near Iten*
**Tel** *020 2039559*
W kerioview.com
Stay in a cottage or a *banda*. The glass-fronted restaurant here has amazing views of the valley. There are mountain bikes for hire.

A pool with a view at Mfangano Island Lodge, Mfangano Island

**KISUMU: Imperial Hotel** $$
City hotel          Road Map A4
*Jomo Kenyatta Avenue*
**Tel** *0734 608111*
W imperialhotelkisumu.com
The hotel has modern rooms and suites, as well as one-bedroom apartments. There is secure parking and a rooftop bar.

**KISUMU: Kiboko Bay Resort** $$
Resort          Road Map A4
*Dunga village, on the lakeshore*
**Tel** *0724 387738*
W kibokobay.com
The only lakeshore option in Kisumu offers comfortable en-suite standing tents under thatch. Tasty food is served by the pool.

**KITALE: Karibuni Lodge** $
Hostel          Road Map A3
*Off Hospital Road*
**Tel** *0706 043618*
W karibunikitale.com
Family-run backpacker's hostel in a pleasant house. Choice of camping, dorm beds and rooms. Good home-cooked meals.

**DK Choice**

**MFANGANO ISLAND: Mfangano Island Lodge** $$$
Luxury lodge          Road Map A4
*In the northeast of the island*
**Tel** *020 2734000*
W governorscamp.com
Exclusive island camp with six stylish thatched rooms shaded by fig trees. The lodge can be reached with a direct flight from the Masai Mara. Exquisite food and excellent service. Spa treatments are available and activities include Nile perch fishing, birdwatching and cultural walks.

**MOLO: Kembu Campsite and Cottages** $
Cottage          Road Map B4
*Between Nakuru and Molo off the A104, 8 km (5 miles) outside Njoro*
**Tel** *0722 725003*
W kembu.com
Spacious cottages on a working old settler farm. Some are self-catering, but meals can be taken in the main house or at the bar. Camping is also permitted.

**MOUNT ELGON NATIONAL PARK: Kapkuro Bandas** $
Self-catering banda Road Map A3
*Near the park headquarters*
**Tel** *020 6000800*
W kws.org
Park accommodation in four basic en-suite *bandas* set in the forest. There is a communal kitchen, but guests need to bring all provisions including drinking water.

**For more information on types of hotels** *see pp360–63*

**RUSINGA ISLAND: Rusinga Island Lodge** $$$
Luxury lodge    **Road Map** A4
*In the northwest of the island*
**Tel** *020 2531314*
W rusinga.com
This remote island lodge, reached by private charter, offers stone and thatch cottages. Aside from relaxing, the main activity is fishing for the giant Nile perch.

## Central Highlands

**ABERDARE NATIONAL PARK: The Ark** $$
Tree hotel    **Road Map** C4
*Eastern slope of the Aberdares*
**Tel** *020 557009*
W thearkkenya.com
Tree hotel overlooking a forest-fringed waterhole, attracting a constant stream of animals. Rooms are in cabins.

**ABERDARE NATIONAL PARK: Treetops Lodge** $$$
Tree hotel    **Road Map** C4
*Eastern slope of the Aberdares*
**Tel** *020 4452095*
W aberdaresafarihotels.co.ke
Founded in 1932, Treetops is the original tree hotel. It overlooks a waterhole, frequented by many animals. Rooms are small, but comfortable.

**LAIKIPIA PLATEAU: Serena Sweetwaters Tented Camp** $$
Tented camp    **Road Map** C4
*Ol Pejeta Conservancy*
**Tel** *020 2842000*
W serenahotels.com
Standing tents with wooden balconies overlooking a waterhole. Facilities include a swimming pool and a game-viewing hide. Meals are superb.

**LAIKIPIA PLATEAU: Lewa House** $$$
Safari lodge    **Road Map** C4
*Lewa Wildlife Conservancy*
**Tel** *0710 781303*
W lewahouse.com
Rooms are in three spacious cottages or in the charming old colonial homestead. Horseback safaris are a speciality.

**LAIKIPIA PLATEAU: Porini Rhino Camp** $$$
Tented camp    **Road Map** C4
*Ol Pejeta Conservancy*
**Tel** *020 7123129*
W porinisafaricamps.com
Isolated camp on a private concession west of Ol Pejeta. Seven classic safari tents are set along a seasonable watercourse. The guiding is excellent.

### DK Choice

**LAIKIPIA PLATEAU: Solio Lodge** $$$
Safari lodge    **Road Map** C4
*Solio Reserve*
**Tel** *0731 914732*
W thesafaricollection.com
Located on a private wildlife sanctuary and a major rhino conservation site, this lodge consists of just five luxurious cottages, individually decorated. Facilities include a fireplace, big modern bathroom with separate bath and shower and vast floor to ceiling windows offering views of Mount Kenya.

**MERU NATIONAL PARK: Elsa's Kopje** $$$
Safari lodge    **Road Map** D4
*Mughwango Hill, Meru National Park*
**Tel** *0730 127000*
W elsakopje.com
Located on the hilltop overlooking the former campsite of Joy and George Adamson. The luxurious open-fronted cottages make the most of the view. Fishing, guided walks and game drives available

### DK Choice

**MERU NATIONAL PARK: Rhino River Camp** $$$
Tented camp    **Road Map** D4
*Meru National Park*
**Tel** *0732 809287*
W rhinorivercamp.com
Set in jungle-like forest along a babbling stream attracting a good selection of birds and small animals, the accommodation here is in six ultra-stylish standing tents set on wooden platforms. There is a riverside infinity pool and the excellent cuisine is Italian-inspired.

Entrance to the The Ark tree hotel, Aberdare National Park

**MOUNT KENYA NATIONAL PARK: Sirimon Bandas** $
Self-catering banda    **Road Map** C4
*Sirimon Gate of Mount Kenya National Park*
**Tel** *020 6000800*
W kws.org
Conveniently located at the start of the ascent route. The two *bandas* each consist of two bedrooms, a kitchen, bathroom and a sitting room.

**MOUNT KENYA NATIONAL PARK: Serena Mountain Lodge** $$
Tree hotel    **Road Map** C4
*In the south of the park, accessed from Kiganjo*
**Tel** *020 2842000*
W serenahotels.com
Enclosed by forest on the foothills of Mount Kenya, this lodge overlooks a busy water-hole. Comfortable rooms.

**NANYUKI: Kongoni Camp** $$
Guesthouse    **Road Map** C4
*2 km (1 mile) north of Nanyuki*
**Tel** *062 2031225*
W kongonicamp.com
Simple accommodation in cottages set in lovely gardens around a swimming pool. A good base for Mount Kenya treks.

**NANYUKI: Fairmont Mount Kenya Safari Club** $$$
Country hotel    **Road Map** C4
*8 km (5 miles) southeast of Nanyuki*
**Tel** *020 2265555*
W fairmont.com
Set in park-like gardens, the main building of the hotel reflects 1950s architecture, while the rooms are in quaint cottages. Activities include golf and horse riding.

**NARO MORU: Naro Moru River Lodge** $$
Country hotel    **Road Map** C4
*2 km (1 mile) west of Naru Moru*
**Tel** *0708 984002*
W naromoruriverlodge.com
Reasonably priced base for Mount Kenya climbs along the western ascent route. The rooms are a bit old-fashioned, but the riverside setting is pleasant.

**NORTHERN LAIKIPIA: Loisaba Koija Starbeds** $$$
Safari camp    **Road Map** C4
*Loisaba Wilderness, 68 km (42 miles) NW of Nanyuki*
**Tel** *0705 202375*
W loisaba.com
Unique and romantic, these are double beds shrouded with mosquito nets that are wheeled on to raised wooden platforms so that guests can sleep under the stars. Meals are prepared by the local Maasai.

**NYAHURURU: Thomson's Falls Lodge** $
Country hotel    Road Map B4
*Next to Thomson's Falls outside town*
**Tel** *065 22006*

**w** thomsonsfallslodge.org
Full of character, this colonial-era hotel dates back to 1934 and has views over the eponymous waterfall. Lovely garden area. There's also a campsite on lush green lawns.

**NYERI: Outspan Hotel** $$
Historical hotel    Road Map C4
*Baden-Powell Road*
**Tel** *020 4452095*
**w** aberdaresafarihotels.co.ke
Founded in 1927, the hotel is mostly a staging post for overnight visits to Treetops. Colonial-style architecture and comfortable rooms set in colourful gardens. Good views of Mount Kenya.

**THIKA: Blue Posts Hotel** $$
Historical hotel    Road Map C5
*On the A2, 2 km (1 mile) N of Thika*
**Tel** *020 529332*
This historical colonial hotel has simple but comfortable rooms with patios in two ivy-clad stone wings. The extensive grounds have viewpoints over the Chania and Thika waterfalls.

# Northern Kenya

**BUFFALO SPRINGS NATIONAL RESERVE: Samburu Simba Lodge** $$$
Safari lodge    Road Map C3
*Eastern end of the reserve*
**Tel** *020 4444401*
**w** simbalodges.com
This is the largest lodge in the Samburu area. The pleasant rooms all have private balconies that offer stunning views over the plains. There are two swimming pools.

**LOIYANGALANI: Oasis Lodge** $$
Lodge    Road Map C2
*Centre of the village*
**Tel** *0729 954672*
**w** oasis-lodge.com
This faded German-run lodge on the shores of Lake Turkana is the only choice in a remote area. It offers basic bungalows and a spring-fed swimming pool.

**MARSABIT: Marsabit Lodge** $$
Safari lodge    Road Map D2
*Marsabit National Park, 8 km (5 miles) from Marsabit Airstrip*
**Tel** *0722 929245*
This colonial lodge offers 24 basic rooms, a campsite and restaurant. The stunning, remote location overlooks a cliff-lined waterhole that attracts game.

Open-air bathroom with stunning views at Desert Rose Lodge, South Horr

**MATTHEWS RANGE: Kitich Camp** $$$
Tented camp    Road Map C3
*34 km (21 miles) northwest of Wamba*
**Tel** *0730 127000*
**w** kitichcamp.com
Exclusive place with six safari tents overlooking the lush gorge of the Ngeng River. Guests can swim in rock pools and go on walks with Samburu guides.

**SAMBURU NATIONAL RESERVE: Samburu Sopa Lodge** $$
Safari lodge    Road Map C3
*Eastern end of the park*
**Tel** *020 3750235*
**w** sopalodges.com
Located on a hilltop away from the river, but arranged around a waterhole. Stay in cottages resembling traditional Samuru homesteads. The swimming pool has a sunken bar.

# DK Choice

**SAMBURU NATIONAL RESERVE: Elephant Watch Camp** $$$
Tented camp    Road Map C3
*In the northwest of the reserve*
**Tel** *020 8048602*
**w** elephantwatchportfolio.com
Owned and managed by elephant experts Oria and Saba Douglas-Hamilton, this exclusive camp consists of six stylish Bedouin tents. The en-suite bathrooms are of the safari bucket style. Its location is on a stretch of river known to be visited by big elephant bulls. Excellent food.

**SAMBURU NATIONAL RESERVE: Samburu Game Lodge** $$$
Safari lodge    Road Map C3
*Near the reserve headquarters*
**Tel** *020 532329*
**w** wildernesslodges.co.ke
This is the oldest lodge in Samburu and it is set in the best

location on the north bank of the Ewaso Nyiro river. Comfortable rooms and buffet-style meals.

**SAMBURU NATIONAL RESERVE: Samburu Intrepids** $$$
Tented camp    Road Map C3
*5 km (3 miles) from the west gate*
**Tel** *020 4446651*
**w** heritage-eastafrica.com
This fabulous camp has luxurious tents with secluded verandas. There is a riverfront dining deck and an open-air lounge area. Children's activities are offered.

**SHABA NATIONAL RESERVE: Joy's Camp** $$$
Tented camp    Road Map C3
*Eastern sector*
**Tel** *0730 127000*
**w** joyscamp.com
A remote camp built on the site of Joy Adamson's Shaba home. The stylish tents have stone bathrooms and verandas with views of a waterhole. There is a swimming pool and spa treatments are offered.

**SHABA NATIONAL RESERVE: Sarova Shaba Game Lodge** $$$
Safari lodge    Road Map C3
*1 km (0.6 miles) north of Natorbe Gate*
**Tel** *020 2767000*
**w** sarovahotels.com
Large lodge with lush grounds and 85 chalet-style rooms that all have views over the Ewaso Nyiro river. Tasty buffet meals.

**SOUTH HORR: Desert Rose Lodge** $$$
Lodge    Road Map C2
*30-minute drive from Kowop airstrip*
**Tel** *020 3864831*
**w** desertrosekenya.com
Isolated, eco-friendly lodge set in a forest grove. It consists of five houses and two cottages with open-air, en-suite bathrooms. The main attraction is Samburu-led camel treks. Dramatic views.

**For more information on types of hotels** *see pp360–63*

# WHERE TO EAT AND DRINK

Nairobi and Mombasa have a wide selection of restaurants offering international fare. Indian food is a firm favourite, although Italian, Chinese and Thai cuisines are also popular. There are some excellent specialist restaurants that make a fine addition to any visitor's itinerary. Safari lodges and beach resorts offer Continental (European) buffets and à la carte menus. Kenyan food, usually stews, curries and some form of starch, can be found at local restaurants and cafés. Fast-food chains are mushrooming all over Kenya and cater to the appetite for fried chicken and ice cream. Snacks such as samosas or fried sausages can be bought from any of the numerous vendors with simple charcoal burners at roadside stalls. Meat is eaten across the country, with the freshwater fish tilapia being preferred in Western Kenya and seafood a speciality along the coast. There is also an excellent choice of fruit and vegetables for vegetarian tastes.

### Places to Eat

Most hotels have restaurants. In fact, some in the upper bracket have several, which are also open to non-guests. At these, visitors can expect international standards, gourmet food and a good, albeit expensive, range of imported wines and champagne. Some of the more exclusive lodges and tented camps are renowned for their cuisine, which is part and parcel of a luxury safari experience. Meals are often taken in the bush or around a crackling fire, and because of the early morning and late afternoon game drives, safaris often feature additional brunch and afternoon tea. On the coast, beach resorts offer sumptuous buffets featuring plenty of seafood and tropical fruit, while smaller regional hotels will attempt some basic but adequate Continental dishes.

There are a number of fine individual restaurants. In Nairobi, Carnivore *(see p377)*, offers a gut-busting meat-eating frenzy, and in the mainland off Mombasa Island, Tamarind *(see p379)* provides a magical seafood banquet on board a dhow. A good choice for vegetarians is Indian cuisine, and Indian restaurants are prolific throughout Kenya and quite often offer good-value all-you-can-eat buffets.

All towns feature simple cafés that offer steaming stews and curries to workers at lunchtime. However, these are rarely open in the evening. South African fast-food chains selling burgers, fried chicken, pizzas and the like can be found in Nairobi and Mombasa.

### Paying and Tipping

Except at the larger hotels or tourist-orientated restaurants that accept credit cards, bills for meals need to be paid in cash. For a large group of customers, a restaurant may well add a 10–15 per cent service charge to the bill. Street vendors do not need to be tipped, but if they cannot give back change of a few shillings, it is polite not to insist.

### Street Food

In urban areas, a number of food items can be purchased from street vendors who usually cook over charcoal burners in roadside shelters known as kiosks. Street food is safe to eat provided it is cooked thoroughly. Items to look out for include *nyama choma*, a feast of roast meat; *mandazi*, a sweet deep-fried dough; egg-bread, a wheat pancake filled with minced meat and fried eggs; samosas, deep-fried pastry triangles filled with meat or vegetables; roasted maize, similar to, but not as sweet as, corn on the cob; *mishkaki*, barbecued meat on skewers; hard-boiled eggs and fried Farmers Choice sausages,

Glorious views of the Indian Ocean from Tamarind restaurant in Nyali, Mombasa *(see p379)*

A display of fresh fruit and vegetables at Nairobi's City Market

a good and hugely popular local brand. Slices of watermelon, mango, papaya and oranges are also on offer, but visitors need to be wary of anything washed in local water. Those who are self-catering can get fruit and vegetables as well as eggs, meat and bread at any of the markets. Imported items can be found in supermarkets in the larger cities.

## Alcoholic Drinks

Kenya Breweries, now part of East African Breweries, produces some very good beer under the labels Tusker, White Cap and Pilsner. The iconic award-winning Tusker lager is served chilled in brown half-litre bottles. Named when one of the Kenya Breweries founders was killed by an elephant in 1923, the distinctive black-and-gold elephant logo can now be found on Tusker souvenirs such as T-shirts and caps.

Imported spirits are available but can be expensive. South African wines are fairly well priced, although these are rarely found away from tourist areas. Cheaper local brands include Kenya Cane, which is similar to rum, and Kenya Gold, a coffee liqueur. A popular and appetizing local cocktail is *dawa*, a mixture of vodka, honey and lime. Home-brewed concoctions such as *pombe* or *chang'aa* are best avoided as they can be contaminated and the latter is also illegal.

## Other Drinks

In terms of the biggest global names, it feels like Kenya has been literally branded by Coca-Cola – there are advertisements everywhere. Coke is sold from giant, bottle-shaped kiosks. Many different flavours of Fanta are also popular, and are sold in shops and on the street, even in remote areas. Soft drinks, or sodas as they are known in Kenya, come in reusable bottles that are returned when empty. Bottled water is widely available, as is fresh fruit juice in season. *Chai* (tea) is usually served in small glasses. The tea, milk and sugar are boiled together, so the brew can be excessively sweet. Kenya is well known for its good coffee but, surprisingly, instant is often used in local restaurants. However, modern coffee-shop chains serving freshly ground coffee feature in the cities.

## Vegetarians

Most people in Kenya are non-vegetarians, and local meals often include red meat, chicken or fish. Sometimes the accompanying vegetable dishes are cooked in meat-based broths. Nevertheless, vegetarians will get by. Most upmarket restaurants offer vegetarian options. Organized safaris cater specifically for vegetarians, as do buffets in hotels and lodges. Peanut butter is a popular addition to dishes, so people with a nut allergy need to enquire whether it has been used in their food.

## Recommended Restaurants

The restaurants featured on the following pages have been carefully selected to give a cross-section of options in every region: you will find everything from fine dining to international buffets and local café fare. The entries are divided into geographical areas corresponding to the chapters in this guide, and then organized by town. Kenyan food tends to be on the bland side and mostly consists of meat or fish on the coast with a starch like *ugali* (maize porridge). Restaurants catering to visitors' tastes often have an international menu with dishes from all over the world (mostly African, Indian and Western). Some are more distinctly Continental (European) or just Western with some more typical American dishes thrown in with the European fare. The larger hotels in the game parks mainly serve buffet style meals. Health restaurants haven't really taken off in Kenya, but there are some exceptions where organic produce is used and vegetarian dishes, salads and smoothies can be ordered. More common is the *grill*, offering grilled meat and chips.

The DK Choice entries highlight exceptional establishments that offer excellent food and more, such as a stunning setting, great atmosphere or good value.

Romantic outside seating area at Hemmingways in Watamu *(see p380)*

# The Flavours of Kenya

Kenyan food has a diversely international history. In the 15th century, the Portuguese introduced crops from newly discovered Brazil, including maize, cassava, bananas and pineapples, as well as citrus fruit from India and China, and pigs. Later, colonists brought potatoes, tomatoes and cucumbers, and indentured labour from India contributed curries and chapatis. The distinctive, spicy Swahili cooking of the coast stems from contact with Arab and other Indian Ocean traders. Tea and coffee were introduced in colonial times and are now important export crops for Kenya.

A pile of chapatis

Kebabs being grilled over a Kenyan barbecue cookstove (*jiko*)

## Kenyan Cuisine

For Kenyans, a key objective of food is to fill one up as efficiently and cost-effectively as possible. Nevertheless, the food is tasty as well as filling. Take a liberal helping of starch, a roasted, grilled or stewed meat and a side dish such as *kachumbari* (a spicy relish) or *sukuma wiki* (stewed greens and tomatoes, the name meaning "stretch the week" in Kiswahili since it helps to extend the weekly food budget), and you have the basic Kenyan meal.

Beer is the favoured accompaniment to meals, and Kenya Breweries has brewed good local bottled beer since 1922. Tusker is the most popular, with its slogan "Bia Yangu, Nchi Yangu", which in Kiswahili translates as "My Beer, My Country".

## Meat and Fish

Kenyan beef, chicken, lamb and pork are all of good quality. Availability and preparation depend on the people and the region. The Maasai, for example, enjoy boiled goat soup, with the meat eaten separately afterwards, while the Kikuyu prefer stewed, boiled or roasted beef and mutton, served with vegetable dishes. Chicken is

Watermelon — Coconut — Pineapple — Mangoes — Bananas — Passion fruits — Guavas — Papaya

Selection of tropical fruits grown in Kenya

## Kenyan Dishes and Specialities

Breakfast in Kenya is generally a simple affair consisting of sugary *chai* (tea), accompanied by *mandazi*, a sweet, doughnut-like flat bread. Another traditional breakfast dish is *uji*, a millet-based porridge served warm with lots of milk and sugar. Some sort of starch accompanies almost every main meal. This might be potato, rice, *matoke* (mashed plantain), *ugali* (a Kikuyu maize and water paste that varies in consistency from porridge-like to a firmish dough), or *irio*. Most are fairly bland on their own but absorb the flavour of the dish that they accompany. The most distinctive Kenyan food is the Swahili cooking found on the coast, in which spices such as cloves and cinnamon feature prominently. Desserts are simple, and include fruit salads, cakes and honey biscuits.

Cloves and cinnamon sticks

**Irio**, a mashed potato, spinach and bean dish, is often used to accompany a vegetable stew such as *githeri*.

Stallholders and their wares at a market in Mombasa

usually cooked in oil with tomatoes and onions. Surprisingly, game is not a traditional part of Kenyan cuisine, although meats such as ostrich and gazelle can be found on restaurant menus.

Coastal waters are rich in seafood, and a fragrant Swahili prawn or fish curry with coconut rice makes a perfect beachside dinner. Inland, freshwater tilapia is popular, and is usually split and dried in the sun. In the far west, Nile perch from Lake Victoria sometimes features on menus, while trout can be found in the Central Highlands.

## Fruit and Vegetables

Kenyan cooking makes excellent use of the country's huge range of fresh vegetables and tropical fruits. The well-watered, fertile soil across the south and centre of the country ensures an endless supply, and every market offers a dazzling display of local produce. Cassava, maize, yams, plantains and pulses are among the all-important starch providers; peppers, pumpkins and tomatoes give dishes flavour and colour; and greens such as kale are plentiful. On the coast, coconuts are abundant, and coconut milk is used in cooking. In the highlands, nuts such as cashews and macadamias are grown.

Right across the country, roadside shacks sell snacks such as barbecue-roasted maize cobs and hunks of cassava, pieces of sugarcane, or oranges and mangoes, halved and scored, to refresh parched travellers with their sweet and sticky juices.

Swahili woman carrying freshly caught fish on the Kenyan shoreline

## ON THE MENU

**Chapati** Flat wheat bread, often served with *githeri*.

**Githeri** Boiled maize and beans or peas, cooked with tomatoes and onions to make a hearty vegetable stew.

**Matoke** Boiled and mashed plantains. When well prepared they taste like buttery, lightly whipped mashed potato.

**Mukimo** Mashed potatoes mixed with green corn, green peas and pumpkin leaves.

**Mursik** Milk that has been fermented and smoked in a gourd before consumption.

**Kachumbari** Spicy relish of chopped tomatoes, onions, cabbage, chillies, cucumber, coriander and lime juice.

**Wali wa nazi** Swahili dish of rice cooked with coconut milk until creamy.

**Ugali with sukuma wiki** is a communal dish in which lumps of dough are used to scoop up the stewed greens.

**Nyama choma**, or marinated, spicy, barbecued chunks of meat, may be served with piquant *kachumbari* relish.

**Mchuzi wa kamba** is a prawn curry with a rich tomato and coconut-milk sauce, served with rice and fried plantain.

# Where to Eat and Drink

## Nairobi

**DAGORETTI CORNER:**
**Mediterraneo Restaurant** $$
Italian
*The Junction Mall, Ngong Road*
**Tel** *020 3878608*
Good range of pasta, pizza and ice cream. The specialities here are home-made pasta and seafood dishes. Decent Italian wine list.

**DAGORETTI CORNER:**
**The Phoenician** $$
Lebanese
*Matundu Lane, off School lane*
*Westlands*
**Tel** *0716 161011*
Offers a wide range of Lebanese, European and Japanese dishes, including *teppanyaki* and pizza. The sushi bar is excellent.

### DK Choice

**DOWNTOWN: Bridges**
**Organic Health Restaurant** $
Organic **Map** 1 C3
*Trust Mansion Building on Tubman Road, off Koinange Steet*
**Tel** *0714 047177* **Closed** *Sun*
Offers organic meals, with plenty of options for vegetarians and a bargain meal of the day. Popular dishes include soups, salads, samosas and butternut chapattis. A big selection of vegetable and fruit juices are available. Farmers' market every Saturday.

**DOWNTOWN: Java House** $
Café **Map** 1 C3
*Mama Ngina Street*
**Tel** *0721 494049*
Head here for excellent freshly brewed Kenyan coffee. There's a good variety of big breakfasts, light meals, cakes, ice-cream sundaes and yogurt smoothies.

**DOWNTOWN: Pasara Café** $
Café **Map** 1 C4
*Lonrho building, Kaunda Street*
**Tel** *020 343696*
An unpretentious café, popular for lunch with office workers. Great for a quick meal – soups, salads and freshly baked baguettes.

**DOWNTOWN: Thorn Tree Café** $
Café **Map** 1 C3
*Sarova Stanley Hotel, Kimathi Street*
**Tel** *020 2767000*
Pavement bistro café, famous for its Thorn Tree message board. The menu features 15 types of coffee, burgers and sandwiches, as well as bigger evening meals. Free Wi-Fi.

**DOWNTOWN: Café Maghreb** $$
Café **Map** 1 A4
*Nairobi Serena Hotel, Kenyatta Avenue*
**Tel** *020 2822000*
A Moroccan-styled, upmarket eatery next to the pool of the Serena Hotel. It offers buffet-style breakfast and lunch, an elaborate à la carte dinner, and a 24-hour brasserie service.

**DOWNTOWN: Thai Chi** $$
Thai **Map** 1 C3
*Sarova Stanley Hotel, Kimathi Street*
**Tel** *020 2767000*
Nairobi's best Thai restaurant offers traditional Thai decor and authentic dishes prepared by chefs from Thailand. Fragrant, hot as well as sweet and sour curries. No children under 12 allowed.

### DK Choice

**DOWNTOWN: Trattoria** $$
Italian **Map** 1 C4
*Kaunda Street*
**Tel** *020 340855*
This is the oldest family-run Italian restaurant in Nairobi. The menu offers specialities from the south of Italy, Rome, Tuscany and Veneto. Everything is prepared with fresh produce including home-made pasta and ice cream. There is a great selection of Italian wines, too.

**DOWNTOWN: Bhandini** $$$
Indian **Map** 1 B4
*InterContinental Hotel, City Hall Way*
**Tel** *020 3200000*
Classy restaurant with impeccable service, pleasant decor and delicious food. Specialities include some sublime Indian desserts. Watch the chef at work through the glass-enclosed kitchen.

**DOWNTOWN: Tatu** $$$
Continental **Map** 1 B2
*Norfolk Hotel, Harry Thuku Road*
**Tel** *020 2265555*
Contemporary restaurant with fantastic service. The dry-aged coal-grilled Angus steak is its speciality, but there is a good range of seafood as well.

**GIGIRI: Village Market**
**Food Court** $
International
*Village Market Mall, Limuru Road*
**Tel** *020 7122488*
A cluster of outdoor tables surrounded by a dozen food counters offering Chinese, Indian, Kenyan *nyama choma*, pizzas and burgers. Cheap and pleasant.

**Price Guide**
Prices are for a two-course meal for one, including a half-bottle of house wine (or equivalent), tax and service.

| | |
|---|---|
| $ | up to US$15 |
| $$ | US$15 to $35 |
| $$$ | over US$35 |

**KAREN: Purdy Arms** $
Continental
*61 Marula Lane*
**Tel** *0712 007001*
This lively, family-friendly pub offers views of the sunset behind the Ngong Hills. The menu features Continental dishes as well as some nostalgic English pub grub.

**KAREN: Talisman** $$
Asian fusion
*320 Ngongo Road*
**Tel** *0705 999997* **Closed** *Mon*
Set in a rambling house with a sprawling garden terrace, this place serves a fusion of Asian, African and Continental cuisines. The bar boasts a long cocktail menu. Live band at weekends.

### DK Choice

**KAREN: Tamambo Karen**
**Blixen** $$$
Seafood
*Karen Blixen Coffee Garden, Karen Road*
**Tel** *0719 346349*
Arguably Nairobi's top seafood restaurant, serving giant prawns, young crabs, juicy lobsters, squid, octopus and oysters. Poultry and steak are also on the menu, as well as some vegetarian dishes. There is a sumptuous dessert menu and a good wine list. The ambience is elegant and the service is attentive.

Bhandini Indian restaurant at the InterContinental Hotel, Nairobi

**KASARANI: Nyama Choma Ranch** $$$
Grill
*Safari Park Hotel, off Thika Road*
**Tel** *020 3633000*
Top restaurant at the Safari Park Hotel, specializing in barbecued meat presented on skewers and carved at the table. Acrobats and the resident band, the Safari Cats, provide entertainment.

**LANGATA: Rangers** $$
Continental
*Entrance of Nairobi National Park, Langata Road*
**Tel** *020 2357470*
Restaurant built on boardwalks at the main gate of Nairobi National Park with views over the animal enclosures in the Safari Walk. Grilled meat is a popular dish. You can order lunch to take away.

### DK Choice

**LANGATA: The Carnivore** $$$
Grill
*Langata Road*
**Tel** *020 6005933*
The ultimate barbecue restaurant. A variety of meat including ostrich, crocodile and beef rump is roasted over charcoal and carved at the table. You can eat as much as you want of the set-menu, which also includes soup and dessert. There is also an à la carte restaurant and a nightclub.

**MILIMANI: China Plate** $$
Chinese
*The Cancery, Valley Road*
**Tel** *020 2727627*
Renowned for its Szechwan Chinese cuisine, the menu includes noodle soup, sizzling meat dishes, fried rice, spring rolls and tom yum. The duck is especially good.

**MOMBASA ROAD: Pampa Churrascaria** $$
Brazilian steakhouse
*Panari Sky Centre, Mombasa Road*
**Tel** *0722 131047*
Lively restaurant with South Brazilian flair. It encompasses an authentic Brazillian rotisserie steakhouse offering a choice of grilled meats. Set menus include one for vegetarians.

**MUTHAIGA: Anghiti** $$
Indian
*Muthaiga Shopping Centre, Limuru Road*
**Tel** *020 4040292* **Closed** Mon
One of Nairobi's best Indian restaurants, serving a broad range of North Indian dishes. Service is attentive and diners can watch the chefs at work behind glass walls.

Mediterraneo Restaurant, Dagoretti Corner, Nairobi

**MUTHAIGA: La Dolce Vita** $$
Italian
*Muthaiga Shopping Centre, Limuru Road*
**Tel** *0734 291670*
This long-standing Italian eatery feels like a transplant from 1960s Europe. It serves great pizzas, pastas and other Italian fare. The desserts are recommended.

### DK Choice

**RUNDA ESTATE: Lord Erroll** $$$
French
*89 Ruaka Road*
**Tel** *020 7122433*
Sophisticated gourmet restaurant set in beautiful gardens. House specialities include flambé dishes, prawns and fillets. The Sunday buffet lunch has an excellent choice. The extensive wine list features imported wines from around the world.

**WESTLANDS: Artcaffe Oval** $
Café
*The Oval, Ring Road, Parklands*
**Tel** *020 2425863*
This café-cum-bakery serves a range of coffees, light snacks, home-made pastries and cakes, as well as hearty meals. The outside seating area on the balcony offers great views. There is also a lounge area and a speciality cocktail bar serving more than 30 cocktails.

**WESTLANDS: Abyssinia** $$
Ethiopian
*Muguga Green Road*
**Tel** *0725 151515*
A great place for the adventurous to try Africa's most distinctive cuisine, a sour-dough pancake-like staple called *injera* eaten with a variety of fiery *wat* stews. The traditional decor adds to the experience.

**WESTLANDS: Bangkok Chinese Restaurant** $$
Chinese
*Parklands Road*
**Tel** *020 3751312*
Great authentic Chinese cuisine, which makes up for the slight lack of atmosphere. The speciality here is seafood and the chef's ginger garlic crab is a must-try.

**WESTLANDS: Haandi** $$
Indian
*The Mall*
**Tel** *020 4448294*
Upmarket restaurant, renowned for its delicately flavoured and traditional food. There is great ambience, with candlelit tables and outstanding service.

**WESTLANDS: Oasis** $$
African fusion
*Southern Sun Mayfair Hotel, Parklands Road*
**Tel** *020 3740920*
Popular and affordable poolside restaurant offering both buffet and à la carte menus in a lovely, relaxed atmosphere. There is usually live music at dinner.

**WESTLANDS: Pepper's Restaurant** $$
Continental fusion
*Parklands Road*
**Tel** *0722 201880*
Set in a large rambling house and garden, this place has a huge menu. The grilled steak, crab and lobster are recommended. There are good wines and cocktails.

**WESTLANDS: Alan Bobbe's Bistro** $$$
French bistro
*Raptha Road*
**Tel** *0727 878783*
Restaurant offering fine dining accompanied by French wines with 18th-century paintings on the walls. Don't miss the crab claws and lobster thermidor.

**For more information on types of restaurants** *see p372*

## Southeastern Savannahs

### AMBOSELI NATIONAL PARK: Ol Tukai Lodge $$
Buffet      **Road Map** C6
*Ol Tukai, near the headquarters*
**Tel** *0726 249697*
Centrally located in Amboseli, this is the obvious place to stop for lunch. It serves the usual lodge-style buffet with a good selection of meat-based dishes. Offers views towards Kilimanjaro.

### TAITA HILLS WILDLIFE SANCTUARY: Chala Restaurant at Sarova Taita Hills Game Lodge $$
Buffet      **Road Map** D7
*1 km (0.5 miles) off Voi–Taveta Road*
**Tel** *0728 608765*
This lodge serves excellent buffet lunches, usually with at least one roast meat dish, fish and salad. Visitors can combine lunch and a game drive on the property.

### TSAVO EAST NATIONAL PARK: Voi Safari Lodge $$
Buffet      **Road Map** D6
*4 km (2 miles) from Voi Gate*
**Tel** *0733 333400*
Overlooking a waterhole regularly visited by elephants and buffalo, this is an ideal lunch stopover in Tsavo East. Lunch is usually a lodge-style buffet, but it can switch to à la carte at quiet times.

### DK Choice

**TSAVO WEST NATIONAL PARK: Kilanguni Serena Safari Lodge $$**
Buffet      **Road Map** D6
*West of Mtiti Andei Gate, off road junction 8*
**Tel** *020 2842000*
The best place to stop for lunch in Tsavo West. The dining room overlooks a waterhole and has views of Kilimanjaro on a clear day. The expansive buffet-style lunch has lots of meat, fish, Continental, Indian and vegetarian options. The dessert counter is especially good.

### VOI: Tembo Restaurant at Voi Wildlife Lodge $$
Buffet      **Road Map** D6
*Immediately outside Voi Gate*
**Tel** *0722 201240*
A good lunchtime spot in Voi for those who don't want to enter Tsavo East National Park. There is a waterhole frequented by elephants and other wildlife. Meals are buffet style with good Indian and vegetarian options as well as the usual meat dishes.

## Southern Coast

### BAMBURI: Il Covo $$
Italian      **Road Map** B6
*Bamburi Beach*
**Tel** *041 5487460*
This place boasts two fabulous beachfront balconies. The menu features meat dishes plus fresh fish, such as tuna and red snapper. There is also a pizza oven.

### BAMBURI: Roberto's $$
Italian      **Road Map** B6
*Indiana Beach Hotel*
**Tel** *0723 223399*
Family-friendly place serving great pasta dishes and wood-oven pizzas. It has an extensive, reasonably priced wine list and a bar offering a variety of cocktails.

### DIANI: African Pot $
African      **Road Map** E7
*Diani Beach Road*
**Tel** *0723 644707*
Simple and unpretentious, this place has a varied selection of Swahili and upcountry dishes, from spicy *pilau* to meat stews with *ugali* (maize meal porridge).

### DIANI: Shan E-Pujab $
Indian      **Road Map** E7
*Diani Beach Road*
**Tel** *078 203012*
The best Indian restaurant in Diani, despite its location in a shopping mall, serves superb meat and vegetarian dishes. Free shuttle to and from nearby hotels.

### DIANI: Aniello's $$
Italian      **Road Map** E7
*Diani Beach Road*
**Tel** *0730 3740408*
Specialities here include fresh pasta, crispy pizza and seafood. The ice cream is recommended.

### DIANI: Forty Thieves Beach Bar and Bistro $$
Bistro      **Road Map** E7
*Diani Beach Road*
**Tel** *0712 294873*
Barefoot bar and restaurant offering breakfast and lunch. Light meals and salads, as well as seafood dishes and pizzas are on the lunch menu. Good selection of fresh juices and cocktails.

### DIANI: Nomad Beach Restaurant $$
Western/Japanese    **Road Map** E7
*Diani Beach Road*
**Tel** *040 3203643*
Located on a beautiful stretch of beach. Aside from the authentic Italian dishes, including wood-fired pizza, there's a Japanese menu offering sushi and tempura.

Seating on the sand at Forty Thieves Beach Bar and Bistro

### DIANI: Sails Beach Bar & Restaurant $$
Seafood      **Road Map** E7
*Diani Beach Road*
**Tel** *0716 863884*
Dine under sweeping canvas and enjoy the stunning beach view. The menu here focuses on fresh seafood and changes weekly.

### DK Choice

**DIANI: Ali Barbour's Cave $$$**
Seafood      **Road Map** E7
*Diani Beach Road*
**Tel** *0714 456131*
One of the most atmospheric eateries on the coast, situated in a natural coral cave that has holes in the ceiling and is illuminated by candles. The focus is on seafood, but pasta, steak and vegetarian options are also available. Free shuttle service.

### MOMBASA: Blue Room $
Fast food      **Road Map** A6
*Haile Selassie Road*
**Tel** *0721 786868*
This bustling, spotless canteen has been serving Mombasa since 1952. The extensive menu offers everything from burgers and pizzas to vegetarian curries.

### MOMBASA: Castle Terrace $
Continental      **Road Map** A6
*Castle Royal Hotel, Moi Avenue*
**Tel** *041 2228780*
The informal street-facing terrace is a great place to watch the busy street life. Grilled meat is the focus here, but there are some fish and seafood options as well.

### MOMBASA: Recoda Restaurant $
Swahili      **Road Map** A6
*Moi Avenue*
**Tel** *041 2223629*
Established in 1942, this restaurant specializes in grilled meat and *pilau* (a spicy local equivalent to risotto). Also serves vegetarian dishes.

**MOMBASA: Singh Restaurant** $
Indian    **Road Map** A6
*Mwembe Tayari Road*
**Tel** *0773 528936*    **Closed** *Mon*
Spacious and centrally located,
this is one of the oldest restaurants
in Mombasa. It serves a wide
selection of Punjabi dishes – the
chicken and seafood options are
particularly recommended.

**MOMBASA: Galaxy Chinese** $$
Chinese    **Road Map** A6
*Mama Ngina Drive*
**Tel** *020 2138611*
This restaurant has ocean views
and offers a good variety of
Chinese dishes. Specialities
include ginger crab, garlic chicken
and an array of satay sizzler dishes.
Vegetarians are also catered for.

**MOMBASA: Shehnai** $$
Indian    **Road Map** A6
*Fatemi House, Maunganu Street*
**Tel** *041 2224801*    **Closed** *Mon*
A stylish restaurant focusing on
Mughlai vegetarian and fish
dishes. It is also famous for its
excellent tandoori menu, which
includes dishes like chicken and
fish tikka baked in a traditional
clay oven. No alcohol is served.

**MTWAPA: The Moorings** $$$
Continental    **Road Map** B6
*Off the Mombasa–Malindi Road*
**Tel** *0736 547923*    **Closed** *Sun*
This thatched floating restaurant
is located on the mangrove-lined
Mtwapa Creek and mainly serves
seafood. It's a great place to
enjoy a cocktail at sunset.

**NYALI: Bollywood Bites** $
Indian vegetarian   **Road Map** B6
*Nyali Cinemax, Nyali Road*
**Tel** *041 470001*
One of the few dedicated vege-
tarian places in the area. The tacky
decor is themed around Bolly-
wood cinema, but the curries
are delicious. Don't miss the 18
varieties of *dosas* (rice pancakes).

**NYALI: Café Mocha** $
Café    **Road Map** B6
*Nyali Cinemax, Nyali Road*
**Tel** *0775 269326*
This café offers Lebanese snacks
including humous, tabbouleh and
*fatoush*. There is also a huge range
of coffees plus tasty desserts.

**NYALI: Roberto's** $$
Italian    **Road Map** B6
*Nyali Cinemax, Nyali Road*
**Tel** *0708 272299*
Known for its extensive and
sensibly priced wine list. Home-
made pizza, pasta and Italian-
style meat dishes are served in
a family-friendly ambience.

**NYALI: La Veranda** $$
Italian    **Road Map** B6
*Mwea Tabere Street, behind
Nakumatt Nyali*
**Tel** *0733 774436*
Head here for delicious home-
made pasta dishes and pizza.
Steaks, seafood and salads also
feature on the menu. The wine
list consists of Italian wines.
Excellent service.

### DK Choice

**NYALI: Tamarind Dhow** $$$
Seafood    **Road Map** B6
*Jetty Tamarind Mombasa*
**Tel** *041 4471747*
A floating companion to the
Tamarind Mombasa, offering
a romantic dinner experience.
Housed in a working dhow,
the restaurant sails twice daily
serving a set menu lunch and
dinner accompanied by traditional Swahili music. There is
usually a choice of seafood
dishes and one meat dish, too.

**NYALI: Tamarind Mombasa** $$$
Seafood    **Road Map** B6
*Cement Silo Road*
**Tel** *041 4471747*
One of the top eateries in
Kenya, with seating on the
terrace overlooking the harbour
or in the Arab-influenced interior.
Seafood is the main fare, but
meat including ostrich and
quail are also available.

**WASINI: Charlie Claw's** $$
Seafood    **Road Map** E7
*Wasini Island*
**Tel** *0722 683860*
Famous for its Swahili seafood
lunches, this is usually visited as
part of an inclusive day tour to
Kisite-Mpunguti Marine Park.
Buffet-style feasts include
barbecued fish in coconut and
ginger-steamed giant crab claws.

## Northern Coast

**LAMU ARCHIPELAGO:
Bush Gardens** $
Seafood    **Road Map** F6
*Waterfront, Lamu town*
This is the pick of several local
eateries on Lamu's waterfront.
Specialities include seafood
dishes, pancakes with banana
and honey, and fresh fruit juices.

**LAMU ARCHIPELAGO:
Hapa Hapa** $
Seafood    **Road Map** F6
*Waterfront, Lamu town*
A thatched restaurant on the
waterfront, offering seafood,
meat and vegetarian dishes.
Breakfasts of omelettes,
pancakes, fruit and yogurt are
good too. No alcohol is served.

**LAMU ARCHIPELAGO:
Lamu Palace** $$
Swahili    **Road Map** F6
*Waterfront, Lamu town*
**Tel** *042 4633164*
A pleasant terrace restaurant
in the hotel of the same name.
It offers a good selection of
Swahili, Indian and seafood
dishes, and serves beer and wine.

### DK Choice

**LAMU ARCHIPELAGO:
Lamu House** $$$
Seafood    **Road Map** F6
*Waterfront, Lamu town*
**Tel** *042 4633491*
This stylish restaurant in a
historical Lamu mansion, which
is also a boutique hotel, offers
some of the best and most
inventive seafood on the island.
Examples include snapper
carpaccio, mussel soup and
seared tuna. Candlelit tables
add to the atmosphere. One of
the few restaurants to offer wine.

Atmospheric dining in a coral cave at Ali Barbour's Cave restaurant

For more information on types of restaurants *see p372*

## DK Choice

### LAMU ARCHIPELAGO: Peponi Hotel $$$
Seafood **Road Map** F6
*Shela, Lamu Island*
**Tel** *0722 203082*
This lovely Shela hotel with waterfront patios and a beautiful Swahili-style dining room offers some of the best seafood in the area. The house speciality is giant prawns either in a traditional Swahili stew, sushi or just grilled. There is a full bar serving wine and delicious cocktails.

### MALINDI: Jahazi Bar & Restaurant $
Continental **Road Map** E6
*Seafront Road*
**Tel** *0720 178982*
Popular restaurant and bar with live entertainment. The large menu features snacks and hearty meals. Pastas, soups and paninis are good. Reasonable prices. The bar has a regular happy hour.

### MALINDI: Baby Marrow $$
Italian **Road Map** E6
*Sabaki Centre, Lamu Road*
**Tel** *0727 581682*
Set under the arms of an enormous tree and thatched roofs, this is a favourite in the expat community. Imaginative pastas are a highlight, but seafood lovers will not be disappointed.

### MALINDI: I Love Pizza $$
Pizzeria **Road Map** E6
*Mama Ngina Road*
**Tel** *042 2120672*
This affordable eatery not only serves great pizza, but seafood, pasta and meat dishes as well. Vegetarians are well catered for and the outside area above street level is great for people-watching.

Waterfront tables at the Peponi Hotel, Lamu Archipelago

### MALINDI: La Malindina $$
Italian **Road Map** F6
*Mtangani Road, off Lamu Road*
**Tel** *042 2120045*
Set in a villa with tables around the swimming pool in a large garden, this stylish restaurant produces great Italian food. Try the seafood from the grill.

## DK Choice

### MALINDI: Old Man and the Sea $$
Seafood **Road Map** E6
*Silversand Road*
**Tel** *042 2131106*
One of Malindi's oldest and most popular seafood restaurants, set in an old beachfront house with a homely atmosphere and a sea-facing terrace. House specials include the grilled seafood platter and grilled king-fish, but meat and chicken dishes are also served. Very popular, so booking in advance is highly recommended.

### MALINDI: La Rosada $$
Seafood **Road Map** E6
*Casuarina Road*
**Tel** *042 308460*
Stylish beach restaurant serving seafood and Italian fare. The lounge area is a perfect spot to sip a cocktail. On Monday night the place transforms into an open-air disco and on Sunday there is a buffet lunch.

### WATAMU: Swahili Café $
Swahili **Road Map** E6
*Watamu Road*
**Tel** *0724 812422*
Small local café serving Swahili food including fresh seafood. Service is slow and the set-up very basic, but it is a cheap and friendly alternative to the surrounding resorts.

### WATAMU: Hemingways $$
Continental **Road Map** E6
*Mida Creek Drive*
**Tel** *020 2649399*
The best bet in Watamu for a light lunch or a buffet dinner, the latter following a different theme every night. Diners can eat outside around the pool.

### WATAMU: Pilipan Restaurant $$
Continental **Road Map** E6
*Beach Road*
**Tel** *0736 724099*
Restaurant with a light and airy interior offering an enticing menu serving meat and vegetarian dishes, as well as some seafood. There are daily specials and seasonal variations to the menu.

# Southern Rift Valley and Masai Mara

### LAKE NAIVASHA: Camp Carnelley's $
International **Road Map** B5
*Moi South Lake Road*
**Tel** *050 50004*
Popular backpackers' resort set in large gardens. The bar and restaurant are furnished with cushions and sofas for relaxation. On offer is an interesting and changing range of dishes using local produce. Boat rides on the lake can be arranged.

## DK Choice

### NAIVASHA: La Belle Inn $
International **Road Map** C4
*Moi Avenue*
**Tel** *020 3510404*
The charming terrace of this old colonial relic is the best place for a meal or a snack in Naivasha town. The menu offers freshly baked pastries and cakes, as well as main meals such as steak and chips or Indian curries. It's a great place to watch life along Naivasha's main street.

### NAKURU: Java Nakuru $
Café **Road Map** B4
*Westside Mall*
**Tel** *0702 811525*
This upcountry branch of the successful Nairobi coffee chain is usefully situated at the junction of Kenyatta Avenue and the Nairobi–Nakuru Highway. It offers freshly brewed Kenyan coffee, a good variety of light meals, outdoor seating, free Wi-Fi and secure parking.

### NAKURU: Midland Hotel $$
International **Road Map** B4
*Geoffrey Kamau Highway*
**Tel** *051 2212125*
Colonial hotel dining room with a reliable choice of main meals such as steaks, pork chops and tilapia, plus some vegetarian dishes and South African wines. The garden bar serves delicious barbecued chicken.

### NAROK: Kenol Petrol Station Restaurant $
Kenyan/Indian **Road Map** B5
*West side of Narok on the way to Masai Mara National Reserve*
Popular truck stop and tourist service station with a shady garden backing onto a riverbank. Simple Kenyan, Chinese and Indian dishes are on offer, as well as snacks and cold drinks.

Colourful, relaxed seating area at Camp Carnelley's, Lake Naivasha

# Western Kenya

**KAKAMEGA: Golf Hotel** $
International     **Road Map** A4
*Khasakhala Road*
**Tel** *0728 833974*
Open to the public, breakfast is served buffet-style here, and the menu offers a wide selection of African and international dishes. The bar shows sports on a big screen.

**KERIO VALLEY: Kerio View** $
International     **Road Map** B3
*Elgeyo Escarpment near Iten*
**Tel** *020 2039559*
This glass-fronted restaurant offers magnificent views over the valley. Items on the menu range from English breakfast to hearty stews and casseroles. Grilled lamb is available from the barbecue.

**KISUMU: The Duke of Breeze** $
International     **Road Map** A4
*Jomo Kenyatta Highway*
**Tel** *0717 105444*
The rooftop bar and restaurant at the Duke of Breeze Hotel has tremendous views across Kisumu and the lake, especially at sunset. Food includes Kenyan dishes, burgers, steaks, stir-fries and salads.

## DK Choice

**KISUMU: Kiboko Bay Resort** $
International     **Road Map** A4
*Dunga village, on the lakeshore*
**Tel** *0724 387738*
A popular resort, with outside tables on the lakeshore serving good Indian and Swahili curries, steak and fish, as well as snacks. The nautical-themed bar is well stocked with lagers and spirits, and cocktails are on offer too. In the dining room, the modern art on the walls is for sale.

**KISUMU: Florence at the Imperial Hotel** $$
International     **Road Map** A4
*Jomo Kenyatta Avenue*
**Tel** *0734 608111*
A fairly formal dining room and one of Kisumu's best options. Highlights on the à la carte menu include fresh grilled fish from the lake, chops and curries.

# Central Highlands

**NANYUKI: Barney's** $
Continental     **Road Map** C4
*Nanyuki Airstrip*
**Tel** *0723 310064*
This popular café serves people waiting at the airfield and is also an ideal stopover for road travellers en route to the reserves. The menu offers filled pancakes, burgers and salads, alongside good coffees and milkshakes.

**NANYUKI: Trout Tree Restaurant** $$
International     **Road Map** C4
*Naro Moru Road*
**Tel** *0726 281704*
Built in an enormous fig tree, this restaurant specializes in trout that is farmed in the surrounding ponds. Items on the menu range from grilled trout to trout masala. Meat and salad dishes are available too.

**NYAHURURU: Thomson's Falls Lodge** $
International     **Road Map** B4
*Next to Thomson's Falls, outside town*
**Tel** *065 22006*
This restaurant is set in large grounds with views of Kenya's most spectacular waterfall. Like the rest of the hotel, it is a bit dated, but the meals are filling and full of flavour. It's the best option in town.

**NYERI: Green Oak Restaurant** $
Kenyan     **Road Map** C4
*Kimathi Way*
Two-storey bar offering decent local fare. Try the *ugali* with *kuku* (maize porridge with chicken) for lunch or *nyama choma* (roast meat) for dinner.

**NYERI: White Rhino Hotel** $
International     **Road Map** C4
*Kenyatta Road*
**Tel** *061 2030944*
Opened in 1913, this colonial hotel is one of the oldest buildings in town. The restaurant offers a menu of international dishes and the bar has a cosy fireplace.

## DK Choice

**NYERI: Outspan Hotel** $$
Continental     **Road Map** C4
*Baden-Powell Road*
**Tel** *061 2032424*
Nyeri's oldest and finest hotel has an excellent lunchtime buffet, an à la carte dinner menu and snacks throughout the day. The hearty food reflects the old-world atmosphere. The large gardens, which have views of Mount Kenya, are good for a stroll and are the venue for regular traditional Kikuyu dance performances after lunch.

# Northern Kenya

**SAMBURU-BUFFALO SPRINGS NATIONAL RESERVES: Samburu Game Lodge** $$
Buffet     **Road Map** C3
*Close to Samburu Reserve Headquarters*
**Tel** *020 532329*
This lodge restaurant, overlooking the river and decorated in a distinct African style, is open to outside visitors for lunch. The large buffet has something for everyone.

## DK Choice

**SHABA NATIONAL RESERVE: Surpelei Restaurant at Sarova Shaba Game Lodge** $$$
Buffet     **Road Map** C3
*1 km (0.5 miles) north of Natorbe Gate*
**Tel** *020 2767000*
Stilted wood-and-thatch restaurant overlooking the gardens and river. Offers a buffet lunch and an à la carte snack menu. Dishes are pan-African, pan-European and pan-Asian. Serves salads from the lodge's own herb and vegetable garden.

**For more information on types of restaurants** *see p372*

# SHOPPING IN KENYA

Kenya has a wide range of locally made items that are ideal as souvenirs and gifts. These include a number of traditional artifacts, precious stones and jewellery, wooden carvings, Maasai beads and blankets, *kikoys* (fabrics) and other textiles, baskets, batiks and paintings, and soapstone figurines and chess boards. There are well-stocked gift shops in Nairobi and along the coast, and dedicated bargain hunters can head for the many outdoor markets and street shops. Most tourist shops in Nairobi are clustered on Koinange Street. In Mombasa, souvenir shops and stalls are located on Moi Avenue and Nyerere Avenue. Hotels, lodges and camps that cater to holiday-makers have craft and curio shops. All airports have duty-free shops that sell high-quality, high-priced items. The art of bargaining has deep roots in Kenyan culture so visitors will often be treated to some good-humoured haggling.

## Opening Hours

Business hours for shops and markets are usually 8am to 5 or 6pm, Monday to Saturday. The smaller shops close for an hour's lunch around 1 to 2pm. Muslim-owned establishments may stay closed all day on Fridays or at least in the afternoons. In Mombasa, opening hours are longer, but many shops and businesses close for a siesta between 2 and 4pm. In places where there are plenty of holiday-makers, such as the coast, shops also open on Sundays. In hotels and lodges, in-house shops usually have their opening times adapted to the times of the day when guests are around. Shopping malls in Nairobi and Mombasa and large supermarkets are also open on Sundays until 1pm.

## How to Pay

Most tourist-orientated shops as well as high-end lodges and hotels accept credit cards, US dollars and, occasionally, cash in other currencies. When purchasing something on a credit card, a 2 to 5 per cent commission is often added, so in some instances it is cheaper to pay for items in cash. Kenya's economy is largely a cash-based one, and in small towns and villages, as well as local bus stations, markets, street-food stalls and other such places, only Kenyan shillings are accepted. Small denomination bills may not be readily available

Swahili goods on display at a souvenir shop near Fort Jesus, Mombasa

and are best kept handy as change or to pay for small items at markets and street stalls.

## Bargaining

Except in upscale shopping malls and shops, bargaining is the expected norm throughout Kenya, and for Kenyan traders it is an essential business skill. It is best to approach bargaining with a sense of humour and a friendly attitude, keeping in mind that it is not just a commercial transaction but a social encounter as well. Opening prices are almost always exaggerated and determined on what the seller thinks the customer can pay – the real price can sometimes be less than half the initial price. However, visitors should keep in mind that a lot of work has gone into making souvenir items, especially good-quality carvings and beaded jewellery. Traders make a living from their sales, so customers should not offer unreasonable prices. Generally, buyers get a good price after a little negotiation and the vendor a reasonable profit. Those who are unsure of what they should be paying should try walking away – if they are called back, there is still room for negotiation; if they are not, it means they did not offer enough and the trader is no longer interested.

## Crafts and Curios

A wide variety of indigenous crafts and curios is available in Kenya, and with careful searching, it is possible to find some of very high quality. Collectors of ethnic artifacts and objects of art will find plenty of traditional and tribal items. The Maasai and northern tribes such as the Gabbra, Turkana, Rendille, Oromo and Samburu are all famous for their beautiful artifacts. Popular items include gourds, stools, neck pillows and drums. Other curios such as

SHOPPING IN KENYA | **383**

Meru outlet of Nakumatt, Kenya's leading chain of supermarkets

wooden salad servers, carved animals and batik paintings are specifically made for the tourist market. Deforestation is a major problem in Kenya. It is best to buy wooden items at high-end stores, because cheap mass-produced objects present the greatest environmental threat, or to buy items that are made from renewable trees such as neem or blue gum.

*A painted mask from Namanga*

## Shops

There are a number of gift shops in urban and tourist localities. Nairobi, in particular, has some fine upmarket galleries. For everyday items, most sizable towns have a supermarket. Nakumatt is the biggest chain of supermarkets and is expanding rapidly. It sells food, household goods, electronics, furniture and – of particular interest to holiday-makers – camping equipment.

The **Nakumatt Mega** in Nairobi and **Nakumatt Likoni** in Mombasa are two of the largest shops in Kenya. Shopping malls are starting to feature all over Africa, and Nairobi now has several. These have cinemas, car parks, supermarkets, food courts, some international chain stores and speciality shops.

Since the building of the Lunatic Line (*see p303*), Asian traders have been operating in the country. Today, many have small shops, selling a wide variety of things, generally clustered around markets or bus stations.

## Markets

Every town in Kenya has a market while the cities have several. All of them feature an array of brilliantly coloured fresh produce, mounds of pulses and grains, pyramids of fresh eggs, live chickens and all sorts of

practical items such as rope, plastic buckets, charcoal burners and brooms.

Some markets are housed in open concrete blocks built for the purpose, while others are nothing more than small congested grids of rickety stalls made from sticks and plastic sheeting. Prices are considerably lower in markets than in shops. They are also an ideal stop for visitors interested in absorbing the busy and lively atmosphere of the place where most Kenyans do their daily shopping.

Urban areas are also home to *mitumba* (second-hand clothes) markets. The clothing available here comes from the USA, Europe and Asia and is sold off in bales to traders – usually to make money for charities. Second-hand Western designer labels and well-known brands can be found here with a little rummaging, which makes these markets hugely popular with Kenyans.

DIRECTORY

## Shops

**Nakumatt Mega**
Uhuru Highway, opposite Nyayo Stadium, Nairobi.
**Tel** 0733 632132.
W nakumatt.net

**Nakumatt Likoni**
Nyerere Avenue, near Likoni Ferry, Mombasa.
**Tel** 0733 632134.
W nakumatt.net

One of the busy fish markets at Homa Bay, on the shores of Lake Victoria

# Shopping in Nairobi

With its modern malls, galleries, downtown trading stores, specialist shops and outdoor markets, Nairobi offers the best shopping experience in Kenya. Apart from the usual wood carvings and soapstone souvenirs, there is a range of handicrafts, textiles, ornaments and paintings for sale here. In addition, there are good bookshops that sell maps of national parks and reference guides to wildlife and birds. The main shopping areas lie between Koinange Street and Moi Avenue, with the malls located further out in the more affluent suburbs of the city. Most shops can organize overseas shipping for larger items.

Busy corner outside a Nakumatt outlet in Downtown Nairobi

## Shopping Malls

Satellite shopping malls have mushroomed all over Nairobi and there are some 20 dotted around the suburbs. Most have a large supermarket serving the local community, specialist shops, restaurants, food courts, banks, bureaux de change, ATMs, post offices, large guarded car parks and additional entertainment such as cinemas. Nairobi's oldest mall is **Sarit Centre**, which has hundreds of shops as well as a cinema, health club and an exhibition centre. It is close to other shops in Westlands including Nakumatt Ukay, a 24-hour supermarket that is part of **Nakumatt**, Kenya's leading supermarket chain. Other shopping malls include **Yaya Centre**, which has a children's play area and a fitness centre, **The Galleria**, which has a food court and children's play area, and **The Junction**, which also features a Nakumatt, a cinema,

casino, and a number of excellent restaurants. The **Village Market** is East Africa's largest shopping mall. It also has a very popular food court on the weekends, a cinema, a ten-pin bowling alley, a children's waterslide park and is surrounded by gardens with cascading waterfalls.

## Markets

For the visitor looking to buy crafts and curios, Nairobi's markets are the ideal places to head to. Among a colourful display of vegetables and fruit, the City Market *(see p160)* in Downtown Nairobi offers a full range of Kenyan souvenirs at reasonable prices, although customers may need to check quality. The **Maasai Market** is held every Sunday at Yaya Centre, every Thursday at The Junction Mall and every Friday at Village Market. Prices are good if

customers bargain hard, and the selection of jewellery, baskets, carvings and other artifacts is excellent. **Kariokor Market** is a huge sprawling open-air market selling everything from fish and vegetables to traditional fabrics and souvenirs. It also has a row of affordable eateries, which are popular at lunchtime with locals.

The **Mitumba Market** near Adams Arcade is one of the best in the city and has stalls piled high with branded clothes from Europe and the USA. When visiting any of these busy markets, it is advisable to leave all valuables at the hotel and to watch out for pickpockets.

## Books and Maps

Nairobi has a number of bookshops selling Kenyan maps, souvenir books and guidebooks. These are not, however, especially cheap as most are imported. Located downtown, **Stanley Bookshop** covers a wide range of subjects despite being a modestly sized store, and has plenty of field guides and maps. There are bookshops in all malls, the best of them being **Bookstop** in Yaya Centre. It offers a wide range of genres from coffee-table books on Africa to romantic novels, and sells a good selection of second-hand books. The National Museum *(see pp162–3)* and Karen Blixen Museum *(see p172)* also have bookshops, which stock titles on a range of

Colourful cloth-paintings and soapstone chess boards at Maasai Market

Kenyan and East African subjects, such as their wildlife, history, literature and culture. Most bookshops sell international newspapers and magazines.

## Specialist Shops

Downtown Nairobi has a dense assemblage of shops catering to visitors and holiday-makers along Muindi Mbingu Street and Kenyatta Avenue. Specialist shops are also scattered around the suburbs and can be visited on the way to attractions such as the Karen Blixen Museum. In town, **Collectors Den** and **Zanzibar Curio Shop** are both crammed with every imaginable Kenyan curio as well as safari clothes. On the outskirts of town, **Spinner's Web** has a good range of wool rugs, jewellery, crafts and weavings, which are outsourced from women's groups. **Kamili Designs** produces a range of hand and screen paintings, many of which have animal designs on them. **Kazuri Beads** (*Kazuri* is Kiswahili for small and beautiful) employs destitute women who use clay-fired, hand-painted beads to make jewellery. These are now sold all

Ceramic ware, bags and pottery items on display

over the world, and in Nairobi there are shops at The Junction or Village Market malls. Visitors to the factory in Karen can also watch them being made.
**Kitengela Glass** is an open-air gallery selling wall panels, glasses and beads made out of recycled glass. They also have outlets in The Junction and Village Market malls. **Utamaduni** near the AFEW Giraffe Centre is home to 18 shops set in a Kikuyu-style house selling Maasai items, fabrics, Kisii stone, baskets and Lamu furniture. **One Way** produces a range of high-quality products made from *kikoy* fabrics, including

Contemporary wood carving

sarongs, tablecloths, bags and clothing. They have several branches in Nairobi including in the Sarit and Yaya centres.
**Matbronze** is a fine art foundry and gallery selling bronze wildlife statues.
**Marula Studios** sells paintings, leather and beaded items and unusual crafts, including sculptures and jewellery, made from recycled plastic flip-flops. They also have a café and playground. Well worth a visit despite its distance from the city is the **House of Treasures**, with its fine pieces of African art for sale as well as decor items from places as far away as Bali and Samarkand.

## DIRECTORY

### Shopping Malls

**The Galleria**
Junction of Langata & Magadi roads.
**Tel** 020 3747408.
W galleria.co.ke

**The Junction**
Dagoretti Corner, Ngong Road.
**Tel** 020 3872881.
W thejunction.co.ke

**Nakumatt**
W nakumatt.net

**Sarit Centre**
Westlands.
**Tel** 020 3747408.
W saritcentre.com

**Village Market**
Limuru Road, Gigiri.
**Tel** 020 7122488.
W villagemarket-kenya.com

### Yaya Centre
Arwings Khodek Road, Hurlingham.
**Tel** 020 2713360.
W yaya-centre.com

### Markets

**Kariokor Market**
Racecourse Road.

**Maasai Market**
Yaya Centre, The Junction and Village Market.

**Mitumba Market**
Behind Adams Arcade, Ngong Road, Kilimani.

### Books and Maps

**Bookstop**
Yaya Centre.
**Tel** 0722 520160.

**Stanley Bookshop**
Kenyatta Ave. **City Map** 1 C3. **Tel** 020 2212776.

### Specialist Shops

**Collectors Den**
Hilton Hotel, Mama Ngina St. **City Map** 1 C3.
**Tel** 020 2226990.

**House of Treasures**
70 Dagoretti Road, Karen.
**Tel** 020 3883224.

**Kamili Designs**
Langata Road, Karen.
**Tel** 020 2430495.

**Kazuri Beads**
Mbagathi Ridge, Karen.
**Tel** 020 2328905.
W kazuri.com

**Kitengela Glass**
Maasai Lodge Road, Muthaiga North.
**Tel** 0732 876507.
W kitengela.com

### Marula Studios
40 Marula Lane, Karen.
**Tel** 0726 248774.
W marulastudios.com

**Matbronze**
2 Kifaru Lane, Langata.
**Tel** 0733 969165.

**One Way**
**Tel** 020 2573918.
W one-way.cc

**Spinner's Web**
Off Peponi Road, Spring Valley. **Tel** 020 2072629.
W spinnerswebkenya.com

**Utamaduni**
Bogoni East Road, Langata.
**Tel** 020 890464.
W utamaduni.com

**Zanzibar Curio Shop**
York House, Moi Ave.
**City Map** 1 C3.
**Tel** 020 2222704.

# What to Buy

Kenya's bustling curio markets and small pavement stalls offer great bargains on a wide range of goods. Handmade items such as batik pictures, soapstone bowls, wood carvings and chess sets are made specifically for visitors. However, the country has a wealth of traditional textiles, artifacts and jewellery that make ideal souvenirs. Nairobi has some excellent upmarket boutiques and galleries selling quality products, with facilities for overseas shipment of large items. Its vibrant street-side stalls also offer the opportunity for some good-humoured bargaining.

Visitors browsing the wide array of handicraft items displayed in the City Market, Nairobi

## Art and Craft

With a wide range of art and crafts produced by its myriad communities, Kenya has grown as a niche market for these items. Popular for interiors themes, African art is very versatile. For instance, a drum can alternate as a coffee table.

**Lamu Chests**
These intricately carved wooden boxes – some studded and inlaid with brass or copper – vary in size from small jewellery boxes to large chests.

**Wooden Giraffes**
One of Kenya's most popular souvenirs, these giraffes can be difficult to cart home. Herds of them, of varying heights, can be seen clustered in shops and markets.

**Wood Carvings**
Produced by the Akamba people of eastern Kenya, these carvings range from exquisite masks and bowls to carved animals and statues of Maasai warriors.

**Handcrafted Toys**
Local artisans shape wire or straw into toys often in the form of miniature vehicles with wheels and steering columns.

**Batiks**
These can be used as cushions, tablecloths or wall hangings. Silk batiks are exclusive to Nairobi's chic galleries, while local markets stock the cheaper cotton ones with village scenes, ethnic and animal motifs.

**Soapstone**
Available in a range of colours such as cream, pink, lavender and black, soapstone is carved into soap dishes, animal statues, vases and unique chess sets with chess pieces fashioned after tribal figures.

## Clothes, Shoes and Accessories

With their primary colours, the traditional textiles of Kenya are extremely versatile. Fabrics are adapted into clothing, bags and cushions, while Maasai beads are used to embellish a host of products.

**Maasai Blankets**
Used by Maasai herdsmen as robes, these blankets have red, blue and purple stripes or checks. They also make good picnic tablecloths and can be used as wraps on a morning safari.

**Kiondo Baskets**
Traditionally woven from sisal, these baskets are now also lined with *kikoy* cloth and dyed in bright colours to make stylish handbags.

**Swahili Sandals**
Found in coastal markets, these beautiful women's sandals have leather straps in floral shapes and are set with cowrie shells or covered with tiny colourful beads.

**Tusker T-shirts**
Served in large brown bottles, Tusker is Kenya's premier beer. The Tusker logo with an elephant's head features in trendy T-shirts sold as popular souvenirs.

**Kikoys**
These striped pieces of cotton, worn by Swahili men on the coast as wraparound skirts, come in bright primary colours and make good sarongs, bags and cushions.

**Maasai Beaded Jewellery**
Jewellery, including the wide collars worn by Maasai brides, earrings, bracelets, necklaces and rings, is available in all tourist areas. Maasai beading also adorns items such as belts, mobile-phone covers and dog collars.

## Tea and Coffee

Tea and coffee are important cash crops and form a substantial chunk of Kenya's exports. Bags of coffee beans, ground coffee, loose tea and locally produced teabags can be bought in supermarkets and even from shops at the airport.

**Tea**
With its strong, heady flavour, the tea grown in the fertile plains of Western Kenya is among the finest in the world.

**Coffee**
The acidic soil near Mount Kenya yields coffee that is easily identified by its full flavour and pleasant aroma.

### What Not to Buy

The purchase of any product derived from wildlife, such as animal pelts and skins, ivory, lion teeth, coral and turtle shell, should be avoided as these are protected under the Convention on International Trade in Endangered Species of Wild Flora and Fauna (CITES). While such products may be seen up for sale, it is a punishable offence to take them out of Kenya. Buying these items also supports the illicit wildlife trade, which should be discouraged.

# ENTERTAINMENT IN KENYA

Nairobi and the coastal strip around Mombasa have the best choice of entertainment in Kenya. Local residents like to party and the popular Tusker beer flows freely at numerous laid-back pubs, upmarket wine bars and formal hotel lounges. There are plenty of nightclubs, and these do not get going until midnight. Away from the cities, most small towns usually feature some basic bars or the town's main hotel may hold a disco on the weekends. There are modern multiscreen cinema complexes in Mombasa and Nairobi. The casinos in Nairobi and the coastal resorts are popular with those wanting a flutter and a late-night drink. Larger nightclubs have stages for live bands, and live music may also be enjoyed in hotel bars and clubs. There are occasional theatre performances at venues such as the Kenya National Theatre or the foreign cultural centres in Nairobi. Many safari lodges and beach resorts provide entertainment such as ethnic dancing and acrobatics.

## Bars

Nairobi has a thriving bar culture and five-star hotels are hugely popular with locals and visitors alike. The **Safari Bar** in the InterContinental has different music themes each night; the **Jockey Pub** in the Hilton has a live duo band on weekends; while the Norfolk (see p364) has the Lord Delamere Terrace, made famous by the gin-and-tonic swilling settler set of early Nairobi. The Aksum Bar in the Nairobi Serena (see p364) offers cocktails and fine wines in elegant surroundings while the Windsor Golf Hotel and Country Club has several bars, including the elegant **Library Bar**, which has a good selection of single malt whiskies and cigars. Other popular bars include the Spanish-themed **Gipsy Bar** that serves tapas and plays flamenco and Latino music, and **Mercury Lounge**, which serves excellent cocktails and sometimes has live jazz nights. **Havanna** has three bars, an outside terrace and chilled salsa music. The **Sierra Lounge**, on the second floor of the Yaya Centre, is an upmarket spot specializing in German beer; **Tamambo** has a variety of cocktails and live music on Fridays and Saturdays.

Most hotels in Mombasa and along the coast have bars catering to holiday-makers. The exceptions are Lamu and downtown Mombasa, both conservative Muslim areas, where alcohol is frowned upon. The spacious Castle Terrace bar at the Castle Royal Hotel (see p378) serves good food. A popular alternative to the hotel bars is **Forty Thieves Beach Bar** on Diani Beach, which has outdoor seating, dancing on some nights, pool tables and a good Sunday lunch buffet with live music. North of Mombasa at Nyali, **Bob's Bar and Murphy's Irish Pub** offers five bars, two discotheques, *nyama choma* and large TVs for watching sports. It is open 24 hours.

A live band performance in one of several bars in Downtown Nairobi

## Nightclubs

Most nightclubs are open Wednesday to Saturday from about 9pm to dawn, although some open every night, especially in peak season. Cover charges vary from 200–1,000 KSh. In Nairobi, **Casablanca** is a sophisticated cocktail lounge and club with dance music. The adventurous can head to Downtown Nairobi, where the **New Florida** and **Florida 2000** nightclubs, going strong since the 1970s, are packed to the gills at weekends. **K1** is a rustically built club with a dance floor and pool hall. **Black Diamond** features a bar and dance floor with DJ. The Simba Saloon at Carnivore Restaurant (see p377) is Nairobi's largest club and can easily accommodate thousands of people.

Mombasa and the coast have a host of clubs situated within close proximity to the major hotels, and many of the big hotels have their own

The cosy interior of Jockey Pub, Hilton Hotel, Nairobi

clubs. With huge dance floors and five bars, **Pirates Beach Club** is perhaps the most popular club along the north coast where virtually all kinds of music is played every night. The **Tembo Disco**, open at weekends, has a dance floor, billiards lounge, restaurant and beer garden, while **Florida Nightclub and Casino** features 24-hour bars, a disco, casino and cabaret shows, and is best visited in a group.

A Maasai dance performance, Alliance Française, Nairobi

## Casinos

There are a few casinos dotted around Nairobi and Mombasa, most of them in the hotels, which offer bars, banks of slot machines and gaming tables. Nairobi's best and most sophisticated is the casino at the **InterContinental**. In Mombasa, the **Golden Key Casino** is located on the roof of the famous **Tamarind Restaurant** *(see p376)*, both of which offer impressive views of the city, its old dhow port and the Indian Ocean.

## Cinemas

Modern cinema complexes in Nairobi and Mombasa show mainstream Hollywood films. In Nairobi, cinema complexes can be found at the Village Market *(see p385)*, The Junction *(see p385)* and the Sarit Centre *(see p385)*. The largest and most central cinema theatre is the **IMAX 20th Century**. The best cinema hall in Mombasa is the **Nyali Cinemax**, which also has a sports bar and regularly showcases Bollywood films.

## Theatre

In Nairobi, occasional theatrical performances are held in the **Kenya National Theatre**. One of the longest-running performance groups is **Phoenix Players**, which has its own intimate, 110-seat theatre and offers a mixed bag of European and African plays. Another popular venue for theatre, comedy, films and art exhibitions is the **Alliance Française**, which has a garden stage popular for concerts.

## DIRECTORY

### Bars

**Bob's Bar and Murphy's Irish Pub**
Links Road, Nyali, Mombasa.
**Tel** 0721 542953.

**Forty Thieves Beach Bar**
Diani Beach, Ukunda.
**Tel** 0712 294873.

**Gipsy Bar**
Woodvale Grove, Westlands, Nairobi.
**Tel** 020 4440964.

**Havanna**
Woodvale Grove, Westlands, Nairobi.
**Tel** 020 4450653.

**Jockey Pub**
Hilton Nairobi, Mama Ngina St, Nairobi.
**City Map** 1 C3.
**Tel** 020 2288000.

**Library Bar**
Windsor Golf Hotel and Country Club, Kigwa Road, Nairobi. **Tel** 020 8647000.

**Mercury Lounge**
ABC Place, Waiyaki Way, Nairobi. **Tel** 020 4450378.

**Safari Bar**
InterContinental Hotel, City Hall Way, Nairobi.
**City Map** 1 B4.
**Tel** 020 3200000.

**Sierra Lounge**
Yaya Centre, Arwings Khodek Road, Hurlingham.
**Tel** 020 556960.

**Tamambo**
Village Market, Gigiri, Nairobi. **Tel** 020 7124005.

### Nightclubs

**Black Diamond**
Mpaka Road, Westlands, Nairobi. **Tel** 0724 592356.

**Casablanca**
Nyangumi Road, Hurlingham. **Tel** 020 2723173.

**Florida 2000**
Commerce House, Moi Ave, Nairobi. **City Map** 2 D4. **Tel** 0706 577009.

**Florida Nightclub and Casino**
Mama Ngina Drive, Mombasa. **Tel** 041 2313127.

**K1 (Klubhouse)**
Ojijo Road, Parklands, Nairobi. **Tel** 0717 969500.

**New Florida**
Koinange St, Nairobi.
**City Map** 1 B3.
**Tel** 020 2215014.

**Pirates Beach Club**
Mombasa–Malindi Road, Nyali, Mombasa.
**Tel** 0716 694817.

**Tembo Disco**
Mombasa–Malindi Road, Bamburi, Mombasa.
**Tel** 041 5485074.

### Casinos

**Golden Key Casino**
Silos Road, Nyali, Mombasa.
**Tel** 041 4471071.

**InterContinental**
City Hall Way, Nairobi. **City Map** 1 B4. **Tel** 020 3200000.

### Cinemas

**IMAX 20th Century**
20th Century Plaza, Mama Ngina St, Nairobi. **City Map** 1 C3. **Tel** 0737 558802. 🔲 imax.or.ke

**Nyali Cinemax**
Nyali Road, Mombasa.
**Tel** 0718 543579.
🔲 nyalicinemax.com

### Theatre

**Alliance Française**
Loita St, Nairobi.
**City Map** 1 B3.
**Tel** 020 4917000
🔲 afkenya.or.ke

**Kenya National Theatre**
Harry Thuku Road, Nairobi. **City Map** 1 B2.
**Tel** 0726 008677

**Phoenix Players**
Professional Centre Parliament Road, Nairobi. **City Map** 1 C4. **Tel** 020 2212661. 🔲 phoenix theatre.co.ke

# OUTDOOR ACTIVITIES

Kenya has an incredible range of landscapes and as such offers plenty of outdoor activities. Kenya is most popular for its safaris, but there are more ways to watch wildlife here than from a safari vehicle, such as game- and bird-walks, animal tracking and floating over herds of wildebeest in a balloon. Also popular is the Kenyan coast, with its full range of water sports as well as excellent snorkelling and scuba-diving facilities. For the adventurous, there is camel trekking in

the remote northern deserts with the Samburu, climbing Mount Kenya and whitewater rafting. There are many annual events, such as the Lewa (Safaricom) Marathon, that are open to international participants, and as a result of the country's colonial history, spectator sports are hugely popular. More relaxed activities include a round of golf on one of the many excellent courses, a gentle sail on a dhow or a relaxing massage in a health spa.

## Cultural Experiences

One of the major highlights of travelling in Kenya is experiencing its immense cultural diversity. In Nairobi, the Bomas of Kenya *(see p165)* showcase tribal dance and music, and has mock-ups of typical villages and homesteads. Visitors on their way to the popular Masai Mara National Reserve *(see pp266–9)* and Amboseli National Park *(see pp198–201)* will discover Maasai *manyattas* on the roads, whose people still follow their traditional ways of life. On the coast, north of Mombasa, the **Bombolulu Workshops and Cultural Centre**, a collection of traditional homesteads and craft centre, produces crafts of a very high standard. Visitors to the north will be able to meet the seminomadic Samburu people – some of whom act as guides on camel treks – and the Pokot people, whose homesteads and markets can be visited from the **Marich Pass Field Studies Centre**.

Hikers to Mount Kenya making their way across Chogoria Route

## Hiking and Climbing

The most favourable areas for hiking in Kenya are Ngong Hills *(see p173)* near Nairobi, Chyulu Hills *(see p184)* in the Southeastern Savannahs, Menengai Crater and Mount Longonot in the Southern Rift Valley *(see pp256–87)*, Mount Elgon and Cherangani Hills *(see pp294–5)* in Western Kenya and the Aberdares *(see pp320–21)* in

the Central Highlands. The most challenging trek in the country is to Mount Kenya *(see pp326–9)*. Of its three main peaks, Lenana can be reached by most trekkers, while Batian and Nelion are attempted only by serious climbers. The three main routes to Lenana – Chogoria, Naro Moru, and Sirimon – all penetrate forest and moorland. A leisurely six days are recommended but the mountain can be climbed in four, and the best time to do so is during the dry season. Travellers arriving from the coast will need at least a few days to acclimatize at a temperate altitude such as Nairobi before attempting the climb. Some of the hotels and lodges around Mount Kenya can organize guided climbs, as can **Mount Kenya Guides and Porters Safari Club**, a community-based organization of guides, porters and cooks in and around Naro Moru. Route details and information can be found on the **Mountain Club of Kenya** website, which also has particulars on other more remote technical rock-climbing destinations around the country. The group is located at the Nairobi Sailing and Sub Aqua Club, and although it does not have a phone number – owing to regular changes in committee members – visitors can email and enquire about attending their weekly club night. Their library has a wide selection of mountaineering books, maps and useful resources for climbing in Kenya.

Traditional dance performance at the Bomas of Kenya, Nairobi

Camel trekking with the Samburu people across the semiarid plains of Maralal

## Camel Trekking

Adventurous camel trekking is available in the drier north and on some of Laikipia Plateau's private ranches *(see pp322–5)*. Camels are used as pack animals for supplies and camping equipment, with travellers walking alongside. Treks are led by expert guides, usually the seminomadic Samburu who proudly show visitors everything of interest in the bush and desert landscape. Trips can last for a few hours from one of the lodges, to several days crossing remote wildernesses and camping out under the stars. Walking is done in the early morning or late afternoon when it is cool and distances of 8 to 20 km (5 to 12 miles) per day are not too strenuous. **Wild Frontiers Kenya**, **Desert Rose** and **Karisia Walking Safaris** can organize multiday treks.

## Bird-Watching

East Africa has one of the richest concentrations of birdlife in the world. Kenya alone is home to some 1,132 species, which represent 12 per cent of the world's bird-species count. Given these figures, it is not unusual to record more than 120 different birds at a particular site on a single day. Even a city such as Nairobi has over 600 resident and migratory species. **Nature Kenya** runs regular bird walks in Nairobi and produces checklists that cover the entire country. There are also a number of tour operators that offer specialist bird-oriented tours. Bird-watching is good all year round, and birds of the bush, such as go-away birds, guinea fowl, rollers and barbets, are always active. For sheer numbers, however, the best time to visit is from October to April, when some 120 migrant species arrive from the northern hemisphere. During the rest of the year, the migrants are replaced by birds from the southern hemisphere, especially Madagascar, but these are no more than 10 or 12 species. Kenya's birding hotspots include the dry-country parks of Samburu *(see pp346–7)* and Tsavo *(see pp186–91)*, the grasslands of the Masai Mara, the Rift Valley lakes and the highland and coastal forests. The coast is especially good during October and December when large flocks congregate at the estuaries.

## Horse Riding

Horse riding is offered in Kenya by a number of country lodges and hotels. Rides vary from short trips for novices through local forests to multiday safaris in wilderness areas for those with experience in the saddle. Riding on the plains past herds of giraffe or zebra is an exhilarating experience and it is possible to get unusually close to wildlife. Most wildlife see horses as non-threatening and humans can go almost unrecognized on top of them. Kenya has a long tradition of rearing horses from the hunter-settler days, and horses reared in the bush are quite accustomed to the presence of wildlife. Usually, the longer trips for experienced riders utilize lodges or mobile tented camps for accommodation and riders are encouraged to look after their steed at night. Vehicles, and in some cases camels, are used to carry equipment and supplies. Popular regions for horseback safaris include the Masai Mara and Amboseli, the Chyulu Hills and the Laikipia Plateau. Most travel agents specializing in equestrian holidays will be able to book a horseback safari in Kenya, as can **Safaris Unlimited** or **Offbeat Safaris**.

Riders get close to a Masai giraffe, Lewa Wildlife Conservancy

Hot-air balloons glide past grazing elephants at the Masai Mara

## Ballooning

Floating over wildlife on the misty plains of the Masai Mara is a magical experience. In Kenya, ballooning is offered by most of the Mara's lodges, and during the high season it is possible to see many candy-striped balloons drifting across the reserve at dawn. The ride usually lasts an hour and is followed by a champagne breakfast in the bush. The best time to go ballooning is during the wildebeest migration *(see pp128–9)* when the sight of thousands of plains animals from the air can be exhilarating, but a graceful and silent float over the Mara to watch the sun rise over the undulating plains is mesmerizing at any time of year. **Transworld Safaris** and **Hot Air Safaris** pick up passengers from several Mara lodges.

## Golf

Long sunny days are a feature of the typical Kenyan weather and are ideal for golf all year round. Thanks to its colonial history, Kenya has over 40 golf courses around the country, which have well-tended greens and popular clubhouses. Many are located in stunning settings where a round of golf can be combined with bird-watching. There are six courses within a 30-km (19-mile) radius of Nairobi, including the Windsor Golf and Country Club, Karen Golf and Country Club, Muthaiga Golf Club and the oldest course in Kenya, the Royal Nairobi Golf Club. The two principal courses along the coast are the Leisure Golf Club and the Nyali Golf and Country Club.

The **Kenya Golf Union**, established in 1928, organizes several tournaments throughout the year, including the Kenya Open. It lists contact details of all Kenya's golf courses on its website, most of which offer temporary membership to visitors for a small fee. Most courses have the luxury of offering caddies who are usually very good players themselves. Unusually, many inland courses are at an altitude of over 1,500 m (5,000 ft), which gives an additional 10 per cent yardage to a golfer's stroke. **Kenya Golf Safaris** can organize packages.

## Water Sports

With soft white sands and a gentle sea breeze, the coast is a veritable playground for water sports. The warm water is ideal for swimming, with none of the health risks associated with Kenya's inland lakes, many of which are infected with the bilharzia parasite, or rivers where there may be the danger of crocodiles. Diving and snorkelling *(see p215)* and boat trips on all manner of craft from traditional fishing boats to luxurious catamarans are all popular, and the resorts along the coast offer parasailing, jet-skiing, sea-kayaking and rides on inflatable banana boats. The Kenyan coast is ideal for windsurfing and kiteboarding. **Kite Beach Kenya** and **H$_2$O Extreme** on Diani Beach offer professionally accredited courses and hire out equipment.

Kitesurfing, an ever-popular water sport at the beaches of Kenya

## Diving and Snorkelling

The clear azure waters of Kenya's Indian Ocean are warm throughout the year and the shallow coral gardens, fringing reefs and blue-water drop-offs are home to some 3,000 species of marine animals and plants. Kenya's reefs, along with Egypt's Red Sea reefs and Australia's Great Barrier Reef, are ranked as some of the most diverse and beautiful in the world. There are a number of protected marine reserves that are alive with myriad species of marine life including manta rays, whale sharks, bottlenose dolphins and turtles. Visibility is excellent for most of the year, though the best time to dive is from October to April before the long rains and subsequent silted river outflows.

Snorkelling can be done by simply walking into the sea or from small local sailing boats called *ngalawa* – none of the dive sites are more than a 30-minute boat ride away. Divers can also explore a number of wrecks such as the MV *Dania*

Game in progress at the well-tended greens of Nyali Golf and Country Club

Snorkelling off the Kenyan coast at Watamu Marine Park

to the north of Mombasa, which was purposely sunk in 2002 to promote diving activities and has become a thriving artificial reef and Kenya's best wreck dive.

Almost all hotels and resorts have diving and snorkelling facilities and rent out equipment. There are many dive schools that run recognized dive courses up to dive master level in several languages. These include **Diving the Crab** and **Diani Marine**, both of which operate from several resorts along Diani Beach, and **Blue Fin Diving** which operates from hotels between Watamu and Malindi.

## Boating

There are a number of ways to enjoy a float on Kenya's innumerable rivers, lakes and even the ocean. On the coast, glass bottom boats are available from the large tourist resorts for viewing underwater life in the offshore coral reefs. A trip on one of the *ngalawa* boats is a relaxing way to be out on the water. Snorkelling is also offered. A popular day-excursion from Diani and Shimoni to the south of Mombasa is the dhow trip to **Wasini Island** *(see p224)* within the Kisite-Mpunguti Marine Park. This usually includes snorkelling and diving and a seafood lunch on the island. It is an ideal way to spend the day and dolphins often accompany the dhows through the reserve. A sail around Mombasa's harbour on

a traditional ocean-going **Tamarind Dhow** is also a lovely romantic way to enjoy a delicious seafood meal at sunset. Further inland, canoes can be taken out on many of the Rift Valley lakes and are a good way to go bird-watching or to get close to hippo. The more adventurous can go whitewater rafting with **Savage Wilderness** on the Tana river, which has rapids up to Grade V and is easily accessible as a day trip from Nairobi. There are longer two- to three-day trips on the Mathioya, Athi or Ewaso Nyiro rivers.

## Fishing

The rich and deep waters off the East African coast are one of the best game-fishing territories in the world. Keen fishermen are permitted to go deep-sea fishing in the Pemba Channel for game fish such as marlin, yellowfin tuna, sailfish, shark, swordfish, barracuda and

Weighing the catch

dorado, which are caught on a tag and release system. Key departure places for boats include the coastal towns of Shimoni, Watamu, Malindi and Kilifi. There are two very definite fishing seasons – the yellowfin tuna season that lasts from August to October, and the marlin season, usually between December and March. Numerous hotels on the coast offer day and overnight trips out to sea. Established operators include the **Pemba Channel Fishing Club** and **Hemingway's**.

Elsewhere in the country, fishing trips are available on motorized *ssese* canoes on Lake Victoria. These are often used to catch the giant Nile perch, and can be hired from the luxury fishing lodges on Mfangano and Rusinga islands *(see pp308–309)*. Some of the upmarket lodges in Aberdare National Park and the foothills of Mount Kenya can arrange trout fishing in nearby rivers and dams.

Brightly coloured fishing boats crowd the port at Mfangano Island

## Spectator Sports

Although athletics is the term most synonymous with Kenyan sports, and there is an active athletics calendar throughout the country, Kenya also features plenty of popular spectator sports, owing to its British and Asian legacy. Cricket, for instance, was first played in Kenya in 1910 in a league known as Officials V Settlers that played up until 1964. A national team was formed in 1951 and the Kenya Cricket Association in 1953. Kenya has since gone on to play at international levels, including participating in the ICC World Cup. The cricketing season lasts from June to February, when league and test matches can be watched at the **Nairobi Gymkhana Club**.

Rugby, too, has its roots in colonial days. The **Kenyan Rugby Football Union Club** was established in 1923. Kenya's Safari Sevens is now a world-recognized tournament in the global sevens rugby series. Kenyans are serious football fans and matches attract plenty of fervent and vocal followers. The Kenya National Football League was established in 1963 and is now today's **Kenyan Premier League**. Details of fixtures can be found on their website or in the local press. The most popular teams are rivals Leopards FC and Gor Mahia FC, while the national team is the Harambee Stars. Part of the European PGA Tour, the annual Kenya Open golf tournament is usually held at Nairobi's prestigious **Muthaiga Golf Club** or **Karen Country Club**

Athletes competing in the annual Lewa (Safaricom) Marathon

in March, and is also a popular event on the social calendar. Polo was introduced in Kenya at the beginning of the 20th century by officers of the King's Africa Rifles. It is still very popular and there are several clubs across the country, including the **Nairobi Polo Club** which was established in 1907. A popular Sunday excursion is the weekly horse race meetings at Nairobi's **Ngong Racecourse**. With three imposing grandstands, the turf course – laid out in the 1950s – also has a golf course at its centre. It is an enjoyable area with plenty of family entertainment, food stalls and a restaurant.

## Marathons

Kenya is host to one of the toughest and most unusual marathons in the world. Generally held in June, the 42-km- (26-mile-) long Lewa (Safaricom) Marathon, which is open to international participants, is the only marathon in the world to run through a region inhabited by wildlife. It has become a hugely popular event and was conceived in 1999. All funds raised by runners through sponsorship go towards various wildlife conservation projects in the Lewa–Il Ngwesi area. The event is also sponsored by mobile-phone giant Safaricom. The course is along dirt roads on the 251-sq-km (97-sq-mile) **Lewa Wildlife Conservancy**

on Laikipia Plateau. This lies at an altitude of 1,670 m (5,500 ft) and is set in stunning scenery in the shadow of Mount Kenya. Lewa is home to all the Big Five and runners are very likely to encounter substantial numbers of rhino, elephant and plains game. To enhance the safety of the event, the course is patrolled by helicopters and armed rangers. Both the full and half marathons are open to runners of all abilities from walkers and fun runners to amateur athletes and international professionals. The event now attracts some 1,000 participants from over 20 countries. There is the added excitement of taking part with Kenya's famous long-distance athletic superstars (see p297).

The **Nairobi Marathon** is the largest athletic event in Kenya attracting more than 25,000 participants. Held in October, it includes a full 42-km (26-mile) marathon, a half marathon, a 10-km (6-mile) fast road race, and a 21 km (13 mile) wheelchair race. It starts on Uhuru Highway outside Nyayo Stadium and goes along Uhuru Highway, Harambee and Haile Selassie avenues, and returns along Mombasa Road in the south. It's fun to watch and international runners can join in.

## Health and Wellness

Kenya's spa and wellness tourism has expanded fast and the country's scenic natural habitat is an ideal place to recharge. Many upmarket lodges and coastal resorts have spas offering massages, scrubs,

Kenya's Maurice Ouma waits for a delivery

wraps, water treatments, facials, baths, manicures and pedicures and other beauty treatments. As in southern Africa, the term "spafari" often features in safari lodge advertising, and a relaxing

massage is certainly welcome after a day bouncing around a game park on the back of a vehicle. For yoga enthusiasts, there are a couple of peaceful yoga retreats in Lamu. Both are

in historic houses in the village of Shela. **Fatuma's Tower** and **Banana House** offer daily yoga classes, as well as meditation, massages and various holistic wellness treatments.

# DIRECTORY

## Cultural Experiences

**Bombolulu Workshops and Cultural Centre**
Malindi Road, Bombolulu, Mombasa.
**Tel** 0723 560933.
W apdkbombolulu.org

**Marich Pass Field Studies Centre**
Kapenguria, West Pokot.
W gg.rhul.ac.uk/MarichPass

## Hiking and Climbing

**Mount Kenya Guides and Porters Safari Club**
6 km (4 miles) east of Naro Moru town on the way to Naro Moru park gate.
W mtkenyaguides.com

**Mountain Club of Kenya**
Nairobi Sailing and Sub Aqua Club, Langata Rd, Nairobi. W mck.or.ke

## Camel Trekking

**Desert Rose**
PO Box 76677, Nairobi 00508. **Tel** 020 3864831.
W desertrosekenya.com

**Karisia Walking Safaris**
PO Box 1716, Nanyuki.
**Tel** 0721 371694.
W karisia.com

**Wild Frontiers Kenya**
PO Box 93, Naro Moru.
W wildfrontierskenya.com

## Bird-Watching

**Nature Kenya**
National Museum of Kenya, Museum Hill, Nairobi.
**Tel** 0771 343138.
W naturekenya.org

## Horse Riding

**Offbeat Safaris**
PO Box 825, Nairobi.
**Tel** 0704 909355.
W offbeatsafaris.com

**Safaris Unlimited**
PO Box 24181, Karen, Nairobi. **Tel** 020 2087296.
W safarisunlimited.com

## Ballooning

**Hot Air Safaris**
**Tel** 0733 300304.
W maraballooning.com

**Transworld Safaris**
**Tel** 020 4451620.
W transworldsafaris.com

## Golf

**Kenya Golf Safaris**
PO Box 20146. Nairobi.
**Tel** 020 2710825.
W kenya-golf-safaris.com

**Kenya Golf Union**
At Muthaiga Golf Club, Kiambu Road, Muthaiga, Nairobi.
**Tel** 0715 457906.
W kgu.or.ke

## Water Sports

**H₂O Extreme**
The Sands at Nomads Beach Bar, Diani Beach.
**Tel** 0712 121974.
W h2o-extreme.com

**Kite Beach Kenya**
Aqualand Water Centre, Galu Kinondo, Diani Beach.
**Tel** 0733 787336.
W kitekenya.com

## Diving and Snorkelling

**Blue Fin Diving**
**Tel** 042 2120444.
W bluefindiving.com

## Diani Marine
Diani Marine Divers Village, Ukunda.
**Tel** 0707 629060.
W dianimarine.com

**Diving the Crab**
Jadini Beach Hotel, Diani Beach.
**Tel** 0712 387617.
W divingthecrab.com

## Boating

**Savage Wilderness**
Sarit Centre, Westlands, 00606, Nairobi.
**Tel** 020 7121590.
W savagewilderness.org

**Tamarind Dhow**
Tamarind Restaurant jetty, Silo Road, Nyali, Mombasa.
**Tel** 041 4474600.
W tamarind.co.ke

**Wasini Island**
Kisite-Mpunguti Marine Park. **Tel** 0722 683860.
W wasini.com

## Fishing

**Hemingway's**
Watamu.
**Tel** 0702 999950.
W hemingways-watamu.com

**Pemba Channel Fishing Club**
Shimoni.
**Tel** 0722 205020.
W pembachannel.com

## Spectator Sports

**Karen Country Club**
Karen Road, Karen, Nairobi. **Tel** 020 3882802.
W karencountryclub.org

**Kenyan Premier League**
W kpl.co.ke

## Kenyan Rugby Football Union Club
Ngong Road, Nairobi.
**Tel** 0724 256179.
W kenyarfu.com

**Muthaiga Golf Club**
Kiambu Road, Karura Forest, Nairobi. **Tel** 020 2368440. W muthaigagolfclub.com

**Nairobi Gymkhana Club**
Desai Road, off Forest Road, Nairobi.
**Tel** 0727 531458.

**Nairobi Polo Club**
Ngong Road, Nairobi.
**Tel** 0725 051012.
W polokenya.com

**Ngong Racecourse**
Ngong Road, Nairobi.
**Tel** 0722 414598.
W ngongracing-kenya.com

## Marathons

**Lewa Wildlife Conservancy**
Lewa Downs.
**Tel** 064 3131405.
W lewa.org

**Nairobi Marathon**
W nairobimarathon.com

## Health and Wellness

**Banana House**
Shela, Lamu.
**Tel** 0721 275538.
W bananahouse-lamu.com

**Fatuma's Tower**
Shela, Lamu.
**Tel** 0722 277138.
W fatumastower.com

# Safari Tours and Bookings

Kenya's single most popular outdoor activity for visitors is going on safari. Many tour operators offer multiday safaris and beach holidays in Kenya. There are essentially two choices. The first is to book with a home-country tour operator or with one in Kenya and the second is to book a scheduled safari or a tailor-made tour to fit specific interests and budgets. Regardless of the various options available, selection should be based on good service and the operator's ability to understand the specific needs of a safarigoer in Kenya.

## Booking Overseas

The advantage of booking with an international agent is that a complete package can be easily organized including flights, safaris, hotel stays, even travel insurance and visa information. There are many specialist agents for travel in Africa who are passionately enthusiastic about their work. Some run their own safaris while others use reputable local ground handlers in Kenya. Another advantage is that many companies are bonded, ensuring that the payment the visitor makes is put in a trust fund until after the holiday is completed. So even if the company goes into liquidation at any time, the visitors' money is safe and can be returned. A good place to start looking is on the **African Travel and Tourism Association (ATTA)** website, which has a full list of operators and agents with plenty of experience of Kenya and good consultants. The list includes specialized tour operators such as **Abercrombie & Kent**, **Africa Travel Centre**,

**Acacia Africa** and **Expert Africa** in the UK. Other agents include the **Africa Adventure Company** in the US, the **Adventure Centre** in Canada, **Go2Africa** and **Rhino Africa** in South Africa, and the **Classic Safari Company** and the **Africa Safari Co** in Australia.

## Booking in Kenya

There are countless agents and tour operators in Kenya offering standard multiday safaris from Nairobi and Mombasa, with coastal add-ons. Usually, it is cheaper to book through a Kenyan operator than through an international agent. The advantage of booking directly is that more flexible itineraries can be organized, which can be changed at short notice to incorporate seasonal variations, of game movement for instance. Much of the money paid remains in Kenya and helps support its economy. Valuable information on booking and itinerary planning can be found on the **Kenya Association of Tour Operators (KATO)** website. Although membership does

not guarantee that the operator is a good one, it does guarantee that it follows a code of conduct and is properly licensed.

Once in Kenya, tourists are often approached in the street by safari company touts offering cheap deals. Avoiding such operators is wise as there is no way of knowing if they will provide value for money or whether they have licensing or insurance. Only the 250 or more established companies that are members of **KATO** are reliable. Of these, the many tour operators that offer regular scheduled departures on safaris to the parks and reserves include **Acacia Safaris**, **Shoor Safaris**, **Gametrackers**, **Go Kenya Tours and Safaris**, **Spurwing Travel & Tours**, **Suntrek Safaris** and **UNIGLOBE Let's Go Travel**.

## Tailor-made Safaris

Most companies, both in Kenya and overseas, offer regular scheduled safaris. These usually range from three to ten days, from a short two-night fly- or drive-in package to Masai Mara National Reserve, to longer trips covering many parks and reserves. On these, people booked together on the same package travel in a group and accommodation is in lodges or camps. Alternatively, many tour operators and agents also offer tailor-made packages designed to suit a couple, a larger family or even a huge group of friends. However, they tend to be more expensive than scheduled safaris because of their exclusivity.

A light aircraft picking up visitors from the Masai Mara National Reserve

A specialized tour operator can carefully tailor a trip to suit special interests, budgets and preferred style of travel. To accommodate the client's specification, some also offer mobile luxury tented camps. Safari vehicles tend to be small 4WDs rather than the larger minibuses used on scheduled tours. Operators specializing in tailor-made safaris include **Origin Safaris**, which offers tours to the more remote places in East and Central Africa, **Basecamp Explorer**, which promotes eco-tourism, **Hoopee Safaris**, which has an excellent commitment to local communities and conservation, and **Kenya One Tours**, **Gamewatchers**, **Muthaiga Travel**, **Safari Travel** and **Southern Cross Safaris**, which cater to smaller groups on safari and offer a choice of other arrangements including beach extensions, trekking and mountain climbing.

# DIRECTORY

## Booking Overseas

### Abercrombie & Kent
St George's House, Ambrose St, Cheltenham, Gloucestershire, GL50 3LG.
Tel 0845 6182200.
W abercrombie kent.co.uk

### Acacia Africa
23 Craven Terrace, Lancaster Gate, London, W2 3QH.
Tel 0207 706 4700.
W acacia-africa.com

### Adventure Centre
Suite 400, 579 Richmond Street West, Toronto, Ontario, M5V 1Y6.
Tel 0416 9227584.
W adventure center.com

### Africa Adventure Company
5353 North Federal Highway, Suite 300, Fort Lauderdale, FL 33308.
Tel 0954 4918877.
W africa-adventure.com

### The Africa Safari Co
Office 1, Commercial Suites, Illawong Shopping Village, 273 Fowler Road, Illawong, NSW 2234.
Tel 02 95414199.
W africasafarico.com.au

### African Travel and Tourism Association (ATTA)
Mailbox 334, 56 Gloucester Road, London, SW7 4UB.
Tel 020 79374408.
W atta.travel

### Africa Travel Centre
227 Shepherds Bush Road, Hammersmith, London, W6 7AS.
Tel 020 7843 3500.
W africatravel.com

### Africa Travel Resource
Milton Heath House, Westcott Road, Dorking, RH4 3NB. Tel 0130 688 0770. W africatravel resource.com

### The Classic Safari Company
124A Queen St, Woollahra, New South Wales 2025.
Tel 02 93270666.
W classicsafari company.com.au

### Expert Africa
10–11 Upper Square, Old Isleworth, Middlesex, TW7 7BJ.
Tel 0208 232 9777.
W expertafrica.com

### Go2Africa
3rd Floor, Longkloof Studios, Darters Road, Cape Town 8001.
Tel 021 4814900.
W go2africa.com

### Rhino Africa
99 Hope St, Gardens, Cape Town 8001.
Tel 021 4692600.
W rhinoafrica.com

## Booking in Kenya

### Acacia Safaris
College House, 4th Floor, University Way, Koinange St, Nairobi.
Tel 020 2050445.
W acaciasafaris.co.ke

### Gametrackers Safaris
Seminary Road, off Magadi Road, Karen, Nairobi.
Tel 020 2003059.
W game trackersafaris.com

### Go Kenya Tours and Safaris
3rd Floor, Vision Plaza, Mombasa Road, Nairobi.
Tel 0723 321938.
W gokenyasafari.com

### Kenya Association of Tour Operators (KATO)
KATO Place, Upper Hill, Nairobi. Tel 020 2713348.
W katokenya.org

### Shoor Safaris
Corner Plaza, Parklands Road, Nairobi.
Tel 0723 202188.
W shoortravel.com

### Spurwing Travel & Tours
326 Dagoretti Road, Karen, Nairobi.
Tel 020 3884412.
W spurwingkenya.com

### Suntrek Safaris
Safari Centre, Waiyaki Way, Nairobi.
Tel 020 4442982.
W suntreksafaris.com

### UNIGLOBE Let's Go Travel
ABC Place, Waiyaki Way, Westlands.
Tel 020 4447151.
W uniglobeletsgo travel.com

## Tailor-made Safaris

### Basecamp Explorer
Seminary Road, off Magadi Road, Karen, Nairobi.
Tel 0733 333909.
W basecampkenya.com

### Gamewatchers Safaris
PO Box 388-00621, Village Market, Nairobi.
Tel 0774 136523.
W porini.com

### Kenya One Tours
PO Box 38423, Nairobi 00623. Tel 020 4453318.
W kenyaonetours.com

### Muthaiga Travel
Muthaiga Shopping Centre, Limuru Road, Nairobi. Tel 020 4050034.
W muthaigatravel.com

### Origins Safaris
5th Floor, Landmark Plaza, Argwings Khodek Road, Nairobi.
Tel 020 2042695.
W originsafaris.info

### Safari Travel
2nd Avenue, Parklands, Nairobi. Tel 020 3747276.
W safaritravel.biz

### Southern Cross Safaris
Nyali Bridge Road, Mombasa.
Tel 020 2434600.
W southerncross safaris.com

# SURVIVAL
# GUIDE

# PRACTICAL INFORMATION

Thanks to its unparalleled natural beauty, abundant wildlife and rich cultural tapestry, Kenya attracts a growing number of visitors each year. The country's tourism infrastructure falls into two extremes. Kenya's safari industry and coastal areas are booming, with plenty of good accommodation, efficient tour operators and a range of outdoor activities to choose from. However, rural Kenya and the more remote regions in the north of the country suffer from bad roads, lack of quality accommodation and poor transport links.

Nevertheless, with a little advanced planning, Kenya can be explored relatively easily. Tour operators are particularly useful for making ground arrangements, and internal air transport is good. Adventurous travellers have the option of getting around by public transport, although a 4WD is needed to get the most out of the national parks and game reserves. There are plenty of affordable safaris on offer from Nairobi and the various coastal resorts, and most visitors combine game viewing with some downtime at the beach.

Hikers on a trail as clouds gather above, Shimba Hills National Reserve

## When to Go

Located on the equator, Kenya experiences subtropical temperatures in the coastal zone and more temperate conditions inland (see pp44–5), with little variation over the year. There are generally two rainy seasons in Kenya, with the rain arriving in short, sharp thunderstorms in the afternoons. The longer rainy spell lasts from March to May and the shorter one from November to December, with two long intervening dry seasons. The long rains may hamper travel through parks as unpaved tracks can become impassable. Constant high temperatures and humidity on the coast are tamed by regular daytime breezes, though it can be sultry at night. The northern region features a typical desert climate with low rainfall and excessive heat. Temperatures are lowest in the Central Highlands, where June to September is the coolest and cloudiest period. The western Rift Valley and Lake Victoria region receive the most

rainfall and there is no real dry season as such, but rain seldom continues over long periods. Wildlife can be seen at all times of year, but the annual migration of wildebeest (see pp128–9) and other wildlife from the Masai Mara National Reserve and Tanzania's Serengeti generally takes place between June and September.

## What to Take

On safari, comfortable cotton clothes in muted colours are most suitable although it is not necessary to wear the old-fashioned safari suits still sold in Nairobi. Evenings and early mornings can be chilly, so it is best to wear layers of clothing to stay warm. Beachgoers must take sunblock, sunglasses and a wide-brimmed hat. Campers will need a sleeping bag, towel and flashlight. Long sleeves and trousers are advised to avoid mosquito bites. Specialized clothing is needed to climb Mount Kenya. Provisions can

also be bought locally, but it is essential to carry a medical first-aid kit if visiting remote areas.

## Visa and Passports

Passports must be valid for at least 6 months after the expected date of departure from Kenya. Visas are required by almost all nationalities and are available on arrival at all land borders and airports. Visitors can use euros, British pounds and US dollars to buy one and may need to show a return ticket or proof of funds. A single-entry visa costs US$50 and is valid for 3 months. It can be extended to 6 months by the Kenya Immigration Department once in the country. A transit visa costs US$20 and is valid for 7 days. Visitors with a Kenya visa who are also travelling to Tanzania and Uganda and then returning to Kenya are not required to get another visa for Kenya. Most visitors need a visa for each of these countries and all standard single-entry visas are valid for up to 3 months even if travelling from one country to another. However, Rwanda is not included in this agreement, so if travelling there and returning to Uganda and Kenya, standard single-entry visas must be purchased again. The East Africa Tourist Visa is a multiple-entry visa and is another option for those travelling between Kenya, Uganda and Rwanda. It allows visitors to move freely within those three countries and costs $100. It is valid for 90 days, but can only be applied for through embassies (not at entry points). Note that Tanzania is not part of the East Africa Tourist Visa initiative, and requires a separate single-entry visa. The cheapest visa option for visitors arriving in Kenya depends on which of the other four East African countries they are visiting too. Always check the latest entry require-ments with the Kenyan embassy in your country before leaving.

## Immunizations

Immigration officials will ask for proof of a yellow fever immunization on arrival if you are coming from an infected region, including Tanzania. While other immunizations are not compulsory for Kenya, the following are recommended: hepatitis A, polio, typhoid and tetanus. The hepatitis B vaccine is essential for minors and health-care workers.

## Visitor Information

The head office of the **Kenya Tourist Board (KTB)** in Nairobi and its offices overseas can provide a few general leaflets on Kenya (see website for details). However, the KTB website is very comprehensive. While Kenya itself has very few tourist information offices, tour operators can provide local information, although travellers should remember that this advice may be biased if they are in the business of selling tours or accommodation. **Kenya Wildlife Service (KWS)** has an office at the entrance of Nairobi

The busy Langoni Road in Mombasa

National Park *(see pp166–9)* and can provide information on national parks and camping fees and also issues and loads Safari Cards *(see p73)* for park entry. The website of the **Kenya Association of Tour Operators (KATO)** is a good source of information on booking a safari.

## Opening Hours

In larger towns, business hours are usually from 8:30am to 5pm, Monday to Friday, while shops stay open from 8am to 6pm from Monday to Saturday. Offices usually stay closed on Saturdays. Muslim-owned establishments may close all day on Friday or at least in the afternoons. In Mombasa, business hours are longer, but many shops and establishments close for a siesta from 2 to 4pm. In rural areas, small shops can have erratic opening hours. Most museums, galleries and curio markets stay open from 9am to 6pm daily. Outdoor attractions, such as parks and reserves, stay open from sunrise to sunset.

## Etiquette

In general, Kenyans are exceptionally polite and helpful. Visitors will soon get used to hearing the Kiswahili words *jambo* (hello) and *hakuna matata* (no worries). It is important to respect local customs by not taking photographs of people without their approval, dressing fairly conservatively in Muslim areas and being sensitive to religious practices. It is illegal in Kenya to smoke in public places and for women to go topless on the beach. If visiting one of the cultural centres, a Maasai village for example, it is gracious to interact with the hosts and ask for permission if you want to take photographs. Kenya has a problem with begging, especially among children, but a better way of helping is to make a donation to a charity or school.

## Tipping

Tipping is not mandatory in Kenya but is customary for good service. Generally 10 per cent of a restaurant bill is considered normal, although in upmarket restaurants a service charge may already be added to the bill. Some lodges and resorts have boxes for tips, which are shared by the service staff. It is customary to tip safari guides and drivers; about US$10–20 a day for both is sufficient. Visitors must bear in mind that excessive tipping can make it difficult for the next customer. Taxi drivers generally do not need tipping and a flat fare is agreed upon before setting off.

A customer making a cash payment, Ol Tukai Lodge bar

Trekking with Samburu in isolated wilderness, Northern Kenya

## Women Travellers

Women travellers should take normal precautions in Kenya such as avoiding secluded places, taking taxis after dark and locking hotel rooms. They may receive unsolicited attention from men, especially on the coast and smaller towns. This is best dealt with by being assertive. Women should dress conservatively in Muslim areas, although swimwear is fine on the beach.

## Disabled Travellers

Kenya, like many other African countries, has few specific facilities for the disabled; there are no special provisions public transport for example. That said, a specialist tour operator will be able to make arrangements for wheelchair-bound travellers. Some hotels have easily accessible ground-floor rooms. Tented camps are also a good option and safaris should not pose too many problems. Tour operators who cater to the disabled include Southern Cross Safaris *(see p397)*, **Go Africa Safaris and Travel** and **Victoria Safaris**. These operators have specially adapted vehicles and suitable accommodation for those with special needs.

## Travelling with Children

Kenya makes a good family destination. Seeing their first animal in the wild is exciting for children, and the beach with its warm, shallow sea and rock pools is ideal. Aside from the wildlife parks and reserves, there are a number of wildlife sanctuaries in Nairobi and along the coast where children can experience closer encounters with animals. However, on long, hot drives younger kids may get bored and irritable if there is no game activity, so bring additional items to keep them occupied and consider a tour operator who specializes in family safaris. In some cases, children under five are not permitted on safaris. Pay attention to the greater risk they run of getting heat exhaustion or diarrhoea and make sure that they drink plenty of water and wear high-factor sunscreen. Also consult a doctor about precautions to take when travelling with youngsters in a malarial zone. Items such as disposable nappies, ready-made puréed food and milk formula are available in the cities, but they are expensive, so consider bringing an adequate supply to last the trip. Most hotel accommodation has family or adjoining rooms and can provide high chairs for dining, cots and, in some cases, babysitting services if required. Away from the popular destinations, such facilities are not easily available.

Children taking a windsurfing lesson at Watamu Beach

## Language

Although there are many indigenous languages spoken in Kenya, almost everyone speaks English and Kiswahili, the Swahili language and the official language of Kenya. Only in the remote areas do people speak in their native tongue. Kiswahili was written down by the colonialists, so words are pronounced just as they are spelt, and as in any country, a few words spoken in the local language is much appreciated.

## Photography

Photographing wildlife in Kenya is very rewarding, but a long lens is needed to get close-up shots of animals. Light in the middle of the day is harsh and is better in the early mornings and late afternoons, which coincide with the best times for game viewing. When photographing individuals or a crowd in a market or village, always ask for permission. In some cases, a payment is expected for taking photographs, but bargain for a better price. In cultural villages and other tourist attractions, a fee for photography is included in the entry fee. Digital cameras can be recharged in hotels but an adapter may be required. Batteries are expensive and not easily available in remote areas. It is forbidden to take photographs of government and military buildings.

## Electrical Supply

Standard switch panel

The standard voltage is 220–240 volts AC and square three-pin British-style plugs and sockets are used. For two-pin and other appliances a travel adapter is needed. Remote lodges and camps often rely on generators which are switched on for a fixed duration.

## Time

Kenya is 3 hours ahead of Greenwich Mean Time (GMT), 8 hours ahead of United States Eastern Standard Time and 6 hours behind Australia's Western Standard Time. As Kenya sits on the equator, there is very little change in the time for sunrise and sunset throughout the year (see pp42–3), usually between 6 and 7am and 6 and 7pm respectively.

## Conversion Chart

**Imperial to Metric**
1 inch = 2.54 centimetres
1 foot = 30 centimetres
1 mile = 1.6 kilometres
1 ounce = 28 grams
1 pound = 454 grams
1 US pint = 0.473 litre
1 US quart = 0.947 litre
1 US gallon = 3.8 litres

**Metric to Imperial**
1 centimetre = 0.4 inch
1 metre = 3 feet 3 inches
1 kilometre = 0.6 mile
1 gram = 0.04 ounce
1 kilogram = 2.2 pounds
1 litre = 1.1 US quarts

(see pp42–3)

# DIRECTORY

## Visas and Passports

**Kenya Immigration Department**
Nyayo House, Kenyatta Ave, Nairobi. **City Map** 1 B4.
**Tel** 020 2222022.
W immigration.go.ke

## Embassies

**Australia**
**Tel** 254 20 427 7100.
W kenya.embassy.gov.au

**Canada**
**Tel** 254 20 3663000.
W kenya.gc.ca

**New Zealand**
W nzembassy.com

**UK**
**Tel** 254 20 2844000.
W gov.uk

**USA**
**Tel** 254 20 3636000.
W nairobi.usembassy.gov

## Visitor Information

**Kenya Association of Tour Operators (KATO)**
KATO Place, Upper Hill, Nairobi.
**Tel** 020 2713348.
W katokenya.org

**Kenya Tourist Board**
Kenya-Re Towers, Ragati Road, Upper Hill, Nairobi.
**Tel** 020 2711262.
W magicalkenya.com

**Kenya Tourist Board in the US and UK**
W magicalkenya.com

**Kenya Wildlife Service**
Nairobi National Park, Langata Rd, Nairobi.
**Tel** 020 6000800.
W kws.org

## Disabled Travellers

**Go Africa Safaris and Travel**
**Tel** 020 2353883.
W go-africa-safaris.com

**Victoria Safaris**
**City Map** 2 D4. Cargen House, Harambee Avenue, Nairobi.
**Tel** 0722 862727.
W victoriasafaris.com

Using a telephoto lens to shoot wildlife, Amboseli National Park

# Personal Health

A number of tropical diseases are present in Kenya, but with immunizations and precautions, the risk of contracting these is fairly remote. The most serious health risk comes from malaria, against which protection is essential. More common conditions include upset stomachs, heat and sun exposure and bites and stings, all of which are easily treated. Nairobi and the coast have excellent hospitals, but facilities in remote areas are few and may be substandard. Treatment is expensive, so comprehensive travel insurance is needed, which should include medical repatriation. In the event of being hospitalized, check that the insurer is satisfied with hospital standards.

## Medical Matters

It is advisable to visit a doctor 6 weeks before departure to Kenya to get the necessary immunizations *(see p401)* and to discuss anti-malaria medication. **MASTA (Medical Advisory for Travellers Abroad)** provides an up-to-date health brief for Kenya on their website. Items to take include insect repellent and sunscreen. Contact-lens wearers need to bring enough solution and may want to take a pair of glasses as dust can be a problem on safari. If going off the beaten track, carrying a basic medical kit is recommended. In Kenya, HIV rates are alarmingly high, so exercise caution in sexual matters and ensure that screened blood is used during medical procedures.

**Antimalarial drugs**

## Malaria

Except at extreme altitudes, malaria is widespread in Kenya and can be fatal within 24 hours of contracting it. It is transmitted by mosquitoes, which are particularly active after dark. A course of antimalarial drugs should be started before arrival in Kenya and continued for the prescribed length of time after returning home. There is as yet no vaccine against malaria. Avoid getting bitten by mosquitoes by using insect repellent, covering exposed flesh and sleeping in an air-conditioned room or under a fan and mosquito net. Symptoms, like lethargy, high fever and headaches, even after arriving back home, should be reported to a doctor immediately.

## Bites and Stings

Mosquitoes can carry other diseases as well as malaria, and insect repellent should be applied every few hours throughout the day to avoid bites and stings. Use antiseptic and antihistamine creams on bites to stop them from itching and becoming infected. Bites from dogs and monkeys can carry rabies and must therefore receive treatment immediately. Visitors travelling deep in the bush need to be wary of ticks and tsetse flies. For those who enjoy walking barefoot, jiggers and sandflies are the main hazard, as they can easily become embedded between the toes. On safari, sturdy shoes are necessary to avoid snake and scorpion bites, although these are rare occurrences. Snakes attack when they feel threatened, so when encountering a snake, it is best to stay put until it slithers away.

## Medical Facilities

Nairobi and the coast are well served with public and private hospitals, clinics and pharmacies. **Nairobi Hospital** is well known for its treatment of tropical diseases and has the best surgeon and specialist facilities in East Africa, with a 24-hour pharmacy. However, rural areas have more basic clinics and those who fall ill should try to reach the cities for medical treatment. It is best to take out medical insurance – covering death, dismemberment and repatriation – before travelling to Kenya. All costs of treatment are payable up front and receipts are required for medical insurance claims. City pharmacies stock a fairly good range of items, although brand names may be unfamiliar and expiry dates need to be checked. Visitors who are on regular medication should

Flying Doctors service, providing medical support in remote areas

Freshwater streams and pools often carry waterborne diseases

come prepared with enough for their stay. Kenya has a **Flying Doctors** service run by the African Medical and Research Foundation (AMREF), which provides air ambulances and medical evacuations from remote destinations to hospitals, as well as medical repatriation to other countries. Visitors can take out a temporary subscription for the service, which covers most of East Africa and is worth considering by those who are not on an organized tour and are going off the beaten track.

### Food and Water

Most people get a bout of traveller's diarrhoea briefly when they arrive in a new country while their bodies adapt to the food and water and local conditions. There are a number of basic safeguards that help reduce the chances of succumbing to diarrhoea and other food- and waterborne diseases, such as typhoid and dysentery. These include washing your hands before a meal, ensuring that your food is prepared and cooked hygienically and avoiding salads and fruit washed in local water. It is best to stick to bottled water and not to take ice in drinks. Tea and coffee are safe to drink as the water is boiled, but unpasteurized milk

and other dairy products should be avoided. Street food is not all risky provided it is fresh and cooked thoroughly and has not been standing around for a while covered in flies. The same can be said for buffets in hotel restaurants. Cooked foods that have been left at room temperature are particularly hazardous.

### Outdoor Hazards

Being on the beach or on safari means that a lot of time is spent outdoors. The sun is strong all year round, so hats and high-factor sunscreen are both indispensable. Ensure that children are lathered up regularly when they go swimming and snorkelling. Beware of coral-cut infections,

which can be nasty. Divers and snorkellers should wear plastic shoes. Drinking from or swimming in freshwater lakes and ponds can be hazardous owing to waterborne diseases such as bilharzia (*Schistosomiasis*), which is transmitted by tiny worms in stagnant water. Lake Victoria and many smaller lakes are infected with this. Swimming in the ocean and swimming pools poses no threat.

Most visitors to Mount Kenya choose a slow ascent to avoid altitude sickness. For those coming up from the coast, a couple of days acclimatizing at over 1,000 m (3,200 ft) is necessary. Dress for the extreme cold to avoid developing hypothermia.

Hikers wearing hats to escape the scorching sun, Shimba Hills

# Personal Security

Kenya has its fair share of security problems and is notorious for high rates of robbery, petty theft and more serious crimes such as armed carjacking and highway banditry. Tourists are easy targets, so they should remain vigilant throughout their stay. However, by taking sensible precautions, most visitors can have a safe and crime-free visit. On an organized tour, the risks are reduced considerably. In general, security is improving in the capital and the popular coastal tourist destinations. In Nairobi, the city centre is monitored by an increased police presence and there is an additional force of tourist police on the coast.

The crowded MacKinnon Market in Mombasa keeps up a frenetic pace

## Personal Safety

The golden rule is not to flash expensive items and to leave anything of monetary or sentimental value at home. Petty crime, bag snatching, mugging and pick-pocketing can occur, but most are opportunist crimes. Money and passport are best kept in a slim money belt concealed beneath clothes. Visitors can use hotel safes to deposit cash or costly items. Day-packs or backpacks have been known to be slashed in crowded areas, so it is best to only take out exactly what you need and to carry bags in front of you. It is not safe, especially for women, to walk alone or anywhere after dark, including on the beach.

Follow local advice about what areas to avoid and be vigilant about the people around you. Hotel doors must

**Keeping bags in front**

be locked as noisy fans or air conditioning can provide cover for thieves. If travelling by public transport, especially buses and *matatus*, guard possessions fiercely and never accept food or drink from strangers as they may be drugged. Visitors should also be cautious of con men posing as tour operators.

Due to unrest caused by Somali militants on the border region north of Lamu, it is advisable to avoid travel within 60 km (37 miles) of the Somali border.

## Information

Located at the Kenya Wildlife Service *(see p403)* headquarters in Nairobi, at the entrance to Nairobi National Park, is the office of the **Safety and Communication Centre**. It is run by Kenya Tourism Federation, a body of tour operators, travel agents, hoteliers and airlines. The staff at this centre can provide information about issues of concern to visitors like road conditions, security, health and travel advisories for the various regions of the country. In the event of a security incident involving visitors to Kenya, the centre can arrange for assistance. It also operates a 24-hour control room and tourist helpline manned by well-trained staff, and has an excellent infrastructure in place, including a countrywide communications radio system. The centre works closely with KWS, the police and the Flying Doctors *(see p405)*.

## Travel Insurance

It is essential to take out a comprehensive travel insurance policy when visiting Kenya. Insurance policies should cover all health requirements, such as treatment for injuries and illnesses, plus medical repatriation to the home country in case of an emergency, as well as provision for theft and loss of luggage. If you're unfortunate enough to be the victim of a crime, you must get a police report and case number from the **Kenya Police**. These are necessary to make a travel insurance claim. Visitors can also approach the helpful

Marine police keeping vigil along the coast, Lamu town

Heavy traffic on Digo Road, Mombasa

tourist police, a division of the regular police that mainly patrols the coastal resorts.

## On the Road

The number of road accidents in Kenya used to be alarmingly high, but the situation has improved greatly thanks to legislation that made wearing of seat belts compulsory and governed the road-worthiness of vehicles, speed limits and over-crowding on public transport. Despite these improvements, visitors should exercise caution on the road and not drive too fast as unexpected potholes or domestic animals on the road can cause accidents. To avoid theft from a parked vehicle, do not leave anything on display inside. Expensive-looking 4WDs are a favourite with carjackers and to avoid any such incident, keep windows rolled up and doors locked at all times. It is also not safe to travel late at night. Importantly, if carjacked at gun-point, it is best not to resist.

Northern Kenya is known for lawlessness and is at its most dangerous near the South Sudanese, Ethiopian and Somali borders, where localized incidents of violent cattle rustling, ethnic conflict and armed banditry occur. Always get local advice about travelling by road to this part of the country and always travel in a convoy of vehicles. The Safety and Communications Centre in

Nairobi offers visitors useful and up-to-date information and advice on issues pertaining to security in all regions of Kenya.

## On Safari

Although incidents of attacks from animals are rare, Kenya's wildlife is exactly that – wild. Many animals are used to being admired by the army of safari vehicles that enter the national parks each day. However, it must never be forgotten that animal behaviour is unpredict-able and it pays to have a healthy respect for wildlife. Use only signposted tracks or ones marked on official maps. Do not get out of a vehicle except in designated areas and never harass or feed the animals or get too close to them. Hippos are said to be among the most dangerous animals in Africa and they attack and trample when

threatened or when their access to water is blocked. Buffalo and elephant are known to charge and attack, usually in self-defence when startled. Rhinos may charge when a vehicle blocks sight of their young. If camping in the wild, food should always be locked away from baboons and hyenas in vehicles and never left in tents. It is preferable not to leave your tent or *banda* during the night. When walking or hiking, it is best to wear sturdy boots and stick to existing paths or flat ground to avoid snakes, and carry a flashlight if it is necessary to move around the bush at night.

## DIRECTORY

### Emergencies

**All Emergencies**
Tel 999.

### Information

**Safety and Communication Centre**
KWS Complex, Nairobi National Park, Langata Road, Nairobi.
Tel 020 2679838
(Tourist Helpline, 24 hrs).
W ktf.co.ke

### Travel Insurance

**Kenya Police**
Emergency
Tel 999.

**Nairobi Central Police Station**
Harambee Avenue.
Map 1 C4.
Tel 020 341411/18.

Visitors on safari maintaining safe distance from a grazing rhino

# Banking and Currency

Banks and bureaux de change are plentiful in urban Kenya. Money can be obtained on arrival, as facilities at Nairobi and Mombasa airports stay open to meet all arriving flights. Small towns have at least one bank that will make foreign transactions, although service is often slow. Hotels, lodges and camps change money for their guests, but the exchange rate may not be competitive. US dollars are the easiest to change, and are accepted by the Kenya Wildlife Service and tour operators. Owing to previous problems of fraud, many places do not take pre-2005 dollar bills. British pounds and euros are also accepted – in fact the euro is quickly replacing the dollar as the standard unit in which prices for tourists are quoted. All three currencies are used to pay for visas on arrival.

ATMs, a facility provided by most of the banks in the country

## Banks and Bureaux de Change

There are branches of **Barclays Bank**, **Kenya Commercial Bank** and **Standard Chartered Bank** across the country, and branch locators can be found on their websites. Banking hours are 8:30am to 3pm on weekdays and 8:30 to 11am on Saturdays. In Mombasa and on the coast, some banks open and close half an hour earlier. In small towns, banks may not open on Saturdays, or open only on one Saturday at the end of the month. Bureaux de change, also known as Forex (foreign exchange bureaus), have longer opening hours, and some, located in the cities and main tourist spots, also open on Sundays. At Nairobi's Jomo Kenyatta International Airport, banks are open 24 hours. Commission is usually charged on changing traveller's cheques and cash. Where commission is not charged, exchange rates are lower and travellers may want to weigh their options. When changing US dollars, lower denomination bills attract a lower exchange rate than higher

denomination bills. Passports must always be presented when changing money and visitors should ensure that they get a competitive rate of exchange. There is no restriction on the amount of foreign currency that visitors can take into Kenya.

## ATMs

Almost all banks have ATMs that accept at least Visa cards. Barclays Bank is the best option, because their ATMs (which can be found in most Kenyan towns) accept Visa, MasterCard, Cirrus and Plus cards. Independent ATMs are also available at places such as petrol stations and modern shopping malls in Nairobi and on the coast. Withdrawals from ATMs offer the most competitive rate of exchange with no commission, but the account-holder's bank at home may charge a fee for withdrawing cash from a foreign ATM and there may be a daily limit. Be vigilant if making a withdrawal from an ATM on the street.

## Currency Cards

Most currency or travel money cards are linked to Visa or Mastercard and can be bought from banks and post offices. They can be pre-loaded (and topped up) with a number of currencies including US dollars, euros and British pounds, and can be used like a debit card to pay for things and withdraw cash from an ATM. As they are not linked to bank accounts, there is no risk of defrauding main home accounts and the risk of identity theft in the event a card is lost or stolen is reduced.

## Credit Cards

Credit cards are widely accepted to pay for accommodation, safaris and curios in upmarket shops. However, they are not taken in budget hotels, markets and small shops, and few restaurants accept them. Visa and Master-Card are the most commonly accepted. A 2 to 5 per cent commission is often added to a credit-card purchase, so in some cases it is cheaper to pay in cash.

## Currency

The currency in Kenya is the Kenyan shilling, with one shilling comprising 100 cents. It is indicated either by the symbol KSh or by the /= notation after the amount, 1,000/= for instance. It is known locally as *bob*. While hotels, tour operators and airlines quote rates in US dollars or euros, Kenyan shillings can also be used. Kenyan shillings are needed in shops, markets and restaurants. Keep the smaller bills for short taxi rides, drinks and inexpensive roadside curios.

The entrance to Barclays Bank at Voi

## Coins

*Kenyan coins come in denominations of 50 c (50 cents) and 1, 5, 10, 20 and 40 KSh. Jomo Kenyatta's head graces one side of the coin and Kenya's coat of arms the other. The word Harambee, Kiswahili for unity, appears in the ribbon of the coat of arms.*

50 c

1 KSh

5 KSh

10 KSh

20 KSh

40 KSh

## Banknotes

*Kenyan banknotes come in denominations of 50, 100, 200, 500 and 1,000 KSh. After Kenya's independence, the face of its first president, Jomo Kenyatta, appeared on all notes and coins. In 1980, it was replaced by the face of the succeeding president, Daniel arap Moi. In 2005, a new series of notes and coins came out with Kenyatta's portrait restored.*

50 KSh

100 KSh

200 KSh

500 KSh

1,000 KSh

# Communications and Media

Kenya's communication facilities are, on the whole, modern and up to date. Mobile phones in particular are hugely popular with Kenyans, and in some cases many people and businesses have abandoned the landline network in favour of mobile phones. Internet access is easily found in cities and tourist places, and even the smaller towns usually feature at least one public place for browsing the web. Wi-Fi is available at many public places such as the airports, and most tourist-orientated accommodation offers it to guests. Much of the country is covered by high-frequency radio, often used by the more remote lodges, as well as Nairobi's Safety and Communication Centre and the Flying Doctors. Postal services are fairly reliable. There is a well-organized Poste Restante in Nairobi, but it is always better to use a courier service for valuable items.

A line of yellow Telkom public telephone booths

## Telephones

Local and international calls can be made from public pay phones, operated by **Telkom Kenya**, that are housed in yellow or red booths on the street or in post offices. These accept coins or phone cards that are available from post offices. Rates are around 12 KSh per minute for a local call, and considerably more for a call to a mobile phone from a landline. International call rates are from US$ 0.40 per minute.

Off-peak times are 6pm to 8am on weekdays and all day at weekends. Calls from Kenya to the neighbouring states of Uganda and Tanzania are charged as long-distance calls and not at international rates. Operator-assisted calls can be made from post offices (for a minimum of 3 minutes). Most hotels add a hefty premium to phone calls, and it is best to avoid calling from satellite phones in remote lodges as they are very expensive.

## Mobile Phones

It is estimated that over a staggering 90 per cent of Kenyans are mobile-phone users. Some 70 per cent of these are also mobile money customers using systems such as M-Pesa (M stands for mobile, and *pesa* is Kiswahili for money). This allows millions of Kenyans to use their phones to buy groceries, pay rent and utility bills or transfer money without the need to maintain a bank account or even carry cash. Kenya has three mobile-phone providers; **Safaricom** is the largest with over 20 million customers, followed by **Airtel** and **Orange** (Telkom Kenya is also owned by Orange).

In Kenya, start-up packs with SIM cards and top-up cards are available everywhere, from shops to street stalls, and hawkers even sell them on public buses. Using a Kenyan SIM card in a mobile phone is the cheapest way to stay connected. Alternatively, roaming on international SIM cards is picked up automatically on arrival in Kenya. Visitors should check with Safaricom, Airtel or Orange that their phone's network is compatible. Visitors need to check their insurance policy in case their phone gets stolen, and keep their network operator's helpline handy for emergencies. Depending on the model of the phone, an adapter may be needed for the charger.

While the northern part of the country has no network access, the southern part – where most tourists stay – has good network coverage. This goes especially for the wide areas around Nairobi, Kisumu and Mombasa, as well as for the whole coast region, the popular safari parks and the Nairobi–Mombasa Highway.

## Internet

Wi-Fi features in many public places including the airports in Nairobi and Mombasa, some of the larger shopping malls and in modern coffee shops. In fact Wi-Fi is becoming so prolific in Kenya that in 2014 Nakuru became the first town in Africa to offer free Wi-Fi to all its residents and visitors. Soon after, Kisumu followed suit – both are university towns. Visitors can access Wi-Fi in almost all accommodation across all budgets – the exception is those without access to Telkom Kenya or other service provider's

### Dialling Codes

- To make any call within Kenya, use the area codes even if in the same area. Useful area codes include Nairobi 020, Mombasa 041, Malindi 042, Diani Beach 040, Lamu 012, Nakuru 051 and Kisumu 057.
- To make an international call to Kenya, first dial the international direct dialling code from that country, followed by the country code for Kenya, 254, then the area code, but drop the first 0, followed by the number.
- To make a direct international call from Kenya, dial 000, then the country code.
- Directory enquiry numbers are different for each mobile-phone network: Safaricom is 191, Airtel is 300 and Orange is 100.

Roadside kiosk displaying popular dailies and magazines

networks such as remote safari lodges or areas like Northern Kenya. In some of the more upmarket places, free Wi-Fi is included in the room rates, but in most cases a voucher with a code to access the network is available to purchase from the reception of hotels and lodges.

Native flora on some of Kenya's colourful postage stamps

## Post and Couriers

Postal services are relatively inexpensive and efficient. Run by Posta Kenya, there are post offices in most towns and urban areas. Postboxes are red and blue, and a letter sent via airmail costs 75 KSh. Post to Europe takes about a week to arrive, and about 10 days to Australia and the USA. Parcels need to be wrapped in brown paper and string. This needs to be done at the post office as contents are checked to see if export duty must be paid. Payment is not normally required for curios and souvenirs. Parcels sent by airmail can weigh up to 32 kg (71 lb) and there is a useful cost calculator to all countries on the website of Posta Kenya.

A courier service is recommended to post valuable items. Posta Kenya offers **EMS**, a reliable local and international courier service for documents and parcels which is available at all post offices. Two international

companies, **Fedex** and **DHL**, are also represented in Kenya. Post office hours are generally 8am to 5pm on weekdays and 9am to noon on Saturdays. Smaller post offices close during lunch hours. **Nairobi Post Office** has an efficient Post Restante service, and post is held alphabetically.

## Newspapers

The most popular English-language daily newspapers are the *Daily Nation* and the *East African Standard*. Both carry news and listings, and the *Daily Nation* has good entertainment and sports listings. The *Kenya Times* is the government-run newspaper, and it tends to have a pro-government bias. The weekly *East African* covers news from Kenya, Uganda and Tanzania. There are also two daily newspapers in Kiswahili. Day-old newspapers from Europe and USA can be found at Nairobi's leading bookshops and the airport.

## DIRECTORY

### Telephones

**Telkom Kenya**
w orange-tkl.co.ke

### Mobile Phones

**Airtel**
w africa.airtel.com

**Orange**
w orange.co.ke

**Safaricom**
w safaricom.co.ke

### Post and Couriers

**DHL**
Tel 0711 017120.
w dhl.co.ke

**EMS**
Tel 020 312291.
w posta.co.ke

**Fedex**
Tel 020 3907000.
w fedex.com/ke

**Nairobi Post Office**
Kenyatta Ave. **City Map** 1 B3.
Tel 020 300500.
w posta.co.ke

## Television and Radio

The Kenya Broadcasting Corporation (KBC) has many radio stations that transmit in English and Kiswahili. Nairobi's Kiss 100 FM station is popular for all kinds of music. KBC's Channel 1 shows sports, news and reruns of US shows, while DSTV (Digital Satellite TV) is a multichannel paid-for service found in most hotels.

The distinctive façade of a Posta Kenya office, Malindi

# TRAVEL INFORMATION

Kenya is East Africa's air transport hub, so there is no shortage of airlines to choose from. Most people arrive in Nairobi on scheduled flights, but some on pre-organized package holidays fly directly from Europe to Mombasa. Domestic flights connect the cities, regional airlines fly from Nairobi to safari destinations throughout East Africa and small planes ferry people in and out of reserves. The train between Nairobi and Mombasa is a slower alternative to flying to the coast. The best way to explore the parks and reserves is on organized safari. Self-drive is a good option on the coast, although roads elsewhere in the country are of varying standards. *Matatus* and buses are not for the timid as they can be driven rather recklessly; nevertheless, they link all the regional centres.

## Arriving by Air

Most European carriers, including **British Airways** and **KLM**, and almost all the Asian, African and Middle Eastern airlines fly to Nairobi, which is 9 hours flying time from London. The national carrier, **Kenya Airways**, has direct links to London, Amsterdam and Paris as well as to destinations in the Middle and Far East, India and Africa. There are no direct flights with North America, however, and airlines fly to Kenya through partnerships with European airlines via London, Frankfurt, Amsterdam or other cities in Europe. Other options for North America visitors include flying through Johannesburg with **South African Airways**, through Dubai with **Emirates**, or through Addis Ababa with **Ethiopian Airlines**.

## International Arrivals

Nairobi's **Jomo Kenyatta International Airport** handles more than 6.5 million passengers annually. After a fire in 2013, the airport has been repaired and part of it has been replaced by a new terminal building with different sections for international arrivals and departures. Facilities include duty-free shops, bars, cafés and airline lounges. Domestic flights have a separate terminal. A new passenger terminal with a capacity of 20 million passengers is due for completion in 2016. A second runway, which will be able to accommodate direct long-haul flights from North America, is also planned.

Visas *(see p400)* can be obtained on arrival at immigration before baggage collection and customs. Visitors boarding connecting flights are directed through the transit procedures. Beyond customs are desks for car hire, tour operators and hotel bookings, plus bureaux de change and ATMs to exchange or obtain Kenyan shillings. Mombasa's **Moi International Airport** is smaller but has the same facilities. It serves domestic

Kenya's flag flying near the Control Tower, Moi International Airport

and regional flights and direct charter flights from Europe carrying people on package holidays to coastal resorts.

## Getting from Airports

Jomo Kenyatta International Airport is 15 km (9 miles) southeast of Nairobi. Allow plenty of time to get to and from the airport through heavy traffic. Taxis are available and it is best to use the official airport

A Kenya Airways Airbus

Jomo Kenyatta International Airport, Nairobi

taxi company **Kenatco Taxis**, which has a desk in the terminal building. Visitors can expect to pay the equivalent of US$20–30 for a ride to the city centre. There is a public bus, but overcrowding leads to problems of luggage theft. Some hotels can arrange pick-ups but this needs to be organized in advance.

Moi International Airport is on the mainland 10 km (6 miles) west of Mombasa's city centre. Inside arrivals is a desk for taxis and shuttle buses. These go to the city centre and all the coastal resorts to the north and south of Mombasa. Rates are published on a board and a fare to the city centre costs in the region of US$12. Public buses also operate between the airport and the city centre.

### Arriving by Road

Kenya has road borders with Uganda, Ethiopia, Tanzania, Sudan and Somalia. Those most commonly used by visitors to Kenya are the Busia and Malaba borders with Uganda, through which regular daily buses run between Kampala and Nairobi, and the Namanga border with Tanzania, through which daily shuttle-bus services operate the 273-km (170-mile) A104. Nairobi is popularly used as a base by tourists on organized safaris to southern reserves and parks in Kenya as well as to the national reserves in Tanzania's Northern Circuit. Owing to the good shuttle-bus links, independent travellers can make their own way between Nairobi and

Arusha and organize safari options from each.

There is another border post between Kenya and Tanzania at Lunga Lunga, south of Mombasa, lying on the 518-km (322-mile) route between Dar es Salaam and Mombasa. Here again, daily buses operate between the two cities. Procedures at these land borders are generally very straightforward and visas are available for each country. Travellers in private vehicles are required to produce a Carnet de Passages en Douane (CPD) – a customs document that identifies a driver's motor vehicle – as well as third-party insurance and other relevant paperwork to drive between countries. Most car hire companies allow vehicles to go to Uganda and Tanzania after prior arrangements have been made. To take a Kenyan registered vehicle out of the country, a log book has to be filled out at the border and the registration documents of the vehicle need to be produced.

Border post in Tanzania, the point of entry into Kenya

# Regional Air Travel

Flying around Kenya is an alternative to long journeys on bumpy and dusty roads. With over 500 airstrips and dozens of flight routes, it is a relatively safe and fairly affordable way to cover a lot of ground. Kenya Airways flies to major cities in Kenya as well as to neighbouring countries, and a number of airlines with smaller planes run scheduled services between Nairobi and the coast and parks. Charter flights operating out of Nairobi's Wilson Airport ferry small groups of people directly to lodges all over the country. All travellers on internal flights are required to carry their passport. Domestic departure taxes are included in ticket or charter costs.

Visitors disembarking at Lamu Airport on the Northern Coast

## Domestic Airports

The **Kenya Airports Authority (KAA)** oversees the management and administration of the airports and covers passenger services as well as cargo handling and freight services for horticultural and agricultural goods, which are a big export earner for Kenya. Information on all domestic airports can be found on the KAA website. While the bigger passenger airlines operate from Nairobi's Jomo Kenyatta International Airport (see p412), other charter flights and airlines from Nairobi fly from **Wilson Airport** on Langata Road, 4 km (2 miles) south of the city centre. This is the heart of all private and commercial light aircraft activities in Kenya, and is also the base of the Flying Doctors (see p405). The airport has an average traffic of 120,000 landings and take-offs annually. There are central facilities and the individual airlines have offices scattered around the hangars. There is also a left luggage facility as some of the smaller planes on flights to the safari lodges have a luggage restriction.

Elsewhere, the other principal domestic airports are Mombasa's Moi International Airport (see p412), 10 km (6 miles) to the west of the city, where the small but orderly domestic terminal serves a regular stream of flights and has a café and shop. Kenya's other domestic airports include **Malindi Airport**, 2 km (1 mile) west of the town on the west side of Mombasa Road, **Kisumu International Airport** on Busia Road about 4 km (2 miles) west of town and **Eldoret International Airport**, 16 km (10 miles) south of town on Kisumu Road. Both Kisumu and Eldoret have international status, but are only served by scheduled domestic flights, and their principal traffic is cargo in the form of flowers and vegetables from the Rift Valley and Western Kenya, destined for European supermarkets. **Lamu Airport** is also known as Manda Airstrip owing to its location on the western side of Manda Island opposite Lamu town. From Manda Jetty, which is reached by a footpath from the edge of the airstrip, passengers are ferried across to Lamu town by motorized dhow, a trip which takes about 15 minutes and provides a delightful first view of the historic waterfront. **Ukunda Airstrip** (also known as Diani Airport), lies between the A14 and Diani Beach Road at the village of Ukunda to the south of Mombasa, and serves visitors to the south coast hotels and resorts.

Light aircraft parked near the hangars of Wilson Airport, Nairobi

An Air Kenya De Havilland Dash 7 landing at Musiara, Masai Mara

## Domestic and Regional Airlines

From Nairobi's Jomo Kenyatta International Airport, Kenya Airways runs daily flights between Nairobi, Mombasa, Malindi, Eldoret and Kisumu, and further afield to Entebbe in Uganda, Kigali in Rwanda, Addis Ababa in Ethiopia and Dar es Salaam, Kilimanjaro, Mwanza, and Zanzibar in Tanzania. Also from Jomo Kenyatta, **Fly540**, a no-frills airline, offers daily flights between Nairobi and Eldoret, Kisumu, Lamu, Lodwar, Malindi and Mombasa and to Zanzibar in Tanzania. **Air Kenya**, based at Wilson Airport, offers daily flights from Nairobi to Amboseli, Lamu, Meru, Diani Beach, Malindi, several airstrips in Masai Mara, Samburu, Lewa Downs, Nakuru and Nanyuki, plus Kilimanjaro in Tanzania. **Safarilink** flies daily between Nairobi and Amboseli, Diani Beach, Lamu, Lewa Downs, Loisaba, Masai Mara, Naivasha, Nanyuki, Samburu, and Tsavo. Again, it also has flights to Kilimanjaro in Tanzania. **Mombasa Air Safari**, based on the coast, has daily flights from Mombasa, Diani Beach, Lamu and Malindi to Wilson Airport in Nairobi and then on to Masai Mara, Amboseli, Lamu, Tsavo, Samburu and Meru, and in Tanzania several airstrips in the Serengeti National Park. Not all of these routes are cheap, but it is worth shopping around the airlines for prices, and good deals can be found thanks to the

Logo of the Fly540 airline

strong competition. For instance, a one-way flight between Nairobi and Mombasa with Fly540 starts from as little as US$99.

## Charter Flights

Apart from the destinations covered on scheduled flights, just about every corner of Kenya can be reached by charter flight. Many of East Africa's more remote tourist destinations, game reserves, ranches, camps and lodges have their own landing strips. There are over 30 charter companies based at Wilson Airport, and most charge a set rate for the flight regardless of the number of passengers. Usually Cessnas, these planes carry up to six people plus the pilot, so the cost can be shared. Tour operators can arrange air charters or visitors can contact the airlines listed under scheduled flights. Some companies such as **Tropic Air** based in Nanyuki also offer helicopters.

## Scheduled Airline Circuits

The smaller airlines generally run services in circuits. Flights may involve many intermediate stops, as the plane drops passengers off at different lodges on each circuit. For example, one of Mombasa Air Safari's routes from Mombasa touches down at Diani Beach, Tsavo West, Amboseli and Masai Mara, and returns in the same

way. Within Masai Mara itself, there can be several "drops", at each of the lodges.

## Baggage

There are no special baggage restrictions on the larger planes, but on smaller ones baggage is restricted to 15 kg (33 lb) and soft-sided bags are preferable. It is possible to leave excess baggage at Wilson Airport, hotels in Nairobi, and storage can also be arranged with airlines and tour operators.

## DIRECTORY

### Domestic Airports

**Eldoret International Airport**
Tel 053 2063377.

**Kenya Airports Authority (KAA)**
Nairobi. **Tel** 020 6611000.
W kaa.go.ke

**Kisumu International Airport**
Tel 057 2531186.

**Lamu Airport**
Tel 042 632018.

**Malindi Airport**
Tel 042 2331201.

**Ukunda Airstrip**
Tel 040 3202126.

**Wilson Airport**
Off Langata Road, Nairobi.
Tel 0724 256837.

### Domestic and Regional Airlines

**Air Kenya**
Wilson Airport, Langata Road, Nairobi. **Tel** 020 3916000.
W airkenya.com

**Fly540**
Jomo Kenyatta International Airport, Nairobi. **Tel** 020 827523.
W fly540.com

**Mombasa Air Safari**
Moi International Airport, Mombasa. **Tel** 0734 400400.
W mombasaairsafari.com

**Safarilink**
Wilson Airport, Langata Road, Nairobi. **Tel** 020 6000777
W flysafarilink.com

**Tropic Air**
Nanyuki. **Tel** 0722 207300.
W tropicairkenya.com

# Travelling by Bus and Train

All regional centres in Kenya are connected by regular buses and *matatus* (minibuses). Generally, larger buses cover the longer distances, have set departure and arrival times, are more comfortable and have more space for luggage. *Matatus* cover shorter distances, have no fixed timetable and simply depart when full. They can stop anywhere on the route to drop off and pick up passengers. Public transport is cheap and efficient, but be aware of petty theft not only on the vehicles but at the bus stands and stations. The overnight train is another option between Nairobi and Mombasa.

## Matatus

A *matatu* is a Toyota or Nissan minibus that usually carries about 15 people. The name derives from the Kiswahili word *tatu* (three), as at one time a flat fee of three coins was charged for the ride. Before the 2004 legislation implemented by Member of Parliament John Michuki – and hence referred to as the Michuki Rules – all kinds of vehicles could serve as *matatus* and they were famously painted and decorated with colourful murals. These older vehicles are now off the road and have been replaced with fleets of white minibuses with yellow stripes. Now, every seat in a *matatu* has to have a seat belt that must be worn by law. The traffic police can, and do, issue on-the-spot fines to violators. *Matatus* can only carry the correct number of passengers the vehicle is designed for and are speed governed not to exceed 80 kmph (50 mph).

Some drivers may still drive irresponsibly, but in general these moves have considerably reduced the number of road accidents in Kenya.

There are set fares and *matatus* running between cities and towns depart only when all the seats have been occupied. They are usually run by a staff of two – the driver and the tout who collects fares and competes with other *matatu* touts over passengers. After all, the sooner a vehicle fills up, the sooner it can depart. However, because of the risk of theft and the necessity to fiercely guard their possessions, most visitors to Kenya still do not use *matatus* very frequently.

## Buses

There are dozens of privately owned buses, and like *matatus*, the stringent traffic rules also apply to them. Standing in the aisle is also no longer permitted.

Large buses cover the longer distances, timetables are fairly reliable and fares are cheap, although these vehicles are slower than *matatus*. They also link Nairobi with Kisumu, Eldoret and Mombasa, and there are bus services across the borders. Tickets are sold at kiosks and should be bought a day in advance to be assured of a seat. Buses generally share the same stages as *matatus*, so again theft can be a problem.

Several companies run shuttle bus services between Nairobi and Arusha in Tanzania, a trip of about 5 hours, including the border crossing. Some services continue further to Moshi for those going to Kilimanjaro. **Riverside Shuttles** offers a good daily service.

A local bus outside the National Archives building, Nairobi

## Trains

The 930-km (578-mile) Mombasa to Kisumu railway was completed in 1901 and extended to Kampala in 1931. Chronic underinvestment has since left the railway a shadow of its former self, with ageing locomotives and carriages and frequent breakdowns. The coming years may see an improvement, as a new consortium has taken over the management of the railways and plans to upgrade its tracks and rolling stock.

For now, overnight passenger trains run three times a week between Nairobi and Mombasa. In theory, the Nairobi–Mombasa run should take 13 hours. However, frequent stops and breakdowns can make the

*Matatus*, a popular means of getting around

*Tuk-tuks* or three-wheel buggies, suitable for short rides within town

actual journey much longer. Indeed, locals have been known to get off the train and catch a bus the rest of the way.

First Class offers two-person compartments, Second Class offers four-person and Third Class is seated and can get very crowded. The First Class carriages are the best bet, and the fare is inclusive of breakfast and dinner. There is a dining car that serves simple dishes, such as soup, beef stew and sponge pudding.

Tickets are available at **Nairobi Railway Station** and **Mombasa Railway Station**, but can also be arranged in advance via a tour operator. Although visitors can fly the distance in an hour for very little more than the cost of a First Class ticket, the journey is a classic and enjoyable way to travel between the two cities and will appeal to anyone with an interest in rail travel. Indeed, spotting big game from the

Nairobi–Mombasa train has always been one of Kenya's great travel experiences.

## City Transport

*Matatus* also ply the streets of any sizable town and city for short urban trips. To hail one, visitors need to just wave with their palm down and a vehicle will pull over to let them in if it is not already full. Again, drivers can be reckless and drive up pavements, footpaths or on the wrong side of the road in order to jump traffic queues.

Nairobi has a fleet of buses, including the pale-blue **Kenya Bus Service** buses, which use a system of numbers and locations to indicate their destination. The main bus terminals are outside the Hilton Hotel on Mama Ngina Street and Nairobi Railway Station, and the website lists bus routes. Nairobi also has a fleet of London-style Hackney cabs.

Mombasa too has red Metro buses that crisscross the island. Taxis are easily available everywhere, some new and some barely serviceable. Some have meters, but for others, it is best to negotiate a fare before getting in.

The latest entrant into the transport scene are *tuk-tuks,* motorized three-wheel buggies seating three people behind the driver. They are cheap over short distances, but not very fast, so it is best to take a taxi for long-distance trips. *Tuk-tuks* are prolific along the coast and cost half the price of a taxi.

*Boda-bodas* are very cheap motorbike and bicycle taxis with a passenger seat behind the rider. They can be hailed on the street and they also wait on corners. Their name is derived from Western Kenya where they were used to ferry people across the Kenya–Uganda border and drivers would shout out *"boda-boda"* ("border border").

The overnight train from Nairobi to Mombasa crossing the Athi Plains

# Travelling by Road

The obvious advantage of self-driving is that visitors can explore at their own pace. However, driving in Kenya can be challenging, and for those without sufficient experience, it is best to stick to organized safaris. The tarred roads in southern Kenya are marred by potholes and crumbling edges but are passable in a normal car. Elsewhere in the country, roads are gravel or dirt and, in the parks, little more than dusty tracks that get muddy in wet weather. A 4WD is essential for off-road driving. Apart from bad road conditions, the biggest threat of road accidents comes from other road users, including reckless *matatu* drivers racing each other, and overloaded trucks swerving to avoid potholes.

## Hiring a Car

Car hire services are available in Nairobi and Mombasa. Most of the international companies are represented, including **Avis**, **Budget** and **Europcar**, which have airport and downtown offices in both cities. Check the websites for locations. There are numerous local car hire companies, and hotels and tour operators can make recommendations. In Nairobi try **Uniglobe Let's Go Travel**, **Central Rent-a-Car** or **Concorde Car Hire**. These can also supply vehicles in Mombasa and Malindi, and rent out safari vehicles with roof hatches. There is also the possibility of hiring a car in Nairobi and dropping it off in Mombasa, or vice versa, for an extra fee.

Depending on the planned itinerary, car hire companies can advise on whether a 4WD is needed. These should be a minimum of 1300cc and in good condition. Land Rovers, Suzuki jeeps or Pajeros are the

A 4WD, highly recommended on muddy forest tracks

favoured vehicles. Visitors must remember to ask what services the company provides in the event of a breakdown or emergency.

## Insurance and Other Documents

Drivers need to be over 23 years of age and have a driving licence printed in English or a translation, or an international driver's permit and a passport. A credit card will be needed for a deposit. Rates are set per day and per kilometre after the daily limit, usually 100 km (60 miles).

Alternatively, drivers can choose an unlimited mileage option for long-distance trips, in which case they should ensure that the quote includes 16 per cent VAT charge.

It is advisable to check the small print of the contract and consider paying extra over the standard insurance that is included in the rate for collision damage, theft protection and excess liability waivers. Also consider personal accident and personal effects cover against having items stolen from a vehicle, although these may already be covered under personal travel insurance policies. With prior arrangement, and for an extra fee required to organize the paperwork, hire cars can be taken into Tanzania and Uganda. Note that some contracts state that if drivers take regular cars off tarred roads or into the game parks and reserves, all waivers may be nullified and the driver financially responsible for any damage caused.

## Rules of the Road

All vehicles are right-hand drive and driving is on the left, but on potholed stretches it is customary to drive all over the road if there is no oncoming traffic.

Speed limits are 100 kmph (62 mph) outside of urban areas, and 40–80 kmph (25–50 mph) in towns and cities. In parks and reserves, the speed limit is 40 kmph (25 mph). Drivers should note that speed bumps, often spaced very closely, are found in even the tiniest of settlements.

Police road blocks are common, but unless a driver is actually breaking the law, such as by not wearing a seat belt, in most cases the vehicle will be waved through. If fined for any reason, insist on going to the nearest police station to make the payment and get a receipt to ensure that it is a genuine fine and not a request for a bribe.

At petrol stations attendants fill up tanks and check oil and water. Most will accept only cash.

One of Nairobi's major thoroughfares, Kenyatta Avenue

A safari vehicle with a roof hatch for game viewing, Amboseli National Park

When parking on the street in any sizable town, a small fee must be paid to a municipal parking attendant, who issues a ticket that must be displayed prominently on the windscreen.

## Road Conditions

Due to erratic traffic and road conditions, it is advisable to keep any long-distance journey to a maximum of 5–6 hours per day. The tarred roads linking the urban centres in the south of the country are generally passable by all cars. The coastal stretch south of Malindi and the loop around the Rift Valley lakes are especially feasible to negotiate for those wanting to explore in a regular hire car for a couple of days. Drivers should watch out for potholes, corrugations and, on hills, deep ruts in the tar made by heavy traffic crawling up and down. It is not safe to drive after dark as other vehicles may have missing headlights

and there is the danger of people and animals on the road, or missing signposts indicating sharp bends or steep hills. Away from the main tarred roads it is advisable to travel in a 4WD.

The north of the country is intersected by stony gravel roads and it is best to travel in a convoy of at least two vehicles carrying adequate fuel and spares. All roads deteriorate in the wet season and some become impassable. Dirt tracks in the parks are very rough so be wary of getting stuck.

Traffic is heavy in Nairobi and Mombasa and drivers must get used to the Kenyan mindset of "me first" to get anywhere at all.

## Road Assistance

For roadside assistance it may be worth considering taking a temporary membership with the **Automobile Association (AA) of Kenya**. The car hire companies can also arrange this.

## DIRECTORY

### Hiring a Car

**Avis**
Tel 020 2213330. W avis.co.ke

**Budget**
Tel 020 652144. W budget.co.ke

**Central Rent-a-Car**
Muindi Mbingu St, Nairobi.
**City Map** 1 C3. **Tel** 020 2222888.
W carhirekenya.com

**Concorde Car Hire**
Sarit Centre, Westlands,
Nairobi. **Tel** 020 3743316.
W concorde.co.ke

**Europcar**
Tel 0722 823455.
W europcar.co.ke

**Uniglobe Let's Go Travel**
Waiyaki Way, Westlands, Nairobi.
**Tel** 020 4447151.
W uniglobeletsgotravel.com

### Road Assistance

**Automobile Association (AA) of Kenya**
Airport North Road, Nairobi.
**Tel** 020 2612300; 0720 227267 (in emergency). W aakenya.co.ke

In the event of a breakdown, it is customary to deposit a bundle of leaves or grass a few metres behind and in front of the vehicle to warn other motorists. To get up-to-date information on road conditions off the beaten track visit the **Safety and Communication Centre** *(see p407)* in Nairobi before setting out.

A local bus travelling on the dusty track leading to Mbita Point, on Lake Victoria

# General Index

# Acknowledgments

Dorling Kindersley would like to thank the many people whose help and assistance contributed to the preparation of this book.

## Main Contributors

Philip Briggs was born in the UK and raised in South Africa, and first backpacked between Nairobi and Cape Town in 1986. In the 1990s, he wrote several Bradt guides to destinations that were then – and in some cases still are – practically uncharted by the travel publishing industry, including South Africa, Ghana, Uganda, Ethiopia, Malawi, Mozambique, Tanzania and Rwanda. Philip has visited more than two dozen African countries and written about most of them, whether for guidebook publishers such as AA, Berlitz, Dorling Kindersley, Frommers, Camerapix, Struik-New Holland, APA-Insight and 30 Degrees South, or magazines such as *Africa Birds & Birding*, *Africa Geographic*, *BBC Wildlife*, *Travel Africa* and *Wanderlust*. He still spends a few months on the road every year, and the rest of his time at home in the mountainous uKhahlamba-Drakensberg region of South Africa.

Lizzie Williams, who originally hails from the UK, worked for several years as a tour leader on overland trucks across Africa before settling in Cape Town to write guidebooks. She has visited more than 20 African countries and is the author of Footprint guides to Namibia, Kenya, South Africa, Zimbabwe and Tanzania. She also wrote the first country guide to Nigeria for Bradt. Her additional work includes writing numerous magazine articles and writing travel content on Africa for websites.

**Fact Checker** Matt Brown

**Proofreader** Deepthi Talwar

**Indexer** Jyoti Dhar

## Design and Editorial

*Publisher* Douglas Amrine
*List Manager* Vivien Antwi
*Managing Art Editor* Jane Ewart
*Project Editor* Michelle Crane
*Senior Project Designer* Paul Jackson
*Project Designer* Kate Leonard
*Senior Cartographic Editor* Casper Morris
*Managing Art Editor (jackets)* Karen Constanti
*Jacket Design* Tessa Bindloss
*DTP Designer* Natasha Lu
*Picture Researcher* Ellen Root
*Production Controller* Linda Dare

## Revisions Team

Richard Czapnik, Fay Franklin, Camilla Gersh, Sylvia Goulding, Susanne Hillen, Maite Lantaron, Jude Ledger, Phoebe Lowndes, Alison McGill, Catherine Palmi, Susie Peachey, Helen Peters, Rada Radojicic, Marisa Renzullo, Preeti Singh, Hollie Teague, Julie Thompson, Richard Trillo, Ajay Verma, Richa Verma, Deepika Verma, Ariadne van Zandbergen.

## Additional Photography

Trish Gant, Frank Greenaway, Mathew Kurien, Ian O'Leary, Harry Taylor, Jerry Young.

## Special Assistance

Dorling Kindersley would like to thank the following for their assistance:

Bike Treks, Dr Dame Daphne Sheldrick at David Sheldrick Wildlife Trust, Alex Millar at Governors' Camp, Peter Kimani at Heritage Hotels, Craig Hilton-Taylor at the IUCN, Raphael Mwangi at Kenya National Archives, Betty Ichan at Kenya Tourist Board, Michael Kipkeu, Evelyn Oroni, Andrew Toboso at Kenya Wildlife Service, LAICO Regency Hotel, Nairobi, Freddie Maruk and Iris Hunt at Mount Kenya Wildlife Conservancy's Animal Orphanage, Simon Gatheru at Nairobi National Museum, Dr Idle Omar Farah, Esther Keige, Dr Mzalendo Kibunjia and Ibrahim Mohamud at National Museums of Kenya, Eve Onduru at Sarova Hotels, Sanjay Shoor at Shoor Travel, Fatma Muses at Sopa Hotels, Torben Rune at Southern Cross Safaris, Mombasa.

## Picture Credits

Key: a-above; b-below/bottom; c-centre; f-far; l-left; r-right; t-top

Works of art have been reproduced with the kind permission of the following copyright holders: *Wings of Love* (1998) © Gakunju Kaigwa 39cb, *Dancing with the Enemy* (2000) © Jimmy Ogonga 39clb; Portrait of Naisuaki Enole Kosen Sarbabi by Joy Adamson, © National Museums of Kenya, Joy Adamson Collection 39cr; *World-Class Black Rhino, Aberdare Forest* (1972) © Peter Beard 39bc.

## Photography Permissions

Dorling Kindersley would like to thank the following for their assistance and kind permission to photograph at their establishments:

African Heritage Centre, Nairobi, Borana Lodge at Laikipia Plateau, Carnivore Restaurant, Colliers Shopping Centre, Elsa's Kopje at Meru National Park, Grand Regency Hotel, Nairobi, Shemina at Galdessa Camp at Tsavo East National Park, Giraffe Manor at Nairobi National Park, Kicheche Camp at the Masai Mara National Reserve, Kisumu Museum, Lamu Guest House, Nairobi Railway Museum, Ol Tukai Lodge Bar, Rondo

Retreat at Kakamega Forest National Reserve, Satao Elerai Camp at Amboseli National Park, Serena Beach Hotel, Serena Mountain Lodge, Elizabeth Nguraru at Shimba Hills Lodge at Shimba Hills National Reserve, Bhavni Satish at Voi Wildlife Lodge.

Works of art have been reproduced with the kind permission of the following copyright holders: *Wings of Love* (1998) © Gakunju Kaigwa 35cb, *Dancing with the Enemy* (2000) © Jimmy Ogonga 35clb; Portrait of Naisuaki Enole Kosen Sarbabi by Joy Adamson, © National Museums of Kenya, Joy Adamson Collection 35cr; *World-Class Black Rhino, Aberdare Forest* (1972) © Peter Beard 35bc.

The publisher would like to thank the following for their kind permission to reproduce their photographs:

**4Corners:** SIME/Schmid Reinhard 181b.
**Aberdare Safari Hotels Ltd:** 81tl, 321bc.
**Africa Image Library:** Ariadne Van Zandbergen 29cl, 34crb, 87ca, 87cr, 90crb, 93tl, 98tr, 107br, 111br,116cla, 127cr, 130cl, 130clb 133tl, 136c, 137tc, 140–41t, 143br, 147cr, 152clb, 187bc, 233bl, 258br, 261crb, 275cr, 275bl, 283c, 336cra, 346bl, 347crb, 356bl.
**African Territories :** 371tl.
**AKG Images:** 51t, 55tr.
**Alamy Images:** A & J Visage 103tr; Ace Stock Limited 106bc; Africa/Tina Manley 25bc, 32cl, 205bl; AfriPics.com 70bl, 89cr,123tl; age fotostock/Larry Dale Gordon 62; Arco Images GmbH 112br, 115cla, /K. Wothe 49cb, /W. Dolder 24cr, 128tr; Robert E. Barber 70cr, Peter Barritt 24crb, 111clb, 149tr, 180; blickwinkel 66tc, 104cr, 135tl, 148tl, Dolder 24clb, 24bc, /Katz 90br, /Layer 115ca, / McPHOTO /BIO 88tr, /McPHOTO/ ZAD 220br, 233cr, 259cra, 341cb, /Poelking 125bl, /Wisniewski 69tl; David Boag 112clb, 144clb, 148tc, 148c; Bon Appetit/Kröger/ Gross 97bc; Mark Boulton 33c, 96br, 234cl, 299bl; James de Bounevialle 125bc; Penny Boyd 118cla, 133cr; Yvette Cardozo 321tl; Gordon Chambers 25fcrb, 149tl; Nick Cobbing 37cb; Gary Cook 349bl; Neil Cooper 261cra; Corbis Premium RF/ Michele Burgess 33cr, 387crb; CreativeAct - Toys/Games series 386br; Tim Davies 64bl,136tl; Danita Delimont 351cl, /Gavriel Jecan 33tr, / David Northcott 102crb, Reinhard Dirscherl 122cla; Discpicture 91bc; Ulrich Doering 195clb; EcoPic 142cr; EggImages 99br; Chad Ehlers 417b; Elvele Images/B J Gadie 314cla, /Fritz Poelking 268cla; Mark Eveleigh 67br, 119br, 266bl; Alissa Everett 113tl; f1 online/Harald Trinkner 127tl; Paul John Fearn 412b; David Fleetham 114ca; FLPA 99crb, 143clb, 280cla, 357tr; fotoshoot 374cla; Fotosonline /Klaus-Peter Wolf 347cl; franzfoto. com 66b; Chris Fredriksson 91cr, 117cr; G&B Images/ Gustav Gonget 96cla; Jason Gallier 147tr; Eddie Gerald 299bc; Angelo Giampiccolo 167tl; Simon de Glanville 138clb; Dacorum Gold 142br; Ken Hackett 24cl;

Martin Harvey 118–19c; Kevin Henshaw 134br; Peter Horree 38cr, 387tr; Friedrich von Hörsten 146tr; David Hosking 149cr; Andre van Huizen 147tc, 147cl; Imagebroker/Stefan Auth 36cr, 95tl,/Klaus-Peter Wolf 149cl; Images & Stories 139cla; Images of Africa Photobank 351clb, 351crb, 351bl, /Friedrich von Horsten 92cla, 299crb, /David Keith Jones 12br, 30crb, 31cl, 34cl, 34cr, 36bc, 65tr, 67cb, 74b, 90tr, 114crb, 118clb, 119bl, 126clb, 127br, 130–31, 131bl, 131br, 136cl, 155tr, 165clb, 233cb, 261tl, 269t, 283br, 302b, 306br, 315crb, 323crb, 326cl, 334cl, 335br, 340tr, 340c, 340–41c, 341tr, 341cra, 341bl, 355tl, 384cl, 386cl, 392tl, 393br, 412cr, 414b, Images of Africa Photobank /Jeremy van Riemsdyke 83ca, /Carla Signorini 258bl, 260tr, 346cl, /Charlotte Thege 29crb; Images & Stories 48bc;  ImageState/ Georgette Douwma 215bl, /Jonathan & Angie Scott 142clb; INTERFOTO Pressebildagentur 315bl; Paul Ives 215crb; Juniors Bildarchiv 128cla, 146c, /F323 98br; John Warburton-Lee Photography/Nigel Pavitt 288, 338; Marion Kaplan 337cb, 345cb, 354bc; Kim Kaminski 84; Mike Lane 148cr, 191bc; Zute Lightfoot 5clb, 327bl, 329t; Andrew Linscott 356c; LMR Group 146cr; Mary Evans Picture Library 53tr, 314tr; David Mbiyu 315cr; Michael Matthews 37cl; Mike Mckavett 299br; Mediacolor's 93cr; Mooch Images 386bl; Philip Mugridge 119tc; Nature Picture Library/Bernard Castelein 116clb, / Jose B. Ruiz 285ca; Nordicphotos/Jörgen Larsson 239bc; North Wind Picture Archives 52br; Chris Pancewicz 386crb; Trevor Payne 137cr,202; Peter Arnold, Inc./Martha Cooper 259bl; Photodisc 117clb, /Anup Shah 111bl, 148cl; PHOTOTAKE Inc./Carolina Biological Supply Company 353cr; Pictorial Press Ltd 40c, 41bl, 113cr; Picture Contact/ Jochem Wijnands 86tr, 115cb, 271tl; Vic Pigula 138cla; Peter Pinnock 141bc; Pixonnet.com/Bo Jansson 92tr; Stu Porter 141cr; Robert Estall Photo Agency //David Coulson 27cr, Angela Fisher 33clb; Robert Harding Picture Library Ltd /Charles Bowman 212br; Malcolm Schuyl 115tr, 142cla, 144br, 146tc; Sean Sprague 55c; Frantisek Staud 314c; Stephen Frink Collection 211tc; Steve Bloom Images 45tr, 125bc, 137tl, 198cl; Stockbyte/Tom Brakefield 134clb, 137c, 309cr; Charles Sturge 410cl;  Stuwdamdorp 58c; Sue Cunningham Photographic 258tr, 258-9c; Trevor Smithers ARPS 375tl;  Jack Sullivan 35br; Bjorn Svensson 28bl; Dawn Swift 117tl; Sylvia Cordaiy Photo Library/ Massimo Piacentino 167bl, /Kjell Sandved 90cla, Kjell Sandved 134cla; Jim Tampin 132br, 135br; tbkmedia.de 260cl; Terry Harris Just Greece Photo Library 396bc; David Tipling 256, 284br; Peter Titmuss 126cla; TNT Magazine 270clb; Charles Tomalin 110bc; Top-Pics TBK 96tr; Travel Ink/ Dave Saunders 211tl; Travelshots.com 231b; Nick Turner 26br, 77t, 289b; David Uney 149c; Ariadne Van Zandbergen 147tl, 248tr, 250b, 261bl, 267tl, 321cra, 341tl, 341br; Miroslava Vilimova 25cl; Vintage Images 48tr; Visions of America, LLC /Joe Sohm 68br, 166clb, 314clb, 323ca, 391br; Ross Warner 112cr;

Maximilian Weinzierl 63b, 66c, 216–17; Westend 61/ Martin Rietze 259br; Terry Whittaker 95cr, 104bl, 113clb, 133bl; Wild Places Photography/Chris Howes 174b; Wildviews/Charles Tomalin 111bc; World Pictures 131bc; World Religions Photo Library/Christine Osborne 37cr; WorldFoto 65bl, 97crb, 128–9c, 139cb, 195br; Karsten Wrobel 94tr; Wyrdlight 93bc; Xinhua 413tl.
**Ali Barbour's Group:** 378tr, 379br.
**Alliance Française de Nairobi:** Christian Randrianampizafy 389tr.
**Ardea:** Mark Boulton 98cla; Piers Cavendish 21bl; Kenneth W. Fink 103cl, 301crb; Clem Haagner 114cb; Michael Neugebauer 353cl.
**Art and Commerce:** Peter Beard 39bc.
**Tom Ashton:** 215cra.
**AWL Images:** Danita Delimont Stock 18, 312; Nigel Pavitt 100, 150–51, 170–71, 196–7, 230, 330–31; Jonathan and Angela Scott 60–61; John Warburton-Lee 2–3.
**Bird Watching Eastafrica:** Chege Wa Kariuki 94cla.
**Bridgeman Images:** British Library, London, *Sloane 197 f.225v-6 Portuguese exploration map of Mombassa, illustration from "Historical Accounts of Portuguese Settlements" 1646 (vellum),* Barretto de Resende, Pedro (fl.1646) 205crb /197 f.9 205cra; Private Collection /© Look and Learn Vasco de Gama (1469-1524) (gouache on paper) Severino Baraldi (b.1930) 46, 204–5c.
**Camerapix:** 29tr, 30cl, 31tr, 35tr, 35clb, 239cr.
**Camp Carnelley's:** 381tl.
**Corbis:** 56crb, 195crb; O. Alamany & E. Vicens 328b; Yann Arthus-Bertrand 123br, 297ca, 354clb, 404b; Bettmann 49bl, 57tc, 57crb, 315tr, 353cla; Tom Brakefield 108cla, 108bc, 109ca, 111cra, 124–5c, 259tl; Ralph A. Clevenger 144tl; Brandon D. Cole 116br; John Conrad 106–7, 129bl; Corbis Sygma/Orban Thierry 48cla; Alissa Crandall 75br; DLILLC 25cr, 32crb, 106cla, 107cb, 108clb, 121crb, 124clb, 131tl, 199tl; Ecoscene/Sally A. Morgan 189tl; EPA 22bl, / Nic Bothma 99bc, /Jon Hrusa 21c, /Stephen Morrison 59tr; Stephen Frink 215cl, 249tl; Gallo Images 105bl, / Nigel J. Dennis 114clb, /Roger De La Harpe 107ca; Louise Gubb 41tc; Martin Harvey 130bc; Rob Howard 130cb; Hulton-Deutsch Collection 56t, 56bc, 319cb; JAI/ Demetrio Carrasco 20bl; Chen Jianli 23bl; Barbra Leigh 110br; Renee Lynn 97tl; Joe McDonald 106br, 124cla, 130cla, 132cr, 138ca; Mary Ann McDonald 105tr; Momatiuk - Eastcott 107bc; Micheline Pelletier 59br; Carl & Ann Purcell 387tl, 407br; Reuters/Antony Njuguna 402bl; Jeffrey L. Rotman 215cb; Kevin Schafer 125tc; Paul Souders 76bl, 108–9; Wendy Stone 402t; Keren Su 22tr; Sygma/William Campbell 58bc; Roger Tidman 93br; Brian A. Vikander 33bl, 128clb; Zefa//Michael Fiala 24tr; Gabriela Staebler 19b,106clb, 109br, /Winfried Wisniewski 109bc.
**Dreamstime.com:** Bryan Busovicki 10br; Byelikova 13tr, 15t; Ebastard129 13br; Edwinmostert 12tr; Ivkuzmin 10cla; Javarman 14br; Lewald168 11tr; Masr 15br; Perseomedusa 246–7.

**East African Educational Publishers Ltd.:** 40bl.
**Fairmont Hotels & Resorts, Kenya:** 332bl.
**FLPA:** Neil Bowman 148tr; Peter Davey 97br; Alan and Linda Detrick 95br; David Hosking 96clb; Imagebroker/ Frank Stober 118bc; Frans Lanting 72b, 88clb, 119bc; Minden Pictures/Tim Fitzharris 118br; Fritz Polking 88cla; Malcolm Schuyl 88br, 119clb; Jurgen & Christine Sohns 89bc; Ariadne Van Zandbergen 33cla, 248bc; Martin B Withers 147c.
**Funzi Keys/About Africa Ltd:** 366tl.
**Steve Garvie:** 102bl.
**Getty Images:** AFP/Deshakalyan Chowdhury 36cl, / Gianluigi Guercia 315tc. Simon Maina 42cra, /Olivier Morin 297crb; Aurora/Robert Caputo 32tr; Steve Bloom 120tl; Digital Vision 71bl, /Paul Souders 71tr; Stu Forster 297bc; Gallo Images/Heinrich van den Berg 131cb; John Gichigi 297clb; Hulton Archive/Anwar Hussein 41cr; Peter Lilja 262cl; S Purdy Matthews 107bl; Miden Pictures/Mark Moffett 89tl; National Geographic/ Kenneth Garrett 48ca; Stan Osolinski 195c; Nigel Pavitt 154, 304–5; Photodisc/Anup Shah 109cb, 122br, 123bc; Photographer's Choice/James Warwick 112cla; Peter Pinnock 24fclb; Kim Steele 375c; Stone/Peter and Stef Lamberti 122bc, /Art Wolfe 266tr; Time & Life Pictures/ William F. Campbell 314bc, /Dmitri Kessel 314–15c, / Mansell 55br, /Terrence Spencer 309cb; Ami Vitale 123tl.
**Governors Camp Collection:** 369bc.
**The Granger Collection, New York:** 54crb, 56bl, 173crb, 225cl.
**Hamill Gallery of African Art, Boston:** 1.
**Hemingways Watamu:** 367br.
**Hilton Nairobi hotel:** 388bl.
**Intercontinental Nairobi:** 376br.
**Jamhuri Wear:** 387cra.
**John Warburton-Lee Photography:** 25tr, 323cl, 326br, 357bl, 391t; Nigel Pavitt 5c, 25cla, 28crb, 31bl, 34bl, 38cb, 43tc, 132clb, 175tr, 175br, 232–3c, 233tr, 253tl, 271br, 274cla, 281tl, 307br, 340clb, 386cra; Susanna Wyatt 394tr.
**Karl Ammann:** 250cl.
**Kenya National Archives:** 54br, 57bl, 57bc.
**Kenya Wildlife Service:** 83cr, Kakamega Forest National Reserve 299tl.
**The Kobal Collection:** Umbrella/BBC/Brit Screen 323tl.
**Last Refuge:** Adrian Warren 27fbl.
**Richard Leakey:** 353bc.
**Lebrecht Music and Arts:** African Pictures 36tr, 37tr, 37cla, 37bl, 37br.
**Luc Lens :** 103bl.
**Lonely Planet Images:** Casey & Astrid Mahaney 215br; Mitch Reardon 153tl.
**Marasa Africa:** 370bc.
**Marketing Worldwide:** 365tl.
**Mary Evans Picture Library:** 53cb, 54tl, 225cr, 225crb, 225br; Illustrated London News Ltd 53br.
**Masterfile:** George Calef 108br; Albert Normandin 20t; Radius Images/Horst Klemm 339b.

Mediterraneo restaurant: 377tr.

Ronald Mulwa: 103crb.

Nairobi National Museum: 162tl, 162tr, 162cl, 162clb, 162br, 163tl, 163cr, 163crb, 163bl.

National Geographic Stock: 49cla, 115cra; Gordan Gahan 48–9c; Kenneth Garrett 48clb, 353clb.

National Museums of Kenya: Fort Jesus Museum/Steve Okoko Ashikoye 233cra.

naturepl.com: Karl Ammann 325br; Peter Blackwell 126br, 139ca, 329c; Bernard Castelein 126cr; Bruce Davidson 145cr, 146cl; Jurgen Freund 99tl; Tony Heald 124bc, 124br, 136cr; Luiz Claudio Marigo 238clb; Hugh Maynard 298bl; Tony Phelps 139tr; Premaphotos 138cra; Mike Read149tc; Jeff Rotman 99clb; Keith Scholey 25bl, 111tl; Anup Shah 109bl, 110crb, 116cr, 123bl, 128br, 129cra, 137cl; Lynne M Stone 110cla; Jeff Vanuga 130br.

NHPA/Photoshot: Daryl Balfour 91tl, 92br; Antony Bannister 114cla, 114cra, 122clb, 139clb, 299fclb; Gerald Cubitt 89br; Nigel J Dennis 115crb, 136tc; Nick Garbutt 115clb; Martin Harvey 125clb; Daniel Heuclin 91br, 301bl; Chris Mattison 138cb; Jean-Louis Le Moigne 25ca; Christophe Ratier 354cl; Kevin Schafer 113br; Jonathan & Angela Scott 353crb; John Shaw 117br; James Warwick 137tr, 143cr.

North Wind Picture Archives: 52tl.

Jimmy Ogonga: 39clb.

OhioRunner.com: 297br.

Ol Pejata Conservancy: Ian Aitken 324bl.

Jochen Ott: 299ca.

Pan Macmillan: Charles Miller 303cr.

Douglas B Paterson: 37cra.

Peponi Hotel Restaurant: 380bc.

Photolibrary: 322tr ; ABPL/Gerald Hinde 122–3c; Roderick Edward Edwards 145br; Nabil Ezz 127cl; OSF/David W Breed 95bc, /Derek Bromhall 295br, /Eliot Neep 69bl, 110–11c, 278–9; Photodisc/Gallo Images/Daryl Balfour 129crb; Photononstop/Yves Talensac 153br; Robert Harding Travel/Julia Bayne 85b.

Photoshot: World Pictures 340br.

Private Collection: 34cra, 52c.

Rahimtulla Museum of Modern Art: 39c.

Reuters: Antony Njuguna 166br; Barry Moody 268br; Radu Sigheti 23tc.

Rhino Ark: 43bl.

Robert Harding Picture Library: 11cr; Michael Boyny 358–9.

Francesco Rovero: 136tr.

Rusinga Island Lodge: www.privatewilderness.com 306cl.

Sarakasi Trust : 36cb.

Sarova Lion Hill Lodge: 81cb.

Sasini Tea & Coffee Ltd: 387cb.

Michael Smith: 413br.

Sopa Lodges: 368tl.

St. Martin's Press: John Henry Patterson, 1907 40tr.

Ronald Sydney Starling: 39cr.

Sam W Stearman: 38crb.

SuperStock: Gallo Images 398–9.

Julie Wieczkowski: 102cra, 102cl.

www.africanpictures.net: Drum Social Histories/Baileys African History 58crb, 59c.

www.bmpix.org: Archives mission 21: Basel Mission 52bc.

www.thesafaricollection.com: 364bl.

Front Endpapers: Alamy Images: age fotostock/Larry Dale Gordon Lbl; Peter Barritt Rbr; Kim Kaminski Lbc; Trevor Payne Rbc; David Tipling Ltc; John Warburton-Lee Photography/Nigel Pavitt Ltl, Rtr; AWL Images: Danita Delimont Stock Rc; Nigel Pavitt Lbr, Rcr; Getty Images: Nigel Pavitt Lcl.

Jacket: Front and spine top Alamy Images: Steve Bloom Images.

All other images © Dorling Kindersley
For further information see: www.dkimages.com

# Phrase Book

Kenya's official language Kiswahili, the language of the Swahili people, belongs to the Bantu group of languages from the Niger-Congo family. Originally spoken by the indigenous people along the East African coast, Kiswahili was greatly influenced by Arabic as well as Persian, Portuguese and English. Standard Kiswahili developed from Zanzibar and although there are many regional variations and dialects present, it is generally recognized throughout East Africa.

Written in the Roman alphabet, the language is spoken in a straightforward manner, the pronunciation of most words being similar to the English equivalent. The stress is nearly always on the penultimate syllable and all vowels in a word are sounded. The consonant **ng** is possibly the only unfamiliar sound for English-speakers. There is also a clear distinction between the English **r** and the softer Kiswahili **r**, which is closer to the sound **d**.

The Swahili system of telling time varies from the international system. Swahili time (*saa za kiswahili*) begins 6 hours after international time and consists of two 12-hour segments –sunrise to sunset and sunset to sunrise.

This phrase book gives the English word or phrase, followed by Kiswahili, then the romanization adapted to aid pronunciation.

## In an Emergency

| | | |
|---|---|---|
| Help! | **Saidia!** | *sa-ee-dee-a* |
| Stop! | **Simama!** | *see-ma-ma* |
| Fire! | **Moto!** | *moh-toh* |
| Call a doctor! | **Mwite daktari** | *m-wee-tay dak-ta-ree* |
| Call an ambulance! | **Ita gari la hospitali!** | *ee-ta ga-ree la ho-spee-ta-lee* |
| Call the police! | **Waite polisi!** | *wa-ee-tay poh lee see* |
| I've been robbed | **Niliibiwa** | *nee-lee-ee-bee-wa* |
| Where is the nearest telephone? | **Simu hapo karibuni iko wapi?** | *see-moo ha-poh-ka-ree-boo-nee ee-koh wa-pee?* |
| Where is the nearest hospital? | **Hospitali hapo karibuni iko wapi?** | *hoh-spee-ta-lee ha-poh ka-ree-boo-nee ee-koh wa-pee?* |

## Communication Essentials

| | | |
|---|---|---|
| Yes | **Ndiyo** | *n-dee-yoh* |
| No | **Hapana** | *ha-pa-na* |
| Please | **Tafadhali** | *ta-fa-dha-lee* |
| Thank you | **Asante** | *a-san-tay* |
| Excuse me | **Samahani** | *sa-ma-ha-nee* |
| Sorry | **Pole** | *poh-lay* |
| Hello | **Habari** | *ha-ba-ree* |
| Goodbye | **Tutaonana** | *too-ta-oh-na-na* |
| Good night | **Usiku mwema** | *oo-see-koo mway-ma* |
| Morning | **Asubuhi** | *a-soo-boo-hee* |
| Afternoon | **Mchana** | *m-cha-na* |
| Evening | **Jioni** | *jee-oh-nee* |
| Yesterday | **Jana** | *ja-na* |
| Today | **Leo** | *lay-oh* |
| Tomorrow | **Kesho** | *kay-shoh* |
| Here | **Hapa** | *ha-pa* |
| There | **Hapo** | *ha-poh* |
| How? | **Vipi?** | *vee-pee* |
| What? | **Nini?** | *nee-nee* |
| When? | **Lini?** | *lee-nee* |
| Why? | **Kwa nini?** | *kwa nee-nee* |
| Where? | **Wapi?** | *wa-pee* |
| Pleased to meet you | **Nafurahi kuku-fahamu** | *na-foo-ra-hee koo-koo fa-ha-moo* |

## Useful Phrases

| | | |
|---|---|---|
| How are you? | **Hujambo?** | *hoo-jam-boh* |
| 'm fine | **Sijambo** | *si-jam-boh* |
| ⁓ you later | **Baadaye tutaonana** | *ba-ada-yay too-ta-oh-na-na* |
| fine | **Ni sawa** | *nee sa-wa* |
| √are...? | **...iko wapi?** | *ee-koh wa-pee* |
| | **Ni umbali gani kwenda...?** | *nee oom-ba-lee ga-nee kwyn-da* |
| ⁓a ⁓nt? | **Unajua hoteli nzuri kula?** | *oo-na-joo-ahoh-tay-lee n-zoo-ree koo-la* |
| | **Unasema Kiingereza? Sielewi** | *oo-na-say-ma kee-een-gay-ray-za see-ay-lay-wee* |
| | **⁓fadhali sema pole?** | *ta-fa-dha-lee say-ma poh-lay poh-lay* |
| | **⁓nikipiga ⁓wewe?** | *ka-ree-boo nee wa-wee-nee-kee-pee-ga pee-cha ya way-way* |

## Useful Words

| | | |
|---|---|---|
| big | **kubwa** | *koob-wa* |
| small | **dogo** | *doh-goh* |
| hot | **joto** | *joh-toh* |
| cold | **baridi** | *ba-ree-dee* |
| good | **nzuri** | *n-zoo-ree* |
| bad | **mbaya** | *m-ba-ya* |
| enough | **ya kutosha** | *ya koo-toh-sha* |
| open | **wazi** | *wa-zee* |
| closed | **ya kufungwa** | *ya koo-foon-gwa* |
| opening hours | **masaa ya kufunguliwa** | *ma-sa ya koo-foon-goo-lee-wa* |
| right | **kulia** | *koo-lee-a* |
| left | **kushoto** | *koo-shoh-toh* |
| straight on | **moja kwa moja** | *moh-ja kwa moh-ja* |
| near | **karibu** | *ka-ree-boo* |
| far | **mbali** | *m-ba-lee* |
| up | **juu** | *joo* |
| down | **chini** | *chee-nee* |
| in front of | **mbele ya** | *m-bay-lay-ya* |
| opposite | **kinyume** | *kee-nyoo-may* |
| behind | **nyuma** | *nyoo-ma* |
| woman | **mwanamke** | *mwan-am-kay* |
| man | **mwanamume** | *mwa-na-moo-may* |
| early | **mapema** | *ma-pay-ma* |
| late | **ya kuchelewa** | *ya koo-chay-lay-wa* |
| now | **sasa** | *sa-sa* |
| soon | **sasa hivi** | *sa-sa hee-vee* |
| more | **zaidi** | *za-ee-dee* |
| less | **chache** | *cha-chay* |
| little | **chache** | *cha-chay* |
| very | **sana** | *sa-na* |
| entrance | **mwingilio** | *mween-gee-lee-oh* |
| exit | **kutoka** | *koo-toh-ka* |
| toilet | **choo** | *choh* |
| free, unoccupied | **kupatikana** | *koo-pa-tee-ka-na* |
| bathroom | **bafu** | *ba-foo* |
| toilet paper | **karatasi ya choo** | *ka-ra-ta-see ya choh* |
| camera | **kemra** | *kaym-ra* |
| batteries | **betri** | *bay-tree* |
| health certificate | **cheti cha afya** | *chay-tee cha af-ya* |
| passport | **pasipoti** | *pa-see-poh-tee* |
| visa | **visa** | *vee-sa* |

## Making a Telephone Call

| | | |
|---|---|---|
| I'd like to place a long-distance call | **Nataka kupiga simu ya mbali** | *na-ta-ka koo-pee-ga see-moo ya m-ba-lee* |
| I want to make a local call | **Nataka kupiga simu jirani** | *na-ta-ka koo-pee-ga see-moo-jee-ra-nee* |
| I'll call again later | **Nitajaribu tene baadaye** | *nee-ta-ja-ree-boo tay-na ba-a-day-yay* |
| Can I leave a message? | **Naomba niache ujumbe?** | *na-ohm-ba nee-a-chay oo-joom-bay* |
| The number is... | **Namba ni...** | *nam-ba ni* |
| Can I speak to...? | **Nataka kuongea na...?** | *na-ta-ka koo-ohn-gay-a na* |

## Shopping

| | | |
|---|---|---|
| How much is it? | **Ni bei gani...?** | *ni bay ga-nee* |
| I would like... | **Nataka...** | *na-ta-ka* |
| Do you have...? | **Mna...?** | *m-na* |
| I'm just looking | **Naangalia tu** | *na-an-ga-lee-a-too* |
| Do you take credit cards? | **Mnakubali kadi ya benki?** | *m-na-koo-ba-lee ka-dee ya bayn-kee* |
| Do you take traveller's cheques? | **Mnakubali hundi ya msafiri?** | *m-na-koo-ba-lee hoon-dee ya m-sa-fee-ree* |
| Can I have it sent overseas? | **Naweza kuipostia kwenye nchi za nje?** | *na-way-za koo-ee-eepoh-stee-a kway-nyay n-chee za n-jay* |
| What time does the shop open? | **Inafungua duka saa ngapi?** | *ee-na-foon-goo-a doo-ka sa n-ga-pee* |
| What time does the shop close? | **Inafunga duka saa ngapi?** | *ee-na-foon-ga doo-ka sa n-ga-pee* |
| This one | **Hii** | *hee* |
| That one | **Hiyo** | *hee-yoh* |
| expensive | **ghali** | *ga-lee* |
| cheap | **rahisi** | *ra-hee-see* |
| bargain | **bei nafuu** | *bay na-foo* |
| size | **saizi** | *sa-ee-zee* |
| white | **nyeupe** | *nyay-oo-pay* |
| black | **nyeusi** | *nyay-oo-see* |
| red | **nyekundu** | *nyay-koon-doo* |
| yellow | **manjano** | *man-ja-noh* |

| green | kijani | kee-ja-nee |
|---|---|---|
| blue | buluu | boo-loo |
| antique shop | duka la vitu vya kizamani | doo-ka la vee-too vya kee za-ma-nee |
| shop | duka | doo-ka |
| bakery | duka la mkate | doo-ka la mkate |
| bank | benki | bayn-kee |
| bookshop | duka la vitabu | doo-ka la vee-ta-boo |
| chemist | duka la dawa | doo-ka la da-wa |
| department store | duka lenye vitu vingi | doo-ka lay-nyay vee-too veen-gee |
| delicatessen | duka la vyakula tayari | doo-ka la vya-koo-la ta-ya-ree |
| fishmonger | duka la samaki | doo-ka la sa-ma-kee |
| gift shop | duka la vitu vya zawadi | doo-ka la vee-too vya za-wa-dee |
| greengrocer | duka la mboga | doo-ka la m-boh-ga |
| grocery | duka la vyakula | doo-ka la vya-koo-la |
| hairdresser | mususi | m-soo-see |
| market | soko | soh-koh |
| store | vitu vingi | vee-too veen-gee |
| newsagent | shirika la habari | shee-ree-ka la ha-ba-ree |
| post office | posta | poh-sta |
| supermarket | duka kubwa | doo-ka koob-wa |
| shoe shop | duka la viatu | doo-ka la vee-a-too |
| tobacconist | duka la tumbaku | doo-ka la tumbaku |
| travel agent | uwakala wa safari | oo-wa-ka-la wa sa-fee-ree |

## Sightseeing

| avenue | barabara | ba-ra-ba-ra |
|---|---|---|
| art gallery | nyumba ya sanaa | nyoom-ba-ya sa-na |
| beach | ufukwe | oo-fook-way |
| boat trip | safari ya boti | sa-fa-ree ya boh-t |
| cathedral | kanisa kuu | ka-nee-sa koo |
| church | kanisa | ka-nee-sa |
| garden | bustani | boo-sta-nee |
| guide | kiongozi | kee-ohn-goh-zee |
| house | nyumba | nyoom-ba |
| highway | barabara | ba-ra-ba-ra |
| map | ramani | ra-ma-nee |
| museum | makumbusho | ma-koom-boo-shoh |
| national park | hifadhi ya wanyama | hee-fa-dhee ya wa-nya-ma |
| night drive | kuzamia wakati wa usiku | koo-za-mee-a wa-ka-tee wa oo-see-koo |
| park | hifadhi | hee-fa-dhee |
| road | barabara | ba-ra-ba-ra |
| square | uwanja | oo-wan-ja |
| street | njia | n-jee-a |
| tourist bureau | uwakala wa safari | oo-wa-ka-la wa sa-fa-ree |

## Safari

| safari/tour | safari | sa-fa-ree |
|---|---|---|
| day trip | safari ya siku moja | sa-fa-ree ya see-koo moh-ja |
| game park | hifadhi ya wanyama | hee-fa-dhee ya wa-nya-ma |
| camel safari | safari ya ngamia | sa-fa-ree ya n-ga-mee-a |
| walking safari | safari ya kutembea | sa-fa-ree ya koo-taym-bay-a |
| park entrance fees | ada za hifadhi | a-da za hee-fa-dhee |
| buffalo | nyati | nya-tee |
| cheetah | duma | doo-ma |
| elephant | ndovu | n-dor-voo |
| leopard | chui | choo-ee |
| lion | simba | seem-ba |
| rhinoceros | kifaru | kee-fa-roo |

## Post Offices and Banks

| bank | benki | bayn-kee |
|---|---|---|
| Bureau de change | mahali pa kubadilisha pesa | ma-ha-lee pa koo-ba-dee-lee-sha pay-sa |
| What is the exchange rate? | Kiwango cha kubadilisha ni nini? | kee-wan-goh cha koo-ba-dee-lee-sha nee nee-nee |
| I want to send a letter | Nataka kupeleka barua | na-ta-ka koo-pay-lay-ka ba-roo-a |
| parcel | kifurushi | kee-foo-roo-shee |
| postcard | postkadi | pohst-ka-dee |
| stamp | stempu | staym-poo |
| draw out money | kuondoa hela | koo-ohn-doh-a hay-la |

## Transport

| When does it leave? | Itaondoka saa ngapi? | ee-ta-ohn-doh-ka saa ngapi |
|---|---|---|
| When's the next train/bus? | Basi/treni ijayo itaondoka lini? | ba-see/tray-nee ee-ja-yoh ee-ta-ohn-doh-ka lee-nee |
| Could you call a taxi for me? | Niitie teksi? | nee-ee-tee-ay tayk-see |
| airport | uwanja wa ndege | oo-wan-ja wa n-day-gay |
| railway station | stesheni ya treni | stay-shay-nee ya tray-nee |
| bus station | stendi ya basi | stayn-dee ya ba-see |
| customs | forodha | foh-roh-dha |
| boarding pass | pasi ya kuingilia | pa-see-ya koo-een-geee-lee-a |
| car hire | gari za kukodi | ga-ree za koo-koh-dee |
| bicycle | baisikeli | ba-ee-see-kay-lee |
| rate | kiasi | kee-a-see |
| insurance | bima | bee-ma |
| fuel station | kituo cha mafuta | kee-too-oh cha ma-foo-ta |
| garage | gereji | gay-ray-jee |
| I have a flat tyre | nina pancha | nee-na pan-cha |

## Health

| I don't feel well | Mimi ni mgonjwa | mee-meee nee m-gohn-jwa |
|---|---|---|
| I have a stomach ache | Nina maumivu ya tumbo | nee-na ma-oo-mee-voo ya toom-boh |
| headache | maumivu ya kichwa | ma-oo-mee-voo ya kee-chwa |
| I've been injured | Nimejeruhiwa | nee-may-jay-roo-hee-wa |
| clinic | kliniki | klee-nee-kee |
| insect repellent | dawa la kufukuza wadudu | da-wa la koo-foo-koo-za wa-doo-doo |

## Staying in a Hotel

| I have a reservation | Nina buking | nee-na boo-keeng |
|---|---|---|
| Are there any rooms available? | Una nafasi ya chumba? | oo-na na-fa-see ya choom-ba |
| How much is per...? | Ni bei gani kwa? | nee bay ga-ne kwa |
| day | siku | see-koo |
| person | mtu | m-too |
| week | wiki | wee-kee |
| double room | chumba cha watu wawili | choom-ba cha wa-too wa-wee-lee |
| double bed | kitanda cha watu wawili | kee-tan-da cha wa-too wa-wee-lee |
| twin beds | vitanda viwili | vee-tan-da vee-wee-lee |
| single room | chumba kwa mtu mmoja | choom-ba kwa m-too m-moh-ja |
| bath, shower | bafu | ba-foo |
| soap | sabuni | sa-boo-nee |
| warm/cold water | ya joto/baridi maji | ya joh-toh/ba-ree-dee ma-jee |
| key | ufunguo | oo-foon-goo-oh |

## Eating Out

| I want to reserve a table | Nataka kuhifadhi meza | na-ta-ka koo-hee-fa-dhee may-za |
|---|---|---|
| Can I see the menu, please? | Naweza kuona, menyu, tafadhali? | na-way-za koo-or-na may-nyoo ta-fa-dha-lee |
| The bill please | Lete bili | lay-tay bee-lee |
| I am a vegetarian | Mimi ni mlaji wa mboga za majani tu | mee-mee nee m-la-jee wa m-boh-ga za ma-ja-nee too |
| menu | menyu | may-nyoo |
| cover charge | bei ya kuingia | bay ya koo-een-gee-a |
| wine list | orodha ya mvinyo | oh-roh-dha ya m-vee-nyoh |
| glass | glasi | gla-see |
| bottle | chupa | choo-pa |
| knife | kisu | kee-soo |
| fork | uma | oo-ma |
| spoon | kijiko | kee-jee-koh |
| breakfast | chai ya asubuhi | cha-ee ya a-soo-boo-hee |

| | | |
|---|---|---|
| lunch | **chakula cha mchana** | cha-koo-la cha m-cha-na |
| dinner | **chakula cha jioni** | cha-koo-la cha jee-oh-nee |
| main course | **chakula kikuu** | cha-koo-la kee-koo |
| starter, first course | **kiamsha hamu** | kee-am-sha ha-moo |
| appetizers | **kiamsha hamu** | kee-am-sha ha-moo |
| main courses | **chakula kikuu** | cha-koo-la-kee-koo |
| bar | **baa** | baa |
| café | **mgahawa** | m-ga-ha-wa |
| rare | **ya kuiva kidogo** | ya koo-ee-va kee-doh-goh |
| medium | **ya kuiva wastani** | ya koo-ee-va wa-sta-nee |
| well done | **ya kuiva sana** | ya koo-ee-va sa-na |

## Menu Decoder

| | | |
|---|---|---|
| **tofaa** | to-fa | apple |
| **ndizi** | n-dee-zee | banana |
| **nyama m'gombe** | nya-ma mg-ohm-bay | beef |
| **wa nyama** | wa nya-ma | beef stew |
| **bia** | bee-a | beer |
| **ya kuchemshwa** | ya koo-chaym-shwa | boiled |
| **mkate** | m-ka-tay | bread |
| **siagi** | see-a-gee | butter |
| **keki** | kay-kee | cake |
| **flat, round Indian bread** | cha-pa-tee | chapati |
| **jibini** | jee-bee-nee | cheese |
| **kuku** | koo-koo | chicken |
| **chipsi** | chee-psee | chips |
| **dafu** | da-foo | coconut (green) |
| **kahawa** | kah-ha-wa | coffee |
| **kitindamlo** | kee-teen-da-m-loh | dessert |
| **maandazi** | man-da-zee | deep-fried doughnut |
| **kavu** | ka-voo | dry |
| **yai** | ya-ee | egg |
| **samaki** | sa-ma-kee | fish |
| **samaki ya kupaka** | sa-ma-kee ya koo-pa-ka | fish cooked in a delicate coconut sauce |
| **tunda safi** | toon-da sa-fee | fresh fruit |
| **nyama ya wanyama pori** | nya-ma ya wa-nya-ma poh-ree | game meat |
| **kitunguu saumu** | kee-toon-goo sa-oo-moo | garlic |
| **sukuma wiki** | soo-koo-ma wee-kee | green vegetables (such as spinach) |
| **ya kuchomwa** | ya koo-chohm-wa | grilled ham |
| **aiskrimu** | a-ee-skree-moo | ice, ice cream |
| **mwanakondoo** | mwa-na-kohn-doh | lamb |
| **limau** | lee-ma-oo | lemon |
| **maji ya ndimu** | ma-jee ya n-dee-moo | lime juice |
| **kamba** | kam-ba | lobster, crayfish |
| **ugali** | oo-ga-lee | maize/cassava flour cooked like porridge |
| **nyama** | nya-ma | meat |
| **nyama choma** | nya-ma choh-ma | meat grilled over charcoal |
| **maziwa** | ma-zee-wa | milk |
| **uji** | oo-jee | millet staple served as a breakfast dish |
| **maji ya madini** | ma-jee ya ma-dee-nee | mineral water |
| **mastadi** | ma-sta-dee | mustard |
| **tambi** | tam-bee | noodles |
| **omlet** | ohm-layt | omelette |
| **mafuta** | ma-foo-ta | oil |
| **zaituni** | za-ee-too-nee | olives |
| **kitunguu** | kee-toon-goo | onions |
| **chungwa** | choon-gwa | orange |
| **maji ya machungwa** | ma-jee ya ma-choon-gwa | fresh orange juice |
| **pilipili** | pee-lee-pee-lee | pepper |
| **nyama nguruwe** | nya-ma n-goo-roo-way | pork |
| | ma-toh-kay | a staple dish of boiled/steamed and mashed plantains |
| | kee-a-zee | potatoes |
| | kam-ba | prawns |

| | | |
|---|---|---|
| **sambusa/ samosa** | sam-boo-sa/ sa-moh-sa | puffed pastry stuffed with meat or vegetables and deep-fried |
| **mchele** | m-chay-lay | rice (uncooked) |
| **wali** | wa-lee | rice (cooked) |
| **skonzi** | skohn-zee | roll |
| **chumvi** | choom-vee | salt |
| **sandwichi** | sand-wee-chee | sandwich |
| **soseji** | soh-say-jee | sausage |
| **konokono** | koh-noh-koh-noh | snails |
| **supu** | soo-poo | soup |
| **mchuzi** | m-choo-zee | spicy sauce served with ugali |
| **mnofu** | m-noh-foo | steak |
| **sukari** | soo-ka-ree | sugar |
| **chai** | cha-ee | tea |
| **slaisi** | sla-ee-see | toast |
| **mboga** | m-boh-ga | vegetables |
| **siki** | see-kee | vinegar |
| **maji** | ma-jee | water |
| **mwekundu** | mway-koon-doo | red wine |
| **mweupe** | mway-oo-pay | white wine |

## Numbers

| | | |
|---|---|---|
| 0 | **sifuri** | see foo ree |
| 1 | **moja** | moh ja |
| 2 | **mbili** | m bee lee |
| 3 | **tatu** | ta too |
| 4 | **nne** | n nay |
| 5 | **tano** | ta noh |
| 6 | **sita** | see ta |
| 7 | **saba** | sa ba |
| 8 | **nane** | na nay |
| 9 | **tisa** | tee sa |
| 10 | **kumi** | koo mee |
| 11 | **kumi na moja** | koo mee na moh ja |
| 12 | **kumi na mbili** | koo mee na m bee lee |
| 13 | **kumi na tatu** | koo mee na ta too |
| 14 | **kumi na nne** | koo mee na n nay |
| 15 | **kumi na tano** | koo mee na ta noh |
| 16 | **kumi na sita** | koo mee na see ta |
| 17 | **kumi na saba** | koo mee na sa ba |
| 18 | **kumi na nane** | koo mee na na see ta |
| 19 | **kumi na tisa** | koo mee na tee sa |
| 20 | **ishirini** | ee shee ree nee |
| 30 | **thelathini** | thay la thee nee |
| 40 | **arobaini** | a roh ba ee nee |
| 50 | **hamsini** | ham see nee |
| 60 | **sitini** | see tee nee |
| 70 | **sabini** | sa bee nee |
| 80 | **themanini** | thay ma nee nee |
| 90 | **tisini** | tee see nee |
| 100 | **mia moja** | mee a moh ja |
| 1,000 | **elfu** | ayl foo |
| 1,000 | **laki** | la kee |

## Time

| | | |
|---|---|---|
| one minute | **dakika moja** | da-kee-ka moh-ja |
| one hour | **saa moja** | sa moh-ja |
| half an hour | **nusu saa** | noo-soo sa |
| Monday | **Jumatatu** | joo ma ta too |
| Tuesday | **Jumanne** | joo ma n nay |
| Wednesday | **Jumatano** | joo ma ta noh |
| Thursday | **Alhamisi** | al ha mee see |
| Friday | **Ijumaa** | ee joo ma |
| Saturday | **Jumamosi** | joo ma moh see |
| Sunday | **Jumapili** | joo me pee lee |

## Swahili Time (saa za kiswahili)

| | | |
|---|---|---|
| 6am (sunrise) | **12 (ST)** | saa kumi na mbili asubuhi |
| 12pm (noon) | **6 (ST)** | saa sita mchana |
| 6pm (sunset) | **12 (ST)** | saa kumi na mbili jioni |
| 12am (midnight) | **6 (ST)** | saa sita usiku |
| morning | **asubuhi** | asubuhi |
| afternoon | **mchana** | m-cha-na |
| evening | **jioni** | jee-oh-nee |
| night | **usiku** | oo-see-kuu |